POLITICS IN ADVANCED NATIONS

POLITICS IN ADVANCED NATIONS:
Modernization, Development, and Contemporary Change

edited by

Norman J. Vig   *Carleton College*

and

Rodney P. Stiefbold   *University of Miami*

PRENTICE HALL, INC.
Englewood Cliffs, New Jersey

0-13-684522-3

Library of Congress Catalog Card Number 73-1486

Printed in the United States of America

10 9 8 7 6 5 4 3 2 1

PRENTICE-HALL INTERNATIONAL, INC., London
PRENTICE-HALL OF AUSTRALIA, PTY. LTD., Sydney
PRENTICE-HALL OF CANADA, LTD., Toronto
PRENTICE-HALL OF INDIA PRIVATE LIMITED, New Delhi
PRENTICE-HALL OF JAPAN, INC., Tokyo

To Our Parents

Contents

Preface

Modernization and political development have become a central focus of scholarship in political science over the past decade. Too often, however, the developmental perspective has been confined to research and teaching on the "underdeveloped" countries of Africa, Asia, and Latin America. The politics of the "developed" nations, on the other hand, are frequently subjected to static comparisons which do little to illuminate either universal processes of change or the special problems which beset societies at the advanced end of the development spectrum. At a minimum this obscures the long-term dynamics of change in highly industrialized nations, while at worst it renders development analysis a tool for Western scholars to pontificate on obstacles to reform in the "Third World" without recognizing the continuing impact of modernization on their own political systems.

This book is an effort to partially remedy such shortcomings in the teaching literature. For the most part we have selected articles by scholars who have turned their attention to comparative study of the developmental patterns which have shaped, and continue to shape, political change in nations currently in advanced phases of modernization. Not all countries in this category are encompassed by the readings—for example, Canada, Australia, Japan, and Israel. Instead, we have attempted by our selection of writings and in our introductory essay to facilitate comparisons between the larger and smaller democracies of Western Europe as well as between them and the Soviet Union and the United States. We have also been selective in placing greatest emphasis on issues related to the development of mass political participation and representation, in both democratic and authoritarian systems.

Much of the inspiration for this volume derives from the late Otto Kirchheimer, whose courses and seminars the editors jointly attended while graduate students at Columbia University a decade ago. Though not a systematic development theorist, Professor Kirchheimer provided unique insights into the emerging dilemmas of "postindustrial" democracy. He was also among the first critics of contemporary modernization theory to emphasize the vital importance of comparative historical inquiry as a foundation for developmental analysis. His selection in this book is sketched against a broad historical canvas and yet captures many of the forebodings which others have come to share over the "quality" of current political life.

We wish to express our gratitude to the many authors who consented to inclusion of their work in this enterprise, and regret that space limitations did not permit us to use several other selections for which permission was graciously given. We also wish to give special thanks to the editors and staff at Appleton-Century-Crofts for their understanding and assistance over the long gestation of this book.

N.J.V.
R.P.S.

INTRODUCTION

Modernization and Political Development in Western Nations: An Overview

Norman J. Vig
Rodney P. Stiefbold

One of the seminal developments in Comparative Politics during the past decade has been a growing re-examination of the history of contemporary advanced nations. Much of this reorientation towards historical patterns of development has been stimulated by studies of countries at the opposite end of the modernization process—nations in Asia and Africa which have only recently emerged as independent states and which are confronted with the most difficult problems of internal order and socio-economic change. Following World War II, and especially in the 1950s and early 1960s, these emerging nations came to occupy a central place in the search for general theories of political development and modernization. The effort to formulate universal models capable of explaining the dynamics of political change in societies at all levels of development rapidly gathered momentum.

For the most part, political scientists and others engaged in this theoretical quest began with inherited assumptions about Western political development. The currently "advanced" nations of Western Europe and North America were generally taken as models for other "developing" societies insofar as these nations represented the "developed" end of the continuum between traditionalism and modernity. Yet these assumptions seldom were examined critically, and often they posited unrealistic or unfounded prerequisites for stable political evolution in societies characterized by wide variations in traditional social structures and cultures. It is primarily this fact which has forced social scientists to pause and re-examine the past circumstances and processes of political change in the Western world in more systematic fashion.

It is evident that the classical theories of previous centuries offer limited insight into the complex processes of change in the modern world. As

3

Gabriel Almond points out,[1] the conditions affecting political development have radically changed in the past several centuries, yet political theories remained rooted in various presumptions of the European enlightenment, especially the belief in a unilinear path of evolution toward popular government. Despite the challenge of 19th century Marxist thought and 20th century totalitarian practices, Western political theory remained essentially ethnocentric, giving little attention to the concrete problems of development in widely differing cultures and societies. From our present viewpoint it is apparent that even a cursory examination of violence and instability in the course of European and American history scarcely supports an optimistic theory of progress toward effective democracy. Not only the rise of Nazi, Fascist, and Communist regimes in the present century, but a host of earlier battles between democratic and authoritarian principles of government, precludes sanguine interpretations of this kind. Thus, as Almond suggests, more realistic, flexible, and open theories of political development are needed if we are to understand the historical experiences of Western nations and their relevance to both the current problems of these countries and to the newer nations of Asia, Africa, and Latin America.

On the other hand, there is increasing skepticism over universal development models which are so generalized as to defy historical and empirical verification. Samuel P. Huntington, for example, argues that there is a growing gap between theory and reality in this field, particularly insofar as political development is seen as an inevitable correlate of general social modernization.[2] Several other scholars have also pointed to the danger in premature "reification" of abstract analytical constructs which may bear little relevance to concrete historical events and experiences, and which may reflect contemporary academic biases more than detached empirical generalization.[3] Nevertheless, most scholars believe that general theory is necessary to stimulate and guide more detailed research, and in the current mood of uncertainty, an argument can be made for the usefulness of multiple approaches at different levels of specificity.

The selections reprinted in this book present a variety of approaches to Western political development. In general, those in Section A suggest broader theoretical perspectives which may be helpful in analyzing universal processes of change. Here we try to explain some of the issues dividing theorists such as Almond and Huntington, as well as some of the intellectual antecedents to their work. The articles in Section B are more detailed studies

---

[1] Almond, "Political Systems and Political Change," reprinted below.

[2] Huntington, "Political Development and Political Decay," reprinted below.

[3] For an excellent general critique of evolutionary theories in contemporary social science, see Robert A. Nisbet, *Social Change and History: Aspects of the Western Theory of Development* (New York: Oxford University Press, 1969). See also A. James Gregor, "Political Science and the Uses of Functional Analysis," *American Political Science Review* 62 (June 1968), pp. 425-439, for problems of reification.

of political change in individual countries over long periods of time, though Huntington also compares American and European patterns of development. These selections are intended to suggest the kind of historical reinterpretation that is possible from the development standpoint. Section C of the readings includes cross-national comparisons of specific problems associated with the emergence of mass political participation in the late 19th and early 20th centuries. Some of the more exciting insights into development processes result from "middle-range" theoretical hypotheses based on more detailed comparisons of this kind. Sections D and E continue the study of development in the post-1945 period, focusing on questions of political representation and participation in advanced industrial society.

A. THE SEARCH FOR DEVELOPMENT THEORY

The past two decades have witnessed a bewildering proliferation of models and theories for explaining social change. In comparative politics, especially, efforts have been made to relate a wide range of socio-economic and cultural variables to the central task of creating effective political institutions.[4] This task is variously referred to as nation-building, political development, or political modernization. Theories concerning this process differ from most earlier writings on politics in that they seek to establish multiple, systematic interrelationships between political change and certain imperatives of modernization.

The general term "modernization" is usually reserved to describe the broadest aspects of social, economic, psychological, and technological change which has taken place over the past several centuries in Western nations and which, by implication, the more recently developing societies must also experience in some form. Economic growth, industrialization, urbanization, education, social mobility, mass communications and transportation, large-scale bureaucratic organization, and rational or universalistic thought processes are all typically considered part of the modernization process.[5]

Perhaps the most comprehensive overview of this process is given by the

[4]The most important pioneering work was Gabriel Almond and James S. Coleman, eds., *The Politics of the Developing Areas* (Princeton: Princeton University Press, 1960). For data collections and methods, see Bruce M. Russett *et al., World Handbook of Political and Social Indicators* (New Haven: Yale University Press, 1964); Arthur S. Banks and Robert B. Textor, *A Cross-Polity Survey* (Cambridge: M.I.T. Press, 1963); and Richard L. Merritt and Stein Rokkan, eds., *Comparing Nations: The Use of Quantitative Data in Cross-National Research* (New Haven: Yale University Press, 1966).

[5]For an extended list of characteristics of modernity, see especially Marius Jansen, ed., *Changing Japanese Attitudes Toward Modernization* (Princeton: Princeton University Press, 1965), pp. 19-23, and the general discussion by John Whitney Hall on pp. 7-41.

historian C. E. Black in his book, *The Dynamics of Modernization*.[6] Black characterizes the present modernization process as a truly epochal revolution beginning with the growth of Western science and technology in the late Middle Ages—a change comparable in significance to the emergence of human beings a million or more years ago or to the appearance of civilized societies some four to seven thousand years ago. What distinguishes the modern era is "the phenomenal growth of knowledge since the scientific revolution and the unprecedented effort at adaptation to this knowledge that has come to be demanded of the whole of mankind."[7] Modernization is thus defined as "the process by which historically evolved institutions are adapted to the rapidly changing functions that reflect the unprecedented increase in man's knowledge, permitting control over his environment. . . ."[8] This process, according to Black and others, is unique in that for the first time a universal set of imperatives or "world culture" affects the development of all societies. Previously, whether in classical Greek and Roman times, or in the Middle Ages, societies and civilizations rose and fell, but without any common intellectual basis or knowledge which made sustained development possible.[9] It is the fundamental unity of this process which demands universal theories of modernization which illuminate the interdependence of change both within separate societies (among different sectors or spheres of social activity) and between societies in the international context (i.e., the transfer of ideas and techniques).

Although modernization theory may offer a genuinely new approach to political development, its roots lie deep in earlier social theory. The functional interdependence of economic, social, and political development was asserted once and for all by Marx, though Marxist philosophy emphasized the primacy of economic forces in generating socio-political revolution. Partly in reaction to this interpretation, other European sociologists in the late 19th and early 20th centuries sought more complex explanations of social change and its political ramifications. For example, Sir Henry Maine, Ferdinand Toennies, Emile Durkheim, and Max Weber all offered comprehensive theories on the transformation of primitive or traditional societies to modern society.[10] The ideas of these European scholars have shaped the major contemporary schools of political sociology and have influenced most of the recent development theories.

[6]New York: Harper & Row, 1966. Black's thesis is discussed further in the article by Bernard Brown reprinted below.

[7]Black, *op. cit.*, p. 4.

[8]*Ibid.*, p. 7.

[9]On this point see also Walter W. Rostow, *Politics and the Stages of Growth* (London: Cambridge University Press, 1971), chap. 2.

[10]For a useful summary of these theories, see Lucian W. Pye, *Aspects of Political Development* (Boston: Little Brown & Co., 1966), pp. 58-62. See also F.X. Sutton, "Social Theory and Comparative Politics," in Harry Eckstein and David E. Apter, eds., *Comparative Politics: A Reader* (New York: Free Press of Glencoe, 1963), pp. 67-81.

Marx and Durkheim, from different perspectives, contributed to the modern conception of societies or nations as interdependent "social systems." In Marx economic relationships determined by the mode of production and resulting class structure established the dynamics and pace of change in the remaining social "superstructure." Durkheim emphasized the interdependence of society brought about by the "division of labor" or differentiation of roles, structures, and functions as social communities advance.[11] The growing specialization of roles must be offset by new forms of social solidarity, which Durkheim saw in the development of broader value consensus and group representation which could integrate society on a new "organic" basis (as opposed to the "mechanical" solidarity of traditional patterns of rule). Thus, while Marx pointed to the class warfare inevitably arising from economic exploitation, Durkheim stressed the growth of over-arching values recognizing the contributions of different social roles and groups. The result is a voluntaristic integration of society, though psychological disorientation might also result when change is especially rapid. But both Marx and Durkheim suggested that politics should be viewed in terms of an interdependent social system in which change in one sector produces tensions and change in all the others. Whether economic relationships or structural-functional differentiation and value integration is seen as the key variable in political development, most contemporary modernization theory assumes close systemic interdependence.[12]

Max Weber, on the other hand, held that relationships between elements of the social structure are something to be proved empirically rather than assumed.[13] Indeed he drew a distinction between "state" and "society," which suggested that the social functions of the two spheres are basically different. Society generally is seen in terms of individual and group competition for power and status, but those achieving control of the state exercise authority of a distinctively greater magnitude than those controlling other social groups. The state was defined as "a compulsory political association with continuous organization" which "upholds a claim to the *monopoly* of the *legitimate* use of physical force" in a given territorial

---

[11] Emile Durkheim, *The Division of Labor in Society* (New York: Free Press of Glencoe, 1933).

[12] Recent functionalist theory goes further in positing that social systems tend toward "equilibrium." That is, if change is introduced in one part of the whole, there is a tendency for other parts to adjust or adapt in such a way as to eliminate the disturbance (which is dysfunctional to the system's stability). Change thus results from the development of strains which upset the equilibrium and require adaptive behavior if the system is to survive. Marxists do not of course accept this evolutionary view of political change, though revolutionary situations can be described in terms of systemic disequilibria.

[13] See Randall Collins, "A Comparative Approach to Political Sociology," in Reinhard Bendix, ed., *State and Society: A Reader in Comparative Political Sociology* (Boston: Little Brown & Co., 1968), pp. 42-66, for an excellent discussion of Weber's approach in contrast to that of Durkheim and the functionalists.

area.[14] Governments are thus distinctive in that they must establish a claim to legitimately exercise domination (or "imperative coordination") over the rest of society. The wider society has other means of achieving coordination for its own purposes—through the economic marketplace and through the many interest groups which people form to improve their "chances in life" or status in society.[15] But political authority inevitably involves domination of some individuals and groups over others.

It was in this connection that Weber made some of his greatest contributions to modern social science. First of all, *authority* was distinguished from *power*, in that authority entails acceptance and voluntary compliance for the most part. Governments do not have the means for stable and effective rule over longer periods of time if they rely on force and coercion alone. This means they must generate authority which is legitimized by some widely accepted belief or agreement in society, and one of Weber's principal concerns was to distinguish different foundations for legitimate types of rule. Secondly, Weber saw one type of authority as perhaps the greatest achievement of Western civilization and culture—what he called "rational-legal" authority, or authority derived from a generalized set of legal procedures and norms. In the excerpt from his *Theory of Social and Economic Organization* reprinted below, he distinguishes this type of authority from two other universal types: "traditional authority," in which legitimacy stems from customary prerogatives and rules of succession handed down from "time immemorial"; and "charismatic authority," by which an individual leader may break with the past and assert a new right to rule on the basis of some extraordinary moral, prophetic, or other mystical qualities which he personally displays.[16] Thirdly, Weber argued that political authority requires (in addition to legitimacy) an organizational apparatus, and contrasted traditional and modern types of administrative structure. Indeed, much of Weber's theory of political development focuses on the *institutionalization* of authority through bureaucratic structures and procedures which he associated with rational-legal order. His ideal of modern, rational bureaucracy stands out as a reference point for contemporary social science.

The point of this brief excursion into the background of current theory is to suggest that many of the basic issues which divided earlier scholars have re-emerged in recent debates over modernization and development. The

---

[14]Weber, *The Theory of Social and Economic Organization*, trans. A. M. Henderson and Talcott Parsons, ed. Talcott Parsons (New York: The Macmillan Co., 1947), p. 154.

[15]Weber did not assume the existence of a general "social value system" common to an entire society, though he did emphasize that people organize to promote idealistic as well as material goals and also stressed the widespread impact of religious values on social behavior (see, e.g., *The Protestant Ethic and the Spirit of Capitalism*).

[16]For a full summary and commentary on Weber's three types of authority, see Reinhard Bendix, *Max Weber: An Intellectual Portrait* (Garden City: Doubleday Anchor Books, 1962), pp. 285-457.

"functional" or "structural-functional" school of political sociology and development theory has built on the concepts of differentiation and value integration pioneered *inter alia* by Durkheim.[17] We shall examine some of Gabriel Almond's ideas as representative of this approach to political development. Weber's emphasis on group competition and political legitimacy is mirrored in a great deal of contemporary political science, but the problem of institutionalizing authority is particularly well represented in the writings of Professor Huntington. The Marxist perspective of revolutionary social conflict has been less fully incorporated in the development theories of Western scholars, although the crucial importance of economic change runs through much of the literature on modernization.[18] Moreover there is a growing concern with the general dynamics of revolution and with the persisting social cleavages which beset advanced political systems.[19]

Gabriel Almond has formulated an approach to political development which combines the work of structural-functional sociologists with recent political systems analysis.[20] Political systems are seen as an integral part of the social order, conditioned at every point by an underlying political culture or set of attitudes, values, and perceptions regarding politics.[21] Yet the political system, though part of a broader social system consisting of society as a whole, is analytically distinct in terms of functions and processes. Essentially, the political system (or subsystem of society) includes mechanisms for channeling demands, personnel, and resources ("inputs") into decision-making processes which convert them into authoritative actions (laws, policies, allocations, etc.) which are the "outputs" of the system (and which by way of feedback again influence the inputs). The input-output conversion model emphasizes the need for differentiation of functions in such a way that the political system has "boundaries"; that is, political structures and processes must develop some degree of autonomy from other social subsystems so that the political system can aggregate the

---

[17]Collins, *op. cit.,* pp. 43-46. The sociologist Talcott Parsons was especially important in introducing functional analysis to the mainstream of American sociology and theories of change; see his *The Social System* (New York: Free Press of Glencoe, 1951), and succeeding works.

[18]See, e.g., the works of W. W. Rostow and Robert Heilbroner.

[19]See Chalmers Johnson, *Revolution and the Social System* (Stanford: Stanford University Press, 1964) and *Revolutionary Change* (Boston: Little Brown & Co., 1966); Ted Gurr, *Why Men Rebel* (Princeton: Princeton University Press, 1970); Barrington Moore, Jr., *Social Origins of Dictatorship and Democracy* (Boston: Beacon Press, 1966).

[20]See Almond's introductory chapter in *The Politics of the Developing Areas,* and Almond and G. Bingham Powell, Jr., *Comparative Politics: A Developmental Approach* (Boston: Little Brown & Co., 1966).

[21]Almond and Sidney Verba, *The Civic Culture* (Boston: Little Brown & Co., 1965); and L. W. Pye and S. Verba, eds., *Political Culture and Political Development* (Princeton: Princeton University Press, 1965).

interests of diverse groups and apply decisions to the entire society. But it is emphasized that different types of structures may perform the same political functions in different systems, and, conversely, that similar institutions may perform quite different functions in different systems.

In Almond's theory, political development results from two basic processes: from the differentiation of social structures which creates political institutions which "mesh" with the social environment yet maintain subsystem boundaries; and secondly, from what is called the secularization (or rationalization) of political culture.[22] The performance of new functions requires an increasing specialization of role structures and political institutions, resulting in growing complexity in the relationships among political actors. Ultimately a developed political system is characterized by a network of semi-autonomous institutional spheres capable of responding independently and relatively harmoniously to new problems which arise. But this process of institutional development cannot succeed without corresponding changes in basic cultural orientations and social behavior. At each stage of political development, therefore, structural specialization must be accompanied by secularization in the political culture, such as development of "achievement" orientations which, for example, permit office-holders to be chosen by merit or ability rather than by ascribed status; the spread of rational or pragmatic outlooks toward the solution of political problems in place of mysticism or fatalism; and emergence of "political competence" (a feeling that one can take part in politics and influence the outcome) among the mass population as well as on the elite level. The political socialization process by which basic political attitudes are shaped from one generation to the next thus becomes a crucial factor in development.

From these basic concepts, Almond goes on to analyze political development in terms of the attainment of broad system capabilities. In "Political Systems and Political Change" he lists four "performance capabilities" which must be developed on the road to modern nationhood: an internal "integrative" or "mobilization" capability, including territorial unification, the development of national identity, and penetration and control of local groups or authorities; an international "acommodative" capability, or achievement of both security in, and responsiveness to, the surrounding international environment; a "participation" capability, involving the admission of wider and wider sectors of the populace into politics and the organization of this participation; and finally, a "distributional" or "welfare" capability which permits more equitable

[22]For a concise discussion of the concepts of structural differentiation and cultural secularization, see Almond and Powell, *op. cit.*, pp. 21-25.

sharing of wealth among all social groups within a mass citizenry. Putting the analysis in these terms allows Almond to relate the development process to the more concrete historical problems which advanced nations have faced—national integration, security, popular involvement, and social welfare. The attainment of political system capabilities—made possible by the underlying processes of structural differentiation and cultural secularization referred to above—thus has enabled societies to confront and resolve a series of major development crises; and the sequence in which these crises arose and the relative timing of their solution has had great impact on the nature of the political systems which emerged.[23] In this case the analysis allows Almond to draw some rather sharp distinctions between the overall development patterns of different European nations. We shall return to this mode of analysis later.

Not surprisingly, many development theorists consider Almond's approach excessively abstract and empirically untestable. Huntington, in his review of recent development literature in the following article, points to a widening gap between theory and reality, especially if one considers the basic problems of the new nations today. He makes several general criticisms of prevailing development theories, the most important of which is that there is no justification for equating overall social modernization with political development. There may be little correlation between various indicators of modernity and the development of effective political systems; indeed, developments in different social spheres may conflict with each other and the general impact of modernization may be political retrogression and "decay" rather than "development." Most contemporary development theories thus err in postulating inevitable progress toward popular democracy or at least improved capacities for dealing with political and social problems as a result of modernization. Even the best of these theories (such as Almond's) tend to become one-way concepts of change which, like earlier theories of social evolution, imply that change is irreversible. Concepts such as structural differentiation and cultural rationalization suggest universal trends toward stable democratic institutions.[24]

Huntington focuses instead on what he regards as the two key variables in political development: growth of participation and level of institutional-

[23]Almond has further elaborated and reformulated the list of system capabilities in "A Developmental Approach to Political Systems," *World Politics* 17 (Jan. 1965), and in Almond and Powell, *op. cit.*, Chap. VIII.

[24]This theme is also developed in Ali A. Mazrui, "From Social Darwinism to Current Theories of Modernization: A Tradition of Analysis," *World Politics* 21 (Oct. 1968), pp. 69-83. Huntington presents a more detailed discussion and critique of modernization theories in "The Change to Change: Modernization, Development, and Politics," *Comparative Politics* 3 (Apr. 1971), pp. 283-322; and the full range of his own ideas is set out in *Political Order in Changing Societies* (New Haven: Yale University Press, 1968).

ization. Following Karl Deutsch, he argues that the principal result of modernization (increased literacy, urbanization, exposure to mass communications, etc.) is "social mobilization" or the readying of non-elites to demand political participation. "Modernization means mass mobilization; mass mobilization means increased political participation; and increased participation is the key element of political development. Participation distinguishes modern politics from traditional politics." The crucial problem, then, is that rapid increases in social mobilization and participation tend to undermine the authority and legitimacy of traditional political institutions (or newly established institutions), and modernization may thus produce disintegration and breakdown. In other words, modernization and political development may correlate negatively rather than positively, and the comparative *rates* of social mobilization and institutional adaptation are the crucial factor—should the rate of mobilization outstrip the rate of institutionalization, political decay is likely. Political development is thus defined as the institutionalization of political organizations and procedures which are sufficiently strong (measured in terms of adaptability, complexity, autonomy, and coherence) to withstand the pressures of mass participation. While this approach differs somewhat from Weber's, in placing less emphasis on the legitimacy of authority and more on order and performance, it nevertheless emphasizes the crucial need for institutionalizing the authority of the state. There are some similarities to Almond's theory also—e.g., in the concern for organizational complexity and autonomy—but the overall implications for development are strikingly different.

As Huntington says, all definitions of development are arbitrary, but some may be more useful than others. In an article on recent changes in the Soviet Union, Alex Inkeles has emphasized much the same point:[25]

> Most social scientists approach the subject they are studying with some kind of conceptual scheme which we may call a model. These models play an enormously important role in deciding what is taken into consideration and what is left out, what weight is assigned to one factor as against another, which sets of interrelationships are assumed to exist and which will go largely unnoticed. There is a great deal of debate about models, most of which deals with the question of whether or not a particular model is right or wrong. In my opinion there is no such thing as a right or wrong sociological model. There are richer and poorer ones.

A particular theoretical approach may thus be more useful for some purposes than for others. For example, Almond's model of input-output conversion and concept of historical capability crises may enrich our understanding of the development of contemporary democratic nations over the

[25]Inkeles, "Models and Issues in the Analysis of Soviet Society," *Survey* 60 (July 1966), p. 3.

past several centuries more than of the more recent revolutionary events which have led to authoritarian regimes or of the problems of new nations which are confronting all the major development crises at once; whereas Huntington's concern with mobilization and institutionalization may be more applicable to the latter context or to certain periods in Western history in which the crisis of mass participation was felt.

Whatever the student's judgment on theoretical models, one thing is certain: more detailed historical research is needed if we are to understand the concrete problems which advanced nations have faced in the past. This is not to say that historical materials have been ignored by social scientists. In other works, C. E. Black, Barrington Moore, Jr., and Huntington—to name but three—have drawn heavily on historical data to support their propositions; and as mentioned at the beginning, there is currently a movement toward greater incorporation of comparative history into the study of modernization.[26] But in the final article in Section A, Val R. Lorwin states that, "Even among those advanced societies we have cheerfully assumed to be well known, systematic empirical knowledge of nation-building and theory on the subject are still underdeveloped, even if developing." Lorwin thus suggests that much more historical research is required, both within the limited cultural area of Western Europe and, more specifically, on individual nations and even their regional and local components. Citing many gaps in knowledge about the fundamental elements of political development, as well as many untapped resources in historical research, he calls for new forms of collaboration between historians and other social scientists to probe the specific sources of political change in different types of societies. This effort must be extended to the smaller European countries as well as the major nations, since the patterns of development and change vary much more widely than has been assumed. In fact the experience of the smaller states may be more relevant to the problems of the new nations than that of the major powers. It is for this reason that we have emphasized developments in some of the smaller democracies in Sections C and D below.

B. CRISES IN POLITICAL MODERNIZATION

In considering the patterns of political development, we are forced to stand back from the welter of particular events, trends, and countertrends which have always preoccupied historians. At the same time,

---

[26]For a review of the work of the authors mentioned and the development of comparative history, see Lester M. Salamon, "Comparative History and the Theory of Modernization," *World Politics,* 23 (Oct. 1970), pp. 83-103.

however, our general concepts must be related to concrete historical changes if comparative modernization theory is to pay off in greater understanding of the actual difficulties of nation-building. Emphasis on specific institutional developments, such as the growth of monarchies, bureaucracies, and parliaments, is one means of closing the gap between general theory and historical specificity, as well as between contemporary and traditional approaches in political science. On the other hand, too narrow a focus on institutional factors also runs the risk of oversimplifying the broader development process, and it may obscure important comparisons between nations which undergo modernization through different types of political structure. Clearly, a wide range of institutional structure and form is compatible with political modernity, and institutional studies may be merely descriptive rather than explanatory.

Another facet of the problem of historical application is to specify general stages of development through which societies have passed and which, by implication, newly developing countries might also face. Analysis of this kind owes much to the familiar concept of the stages of economic growth propounded by development economists, notably W. W. Rostow.[27] Rostow's classic work is subtitled "A Non-Communist Manifesto" and is intended to refute the Marxist theory of economic, social, and political change through successive revolutionary stages.[28] Other social scientists have sought to reduce political change to analogous stages of evolution. Black, for example, defines four general "phases" of political development,[29] and A. F. K. Organski discusses four stages of political economy culminating in "the politics of abundance."[30] Indeed all development theorists rely on some concept of sequential transformation or stages, as do we in our conception of advanced nations.

However, there are a number of critical problems in seeking to analyze political development in terms of discrete historical or evolutionary stages. The historical experiences from which sequential patterns of development

[27]Rostow, *The Stages of Economic Growth: A Non-Communist Manifesto* (Cambridge: Cambridge University Press, 1960), and *Politics and the Stages of Growth.*

[28]Marx of course distinguished five general stages or eras of social and political development: the ancient slave states, feudalism, capitalism, socialism, and communism. But it is questionable whether he intended his analysis (based on Western history) to apply on a universal scale, that is, to non-Western colonial areas and traditional societies generally. See Schlomo Avineri, *Karl Marx on Colonialism & Modernization* (Garden City: Doubleday Anchor Books, 1969), pp. 1-31.

[29]Black, *op. cit.*, pp. 67-89. He discusses "the challenge of modernity," "the consolidation of modernizing leadership," "economic and social transformation," and "integration of society."

[30]Organski, *The Stages of Political Development* (New York: Alfred A. Knopf, 1967). The four stages are "primitive unification," "industrialization," "national welfare," and "abundance."

are abstracted may be far too restricted to encompass the varieties of political innovation found in widely differing societies at different time periods. Again, there may be a tendency to reify abstract models of institutional and social change in totally different circumstances, with profoundly unhistorical results. More specifically, even within areas of relatively equal socioeconomic and technological development (such as Western Europe), political systems have diverged greatly at any given point in time; for example, there is obviously no immediate correlation between economic level and democratic stability. Furthermore, attention to chronological developments within a particular nation may result in artificial periodization of complex changes which occur simultaneously and gradually rather than sequentially or abruptly. In his article on "The French Experience of Modernization," for example, Bernard Brown criticizes several recent studies of French development (including those of Black and Huntington) on grounds that they oversimplify the complexity of modernization by imposing overly rigid periodization schemes which misrepresent the essential continuity of political and social change.

Brown's reservations about stage analysis serve as a warning that sequential models of development must be handled carefully if they are to withstand the test of historical verification. But they do not vitiate all periodization scales or concepts of sequential change. There would be no modernization and development theory without some idea of sequential order. What must be avoided, as Brown indicates, is overly rigid distinctions between "traditional" and "modern" features, and all that this implies. The same point has been made by Almond in regard to what he calls the "dualism" of all political systems and cultures—they are all partially mixed in terms of traditionality and modernity.[31] Careful attention must therefore be paid to subtle transitional processes which rarely result in sudden "qualitative" transformations. Even transition points as dramatic as the French and Russian revolutions reflect broad continuities of experience.

Perhaps the most useful method of reconciling general theory and historical experience, then, is to concentrate on frequently observed crises of development and their relationships to the broader processes of modernization. That is, if political development cannot be reduced to clearcut evolutionary stages, we can nevertheless focus on certain critical situations which result from the accumulation of development problems requiring systemic changes such as those discussed by Almond. He points out that the general characteristics of political systems depend a great deal on the manner in which problems of acquiring new performance capabilities are confronted and resolved. Where these problems are solved sequentially and incrementally, as in Britain, development crises may be minimized and

---

[31]Almond and Coleman, *op. cit.*, pp. 20-25. Cf. Pye and Verba, *op. cit.*, pp. 19-21.

system adaptation may proceed with relative stability. But if the different problems are allowed to accumulate, or are confronted simultaneously because of delayed pressures for rapid modernization, severe crises may ensue from the clustering of multiple adaptation difficulties which feed upon each other.[32]

In general, it may be hypothesized that if national integration (or formation of a national identity) precedes the institutionalization of specialized and centralized governmental structures, and if this in turn pre-dates the formation of organized partisan groups and extension of mass participation, the chances for stable democratic development are greatest.[33] Conversely, and more typically, where these developments coincide in time or are forced at a rapid rate, the system may be "overloaded" (cf. Huntington's "decay") and authoritarian responses to resulting tensions are likely. Thus as Almond indicates, much of recent German and Italian history can be explained by the fact that late unification forced these systems to confront the problems of international accommodation and national integration in the latter part of the 19th century, at the same time as pressures for popular participation and national welfare distribution arose. The unsolved problem of national identity blocked resolution of the latter problems and resulted in severe political crises which contributed much to the failure of democratic regimes after World War I and consequently to the rise of Nazism and Fascism.

The *timing, sequence,* and *intensity* of modernization pressures are thus crucial factors in the explanation of development crises. On the whole, the intensity and contiguity of such pressures have increased greatly over the past century and continue to accelerate in newly developing nations today. The rate of expected change now far exceeds the capabilities of most emerging nations. Yet the scope of these problems is not entirely unprecedented, nor do quantitative differences in the contemporary Third World necessarily amount to qualitative ones. Much of the difference between past and present patterns of modernization lies in the timing and rates of change.

In the first article in Section B, "Political Modernization: America vs. Europe," Huntington expands his concept of institutionalization into a broader theory of political modernization. This, he suggests, involves three

[32]This is generally the approach taken by the Committee on Comparative Politics of the Social Science Research Council which has sponsored a seven-volume series on political development published by Princeton University Press, beginning with Almond and Coleman's *Politics of the Developing Areas* and culminating with Leonard Binder et al.. *Crises and Sequences in Political Development* (1971). See especially the summary chapters by Coleman and Verba in the latter volume. The five crises discussed are identity, legitimacy, penetration, participation, and distribution.

[33]In addition to the chapter by Verba noted in the previous reference, see Eric A. Nordlinger, "Political Development: Time Sequences and Rates of Change," *World Politics* 20 (Apr. 1968), pp. 494-520, which we have drawn upon in this paragraph.

developments: the rationalization of authority, or growth of a single legal and administrative center which exercises sovereignty internally and externally; the differentiation of political functions and specialization of structures; and increased participation by groups and the mass public. Clearly these concepts are closely related to those of Almond.

Not only does structural-functional differentiation reappear as a basic development variable, but Huntington's conception of rationalized authority encompasses most of Almond's integrative and international accommodative capabilities. In the Weberian tradition, however, Huntington gives more attention to the manner in which central authority was institutionalized in the different areas considered. In this respect he differentiates between Continental European, British, and American patterns of institutionalization.

Huntington places the crucial stage of rationalization and differentiation of institutions in the 17th century, some two centuries before the development of mass participation in Europe. It was in this period, he suggests, that the decentralized and diffuse structures of feudalism were broken down by the centralizing absolute monarchies on the Continent, and, after the civil war in Stuart England, by the development of parliamentary sovereignty in Britain. In both cases there was a marked growth in the capabilities of governments and their legal, administrative, and military services which changed essentially feudal polities into modern nation states. Huntington thus argues that the new constitutional and absolute monarchies played a crucial role in adapting traditional institutions to the needs of modernization.

In America, on the other hand, the colonists who came in the early 17th century brought with them older concepts of fundamental or natural law and diffused, unspecialized, and essentially feudalistic authority which were institutionalized in the colonial organs of government and subsequently in the 1789 constitution. In terms of the rationalization or centralization of authority and the differentiation of structures the United States therefore remained less developed, with earlier Tudor theories and practices mixed with more modern participatory attributes. This unique fusion of traditional and modern elements may not be possible elsewhere, since American society itself was already relatively advanced and required no fundamental restructuring to achieve rapid development, but it accounts for many of the basic differences in national politics in this country as opposed to Britain and the rest of Europe over the past three centuries. Huntington is thus able to show how the earlier phases of institutional development affected later stages of modernization quite apart from broader social and economic conditions which are often thought to determine the patterns of institutionalization. In this sense political development again emerges as a relatively independent variable, brought about by essentially political revolutions during the 17th century transition to modern statehood. Bernard Brown takes issue with this approach in the article which follows.

In the case of France, a strong case is made by Professor Brown that modern political development can be traced as far back as the 11th century. Indeed, the feudalization of Gaul which followed the breakup of the Roman Empire already contained important elements of "modernity." Over the following centuries the urbanization and secularization of life gradually eroded feudal institutions and values, culminating in the revival of centralized authority under Louis XIV. Yet if divine-right monarchies accelerated the demise of the feudal nobility, they also sought to retard social modernization and ultimately failed to develop a rational basis for authority. The legitimacy of the Old Regime was thus undermined long before 1789 by Enlightenment ideas of popular sovereignty, and the revolution only completed an extremely long and complicated phase of multi-faceted intellectual and social modernization.

However, the subsequent history of France also illustrates the accumulation of unsolved problems associated with development crises in other parts of Europe. The French Revolution destroyed feudal privileges and legal constraints on social mobility but did not solve the problem of political legitimacy. Despite a rationalized bureaucracy and new legal order, the political community remained fragmented on the question of secularization versus maintenance of clerical prerogatives, as well as over the basic structure of national government. The unresolved question of "the regime" produced frequent political crises through the 19th century and delayed response to further modernization pressures. As Brown indicates, industrialization was itself retarded by the persistence of pre-revolutionary values, though a basis for economic modernization was gradually laid amidst fluctuating government policies. More importantly, however, the delayed timing and fitful pace of French economic development, together with continuing divisions over parliamentary institutions, enormously complicated the emerging problems of mass participation and social welfare reforms throughout the Third Republic (1875-1940). In Almond's terms, France was caught in the grip of cumulative development crises which have continued down to the Fifth Republic.

An important difference in perspective is thus brought out in the contributions by Huntington and Brown. Huntington emphasizes the importance of a relatively brief transitional period in which central institutional patterns were established, while Brown stresses the broader continuities of national experience as well as the general impact of social modernization on political change. Among other things, this raises the question of how revolutionary events are to be interpreted. Few would disagree with Huntington's emphasis on the institutional continuities in the United States following the revolutionary break with England, but more complete breaks with the past such as occurred during the French and Russian Revolutions raise questions about the importance of the initial patterns of institutionalization described in his article. Brown stresses the failure of the French monarchy to establish a lasting basis for authority or to adapt to the pressures of modernization. The collapse of the Old Regime thus reflected growing institutional rigidity or decay which could only be reversed by violent upheaval against the system. The old order was by no means fully liquidated, but the breakthroughs achieved ushered in a new period of transition marked by further changes in the regime in 1830 and 1848. Indeed the entire period of European revolutions between 1789 and 1848 may be regarded as a transitional one in which earlier (but by no means traditional in the medieval sense) legal and administrative patterns were upset by new concerns for national efficiency and development brought about by more educated segments of the population who found no place in the established bureaucratic and aristocratic structure of government. John Gillis has demonstrated that, both in France prior to 1789 and Prussia before the 1848 revolution, substantial elements among the relatively privileged and educated elites joined and led the popular forces for reform out of a sense of frustration with the inflexible and corrupt nature of established administrative services.[34] It must be kept in mind, therefore, that the particular structures of authority and administration established in the earlier phases of nation-building analyzed by Huntington were themselves subject to decay and breakdown in the 18th and 19th centuries as new considerations of national power and efficiency came to the fore.

This does not mean that the basic principles of state sovereignty and centralized administration mentioned by Huntington were changed, but that further rationalization and specialization were necessary throughout later periods of development, even before mass political participation began to place new demands for efficiency and equity on the state. In support of Huntington, the foregoing discussion does suggest that central institutional development was in part an autonomous variable which itself divided the elites and brought about revolutionary changes which cannot be explained in terms of generalized social discontent or class conflict. As Gillis points out, the revolutions of 1848 were in large part fought over political institutional development rather than broader social or economic issues. Pressures for general modernization in society were a factor, but deteriorating social conditions did not in themselves result in upheaval. The disequilibrium between the Old Regime and social modernization described by Brown was no doubt present, but in our opinion the decay or retrogression of central governmental structures contributed more directly to the revolutions which occurred in this period, which preceded general mobilization of the populace. Huntington's analysis, if extended to cover later phases of institutional decay and reform, thus provides a valuable complement to

---

[34]John R. Gillis, "Political Decay and the European Revolutions, 1789-1848," *World Politics* 22 (Apr. 1970), pp. 344-70. This article proved very helpful for the discussion which follows.

broader theories of socio-economic modernization which place primary emphasis on disequilibria between political and social conditions.

The same issue arises in relation to the Russian Revolution, which may be regarded as a delayed consequence of other European revolutions which involved many of the same issues of institutional development. The Russian Empire which had grown up under the Muscovite Czars in the 16th and 17th centuries bore many resemblances to the absolute monarchies of Western Europe. Supreme authority was vested in the Czar (Tsar) by virtue of conquest and divine right, and by the 17th century the traditional landed nobility was decimated and replaced by a new class of state bureaucrats and servitors. During the 18th and 19th centuries official obligations to the state began to be reduced and the more enlightened czars initiated programs of "westernization" to improve the efficiency of administrative and military services. But the new institutional structures—comparable in many ways to the pre-revolutionary, transitional bureaucracies in Western Europe— proved even more resistant to change and reform in the century preceding the Russian Revolution.

Historian Richard Pipes discusses these failures of institutional adaptation in the next selection below. Pipes notes that in the wake of the French Revolution, pressures for political reforms spread to Russia as to other parts of Europe. A process of social emancipation from services required by the state had already begun, and it culminated in the formal abolition of serfdom in 1861. But from then on political development was severely constricted, and in some respects reversed, by reactionary government policies. As the author puts it, "Centuries of treating the country as a 'command' and its inhabitants as servitors had accustomed the government to regard any sign of vitality on the part of its subjects as a threat to its existence."[35] At the same time, however, the Czarist regime committed itself to an accelerating program of westernization in military, industrial, and educational matters. This combination of delayed institutional and social modernization, coupled with rigidly constricted political reforms, alienated major sectors of the traditional elite as well as broader social groups affected by modernization. Pipes thus argues that, "Whether a given country will or will not go Communist (or, for that matter, Fascist) seems ultimately to depend on its capacity to absorb and assimilate the shocks engendered by 'modernization'—in other words, on its vitality." The lack of vitality or adaptive capacity in this case reflected the institutional decay of the bureaucratic oligarchy brought into being during the earlier expansion and consolidation of the empire. Its collapse in World War I left few alternatives to the revolutionary seizure of power by the Bolsheviks.

Imperial Germany, like Russia, also presents a case of delayed

---

[35]Cf. T. H. Rigby, "Traditional, Market, and Organizational Societies in the USSR," *World Politics* 16 (July 1964), pp. 539-557.

industrialization and constricted political development. To be sure, industrial growth began earlier and proceeded much more rapidly in the latter half of the 19th century, and the Prussian civil service was revitalized during and after the unification process culminating in formation of the Second Empire (1871). The new German state, under the aegis of Bismarck, also made various political concessions to the democratic reformers, though the state retained Prussian traditions of bureaucratic rule and was never subject to parliamentary or popular control. Indeed, the prior integration and bureaucratization of Prussia solidified power in the hands of conservative landowning, military, and administrative elites. This pattern of institutionalization, combining traditional status privileges with rationalized administrative services under rigid codes of law, determined the manner in which further social and economic modernization was carried out.

As the German sociologist, Ralf Dahrendorf, indicates in the concluding essay in this section, the development of state capitalism under the Bismarckian oligarchy hampered the formation of an independent middle class, and left Germany with the paradox of a "feudal-industrial society" down to World War I. But, unlike Russia, the upheavals of 1918 failed to destroy the established conservative elites. Dahrendorf thus argues that it was not until the rise of National Socialism that Germany entered the era of modern mass politics—"in its ugliest, totalitarian form"—and that it is only since World War II that German society has finally escaped its autocratic traditions, though only in the west. In East Germany the Communist leadership has established a new social basis for authoritarian rule.

Dahrendorf's essay reminds us of several additional points concerning political modernization. First, it is evident that traditional social forces had considerable staying power when older forms of bureaucratic administration could be adapted to perform new functions such as capital investment in industrialization and provision of minimal social services. The transition to modern statehood in this case stopped short of political democracy despite the growth of mass parties and other organs of representation. The early subjugation of both rural gentry and urban commercial classes to the hereditary Junker nobility allied with the state largely prevented the emergence of an autonomous bourgeoisie. The middle classes absorbed hierarchical values and ultimately rallied to conservative elites against the lower strata, thus subordinating their own interests to reactionary forces while helping to isolate the growing industrial working class from effective political involvement.[36] We shall discuss the malintegration of the lower

---

[36]On the pattern of "conservative modernization" in Germany and emergence of a "fascist" class alliance of aristocracy and bourgeoisie, see Moore, *op. cit.*, pp. 435-442. From the perspective of comparative social values, see Seymour M. Lipset, *The First New Nation* (New York: Basic Books, 1963), chap. 6, especially pp. 266-78 on Germany; and Talcott Parsons, "Democracy and Social Structure in Pre-Nazi Germany," in Parsons, *Politics and Social Structure* (New York: Free Press, 1969), pp. 65-81.

classes in the section which follows, but it is important to remember that earlier political institutionalization affected the demands of different social classes. Secondly, Dahrendorf reminds us of the crucial role of political leadership. If social forces ultimately shape the broader contours of political modernization, political elites may also mold social institutions to support a particular type of regime. Social engineering from above characterized both Bismarckian Germany and the new regimes established after World War II. In a more general sense, however, the particular structure and orientation of elites is an independent variable throughout the development process. Finally, Dahrendorf emphasizes that the process of nation-building is still going on in the two halves of Germany, and the same must be said of other Western societies. Not only the threats to national security which continued after 1945, but the tensions generated by socio-economic and technological modernization, have deeply influenced further political developments.

Thus far, however, we have concentrated on the earlier phases of institutionalization and reform which established pre-democratic structures. With some exceptions (notably the United States), political development prior to the latter half of the nineteenth century involved the centralization and rationalization of authority, accompanied by growing specialization in the functions and services of the state. In Russia the transitional bureaucratic structures proved so brittle that the system collapsed entirely; in Germany such institutions were adapted to modern functions while preserving the interests of traditional elites against the rising industrial classes; in France a series of revolutions culminated in parliamentary government in 1875 but traditional values and political cleavages continued to slow modernization. In the United States the civil war was fought in part over the legitimacy of central political authority, and rapid industrialization followed in the last decades of the century. In Britain and in some of the smaller European democracies political development was more orderly and evolutionary, though rarely without some violent disruptions.

If critical changes in the structure and operation of governments took place before the era of mass political involvement, the transition to mass participation in the late 19th and early 20th centuries marks a further stage of development. At this point the effects of social modernization, especially industrialization, were felt everywhere in Europe and led to wholly new demands for legal, political, and social rights on behalf of the lower classes. Insofar as all modern politics involves mobilization of human and material resources on an unprecedented scale, the manner in which the participation crisis was handled in different countries had profound effects on the further course of development. We have already indicated that in Russia and Germany mass participation was delayed until the imperial regimes were destroyed in World War I, with immense consequences for the types of mobilization which followed. Elsewhere mass participation was achieved through the organization of new political parties and social groups which attained representation and integration in the state. But the struggle for citizenship rights was difficult and requires more detailed scrutiny in the section which follows.

C. THE EMERGENCE OF MASS POLITICS

It is well to recall Huntington's statement that "participation distinguishes modern politics from traditional politics." The changes involved in democratization or in the establishment of totalitarian regimes of controlled participation are most fundamental and far-reaching. The traditional associational ties and basic social perspectives of millions of individuals must be altered as they are transformed into active citizens or mobilized subjects. New, more specialized decision-making procedures must be added to pre-existing or revolutionary executive organs. The general process of political integration takes on a new dimension as state and society are bound together by innumerable reciprocal linkages. The effectiveness of these linkages and the directional flow of political influence depend of course on the particular type of regime which emerges. Nonetheless, the sheer force of mass involvement and interpenetration of government and society presents many common problems in the modern participatory state.

In its broadest outlines, mass participation has taken one of two general forms: either it has provided some basis for the representation of pluralistic social interests through free elections, competitive parties, and responsible legislative bodies; or it has been controlled from above by essentially autonomous political elites through plebiscitary election techniques, manipulated mass organizations, and more or less rigid suppression of political opposition to state policies. This familiar distinction between democratic and authoritarian regimes pre-dates the establishment of totalitarian states in the 20th century, though Communism and Fascism completed the breach and developed entirely novel technologies for social mobilization and control; indeed the Stalinist and Hitlerian regimes were the first to achieve relatively total mobilization of society.[37] In this connection it is vital to understand that totalitarianism is a modern response to the potentials of mass participation, which was rendered possible by earlier forms of mobilization. Totalitarianism has thus been characterized as a

[37]The classic works on the novelty of totalitarianism are Hannah Arendt, *The Origins of Totalitarianism*. 3d ed. (New York: Harcourt, Brace & World, 1966); and Carl J. Friedrich and Zbigniew K. Brzezinski, *Totalitarian Dictatorship and Autocracy*. rev. ed. (Cambridge: Harvard University Press, 1965).

"post-democratic" phenomenon, reaching its full expression in the 1930s in the wake of both mobilization potentials demonstrated by democratic systems and the breakdown or decay of many of these systems.[38] But the polarization between democratic and totalitarian views of government since the 1930s conceals many earlier variations in system adaptation as well as general similarities in the transition to mass politics.

Hans Daalder discusses several specific variables which affected the style of participatory adaptation in Western European countries. Again, the previous course of political development is a crucial factor, especially what he refers to as the "earlier elite setting." By the 18th century, he argues, a fundamental division had appeared between those societies which had hardened along autocratic lines and those which had gradually come to accept the representation in government of plural interests. These basic differences had profound effects on the subsequent role of elites. In some countries (Britain, Sweden, the Netherlands, Switzerland) political competition among elite groups in parliamentary or conciliar government organs long preceded demands for mass participation and provided a basis for initial partisan organization. These proto-parties stimulated wider political activity and led to elite acceptance of partisan competition and voluntary extension of the suffrage during the 19th century. Where such traditions were lacking at the elite level, as in France and Germany, the transition to democratic politics was much more difficult. Traditional elites sought to maintain power through the influence of non-representative institutions (the church, army, state bureaucracy, or business) and diffuse conservative movements (clericalism, militarism, nationalism). Or, if political concessions were made, they might be nullified by the subordination of representative bodies to independent executive cabals and bureaucratic agencies, by manipulation of the franchise, and by police harrassment of opposition groups (as in Imperial Germany and Russia). The behavior of elites in turn affected the actions of other social groups.

In general, the 19th century brought the European middle classes and subsequently the industrial working force to socio-economic positions requiring political influence. The manner in which traditional elites responded to the mobilization of the middle sectors affected their attitudes toward further extension of democratic rights to the lower classes. Where the new business and commercial groups gradually achieved political as well as economic power (as in Britain) they tended to accept representation of the lower strata; the working class in turn then found it easier to adapt to established forms of parliamentary politics. In France and Germany, on the other hand, the grudging acceptance of bourgeois influence by aristocratic

[38]Friedrich and Brzezinski, pp. 25-26; and William Kornhauser, *The Politics of Mass Society* (New York: Free Press of Glencoe, 1959), *passim.*

elites undermined the security of the middle classes and produced deeply negative reactions to further sharing of power with the laboring classes. In Germany the middle class remained dependent on state policies and allied with traditional elites against effective working-class participation, while in France the commercial bourgeoisie and independent farmers reacted against all concentrations of power in representative bodies and labor organizations.

Like previous contributors, Daalder points out that the general timing and pace of modernization (especially industrialization) affected the problem of entry for new social groups. While the Industrial Revolution produced massive dislocations and new political alignments everywhere in Europe, the effects upon specific social groups varied greatly. Some social groups declined or grew in influence more rapidly than others. Where industrialization was relatively late or restricted to particular economic or geographical sectors (as in the industrial belt around Paris and in the northern parts of France), great disparities developed between the prevailing style of national politics and the specific demands of different socio-economic groups and sectional interests. In France the continuing predominance of traditional family businesses, small shopkeepers and farmers, and local provincial elites in parliament resulted in an enormous political lag in the representation of new industrial interests. Despite universal suffrage, therefore, French labor leaders and socialist intellectuals were deeply alienated from the parliamentary game of politics.

These factors affected not only the pattern of class relationships, but the entire nature of the party systems which emerged and the broader social cleavages they reflected. Daalder reminds us that party representation is only one mode of political influence and that the "reach" and "permeation" of parties depended upon their relationship to other political organizations. Where traditional political elites resisted incorporation into the party system or sought to undermine it through reactionary counter-movements, the development of responsible party government was delayed. The relative power of pre-democratic bureaucratic or administrative officials also determined the effective control over policymaking that partisan leaders were able to attain through parliamentary channels. Such counter-pressures thus affected the degree to which parties succeeded in achieving effective political integration for their respective clienteles. Many social, religious, and sectional groups were only partially or weakly incorporated in national political life through ineffectual party organizations and others remained essentially outside the political system. In addition to the question of relative access of different major interests to government, there was the problem of persisting local isolation in small towns and rural areas. Parties tended to develop at the political center (the capital and other large cities where population was concentrated) and gradually expand to regional and local peripheries. The extent to which national parties penetrated to the grass roots of local politics thus varied considerably.[39]

When viewed from the perspective of elite/mass and center/local integration, the number of parties in the system is less important than the degree to which diverse outgroups achieved effective access to national political life. Whether new social groups and interests formed separate parties or sought representation through existing organizations or broader alliances depended a great deal on specific circumstances (see discussion below). While in some cases extreme fragmentation of partisan activity no doubt weakened the representation of all sectors, no categorical statement can be made about the relative effectiveness of two-party versus multiparty systems. As Daalder indicates, multiple parties can either isolate or integrate social groups depending upon the relationship of their leaders to other political elites and the responsiveness of the rest of the system to their demands. Moreover, as will be seen later, the nature and depth of underlying social cleavages required different types of partisan alignments at the mass membership level.

As Stein Rokkan puts it in the second article, "The twin processes of urbanization and industrialization have tended to increase the comparability of occupational structures across the nations but have not produced anything approaching uniformity in the *structures of political alternatives* confronting the citizens of different polities." What is needed therefore is more detailed historical study to determine the configuration of factors present in each nation which shaped the emergence of partisan alignments. How were social cleavages translated into parties and voting alignments, and how was the sequence of institutional developments in each country related to these divisions? In the essay below, Rokkan constructs a precise historical-configurational typology of institutional reforms and their relationship to the structuring of electoral politics in eleven of the smaller countries of Western Europe.[40] These nations have much in common: besides being smaller than the major powers usually studied, they all have long parliamentary traditions, all developed multiparty systems representing

---

[39]For a discussion of center/periphery relations and the lag in rural mobilization in Norway, see Stein Rokkan, "Electoral Mobilization, Party Competition, and National Integration," in Joseph LaPalombara and Myron Weiner, eds., *Political Parties and Political Development* (Princeton: Princeton University Press, 1966), pp. 241-65; also chaps. 6-7 in Rokkan, *Citizens, Elections, Parties* (New York: David McKay Co., 1970).

[40]In the remainder of the article not reprinted here, Rokkan constructs a second, complementary typology for the timing and nature of social cleavage "inputs" which developed in these countries, to be related in further research to the institutional "output" typology discussed here. For a more detailed elaboration, incorporating some sophisticated Parsonian theory, see S. M. Lipset and S. Rokkan, "Cleavage Structures, Party Systems, and Voter Alignments," in their jointly edited volume, *Party Systems and Voter Alignments: Cross-National Perspectives* (New York: Free Press, 1967), pp. 1-64; and Rokkan, *Citizens, Elections, Parties,* chap. 3.

diverse social and cultural groups, and all introduced mass suffrage and election systems based on proportional representation (PR) by the 1920s. That they followed somewhat different paths of development from those of the larger nations is thus a crucial historical fact; yet they too produced different partisan choices or electoral alternatives for their respective populations.

Without entering into detailed discussion of Rokkan's typology—which covers a broad range of variables from medieval traditions to the international status of emerging states—it should be noted that Rokkan suggests that the process of democratization required the surmounting of four institutional thresholds: legitimation of dissent and opposition; incorporation of opposition groups through extension of the suffrage; representation of new groups through parties and in the legislature; and finally the attainment of actual executive power by these groups and hence of full majority rule. Each of these changes involved a lowering of barriers to mass participation and influence, and the multiple problems encountered affected the timing and sequence of institutional reforms. In general, the manner in which the first two barriers (legitimation of opposition and extension of the vote) were crossed established the opportunities for parliamentary representation and party government. The way in which the vote was extended had especially important consequences for the type of partisan activity which developed. The smaller nations fell along a continuum in this respect between the British model of gradual, step-by-step expansion of citizenship rights and the French pattern of sudden mass enfranchisement (in 1848) followed by plebiscitarian elections and reversals of voting privileges. But nowhere did formal equality in electoral participation lead automatically to effective political representation, and in many cases enfranchisement of the rural population increased the hold of conservative forces on government.[41]

What is particularly significant in the smaller democracies is the manner in which election systems were altered in the later stages of mass mobilization in order to provide proportional representation of all partisan interests. Rokkan traces this development and offers a number of hypotheses as to why this type of representation was more readily adaptable to small systems than in the larger European nations. In some cases (the Netherlands, Belgium, Austria, Switzerland) these societies were so deeply segmented into ethnic-linguistic-religious communities that parliamentary accommodation perhaps demanded mechanical safeguards for minority representation, but the universal adoption of proportional representation in the eleven nations after 1890 suggests deeper psychological motives among partisan elites

---

[41] See Bendix and Rokkan's "The Extension of Citizenship to the Lower Classes," in Reinhard Bendix, *Nation-Building and Citizenship* (Garden City: Doubleday Anchor Books, 1969), pp. 89-126; and T. H. Marshall's classic study of British citizenship, "Citizenship and Social Class," in *Class, Citizenship, and Social Development: Essays by T. H. Marshall*, Intro. S. M. Lipset (Garden City: Doubleday Anchor Books, 1965), pp. 71-134.

operating in the context of limited national resources in smaller states. In any event, the general effect of partisan accommodation through PR between 1890 and 1920 was to freeze the party alternatives which had emerged at this stage in the development of parliamentary representation. While helping to stabilize political development at this critical juncture, proportional representation also tended to maintain existing subcultural cleavages and to "ossify" the electoral choices available to different segments of the population.

But the stability of these systems depended ultimately on the opportunities for parties to convert electoral votes and parliamentary seats into effective control over executive organs. Much depended here on specific constitutional reforms which came at different stages of mass mobilization and party formation. In some cases (Belgium, Holland) cabinet responsibility to parliamentary majorities was established early, as in Britain (after 1832); in others parliamentary control was delayed until long after suffrage was broadened, as in Germany (after 1918); and in still others responsible party government followed quickly upon the expansion of citizenship rights and adoption of PR in the early 20th century. All had responsible cabinet executives by 1920, requiring in theory the support of a numerical parliamentary majority (except in Switzerland where minority parties were also given a share of government posts). In practice, however, these countries maintained multiparty systems of various types which necessitated coalition governments of sub-majoritarian parties through most of their subsequent histories. The success of these "bargaining partnerships" depended on the size and distribution of partisan configurations established by PR as well as deeper political cultural factors.[42] In general (with the notable exception of Austria, which hovered on the brink of civil war in the 1930s) the record of political stability and achievement of social justice in these countries has been better than that of the larger industrial nations.

The analyses of Daalder and Rokkan indicate the complex interactions of socio-economic, cultural, and institutional factors which established widely different bases for political participation in European nations. At this point we might summarize some of the key variables which appeared to affect the transition to mass participation most directly:

A.   Factors present before mass mobilization
     1.   Degree of political centralization under pre-democratic authorities (monarchies, parliaments, administrative bureaucracies, etc.)
     2.   Attitudes of traditional elites toward political competition and popular involvement

---

[42]See Robert A. Dahl, ed., *Political Oppositions in Western Democracies* (New Haven: Yale University Press, 1966), which includes chapters on Belgium, the Netherlands, and Austria as well as several other countries.

      3. Pre-existing social cleavages (religious, cultural, regional, economic, etc.)

B. The dynamics of mobilization

      4. Speed and timing of industrialization

      5. How traditional and newer cleavages were translated into party organizational alignments

      6. How and in what form voting and other citizenship rights were extended to the mass population

C. Institutionalized results

      7. Range of electoral choices open to voters and relative integration of different groups

      8. Degree of control by parliamentary parties over executive organs and policy-making

      9. Success in achieving social justice or other indicators of effective representation

    10. Relative stability or instability

This list does not include all possible factors affecting development (e.g., wars and other international events, as well as imponderables such as the skill of individual leaders), nor does stability inevitably result from equitable group representation and social welfare. But in European historical experience it appears to encompass the principal conditions and criteria for development during the transition to mass participation.

In this connection, brief reference might also be made to the United States. As noted earlier by several authors (Almond, Huntington, Daalder), the general pattern of political development was markedly different than in Europe. Not only was institutional theory and practice different from the beginning (Huntington), but problems of internal mobilization and international security were greatly mitigated by American isolation and domestic social opportunities (Almond). But perhaps the most distinctive feature of American development was the general absence of elite resistance to mass participation and the early expansion of mass suffrage (to adult white males in most states by the 1830s). As Daalder points out, representative government and mass suffrage preceded urbanization and the formation of an industrial working class—a sequence repeated nowhere in Europe (Switzerland perhaps came closest, but its form of cantonal representation and collegial executive were equally unique). Nowhere were parties formed earlier on a popular basis, or so directly responsible for electing officials at all levels. As Huntington put it, in Europe electoral rights were extended to groups of people or social strata, whereas in the U.S. the vote was extended to new elective offices and institutions. At the same time, the electoral functions of American parties reflected the more limited role they played as agents of social integration and fundamental sources of change. With some notable exceptions, new social classes and minority groups were easily incorporated by the loose two-party systems which emerged in the 1790s,

1830s, and 1860s. The absorption of the new industrial working class by mass parties already established on a diverse agrarian and urban capitalist base was entirely unique, as was the initial emergence of parties as electoral institutions prior to 1800.[43] After the Civil War national integration proceeded gradually through sectional alliances among regional party leaders and interests (Northern and Southern Democrats, big business and small farmers, Eastern capital and Western mining and ranching interests, etc.) and through the unifying impact of national presidential elections. Indeed from the beginning mass political mobilization involved the periodic formation of coalitions to win the presidency.

With the exception of the battles fought between sectional interests in the Civil War, the issues dividing American parties were thus of a lesser magnitude than those in Europe. On the Continent, and to a lesser extent in Britain, the partisan competition of the late 19th century raised fundamental questions of citizenship rights and social justice for different sectors of the population. As often as not, parties were formed to win political access rather than to defend established interests. In this light two questions are of paramount importance: what were the alternative ways in which parties could organize their constituents vis-à-vis the established elites and the state? And under what conditions did mass party competition result in political decay or the breakdown of democratic institutions and rise of totalitarianism?

The legacy of Marxian sociology has greatly influenced our thinking on these matters. In this essay we have already mentioned the rise of the middle classes and then the working class and their demands for participation, and class analysis of this kind is not without foundation. But organization of parties on the basis of functional economic interests or class consciousness was only one of the options open to partisan leaders and their followers. For one thing, the majority of people were not industrial workers or middle-class entrepreneurs but small farmers or peasants, and rural people have typically been ambiguous about their class interests. Moreover even among urban industrial workers there has been a good deal of schizophrenia between concrete material interests and a broader sense of class solidarity or consciousness. Thus, as Val Lorwin has pointed out elsewhere, there were at least three basic alternatives:[44]

> When, in the nineteenth century, European workers, peasants, and lower-middle-class elements began to organize for representation of their group interests, they had the choice of three basic frameworks: that of an existing

[43]Lipset, *The First New Nation*, chaps. 1 and 2; and William N. Chambers, "Parties and Nation-Building in America," in LaPalombara and Weiner, *Political Parties and Political Development* pp. 79-106. For a differing viewpoint see Moore, *Social Origins of Dictatorship and Democracy*, chap. 3, "The American Civil War: The Last Capitalist Revolution."

[44]Lorwin, "Segmented Pluralism: Ideological Cleavages and Political Cohesion in the Smaller European Democracies," *Comparative Politics* 3 (Jan. 1971), p. 145.

framework of religious organization, the 'functional' framework of socio-economic interests alone, or that offered by some form of the new doctrines and organization of socialism. Politically, the most important organizations were to be those of peasants and of workers, the latter being the more important, because they were a growing class, more dynamic and more open to conflicting appeals.

The organizational framework chosen depended on a number of factors, including the nature and strength of pre-existing social and religious cleavages, the response of the established regime to new demands, and the availability of new functional interest organizations to articulate these demands.

Where religious cleavages or the position of the church were particularly strong, religious organizations provided a ready basis for political mobilization. In most of the countries of northern and central Europe, religion combined with agrarian and small town interests in the formation of mass peasant parties in the latter half of the 19th century. In other cases where one church was dominant (notably the Catholic Church in France and Italy) mobilization of the faithful through religious organizations was complicated by the quasi-official status of the church and the question of clerical influence in the state, which split the religious base into conservative-clerical and liberal or socialist anti-clerical fragments. Where this happened the working class, especially, was drawn toward an ideological form of socialism. But only in very few cases—notably Britain and the United States—did religion not come to account for major political cleavages (and, even in these cases, religious associations have significantly influenced partisan preferences).[45]

The response of established elites toward new political organizations deeply affected partisan goals and ideologies. As Bendix and Rokkan have pointed out, the most fundamental political right (as a precondition for all others) is the right to associate and combine for political ends.[46] The extent to which organizations such as trade unions and parties were legally permitted to function was a crucial variable. In at least one instance (Czarist Russia) the basic right of association was never fully granted, and in another (Imperial Germany) the new workers' organizations were suppressed or harrassed by the police and then entitled to function within carefully circumscribed limits. In both cases partisan activity was submerged in a welter of legal and bureaucratic controls, resulting in what Otto Kirchheimer has called fundamental "opposition of principle" on the part of emerging partisan organizations; that is, party leaders came to demand the overthrow

---

[45]See Richard Rose and Derek Urwin, "Social Cohesion, Political Parties and Strains in Regimes," *Comparative Political Studies* 2 (Apr. 1969), pp. 7-67, for statistical evidence on the continuing influence of religion on party cohesion.

[46]Bendix, *Nation-Building and Citizenship.* pp. 96-105.

of the political regime itself.[47] In other instances restrictions on interest group and party organization were minimal (United States) or went unenforced until repealed at the time that mass parties began to organize (the British Combination Laws), and little opposition to the basic constitutional order developed. Other countries fell in between, with what Rokkan calls the legitimation of opposition being a significant barrier to be crossed in early organizational efforts.

The number of parties which emerged in any given system was more a consequence of such institutional variables than of the inherent diversity of interests in different societies. Two-party competitive systems developed in the United States and Britain (and then only in certain periods and, in the U.S., in states where neither party was dominant).[48] Multiparty systems were the rule elsewhere, and these may be divided into three general types:

1. *Ideologically fragmented* systems (as in France, Germany, and Italy). In these systems multiple cleavages—religious, economic, regional, and constitutional—were on the whole translated into ideologically rigid parties. Some parties, notably the Socialists, sought to isolate their constituents from other groups and called for revolutionary changes in the regime (although generally willing to collaborate with government on specific reforms and in times of national crisis). Other parties, especially the various liberal groups, were loose associations of local, parliamentary, and intellectual notables which had little permanent organization but expressed dogmatic ideological positions on many issues. The interest groups affiliated with parties tended to be weak or divided among different partisan camps, though in Germany the socialist labor unions became a strong arm of the party (see below). Party coalitions at the parliamentary and cabinet level (whether in control of government or not) were usually temporary and unstable, giving particular advantage to center groups which most easily allied with other parties. Political instability contributed to the growth of movements expressing opposition of principle (the Nazis and Communists in Germany, the Fascists and Communists in Italy, and the Communists and various semi-fascist groups in France).[49]

2. *Culturally segmented* systems. In several of the smaller democracies described by Rokkan and Daalder (the Netherlands, Belgium, Switzerland, and Austria) parties came to be divided on the basis of what has

[47]Otto Kirchheimer, "The Waning of Opposition in Parliamentary Regimes," *Social Research* 24 (Summer 1957), pp. 127-56.

[48]See Dahl, *op. cit.*, 333ff.

[49]The best discussion of party systems of this type is found in Sigmund Neumann, ed., *Modern Political Parties* (Chicago: University of Chicago Press, 1955), especially in Neumann's chapter on Germany and in his classification of parties at pp. 400ff. See also Dahl, chaps. 7, 9, 10 and conclusions.

been called "segmented pluralism." In this case religious organization provided the most important vehicle for mobilization, but economic, regional, and in some countries ethnic-linguistic differences also contributed to the hardening of lines between subcultural groupings within the basic political-religious framework. The result was typically the emergence of several cohesive subcultural blocs or "pillars" (vertical organizational networks), within which multiple political and social organizations were formed—not only political parties, but separate labor and farmers' organizations, cultural associations, schools, communications media, and so on. Although each bloc developed a distinctive political and cultural ideology, and insulated its members from broader social contacts with other pillars, the parties established working coalitions in parliament through which leaders representing all major segments of society were able to bargain for mutually acceptable policies. This type of system in which stability was possible through inter-elite collaboration despite segmented social life has been termed "consociational."[50]

3. *Functionally integrated* systems. As the term is used here, we have in mind multiparty systems which on the whole came to reflect the major socio-economic or functional interests in society (as in the Scandinavian countries). Religious cleavages were less important than in the aforementioned systems, and parties developed close linkages to the major economic organizations and interests which supported them (farmers, business, labor, and professional groups). The interest groups were well organized and gradually extended across partisan lines so that parties were not confined to narrow segments of the population. Although radical socialist movements threatened to develop in the early part of this century (and a large Communist party eventually emerged in Finland), bargaining relationships with corporate interest groups had the effect of moderating ideological appeals. Moderate socialist parties gradually achieved predominance and were able to consolidate reforms which came to be associated with the Welfare State in Europe.[51]

Thus far we have said relatively little about the role of associational groups other than parties in the development process. Certainly the early growth of voluntary associations and organized interest groups in the United States facilitated the development of loosely aggregative parties and direct

---

[50]See Lorwin, "Segmented Pluralism"; and Arend Lijphart, "Consociational Democracy," *World Politics* 21 (Jan. 1969), pp. 207-255. This type of system is discussed further in Section D below.

[51]See Dankwart A. Rustow, "Scandinavia: Working Multiparty Systems," in Neumann, *op. cit.*, pp. 169-93. Cf. Lijphart's typology of democratic systems—distinguishing "centrifugal," "consociational," and "centripital" types—in "Typologies of Democratic Systems," *Comparative Political Studies* 1 (Apr. 1968), p. 31.

representation of economic interests in legislative decision-making. In Europe the development of interest group infrastructures was generally slower and encountered greater obstacles in gaining direct political influence. Organized interests were more closely tied to party government, and, indeed, were themselves responsible for the initial formation of new parties in some cases. As the analysis above suggests, the nature of linkages between interest groups and parties was an important intervening variable in the type of socio-political mobilization achieved. This was particularly true in the mobilization of the European working classes, which gave rise to the first large-scale associational groups (trade unions) as well as the first highly organized mass parties.

In the third article below, Arnold Heidenheimer indicates how specific circumstances in the formative period of trade union organization in Britain and Germany (1890-1914) affected the basic relations between unions and parties and the consequent style of mobilization which these parties achieved. The relative timing and sequence of party formation, union organization and growth, and state social reforms was important in shaping labor strategies and options. In Britain, localized Friendly Societies were established to provide minimal health insurance benefits for workers before national trade unions gained full rights of organization (1871-1875). Unions in turn developed on a decentralized basis before the bulk of the working class was granted the right to vote (1884), and attained sizable memberships before they joined a variety of socialist societies and other groups to form the Labour Party (1900-1906). As Heidenheimer suggests, these circumstances favored loose organization within the labor movement and a bifurcated concern between local collective bargaining and partisan legislative strategies at the national parliamentary level. Passage of the National Insurance Act in 1911 generally reduced the role of labor organizations in providing primary social security benefits for their memberships, thus further eliminating a potential source of partisan recruitment through what Heidenheimer calls "exclusive" services.

In Germany, on the other hand, the sequence was almost the reverse. Electoral rights (however circumscribed and ineffective in practice) were granted to the working classes at the outset of the Bismarckian Empire, resulting in formal organization of the Social Democratic Party (SPD) in 1875. After abortive attempts to suppress the socialist movement, Bismarck sought to deflect its growth by passage of the first compulsory state social insurance program in Europe (1883-1885). This early "collectivization of welfare" under state agencies (Sickness Funds) influenced the subsequent role of trade unions. After relatively slow growth up to 1900 (some 600,000 members compared to over two million in Britain), the German unions adopted a strategy of recruitment based on competition with the Sickness Funds in the provision of primary social insurance benefits. This preoccupation of union leaders, together with rapid expansion of membership and finances during 1900-1912, affected the basic structure of the unions as well as their role in mobilizing workers for the Social Democratic Party. Thus both British and German unions played an important part in the induction of new recruits into political parties and political life generally. However, the mobilization styles were quite different, with far-reaching effects on the type of integration achieved and the subsequent nature of these parties. In Britain unionists were drawn into the Labour Party more on the basis of collective legislative goals than by promises of exclusive union benefits, and the relations between local union action (such as shop-floor bargaining or strikes) and the national party remained relatively weak (later producing great resistance of the rank-and-file to Labour Government policies). In Germany the unions themselves became highly centralized and professionalized; in fact the union bureaucracy became a separate pillar in the labor movement alongside the Social Democratic Party (and the State Funds as well, once unions had organized to control their supervisory boards). Insofar as the unions served to recruit members for the SPD (close links were established at the national level), this partisan recruitment was heavily rooted in union provision of exclusive benefits rather than in broader legislative and ideological goals. As a result, recruitment to the SPD was greatest among the wealthier craft unions most successful in raising dues and providing insurance benefits, while the weaker unions in lower industrial occupations were less likely to provide a conveyor belt to the SPD. Not only were the lower working strata poorly represented in the party, but the SPD-union bureaucracy became increasingly oriented toward exploitation of narrow interests and protection of the status of better-off workers against both the middle classes and the lower proletariat (while at the same time maintaining ideological opposition toward other parties and the political system generally).[52]

In broader perspective, it has been argued that the authoritarian nature of the Imperial Government and the limited sphere of permissable labor activities resulted in the development of a German working-class subculture which was only partially or "negatively" integrated into the political and social system.[53] The working classes remained in relative isolation (while sharing in certain economic benefits) until the establishment of the Weimar

[52]Cf. Lipset's statement in *The First New Nation* (p. 333): "The split within the working class between Socialists and Communists in Weimar Germany was also partly due to this status consciousness of the skilled workers in the Social-Democratic Party, who left the more depressed sector to be recruited by the Communists. Robert Michels has pointed out how their sense of superiority was reflected in party literature, which attacked the Communists by arguing that their supporters were largely the shiftless *Lumpenproletariat*." For the classic statement on bureaucratization in the German labor movement and SPD ("the iron law of oligarchy"), see Michels, *Political Parties*, 1915 (various recent editions).

[53]Guenther Roth, *The Social Democrats in Imperial Germany: A Study in Working-Class Isolation and National Integration* (Totowa, N.J.: Bedminster Press, 1963), esp. pp. 315-16.

Republic in 1919. But negative, defensive attitudes had inhibited the development of positive reform programs and politically experienced leadership capable of working compromises with other parties in the 1920s. In Southern Europe labor movements were denied effective access to national government even longer, provoking more complete isolation and alienation of socialist countercultures (as in France, where a large Communist Party absorbed most industrial workers and where effective access might be dated at the formation of the Popular Front government in 1936). In general, however, malintegration of the lower classes exacerbated social tensions and contributed to the turbulent conditions producing both Communist and Fascist movements in the interwar period.[54]

Much has been written about the origins of totalitarian movements in efforts to determine universal causes for their development. However, with greater historical perspective it appears that no single answer will suffice, that the causes were indeed multiple within individual societies and across national boundaries. Some scholars have sought to relate totalitarian ideologies to earlier utopian philosophies of political equality and direct representation in the state;[55] others have traced such movements to the breakup of the traditional class structure and emergence of "mass society" in the twentieth century;[56] and still others have sought explanations in the psychological traits (authoritarian personality) of people in certain national cultures or socio-economic classes.[57] All of these explanations have relevance, but it is more likely that the configuration of historical circumstances in each society that gave rise to totalitarianism was fundamentally different. The emergence of the Bolsheviks in Russia was the product of an autocratic regime, incessant police repression, failures of economic and political modernization, a disastrous defeat in war, and the ideological leadership of Lenin himself. In this case mass mobilization was carried out only during the civil war and under the political regime which followed. In Germany the specific causes of the Nazi (and Communist) movements were equally diverse: the psychology of defeat following World War I, a disastrous and worsening economic situation, partisan and ideological hostility among the new parliamentary leaders, an unworkable constitutional system, the growing insecurity of all economic class interests, and a leader who succeeded in mobilizing national fears and prejudices. In Italy Mussolini's 1922 march on Rome occurred amidst political chaos following an indecisive war effort and polarization among groups contending for influence in an unrepresentative constitutional monarchy; the Fascist appeal for national unity and order was perhaps paramount.

[54]S. M. Lipset, *Political Man* (New York: Doubleday & Co., 1960), chaps. 4-5.
[55]J. L. Talmon, *The Origins of Totalitarian Democracy* (New York: Frederick A. Praeger, 1960).
[56]Arendt, *op. cit.;* Kornhauser, *op. cit.*
[57]Theodore Adorno et al., *The Authoritarian Personality* (New York: Harper & Bros., 1950); and Lipset, *Political Man,* chaps. 4-5.

With this said, it is nevertheless evident that totalitarian opposition of principle reflected failures of adaptation in the relevant political systems, particularly the failure to integrate groups effectively in the transition to modern mass politics. In Russia only feeble attempts were made to represent the interests of diverse groups (e.g., in the parliamentary Duma after 1905), and the general rights of opposition and participation were never fully granted. In Germany the breakdown must be traced in part to the failure to allow effective representation through the Reichstag before 1919 and to the fragmentation of partisan and group interests brought about by the authoritarian controls of the Imperial Regime; partisan hostilities as well as the traditional autonomy of bureaucratic and official elites carried over into the Weimar Republic. In Italy the transition to representative government had not fully occurred, and both there and in France the lower classes had yet to be integrated into national parliamentary decision-making. Thus failures to achieve mass participation through extension of citizenship rights and new forms of group representation seem to provide one proximate and necessary (if not sufficient) cause for the development of totalitarian forms of mobilization.

Not only the origins (both situational and philosophical), but the ideologies and fundamental goals of the totalitarian regimes were different. In terms of basic values, there is no ready equation between the Marxist drive for socialist reconstruction to achieve a classless society and the Nazi goal of racial superiority and world conquest, although both ideologies demanded international expansion and brought immense human suffering in their wake. The greatest similarities between such regimes lay in the methods used to attain mass political mobilization and controlled participation to further the interests of a supreme leader and elite party.[58] Perhaps the best-known model of totalitarian organization and methods is that of Friedrich and Brzezinski, which includes a syndrome of the six following traits:[59]

1. An elaborate ideology or official body of doctrine calling for radical change in the existing order
2. A single mass party typically led by one man
3. A system of terror, whether physical or psychic, directed against arbitrarily selected classes of the population
4. A near-complete monopoly on the means of mass communication
5. A similar monopoly on all weapons of armed combat
6. Central control and direction of the entire economy.

---

[58]See Leonard Schapiro, "The Concept of Totalitarianism," *Survey* 73 (Autumn 1969); and Herbert Spiro, "Totalitarianism," in *International Encyclopedia of the Social Sciences*, 1968 ed., vol. XVI.

[59]Condensed from Friedrich and Brzezinski, *op. cit.*, p. 22.

Friedrich and Brzezinski emphasize that these methods of control are only feasible in societies characterized by relatively advanced science and technology.

While this model has been widely used to describe the "classic" totalitarian systems (Hitler Germany, Stalinist Russia, and, to a lesser extent, Mussolini's Italy), it has also been criticized in recent years for failing to account for important differences between these regimes as well as their potentials for adaptability and development.[60] In the final selection below, Alexander Groth considers the social bases and organizational reforms of the three regimes, and suggests that the mobilization style in each case was quite different. While similar in general structure and coercive techniques, Groth argues that the internal dynamics and development potentials of these modern dictatorships scarcely justifies a "unitotalitarian" approach. As he puts it, "We need to know the group physiognomy of the regime, its impact upon the group structure of the society it rules, and what sorts of changes capable of influencing the social structure the regime sponsors or fosters." In this perspective, Soviet Russia (and Communist systems generally) differ fundamentally from the defunct Nazi and Fascist systems. While Communist governments have carried out "total" socio-economic revolutions and established entirely new social and elite organizations to support the regime (cf. earlier comments by Dahrendorf), the German and Italian systems were counter-revolutionary in the sense that they were largely built on the pre-existing class and elite structures. Groth suggests that the demands and constraints of the underlying group interests limited the development potentials of these regimes and led to increasing internal instability. While primarily concerned with the impact of social structure on the disintegration of the Hitler and Mussolini regimes during the war, Groth's analysis also raises questions about the effects of continuing social change on the stability of Communist systems.

Whether democratic or totalitarian mobilization ultimately occurred, the transition to mass involvement strengthened the potential capabilities of governments. The resources available for political direction were greatly enlarged as the state penetrated society and vice-versa. Mass participation thus had a dual effect: while it gave citizenship rights and a degree of political equality to the previously excluded masses and opened the way to greater social justice, it also increased the chances for domination of some groups or elites over others. In the case of totalitarian mobilization, control

[60]For a useful critique of both Arendt and Friedrich and Brzezinski, see Robert Burrowes, "Totalitarianism: the Revised Standard Version," *World Politics* 21 (Jan. 1969), pp. 272-294. Revisionist interpretations are given in Chalmers Johnson, ed., *Change in Communist Systems* (Stanford: Stanford University Press, 1970); and Samuel P. Huntington and Clement E. Moore, eds., *Authoritarian Politics in Modern Society: The Dynamics of Established One-Party Systems* (New York: Basic Books, 1970).

by a single party elite reached extreme proportions, but in the democratic countries the stakes of political competition were also raised appreciably as contending parties sought to assert their interests and ideologies. In the interwar period, especially, partisan conflict over social and economic reforms threatened to disrupt the national integration attained by the previous extension of representation. The resulting political instability delayed the potentials for social reform and state planning or regulation into the postwar period in most European countries. The accumulation of unsolved social problems, together with the shocks and hardships of the war itself, led to the postwar "welfare state."

D. SOCIAL CLEAVAGES, PARTY COMPETITION AND GROUP INTERESTS IN THE WELFARE STATE

The major theme of studies on political change in advanced nations since World War II is that they have entered a new phase of politics, often characterized as postindustrial in the sense that political competition no longer reflects the basic cleavages resulting from earlier stages of industrialization and modernization. The working class, in particular, is no longer the driving force in politics, having been integrated into the bargaining processes of the welfare state or having been surpassed in importance by the new white-collar and service strata in advanced societies. New types of integration have been achieved through economic planning and social service bureaucracies, reducing the significance of partisan and parliamentary competition for office. The lines of party conflict have further been blurred by the growing affluence of citizens who react to politics as consumers rather than as producers and whose special interests are increasingly promoted by organized pressure groups and lobbies. Consequently pragmatic bargaining and consensual elections fought through the mass advertising media have come to replace the bitter ideological struggles of the pre-war period.

If this is the conventional wisdom on postwar development in the advanced democratic nations, it has not gone unchallenged in recent years. There has been a flood of radical criticism of the postindustrial convergence theories and of the basic nature of advanced industrial societies themselves.[61]

---

[61]For the radical critique, see especially Herbert Marcuse, *One Dimensional Man* (Boston: Beacon Press, 1964); and Norman Birnbaum, *The Crisis of Industrial Society* (New York: Oxford University Press, 1969). From a more conservative perspective, Raymond Aron attacks convergence theories and the concept of "postindustrial" society in *Industrial Society* (New York: Frederick A. Praeger, 1967), and *Progress and Disillusion: The Dialectics of Modern Society* (New York: Frederick A. Praeger, 1968).

Both political activists of the New Left and social scientists concerned with mounting evidence of persisting inequalities and seemingly insoluble problems have questioned the fundamental premises of the aforementioned thesis. Neo-Marxists deny that the basic social conflicts have ever been resolved and look for new revolutionary changes, while others argue that a host of new problems and issues arose in the 1960s that rendered the previous analysis obsolete. Still others accept the main lines of the argument given above but arrive at different conclusions about its significance—the submergence of traditional kinds of political conflict and older ideological values may be a sign of stasis and decay. Indeed in the new social conditions—with accelerated technological innovation touching every sphere of life, with mass private abundance and deteriorating public environments, and constantly evolving styles of leisure, education, and communication—it is sometimes questionable whether modern political systems are capable of meeting new demands and needs which arise. It is possible that growing lags between social change and political adaptation will yet result in untold crises at the advanced end of the development process, much as in earlier periods when multiple pressures and problems were allowed to accumulate and overload pre-democratic structures.

Whatever outlook one takes, one thing is certain: political change and development has continued into the current period. Social, economic, and technological modernization has, if anything, accelerated in the postwar years, and perpetual change and improvement has come to be expected by increasingly mobile citizenries everywhere. The phenomenon of rising expectations is not confined to the poorer nations, and in advanced societies economic abundance and the public services provided by governments have stimulated new demands for equitable distribution and participation in decision-making. These demands thus reflect both the success of governments in promoting social welfare and new allocational disparities brought about by greatly increased public spending. They also reflect a communications revolution which frequently brings instant awareness of political problems to the electorate and provides new opportunities for mass mobilization and integration. It is this conundrum of expected change, increased awareness, and potential for new types of mobilization which raises once again Huntington's specter of political decay.[62]

---

[62]For a brilliant application of Huntington's theory to contemporary conditions, see Mark Kesselman, "Overinstitutionalization and Political Constraint: The Case of France," *Comparative Politics* 3 (Oct. 1970), pp. 21-44. Kesselman turns Huntington's argument upside down and argues that the problem in advanced societies may be the overinstitutionalization of political organizations inherited from the past.

Modernization, Social Structure, and the Convergence Theory

A good deal has been written about the beneficial impact of economic development on partisan politics. In its most general form, it has been argued by American social scientists that economic growth and modernization tend to provide conditions for stable democratic politics—a more complex economic and social group structure, a larger middle-class and more equitable distribution of income, and new, more rational attitudes toward political competition and reform.[63] This body of theory rests partly on retrospective generalizations deriving from the experience of countries such as the United States and Britain; partly on demonstrable statistical correlations between general levels of socio-economic modernization and gross indicators of democracy and stability; and partly on more elaborate hypotheses concerning the intervening variables through which basic social and economic changes are translated into particular types of organizational and attitudinal patterns which are conducive to democratic political processes.

Political development theories which emphasize the problem of integrating different social groups and classes often imply the attainment of social stability once equal citizenship and mass participation are achieved. The crucial difficulties are seen as developing historically at the points at which new groups gain access to the political system, as in the studies discussed in part C above. But then, as Reinhard Bendix put it in a slightly different context,[64]

> Under these circumstances politics are no longer a struggle over the distribution of the national sovereignty; instead they have tended to become a struggle over the distribution of the national product and hence over the policies guiding the administration of centralized functions.

That is, once political integration is more or less complete, the social pressures which gave rise to radical social movements and class conflicts are progressively dissipated and replaced by what is essentially peaceful economic competition for material benefits in the centralized welfare state.

[63] S. M. Lipset, "Some Social Requisites of Democracy," *American Political Science Review* 53 (Mar. 1959), pp. 69-105; Lipset, *Political Man*, chaps. 2-3; Philips Cutright, "National Political Development: Its Measurement and Social Correlates," in Nelson W. Polsby, Robert A. Dentler, and Paul A. Smith, eds., *Politics and Social Life* (Boston: Houghton-Mifflin, 1963); and James S. Coleman, "Conclusion: the Political Systems of Developing Areas," in Almond and Coleman, *op. cit.*, pp. 538-544 and appendix.

[64] Bendix, "Social Stratification and Political Community," *European Journal of Sociology* 1 (1960), as quoted by Robert Alford in *Party and Society* (Chicago: Rand McNally & Co., 1963), p. 338.

Indeed, although institutions of government may remain quite different, there is an inevitable convergence of economic and bureaucratic service functions in modern societies, and consequently a growing similarity in the political life of advanced nations. This is implied by Almond's fourth-stage welfare or distribution capability[65] and by most other structural functional analyses.

The assumption that industrial or modern societies are moving towards convergence is not new.[66] In contemporary modernization theory, however, there has been a reluctance to suggest *structural* convergence except in certain areas where technical factors are paramount, such as factory organization, occupational stratification, and perhaps general management practices.[67] The latter fields, of course, imply other structural similarities, as well as a considerable degree of psychological convergence through what has been called cultural rationalization and secularization. But few have been willing to state, as does Marion Levy, Jr., that "the level of structural uniformity among relatively modernized societies continually increases regardless of how diverse the original basis from which change took place in these societies may have been."[68] Other structural-functional theorists have sought to avoid the stigma of evolutionary determinism by stressing functional rather than structural convergence.

We do not wish to enter this theoretical dispute, which lies at the base of current social science. It seems to us, however, that at a minimum one might distinguish between "internal" and "external" or universal convergence. That is, it is not necessary to posit a universal process of external convergence *between* different types of socio-political systems (as between those of the U.S. and the Soviet Union) in order to recognize *parallel* tendencies within individual nations which result from modernization. As national integration takes place, internal convergence in the sense of movement towards the political "center" or reduction in intergroup tensions is likely. At the same time, there may be common trends towards declining popular opposition to the norms of the system and a lessening of ideological controversy as economic distribution issues become the central focus of politics. Thus there may be parallel trends within different types of advanced societies without implying similar consequences or overall, systemic convergence. It is with theories of internal convergence of this kind that we are concerned in this section.

[65]Cf. Almond, "Political Systems and Political Change," below.

[66]For a review of the literature, see Ian Weinberg, "The Problem of Convergence of Industrial Societies: A Critical Look at the State of a Theory," *Comparative Studies in Society and History* 11 (Jan. 1969), p. 1ff.

[67]*Ibid.*, pp. 4-8.

[68]Levy, *Modernization and the Structure of Societies* (Princeton: Princeton University Press, 1966), vol. II, p. 709, quoted by Weinberg, p. 7. Cf. also Samuel P. Huntington and Zbigniew Brzezinski, *Political Power: USA/USSR* (New York: Viking Press, 1964), pp. 419-436.

Of more immediate consequence than this long-run shift in the focus of domestic politics has been the rapid economic growth in all currently advanced nations after World War II. The effect of this growth is not easy to distinguish from that of other social changes, and particular growth rates do not obviously account for differences in political development within this group of countries. In nations such as Germany and France, for example, the experience of war itself produced critical changes of attitude which were in some sense prerequisites for the success of economic policies in the postwar years, as were American occupation and aid. Moreover such things as the extension of mass communication and education are not strictly attributable to recent economic progress. What does seem fundamental, when viewed in historical perspective, is the sheer improvement in material living standards for the majority of citizens in advanced nations since the 1940s, and the new patterns of mass consumption which this improvement has entailed. It is this relative abundance of consumer goods available to the average citizen—and the reorientation of social life around private family consumption—that seems most central to postwar economic affluence in the West. On the other hand, there has also been substantial improvement in the public social services which have provided basic economic security in all advanced nations (though the United States, for example, has lagged significantly behind in minimum income standards, and Communist states continue to limit consumption generally). The result of both forms of mass consumption—private and public—has been, according to most observers, a further erosion of social cleavages and blurring of class distinctions as common patterns of consumption produce increasingly similar life styles.

In the first article reprinted below, Seymour Martin Lipset discusses the effects of postwar economic prosperity in Western Europe on several levels. This relative affluence has contributed to a new consensus favoring social democratic welfare programs and better management-labor relations. In a broader sense, the trend toward stability and moderation in European political life reflects the culmination of long-term social structural changes which have altered the class system, permitted final integration of the lower strata into the political system, and shaped a new political culture generally. This culture, which is scientific or rational, pragmatic, and supportive of professional expertise and planning, seems to be the most important connecting link between social change and political behavior. Thus, if socio-economic modernization has not produced societies which are truly egalitarian, it has at least resulted in a set of prevailing attitudes which allow mutual accommodation of interests through pragmatic cooperation and compromise. Carried to its logical conclusion, the implication of such changes in social psychology and intergroup relations is that politics loses its moralistic and ideological character and becomes increasingly instrumental and consensual. The result in Western Europe has been what Lipset calls the "politics of collective bargaining," in which partisan competition is largely reduced to haggling over marginal increments to one's share of the national wealth. In practice there have been exceptions to this general pattern— particularly the continued strength of large Communist parties in France and Italy, and new sources of group cleavage stemming from persisting inequalities or relative deprivation in many areas of social opportunity (such as access to higher education). But on the whole, traditional cleavages between social classes and their party organizations have been undermined by cumulative economic advance.

Most development theorists have also argued that modernization produces an increasingly complex, differentiated, and specialized organizational and group infrastructure, and that representation through diffuse social movements tends to give way to membership in "functionally specific" voluntary associations, professional organizations, and political interest groups. In the United States, political theorists from Alexis de Tocqueville to Arthur Bentley and David Truman have lauded the role of voluntary associations and pressure groups in establishing a stable, pragmatic, bargaining style of politics.[69] Truman's theory that American political behavior has remained stable and orderly because citizens hold multiple, overlapping memberships in organized and informal interest groups of different kinds has had a particularly great influence on political scientists and sociologists seeking to explain the general conditions needed for stable democratic politics. Lipset himself has argued in a similar vein that,[70]

> Multiple and politically inconsistent affiliations, loyalties, and stimuli reduce the emotion and aggressiveness involved in political choice. . . . The available evidence suggests that the chances for stable democracy are enhanced to the extent that groups and individuals have a number of crosscutting, politically relevant affiliations. To the degree that a significant proportion of the population is pulled among conflicting forces, its members have an interest in reducing the intensity of political conflict.

Lipset thus comments favorably on the growing role of organized interest groups in postwar European politics, and, together with blurring social stratification and the secularization of political cultural attitudes, this trend on the institutional level has presumably contributed to the stabilization of political competition and bargaining.

Although these conclusions are primarily derived from Western democratic experience, there is a growing tendency to interpret political trends in

[69]Tocqueville, *Democracy in America* (1835), esp. Book 4, chap. 7; Arthur F. Bentley, *The Process of Government* (Chicago: University of Chicago Press, 1908); David B. Truman, *The Governmental Process* (New York: Alfred A. Knopf, 1951).

[70]Lipset, *Political Man*, pp. 77-78. For a concise summary of different theories of crosscutting cleavages, see the opening pages of Michael Taylor and Douglas Rae, "An Analysis of Crosscutting between Political Cleavages," *Comparative Politics* 1 (July 1969).

the Soviet Union and other advanced authoritarian systems in much the same manner. It is argued that the forces of cultural secularization and group specialization have undercut both the relevance of official ideologies and the possibilities for monolithic control of political life by single parties or dictators. In part this reflects the inadequacies of earlier interpretations based on essentially static concepts of totalitarianism (cf. article by Groth), but also a mounting volume of more detailed comparative evidence on the diversities and problems of contemporary Communist states.[71]   More generally, Robert Tucker and others have argued that Marxist movements undergo a process of deradicalization once they are forced to confront the realities of exercising power.[72]

The major exception to the trend towards consensual bargaining politics in the early 1960s noted by Lipset was the continuing existence of large Communist parties in two Western countries, France and Italy. Like the major socialist or labor parties in Europe, the Communist parties have maintained (and in the case of Italy even enlarged) their electoral support despite the apparent decline in revolutionary aspirations and ideology suggested by Tucker. How does one account for this anomaly and, indeed, for the continuing success of other working-class parties amidst growing bourgeois prosperity? Has the class structure fundamentally changed or not? If so, how does one explain the persisting organizational strength of leftist parties?

Lipset suggests that the postwar Social Democratic parties have broadened their electoral bases by further diluting the doctrinal and programmatic content of their platforms; that is, by dropping most of the socialist rhetoric and adapting their electoral appeals to the new white-collar groups resulting from advanced industrial modernization. This movement from the left has been matched by a similar trend toward the center among the Christian Democratic and other conservative mass parties in Europe since 1945. Nevertheless, electoral statistics indicate a persisting tendency toward voting along objective class lines, at least into the early 1960s.[73] One general reason seems to be that labor organizations were built up in heavily industrialized areas with large factories and other conditions which facilitate associational ties that perpetuate established working-class values and

[71]See especially Johnson, *Change in Communist Systems*; and Robert C. Tucker, "On the Comparative Study of Communism," *World Politics* 19 (Jan. 1967), pp. 242-257.

[72]Tucker, "The Deradicalization of Marxist Movements," *American Political Science Review* 61 (June 1967), pp. 343-358, and *The Marxian Revolutionary Idea* (New York: W. W. Norton & Co., 1969), esp. chaps. 4, 6; Alfred Meyer, "Authority in Communist Political Systems," in Lewis J. Edinger, ed., *Political Leadership in Industrialized Nations* (New York: John Wiley & Sons, 1967), pp. 84-107.

[73]On this point see especially Alford, *Party and Society,* chaps. 4-5. For a summary and some additional data, cf. Alford, "Class Voting in the Anglo-American Political Systems," in Lipset and Rokkan, *Party Systems and Voter Alignments,* pp. 67-94.

habits. In the case of Communist parties, Lipset argues that deliberate efforts to maintain subcultural isolation in lower-class neighborhoods through such organizational networks are a major obstacle to political modernization. At the same time, because France and Italy have been relatively less industrialized and urbanized than some of the other European countries, it is suggested that the dislocations of economic development have continued to provide a basis for Communist recruitment among newly mobilized workers in these nations. Finally, Lipset offers the more speculative hypothesis that, due to their oppositional role, the Communist parties are increasingly a reservoir for protest votes from marginal strata of the population and from declining or stagnant sectors of the economy. Thus for various reasons Communist voting may not involve commitment to Marxist principles or even to the major goals of the party, and the broader trend towards *déideologisation* continues among the rank-and-file supporters if not among active cadres and militants.[74]

In fact the French Communist Party (PCF) has been much slower in shifting to reformist parliamentary politics than the Italian party (PCI), having chosen a strategy of militant opposition in 1947-1948 after an unsuccessful bid for power through coalition with the Socialists and Popular Republicans. This strategy of isolated, total opposition began to change only under pressure for a new popular front against Gaullist domination of the Fifth Republic in the early 1960s. In recent years the PCF has sought to regain influence through a variety of temporary electoral alliances with other leftist parties, and in 1968 refused to support the student-worker revolt beyond concrete wage negotiations for fear of endangering its parliamentary tactics.[75] This strategy appears to have paid off as the PCF was able to formulate a joint program with the Socialists for the parliamentary elections of March, 1973, and seriously threatened the governing coalition.[76]

We have focused on Western Communist parties not only because they remain the principal alternative to present governments in France and Italy, but because their continuing organizational strength has broader implications for the nature of politics in the contemporary era. For example, there is a good deal of evidence that raises doubts about the general thesis that economic affluence makes political conservatives or middle-class moderates of industrial workers and their families. Richard F. Hamilton, in his study on *Affluence and the French Worker in the Fourth Republic*, concluded that

[74]For some striking data see Philip E. Converse and Georges Dupeux, "Politicization of the Electorate in France and the United States," *Public Opinion Quarterly* 26 (Spring 1962), pp. 1-23.
[75]Arthur P. Mendel, "Why the French Communists Stopped the Revolution," *The Review of Politics* 31 (Jan. 1969), pp. 3-27.
[76]See also Thomas H. Green, "The Communist Parties of Italy and France: A Study in Comparative Communism," *World Politics* 21 (October 1968), pp. 1-38.

economic development (including significant increases in real income) had relatively little impact on the radicalism of French working-class politics in the 1950s since Communist militants continued to control the trade unions and other industrial organizations. In this situation economic growth and industrialization continued to strengthen the industrial base of the PCF rather than weakening it.[77] In a study of German workers he similarly found that working-class political allegiances as well as social habits remained remarkably impervious to middle-class styles despite higher income and consumption.[78] More recent analyses of new working-class neighbourhoods in England suggest much the same thing—that occupational mobility and new consumption opportunities have not generally resulted in the socio-political *embourgeoisement* of traditional Labour Party supporters. A group of political sociologists has suggested some of the reasons in this case:[79]

> While the nature of the relationship between trade union membership and voting for the Labour Party is in need of further study, it is not difficult to understand how both have a common basis in the work situation of the indus-trial employee. For, despite his affluence, the workers's experience of the social divisions of the work-place, of the power and remoteness of management, and of his own inconsiderable chances of ever being anything but a manual wage-earner all generally dispose him to think of himself as a member of the class of 'ordinary workers', and to seek collective rather than individualistic solutions to his problems. Although the 'new' worker's class consciousness may not extend much beyond his own particular work-place, it is probably still the most powerful single influence affecting his sense of social identity. And this is perhaps all the more likely to be so since members of the new working class tend to live a relatively privatized social life outside of work. For while they are no longer involved in working class communities of the traditional type, they do not appear to have become integrated to any great extent into middle-class society either. In our own study, for example, we found that while our affluent workers enjoyed a standard of living comparable to that of many white-collar families, their worlds are still, in the majority of cases, separate from those of the latter. Nor was there much indication that affluence had encouraged a

[77]Hamilton, *Affluence and the French Worker in the Fourth Republic* (Princeton: Princeton University Press, 1967). For a superb detailed comparison of France and Italy relevant to this point, see Mattei Dogan, "Political Cleavage and Social Stratification in France and Italy," in Lipset and Rokkan, *op. cit.,* pp. 129-196.

[78]Hamilton, "Affluence and the Worker: the West German Case," *American Journal of Sociology* 71 (1965), pp. 144-152. Cf. also David R. Segal, "Classes, Strata and Parties in West Germany and the United States," *Comparative Studies in Society and History* 10 (Jan. 1968), pp. 66-84, which brings out the persistence of voting alignments.

[79]John H. Goldthorpe, David Lockwood, Frank Bechhofer, and Jennifer Platt, *The Affluent Worker: Political Attitudes and Behaviour* (Cambridge: Cambridge University Press, 1968), pp. 78-79. The survey referred to was conducted in Luton, England, a modern and progressive industrial center with a mobile, well-paid work force.

desire on the part of these workers to *seek* acceptance in this new social *milieux* at higher status levels. Thus, although the division between 'us' and 'them' may have become less evident in terms of income and living standards, and at the same time less dominant in the workers' 'image' of the social order, it is nonetheless one which still in fact persists in the relationships of both work and community life.

Thus, as Robert Alford put it, class behavior patterns (such as voting for a workers' party) may persist and even increase in strength as classes themselves are transformed from "great diffuse blocs of people in generalized conflict" to "groups in similar objective situations organizing to pursue collective interests." [80]

The enhanced role of organized pressure groups may have little impact on the individual member's attitudes or sense of involvement in politics. Although citizens are more likely to belong to such groups than in the past, the increasing professionalization of special-interest organizations may inhibit rank-and-file participation and influence. Moreover there is some evidence to suggest that cross-pressures generated by multiple group affiliations lower active involvement or may simply be irrelevant to broader political orientations. For example, a comparative study of attitudes among American and Italian group members turned up little evidence that cross-cutting affiliations moderated political values or intolerance of others, although Italians who belonged to several organizations of the same political orientation seemed to have their attitudes reinforced by homogeneous contacts.[81] Thus it appeared that the intensifying effects of cumulative, homogeneous associations are more significant than the moderating impact of heterogeneous affiliations.

This tentative conclusion is significant not only in raising doubts about a major developmental hypothesis—that increasingly complex group life moderates political behavior—but in suggesting some of the reasons for the perpetuation of established party preferences or divisions in the current period. On the one hand, it appears that multiple associational involvement may have no effect on party preferences since partisan discussion is studiously avoided in most groups or else may lead to withdrawal. On the other hand, where intermediary organizations are strongly politicized or restricted to separate subcultural blocs, they may function as ideological forums and auxiliary party bodies. Either way the associational linkages at this level may serve to support existing partisan alignments.[82] In any event it is necessary to re-examine the nature of partisanship and group competition in light of the continuity of many organizational alignments.

---

[80]Alford, *Party and Society,* pp. 337.

[81]Sidney Verba, "Organizational Membership and Democratic Consensus," *Journal of Politics* 27 (Aug. 1965), pp. 464-497.

[82]*Ibid.*

Continuity and Change in Partisan Politics

Most systematic comparisons of partisan politics in Western nations have focused either on ideal types of party organization and structure or on some classification of party systems based on the number and range of competing parties (usually one-party, two-party, and multiparty).[83] Although such comparisons are useful, they often fail to explain the changing relationships between party elites, party members, the broader electorate, and outside interest groups. There have been various efforts in recent years to remedy these shortcomings, notably through studies of the foundations of partisanship in national political cultures[84] and development of new typologies which cover a wider range of variables and situations.[85] Other gaps such as comparative analyses of the attitudes and strategies of party leaders at different levels are only beginning to be filled. Consequently we can only discuss a number of issues relating to the current nature of partisan politics, but we believe the selections reprinted below illustrate the principal types of interparty competition and accommodation which

[83] The best known classifications of this kind are those of Maurice Duverger and Sigmund Neumann; see Duverger, *Political Parties*, trans. Barbara and Robert North (New York: John Wiley & Sons, 1963), pp. 62-71, 206-280, and Neumann, *Modern Political Parties*, pp. 400-405. Duverger distinguishes between "cadre" parties (created and dominated by parliamentary leaders and financial and professional "notables" for the purpose of conducting election campaigns as the suffrage was extended) and "mass" parties (parties largely established outside parliament in which mass membership and dues were utilized to integrate a maximum number of individuals from a given social sector into a permanent organizational structure). He also mentions the possibility of a third type, the "devotee" party, in which organizational membership takes on a different character as it is restricted to an elite segment or vanguard of the most fanatical elements of the population (as in Communist and Fascist parties); the party then becomes an elite "order." He also develops a typology of two-party, multiparty, and single-party systems in the latter part of his book. Neumann distinguishes between "parties of individual representation" and "parties of integration" in much the same way, but places greater emphasis on the latter as a characteristic modern type. He further distinguishes between "parties of democratic integration" (e.g., Socialist and Catholic parties) and "parties of total integration" (Communist and Fascist varieties). For a general discussion, see Harry Eckstein, "Political Parties," in *International Encyclopedia of the Social Sciences*, 1968.

[84] Almond and Verba, *The Civic Culture;* and Almond and Powell, *Comparative Politics*, pp. 217, 259-298. Cf. also Harry Eckstein, *Division and Cohesion in a Democracy: A Study of Norway* (Princeton: Princeton University Press, 1966); and Eric Nordlinger, *The Working Class Tories* (Berkeley and Los Angeles: University of California Press, 1967), esp. pp. 210-252.

[85] Among the most significant are Arend Lijphart, "Typologies of Democratic Systems," *Comparative Political Studies* 1 (Apr. 1968), pp. 3-44; Giovanni Sartori, "The Typology of Party Systems—Proposals for Improvement," in Eric Allardt and Stein Rokkan, eds., *Mass Politics: Studies in Political Sociology* (New York: Free Press, 1970), pp. 322-352; and J. LaPalombara and M. Weiner, *Political Parties and Political Development*, pp. 33-41. Cf. also the article cited in note 45 above, and, for a useful compilation of data on the voting strengths and governmental role of most Western parties, Jean Blondel, "Party Systems and Patterns of Government in Western Democracies," *Canadian Journal of Political Science* 1 (June 1968), pp. 180-203.

presently exist. In the concluding part of this section we also discuss the potentials for increasing pluralism in Communist one-party systems.

It should be noted that we have focused on criteria other than formal organizational structures and the number of competing units in drawing up the following list of issues and patterns of party competition. However, it should be kept in mind that different types of party systems represent differing patterns of institutionalization which have evolved from the earlier paths to social integration discussed in Sections B and C. Thus current systems reflect both organizational continuity and new styles of leadership and mobilization that have emerged from recent social, economic, and technological change.

1. *Parties as interest group aggregations.* Although the general effect of associational membership on the partisanship of citizens may be ambiguous, it can be argued that party leaders are required to pay increasing attention to the claims of organized interests if they are to form winning coalitions at election time. One of the principal differences between party systems is then the extent to which an institutional substructure of organized interest groups has come to dominate the partisan superstructure. According to this model, the primary function of modern parties (along with leadership recruitment for elective offices) is to aggregate the claims of disparate groups into broad programs and policies after they have been articulated by the various groups concerned. Where such patterns of articulation and aggregation are well-developed and synchronized (as in the U.S. and Britain), party systems are likely to be stable and responsive; where they are not (as in France) parties are likely to remain fragmented and ineffective.[86]

Samuel H. Beer discusses what he calls the new group politics in Britain in the excerpt from *British Politics in the Collectivist Age* reprinted below. He argues that British postwar politics has been characterized by close inter-party competition which depends in good part on the mobilization of interest groups. The participation of groups has been greatly enhanced by government intervention in the economy and its growing responsibility for the allocation of social welfare benefits. But the managed economy and welfare state have also resulted in a more complex pattern of party-interest group relations. On the one hand, the realities of controlling the economic system have required political elites (in both official and partisan capacities) to bargain for "advice, acquiescence, and approval" from organized producer groups which hold important sanctions of non-cooperation in the postwar mixed economy (as in massive labor strikes in recent years over inflationary controls and trade union reforms). At the same time, in order to win power, party leaders must constantly bid for support from the new

---

[86]This model is based primarily on Almond and Coleman, *The Politics of the Developing Areas,* pp. 33-45.

consumer groups brought into being by state welfare programs and increased affluence. These two obligations are closely intertwined since producers are also consumers and since both types of groups desire a stable, expanding economy; but they may also be brought into sharp conflict when economic advance falters (as it has over much of the past two decades) or when specific interests seek concrete rewards for political support given.

More broadly, long-term patterns of institutionalization have led in Britain to a concentration of organized economic interests in each sector represented by peak associations which act as supreme bargaining agents. Moreover the postwar expansion of administrative bureaucracy has provided them with channels of access to government which bypass parties and parliament. In these circumstances the major parties must try to facilitate individual and group claims against the bureaucracy and to mobilize key groups of dissatisfied citizens who might be persuaded to support a new administration in order to improve the efficiency or equity of state services. However, Beer argues that the parties are not powerless and do not simply aggregate interest group claims. They can mobilize the organizational resources of groups in effective campaigns, and in fact stimulate the formation of groups and the articulation of demands through active propaganda activities. In the consumer sector especially, parties use increasingly sophisticated public relations techniques to anticipate and shape the pattern of demands. This two-way communication between parties and the public means that each party projects a different image of the collective interest which reflects underlying differences of philosophy.

Indeed the 1970 election in Britain took on a more overtly ideological cast than any in recent years as the two major parties prepared for battle over trade union reform, inflation, guarantees for entry to the Common Market, decontrol of private business and the nationalized industries, and a host of other issues related to economic stagnation. New issues of this kind have cut across older party and interest group alignments and appear to require increasingly firm leadership on the part of political elites.

2. *"Catch-all" party competition.* This view of contemporary partisan politics was best expressed by the late Otto Kirchheimer, who was among the first to warn of a long-term decay of interparty competition in Western parliamentary systems.[87] In the first section of the article reprinted here, Kirchheimer reviews the past failures of democratic parties and then goes on to discuss the transformation of these parties into what he calls catch-all people's parties in the postwar decades. Since the old bourgeois individualistic parties were largely unable to compete with the major

[87]Kirchheimer, "The Waning of Opposition in Parliamentary Regimes." For Kirchheimer's collected writings, see Frederic S. Burin and Kurt L. Shell, eds., *Politics, Law, and Social Change: Selected Essays of Otto Kirchheimer* (New York: Columbia University Press, 1969).

organized forces in the reconstruction effort, this transformation primarily involves the development of new functions and modes of competition by the revived socialist mass parties (Social Democrats) and the denominational popular parties (Christian Democrats). To a considerable extent, however, the major premises of his argument might be applied wherever two major parties compete for office (the U.S. and Britain). Where competition tends towards dualism but the major opposition party remains the Communists (France and Italy) the catch-all style is more limited and is most characteristic of the governing party (the Gaullist UNR-UDR and Italian Christian Democrats).

Kirchheimer suggests that ideology and organization are no longer sufficient to win and hold power in the mass consumption, mass communications era. Rather it becomes necessary to offer programs or solutions which are designed to appeal to the widest possible spectrum of public opinion. Groups and individuals who are the beneficiaries of the welfare state must be impressed with the general managerial capacity of the competing leadership teams.[88] More broadly, the party must convey a "safe" image to the mass electorate via modern marketing and public relations media. This means, among other things, that divisive issues are avoided in favor of consensual items and that promises to specific groups must be limited so as to alienate as few other potential supporters as possible. On the other hand, the parties compete vigorously at election time to capture the same clienteles in the center and to rally a maximum share of the *unorganized* vote. But their campaigns are likely to revolve around immediate problems elevated to the electoral stage by opposition charges or by fortuitous scandals or international events; there is no longer much attempt by the catch-all parties to shape the deeper "action preferences" of the public.

This competitive style reflects a change in functions by postwar parties. They no longer seek to isolate and integrate large sectoral subgroupings in society, or to enroll a maximum of individuals as official party members. While shaping public commitments in this way declines in significance, the "expressive" function of parties (the function of representing popular grievances and acting as critic of government) is de-emphasized in favor of tactical office-holding considerations. Indeed it is mainly the governmental functions that have expanded along with increased opportunities for sharing in the distribution of economic and social benefits in the public domain. In

---

[88]For the classic statement on trends in this direction, see Joseph A. Schumpeter, *Capitalism, Socialism and Democracy* (London: George Allen & Unwin, 1943), chap. 22. Cf. also Carl J. Friedrich, *Constitutional Government and Democracy*, 4th ed. (Waltham, Mass.: Blaisdell Publishing Co., 1968), chap. XX, esp. at pp. 434-439; and Erwin C. Hargrove, "Political Leadership in the Anglo-American Democracies," in Edinger, *Political Leadership in Industrialized Societies*, pp. 182-219.

support of this goal, the party must develop new capabilities for mobilizing transient opinion (as opposed to integrating and educating people) and concentrate on nominating successful candidates for office (the leadership selection function). The government party (or parties) is then in a position to arbitrate among the various interest group claims for service and to coordinate to some extent the actions of other power-holding elites. But there appears little potential for basic policy changes as parties lose their representative functions and organizational base. They may offer neither effective channels for integrating social interests nor meaningful opportunities for mass participation in future.

If Kirchheimer's interpretation is correct, and parties are increasingly "purveyors of consensus" or professional electoral machines, then partisan competition contributes relatively little to the capability for conflict resolution in a society. Although party leaders in and out of office may be willing to bargain for favors and cooperate on particular legislative enactments, they may have little direct connection with the social groups which are the subject of policy. They may also succeed in delaying or avoiding the resolution of issues which do not fit the normal categories of interparty rivalry or which activate negative feelings about party and governmental leadership in general. With neither ideological nor organizational constraints on their actions, party elites may no longer be responsive to broader social pressures, and demands for change may be forced into new ideological counter-movements outside the party system. Hence the old problems of partisan representation and integration may be developing in new form in the postindustrial state.

Kirchheimer's view was undoubtedly influenced by the increasingly moderate and pragmatic character of party competition in West Germany, which culminated in the Grand Coalition government of the two major parties in 1966. The nebulous programs and professional campaign techniques of many parties in the mid-1960s may have led him to overstate his case, but clearly there are dangers that parties have become overly bureaucratic and insensitive to the changing needs of the electorate. The "loose integration" achieved by electoral mobilization may no longer provide a basis for either consistent action on the part of elites or public commitment to the programs which result from interparty compromise. Insofar as party accountability diminishes, public opinion may shift erratically from one election to the next with little sense of direction.

3. *Ideological versus organizational competition.* One of the principal themes mentioned earlier was the common assertion that political ideologies have lost their relevance. Particularly in regard to Continental Europe, it was vigorously argued in the early 1960s that affluence and the changing class structure had produced a sharp decline in doctrinal conflict as socialist and other parties sought to accommodate themselves to the existing order. The

French term *dépolitisation* gained currency to describe not only the waning intensity of ideological commitment but a general loss of vitality in political life and a growing tendency to seek expert or technocratic solutions to social problems. While others argued that such tendencies were more appearance than reality since civic involvement in specialized groups and other channels of influence was greater than ever, there was nonetheless a widespread feeling that principled interparty politics had undergone a substantial evolutionary decline since World War II.

The result was a vigorous theoretical and terminological debate on the "end of ideology," but, as in the concurrent "Is God dead? " dispute, much of the argument was semantic. Quite clearly evidence could be adduced on either side of the issue depending on how ideology was defined. Thus several scholars sought to refute the end of ideology thesis by widening the concept of ideology to include almost any kind of political attitudes or beliefs. Joseph LaPalombara, for example, in contesting Lipset's position implied that ideology could include "any given set of values, preferences, expectations and prescriptions regarding society," and made the important point that ideology need not be utopian, dogmatic, passionately articulated, or even fully believed in order to affect political behavior.[89] James B. Christoph made much the same argument in regard to Britain, suggesting that one could speak of an ideology of pragmatism.[90] Lipset himself did not seem to disagree with these arguments and made it clear that the end of "total" ideologies does not mean the end of all ideologies; indeed he notes that commitment to the politics of collective bargaining is itself the basis for a common ideological perspective which he characterized as "conservative socialism."

It is in this context of semantic confusion that we believe the article below by Samuel H. Barnes is especially helpful in assessing the changing role of ideology in interparty competition. Barnes adopts the general term "belief systems," and limits the term "ideology" to belief systems which are internally consistent (or involve constraint among different elements) and which are consciously held. In this way he allows for the fact that a great deal of survey evidence indicates that mass publics do not demonstrate much ideological sophistication, while at the same time it appears that significant numbers of citizens are still motivated by relatively fixed attitudes and habits. The level of ideology in the sense defined is then a problem for

[89]LaPalombara, "Decline of Ideology: A Dissent and Interpretation," *American Political Science Review* 60 (Mar. 1966), pp. 7-8. Cf. reply by Lipset and rejoinder by LaPalombara in the same issue. LaPalombara argues that in postwar Italy ideological competition has increased, and that social scientists who insist on the end of ideology are themselves ideologues in a pure sense.

[90]Christoph, "Consensus and Cleavage in British Political Ideology," *American Political Science Review* 59 (Sept. 1965), pp. 629-642. A collection of writings on the subject is available in Chaim I. Waxman, ed., *The End of Ideology Debate* (New York: Funk & Wagnalls, 1968).

empirical investigation, but the more interesting question is how constraints enter the belief systems of individuals below the threshold of ideological awareness. Professor Barnes argues that organizations such as parties are a primary source of non-ideological constraints, despite the greater ideological sophistication of partisan elites. That is, although the ideologies of leaders are partially transmitted to the rank and file, both elites and mass membership tend to develop sets of ideas which owe more to the organizational milieu than to ideology *per se*. Furthermore, the nature of partisan conflict in a society depends more on the institutional network than on the distribution of ideologies among intellectual elites; it is the political organizations which structure the conflict, and ideologies are relevant insofar as the leaders holding them have an organizational base. This means, paradoxically, that successful organizational elites may perpetuate ideological conflict on the system level long after ideology has lost its hold on the mass public and party members, while access to institutional power may be the crucial requirement for exponents of deviant beliefs.

The most striking conclusion of Barnes' study, however, is perhaps that although on the "micro" level (that of the individual) ideology is increasingly irrelevant (especially on economic matters), on the "macro" (organizational and structural) level ideological or value conflicts continue to shape political conflict because they have been institutionalized. Hence growing popular consensus on some ideological dimensions—notably economic development issues or class values—does not necessarily lead to convergence on other dimensions. In fact this may enhance the significance of other structural cleavages such as religious, regional, ethnic, and linguistic differences. The principal weakness in most ideological convergence theories is that they are focused almost entirely on the waning of economic or class hostilities. More recent studies suggest that this approach to ideological and structural change is not justified. Richard Rose and Derek Urwin, for example, examined 76 parties in 17 advanced countries and found that "religious divisions, not class, are the main social basis of parties in the Western world today."[91] Their data suggest that 35 of the 76 parties owe their electoral support primarily to common religious or antireligious outlooks among their supporters, while occupational class is the principal cohesive factor in only 33 of the cases. In most of the remaining parties regional or communal (linguistic and ethnic) identifications were foremost.

Hence in considering the potentials for ideological convergence and the nature of party systems generally, it is necessary to recognize the multiple bases of party support and the degree to which non-economic cleavages have been institutionalized. The data presented by Rose and Urwin do not suggest that socio-economic changes in Western societies have caused a decline in the support of religious, working-class, communal, or regionally based

[91]Rose and Urwin, *op. cit.*, *p. 12.*

parties, or that such changes have resulted in the general development of heterogeneous parties of the American type. On the other hand, this does not preclude the possibility that the functions of ideology are changing in modern society, or that ideology is important to some kinds of party organizations and not to others. Ulf Himmelstrand has suggested that ideology serves different purposes—if no longer aimed at utopian goals, it may still provide practical guidance for party action or an important source of symbolic gratification which engenders emotional loyalty to party leaders at election time.[92] The latter function of ideology, which he terms the "expressive" function, may be far from dead in modern politics. Although policy-making between elections may be highly pragmatic and "depoliticized," expressive party symbolism may be intensified by organizational elites at election time to rekindle partisan emotions.

In any case, there was a revival of ideological symbolism and movements in most advanced nations during the late 1960s. The 1968 student-worker revolt in France and the ensuing parliamentary elections produced an obvious recrudescence of the old polarization between radical utopianism and the forces of anti-Communism and order.[93] In West Germany the neo-fascist National Democratic Party threatened to upset the growing consensus in public life prior to the 1969 elections, as did the radical student opposition.[94] The politicization of communal ties among Flemish and Wallonian segments in Belgium brought near collapse in the late 1960s,[95] while ethnic nationalism also grew in French-speaking Canada, Scotland, and Wales, and religious animosities culminated in a tragic civil war in Northern Ireland.[96] But even in the most stable and consensual systems such as Sweden, Britain, and the United States there has been renewed ideological conflict. In Sweden Himmelstrand noted a "renewed emphasis and a sharper articulation of ideological differences between the political parties of the left

[92]Himmelstrand, "Depoliticization and Political Involvement: A Theoretical and Empirical Approach," in Allardt and Rokkan, *Mass Politics,* pp. 64-92.

[93]See David B. Goldey, "The Events of May and the French General Election of June 1968," *Parliamentary Affairs* 21-22 (Autumn 1968 and Spring 1969), pp. 307-337, 116-133; and Stanley Hoffmann, "The French Psychodrama: De Gaulle's Anti-Communist Coup," *New Republic* (Aug. 31, 1968), pp. 15-21.

[94]See Kurt Shell, "Extraparliamentary Opposition in Postwar Germany," *Comparative Politics* 2 (July 1970), pp. 653-680, and other articles on the 1969 West German elections in this issue.

[95]George A. Kelly, "Belgium: New Nationalism in an Old World," *Comparative Politics* 1 (Apr. 1969), pp. 343-365.

[96]See, e.g., John E. Schwarz, "The Scottish National Party: Nonviolent Separatism and Theories of Violence," *World Politics* 22 (July 1970), pp. 496-517; Frank L. Wilson, "French-Canadian Separatism," *Western Political Quarterly* 20 (Mar. 1967); and, more generally, Walker Connor, "Self-Determination: the New Phase," *World Politics* 20 (Oct. 1967), pp. 30-54.

and the right,"[97] and the 1970 British and 1968 and 1972 American elections resulted in some of the bitterest symbolic confrontations in decades. Although much of the revived ideological opposition has emanated from outside the established party systems, there would appear to be no solid foundation for the general end of ideology thesis. The problem may rather be that ideological sentiments can easily be revived by the course of events or by symbol manipulation but that the values expressed may have little impact on policy processes. As Himmelstrand puts it,[98]

> . . . If depoliticization gathers momentum in the political bodies while at the same time large or crucially important part[s] of the public retain much of an expressive concern for political matters, this kind of dualism of political culture may give rise to wavering and irrationally unstabilizing changes of political involvement. Between elections when the factual, technical, and economical issues of depoliticized politics are most prominent, politics may seem very dull indeed to the expressive ideologists in the public. In this period reforms and legislation, however, may be accepted as we accept most of the helpful gadgets which become part of our lives. But when election time comes, and the honorific symbols of ideology once again are in the air, all this can be drastically changed. Politics becomes important—but in a way disconnected from life between elections. Reforms and legislation recently accepted in a matter-of-fact way now may be perceived as sinister manipulations with the freedom or with the welfare of the individual, or lost out of sight completely in the glaring light of party symbolism.

Thus there is no easy answer to the question of what role ideology will play in the future of democratic politics. What does seem evident is that organizational elites in Barnes' sense will have a crucial impact on the structuring of political competition. The following discussion elaborates this theme further in the context of one of the smaller nations.

4. *Consociational party competition.* Among the limitations on catch-all electoral competition noted by Kirchheimer were tendencies toward circumscribed competition or interparty collaboration in the smaller European countries. In Austria, for example, a novel form of government by "party cartel" had emerged in the postwar period, by which the two largest parties formed a permanent coalition under which offices were shared according to electoral results.[99] More recently, Arend Lijphart of the Netherlands has set out a general theory of "consociational democracy" which incorporates such tendencies toward cooperation into a broader pattern of interparty

---

[97]Himmelstrand, *op. cit.,* p. 70.
[98]*Ibid.,* pp. 90-91.
[99]Kirchheimer, "The Waning of Opposition in Parliamentary Regimes."

relations characterizing the smaller democracies of Austria, the Netherlands, Belgium, and Switzerland.[100]

It will be recalled that these countries are distinguished by proportional representation of social cleavages referred to as "segmented pluralism." That is, each party has tended to represent a distinct subcultural grouping or social pillar, with relatively few crosscutting organizational ties. Yet the result in terms of governmental stability and conflict resolution has been favorable. Not only have the governments of these nations been extremely stable but (until recently at least) they have been most successful in promoting rapid economic growth without social disruption. How has this been possible within a framework of deep-set ethnic, religious, class, and even ideological divisions?

In the paper below, Rodney Stiefbold summarizes and elaborates Lijphart's model, utilizing the Second Republic of Austria as a case study in consociational politics. According to Lijphart, a consociational system is one in which party leaders, as a deliberate response to cultural segmentation, agree to cooperate on a continuing basis so as to constitute a formal or informal coalition or partnership, whatever the electoral results. This collaboration is in turn possible because the parties are able to speak for discrete social segments which together encompass all major sectors of the population. In other words, the segregation of social groups into exclusive subcultural blocs and organizational hierarchies limits intergroup political contacts to top partisan elites who are able to bargain effectively on behalf of their sector. This, of course, assumes a good deal of overarching consensus on national goals and basic policy issues among top subcultural elites. But where such patterns of elite accommodation exist—whether through long traditions or recent responses to national crises—the perpetuation of fundamental social cleavages may actually facilitate political compromise and agreement. In this sense Lijphart adds an important amendment to conventional pluralist doctrines which assume that such cleavages are inherently antagonistic and destabilizing.[101]

Stiefbold's study of Austria under the Great Coalition of 1945-1966 brings out the reality of this situation but also reveals further dimensions of its operation and additional conditions for its success. Empirical survey data on mass and elite opinion structures indicate that the two interact in a considerably more complex fashion than implied in Lijphart's model. On the mass level there is a good deal of evidence that subcultural blocs (Lager), while organizationally and sociologically distinctive, do not constitute watertight compartments in attitudinal terms; instead, there is a common

[100]Lijphart, "Consociational Democracy," and "Typologies of Democratic Systems."

[101]See Lijphart, *The Politics of Accommodation: Pluralism and Democracy in the Netherlands* (Berkeley and Los Angeles: University of California Press, 1968), chaps. I and X, for a fuller exposition of his amendments to pluralist theory.

pan-Lager tendency toward passive support of the system and relatively little disagreement on specific issues. However, if mass opinion is not ordinarily polarized or very deeply engaged in politics, party activities have the effect of isolating sectors organizationally, and of rekindling hostilities at election time. Electoral campaigns are divisive, rather than conciliatory or catch-all in nature. This intentional disharmony is explained by the existence of different types of elites at different levels of party organization. While the top party leaders are responsible for consociational arrangements and policy-making, most electoral communication is in the hands of middle-level party officials who are far more ideological than either the top party leaders or their middle-level counterparts in socio-economic interest groups. Thus, throughout the era of consociational rule (1945-1966), while policy advice flowed primarily upwards from middle-level socio-economic elites, elite-mass communication was essentially through party militants who perpetuated Austria's traditional Lager mentality, especially at election time. This disjuncture of middle and top elite roles prevented evolution toward overall political convergence and constituted the principal reason for the continuation of segmented, consociational politics long after "objective" conditions—peace, prosperity, and growing consensus among adherents of the Lager on a wide range of issues—which had ostensibly given rise to government by elite cartel had faded from prominence.

The broader theoretical significance of Stiefbold's study lies in the fact that it further illustrates how ideological and organizational variables may interact with and severely constrain elite political strategies. Whereas in catch-all competition ideology and organization may be de-emphasized in favor of direct attempts by leaders to influence opinion through mass communications media, in consociational regimes consensus-building at the top has proceeded despite (and because of) continuing interorganizational hostility at the popular level. Thus in the Austrian case consociation among elites was not only a deliberate effort to overcome subcultural cleavages but part of a party system which nurtured and sustained underlying political-cultural divisions. This apparent contradiction of party functions is only understandable in terms of the roles of leaders at different organizational levels. Needless to say, role structures in this sense may themselves be subject to change over time (as partly reflected in dissolution of the Austrian Great Coalition in 1966, though consociational bargaining continued behind the scenes). More generally, however, new pressures for change may result in a shifting balance among intraorganizational elites which upsets established patterns of interparty accommodation in government.

5. *One-party pluralism?*   This potential for shifting organizational and elite roles is especially important in single-party totalitarian or authoritarian systems since any movement toward greater competition or pluralism is

likely to occur within the established institutional framework.[102] Most observers agree that in the Soviet Union, for example, the Communist Party is not likely to relinquish its ultimate monopoly of decision-making, and the brutal repression of Czechoslovak party reforms in 1968 is vivid testimony of the continuing commitment to established organizational principles. However, as one-party rule matures and a substantial degree of socio-economic modernization is achieved, there may be unintended developmental consequences.[103] Among these are increasing differentiation of functions and specialization of roles and the growth of new organizations and elites which are essential for rational decision-making and for the continuing development of the system. The new organizational elites may become part of the "ruling class,"[104] but they also develop their own professional and bureaucratic interests which may not coincide with previous dictates of the party. The consequence according to many scholars is growing internal conflict and the emergence of a new kind of intrabureaucratic interest group politics.[105] The potentials for competition and pluralism may be considerably wider than this. Huntington, for example, has recently suggested that established one-party systems must confront four major challenges:[106]

> (1) the emergence of a new, innovative, technical-managerial class; (2) the development of a complex group structure, typical of a more industrial society, whose interests have to be related to the political sphere; (3) the reemergence of a critical intelligentsia apart from and, indeed, increasingly alienated from the institutionalized structures of power; and (4) the demands by local and popular groups for participation in and influence over the political system.

The complete resolution of these problems might indeed entail democratization of such systems, but thus far there is no evidence that adaptation of this kind is inevitable or likely. Whether the alternative in countries such as the Soviet Union is developmental stagnation or degeneration remains to be seen.[107]

[102]See especially Samuel Huntington, "Social and Institutional Dynamics of One-Party Systems," in Huntington and Moore, *Authoritarian Politics in Modern Society*, pp. 3-47.

[103]Chalmers Johnson, "Comparing Communist Nations," in Johnson, *Change in Communist Systems*, pp. 1-32.

[104]The now-classic statement on this is Milovan Djilas, *The New Class* (New York: Frederick A. Praeger, 1957).

[105]The definitive work is H. Gordon Skilling and Franklyn Griffiths, eds., *Interest Groups in Soviet Politics* (Princeton: Princeton University Press, 1971). See also Sidney Ploss, "Interest Groups," in Allen Kassof, ed., *Prospects for Soviet Society* (New York: Frederick A. Praeger, 1968), pp. 76-103; and Andrew C. Janos, "Group Politics in Communist Society: A Second Look," in Huntington and Moore, *op. cit.*, pp. 437-50.

[106]Huntington, in Huntington and Moore, p. 33.

[107]The argument that failure to institutionalize group representation in the U.S.S.R. will lead to political decay is made by Z. Brzezinski in "The Soviet Political System: Transformation or Degeneration," *Problems of Communism* 15 (Jan.-Feb. 1966), pp. 1-15, also in Brzezinski, ed., *Dilemmas of Change in Soviet Politics* (New York: Columbia University Press, 1969), pp. 1-34.

The most tangible evidence of growing pluralization in the Soviet Union concerns policy disputes which are linked to the interests of specialized groups and elites. Joel Schwartz and William Keech analyze the Soviet educational reforms of 1958 and demonstrate that, at least in certain circumstances, social groups and technical elites may indeed influence decisional outputs at the highest level. In this case Khruschev's personal plans for revision of the secondary educational system appear to have been negated by widespread opposition from interested groups. Teachers, parents, scientists, industrial managers, and education bureaucrats all expressed dissent through specialized communications media. But how was such opposition converted into decisional influence in the higher councils of Soviet government? Schwartz and Keech suggest that the crucial factor in defeating Khruschev's proposal was actually disagreement within the party leadership itself; when the dispute could not be settled within the highest party organs, the First Secretary's opponents mobilized the different educational groups to support their arguments by airing their views in public. In such circumstances, groups having recognized expertise may be important in reinforcing the positions of the higher authorities, but their communications to political leaders may also have an independent effect on the outcome. Thus, while functional representation of differential group interests may not be regarded as legitimate, it is likely that expert opinion from relevant "skill groups" or "issue publics" is accorded legitimacy in policy conflicts of this kind.[108] Moreover such expert judgments inevitably reflect the self-interests of the participants to some extent.

On the other hand, it appears that even expert participation is heavily contingent upon leadership conflicts which generate wider public debate. Have such leadership disputes themselves been institutionalized in the period of greater collective leadership? In offering a number of suggestive hypotheses concerning potentials for group influence, Schwartz and Keech conclude that socio-economic modernization, de-Stalinization, and collective decision-making have all increased the chances for policy disagreements which permit wider debate. Under conditions of diminished terror and broadening consensus on general social goals, policy disputes are less likely to involve power struggles which seriously endanger the participants; hence the costs of involvement have been lowered. Other evidence suggests that Soviet specialized elites increasingly view their roles as instrumental policy participants, although party elites remain less willing to recognize autonomous influences of this kind. A general division between instrumental and ideological modes of thought may thus be developing.[109] However, the primary problem would appear to be that group competition and representa-

[108]Cf. Philip D. Stewart, "Soviet Interest Groups and the Policy Process: the Repeal of Production Education," *World Politics* 22 (Oct. 1969), pp. 29-50.

[109]See Milton Lodge, "Soviet Elite Participatory Attitudes in the Post-Stalin Period," *American Political Science Review* 62 (Sept. 1968), pp. 827-839.

tion have not yet been structured or formally recognized in most Communist systems.[110] In essence, it remains dependent on the ability of the political leadership to maintain unity and control, or to manage conflicts so as to limit their impact on the general goals of the regime and preserve the preeminent status of the party leaders.[111]

E. MASS PARTICIPATION, REPRESENTATION, AND SUPPORT

The various studies in Section D make one point in common: whatever the party system and cultural milieu, whether divisive multi-partyism in France and Italy, two-party consensual competition in the United States and West Germany, interest group partisanship in Britain and Scandinavia, segmented interparty collaboration in Austria and the Low Countries, or submerged intraparty pluralism in the Soviet Union, the nature of partisan relations at the policy-making level is largely in the hands of party elites. In democratic systems there seems to be a considerable gap between what goes on at the polls as a result of the distribution and intensity of partisan preferences among the mass electorate, and what happens the rest of the time within each party's leadership and between the different party elites in the system. In mature Communist systems the imperatives of functional differentiation and rational management have not destroyed the hegemony of party leaders. It thus appears that the modern citizen has little influence other than in casting his lot for one or another competing leadership team or relying on interest group elites to defend his position by proxy. Is the citizen's role as participant then meaningless?

[110]The only clear exception appears to be Yugoslavia. On functional representation of socio-economic and ethnic groups in the Federal Assembly, see M. George Zaninovich, *The Development of Socialist Yugoslavia* (Baltimore: Johns Hopkins Press, 1968), esp. pp. 116-117.

[111]A rather skeptical view is taken by H. Gordon Skilling in the concluding chapter of *Interest Groups in Soviet Politics,* especially at pp. 403-405. Skilling argues that, while social and economic forces may enhance the status of interest groups, their increased activity under Khruschev reflected "a purposeful act of leadership, designed to remove some of the defects of the system and hence to prevent its disintegration or breakdown." He goes on to note that "the consultative process was not embodied in institutional form and was restricted to the elite sectors of Soviet society. Moreover, the activity of groups continued to be regarded as illegitimate and to be hemmed in by many restrictions, increasingly so under Khruschev's successors." The role of groups may thus vary erratically with the felt needs and attitudes of the leadership, and there is no assurance that the process will lead to greater pluralism or democracy. Cf. also the discussion of cleavages *within* groups and potentials for alliances *between* segments of groups (*ibid.,* pp. 384-389), and the critical comments on evidence presented by Lodge *ibid.,* pp. 408-409). Skilling's conclusions about the role of groups in this work are a good deal more circumspect than in his initial path-breaking article, "Interest Groups and Communist Politics," *World Politics* 18 (Apr. 1966), pp. 435-451.

Development theory is, in general, silent on the question of mass participation once political integration has been achieved through party and group representation. It is normally assumed that centralized parliamentary or presidential offices and expanded administrative services, together with modern mass communications and higher education, have brought government in ever more intimate contact with society. In comparison with earlier stages of modernization, people are highly mobilized and capable of collective political action. Yet here we are immediately confronted with a mass of recent survey evidence which indicates that the average modern citizen has little concern about politics. Indeed, the most striking conclusions of public opinion research have been in documenting the low level of political involvement, interest, and knowledge which prevails among the mass population in advanced democratic nations, and there is little reason to believe it is different in the Soviet Union.[112] Much of this evidence is summarized in the article by John C. Wahlke below, but suffice it to say at this point that political integration and mobilization do not necessarily imply active citizen roles. The specialization of roles and functions attendant upon modernization may reduce the salience of politics for the average person except when he is called on to cast his vote or to defend some immediate interest.

The other side of the coin is that there also appear to be substantial cross-national differences in the potentials for mass political involvement, and it can be argued that potential as well as actual participation affects the behavior of elites in democratic systems. This is essentially the position taken by Gabriel Almond and Sidney Verba in their five-nation political culture study entitled *The Civic Culture.* The find significant differences in the sense of awareness and involvement among citizens of the United States and Britain as compared with those of Italy and Mexico, with West Germans occupying an intermediate position on most indices. In the first essay in Section E Verba sets out some of the preliminary findings of this study relating to the concept of relative "subjective competence" for which *The Civic Culture* is perhaps known best. This concept holds that despite normal passivity, it makes a great deal of difference whether the citizens of a country *think* they can participate actively and influence political elites, for belief in the possibility of exerting influence (a sense of competence) tends to increase *actual* participation and, even more importantly, is likely to force government officials to respond to civic demands by anticipating potential "deprivations" at the hands of an aroused citizenry. In other words,

[112]For a useful compendium of data and hypotheses on civic involvement, see Lester W. Milbraith, *Political Participation* (Chicago: Rand McNally & Co., 1965); and for some evidence on civic apathy in the U.S.S.R., Jerome M. Gilison, "Soviet Elections as a Measure of Dissent: the Missing One Percent," *American Political Science Review* 62 (Sept. 1968), pp. 814-826. The best general study is Giuseppe di Palma, *Apathy and Participation: Mass Politics in Western Society* (New York: Free Press, 1970).

although subjective competence does not measure actual involvement and influence, it is alleged to have important operational consequences for both, and hence for the general extent of democracy in a society. One can thus draw important conclusions by asking national samples of citizens how they *might* act in different circumstances, particularly in hypothetical stress situations.

The results of this survey are striking in several respects, but especially in showing large variations in overall levels of competence (even in local politics) between the countries, and in suggesting similar differences in the means or strategies of influence which citizens of these countries would follow. In the latter regard it is perhaps most interesting that political "competents" in all countries are far more likely to attempt to exert influence through informal group cooperation than through political parties, interest groups, or other formal organizations. However, the cross-cultural differences here—which are taken as a rough index of capabilities to act cooperatively and hence effectively in practice—indicate very substantial differences in national political styles. Moreover these differences are not fully accounted for by the different level of socio-economic development in the five countries; and, while higher education correlates with increasing political competence in each nation, it has less impact on this potential for cooperative civic action than do intangible cultural factors.

The next selection, by Nie, Powell and Prewitt, reports the results of a much more extended and sophisticated analysis of the *Civic Culture* data on participatory attitudes in relation to economic modernization. The authors conclude that economic development produces higher rates of political participation through two primary variables: changes in social stratification which raise the socio-economic status (SES) of individuals, and the development of more complex organizational structures. These two variables account for most of the difference in rates of actual participation between the five nations studied, and the article carries the analysis a step further by tracing the intervening attitudinal changes (secondary variables) through which higher status and organizational involvement are directly linked to increased participation. Using new techniques of analysis, they are able to demonstrate that SES and organizational membership affect participation in quite different ways. Whereas belonging to an organization tends to increase political activity directly, without basic change in the attitudes or knowledge of the individual, most of the impact of higher social status is through intervening psychological or cognitive changes—that is, not higher SES *per se,* but greater sense of obligation to participate, greater competence or sense of efficacy, higher awareness and knowledge of government, and so on. This is most striking in that it leads to the hypothesis that, in democratic systems generally, organizational development and the socializing effects of individual socio-economic achievement are to a considerable extent *alternative* processes for enlarging mass political participation. If this is so, the consequences are profound for the amount of participation and influence which different social groups are able to attain in different societies. In particular, it becomes clear how economically disadvantaged or low status groups have been able to attain much higher levels of political involvement in some nations than in others through organizational mobilization.

In all countries the lower classes are significantly under-represented among the politically active citizens, but the particular mix of stratification and organizational factors may exacerbate or ameliorate this imbalance. Thus in the United States the lower social strata have proportionally less representation than in any of the five nations studied since organizational affiliations are themselves concentrated in the middle and upper classes, thereby compounding the status advantages which these groups already enjoy in the form of attitudinal resources. In Europe, on the other hand, organizational resources are more evenly distributed due to the earlier mobilization of the working classes by socialist political parties. The broader implication for social reform is, of course, that organizational strength is a primary requisite if lower SES groups are to improve their condition in this country. The authors warn, however, that there are still many unknowns in this analysis, including the quality of organizational participation and the effects of greater participation in different types of systems.

This study raises some doubts about the significance of the earlier subjective competence scale since it appears that several other variables are involved which may be more important for actual participation rates. What is here termed "political efficacy" is only one intervening factor, which other studies have shown to be heavily dependent on early socialization experiences.[113] But the broader question which comes to mind is whether Almond and Verba's subjectively competent citizen is an activist at all. That is, the *Civic Culture* survey may have measured recognition of the *norm* of participatory democracy without coming to grips with the actual willingness of individuals in different cultures to assert their rights. Put another way, subjective competence may be a better indicator of regime *support* than of the relative extent to which citizen *demands* are made or anticipated by those in power. We shall return to this point shortly, but suffice it to say here that perceived discrepancies between the general norm of competence or efficacy and one's actual ability to participate effectively may result in feelings of anger, frustration, or cynicism among the young and well educated as well as among underprivileged groups whose experience contradicts expectations.

The Nie, Powell, and Prewitt study also pulls together several themes discussed earlier in this essay. For one thing, it throws further light on the

---

[113]See David Easton and Jack Dennis, "The Child's Acquisition of Regime Norms: Political Efficacy," *American Political Science Review* 61 (Mar. 1967), pp. 25-38.

question of changing social stratification by suggesting how unequal political representation is a continuing facet of status inequalities in advanced democratic nations. However diffused the historic class struggle may have become, there are still social hierarchies of participation, access, and influence. Secondly, the crucial importance of the organizational infrastructure is again brought out. As suggested earlier, the ideological or psychological impact of organizational involvement may be ambiguous for the average member, but organizational elites nevertheless speak with authority by virtue of their position. Once again, however, the weight of earlier patterns of institutionalization becomes apparent, since the existing organizational structure is difficult to change. Finally, the high costs of active political participation again point to relative autonomy of elites in structuring policy alternatives and defining the opportunities for electoral choice.

Looked at from the perspective of much of recent behavioral research, the model of the active, involved citizen and responsible party government is indeed questionable. Professor Wahlke summarizes numerous empirical studies on the linkages between elites and masses in political decision-making and concludes that the primary function of citizens in the modern state is not to make demands on government but to support the system. But it is noteworthy that Wahlke questions not only simplistic "rational-activist" and "responsible party" models of citizen representation and influence, but "polyarchical" (group pluralist) and elitist theories as well. That is, none of the conventional demand-input models provides convincing evidence of effective linkages between citizen interests and aspirations and the policy-making processes of government.

Wahlke's analysis rests heavily on a distinction made earlier by David Easton between demand inputs and support inputs.[114] The former category includes specific requests for policy actions by individuals and groups to which the political authorities respond (hence it encompasses the demand-response premises of traditional liberal democratic theory). The latter (support inputs) recognizes that political systems require and obtain overarching feelings of support if they are to maintain legitimacy. Easton distinguished three levels at which support may be required for political stability:[115]

[114]This was originally set out by Easton in "An Approach to the Analysis of Political Systems," *World Politics* 9 (1956-57), pp. 383-400.

[115]David Easton, *A Systems Analysis of Political Life* (New York: John Wiley & Sons, 1965), chaps. 11-13. The summary here is quoted from Edward N. Muller, "The Representation of Citizens by Political Authorities: Consequences for Regime Support," *American Political Science Review* 64 (Dec. 1970), p. 1151 (emphasis added). The opening pages of this article contain an excellent discussion of Wahlke's and Easton's ideas.

(1) the *political community* or that group of persons bound together by the fact that they participate in a common political enterprise;

(2) the *regime*, or the constitutional order, broadly interpreted to include the values, norms, and structures of authority; and

(3) the *authorities*, or those actors occupying roles in the authority structure—the rulers.

Demand and support attitudes come together at the level of the authorities, because it is to them that demands are actually made. If demands are not met—and citizens become dissatisfied with the performance of public officials—they may deny "specific support" to these leaders. This denial may consequently result in a loss of "diffuse support" for the regime and political community if allowed to continue. Hence the ultimate stability of political systems depends on the performance of government officials in satisfying the demand inputs of citizens, though in the short run support inputs may be crucial.

The difficulty with this model is that it assumes (more or less) that citizens have clear policy preferences and that they react in support behavior according to perceptions of demand satisfaction. Wahlke marshals a host of evidence which suggests that neither of these premises is valid. He thus recommends that political scientists recognize the facts and focus on the citizen's role as "supporter" rather than "influencer" of government. His argument is buttressed by studies of legislative behavior which fail to demonstrate close connections between the motives of representatives and the opinions of their constituents, and a variety of other research which appears to suggest that the particular character of representative structures makes little difference for the general policy outcomes.

Even if some of these findings are taken with a grain of salt, Wahlke's conclusions are disturbing:

> The foregoing arguments are not especially 'anti-democratic' or 'anti-representative'. They are just as damaging to much antidemocratic theory and to elitist criticisms of representative democracy. It is not only policy-opinions of citizens in the mass public which are demoted in the rank order of policy determinants but policy opinions of elites and group leaderships as well. The principal implication is that 'policy-process' studies whose aim is primarily to discover the political bases of policy decisions conceived of as choices between policy alternatives contended for by divergent political forces, or to explain why a particular decision went one way instead of another, comprehend too little of the political life of man, and that the part they do comprehend is probably not its most vital. The appropriate conclusion is not the grandiose notion that representative democracy is chimerical but the limited recognition that our conceptions of government, politics, and representation are somehow deficient, that 'policy making' plays a different and evidently smaller role in the governance of society than we thought.

What then is left for politics? The answer, of course, is maintenance of diffuse civic support for on-going systems of government. Such generalized support is less dependent upon satisfaction of specific citizen or group demands than on psychic or symbolic gratifications. The role of the legislature and other representative agencies is reduced to latent functions such as "legitimization of decisions made elsewhere" and "mobilizing consent."

The important argument here is not only that socialization to support at all levels of government becomes the primary determinant of political legitimacy (and Wahlke performs a valuable service in challenging socialization studies which imply that the result of socialization is participatory rather than supportive orientations), but that system maintenance or persistence is the basic problem of modern democracy.[116] In this light, the fundamental problems of advanced nations do not appear to be analytically different from those of newly developing nations in Africa and Asia plagued by political instability. That is, the overriding problem in the modern industrial state may be that of maintaining (or generating) sufficient popular respect for political institutions which are increasingly remote from direct citizen involvement. Paradoxically, if one follows Wahlke's line of thought, the issue remains one of legitimacy of authority despite the apparent decline in political opposition discussed earlier. This would appear to be the case in advanced Communist systems as well—indeed one assumes that the problem of legitimacy is compounded in the single-party state which suppresses opposition to the authorities and regime and seeks to enforce an overall sense of community.

In the selection following Wahlke's, James H. Oliver employs Easton's demand-support model in analyzing the responses of Soviet officials to citizen complaints and requests. The absence of organized interest groups and party competition, he suggests, has meant that popular demands and grievances are primarily articulated by individual "citizen gatekeepers" and channeled through local bureaucratic officials. Whether in the form of personal representations or collective electoral mandates which party candidates espouse, these demands require a good deal of official attention and are generally taken seriously by the regime. In fact, higher authorities

[116]In addition to the references given in Wahlke, see D. Easton and Jack Dennis, *Children in the Political System: Origins of Political Legitimacy* (New York: McGraw-Hill, 1969), esp. chaps. 2-3. Suffice it to say here that Easton and Dennis distinguish between "system maintenance" and "systems persistence" theories, and view the latter as more relevant. While functional systems maintenance theory tended to imply a continuation of the status quo, systems persistence assumes change and focuses on sources of stress and instability. In other words, systems persistence theory concentrates on the *minimal conditions* which allow a system to operate rather than on optimum conditions for stability. Whether political socialization can then preserve the existence of a system becomes problematical.

have encouraged citizen demands both as a check on the performance of local officials and as an indicator of support for the regime. Since the harrassed official may have limited resources for satisfying these claims and has his own interests to protect, he may in practice tolerate deviant behavior or otherwise seek to avoid citizen pressures. Thus some collusion in illegal activities, together with the demands which are favorably processed, serves to reduce the buildup of dissatisfactions which might otherwise threaten the regime and at the same time (insofar as popular feelings are known) provides the higher leadership with information that is useful in mobilizing broader support. This is not to deny the overall rigidity of the Soviet system or the suppression of undesirable demands and outright political dissent, but it does suggest that citizen participation is a more significant input than has generally been recognized by outside scholars and that this participation is not unrelated to acceptance of the regime. On the other hand, the relatively low level of direct policy influence resulting from this participation bears out the conclusion that mass support does not require effective representation or aggregation of demands so long as immediate needs are met. In the Soviet case, citizen participation is functional to the authority system in that it helps define the rules of the game, generates some feelings of efficacy, and furnishes the leaders with information needed in mobilizing opinion against those who would challenge the regime.

The foregoing discussion suggests that mass political participation remains one of the most problematic aspects of modern society. It has recently been argued that in the Soviet Union and other mature Communist systems, politics have entered the "post-mobilization" stage in which the party elites are no longer capable of directing fundamental social changes from above.[117] Yet demobilization in this sense has not entailed a significant increase in popular representation and influence, and in the democratic countries mobilization appears to revolve as much around symbolic gratification as opposing social and political interests. Most empirical studies have shown low issue awareness and sense of involvement in postwar democratic elections, and some suggest that voting in Western democracies (as in the Soviet Union) amounts to ritualistic affirmation of system support by the majority of citizens.[118] What may occur as societies become more fully integrated structurally and functionally—through the growth of governmental services and regulation, the blurring of lines between public and private sectors, the universal penetration of mass communications media, and the development of innumerable specialized organizations and

[117]See Johnson, *Change in Communist Systems,* especially Richard Lowenthal, "Development vs. Utopia in Communist Policy," pp. 33-116.
[118]This is argued in Richard Rose and Harve Mossawir, "Voting and Elections: A Functional Analysis," *Political Studies* 15 (1967), pp. 173-201.

institutions—is that *political* systems lose relevance in the management and resolution of social conflicts. Other social relationships or subsystems may be more salient for the average citizen than political representation, and political elites may be increasingly circumscribed (apart from electoral mobilization) by established governmental structures and other social institutions. A degree of political demobilization and disintegration on the mass level thus seems present in the advanced stages of modernization.

On the elite level, the people's representatives may be increasingly immobilized by lack of active public support and by the complexity of contemporary political and social issues. The welfare state, whether under democratic or authoritarian leadership, is also highly specialized and bureaucratized in its policy-making and administrative functions. As Max Weber pointed out in the passage reprinted below, bureaucracy is the hallmark of rational-legal authority because it institutionalizes technical competence in the affairs of government. Bureaucratic administration "means fundamentally the exercise of control on the basis of knowledge." Thus Weber foresaw a central characteristic of advanced societies—that decision-making depends increasingly on the command of technical expertise. That he considered this a basic problem for democratic parliamentary systems is suggested in the following excerpt:

> The question is always who controls the existing bureaucratic machinery. And such control is possible only in a very limited degree to persons who are not technical specialists. Generally speaking, the trained permanent official is more likely to get his way in the long run than his nominal superior, the Cabinet minister, who is not a specialist.

Hence while "monocratic" control by a single supreme authority is not likely in modern states divided by numerous political and social interests, democratic control of government may be undermined by the emergence of an administrative class or superior "status groups" whose command of technical resources surpasses that of elected officials.[119] Among other things, the consequence may be growing secrecy in government as possession of esoteric knowledge becomes the basis of decisional influence and power.[120] Insofar as such knowledge is concentrated in the professional bureaucracy it becomes an important element in policy formulation as well as policy execution.

In the final article, Karl D. Bracher focuses on the impact of technical knowledge and executive direction on the functions of parliamentary institutions. He argues that it is "opposition between highly specialized

[119]See *From Max Weber: Essays in Sociology,* ed. H. H. Gerth and C. Wright Mills (New York: Oxford University Press, 1946), chap. VIII, especially pp. 214-216, 232-244.
[120]*Ibid.,* pp. 233-235.

expertise and the principle of democratic participation that appears as the central structural problem of all western parliamentary democracies," since elected representatives are increasingly bypassed in decision-making due to sheer technical incompetence. While legislative committees and party elites may continue to influence specific policies, parliament as a whole is largely irrelevant.

Overtaxed in its assignments, the parliment limits itself to topics that have an effect on the elections and abandons important decisions in practice to the planning and formulating bureaucracy. Thus their roles are often exactly reversed. Lawgiving is transferred to the apparatus of administration and parliament loses its authority to a quasidictatorship of the executives.

Technical assistance and research services are being developed by legislative bodies everywhere, but none (with the possible exception of the facilities available to some American congressional committees) begin to approach parity with those of executive and administrative agencies. Moreover there is the danger that parliamentary experts will themselves become unrepresentative bureaucratic functionaries. Thus Bracher raises the dilemma of how representative institutions might be reformed and participation in decision-making broadened without further isolating elected officials from their constituents.

The erosion of principled party politics is significant in this regard, but must be distinguished from broader ideological or value conflicts in society. It appears increasingly difficult for citizens to identify closely with the political parties which solicit their vote, despite persisting differences of philosophy over government and its functions. Consequently much of the ferment over public affairs in recent years has taken place outside the established partisan frameworks. Student protests and demonstrations, ethnic and racial antagonisms, strikes by public as well as private employees, demands for consumer protection and environmental quality, all have largely bypassed existing party and interest group channels of representation. The growing prerogatives of executive and bureaucratic elites in the field of international affairs has obviously contributed to public alienation and dissent.[121] But on domestic issues as well, it remains to be seen whether new avenues of representation can be institutionalized in advanced political systems. Otherwise, as Robert Dahl put it, democratic opposition may come to focus primarily on the "Leviathan" state itself.[122]

[121]On this point see Wilson C. McWilliams, "Democracy, Publics and Protest: the Problem of Foreign Policy," *Journal of International Affairs* 23 (1969), pp. 189-209.
[122]Dahl, *Political Oppositions in Western Democracies,* pp. 399-401.

CONCLUSION

We have sought to emphasize six general themes in this essay. First, we argued that if modernization theory is to result in greater understanding of the processes by which nations develop it must be infused with more detailed historical research on the developmental problems of currently advanced societies. Second, that on the basis of available evidence modernization has not only contributed to greater opportunities for social integration and political achievement, but has created immense problems of institutional adaptation and reform. Third, that the manner in which crises of adaptation have been met in the past—especially during the transition to mass participation—has had great impact on the institutional and organizational structures of modern politics, which continue to shape the alternatives open to the people. Fourth, that the effects of rapid economic growth and material welfare in recent decades are ambiguous so far as the reduction of socio-political conflict is concerned, since organizational elites may continue to determine the nature of competition. Fifth, that despite the potentials for mass mobilization and civic involvement in advanced societies, the continuing specialization of political functions may have lowered the impact of mass participation on decision-making. Finally, that questions of institutional legitimacy and support remain vital and may yet lead to severe developmental crises in advanced nations.

The latter points raise serious questions concerning democratic theory and practice at the advanced stages of modernization, as well as about the value of currently developed nations as models for the non-Western world. Modernization has been too easily accepted as a universal harbinger of progress and goal to be emulated in the less-developed countries. Yet there is no denying the impact of modernization on societies, both in the past and at present. The problem is that the multiple and reciprocal linkages between change in different sectors or subsystems of society are still only partially understood, and that change itself provides alternative choices at each stage of development. The process of change is therefore not determined by any given set of circumstances so much as by the actions and decisions taken by individual leaders and groups within broad constraints established by modernization. The influence of ideas and values which affect such choices can never be fully explained by reference to empirical indicators of modernity, nor can the expectations and aspirations of the individual citizen.

But social science cannot escape the task of generalizing about past human relationships and experiences. The scope and utility which general theory will ultimately attain is an open question. Whether any one set of universal laws or propositions regarding political development and change will ever be fully accepted by scholars is doubtful, yet the academic mind cannot rest until it has made the effort. Moreover the potential benefits may extend beyond the need to fathom our own historical predicament. As one percipient scholar recently concluded,[123]

Thinking through the value assumptions implicit in assessing changes within modernized societies, particularly our own, may help to clarify value assumptions involved in studying transitional societies at various distances from the threshold of modernization. Such an exercise can also usefully call attention to the extent to which societies which take different paths in transition to modernity may also take different paths out of this category to other stages of development. Conceivably, some transitional societies might attain non-materialistic features characterizing 'post-modern' societies by leapfrogging past some of the less desirable or more ephemeral characteristics of modern societies today.

[123]Richard Rose, "Modern Nations and the Study of Political Modernization," in Stein Rokkan, ed., *Comparative Research Across Culture and Nations* (Paris: Mouton, 1968), pp. 126-127.

A

THE SEARCH FOR DEVELOPMENT THEORY

1

Types of Authority and Legitimacy

Max Weber

I. THE BASIS OF LEGITIMACY [1]

1: The Definition, Conditions, and Types of Imperative Control

'Imperative co-ordination' was defined above [2] as the probability that certain specific commands (or all commands) from a given source will be obeyed by a given group of persons. It thus does not include every mode of exercising 'power' or 'influence' over other persons. The motives of obedience to commands in this sense can rest on considerations varying over a wide range from case to case; all the way from simple habituation to the most purely rational calculation of advantage. A criterion of every true relation of imperative control, however, is a certain minimum of voluntary submission; thus an interest (based on ulterior motives or genuine acceptance) in obedience.

Not every case of imperative co-ordination makes use of economic means; *still less* does it always have economic objectives. But normally (not always) the imperative co-ordination of the action of a considerable number

Reprinted with permission of The Macmillan Company from *The Theory of Social and Economic Organization* by Max Weber, translated by A. M. Henderson and Talcott Parsons. Edited by Talcott Parsons. Copyright 1947 by Talcott Parsons.

[1] In this chapter Weber departs from his previous practice and, in addition to the usual division into numbered sections, has a system of somewhat more comprehensive subdivisions. These will be designated by capital letters.—Ed.

[2] Chap. i, p. 152. The translation problem raised by the term *Herrschaft* was commented upon at that point.—Ed.

of men requires control of a staff of persons.[3] It is necessary, that is, that there should be a relatively high probability that the action of a definite, supposedly reliable group of persons will be primarily oriented to the execution of the supreme authority's general policy and specific commands.

The members of the administrative staff may be bound to obedience to their superior (or superiors) by custom, by affectual ties, by a purely material complex of interests, or by ideal (*wertrational*) motives. *Purely* material interests and calculations of advantage as the basis of solidarity between the chief and his administrative staff result, in this as in other connexions, in a relatively unstable situation. Normally other elements, affectual and ideal, supplement such interests. In certain exceptional, temporary cases the former may be alone decisive. In everyday routine life these relationships, like others, are governed by custom and in addition, material calculation of advantage. But these factors, custom and personal advantage, purely affectual or ideal motives of solidarity, do not, even taken together, form a sufficiently reliable basis for a system of imperative co-ordination. In addition there is normally a further element, the belief in legitimacy.

It is an induction from experience that no system of authority voluntarily limits itself to the appeal to material or affectual or ideal motives as a basis for guaranteeing its continuance. In addition every such system attempts to establish and to cultivate the belief in its 'legitimacy.' But according to the kind of legitimacy which is claimed, the type of obedience, the kind of administrative staff developed to guarantee it, and the mode of exercising authority, will all differ fundamentally. Equally fundamental is the variation in effect. Hence, it is useful to classify the types of authority according to the kind of claim to legitimacy typically made by each. . . .

2: The Three Pure Types of Legitimate Authority

There are three pure types of legitimate authority. The validity of their claims to legitimacy may be based on:

1. Rational grounds—resting on a belief in the 'legality' of patterns of normative rules and the right of those elevated to authority under such rules to issue commands (legal authority).

2. Traditional grounds—resting on an established belief in the sanctity of immemorial traditions and the legitimacy of the status of those exercising authority under them (traditional authority); or finally,

3. Charismatic grounds—resting on devotion to the specific and exceptional sanctity, heroism or exemplary character of an individual person, and

[3]An "administrative staff." See chap. i, p. 12.

of the normative patterns or order revealed or ordained by him (charismatic authority).

In the case of legal authority, obedience is owed to the legally established impersonal order. It extends to the persons exercising the authority of office under it only by virtue of the formal legality of their commands and only within the scope of authority of the office. In the case of traditional authority, obedience is owed to the *person* of the chief who occupies the traditionally sanctioned position of authority and who is (within its sphere) bound by tradition. But here the obligation of obedience is not based on the impersonal order, but is a matter of personal loyalty within the area of accustomed obligations. In the case of charismatic authority, it is the charismatically qualified leader as such who is obeyed by virtue of personal trust in him and his revelation, his heroism or his exemplary qualities so far as they fall within the scope of the individual's belief in his charisma.

1. The usefulness of the above classification can only be judged by its results in promoting systematic analysis. The concept of 'charisma' ('the gift of grace') is taken from the vocabulary of early Christianity. For the Christian religious organization Rudolf Sohm, in his *Kirchenrecht,* was the first to clarify the substance of the concept, even though he did not use the same terminology. Others (for instance, Hollin, *Enthusiasmus und Bussgewalt*) have clarified certain important consequences of it. It is thus nothing new.

2. The fact that none of these three ideal types, the elucidation of which will occupy the following pages, is usually to be found in historical cases in 'pure' form, is naturally not a valid objection to attempting their conceptual formulation in the sharpest possible form. In this respect the present case is no different from many others. Later on (§ 11 ff.) the transformation of pure charisma by the process of routinization will be discussed and thereby the relevance of the concept to the understanding of empirical systems of authority considerably increased. But even so it may be said of every empirically historical phenomenon of authority that it is not likely to be 'as an open book.' Analysis in terms of sociological types has, after all, as compared with purely empirical historical investigation, certain advantages which should not be minimized. That is, it can in the particular case of a concrete form of authority determine what conforms to or approximates such types as 'charisma,' 'hereditary charisma' (§ 10, 11), 'the charisma of office,' 'patriarchy' (§ 7), 'bureaucracy' (§ 4), the authority of status groups,[4] and in doing so it can work with relatively unambiguous concepts. But the idea that the whole of concrete historical reality can be exhausted in the conceptual scheme about to be developed is as far from the author's thoughts as anything could be.

---

[4] *Ständische.* There is no really acceptable English rendering of this term.—Ed.

II. LEGAL AUTHORITY WITH A BUREAUCRATIC ADMINISTRATIVE STAFF[5]

3: Legal Authority: The Pure Type with Employment of a Bureaucratic Administrative Staff

The effectiveness of legal authority rests on the acceptance of the validity of the following mutually inter-dependent ideas.

1. That any given legal norm may be established by agreement or by imposition, on grounds of expediency or rational values or both, with a claim to obedience at least on the part of the members of the corporate group. This is, however, usually extended to include all persons within the sphere of authority or of power in question—which in the case of territorial bodies is the territorial area—who stand in certain social relationships or carry out forms of social action which in the order governing the corporate group have been declared to be relevant.

2. That every body of law consists essentially in a consistent system of abstract rules which have normally been intentionally established. Furthermore, administration of law is held to consist in the application of these rules to particular cases; the administrative process in the rational pursuit of the interests which are specified in the order governing the corporate group within the limits laid down by legal precepts and following principles which are capable of generalized formulation and are approved in the order governing the group, or at least not disapproved in it.

3. That thus the typical person in authority occupies an 'office.' In the action associated with his status, including the commands he issues to others, he is subject to an impersonal order to which his actions are oriented. This is true not only for persons exercising legal authority who are in the usual sense 'officials,' but, for instance, for the elected president of a state.

4. That the person who obeys authority does so, as it is usually stated, only in his capacity as a 'member' of the corporate group and what he obeys is only 'the law.' He may in this connexion be the member of an association, of a territorial commune, of a church, or a citizen of a state.

5. In conformity with point 3, it is held that the members of the corporate group, in so far as they obey a person in authority, do not owe this obedience to him as an individual, but to the impersonal order. Hence, it

[5]The specifically modern type of administration has intentionally been taken as a point of departure in order to make it possible later to contrast the others with it.

follows that there is an obligation to obedience only within the sphere of the rationally delimited authority which, in terms of the order, has been conferred upon him.

The following may thus be said to be the fundamental categories of rational legal authority:—

(1) A continuous organization of official functions bound by rules.

(2) A specified sphere of competence. This involves (a) a sphere of obligations to perform functions which has been marked off as part of a systematic division of labour. (b) The provision of the incumbent with the necessary authority to carry out these functions. (c) That the necessary means of compulsion are clearly defined and their use is subject to definite conditions. A unit exercising authority which is organized in this way will be called an 'administrative organ.' [6]

There are administrative organs in this sense in large-scale private organizations, in parties and armies, as well as in the state and the church. An elected president, a cabinet of ministers, or a body of elected representatives also in this sense constitute administrative organs. This is not, however, the place to discuss these concepts. Not every administrative organ is provided with compulsory powers. But this distinction is not important for present purposes.

(3) The organization of offices follows the principle of hierarchy; that is, each lower office is under the control and supervision of a higher one. There is a right of appeal and of statement of grievances from the lower to the higher. Hierarchies differ in respect to whether and in what cases complaints can lead to a ruling from an authority at various points higher in the scale, and as to whether changes are imposed from higher up or the responsibility for such changes is left to the lower office, the conduct of which was the subject of complaint.

(4) The rules which regulate the conduct of an office may be technical rules or norms. [7] In both cases, if their application is to be fully rational, specialized training is necessary. It is thus normally true that only a person who has demonstrated an adequate technical training is qualified to be a member of the administrative staff of such an organized group, and hence only such persons are eligible for appointment to official positions. The administrative staff of a rational corporate group thus typically consists of 'officials,' whether the organization be devoted to political, religious, economic—in particular, capitalistic—or other ends.

---

[6] *Behörde.*

[7] Weber does not explain this distinction. By a "technical rule" he probably means a prescribed course of action which is dictated primarily on grounds touching efficiency of the performance of the immediate functions, while by "norms" he probably means rules which limit conduct on grounds other than those of efficiency. Of course, in one sense all rules are norms in that they are prescriptions for conduct, conformity with which is problematical.—Ed.

(5) In the rational type it is a matter of principle that the members of the administrative staff should be completely separated from ownership of the means of production or administration. Officials, employees, and workers attached to the administrative staff do not themselves own the non-human means of production and administration. These are rather provided for their use in kind or in money, and the official is obligated to render an accounting of their use. There exists, furthermore, in principle complete separation of the property belonging to the organization, which is controlled within the sphere of office, and the personal property of the official, which is available for his own private uses. There is a corresponding separation of the place in which official functions are carried out, the 'office' in the sense of premises, from living quarters.

(6) In the rational type case, there is also a complete absence of appropriation of his official position by the incumbent. Where 'rights' to an office exist, as in the case of judges, and recently of an increasing proportion of officials and even of workers, they do not normally serve the purpose of appropriation by the official, but of securing the purely objective and independent character of the conduct of the office so that it is oriented only to the relevant norms.

(7) Administrative acts, decisions, and rules are formulated and recorded in writing, even in cases where oral discussion is the rule or is even mandatory. This applies at least to preliminary discussions and proposals, to final decisions, and to all sorts of orders and rules. The combination of written documents and a continuous organization of official functions constitutes the 'office'[8] which is the central focus of all types of modern corporate action.

(8) Legal authority can be exercised in a wide variety of different forms which will be distinguished and discussed later. The following analysis will be deliberately confined for the most part to the aspect of imperative co-ordination in the structure of the administrative staff. It will consist in an analysis in terms of ideal types of officialdom or 'bureaucracy.'

In the above outline no mention has been made of the kind of supreme head appropriate to a system of legal authority. This is a consequence of certain considerations which can only be made entirely understandable at a

[8]*Bureau.* It has seemed necessary to use the English word "office" in three different meanings, which are distinguished in Weber's discussion by at least two terms. The first is *Amt.* which means "office" in the sense of the institutionally defined status of a person. The second is the "work premises" as in the expression "he spent the afternoon in his office." For this Weber uses *Bureau* as also for the third meaning which he has just defined, the "organized work process of a group." In this last sense an office is a particular type of "organization," or *Betrieb* in Weber's sense. This use is established in English in such expressions as "the District Attorney's Office has such and such functions." Which of the three meanings is involved in a given case will generally be clear from the context.—Ed.

later stage in the analysis. There are very important types of rational imperative co-ordination which, with respect to the ultimate source of authority, belong to other categories. This is true of the hereditary charismatic type, as illustrated by hereditary monarchy and of the pure charismatic type of a president chosen by plebiscite. Other cases involve rational elements at important points, but are made up of a combination of bureaucratic and charismatic components, as is true of the cabinet form of government. Still others are subject to the authority of the chief of other corporate groups, whether their character be charismatic or bureaucratic; thus the formal head of a government department under a parliamentary regime may be a minister who occupies his position because of his authority in a party. The type of rational, legal administrative staff is capable of application in all kinds of situations and contexts. It is the most important mechanism for the administration of everyday profane affairs. For in that sphere, the exercise of authority and, more broadly, imperative co-ordination, consists precisely in administration.

4: Legal Authority: The Pure Type with Employment of a Bureaucratic Administrative Staff—(Continued)

The purest type of exercise of legal authority is that which employs a bureaucratic administrative staff. Only the supreme chief of the organization occupies his position of authority by virtue of appropriation, of election, or of having been designated for the succession. But even *his* authority consists in a sphere of legal 'competence.' The whole administrative staff under the supreme authority then consists, in the purest type, of individual officials who are appointed and function according to the following criteria:[9]

(1) They are personally free and subject to authority only with respect to their impersonal official obligations.

(2) They are organized in a clearly defined hierarchy of offices.

(3) Each office has a clearly defined sphere of competence in the legal sense.

(4) The office is filled by a free contractual relationship. Thus, in principle, there is free selection.

(5) Candidates are selected on the basis of technical qualifications. In the most rational case, this is tested by examination or guaranteed by diplomas certifying technical training, or both. They are *appointed*, not elected.

[9]This characterization applies to the "monocratic" as opposed to the "collegial" type, which will be discussed below.

(6) They are remunerated by fixed salaries in money, for the most part with a right to pensions. Only under certain circumstances does the employing authority, especially in private organizations, have a right to terminate the appointment, but the official is always free to resign. The salary scale is primarily graded according to rank in the hierarchy; but in addition to this criterion, the responsibility of the position and the requirements of the incumbent's social status may be taken into account.[10]

(7) The office is treated as the sole, or at least the primary, occupation of the incumbent.

(8) It constitutes a career. There is a system of 'promotion' according to seniority or to achievement, or both. Promotion is dependent on the judgment of superiors.

(9) The official works entirely separated from ownership of the means of administration and without appropriation of his position.

(10) He is subject to strict and systematic discipline and control in the conduct of the office.

This type of organization is in principle applicable with equal facility to a wide variety of different fields. It may be applied in profit-making business or in charitable organizations, or in any number of other types of private enterprises serving ideal or material ends. It is equally applicable to political and to religious organizations. With varying degrees of approximation to a pure type, its historical existence can be demonstrated in all these fields. . . .

5: The Monocratic Type of Bureaucratic Administration

Experience tends universally to show that the purely bureaucratic type of administrative organization—that is, the monocratic variety of bureaucracy—is, from a purely technical point of view, capable of attaining the highest degree of efficiency and is in this sense formally the most rational known means of carrying out imperative control over human beings. It is superior to any other form in precision, in stability, in the stringency of its discipline, and in its reliability. It thus makes possible a particularly high degree of calculability of results for the heads of the organization and for those acting in relation to it. It is finally superior both in intensive efficiency and in the scope of its operations, and is formally capable of application to all kinds of administrative tasks.

The development of the modern form of the organization of corporate groups in all fields is nothing less than identical with the development and continual spread of bureaucratic administration. This is true of church and state, of armies, political parties, economic enterprises, organizations to

[10]See below, chap. iv.

promote all kinds of causes, private associations, clubs, and many others. Its development is, to take the most striking case, the most crucial phenomenon of the modern Western state. However many forms there may be which do not appear to fit this pattern, such as collegial representative bodies, parliamentary committees, soviets, honorary officers, lay judges, and what not, and however much people may complain about the 'evils of bureaucracy,' it would be sheer illusion to think for a moment that continuous administrative work can be carried out in any field except by means of officials working in offices. The whole pattern of everyday life is cut to fit this framework. For bureaucratic administration is, other things being equal, always, from a formal, technical point of view, the most rational type. For the needs of mass administration to-day, it is completely indispensable. The choice is only that between bureaucracy and dilletantism in the field of administration.

The primary source of the superiority of bureaucratic administration lies in the role of technical knowledge which, through the development of modern technology and business methods in the production of goods, has become completely indispensable. In this respect, it makes no difference whether the economic system is organized on a capitalistic or a socialistic basis. Indeed, if in the latter case a comparable level of technical efficiency were to be achieved, it would mean a tremendous increase in the importance of specialized bureaucracy.

When those subject to bureaucratic control seek to escape the influence of the existing bureaucratic apparatus, this is normally possible only by creating an organization of their own which is equally subject to the process of bureaucratization. Similarly the existing bureaucratic apparatus is driven to continue functioning by the most powerful interests which are material and objective, but also ideal in character. Without it, a society like our own—with a separation of officials, employees, and workers from ownership of the means of administration, dependent on discipline and on technical training—could no longer function. The only exception would be those groups, such as the peasantry, who are still in possession of their own means of subsistence. Even in case of revolution by force or of occupation by an enemy, the bureaucratic machinery will normally continue to function just as it has for the previous legal government.

The question is always who controls the existing bureaucratic machinery. And such control is possible only in a very limited degree to persons who are not technical specialists. Generally speaking, the trained permanent official is more likely to get his way in the long run than his nominal superior, the Cabinet minister, who is not a specialist.

Though by no means alone, the capitalistic system has undeniably played a major role in the development of bureaucracy. Indeed, without it capitalistic production could not continue and any rational type of socialism would have simply to take it over and increase its importance. Its development, largely under capitalistic auspices, has created an urgent need for stable, strict, intensive, and calculable administration. It is this need which gives bureaucracy a crucial role in our society as the central element in any kind of large-scale administration. Only by reversion in every field—political, religious, economic, etc.—to small-scale organization would it be possible to any considerable extent to escape its influence. On the one hand, capitalism in its modern stages of development strongly tends to foster the development of bureaucracy, though both capitalism and bureaucracy have arisen from many different historical sources. Conversely, capitalism is the most rational economic basis for bureaucratic administration and enables it to develop in the most rational form, especially because, from a fiscal point of view, it supplies the necessary money resources.

Along with these fiscal conditions of efficient bureaucratic administration, there are certain extremely important conditions in the fields of communication and transportation. The precision of its functioning requires the services of the railway, the telegraph, and the telephone, and becomes increasingly dependent on them. A socialistic form of organization would not alter this fact. It would be a question whether in a socialistic system it would be possible to provide conditions for carrying out as stringent bureaucratic organization as has been possible in a capitalistic order. For socialism would, in fact, require a still higher degree of formal bureaucratization than capitalism. If this should prove not to be possible, it would demonstrate the existence of another of those fundamental elements of irrationality in social systems—a conflict between formal and substantive rationality of the sort which sociology so often encounters.

Bureaucratic administration means fundamentally the exercise of control on the basis of knowledge. This is the feature of it which makes it specifically rational. This consists on the one hand in technical knowledge which, by itself, is sufficient to ensure it a position of extraordinary power. But in addition to this, bureaucratic organizations, or the holders of power who make use of them, have the tendency to increase their power still further by the knowledge growing out of experience in the service. For they acquire through the conduct of office a special knowledge of facts and have available a store of documentary material peculiar to themselves. While not peculiar to bureaucratic organizations, the concept of 'official secrets' is certainly typical of them. It stands in relation to technical knowledge in somewhat the same position as commercial secrets do to technological training. It is a product of the striving for power.

Bureaucracy is superior in knowledge, including both technical knowledge and knowledge of the concrete fact within its own sphere of interest, which is usually confined to the interests of a private business—a capitalistic enterprise. The capitalistic entrepreneur is, in our society, the only type who has been able to maintain at least relative immunity from subjection to the control of rational bureaucratic knowledge. All the rest of the population have tended to be organized in large-scale corporate groups which are inevitably subject to bureaucratic control. This is as inevitable as the dominance of precision machinery in the mass production of goods.

The following are the principal more general social consequences of bureaucratic control:—

(1) The tendency to 'levelling' in the interest of the broadest possible basis of recruitment in terms of technical competence.

(2) The tendency to plutocracy growing out of the interest in the greatest possible length of technical training. To-day this often lasts up to the age of thirty.

(3) The dominance of a spirit of formalistic impersonality, '*Sine ira et studio,*' without hatred or passion, and hence without affection or enthusiasm. The dominant norms are concepts of straightforward duty without regard to personal considerations. Everyone is subject to formal equality of treatment; that is, everyone in the same empirical situation. This is the spirit in which the ideal official conducts his office.

The development of bureaucracy greatly favours the levelling of social classes and this can be shown historically to be the normal tendency. Conversely, every process of social levelling creates a favourable situation for the development of bureaucracy; for it tends to eliminate class privileges, which include the appropriation of means of administration and the appropriation of authority as well as the occupation of offices on an honorary basis or as an avocation by virtue of wealth. This combination everywhere inevitably foreshadows the development of mass democracy, which will be discussed in another connexion.

The 'spirit' of rational bureaucracy has normally the following general characteristics:

(1) Formalism, which is promoted by all the interests which are concerned with the security of their own personal situation, whatever this may consist in. Otherwise the door would be open to arbitrariness and hence formalism is the line of least resistance.

(2) There is another tendency, which is apparently in contradiction to the above, a contradiction which is in part genuine. It is the tendency of officials to treat their official function from what is substantively a utilitarian point of view in the interest of the welfare of those under their authority. But this utilitarian tendency is generally expressed in the enactment of corresponding regulatory measures which themselves have a formal character and tend to be treated in a formalistic spirit.[11] This tendency to substantive rationality is supported by all those subject to authority who are not included in the class mentioned above as interested in the security of advantages already controlled. The problems which open up at this point belong in the theory of 'democracy.'

[11] This will be further discussed in the Sociology of Law.

III. TRADITIONAL AUTHORITY

6: Traditional Authority

A system of imperative co-ordination will be called 'traditional' if legitimacy is claimed for it and believed in on the basis of the sanctity of the order and the attendant powers of control as they have been handed down from the past, 'have always existed.' The person or persons exercising authority are designated according to traditionally transmitted rules. The object of obedience is the personal authority of the individual which he enjoys by virtue of his traditional status. The organized group exercising authority is, in the simplest case, primarily based on relations of personal loyalty, cultivated through a common process of education. The person exercising authority is not a 'superior,' but a personal 'chief.'[12]

His administrative staff does not consist primarily of officials, but of personal retainers.[13] Those subject to authority are not 'members' of an association, but are either his traditional 'comrades' or his 'subjects.' What determines the relations of the administrative staff to the chief is not the impersonal obligation of office, but personal loyalty to the chief.

Obedience is not owed to enacted rules, but to the person who occupies a position of authority by tradition or who has been chosen for such a position on a traditional basis. His commands are legitimized in one of two ways: (a) partly in terms of traditions which themselves directly determine the content of the command and the objects and extent of authority. In so far as this is true, to overstep the traditional limitations would endanger his traditional status by undermining acceptance of his legitimacy. (b) In part, it is a matter of the chief's free personal decision, in that tradition leaves a certain sphere open for this. This sphere of traditional prerogative rests primarily on the fact that the obligations of obedience on the basis of personal loyalty are essentially unlimited.[14] There is thus a double sphere: on the one hand, of action which is bound to specific tradition; on the other hand, of that which is free of any specific rules.

In the latter sphere, the chief is free to confer 'grace' on the basis of his personal pleasure or displeasure, his personal likes and dislikes, quite arbitrarily, particularly in return for gifts which often become a source of regular income. So far as his action follows principles at all, these are

[12] *Herr.*
[13] *Diener.*
[14] This does not seem to be a very happy formulation of the essential point. It is not necessary that the authority of a person in such a position, such as the head of a household, should be unlimited. It is rather that its extent is unspecified. It is generally limited by higher obligations, but the burden of proof rests upon the person on whom an obligation is laid that there is such a conflicting higher obligation.—Ed.

principles of substantive ethical common sense, of justice, or of utilitarian expediency. They are not, however, as in the case of legal authority, formal principles. The exercise of authority is normally oriented to the question of what the chief and his administrative staff will normally permit, in view of the traditional obedience of the subjects and what will or will not arouse their resistance. When resistance occurs, it is directed against the person of the chief or of a member of his staff. The accusation is that he has failed to observe the traditional limits of his authority. Opposition is not directed against the system as such.

It is impossible in the pure type of traditional authority for law or administrative rules to be deliberately created by legislation. What is actually new is thus claimed to have always been in force but only recently to have become known through the wisdom of the promulgator. The only documents which can play a part in the orientation of legal administration are the documents of tradition; namely, precedents.

7: Traditional Authority—(Continued)

A traditional chief exercises authority with or without an administrative staff. The typical administrative staff is recruited from one or more of the following sources:

(a) From persons who are already related to the chief by traditional ties of personal loyalty. This will be called 'patrimonial' recruitment. Such persons may be kinsmen, slaves, dependents who are officers of the household, clients, coloni, or freedmen.

(b) It may be recruited from other sources on an 'extra-patrimonial' basis. This category includes people in a relation of purely personal loyalty, such as all sorts of 'favourites,' people standing in a relation of fealty to their chief—'vassals'—and, finally, those who have of their own free will entered into a relation of personal loyalty as officials.

In traditionalistic organizations, it is very common for the most important posts to be filled with members of a ruling family or clan.

In patrimonial administrations, it is common for slaves or freedmen to rise even to the highest positions. It has not been uncommon even for Grand Viziers to have been at one time slaves.

The typical household officials have been the following: the senechal, the marshal (once in charge of horses), the chamberlain, the carver, the steward, who was the head of the service personnel and possibly even of the vassals. These are to be found everywhere in Europe. In the Orient, in addition, the head eunuch, who was in charge of the harem, has been particularly important. In the African kingdoms, the executioner is often included. Universally, the body physician, the astrologer, and various others have been common.

In China and in Egypt, the principal source of recruitment for patrimonial officials lay in the clientele of the king. Armies of coloni have been
known throughout the Orient and were typical of the Roman nobility. Even
in modern times, in the Mohammedan world, armies of slaves have existed.

The regime of 'favourites' is characteristic of every patrimonial system
and has often been the occasion for 'traditionalistic' revolutions.

The status of 'vassal' will be dealt with separately.

Bureaucracy has first developed in patrimonial states with a body of
officials recruited from extra-patrimonial sources; but, as will be shown
presently, these 'officials' have originally been personal followers of their
chief.

In the pure type of traditional authority, the following features of a
bureaucratic administrative staff are absent: (a) a clearly defined sphere of
competence subject to impersonal rules, (b) a rational ordering of relations of
superiority and inferiority, (c) a regular system of appointment and promotion on the basis of free contract, (d) technical training as a regular
requirement, (e) fixed salaries, in the type case paid in money.

In place of a well-defined impersonal sphere of competence, there is a
shifting series of tasks and powers commissioned and granted by a chief
through his arbitrary decision of the moment. They then tend to become
permanent and are often traditionally stereotyped. An important influence is
exerted by competition for sources of income and advantage which are at the
disposal of the persons acting on behalf of the chief or of the chief himself. It
is often in the first instance through these interests that definite functional
spheres are first marked off and, with them, genuine administrative organs.

In the first instance, those with permanent functions are household
officials of the chief. Their functions outside the administration of the
household itself are often in fields of activity which bear a relatively
superficial analogy to their household function, or even which have originated in a completely arbitrary act of the chief, and have later become
traditionally stereotyped. In addition to household officers, there have
existed primarily only persons with *ad hoc* specific commissions.

The absence of clear spheres of competence is clearly evident from a
perusal of the list of the titles of officials in any of the Ancient Oriental
states. With rare exceptions, it is impossible to associate with these titles a
set of functions rationally delimited in the modern Western sense which has
remained stable over a considerable period.

The process of defining permanent functions in terms of competition
among and compromise between interests seeking favours, income, and
other forms of advantage is especially clearly evident in the Middle Ages.
This phenomenon has had very important consequences. The interests in
fees of the powerful Royal courts and of the powerful legal profession in
England was largely responsible, partly for breaking the influence of Roman
and Canon law, partly for limiting it. Existing irrational divisions of official

functions have frequently in all periods been stereotyped by the existence of an established set of rights to fees and perquisites.

In contrast to the rational hierarchy of authority in the bureaucratic system, the question who shall decide a matter—which of his officials or the chief himself—or who shall deal with complaints, is, in a traditional regime, treated in one of two ways. (1) Traditionally, on the basis of the authority of particular received legal norms or precedents. (2) Entirely on the basis of the arbitrary decision of the chief. Whenever he intervenes personally, all others give way to him.

In Germanic law, apart from the traditionalistic system of adherence to precedent, there is a principle which is derived from the arbitrary power of the political chief; namely, that in the presence of the chief himself the jurisdiction of any court is suspended. This principle has the same source as the *jus avocandi,* in the arbitrary grace of a monarch and its modern derivative, chamber justice. A court rendering judgment in terms of precedents was in the Middle Ages very often the agency which declared and interpreted the law and was thus the principal source from which the law of a locality was taken.

As opposed to the bureaucratic system of free appointment, household officials and favourites are very often recruited on a purely patrimonial basis from among the slaves or serfs of the chief. If, on the other hand, the recruitment has been extra-patrimonial, they have tended to be holders of benefices which he has granted as an act of grace without being bound by any formal rules. A fundamental change in this situation is first brought about by the rise of free vassals and the filling of offices by a contract of fealty. Since, however, such relations of fealty have been by no means primarily determined by considerations of objective function, this has not altered the situation with respect to definite spheres of competence or clearly determined hierarchical relationships. Except under certain circumstances when the administrative staff is organized on a basis of praebends, there is such a thing as 'promotion' only according to the arbitrary grace of the chief.

Rational technical training as a basic qualification for office is scarcely to be found at all among household officials or the favourites of a chief. Where there is even a beginning of technical training for appointees, regardless of what it consists in, this fact everywhere makes for a fundamental change in the development of administrative practice.

For many offices a certain amount of empirical training has been necessary from very early times. This is particularly true of the 'art' of reading and writing which was originally truly an art with a high scarcity value. This has often, most strikingly in China, had a decisive influence on the whole development of culture through the mode of life of persons with a literary education. Among other things, it has eliminated the recruiting of officials from intra-patrimonial sources and has thus limited the power of the chief by making him dependent on a definite social group.

In place of regular salaries, household officials and favourites are usually supported and equipped in the household of the chief and from his personal stores. Generally, their exclusion from the lord's own table means the creation of benefices, at first usually benefices in kind. It is easy for these to become traditionally stereotyped in amount and kind. Along with the elements supported by benefices or in place of them, there are various agencies commissioned by the lord outside his own household, as well as various fees which are due him. The latter are often collected without any regular rate or scale, being agreed upon from case to case with those seeking favours. . . .[15]

IV. CHARISMATIC AUTHORITY

10: The Principal Characteristics of Charismatic Authority and Its Relation to Forms of Communal Organization

The term 'charisma' will be applied to a certain quality of an individual personality by virtue of which he is set apart from ordinary men and treated as endowed with supernatural, superhuman, or at least specifically exceptional powers or qualities. These are such as are not accessible to the ordinary person, but are regarded as of divine origin or as exemplary, and on the basis of them the individual concerned is treated as a leader. In primitive circumstances this peculiar kind of deference is paid to prophets, to people with a reputation for therapeutic or legal wisdom, to leaders in the hunt, and heroes in war. It is very often thought of as resting on magical powers. How the quality in question would be ultimately judged from any ethical, aesthetic, or other such point of view is naturally entirely indifferent for purposes of definition. What is alone important is how the individual is actually regarded by those subject to charismatic authority, by his 'followers' or 'disciples.'

For present purposes it will be necessary to treat a variety of different types as being endowed with charisma in this sense. It includes the state of a 'berserker' whose spells of maniac passion have, apparently wrongly, sometimes been attributed to the use of drugs. In Medieval Byzantium a group of people endowed with this type of charismatic war-like passion were maintained as a kind of weapon. It includes the 'shaman,' the kind of magician who in the pure type is subject to epileptoid seizures as a means of

[15]The concept of "benefices" will be taken up presently.

falling into trances. Another type is that of Joseph Smith, the founder of Mormonism, who, however, cannot be classified in this way with absolute certainty since there is a possibility that he was a very sophisticated type of deliberate swindler. Finally it includes the type of intellectual, such as Kurt Eisner,[16] who is carried away with his own demagogic success. Sociological analysis, which must abstain from value judgments, will treat all these on the same level as the men who, according to conventional judgments, are the 'greatest' heroes, prophets, and saviours.

1. It is recognition on the part of those subject to authority which is decisive for the validity of charisma. This is freely given and guaranteed by what is held to be a 'sign' or proof,[17] originally always a miracle, and consists in devotion to the corresponding revelation, hero worship, or absolute trust in the leader. But where charisma is genuine, it is not this which is the basis of the claim to legitimacy. This basis lies rather in the conception that it is the *duty* of those who have been called to a charismatic mission to recognize its quality and to act accordingly. Psychologically this 'recognition' is a matter of complete personal devotion to the possessor of the quality, arising out of enthusiasm, or of despair and hope.

No prophet has ever regarded his quality as dependent on the attitudes of the masses toward him. No elective king or military leader has ever treated those who have resisted him or tried to ignore him otherwise than as delinquent in duty. Failure to take part in a military expedition under such leader, even though recruitment is formally voluntary, has universally been met with disdain.

2. If proof of his charismatic qualification fails him for long, the leader endowed with charisma tends to think his god or his magical or heroic powers have deserted him. If he is for long unsuccessful, above all if his leadership fails to benefit his followers, it is likely that his charismatic authority will disappear. This is the genuine charismatic meaning of the 'gift of grace.'[18]

Even the old Germanic kings were sometimes rejected with scorn. Similar phenomena are very common among so-called 'primitive' peoples. In China the charismatic quality of the monarch, which was transmitted unchanged by heredity, was upheld so rigidly that any misfortune whatever, not only defeats in war, but drought, floods, or astronomical phenomena which were considered unlucky, forced him to do public penance and might even force his abdication. If such things occurred, it was a sign that he did not possess the requisite charismatic virtue, he was thus not a legitimate 'Son of Heaven.'

---

[16] The leader of the communistic experiment in Bavaria in 1919.—Ed.

[17] *Bewährung.*

[18] *Gottesgnadentum.*

3. The corporate group which is subject to charismatic authority is based on an emotional form of communal relationship.[19] The administrative staff of a charismatic leader does not consist of 'officials'; at least its members are not technically trained. It is not chosen on the basis of social privilege nor from the point of view of domestic or personal dependency. It is rather chosen in terms of the charismatic qualities of its members. The prophet has his disciples; the war lord his selected henchmen; the leader, generally, his followers. There is no such thing as 'appointment' or 'dismissal,' no career, no promotion. There is only a 'call' at the instance of the leader on the basis of the charismatic qualification of those he summons. There is no hierarchy; the leader merely intervenes in general or in individual cases when he considers the members of his staff inadequate to a task with which they have been entrusted. There is no such thing as a definite sphere 'of authority and of competence, and no appropriation of official powers on the basis of social privileges. There may, however, be territorial or functional limits to charismatic powers and to the individual's 'mission.' There is no such thing as a salary or a benefice. Disciples or followers tend to live primarily in a communistic relationship with their leader on means which have been provided by voluntary gift. There are no established administrative organs. In their place are agents who have been provided with charismatic authority by their chief or who possess charisma of their own. There is no system of formal rules, of abstract legal principles, and hence no process of judicial decision oriented to them. But equally there is no legal wisdom oriented to judicial precedent. Formally concrete judgments are newly created from case to case and are originally regarded as divine judgments and revelations. From a substantive point of view, every charismatic authority would have to subscribe to the proposition, 'It is written . . . , but I say unto you. . . .'[20] The genuine prophet, like the genuine military leader and every true leader in this sense, preaches, creates, or demands *new* obligations. In the pure type of charisma, these are imposed on the authority of revolution by oracles, or of the leader's own will, and are recognized by the members of the religious, military, or party group, because they come from such a source. Recognition is a duty. When such an authority comes into conflict with the competing authority of another who also claims charismatic sanction, the only recourse is to some kind of a contest, by magical means or even an actual physical battle of the leaders. In principle, only one side can be in the right in such a conflict; the other must be guilty of a wrong which has to be expiated.

Charismatic authority is thus specifically outside the realm of everyday

---

[19]Weber uses the term *Gemeinde*, which is not directly translatable.—Ed.

[20]Something contrary to what was written, as Jesus said in opposition to the Scribes and Pharisees.—Ed.

routine and the profane sphere.[21] In this respect, it is sharply opposed both to rational, and particularly bureaucratic, authority, and to traditional authority, whether in its patriarchal, patrimonial, or any other form. Both rational and traditional authority are specifically forms of everyday routine control of action; while the charismatic type is the direct antithesis of this. Bureaucratic authority is specifically rational in the sense of being bound to intellectually analysable rules; while charismatic authority is specifically irrational in the sense of being foreign to all rules. Traditional authority is bound to the precedents handed down from the past and to this extent is also oriented to rules. Within the sphere of its claims, charismatic authority repudiates the past, and is in this sense a specifically revolutionary force. It recognizes no appropriation of positions of power by virtue of the possession of property, either on the part of a chief or of socially privileged groups. The only basis of legitimacy for it is personal charisma, so long as it is proved; that is, as long as it receives recognition and is able to satisfy the followers or disciples. But this lasts only so long as the belief in its charismatic inspiration remains.

The above is scarcely in need of further discussion. What has been said applies to the position of authority of such elected monarchs as Napoleon, with his use of the plebiscite. It applies to the 'rule of genius,' which has elevated people of humble origin to thrones and high military commands, just as much as it applies to religious prophets or war heroes.

4. Pure charisma is specifically foreign to economic considerations. Whenever it appears, it constitutes a 'call' in the most emphatic sense of the word, a 'mission' or a 'spiritual duty.' In the pure type, it disdains and repudiates economic exploitation of the gifts of grace as a source of income, though, to be sure, this often remains more an ideal than a fact. It is not that charisma always means the renunciation of property or even of acquisition, as under certain circumstances prophets and their disciples do. The heroic warrior and his followers actively seek 'booty'; the elective ruler or the charismatic party leader requires the material means of power. The former in addition requires a brilliant display of his authority to bolster his prestige. What is despised, so long as the genuinely charismatic type is adhered to, is traditional or rational everyday economizing, the attainment of a regular income by continuous economic activity devoted to this end. Support by gifts, sometimes on a grand scale involving foundations, even by bribery and grand-scale honoraria, or by begging, constitute the strictly voluntary type of support. On the other hand, 'booty,' or coercion, whether by force or by other means, is the other typical form of charismatic provision for needs.

---

[21]Weber used the antithesis of *Charisma* and *Alltag* in two senses. On the one hand, of the extraordinary and temporary as opposed to the everyday and routine; on the other hand, the sacred as opposed to the profane. See the editor's *Structure of Social Action*, ch. xvii.—Ed.

From the point of view of rational economic activity, charisma is a typical anti-economic force. It repudiates any sort of involvement in the everyday routine world. It can only tolerate, with an attitude of complete emotional indifference, irregular, unsystematic, acquisitive acts. In that it relieves the recipient of economic concerns, dependence on property income can be the economic basis of a charismatic mode of life for some groups; but that is not usually acceptable for the normal charismatic 'revolutionary.'

The fact that incumbency of church office has been forbidden to the Jesuits is a rationalized application of this principle of discipleship. The fact that all the 'virtuosi' of asceticism, the mendicant orders, and fighters for a faith belong in this category, is quite clear. Almost all prophets have been supported by voluntary gifts. The well-known saying of St. Paul, 'If a man does not work, neither shall he eat,' was directed against the swarm of charismatic missionaries. It obviously has nothing to do with a positive valuation of economic activity for its own sake, but only lays it down as a duty of each individual somehow to provide for his own support. This because he realized that the purely charismatic parable of the lilies of the field was not capable of literal application, but at best 'taking no thought for the morrow' could be hoped for. On the other hand, in such a case as primarily an artistic type of charismatic discipleship, it is conceivable that insulation from economic struggle should mean limitation of those who were really eligible to the 'economically independent'; that is, to persons living on income from property. This has been true of the circle of Stefan George, at least in its primary intentions.

5. In traditionally stereotyped periods, charisma is the greatest revolutionary force. The equally revolutionary force of 'reason' works from without by altering the situations of action, and hence its problems finally in this way changing men's attitudes toward them; or it intellectualizes the individual. Charisma, on the other hand, may involve a subjective or internal reorientation born out of suffering, conflicts, or enthusiasm. It may then result in a radical alteration of the central system of attitudes and directions of action with a completely new orientation of all attitudes toward the different problems and structures of the 'world.'[22] In prerationalistic periods, tradition and charisma between them have almost exhausted the whole of the orientation of action.

---

[22]Weber here uses *Welt* in quotation marks, indicating that it refers to its meaning in what is primarily a religious context. It is the sphere of "worldly" things and interests as distinguished from transcendental religious interests.—Ed.

2

Political Systems
and Political Change

Gabriel A. Almond

Concern with the problem of political development and change has acquired a new impetus in recent decades. This is primarily a response to the emergence in the contemporary world of the new nations, and the efforts of many of the older ones to modernize themselves. Students of politics seeking to explain and order these phenomena have found little help in the concepts and insights of political theory. This is not to say that political theorists have neglected the theme of political change.

CONCEPTS OF POLITICAL CHANGE IN POLITICAL HISTORY

Plato and Aristotle placed political stability and change at the very center of their theories. Their conception of the three pure forms of government—aristocracy, monarchy, and democracy—the principles embodied in these forms, the causes of their perversion, and the sequences of change which they are alleged to undergo, has been one of the most influential conceptual schemes in the history of political theory. These ideas are to be found repeated, elaborated, and modified in Polybius, Cicero, Machiavelli, Bodin, Locke, Montesquieu, and the Federalist Papers.[1] Simi-

"Political Systems and Political Change," by Gabriel Almond is reprinted from *American Behavioral Scientist,* Volume VI, Number 10 (June 1963), pp. 3-10, by permission of the Publisher, Sage Publications, Inc. Abridged by permission of the author.
    [1]See W. A. Dunning, *A History of Political Theories: Ancient and Medieval* (New York: Macmillan, 1923), chaps. II, III, IV; Dunning, *Political Theories from Luther to Montesquieu,* chaps. III, X, XII; and C. E. Merriam, *American Political Theories* (New York; Macmillan, 1920), chap. III.

larly, Aristotle's and Polybius' formula for obtaining the best and most stable form of government by mixing the pure forms, elaborated in a more modern context and with variations by Montesquieu, was one of the chief theoretical tools employed by the Founding Fathers in framing the American Constitution.

In this conception of political development as it was formulated in the Enlightenment, change was seen as inevitably progressive, as political institutions became more congruent with man's nature as a reasoning, choosing being with inalienable rights. The more conservative Enlightenment tradition took a more qualified view of man's nature and stressed the importance of institutional arrangements which would mitigate the impact of transient popular passions on institutions and public policy. The Radical tradition in England and the Populist tendency in America rejected these qualifications, unequivocally favored popular participation in governmental processes, and postulated a trend of political change in which these principles would imminently be realized. Whether in its qualified or extreme form, the Enlightenment theory of political change was a unilinear evolutionary theory of progress toward more popular government.

A variant of this Enlightenment approach to political change was manifested in the continental European social revolutionary movements of the nineteenth century, and particularly in Marxism. Marxism was pre-eminently a theory of economic-social and political change, in which the latter was assumed to follow upon the former. Quite in contrast with Radicalism and Populism, which assumed that equitable distribution and social justice would follow upon popular political participation, Marxism assumed that the revolutionary elimination of economic privilege was the inevitable precursor and the only possible avenue to genuine democratic participation.

Thus, the theme of political change is a very central concern of political theory; and yet the contemporary student of politics finds these conceptions unsuitable for the explanation and ordering of the problems and patterns of change in the modern world.

There are perhaps two aspects of the traditional theories which create these problems. In the first place, the Enlightenment theories were conceived, and in general applied, within the Western world with its common Christian and Greco-Roman culture, and with the nation-state as the dominant political form. Hence its conception of the starting point of political change was culture-bound, so to speak. The starting point of political change in the contemporary world is immensely varied in both culture and structure. A contemporary theory of political change must explain not only Western patterns, but those of a Japan, an Indonesia, an India, a Yemen, and a Uganda.

In the second place, the concepts of change in political theory assume an inevitable and unilinear course of development. When Western political scientists, in the Enlightenment tradition, view the variety and instability of political systems in the modern world, they may retain their faith in or hope for such an outcome but they can hardly believe with conviction in the general triumph of effective democracy in the foreseeable future.

INTERPRETATION OF EUROPEAN POLITICAL SYSTEMS

We are searching for a theory of change more sober in spirit, more open in concept, and more versatile in its explanatory capacity than those made available to us in traditional political theory. One way of approaching the problem stems from the body of knowledge and interpretation dealing with the political systems of Europe and particularly continental Europe. Events in the analyses of the political histories and processes of France, Germany, and Italy—countries in the very center of the Greco-Roman-Christian tradition—have raised the most serious question about the Enlightenment theory of democratic progress. How explain the instability of French politics, or the failures of the democratic systems of Germany and Italy, in contrast with the steady consolidation of democracy in Britain, the United States, and the Old Commonwealth? In France a whole series of historians and political scientists including Siegfried, Thomson, Micaud, Philip Williams, Luethy, and others have concerned themselves with this problem.[2]

In one form or another, these students of French politics have pointed out that French political movements and ideologies since the French Revolution have been fragmented along two lines of cleavage. The first of these is the classic French revolutionary cleavage between left and right—the first republican, democratic, and rational-anti-clerical in spirit; the second royalist, aristocratic, and traditional-clerical in tendency. The second line of cleavage, based on demands for an equitable distribution and economic and social values and opportunities, emerged before consensus and stable institutions were establised in response to the first challenge. Thus, France in the nineteenth and twentieth centuries has been seeking to solve two basic probems of growth simultaneously, that of political participation and that of socio-economic distribution. French immobilism and constitutional in-

---

[2]See André Siegfried, *France: A Study in Nationality* (New Haven: Yale University Press, 1933); David Thomson, *Democracy in France* (New York: Oxford University Press, 1958); Charles Micaud, "The Bases of Communist Strength in France," *World Politics* (Sept. 1955), p. 354 ff.; Micaud, "French Intellectuals and Communists," *Social Research* (Autumn 1954), p. 286 ff.; Philip Williams, *Politics in Post-War France* (London: Longmans, 1958); Herbert Luethy, *France Against Herself* (New York: Praeger, 1955).

stability is explained in terms of political structure and culture incapable of producing positive and stable majority coalitions. An anti-clerical left consisting of Communists, Socialists, and Radicals polarizes a clerical-conservative right consisting of working and middle and upper class Catholics, and the economically conservative middle and upper classes fearful of social revolution. The left, collectivist and social welfare-oriented, loses its middle class republican allies and polarizes a coalition of the conservative middle and upper classes and peasantry.

This pattern of political culture and infrastructure explains the classic sequence of French political history—the immobilist, heterogeneous center coalitions incapable of decisive action in either the constitutional or social policy direction, followed by "crisis-liquidation" cabinets such as the *Union-Sacrée* of World War I or the brief Mendès-France interlude in the 1950's, when a grave national emergency creates a temporary consensus. It also explains the latent "Caesarism" and authoritarianism of French politics. Immobilism and cabinet instability create a widespread cynicism toward democratic politics. From the French Revolution right on through MacMahon, Boulanger, and de Gaulle, the alternative of national unity, authority, dignity and order consistent with the glorious Napoleonic and monarchic past has exerted great attraction not only among French traditionalists, but among disillusioned democrats. The fragility and ineffectiveness of French politics becomes especially manifest in periods when the French political process has been loaded with fateful problems of national accommodation, as in the present period of decolonization. The pathetic life and the sudden and almost voluntary death of the Fourth Republic was a consequence of the impact of three grave problems which that Republic was unable to solve—the problems of participation and governmental organization, welfare distribution, and international accommodation.

The introduction of the international problem turns our attention to the experience of Germany and Italy, for in a special degree—in a degree far greater than in the case of France—Germany and Italy were hit by problems both of international accommodation and integration at the same time that they were seeking solutions to the problems of political participation and welfare distribution. Indeed, Fascism and Nazism as the manifestation of Italian and German authoritarianism, in contrast with the more moderate and traditional authoritarianism of France, may in part be explained by the special impact of the problem of national accommodation and integration on the politics of those countries. At the same time that both Germany and Italy were seeking solutions to the problems of political participation and social distribution, they were confronted in the very basic sense by the problems of establishing national identities through the integration of their parochial components and through accommodation in an international political system, already well established and not providing much freedom of maneuver vis-a-vis the older great powers.

Here again we are not saying anything new but simply explicating, as an analytical tool, explanations of political system characteristics and performance which are to be found in the literature dealing with German and Italian politics.[3] Thus, the late arrival of the German Reich at nationhood has often been viewed as an explanation of the failure of the German middle classes to carry through a participation revolution and as an explanation of the special virulence and sensitivity of German nationalism. The failure of the German Reich to democratize itself has been offered as an explanation of the radicalization of the German left. The strength of Marxism in Germany is attributed to pessimism regarding the responsiveness of German political institutions to popular demands for democracy and social welfare. The rise and popularity of National Socialism is attributed in part to the political fragmentation of the Weimar Republic along traditional authoritarian and democratic lines, religious lines, socialist-antisocialist, and nationalist-cosmopolitan lines. The national humiliation of the Weimar Republic, its political instability and fragmentation, and its related failures to solve the distribution and welfare problems of the inflation and depression are the chief situational reasons cited for the rise of National Socialism.

The German and Italian patterns of political development, similar though they were in some respects, may be explained in terms of the different impacts of these unsolved problems. Germany came into the period of national unification with its largest constituent unit, Prussia, thoroughly integrated in the sense of national identity and penetration of parochial, regional, and pluralistic status groups. Indeed, the breaking of the civic will of the German middle classes had begun long before the national unification which followed the Franco-Prussian War. As one writer put it, the Prussian middle classes had begun to be infeudated by the aristocratic and bureaucratic-authoritarian regime in the course of the eighteenth and first part of the nineteenth centuries.[4] At the time of national unification, it was the culture and socio-political structure of Prussia which was quickly imprinted on the whole of Germany. Thus Germany began its career as a nation as a "disziplin-volk," as Max Weber expressed it, and with a widespread, though insecure, sense of national identity. To be sure there were separatist and pluralist tendencies, but the dominant model for German integration was that of Prussia.

In Italy, national unification was superficial in both a structural and cultural sense. The historic particularities of Italy, and especially the Church, retained substantial autonomy, and while Fascism sought to break

[3]See, for example, K. S. Pinson, *Modern Germany* (New York: Macmillan, 1954); Sigmund Neumann, "Germany: Changing Patterns and Lasting Problems" in Neumann, ed., *Modern Political Parties* (Chicago: University of Chicago Press, 1956), p. 354 ff.; Joseph LaPalombara, *Pressure Groups and Bureaucracy in Italy* (Princeton: Princeton University Press, 1964), chap. I.

[4]See Hans Rosenberg, *Bureaucracy, Autocracy, and Aristocracy.*

through these autonomies and create an aggressive sense of national identity, it was only partially successful at best. Thus, Italian Fascism was dilettantish in its efforts to mobilize Italian resources and to create an aggressive nationalism, by comparison with the gruesome pedantry and demonic aggressiveness of National Socialism.

If we contrast British political experience in recent centuries with that of France, Germany, and Italy, it is evident that we are dealing with a radically different historic pattern. With the exception of the problem of Ireland, which was to plague Britain and disrupt its political process in the last decades of the nineteenth century and the first decades of the twentieth, Britain had attained a stable integration of its constituent parts by the early seventeenth century. Its sense of national identity was well established and widely distributed as early as the Elizabethan era, was sustained by success in the international political system in the whole of the modern era, and now seems to be adapting to a radical lessening and restructuring of its international position without significant disruptive political consequences. Its problem of political participation was solved incrementally in a historical process beginning in the thirteenth century and continuing step by step into the post-World War II period, with only one discontinuous episode. Its problem of social distribution, though in part solved in the same incremental, continuous manner, is still in many respects unsolved. This issue of the distribution of social opportunity in Britain and accommodation to its new international position are the chief unsolved problems of contemporary British politics. The probability that they will be dealt with without radically altering the British political system is high, in view of the widespread and secure sense of national identity and the general acceptance among Britons of the legitimacy of their political system.

A DEFINITION OF POLITICAL CHANGE

This body of historical interpretations of European political systems suggests a theoretical insight: a conception of political change which may be formulated in terms of the performance capabilities of political systems. The British pattern of political change was one in which these fundamental problems of system adaptation were solved with appropriate structural and cultural adaptations, so that the system "grew," so to speak, from monarchy to aristocratic oligarchy, from aristocratic oligarchy to a welfare democracy. In France by contrast, the problem of political participation was not solved but rather continued through the nineteenth and twentieth centuries as a basically unsolved problem of system adaptation. France was fixated, so to speak, in a state of fragmented political culture and structure, a fragmentation which was compounded in the nineteenth and twentieth centuries by her inability to solve the problem of social distribution. Thus, France became neither a stable democracy nor a welfare democracy, but was caught in conflicting impulses to carry through these systemic changes, or to suppress them; became, in other words, an immobilist, unstable, democratic-authoritarian system. The immobility and instability of Germany and Italy, on the other hand, were compounded by the fact that these two countries were unable to solve satisfactorily the problems of national integration and national identity, in other words, were ambivalent in the national sense. How else can we explain the contrast between the intense nationalism of National Socialism and Fascism, and the apparent absence of national feeling in contemporary Germany and Italy? We may say of France, Germany, and Italy in the last century that they were caught in the grips of cumulative revolutions, unable to solve any one of them through appropriate systemic adaptations, in considerable part *because of the simultaneity* of their impact.[5]

It should be clear that we are defining political change in a special sense. We are not using it here to refer to the general phenomenon of change, the sense in which all political systems undergo change. We mean by political change the acquisition by a political system of some new capability. For example, we may say that when a tribal elite develops an officialdom capable of penetrating the tribal villages, extracting tribute and manpower, the tribe develops an integration and mobilization capability, and has changed systemically from its earlier essentially kinship and religious cohesion to a specifically political cohesion. If such a tribal political system uses the resources which it now can mobilize as a means of accommodating itself in its relations to other political systems in the international arena (whether by regular military defense or aggression or by diplomatic negotiation), we may say that it has acquired an *international accommodative capability*. It has changed systemically. It has acquired the familiar attributes of the nation-state: effective internal political integration, territorial boundaries, and more or less regularized exchanges with other nation-states. If such a political system develops a culture and a structure which enables its population or a substantial part of it to participate in the recruitment of elites and formulation of public policy, we can say that it has acquired a *participation capability*. It has changed from some sub-species of authoritarian state to a participant, or democratic one. Similarly, if such a

---

[5] I am indebted for this concept of the simultaneity or cumulativeness of revolutions to Sigmund Neumann, "Toward a Comparative Study of Political Parties," in *Modern Political Parties*, but more particularly to his oral presentation of this concept on a number of occasions. In applying this analysis in the non-Western world, let me acknowledge my debt to Lucian Pye's *Politics, Personality, and Nation Building* (New Haven: Yale University Press, 1962), and in particular to his concept of role conflict and the identity crises in the new nations.

political system develops a capability of penetrating the economy and social structure in such a way as to respond regularly or recurrently to demands for the distribution of the social product, we may say that it has acquired a *welfare* or a *distribution capability.*

We call each one of these changes "systemic" changes because the acquisition of the new capability is associated with fundamental changes in political culture and structure. Thus, the development of the integrative capability is accompanied by the development of a sense of national identity and the emergence of a specialized central bureaucracy. The development of an international accommodative capability is associated with the development of a more open, cosmopolitan culture supportive of regular exchanges across national boundaries, and the further development of bureaucracy —foreign offices, diplomats, armed services. The development of a participation capability is associated with the development and spread of a political culture of civic obligation and competence, and the elaboration of the various components of the democratic infrastructure—political parties, associational interest groups, and autonomous media of communication. The development of a distribution capability is associated with the development and widespread dissemination of a welfare culture; further special bureaucratic changes; and emergence of a pattern of accommodation between the political structure and process, and the socal structure and process.

THE PROBLEM OF UNILINEARITY

Stated in this simple way, we seem to be falling victim to the same unilinear evolutionary theory, from which we are seeking to escape. But this is not the import nor the intention of this concept of change. In the first place, political systems may not encounter these problems or may not encounter them in the same order, form, or intensity, or having encountered them in some special way, they may solve them differently. What we are arguing is that the systemic characteristics of political systems—their structural, cultural, and performance properties—are determined by the way in which these problems or challenges are encountered and experienced. The sources of tendencies toward political system change are either indigenous or from the international environment, or both. The kind of impulses which emerge from these sources, their order, and intensity are capable of great variation.

If we focus for a moment on man's historical experience with political systems prior to the Renaissance and the emergence into international dominance of the Western state system, the impact of these problems and their solution in various parts of the world was relatively compartmented and independent. Thus, what happened in Japan was independent of what happened in India or in Africa. Furthermore, political systems acquired and lost capabilities and their associated cultural, structural, and performance characteristics in anything but a unilinear, evolutionary way. Within the confines of the Greek city states, Aristotle and Plato could respond to the patterns of political change which they observed only by positing a cyclical theory of political change, and Machiavelli, observing the Italian principalities and city states, was drawn to a similar model. In ancient and even recent Asia and Africa, nations and empires formed in response to these challenges, then reverted to the closure and parochialism of less versatile political systems, and then formed up again into larger and more capable systems without any apparent regularity or order.

But we have to argue that since the Renaissance, the Enlightenment, and the industrial revolution some of the independence of man's political experiments has been lost, that the course of recent history supports the idea of the emergence of world culture.[6] We would argue that recent centuries have seen a fundamental change in the world historical process. In a sense political systems have increasingly been losing their uniqueness with respect to the kinds of problems they encounter, and in the ways in which they may solve these problems. The technological and communications revolutions have fundamentally changed the speed and the direction of cultural diffusion. Communication, industrialization and urbanization force the problems of national integration, international accommodation, political participation, and welfare distribution on the new nations and the traditional older ones. They are confronted inescapably with the simultaneous or cumulative revolutions of which Neumann speaks, and which Lucian Pye has analyzed so cogently in his Burmese study. The structure, culture, and performance characteristics of the new nations and the rapidly changing older ones will be determined by the way they encounter these four problems and the way in which they seek to solve them. However, the implications of this modification in the patterns of cultural diffusion and cultural change are far from unilinear. We still begin with the enormous variety of cultural and structural starting points in the emerging nations, and even though they are confronted with all four problems of political growth simultaneously, the dosages of each vary from case to case, and the responses of elites to these challenges differ from one country to the next. Thus, while we can say that there will be *some common content* in the outcomes of these processes of change, this is far from arguing that there will be *one common outcome.*

[6]See C. P. Snow, *The Two Cultures and the Scientific Revolution* (New York: Cambridge University Press, 1961), p. 47 ff.; and as applied in the specific context of the theory of political development, Lucian Pye, *op. cit.*. p. 10 ff.; and *The Political Context of National Development.* unpublished ms. (Center for International Studies, MIT, Cambridge, Mass., 1962).

TYPES OF POLITICAL SYSTEMS AND
POLITICAL CHANGE

We have suggested that political systems change, in the sense in which we have defined the term, when they acquire new capabilities in relation to their social and international environments. This in turn suggests an approach to political classification in terms of such a concept of political change. Differences among political systems may be put in terms of their acquisition of capabilities, their failure to have developed these capabilities, or their having become fixated in the process of acquiring them. But first several points must be made, regarding the nature of political capabilities, the relations between capabilities and the structural and cultural aspects of political systems, and the interrelationships among capabilities.

The difference between simple and complex political systems is not that the latter possess capabilities and the former lack them. In both a functional and a structural sense all the capabilities present in "modern" political systems are present in primitive ones. The sole exception would be the international accommodative capability in those cases of genuine isolation as in oceanic island communities, and even here the evidence would seem to suggest that complete isolation over long periods of time is very rare. Aside from this possible exception, we may say that all political systems somehow cope with the problems of international accommodation, internal integration, and resource mobilization, participation, and distribution. At the other extreme, we have to say that no political system ever develops its capabilities to the point where they become fully stabilized at optimum levels of performance. The best-ordered and most stable political system may be shaken or destroyed by a change in the structure of the international environment, or some internal disruptive development. Thus, most if not all contemporary traditional systems—some of them stable for centuries—are undergoing rapid internal transformation as a consequence of their efforts to accommodate and respond to the international environment. A Britain having served for a century as the leading power in the international political system now has to respond to a fundamentally changed international political system, and cannot escape the internal systemic strains resulting from it.

The integrative, accommodative, participant, and distribution capabilities of political systems, even when we can speak of them as being "developed," still confront "issues" and undergo structural and cultural change. What do we mean then by the acquisition of a performance capability? We mean that the new performance capability is expressed in a specialized structure and related differentiated psychological orientations or culture. The capability acquires a kind of autonomy. The political system now can respond to problems of integration, accommodation, participation, or distribution in their own terms. Thus, one way of explaining the instabilities of the ancient empires of the Near East is to point out that most of them failed to differentiate accommodative capabilities from their integrative capabilities. They were neither structurally nor culturally capable of coping with other nations in the international environment in accommodative terms. They sought rather for unlimited empire by integrating other nations into their own political systems.

In more recent times nations such as Japan, Germany and Russia have had similar problems in adjusting to participation in the international political system, *i.e.*, in developing a specialized accommodative structure and the relatively open culture which stable membership in the international political system requires. The criterion of political change, then, is the acquisition of a new capability, in the sense of a specialized role structure and differentiated orientations which together give a political system the possibility of responding efficiently, and more or less autonomously, to a new range of problems.

The order in which political systems encounter particular problems of change, and the way in which they solve them greatly limits their freedom in responding to and solving problems which arise later. Thus, Germany and Japan, late arrivals in the international political system, concentrated on integration and resource mobilization, and finding a satisfactory place in the international political system, and responded by subordinating their participation capabilities, or better, repressing their tendencies to acquire an autonomous culture and structure. An America, on the periphery of the international political system and under little pressure to integrate and mobilize its resources, developed a participation capability which limited its capacity for integration and resource mobilization, a pattern of growth almost the converse of that which occurred in Japan and Germany. But this question of the relations among capabilities may be treated more systematically by examining a variety of different types of political systems. . . .[7]

In the remainder of the article not reprinted here, Prof. Almond develops a sevenfold classification of political systems based on acquisition of the capabilities mentioned.—Ed.

3

Political Development
and Political Decay

Samuel P. Huntington

"Among the laws that rule human societies," de Tocqueville said, "there is one which seems to be more precise and clear than all others. If men are to remain civilized or to become so, the art of associating together must grow and improve in the same ratio in which the equality of conditions is increased."[1] In much of the world today, equality of political participation is growing much more rapidly than is the "art of associating together." The rates of mobilization and participation are high; the rates of organization and institutionalization are low. De Tocqueville's precondition for civilized society is in danger, if it is not already undermined. In these societies, the conflict between mobilization and institutionalization is the crux of politics. Yet in the fast-growing literature on the politics of the developing areas, political institutionalization usually receives scant treatment. Writers on political development emphasize the processes of modernization and the closely related phenomena of social mobilization and increasing political participation. A balanced view of the politics of contemporary Asia, Africa, and Latin America requires more attention to the "art of associating together" and the growth of political institutions. For this purpose, it is useful to distinguish political development from modernization and to identify political development with the institutionalization of political

"Political Development and Political Decay" by Samuel P. Huntington is reprinted by permission from *World Politics* 17 (April 1965), pp. 386-430. Article and footnotes abridged by permission of the author.

The author wishes to thank the Center for International Affairs, Harvard University, for the support which made this article possible, and Edward C. Banfield, Mather Eliot, Milton J. Esman, H. Field Haviland, Jr., and John D. Montgomery, for their helpful written comments on an earlier draft.

[1] *Democracy in America* (Phillips Bradley edn., New York 1955), vol. II, pp. 118.

organizations and procedures. Rapid increases in mobilization and participation, the principal political aspects of modernization, undermine political institutions. Rapid modernization, in brief, produces not political development, but political decay.

I. POLITICAL DEVELOPMENT AS MODERNIZATION

Definitions of political development are legion. Most, however, share two closely related characteristics. First, political development is identified as one aspect of, or as intimately connected with, the broader processes of modernization in society as a whole. Modernization affects all segments of society; its political aspects constitute political development. Indeed, many authors seem to prefer the phrase "political modernization" as more descriptive of their primary concern. Second, if political development is linked with modernization, it is necessarily a broad and complex process. Hence most authors argue that political development must be measured by many criteria. The "multi-function character of politics," Lucian Pye has said, ". . . means that no single scale can be used for measuring the degree of political development."[2] It thus differs from economic development, on the character of which there seems to be more general agreement and which is measurable through fairly precise indices such as per capita, national income. Definitions of political development hence tend to itemize a number of criteria. Ward and Rustow list eight characteristics of the modern polity; Emerson has five. Pye identifies four major aspects of political development plus half a dozen additional "factors." Eisenstadt finds four characteristics of political modernization.[3]

The definitions are many and multiple; but, with a few exceptions, the characteristics which they identify with political development are all aspects of the processes of modernization. Four sets of categories recur continuously in the definitions. One set, focusing on the Parsonian pattern variables, can perhaps best be summed up as *rationalization*. This involves movement from particularism to universalism, from diffuseness to specificity, from ascription to achievement, and from affectivity to affective neutrality. In terms of political development, functional differentiation and achievement criteria are particularly emphasized.[4] A second set of characteristics

[2]Lucian W. Pye, ed., *Communications and Political Development* (Princeton 1963), p. 16.

[3]Robert E. Ward and Dankwart A. Rustow, eds., *Political Modernization in Japan and Turkey* (Princeton 1964), pp. 6-7; Rupert Emerson, *Political Modernization: The Single-Party System* (Denver 1963), pp. 7-8; Pye, ed., *Communications and Political Development*, pp. 17-18; S. N. Eisenstadt, "Bureaucracy and Political Development," in Joseph LaPalombara, ed., *Bureaucracy and Political Development* (Princeton 1963), p. 99.

[4]James S. Coleman, in Gabriel A. Almond and Coleman, eds., *The Politics of the Developing Areas* (Princeton 1960), p. 532; Fred W. Riggs, "Bureaucracy and Political Development: A

identified with development involves nationalism and *national integration.*
Almost all writers recognize the problem of the "crisis of national identity"
and the necessity of establishing a firmly delimited ethnic basis for the
political community.[5] A developed polity, it is usually assumed, must, with
rare exception, be a nation-state. "Nation-building" is a key aspect of
political development. A third approach focuses on *democratization:*
pluralism, competitiveness, equalization of power, and similar qualities.
"Competitiveness," says Coleman, "is an essential aspect of political
modernity. . . ." Hence, "the Anglo-American polities most closely approximate the model of a modern political system. . . ."[6] Frey argues that "the
most common notion of political development in intellectual American
circles is that of movement towards democracy." He finds this a congenial
notion and offers his own definition of political development as "changes in
the direction of greater distribution and reciprocity of power. . . ."[7]

Rationalization, integration, and democratization thus commonly
appear in definitions of political development. The characteristic of political
development or political modernization which is most frequently
emphasized, however, is *mobilization, or participation.* Modernization, Karl
Deutsch has emphasized, involves social mobilization, and "this complex of
processes of social change is significantly correlated with major changes in
politics." Increases in literacy, urbanization, exposure to mass media,
industrialization, and per capita income expand "the politically relevant
strata of the population," multiply the demands for government services,
and thus stimulate an increase in governmental capabilities, a broadening of
the elite, increased political participation, and shifts in attention from the
local level to the national level.[8] Modernization means mass mobilization;
mass mobilization means increased political participation; and increased
participation is the key element of political development. Participation
distinguishes modern politics from traditional politics. "Traditional
society," says Lerner, "is non-participant—it deploys people by kinship into
communities isolated from each other and from a center. . . ." Modern
society, in contrast, is "participant society."[9] The "new world political
culture," say Almond and Verba, "will be a political culture of participation.
If there is a political revolution going on throughout the world, it is what

Paradoxical View," in LaPalombara, ed., *Bureaucracy and Political Development,* p. 122;
Eisenstadt, in *ibid.,* p. 99; Ward and Rustow, eds., *Political Modernization,* p. 7.
[5]See, e.g., Gabriel A. Almond, "Political Systems and Political Change," [reprinted above];
Ward and Rustow, eds., *Political Modernization,* p. 7.
[6]Coleman, in Almond and Coleman, eds., *Politics of Developing Areas,* p. 533.
[7]Frederick W. Frey, "Political Development, Power, and Communications in Turkey," in
Pye, ed., *Communications and Political Development,* p. 301.
[8]Karl W. Deutsch, "Social Mobilization and Political Development," *American Political
Science Review* 55 (Sept. 1961), p. 493 ff.
[9]Daniel Lerner, *The Passing of Traditional Society* (Glencoe 1958), pp. 48-50.

might be called the participation explosion. In all the new nations of the world the belief that the ordinary man is politically relevant—that he ought to be an involved participant in the political system—is widespread. Large groups of people who have been outside politics are demanding entrance into the political system."[10] Political development, Rustow argues, may be defined as "(1) an increasing national political unity plus (2) a broadening base of political participation. . . ." Similarly, Riggs declares that political development "refers to the process of politicization: increasing participation or involvement of the citizen in state activities, in power calculations, and consequences."[11]

All definitions are arbitrary. These definitions of political development as some combination or permutation of participation, rationalization, democratization, and nation-building are just as legitimate as any other definition. While all definitions may be equally arbitrary and equally legitimate, they do vary greatly, however, in their relevance to particular problems and their usefulness for particular ends. Presumably one major purpose of concepts of political development is to facilitate understanding of the political processes in contemporary Asian, African, and Latin American societies. To be analytically useful, a concept must be precise and relevant. It must also have sufficient generality of application to permit comparative analysis of differing situations. Many approaches to political development suffer from one or more of the following difficulties.

First, the identification of political development with modernization or with factors usually associated with modernization drastically limits the applicability of the concept in both time and space. It is defined in parochial and immediate terms, its relevance limited to modern nation-states or the emergence of modern nation-states. It becomes impossible to speak of a politically developed tribal authority, city-state, feudal monarchy, or bureaucratic empire. Development is identified with one type of political system, rather than as a quality which might characterize any type of political system. All systems which are not modern are underdeveloped, including presumably fifth-century Athens, the third-century B.C. Roman republic, the second-century A.D. Roman empire, the Han and T'ang empires in China, or even eighteenth-century America. None of these political systems was modern. Is it also useful to consider them underdeveloped? Would it not be more appropriate to consider development or underdevelopment as a characteristic which might be found in any type of political system? City-states could be developed or underdeveloped; so also could be bureaucratic empires or modern nation-states. This approach would cast additional light on contemporary modernizing societies by furnishing a second set of

[10]Gabriel A. Almond and Sidney Verba, *The Civic Culture* (Princeton 1963), p. 4.
[11]Dankwart A. Rustow, "The Vanishing Dream of Stability," *AID Digest* (Aug. 1962), p. 13; Riggs, in LaPalombara, ed., *Bureaucracy and Political Development*, p. 139.

categories (in addition to the traditional-modern set) for comparing the processes of change in those societies with the processes of change in other types of societies. Such an approach, of course, would also liberate the concept of development from the even more limited identification of it with the Western, constitutional, democratic nation-state.

The second problem with many definitions of political development is the obverse but also the corollary of the first. On the one hand, development is limited to the characteristics of the modern nation-state. On the other, it is also broadened to include almost all politically relevant aspects of the modernization process. It acquires comprehensiveness at the cost of precision. There is a natural tendency to assume that political development is all of a piece, that one "good thing" is compatible with another. In addition, studies of modernization have shown a very high degree of correlation among such indices as literacy, urbanization, media participation, and political participation.[12] Hence, it is easy to assume that a similar correlation exists among the various elements identified as contributing to political development. In fact, however, the four, eight, or twelve criteria of development may or may not have any systematic relation to each other. They may indeed be negatively correlated. There is no particular reason, for instance, why more participation and more structural differentiation should go together; in fact, there is some a priori reason to assume that more of one might mean less of the other. If this be the case, two contradictory tendencies (A, —B; —A, B) could both be labeled "political development." The broader the definition of development, moreover, the more inevitable development becomes. The all-encompassing definitions make development seem easy by making it seem inescapable. Development becomes an omnipresent first cause, which explains everything but distinguishes nothing. Almost anything that happens in the "developing" countries—coups, ethnic struggles, revolutionary wars—becomes part of the process of development, however contradictory or retrogressive this may appear on the surface. Political development thus loses its analytical content and acquires simply a geographic one. At the extreme, it becomes synonymous with the political history of Asia, Africa, and Latin America.

Thirdly, many definitions of political development fail to distinguish clearly the empirical relevance of the components going into the definition. Concepts of "developed" and "undeveloped" as ideal types or states of being are confused with concepts of "development" as a process which are, in turn, identified with the politics of the areas commonly called "developing." The line between actuality and aspiration is fogged. Things which are in fact occurring in the "developing" areas become hopelessly intertwined with things which the theorist thinks should occur there. Here again the tendency has been to assume that what is true for the broader processes of social

[12]Lerner, *Passing of Traditional Society.* chap. 2.

modernization is also true for political changes. Modernization, in some degree, is a fact in Asia, Africa, Latin America: urbanization is rapid; literacy is slowly increasing; industrialization is being pushed; per capita gross national product is inching upward; mass media circulation is expanding; political participation is broadening. All these are facts. In contrast, progress toward many of the other goals identified with political development—democracy, stability, structural differentiation, achievement patterns, national integration—often is dubious at best. Yet the tendency is to think that because modernization is taking place, political development also must be taking place. As a result, many of the sympathetic Western writings about the underdeveloped areas today have the same air of hopeful unreality which characterized much of the sympathetic Western writing about the Soviet Union in the 1920's and 1930's. They are suffused with what can only be described as "Webbism": that is, the tendency to ascribe to a political system qualities which are assumed to be its ultimate goals rather than qualities which actually characterize its processes and functions.

In actuality, only some of the tendencies frequently encompassed in the concept "political development" appear to be characteristic of the "developing" areas. Instead of a trend toward competitiveness and democracy, there has been an "erosion of democracy" and a tendency to autocratic military regimes and one-party regimes. Instead of stability, there have been repeated coups and revolts. Instead of a unifying nationalism and nation-building, there have been repeated ethnic conflicts and civil wars. Instead of institutional rationalization and differentiation, there has frequently been a decay of the administrative organizations inherited from the colonial era and a weakening and disruption of the political organizations developed during the struggle for independence.[13] Only the concept of political development as mobilization and participation appears to be generally applicable to the "developing" world. Rationalization, competitiveness, and nation-building, in contrast, seem to have only a dim relation to reality.

This gap between theory and reality suggests a fourth difficulty in many concepts of political development. They are usually one-way concepts. Little or no provision is made for their reversibility. If political development is thought to involve the mobilization of people into politics, account should also be taken of the possibility that political de-development can take place and people can be demobilized out of politics. Structural differentiation may occur, but so also may structural homogenization. National disintegration is a phenomenon as much as national integration. A concept of political development should be reversible. It should define both political development and the circumstances under which political decay is encouraged.

[13] On the "erosion of democracy" and political instability, see Rupert Emerson, *From Empire to Nation* (Cambridge, Mass., 1960), chap. 15; and Michael Brecher, *The New States of Asia* (London 1963), chap. 2.

The failure to think of political development as a reversible process apparently stems from two sources. Insofar as development is identified with modernization, many aspects of modernization do appear to be practically irreversible. Urbanization is not likely to give way to ruralization. Increases in literacy are not normally followed by sharp declines. Capital once invested in factories or power plants stays invested. Even increases in per capita gross national product are, more often than not, permanent, except for minor dips or destruction caused by war or natural catastrophe. With varying slopes, with hesitancy in some sectors but with strength and steady progress in others, virtually all the indices of modernization progress steadily upward on the charts. But political changes have no such irreversibility.

In other instances, one feels that an underlying commitment to the theory of progress is so overwhelming as to exclude political decay as a possible concept. Political decay, like thermonuclear war, becomes unthinkable. Almond, for instance, measures not just political development but *political change* by "the acquisition by a political system of some new capability."[14] The specific capabilities he has in mind are those for national integration, international accommodation, political participation, and welfare distribution. Before the Renaissance, Almond argues, political systems "acquired and lost capabilities . . . in anything but a unilinear, evolutionary way." Modernization, however, reduces "the independence of man's political experiments." Change is "far from unilinear," but it is toward "the emergence of world culture." Surely, however, modern and modernizing states can change by losing capabilities as well as by gaining them. In addition, a gain in any one capability usually involves costs in others. A theory of political development needs to be mated to a theory of political decay. Indeed, as was suggested above, theories of instability, corruption, authoritarianism, domestic violence, institutional decline, and political disintegration may tell us a lot more about the "developing" areas than their more hopefully defined opposites.

II. POLITICAL DEVELOPMENT AS INSTITUTIONALIZATION

There is thus much to be gained (as well as something to be lost) by conceiving of political development as a process independent of, although obviously affected by, the process of modernization. In view of the crucial importance of the relationship between mobilization and participation, on the one hand, and the growth of political organizations, on the other, it is useful for many purposes to define political development as the institutionalization of political organizations and procedures. This concept

[14]Almond, *American Behavioral Scientist* 6, p. 6.

liberates development from modernization. It can be applied to the analysis of political systems of any sort, not just modern ones. It can be defined in reasonably precise ways which are at least theoretically capable of measurement. As a concept, it does not suggest that movement is likely to be in only one direction: institutions, we know, decay and dissolve as well as grow and mature. Most significantly, it focuses attention on the reciprocal interaction between the on-going social processes of modernization, on the one hand, and the strength, stability, or weakness of political structures, traditional, transitional, or modern, on the other.[15]

The strength of political organizations and procedures varies with their *scope of support* and their *level of institutionalization*. Scope refers simply to the extent to which the political organizations and procedures encompass activity in the society. If only a small upper-class group belongs to political organizations and behaves in terms of a set of procedures, the scope is limited. If, on the other hand, a large segment of the population is politically organized and follows the political procedures, the scope is broad. Institutions are stable, valued, recurring patterns of behavior. Organizations and procedures vary in their degree of institutionalization. Harvard University and the newly opened suburban high school are both organizations, but Harvard is much more of an institution than is the high school. The seniority system in Congress and President Johnson's select press conferences are both procedures, but seniority is much more institutionalized than are Mr. Johnson's methods of dealing with the press. Institutionalization is the process by which organizations and procedures acquire value and stability. The level of institutionalization of any political system can be defined by the adaptability, complexity, autonomy, and coherence of its organizations and procedures. So also, the level of institutionalization of any particular organization or procedure can be measured by its adaptability, complexity, autonomy, and coherence. If these criteria can be identified and measured, political systems can be compared in terms of their levels of institutionalization. Furthermore, it will be possible to measure increases and decreases in the institutionalization of particular organizations and procedures within a political system.

Adaptability-Rigidity

The more adaptable an organization or procedure is, the more highly institutionalized it is; the less adaptable and more rigid it is, the lower its level of institutionalization. Adaptability is an acquired organizational characteristic. It is, in a rough sense, a function of environmental challenge

[15]The concept of institutionalization has, of course, been used by other writers concerned with political development— most notably, S. N. Eisenstadt. His definition, however, differs significantly from my approach here. See, in particular, his "Initial Institutional Patterns of Political

and age. The more challenges which have arisen in its environment and the greater its age, the more adaptable it is. Rigidity is more characteristic of young organizations than of old ones. Old organizations and procedures, however, are not necessarily adaptable if they have existed in a static environment. In addition, if over a period of time an organization has developed a set of responses for dealing effectively with one type of problem, and if it is then confronted with an entirely different type of problem requiring a different response, the organization may well be a victim of its past successes and be unable to adjust to the new challenge. In general, however, the first hurdle is the biggest one. Success in adapting to one environmental challenge paves the way for successful adaptation to subsequent environmental challenges. If, for instance, the probability of successful adjustment to the first challenge is 50 per cent, the probability of successful adjustment to the second challenge might be 75 per cent, to the third challenge 87½ per cent, to the fourth 93¾ per cent, and so on. Some changes in environment, moreover, such as changes in personnel, are inevitable for all organizations. Other changes in environment may be produced by the organization itself; if, for instance, it successfully completes the task which it was originally created to accomplish. So long as it is recognized that environments can differ in the challenges which they pose to organizations, the adaptability of an organization can in a rough sense be measured by its age. Its age, in turn, can be measured in three ways.

One is simply chronological: the longer an organization or procedure has been in existence, the higher the level of institutionalization. The older an organization is, the more likely it is to continue to exist through any specified future time period. The probability that an organization which is one hundred years old will survive one additional year, it might be hypothesized, is perhaps one hundred times greater than the probability that an organization one year old will survive one additional year. Political institutions are thus not created overnight. Political development, in this sense, is slow, particularly when compared with the seemingly much more rapid pace of economic development. In some instances, particular types of experience may substitute for time: fierce conflict or other serious challenges may transform organizations into institutions much more rapidly than normal circumstances. But such intensive experiences are rare, and even with such experiences time is still required. "A major party," Ashoka Mehta has observed, in commenting on why communism is helpless in India, "cannot be created in a day. In China a great party was forged by the revolution. Other major parties can be or are born of revolutions in other countries.

Modernisation," *Civilisations* 12 (No. 4, 1962), pp. 461-472, and 13 (No. 1, 1963), pp. 15-26; "Institutionalization and Change," *American Sociological Review* 29 (Apr. 1964), pp. 235-247; "Social Change, Differentiation and Evolution," *ibid.* 29 (June 1964), pp. 375-386.

But it is simply impossible, through normal channels, to forge a great party, to reach and galvanize millions of men in half a million villages."[16]

A second measure of adaptability is generational age. So long as an organization still has its first set of leaders, so long as a procedure is still performed by those who first performed it, its adaptability is still in doubt. The more often the organization has surmounted the problem of peaceful succession and replaced one set of leaders with another, the more highly institutionalized it is. In considerable measure, of course, generational age is a function of chronological age. But political parties and governments may continue for decades under the leadership of one generation. The founders of organizations—whether parties, governments, or business corporations—are often young. Hence the gap between chronological age and generational age is apt to be greater in the early history of an organization than later in its career. This gap produces tensions between the first leaders of the organization and the next generation immediately behind them, which can look forward to a lifetime in the shadow of the first generation. In the middle of the 1960's the Chinese Communist Party was forty-five years old, but in large part it was still led by its first generation of leaders. An organization may also change leadership without changing generations of leadership. One generation differs from another in terms of its formative experiences. Simple replacement of one set of leaders by another, i.e., surmounting a succession crisis, counts for something in terms of institutional adaptability, but it is not as significant as a shift in leadership generations, i.e., the replacement of one set of leaders by another set with significantly different organizational experiences. The shift from Lenin to Stalin was an intra-generation succession; the shift from Stalin to Krushchev was an inter-generation succession.

Thirdly, organizational adaptability can be measured in functional terms. An organization's functions, of course, can be defined in an almost infinite number of ways. (This is a major appeal and a major limitation of the functional approach to organizations.) Usually an organization is created to perform one particular function. When that function is no longer needed, the organization faces a major crisis. It either finds a new function or reconciles itself to a lingering death. An organization which has adapted itself to changes in its environment and has survived one or more changes in its principal functions is more highly institutionalized than one which has not. Not functional specificity but functional adaptability is the true measure of a highly developed organization. Institutionalization makes the organization more than simply an instrument to achieve certain purposes.[17] Instead

---

[16]Ashoka Mehta, in Raymond Aron, ed., *World Technology and Human Destiny* (Ann Arbor 1963), p. 133.

[17]See the very useful discussion in Philip Selznick's small classic, *Leadership in Administration* (New York 1957), p. 5 ff.

its leaders and members come to value it for its own sake, and it develops a life of its own quite apart from the specific functions it may perform at any given time. The organization triumphs over its function.

Organizations and individuals thus differ significantly in their cumulative capacity to adapt to changes. Individuals usually grow up through childhood and adolescence without deep commitments to highly specific functions. The process of commitment begins in late adolescence. As the individual becomes more and more committed to the performance of certain functions, he finds it increasingly difficult to change those functions and to unlearn the responses which he has acquired to meet environmental changes. His personality has been formed; he has become "set in his ways." Organizations, on the other hand, are usually created to perform very specific functions. When the organization confronts a changing environment, it must, if it is to survive, weaken its commitment to its original functions. As the organization matures, it becomes "unset" in its ways.

In practice, organizations vary greatly in their functional adaptability. The YMCA, for instance, was founded in the mid-nineteenth century as an evangelical organization to convert the single young men who, during the early years of industrialization, were migrating in great numbers to the cities. With the decline in need for this function, the Y successfully adjusted to the performance of many other "general service" functions broadly related to the legitimizing goal of "character development." Concurrently, it broadened its membership base to include first non-evangelical Protestants, then Catholics, then Jews, then old men as well as young, and then women as well as men.[18] As a result, the organization has prospered although its original functions disappeared with the dark satanic mills. Other organizations, such as the WCTU and the Townsend Movement, have had greater difficulty in adjusting to a changing environment. The WCTU "is an organization in retreat. Contrary to the expectations of theories of institutionalization, the movement has not acted to preserve organizational values at the expense of past doctrine."[19] The Townsend Movement has been torn between those who wish to remain loyal to the original function and those who put organizational imperatives first. If the latter are successful, "the dominating orientation of leaders and members shifts *from the implementation of the values the organization is taken to represent* (by leaders, members, and public alike), *to maintaining the organizational structure as such*, even at the loss of the organization's central mission."[20] The conquest

[18]See Mayer N. Zald and Patricia Denton, "From Evangelism to General Service: The Transformation of the YMCA," *Administrative Science Quarterly* 8 (Sept. 1963), p. 214 ff.
[19]Joseph R. Gusfield, "Social Structure and Moral Reform: A Study of the Woman's Christian Temperance Union," *American Journal of Sociology* 61 (Nov. 1955), p. 232; and Gusfield, "The Problem of Generations in an Organizational Structure," *Social Forces* 35 (May 1957), p. 323 ff.
[20]Sheldon L. Messinger, "Organizational Transformation: A Case Study of a Declining Social Movement," *American Sociological Review* 20 (Feb. 1955), p. 10; italics in original.

of polio posed a similar acute crisis for the National Foundation for Infantile Paralysis. The original goals of the organization were highly specific. Should the organization dissolve when these goals were achieved? The dominant opinion of the volunteers was that the organization should continue. "We can fight polio," said one town chairman, "if we can organize people. If we can organize people like this we can fight anything." Another felt that: "Wouldn't it be a wonderful story to get polio licked, and then go on to something else and get that licked and then go on to something else? It would be a challenge, a career."[21]

The problems of functional adaptability are not much different for political organizations. A political party gains in functional age when it shifts its function from the representation of one constituency to the representation of another; it also gains in functional age when it shifts from opposition to government. A party which is unable to change constituencies or to acquire power is less of an institution than one which is able to make these changes. A nationalist party whose function has been the promotion of independence from colonial rule faces a major crisis when it achieves its goal and has to adapt itself to the somewhat different function of governing a country. It may find this functional transition so difficult that it will, even after independence, continue to devote a large portion of its efforts to fighting colonialism. A party which acts this way is less of an institution than one, like the Congress Party, which after achieving independence drops its anti-colonialism and quite rapidly adapts itself to the tasks of governing. Industrialization has been a major function of the Communist Party of the Soviet Union. A major test of the institutionalization of the Communist Party will be its success in developing new functions now that the major industrializing effort is behind it. A governmental organ which can successfully adapt itself to changed functions, such as the British Crown in the eighteenth and nineteenth centuries, is more of an institution than one which cannot, such as the French monarchy in the same period.

Complexity-Simplicity

The more complicated an organization is, the more highly institutionalized it is. Complexity may involve both multiplication of organizational subunits, hierarchically and functionally, and differentiation of separate types of organizational subunits. The greater the number and variety of subunits, the greater the ability of the organization to secure and maintain the loyalties of its members. In addition, an organization which has many purposes is better able to adjust itself to the loss of any one purpose

---

[21]David L. Sills, *The Volunteers* (Glencoe 1957), p. 266. Chap. 9 of this book is an excellent discussion of organizational goal replacement with reference to the YMCA, WCTU, Townsend Movement, Red Cross, and other case studies.

than an organization which has only one purpose. The diversified corporation is obviously less vulnerable than that which produces one product for one market. The differentiation of subunits within an organization may or may not be along functional lines. If it is functional in character, the subunits themselves are less highly institutionalized than the whole of which they are a part. Changes in the functions of the whole, however, are fairly easily reflected by changes in the power and roles of its subunits. If the subunits are multifunctional, they have greater institutional strength, but they may also, for that very reason, contribute less flexibility to the organization as a whole. Hence, a political system with parties of "social integration," in Neumann's terms, has less institutional flexibility than one with parties of "individual representation."[22]

Relatively primitive and simple traditional political systems are usually overwhelmed and destroyed in the modernization process. More complex traditional systems are more likely to adapt to these new demands. Japan, for instance, was able to adjust its traditional political institutions to the modern world because of their relative complexity. For two and a half centuries before 1868, the emperor had reigned and the Tokugawa shogun had ruled. The stability of the political order, however, did not depend solely on the stability of the shogunate. When the authority of the shogunate decayed, another traditional institution, the emperor, was available to become the instrument of the modernizing samurai. The collapse of the shogun involved not the overthrow of the political order but the "restoration" of the emperor.

The simplest political system is that which depends on one individual. It is also, of course, the least stable. Tyrannies, Aristotle pointed out, are virtually all "quite short-lived." A political system with several different political institutions, on the other hand, is much more likely to adapt. The needs of one age may be met by one set of institutions; the needs of the next by a different set. The system possesses within itself the means of its own renewal and adaptation. In the American system, for instance, President, Senate, House of Representatives, Supreme Court, and state governments have played different roles at different times in history. As new problems arise, the initiative in dealing with them may be taken first by one institution, then by another. In contrast, the French system of the Third and Fourth Republics centered authority in the National Assembly and the national bureaucracy. If, as was frequently the case, the Assembly was too divided to act and the bureaucracy lacked the authority to act, the system was unable to adapt to environmental changes and to deal with new policy problems. When in the 1950's the Assembly was unable to handle the dissolution of the French Empire, there was no other institution, such as an independent executive, to step into the breach. As a result, an extraconstitutional force,

---

[22]Sigmund Neumann, "Toward a Comparative Study of Political Parties," in Neumann, ed., *Modern Political Parties* (Chicago 1956), pp. 403-405.

the military, intervened in politics, and in due course a new institution, the de Gaulle Presidency, was created which was able to handle the problem. "A state without the means of some change," Burke observed of an earlier French crisis, "is without the means of its conservation." The classical political theorists, preoccupied as they were with the problem of stability, arrived at similar conclusions. The simple forms of government were most likely to degenerate; the "mixed state" was more likely to be stable. Both Plato and Aristotle suggested that the most practical state was the "polity" combining the institutions of democracy and oligarchy. A "constitutional system based absolutely, and at all points," Aristotle argued, "on either the oligarchical or the democratic conception of equality is a poor sort of thing. The facts are evidence enough: constitutions of this sort never endure." A "constitution is better when it is composed of more numerous elements." Such a constitution is more likely to head off sedition and revolution. Polybius and Cicero elaborated this idea more explicitly. Each of the "good" simple forms of government—kingship, aristocracy, and democracy—is likely to degenerate into its perverted counterpart—tyranny, oligarchy, and mobocracy. Instability and degeneration can be avoided only by combining elements from all the good forms into a mixed state. Complexity produces stability. "The simple governments," Burke echoed two thousand years later, "are fundamentally defective, to say no worse of them."

Autonomy-Subordination

A third measure of institutionalization is the extent to which political organizations and procedures exist independently of other social groupings and methods of behavior. How well is the political sphere differentiated from other spheres? In a highly developed political system, political organizations have an integrity which they lack in less developed systems. In some measure, they are insulated from the impact of nonpolitical groups and procedures. In less developed political systems, they are highly vulnerable to outside influences.

At its most concrete level, autonomy involves the relations between social forces, on the one hand, and political organizations, on the other. Social forces include the groupings of men for social and economic activities: families, clans, work groups, churches, ethnic and linguistic groupings. Political institutionalization, in the sense of autonomy, means the development of political organizations and procedures which are not simply expressions of the interests of particular social groups. A political organization which is the instrument of a social group—family, clan, class—lacks autonomy and institutionalization. If the state, in the traditional Marxist claim, is really the "executive committee of the bourgeoisie," then it is not much of an institution. A judiciary is independent to the extent that it adheres to distinctly judicial norms and to the extent that its perspectives and behavior are independent of those of other political institutions and social groupings. As with the judiciary, the autonomy of political institutions is measured by the extent to which they have their own interests and values distinguishable from those of other social forces. As with the judiciary, the autonomy of political institutions is likely to be the result of competition among social forces. A political party, for instance, which expresses the interests of only one group in society—whether labor, business, or farmers— is less autonomous than one which articulates and aggregates the interests of several social groups. The latter type of party has a clearly defined existence apart from particular social forces. So also with legislatures, executives, and bureaucracies. Political procedures, like political organizations, also have varying degrees of autonomy. A highly developed political system has procedures to minimize, if not to eliminate, the role of violence in the system and to restrict to explicitly defined channels the influence of wealth in the system. To the extent that political officials can be toppled by a few soldiers or influenced by a few dollars, the organizations and procedures lack autonomy. Political organizations and procedures which lack autonomy are, in common parlance, said to be corrupt.

Political organizations and procedures which are vulnerable to non-political influences from within the society are also usually vulnerable to influences from outside the society. They are easily penetrated by agents, groups, and ideas from other political systems. Thus, a *coup d'état* in one political system may easily "trigger" a *coup d'état* by similar groups in other less-developed political systems.[23] In some instances, apparently, a regime can be overthrown by smuggling into the country a few agents and a handful of weapons. In other instances, a regime may be overthrown by the exchange of a few words and a few thousand dollars between a foreign ambassador and some disaffected colonels. The Soviet and American governments presumably spend substantial sums attempting to bribe high officials of less well-insulated political systems which they would not think of wasting in attempting to influence high officials in each other's political system.

In every society affected by social change, new groups arise to participate in politics. Where the political system lacks autonomy, these groups gain entry into politics without becoming identified with the established political organizations or acquiescing in the established political procedures. The political organizations and procedures are unable to stand up against the impact of a new social force. Conversely, in a developed political system, the autonomy of the system is protected by mechanisms which restrict and moderate the impact of new groups. These mechanisms either slow down the

[23]See Samuel P. Huntington, "Patterns of Violence in World Politics," in Huntington, ed., *Changing Patterns of Military Politics* (New York 1962), pp. 44-47.

entry of new groups into politics or, through a process of political socialization, impel changes in the attitudes and behavior of the most politically active members of the new group. In a highly institutionalized political system, the most important positions of leadership can normally be achieved only by those who have served an apprenticeship in less important positions. The complexity of a political system contributes to its autonomy by providing a variety of organizations and positions in which individuals are prepared for the highest offices. In a sense, the top positions of leadership are the inner core of the political system; the less powerful positions, the peripheral organizations, and the semi-political organizations are the filters through which individuals desiring access to the core must pass. Thus the political system assimilates new social forces and new personnel without sacrificing its institutional integrity. In a political system which lacks such defenses, new men, new viewpoints, new social groups may replace each other at the core of the system with bewildering rapidity.

Coherence-Disunity

The more unified and coherent an organization is, the more highly institutionalized it is; the greater the disunity of the organization, the less its institutionalization. Some measure of consensus, of course, is a prerequisite for any social group. An effective organization requires, at a minimum, substantial consensus on the functional boundaries of the group and on the procedures for resolving disputes on issues which come up within those boundaries. The consensus must extend to those active in the system. Non-participants or those only sporadically and marginally participant in the system do not have to share the consensus and usually, in fact, do not share it to the same extent as the participants.[24] In theory, an organization can be autonomous without being coherent and coherent without being autonomous. In actuality, however, the two are often closely linked together. Autonomy becomes a means to coherence, enabling the organization to develop an esprit and style which become distinctive marks of its behavior. Autonomy also prevents the intrusion of disruptive external forces, although, of course, it does not protect against disruption from internal sources. Rapid or substantial expansions in the membership of an organization or in the participants in a system tend to weaken coherence. The Ottoman Ruling Institution, for instance, retained its vitality and coherence as long as admission was restricted and recruits were "put through an elaborate education, with selection and specialization at every stage." The Institution

[24]See, e.g., Herbert McCloskey, "Consensus and Ideology in American Politics," *American Political Science Review* 18 (June 1964), p. 361 ff.; Samuel Stouffer, *Communism, Conformity, and Civil Liberties* (New York 1955), *passim*.

perished when "everybody pressed in to share its privileges. . . . Numbers were increased; discipline and efficiency declined."[25]

Unity, esprit, morale, and discipline are needed in governments as well as in regiments. Numbers, weapons, and strategy all count in war, but major deficiencies in any one of those may still be counterbalanced by superior coherence and discipline. So also in politics. The problems of creating coherent political organizations are more difficult but not fundamentally different from those involved in the creation of coherent military organizations. "The sustaining sentiment of a military force," David Rapoport has argued, "has much in common with that which cements any group of men engaged in politics—the willingness of most individuals to bridle private or personal impulses for the sake of general social objectives. Comrades must trust each other's ability to resist the innumerable temptations that threaten the group's solidarity; otherwise, in trying social situations the desire to fend for oneself becomes overwhelming."[26] The capacities for coordination and discipline are crucial to both war and politics, and historically societies which have been skilled at organizing the one have also been adept at organizing the other. "The relationship of efficient social organization in the arts of peace and in the arts of group conflict," one anthropologist has observed, "is almost absolute, whether one is speaking of civilization or subcivilization. Successful war depends upon team work and consensus, both of which require command and discipline. Command and discipline, furthermore, can eventually be no more than symbols of something deeper and more real than they themselves."[27] Societies, such as Sparta, Rome, and Britain, which have been admired by their contemporaries for the authority and justice of their laws have also been admired for the coherence and discipline of their armies. Discipline and development go hand in hand.

One major advantage of studying development in terms of mobilization and participation is that they are measurable. Statistics are readily available for urbanization, literacy, mass media exposure, and voting. Hence, comparisons are easily made between countries and between different stages of the same country. What about institutionalization? Are the criteria of adaptability, complexity, autonomy, and coherence also measurable? Quite obviously the difficulties are greater. The UN has not conveniently collected in its *Statistical Yearbook* data on the political institutionalization of its members. Nonetheless, no reason exists why with a little imagination and effort sufficient information could not be collected to make meaningful comparisons of the levels of political institutionalization of different countries or of the same country at different times. Adaptability can be

[25]Arnold J. Toynbee, *A Study of History* (Abridgement of Vols. I-VI by D. C. Somervell, New York 1947), pp. 176-177.

[26]David C. Rapoport, "A Comparative Theory of Military and Political Types," in Huntington, ed., *Changing Patterns of Military Politics,* p. 79.

[27]Harry Holbert Turney-High, *Primitive War* (Columbia, S.C., 1949), pp. 235-236.

measured by chronological age, leadership successions, generational changes, and functional changes. Complexity can be measured by the number and diversity of organizational subunits and by the number and diversity of functions performed by the organizations. Autonomy is perhaps the most difficult of the criteria to pin down: it can, however, be measured by the distinctiveness of the norms and values of the organization compared with those of other groups, by the personnel controls (in terms of cooptation, penetration, and purging) existing between the organization and other groups, and by the degree to which the organization controls its own material resources. Coherence may be measured by the ratio of contested successions to total successions, by the cumulation or non-cumulation of cleavages among leaders and members, by the incidence of overt alienation and dissent within the organization, and, conceivably, by opinion surveys of the loyalties and preferences of organization members.

Experience tells us that levels of institutionalization differ. Measuring that difference may be difficult, but it is not impossible. Only by measuring institutionalization will we be able to buttress or disprove hypotheses about the relation between social, economic, and demographic changes, on the one hand, and variations in political structure, on the other.

Political Institutions and Public Interests

A society with weak political institutions lacks the ability to curb the excesses of personal and parochial desires. Politics is a Hobbesian world of unrelenting competition among social forces—between man and man, family and family, clan and clan, region and region, class and class—a competition unmediated by more comprehensive political organizations. The "amoral familism" of Banfield's village has its counterparts in amoral clanism, amoral groupism, and amoral classism. Without strong political institutions, society lacks the means of defining and realizing its common interests. The capacity to create political institutions is the capacity to create public interests.

Traditionally the public interest has been approached in three ways.[28] It has been identified either with abstract, substantive ideal values and norms such as natural law, justice, or right reason; or with the specific interest of a particular individual ("L'état, c'est moi"), group, class (Marxism), or majority; or with the result of a competitive process among individuals (classic liberalism) or groups (Bentleyism).

*   *   *

[28]See, in general, Glendon Schubert, *The Public Interest* (Glencoe 1960); Carl J. Friedrich, ed., *Nomos V: The Public Interest* (New York 1962); Douglas Price, "Theories of the Public Interest," in Lynton K. Caldwell, ed., *Politics and Public Affairs* (Bloomington, Ind., 1962), pp. 141-160.

The problem in all these approaches is to arrive at a definition which is concrete rather than nebulous and general rather than particular. Unfortunately, in most cases what is concrete lacks generality and what is general lacks concreteness. One partial way out of the problem is to define the public interest in terms of the concrete interests of the governing institutions. A society with highly institutionalized governing organizations and procedures is, in this sense, more able to articulate and achieve its public interests. "Organized (institutionalized) political communities," as Friedrich argues, "are *better adapted* to reaching decisions and developing policies than unorganized communities."[29] The public interest, in this sense, is not something which exists *a priori* in natural law or the will of the people. Nor is it simply whatever results from the political process. Rather it is whatever strengthens governmental institutions. The public interest is the interest of public institutions. It is something which is created and brought into existence by the institutionalization of government organizations. In a complex political system, many governmental organizations and procedures represent many different aspects of the public interest. The public interest of a complex society is a complex matter.

We are accustomed to think of our primary governing institutions as having representative functions—that is, as expressing the interests of some other set of groups (their constituency). Hence, we tend to forget that governmental institutions have interests of their own. These interests not only exist; they are also reasonably concrete. The questions, "What is the interest of the Presidency? What is the interest of the Senate? What is the interest of the House of Representatives? What are the interests of the Supreme Court?" are difficult but not completely impossible to answer. The answers would furnish a fairly close approximation of the "public interest" of the United States. Similarly, the public interest of Great Britain might be approximated by the specific institutional interests of the Crown, Cabinet, and Parliament. In the Soviet Union, the answer would involve the specific institutional interests of the Presidium, Secretariat, and Central Committee of the Communist Party.

Institutional interests differ from the interests of individuals who are in the institutions. Keynes's percipient remark that "In the long run, we are all dead" applies to individuals, not institutions. Individual interests are necessarily short-run interests. Institutional interests, however, exist through time: the proponent of the institution has to look to its welfare through an indefinite future. This consideration often means a limiting of immediate goals. The "true policy," Aristotle remarked, "for democracy and oligarchy alike, is not one which ensures the greatest possible amount of either, but one which will ensure the longest possible life for both." The official who attempts to maximize power or other values in the short run often weakens

[29] Carl J. Friedrich, *Man and His Government* (New York 1963), p. 150; italics in original.

his institution in the long run. Supreme Court justices may, in terms of their immediate individual desires, wish to declare an act of Congress unconstitutional. In deciding whether it is in the public interest to do so, however, presumably one question they should ask themselves is whether it is in the long-term institutional interest of the Supreme Court for them to do so. Judicial statesmen are those who, like John Marshall in *Marbury vs. Madison*, maximize the institutional power of the Court in such a way that it is impossible for either the President or Congress to challenge it. In contrast, the Supreme Court justices of the 1930's came very close to expanding their immediate influence at the expense of the long-term interests of the Court as an institution.

The phrase "What's good for General Motors is good for the country" contains at least a partial truth. "What's good for the Presidency is good for the country," however, contains more truth. Ask any reasonably informed group of Americans to identify the five best Presidents and the five worst Presidents. Then ask them to identify the five strongest Presidents and the five weakest Presidents. If the identification of strength with goodness and weakness with badness is not 100 per cent, it will almost certainly not be less than 80 per cent. Those Presidents—Jefferson, Lincoln, the Roosevelts, Wilson—who expanded the powers of their office are hailed as the beneficent promoters of the public welfare and national interest. Those Presidents, such as Buchanan, Grant, Harding, who failed to defend the power of their institution against other groups are also thought to have done less good for the country. Institutional interest coincides with public interest. The power of the Presidency is identified with the good of the polity.

The public interest of the Soviet Union is approximated by the institutional interests of the top organs of the Communist Party: "what's good for the Presidium is good for the Soviet Union." Viewed in these terms, Stalinism can be defined as a situation in which the personal interests of the ruler take precedence over the institutionalized interests of the Party. Beginning in the late 1930's Stalin consistently weakened the Party. No Party Congress was held between 1939 and 1952. During and after World War II the Central Committee seldom met. The Party secretariat and Party hierarchy were weakened by the creation of competing organs. Conceivably this process could have resulted in the displacement of one set of governing institutions by another, and some American experts and some Soviet leaders did think that governmental organizations rather than Party organizations would become the ruling institutions in Soviet society. Such, however, was neither the intent nor the effect of Stalin's action. He increased his personal power, not the governmental power. When he died, his personal power died with him. The struggle to fill the resulting vacuum was won by Khrushchev, who identified his interests with the interests of the Party organization, rather than by Malenkov, who identified himself with the governmental bureaucracy. Khrushchev's consolidation of power marked the reemergence and revitalization of the principal organs of the Party. While they acted in very different ways and from different motives, Stalin weakened the Party just as Grant weakened the Presidency. Just as a strong Presidency is in the American public interest, so also a strong Party is in the Soviet public interest.

In terms of the theory of natural law, governmental actions are legitimate to the extent that they are in accord with the "public philosophy." [30] According to democratic theory, they derive their legitimacy from the extent to which they embody the will of the people. According to the procedural concept, they are legitimate if they represent the outcome of a process of conflict and compromise in which all interested groups have participated. In another sense, however, the legitimacy of governmental actions can be sought in the extent to which they reflect the interests of governmental institutions. In contrast to the theory of representative government, under this concept governmental institutions derive their legitimacy and authority not from the extent to which they represent the interests of the people or of any other group, but from the extent to which they have distinct interests of their own apart from all other groups. Politicians frequently remark that things "look different" after they obtain office than they did when they were competing for office. This difference is a measure of the institutional demands of office. It is precisely this difference in perspective which legitimizes the demands which the officeholder makes on his fellow citizens. The interests of the President, for instance, may coincide partially and temporarily first with those of one group and then with those of another. But the interest of the Presidency, as Neustadt has emphasized,[31] coincides with that of no one else. The President's power derives not from his representation of class, group, regional, or popular interests, but rather from the fact that he represents none of these. The Presidential perspective is unique to the Presidency. Precisely for this reason, it is both a lonely office and a powerful one. Its authority is rooted in its loneliness.

The existence of political institutions (such as the Presidency or Presidium) capable of giving substance to public interests distinguishes politically developed societies from undeveloped ones. The "ultimate test of development," as Lucian Pye has said, "is the capacity of a people to establish and maintain large, complex, but flexible organizational forms." [32] The level of organization in much of the world, however, is low. "Except in Europe and America," Banfield notes, "the concerting of behavior in political associations and corporate organizations is a rare and recent

---

[30]See Walter Lippmann, *The Public Philosophy* (Boston 1955), especially p. 42, for his definition of the public interest as "what men would choose if they saw clearly, thought rationally, acted disinterestedly and benevolently."

[31]See Richard E. Neustadt, *Presidential Power* (New York 1960), *passim*, but especially pp. 33-37, 150-51.

[32]Pye, *Politics, Personality and Nation Building,* p. 51.

thing."[33] The ability to create public organizations and political institutions is in short supply in the world today. It is this ability which, above all else, the Communists offer modernizing countries.

Degeneration and the Corrupt Polity

Most modernizing countries are buying rapid social modernization at the price of political degeneration. This process of decay in political institutions, however, has been neglected or overlooked in much of the literature on modernization. As a result, models and concepts which are hopefully entitled "developing" or "modernizing" are often only partially relevant to the countries to which they are applied. More relevant in many cases would be models of corrupt or degenerating societies, highlighting the decay of political organization and the increasing dominance of disruptive social forces. Who, however, has advanced such a theory of political decay or a model of a corrupt political order which might be useful in analyzing the political processes of the countries that are usually called "developing"? Perhaps the most relevant ideas are the most ancient ones. The evolution of many contemporary new states, once the colonial guardians have departed, has not deviated extensively from the Platonic model. Independence is followed by military coups as the "auxiliaries" take over.[34] Corruption by the oligarchy inflames the envy of rising groups. Conflict between oligarchy and masses erupts into civil strife. Demagogues and street mobs pave the way for the despot. Plato's description of the means by which the despot appeals to the people, isolates and eliminates his enemies, and builds up his personal strength is a far less misleading guide to what has taken place in Ghana and other new states than many things written yesterday.[35]

Plato is one of the few theorists, ancient or contemporary, with a highly explicit theory of political degeneration.[36] The concept of a "corrupt

[33]Edward C. Banfield, *The Moral Basis of a Backward Society* (Glencoe, Ill., 1958), pp. 7-9, 15 ff.

[34]For comments on the short time lag between independence and the first coup, see Dankwart A. Rustow, "The Military in Middle Eastern Society and Politics," in Sydney N. Fisher, ed., *The Military in the Middle East: Problems in Society and Government* (Columbus, Ohio, 1963), p. 10.

[35]See, in general, *The Republic*, Book VIII, and especially the description of the despotic regime (Cornford trans., New York 1945), pp. 291-293.

[36]Perhaps the closest contemporary model comes not from a social scientist but from a novelist: William Golding. The schoolboys (newly independent elites) of *The Lord of the Flies* initially attempt to imitate the behavior patterns of adults (former Western rulers). Discipline and consensus, however, disintegrate. A demagogic military leader and his followers gain or coerce the support of a majority. The symbol of authority (the conch) is broken. The voices of responsibility (Ralph) and reason (Piggy) are deserted and harassed, and reason is destroyed. In the end, the naval officer (British Marine Commandos) arrives just in time to save Ralph (Nyerere) from the "hunters" (mutinous troops).

society," however, is a more familiar one in political theory. Typically it refers to a society which lacks law, authority, cohesion, discipline, and consensus, where private interests dominate public ones, where there is an absence of civic obligation and civic duty, where, in short, political institutions are weak and social forces strong. Plato's degenerate states are dominated by various forms of appetite: by force, wealth, numbers, and charisma. "Those constitutions," says Aristotle, "which consider only the personal interest of the rulers are all wrong constitutions, or perversions of the right forms." So also, Machiavelli's concept of the corrupt state, in the words of one commentator, "includes all sorts of license and violence, great inequalities of wealth and power, the destruction of peace and justice, the growth of disorderly ambition, disunion, lawlessness, dishonesty, and contempt for religion."[37] Modern equivalents of the classical corrupt society are Kornhauser's theory of the mass society (where, in the absence of institutions, elites are accessible to masses and masses are available for mobilization by the elite) and Rapoport's concept of the praetorian state where "private ambitions are rarely restrained by a sense of public authority; [and] the role of power (i.e., wealth and force) is maximized."[38] Typical of the corrupt, praetorian, or mass societies is the violent oscillation between extreme democracy and tyranny. "Where the pre-established political authority is highly autocratic," says Kornhauser, "rapid and violent displacement of that authority by a democratic regime is highly favorable to the emergence of extremist mass movements that tend to transform the new democracy in anti-democratic directions."[39] Aristotle and Plato saw despotism emerging out of the extremes of mob rule. Rapoport finds in Gibbon an apt summary of the constitutional rhythms of the praetorian state, which "floats between the extremes of absolute monarchy and wild democracy."[40] Such instability is the hallmark of a society where mobilization has outrun institutionalism. . . .

[37]George H. Sabine, *A History of Political Thought* (rev. edn., New York 1950), p. 343.

[38]Kornhauser, *Politics of Mass Society, passim*; David C. Rapoport, "Praetorianism: Government Without Consensus" (Ph.D. dissertation, University of California, Berkeley 1959); and Rapoport in Huntington, ed., *Changing Patterns of Military Politics*, p. 72, where the quotation occurs.

[39]Kornhauser, *Politics of Mass Society*, p. 125.

[40]Edward Gibbon, *The Decline and Fall of the Roman Empire* (New York 1899), vol. I, p. 235, quoted by Rapoport in Huntington, ed., *Changing Patterns of Military Politics*, p. 98.

4

Historians and Other Social Scientists: The Comparative Analysis of Nation-Building in Western Societies

Val R. Lorwin

This paper attempts to do four simple things. First, it recalls the utility of more historical studies as the basis for continuing comparative research and theory concerning the processes of nation-building and, more specifically, the utility of work within one cultural area, that of Western Europe. Second, it discusses various kinds of 'one-nation studies' which are needed for further international comparisons. Third, it looks at a few characteristics of the work of professional historians in relation to the possibilities of more, and more effective, cooperation between historians and other social scientists. Finally, the paper describes a series of comparatively oriented interdisciplinary studies, now under way, dealing with the smaller European democracies.

The term 'nation-building' is now being used to cover the historical processes of both nation-state formation and civic integration within the national life. The two processes are of course related and in some cases overlapping, notably in many new states that would be nations. For the Western nations, mostly older creations, we can usually separate the two processes. It is with national integration, the extension of civic, political, and socioeconomic rights and participation, in the sense of T. H. Marshall's classic essay 'Citizenship and Social Class',[1] that I shall be chiefly concerned, rather than with the nation-state's territorial formation or consolidation.

"Reprinted by permission from *Comparative Research Across Cultures and Nations,* Stein Rokkan, ed. (Paris: Mouton, 1968). The original version of this article entitled "The Comparative Analysis of Historical Change: Nation-Building in the Western World," appeared in *International Social Science Journal,* Vol. XVII, No. 4 (1965), published by UNESCO. Article and footnotes abridged by permission of UNESCO."

[1]Reprinted in T. H. Marshall, *Class, Citizenship, and Social Development* (Garden City, N.Y.: Doubleday, Anchor Books, 1965), pp. 71-134.

1. STUDIES OF WESTERN SOCIETY

In the study of national integration, we should not linger too long over the dichotomies between developed and underdeveloped societies. These dichotomies blur the vital differences among nations in the group labeled 'developed' (sometimes quaintly called 'fully developed') as well as among those labeled 'developing'. They deny us some of the most significant dimensions of comparative analysis. It is essential, as Lipset has urged, 'to move beyond the pointing out of gross variations at different levels of technical development and to specify the key sources of differences among nations at comparable levels' of development.[2]

Even among those advanced societies we have cheerfully assumed to be well known, systematic empirical knowledge of nation-building and theory on the subject are still underdeveloped, even if developing. Western political science, as Almond and Verba have pointed out, 'has only begun to codify the operating characteristics of the democratic polity itself'.[3] No doubt historians have already produced more materials than have yet been absorbed by those engaged in the tasks of 'codification'. Yet for Western society, we are still in the early stages of comparative research on the processes of nation-building.

Western society has the richest history of national achievement and of pathological nationalism. It is also richest in trans-national associations and in attempts at supra-national political organization. The vocabulary and concepts of the discussions of nation-building and national integration —even in the developing nations—are derived from Western experience, chiefly by way of Western social science. Although we are still redefining the concepts of nation-building and national integration, research and communication on these problems in Western society suffer less from terminological ambiguity and conceptual uncertainty than do discussions which combine the experiences of developed and developing societies. There is enough common historical experience and common cultural context in Western society to make comparisons realistic and fruitful. On the other hand, there are differences enough, among the Western nations, to make comparisons exciting and significant.

[2]S. M. Lipset, "Democracy and the Social System," in Harry Eckstein, ed., *Internal War, Problems and Approaches* (Glencoe, Ill.: The Free Press, 1964), p. 317.

[3]Gabriel A. Almond and Sidney Verba, *The Civic Culture: Political Attitudes and Democracy in Five Nations* (Princeton, N.J.: Princeton University Press, 1963), p. 5.

2. ONE-NATION STUDIES

International studies alone will not sustain international comparisons. To compare the nations, we need more knowledge of processes and institutions and social forces within the nations. One would be happy to learn that it is breaking through an open door to plead the case of one-nation studies. But it often looks as if, in our anxiety to compare sequences of historic change, we are trying to skip sequences of needed historical research.

There are reasons for dissatisfaction with much of the existing single-country specialization in Western societies. Ideally, single-country studies should be informed by a lively sense both of the varieties of historical experience within the nation and of some of the relevant experience beyond present national frontiers. They should separate the workings of factors specific to the nation and those which are characteristic of many nations. Ideally, no doubt, historical researches on nation-building should be related to explicit hypotheses about nation-building in general, with the hypotheses in turn being reformulated in the light of research findings. So much for the ideal.

The mills of comparison, however, must rely for grist on many sources, including some which will seem parochial indeed. Most of the information for international comparison is likely, for some time, to come from single-nation studies, unrelated to any trans-national hypotheses. We can hope and we can work for a comparative framework in the basic national studies; we cannot expect it. Now we must be at once grateful for materials produced out of concerns remote from our own and critical in our handling of such materials in comparative research.

Hopeful of getting more materials for comparison, one may list some of the major themes on which, for so many Western nations, we still need historical studies: the formation, attitudes, and behavior of political parties, social movements, interest groups, regional associations, and patriotic societies; crises in national identity and in civic cohesion; the interaction of local and national politics; the growth of the public administration at various levels; the role of national and local police forces and popular images of them; the recruitment of elites; the adjustment of old elites to the increasing importance of the masses; the absorption of immigrants.

Nobody doubts the existence of national character who knows anything about schools and armies, said Lord Acton. But we need to know a great deal more about the role of schools and armies—and churches and other voluntary organizations—in political socialization. We need to know a great deal more about popular literature and folk art, the nature of folk heroes, national symbols and the language of national identification (positive and negative), popular mythology and popular conceptions of fundamental law.

Such studies call upon the materials and methods of intellectual history and cultural anthropology, as well as upon more traditional historical sources and styles of research. There is nothing new in this sort of an agenda, but most of the work remains to be done.

The study of nation-building in Western society is not a set of historical variations on a swelling theme of widening and deepening community. So eminent a historian as Halvdan Koht could speak of 'a constant progress toward national unity through the rise of successive classes' toward a 'fuller and richer national solidarity'.[4] But that was over half a century ago, and we know now, if we did not then, that the progress is not 'constant' and the solidarity not always 'fuller and richer'. Although Koht's vision has not been nation-bound, what a Norwegian might see around him would be more reassuring than what a German or a Spaniard saw.

Pathology is a well-known aid to the study of physiology, as Durkheim reminded us. We must give more study to the discontinuities and the retrogressions of civic integration, to xenophobia and nativism as well as assimilation; the loss of spontaneity and liberating purpose in social movements; the apathy in the exercise of rights which often follows the struggle for equality; the vapidity as well as the virtues of high-consensus societies. . . .

To understand the present, we must—to quote Durkheim again—from time to time stand back from it. To understand the nation, we must from time to time stand back from its center and study its components and its peripheries. If the nation is more than the sum of its parts, the parts are more than fractions of the whole. Sometimes national aggregates cancel out, rather than sum up, important local and regional, class or occupational, ethnic and cultural developments. The history of political parties and of trade unions, for example—in fact, the history of the nation itself—has too often been written and rewritten only on a national basis. Even for national history and international comparison, we must disaggregate the national data by studies of the nation's geographic or occupational or cultural and other components. We need studies of limiting as well as more or less typical cases. Local studies, moreover, permit the testing of hypotheses of national behavior, for example, phenomena of mass behavior which, as a historian of Jacksonian democracy has said, are 'better assayed by increasing the precision of research than by widening its geographic scope'.[5]

Some medieval communes are better known than their nineteenth-century successors. 'Social history is local history', Dorothy George has remarked.[6] So is a good deal of political and economic and cultural history, if the local is also seen in its larger context. The processes of political

---

[4]Cited by Halvdan Koht in his *Driving Forces in History*, trans. by Einar Haugen (Cambridge, Mass.: Belknap Press, 1964), pp. 120-121.

[5]Lee Benson, *The Concept of Jacksonian Democracy* (Princeton, N.J.: Princeton University Press, 1961), p. vii.

[6]Dorothy George, *England in Transition* (Harmondsworth: Pelican Books, 1953), p. 41.

socialization, for example, often revolve about the local political scene. So begins, and sometimes continues, the *cursus honorum* for many a national politician: a Joseph Chamberlain or a Theodore Roosevelt or a Camille Huysmans (to cite an internationalist who remained a local potentate while becoming a national figure).

We must be grateful for the chance to utilize what local history we have, even when it offers erroneous local causations. If it is written in the broader context of comparison, within the nation or beyond it, it is of course likely to be more interesting, sounder and more meaningful. Asa Briggs has shown how one may write modern urban history, and compare community with local community, within the same and in another country, to illuminate the relations between politics and social structure at a crucial period of class relations and political ferment.[7]

Regional studies furnish essential information and bases of comparisons. One may study the region, or another administrative or political or cultural or economic unit below the nation, for its own sake, as the scholars of French electoral geography and electoral sociology have been studying the political history and public opinion of *département* after *département*. Or one may compare periphery and center and their relations to each other, as Rokkan and Valen have done for Norway,[8] Erik Allardt for Finland,[9] and Juan Linz for Spain.[10] Charles Tilly has recently shown how a regional historical study may use social science techniques for systematic comparisons within the region and thereby clarify its long mythical relationship to the national regime in a crisis period.[11] One may compare different kinds of urban and industrial environments in which members of a social class have played their life roles, as Georges Duveau has done with sensitive attention and sympathy for the workers of the Second Empire in France.[12]

[7]Asa Briggs, "The Background of the Parliamentary Reform Movement in Three English Cities, 1830-1832," *Cambridge Historical Journal* 10 (1952), pp. 293-317, and "Social Structure and Politics in Birmingham and Lyons (1825-1848)," *British Journal of Sociology* 1: 1 (1950), pp. 67-80.

[8]Stein Rokkan and Henry Valen, "Regional Contrasts in Norwegian Politics: A Review of Data from Official Statistics and from Sample Surveys," in Erik Allardt and Yrjö Littunen, eds., *Cleavages, Ideologies and Party Systems: Constributions to Comparative Political Sociology.* Transactions of the Westermarck Society, vol. X, Helsinki, 1964, pp. 162-238, and a number of other studies cited therein.

[9]Erik Allardt, "Patterns of Class Conflict and Working Class Consciousness in Finnish Politics," in Allardt and Littunen, eds., *op. cit.,* pp. 97-131.

[10]See especially Juan Linz and Amando de Miguel's chapter in Richard Merritt and Stein Rokkan, eds., *Comparing Nations* (New Haven, Conn.: Yale University Press, 1966) and a number of articles cited therein.

[11]Charles Tilly, *The Vendée* (Cambridge, Mass.: Harvard University Press, 1964). Note the comment of the reviewer in *The Economist* (March 6, 1965), p. 1026: ". . . as the book proceeds . . . Mr. Tilly has evidently begun to wonder if historical study should not be prescribed for sociologists rather than sociology for historians."

[12]Georges Duveau, *La Vie ouvrière en France sous le Second Empire* (Paris: Gallimard, 1946), pp. 225-230 and *passim.* These pages are translated in Val R. Lorwin, ed., *Labor and Working Conditions in Modern Europe* (New York: Macmillan, 1967).

3. HISTORIANS AND OTHER SOCIAL SCIENTISTS

Some of the most valuable of the historical work I have been discussing is by men and women whose formal attachment is to another discipline. 'History, it is clear, has no monopoly on the study of the past'.[13] Now I should like to turn to historical work by members of the guild of historians, qualified to publish, as it were, under the *appélation contrôlée*. How can we help make available more of the historical data and evoke more of the basic historical studies which are still needed, even for the comparatively well studied nations of Western Europe, as we go forward to the fullness of systematic comparisons within nations and among nations? Clearly a closer and freer cooperation between historians and other social scientists is needed. Theorists of nation-building must rely chiefly on secondary authorities.[14] 'Life is too short to do anything else when using the comparative method', as T. H. Marshall reminds us.[15] And, he adds with an irony authorized by a rare mastery of both disciplines, surely historians 'will not rebuke the sociologist for putting his faith in what historians write'. . . .

Most of us do not work in a comparative perspective. Historians, it is true, have been making analogies and comparisons, first across space and then across time, since Thucydides compared the politics of Athens and Sparta. They have embodied implicit comparisons in their terminology and in the moral lessons they have drawn from man's experience. But comparisons are not necessarily comparative history. As a whole, the historical fraternity has not paid much attention to the methods and opportunities of explicit and more or less systematic comparative study. The comparative method is an integral part of linguistic studies, art and religious history, law, sociology, and political science. But history, as Bert Hoselitz gloomily observed, has been 'outstanding among the social sciences in rejecting longest the application of this method'.[16] This continues to be true despite the interesting discussions of philosophy and method, and applications of method, not only in books and old-established journals, such as *Annales* and the *Journal of the History of Ideas*, but in such new journals as *Comparative Studies in Society and History, History and Theory*, and the

[13]Carey B. Joynt and Nicholas Rescher, "The Problem of Uniqueness in History," *History and Theory* 1 (1961), p. 151.

[14]See for example the excellent work of Reinhard Bendix, with one chapter in collaboration with Stein Rokkan, *Nation-Building and Citizenship* (New York: J. Wiley, 1964). It shows the utilization of, and reflection on, a vast body of historical material, as well as Bendix's usual shrewd theoretical analysis. But, at least by implication, it also calls attention to the lack of information on many problems in many countries.

[15]T. H. Marshall, *op. cit.* (cited in note 1 above), p. 38.

[16]"On Comparative History," review of Rushton Coulborn, ed., *Feudalism in History* (Princeton, N.J.: Princeton University Press, 1956), in *World Politics* (Jan. 1957), p. 267.

Archives Européennes de Sociologie. For these discussions only very slowly and indirectly affect the writing of most historians. . . .

'Historical research does not permit autarchy', said Marc Bloch. But most historians study a problem or an institution, a personality or an event, within a single country, usually their own.

The reasons for a national focus are many: to begin with, the roots of national history in national culture, and then the facts of organization of school curricula and documentary administration. The nation-state produces vast quantities of materials out of its internal political processes, its dealings with its *administrés,* and its external relations. It also shapes the scope and direction—hence the documents—of voluntary organizations, interest groups, and social movements, as well as cultural activities of the modern era. Authority is responsible even for many of the materials of protest against authority: the police archives contain essential materials for the history of labor and radical movements.

The modern historian who is a teacher is likely to be teaching the history of his own country; if not, the history of another, a leading, nation. If he is an archivist, he is likely to be organizing or administering archives of his own nation, at the national or local level. He meets his colleagues in national organizations for the promotion of scholarship, teaching, and professional interests. Language facility and access to materials in the homeland direct the historian to the study of his own country. He may expect to find more of a public for works on his own country, whether among the general reading public or his professional colleagues or in those local history societies so congenial in their blend of disinterested scholarship and antiquarianism, local and family piety.

More or less consciously the guardians of their nation's traditions, historians, in their finest hours, revivify those traditions and bring the best in them to bear upon the problems of the present. But most, said Pirenne, 'behave toward the nation like the architect toward his client'; they 'seek above all to furnish him a history in conformity with his tastes and his customs, in short, a *habitable* history'. Pirenne was well placed to speak, for he was one of the few men to have become a 'national historian' in the sense of a national institution or symbol.

Yet historians are not perforce any more ethnocentric than the many economists, political scientists and sociologists, who—despite the canons of their crafts—do not hesitate to generalize about all human behavior from their study of some of their own countrymen's behavior. 'Economic teaching and research in the United States have suffered from a myopic pre-occupation with Anglo-American ideas, institutions, and problems', a leading American economist recently found. He called for a 'geophysical stretching' of the scope of economics, which is 'at least as necessary as the "historical stretching" that is rightly urged by historians and others'.[17]

[17]Lloyd Reynolds, in National Bureau of Economic Research, *The Comparative Study of*

Obviously, economics is not the only discipline, nor are Americans the only people, to fall short in this regard.

Individual labor comes more easily to historians than collective enterprise, except for such work as the editing of national series of documents or war histories. Small-scale enterprise is more natural than large; 'they reject frescoes in favor of portraits'. International projects are likely to be more collective and larger in scale than the work most historians envisage. Moreover, most of us are more accustomed to looking down the corridors of time than across space. We are modest about our capacity to comprehend many cultures, and loath to compare without at least the illusion of such comprehension. Our literary canons do not induce tolerance among historians for the specialized vocabularies in which some behavioral scientists seek to give greater precision to their ideas. Reluctant to study languages used by only a few million people, historians are even less eager to make an effort for vocabularies which they (perhaps hastily) conclude are destined to remain the vehicles of a few dozen.

Another source of difficulty in cooperation with other social scientists is the reluctance of historians to accommodate themselves to explicit models. Abstraction from the complexities they know or would know is a wrench of the spirit. They tend therefore to look upon model-builders with a skepticism even deeper than that of the social psychologist who spoke of 'the authors who seem to entertain their models because the models entertain them'.[18] Yet this skepticism cannot prevent us from seeing our evidence in relation to our own implicit models, usually as cherished as unexamined. . . .

'The art of theorizing, like that of fiction, largely consists in knowing what to leave out', as Michael Balfour says. Historians usually want to find out more about what needs to be put in, before they rigorously leave out. For their colleagues in the social sciences as for themselves, they have a wholesome fear of what T. H. Huxley called the greatest tragedy, a beautiful theory killed by a simple fact.

The less sophisticated historians have not acquired a proper respect for the processes by which stimulating theoretical formulations may arise out of summary and imperfect perception of the historical evidence. Nor do they always appeciate the virtue of the 'outrageous hypothesis' in generating useful inquiry.

About the use of the material they have amassed and analyzed and qualified, historians often feel as psychologists and anthropologists do about sociologists' use of their data. They have an innocent capacity for being shocked by inattention to, or careless handling of, facts in works of greater

Economic Growth and Structure: Suggestions on Research Objectives and Organization (New York: NBER, 1959), p. 177.

[18]Gordon W. Allport, *Personality and Social Encounter: Selected Essays* (Boston: Beacon, 1960), p. 67, n.10.

theoretical range than their own. They may not be charmed when a well-known sociologist gracefully asks 'the reader's indulgence if the next few pages leave much to be desired in terms of historical accuracy and detail'. They are likely to worry, not about absence of factual detail, but about carelessness of broad statements of presumed fact. They will not be reassured, even if they are grateful, when they read that 'All too often the societies that appear in the work of sociologists are merely historical constructions borrowed from earlier works or even invented in order to provide an impressive contrast for contemporary data.'[19]

Short-run time sequences may concern the historian more than other social scientists. But those concerned with grand sequences of social change cannot disregard the short-run sequences in periods of crisis and decision. John Plamenatz has stated this concern with his usual cogency, in warning us against the reification of the concept of 'revolution'.[20] (In the study of nation-building the traps of reification are many.)

There is a constant tension in the work of most historians between the claim that they alone are serious in the handling of the facts of the recorded past and—on the other hand—the disclaimer of the aims of science for their work because theirs is not a discipline of regularities and laws and predictions. The claim is exaggerated; the disclaimer out of place. As Max Weber observed, 'The professional historians, unfortunately, have contributed not a little to the strengthening of the prejudice that "historical work" is something qualitatively different from "scientific work" because "concepts" and "rules" are of "no concern" to history.'[21] Since Weber wrote, moreover, we have learned much more about indeterminism in the natural and physical sciences, about the role of description in the generalizing disciplines, and about 'the circumstantial, the irrational, and nonrational, as well as the logical and systematic nature of social research'.[22] Historians may come to lose some of the feeling of uniqueness in their intellectual processes and in the findings of their discipline. Meanwhile, the social sciences not being very scientific, Bertrand de Jouvenel has suggested, they ought to be very social.

A contemporary economist distinguished for his work in economic history once deplored the separation of the two disciplines in that field: the economists seemed to have all the problems and the historians all the data. Surely, by now, in our work on nation-building, as on economic growth and

[19]Ralf Dahrendorf, *Class and Class Conflict in Industrial Society* (Stanford, Calif.: Stanford University Press, 1959), pp. 241 and 242.

[20]John Plamenatz, *The Revolutionary Movement in France, 1815-1871* (London: Longmans, Green and Co., 1952), pp. xii-xiii.

[21]Max Weber, *The Methodology of the Social Sciences*, E. A. Shils and H. A. Finch, transls. and eds., (Glencoe, Ill.: Free Press, 1949), p. 115.

[22]Phillip E. Hammond, ed., *Sociologists at Work* (New York: Basic Books, 1964), Introduction, especially p. 2.

other problems of social change, enough people within the relevant disciplines have enough realization of mutual interest and interdependence to call more upon the historians in the formulation of the problems and upon other social scientists in the pursuit of the historical data?

At a conference on the study of comparative politics,[23] an American political scientist demanded, with asperity, 'Must we all become sociologists, or whatever the most general field of study is?' In the dozen years or so since that conference, an answer has come from some of the most effective contributions, empirical and theoretical, to comparative politics. Now members of the more theoretically and behaviorally oriented disciplines may ask, in their work on nation-building: Must we all become historians?

Clearly, history is too important to be left to the professional historians alone. We all mine the endlessly complex seams of a fascinating and frequently tragic human experience. We have everything to gain by making the confrontations of historians and other social scientists in that work more frequent and—to use a word dear to Marc Bloch—fraternal.

4. AN EXAMPLE OF COMPARATIVE STUDIES: THE POLITICS OF THE SMALLER EUROPEAN DEMOCRACIES

This communication may be of most practical use (its writer's modest aim) if it now turns to a fraternal research undertaking of an international and interdisciplinary nature. The series of studies recently launched on the Politics of the Smaller European Democracies will, we hope, indicate something of the possibilities of a cooperative project which combines the national specializations of individual authors with comparative and theoretical concerns from the outset. It also combines the autonomy of the individual scholar with the stimuli of continuing confrontation and mutual criticism. The collaborating authors are people whose training and interests include history and behaviorally oriented disciplines. Steeped in the development and problems of the countries they are working on, many of them also have a 'built-in' comparative focus because of their research on other countries than their own. The initiators of the project[24] have had an experience of candid collaboration on a volume of country studies and comparative analysis, launched by Robert A. Dahl, on *Political Oppositions*

[23]Roy C. Macridis, "Research in Comparative Politics: A Seminar Report," *American Political Science Review* 47 (1953), pp. 641-675.

[24]Hans Daalder of the University of Leiden, Stein Rokkan of the Christian Michelsen Institute and the University of Bergen, Norway, Robert A. Dahl of Yale University, and the author of this paper.

in Western Democracies,[25] which includes both large and small democracies. In working conferences, the authors have hammered out a common outline and a set of priorities for the types of information they hope to bring together on most of the countries, at various historic periods, for the individual country studies and for comparisons. One result of these meetings has been to show us how serious are some of the gaps in the availability of basic historic information for countries of advanced political, cultural, and administrative development. Departures from the common outline will of course be necessary because of the contrasts in national experiences. These contrasts give us some of the dimensions of comparison against the background of common characteristics. The small democracies include old states and newly independent ones; old monarchies and republics old and new; unitary states and federal; unilingual nations and multilingual; religious homogeneity and religious pluralism; nations with experiences of ruling other peoples and nations with memories of being ruled. Economic development came early to some countries and only very recently to others.

The similarities and the differences among these states—the five Scandinavian nations, the three Benelux countries, Ireland, Austria, and Switzerland—indicate something of the historical and comparative interest of the individual country studies and the later more theoretical analysis. The smaller European democracies show a number of different styles—perhaps later we can speak of 'types'—of civic participation. One need only contemplate the differences between The Netherlands and Belgium: states of the same degree of economic and cultural development, similar in size and exposed international position, and of similar cultural values. The Dutch show a striking civic cohesion despite all the rigidities of religious, social, political, and cultural particularisms to which they have given their own name: *verzuiling.* The Belgians have achieved a high degree of social organization but a less orderly relation of particularistic groupings to national political life; their civic culture has more of the *frondeur* tone of France and less of the rational tone of the Northern countries. Within Belgium the differences among Flemings and Walloons and Bruxellois are at least as striking as those between Belgium as a whole and The Netherlands. Both countries show the importance in the processes of national integration of the pre-national and even medieval collectivities, institutions, and traditions: church, 'estates', universities, and—in Belgium—linguistic groupings. These make a rich field for the study of continuities and of change in societies whose complexity is so much greater than their size.

Some of our concerns are basic to the history and analysis of the consolidation, governing, and civic integration of all national states in a

[25]Robert A. Dahl, ed., *Political Oppositions in Western Democracies* (New Haven, Conn.: Yale University Press, 1966). The volume contains chapters on Austria, Belgium, France, Germany, Italy, The Netherlands, Norway, Sweden, Great Britain, and the United States.

fairly advanced cultural setting. Others are questions specific to small nations. How has smallness of population-and-area affected the substance and intensity of national life? Are there—for example—national political myths and ideologies linked to smallness? What has smallness meant for the character of relationships among elites? For relationships between leaders and led in government and in social movements and interest groups? How has it affected the degree of dependence on power resources outside the national system? Accessibility to international economic penetration and vulnerability to international economic changes? What have been the consequences of smallness for governments and voluntary organizations in relation to regional, European, and global international cooperation?

Following an understandable bias in research and teaching, Western theorists of democratic politics have tended to take account only of the experiences of the main 'Anglo-Saxon' states, France, and Germany, with occasional reference to Italy or Sweden or Switzerland. The rich diversity of experiences in the smaller European democracies has been almost lost to comparative theory, or confused in its occasional exploitation, for lack of available information. Yet each of the smaller democracies offers fascinating historical and current evidence, on nation-building among other subjects, which needs assembly and modern analysis, comparison with the larger democracies and with existing theories of democratic political behavior.

If human history is permitted to continue, the West will not forever furnish the models (whether in an analytical or normative sense) of nation-building. As long as it does, however, the models need not be based only on England and France and the United States. Through the smaller European democracies, we can see experiences significantly different from those of the large nations.

A distinguished Swedish economic historian remarked that no citizen of a small country should expect other people to study his country's history merely because it happened. May we not turn his modest statement around and say that no scholar of a larger country should ignore the history of another country simply because it is a small country? Let us not yield to the snobbishness of size, which is unlovely and, like all snobbishness, stifling to the intellect as well as to the heart. The value of human experience is not in the size of the political community. Ancient Athens knew cultural greatness among a body of citizens no more numerous than that of Iceland today. Shakespeare's England had a population no greater than that of Switzerland now.

One speaks softly in suggesting that any academic studies have utility for the tasks of statesmanship. But in the life of many of today's new nations, smallness of population-and-power is a crucial characteristic. Many of their nation-builders find much of the experience of the large nations apparently unrelated to their own problems simply because of the differences in numbers of electorate and of elites, in weight of national resources and power. Some of the people in the new nations and their friends have therefore turned with interest to the social, political, and administrative experiences of the smaller European democracies.

However differently we may evaluate the elements of human freedom, we must remain sensitive to its forms and uses in our discussions of modernization and nation-building. Nowadays other objectives, no doubt worthy and pressing, generally take pride of place, and push individual freedom out of sight or hearing, in discussions of the 'political alternatives of development'. Is it unreasonable to hope that study and comparison of the development of the smaller European democracies will throw light on the conditions under which peoples may—at least for a historic moment—harmonize the often contradictory goals of freedom and discipline, spontaneity and order, compassion and justice, growth and stability, national integrity and international cooperation?

B

CRISES IN POLITICAL MODERNIZATION

5

Political Modernization: America vs. Europe

Samuel P. Huntington

I. THREE PATTERNS OF MODERNIZATION

Political modernization involves, let us assume, three things. First, it involves the rationalization of authority: the replacement of a large number of traditional, religious, familial, and ethnic political authorities by a single, secular, national political authority. This change implies that government is the product of man, not of nature or of God, and that a well-ordered society must have a determinate human source of final authority, obedience to whose positive law takes precedence over other obligations. Rationalization of authority means assertion of the external sovereignty of the nation-state against transnational influences and of the internal sovereignty of the national government against local and regional powers. It means national integration and the centralization or accumulation of power in recognized national law-making institutions. Secondly, political modernization involves the differentiation of new political functions and the development of specialized structures to perform those functions. Areas of peculiar competence—legal, military, administrative, scientific—become separated from the political realm, and autonomous, specialized, but subordinate, organs arise to discharge those tasks. Administrative hierarchies become more elaborate, more complex, more disciplined. Office and power are distributed more by achievement and less by ascription. Thirdly, political modernization involves increased participation in politics

"Political Modernization: America vs. Europe" by Samuel P. Huntington is reprinted by permission from *World Politics* 18 (April 1966), pp. 378-414. Footnotes abridged by permission of the author.

by social groups throughout society and the development of new political institutions—such as political parties and interest associations—to organize this participation. Broadened participation in politics may increase control of the people by the government, as in totalitarian states, or it may increase control of the government by the people, as in some democratic ones. But in all modern states the citizens become directly involved in and affected by governmental affairs. Rationalized authority, differentiated structure, and mass participation thus distinguish modern polities from antecedent polities.

The political modernization of Western Europe and North America was, of course, spread over many centuries. In general, the broadening of participation in politics came after the rationalization of authority and the differentiation of structure. Significant broadened participation dates from the latter half of the eighteenth century. The rationalization of authority and the differentiation of structure got under way in earnest in the seventeenth century. This article will be primarily concerned with these earlier phases of political modernization in Europe and America.[1]

Three distinct patterns of political modernization can be distinguished: Continental, British, and American. On the Continent the rationalization of authority and the differentiation of structures were dominant trends of the seventeenth century. "It is misleading to summarize in a single phrase any long historical process," Sir George Clark observes, "but the work of monarchy in the seventeenth century may be described as the substitution of a simpler and more unified government for the complexities of feudalism. On one side it was centralization, the bringing of local business under the supervision or control of the government of the capital. This necessarily had as its converse a tendency toward uniformity."[2] It was the age of the great simplifiers, centralizers, and modernizers: Richelieu, Mazarin, Louis XIV, Colbert, and Louvois in France; the Great Elector in Prussia; Gustavus Adolphus and Charles XI in Sweden; Philip IV and Olivares in Spain; and their countless imitators among the lesser realms of the Continent. The modern state replaced the feudal principality; loyalty to the state superseded loyalty to church and to dynasty. "I am more obligated to the state," Louis XIII declared on the famous "Day of Dupes," November 11, 1630, when he rejected the Queen Mother and her claims for family in favor of the Cardinal and his claims for the state. "More than any other single day," Friedrich

---

[1] For the sake of clarity, let me make clear the geographical scope I give these terms. With appropriate apologies to Latin Americans and Canadians, I feel compelled by the demands of brevity to use the term "America" to refer to the thirteen colonies that subsequently became the United States of America. By "Europe" I mean Great Britain and the Continent. By "the Continent" I refer to France, the Low Countries, Spain, Portugal, Sweden, and the Holy Roman Empire.

[2] *The Seventeenth Century* (New York 1961), p. 91.

argues, "it may be called the birthday of the modern state."[3] With the birth of the modern state came the subordination of the church, the suppression of the medieval estates, and the weakening of the aristocracy by the rise of new groups. In addition, the century witnessed the rapid growth and rationalization of state bureaucracies and public services, the origin and expansion of standing armies, and the extension and improvement of taxation. In 1600 the medieval political world was still a reality on the Continent; by 1700 it had been replaced by the modern world of nation-states.

The British pattern of evolution was similar in nature to that on the Continent but rather different in results. In Britain, too, church was subordinated to state, authority was centralized, sovereignty asserted internally as well as externally, legal and political institutions differentiated, bureaucracies expanded, and a standing army created. The efforts of the Stuarts, however, to rationalize authority along the lines of continental absolutism provoked a constitutional struggle, from which Parliament eventually emerged the victor. In Britain, as on the Continent, authority was centralized but it was centralized in Parliament rather than in the Crown. This was no less of a revolution than occurred on the Continent and perhaps even more of one.

In America, on the other hand, the political system did not undergo any revolutionary changes at all. Instead, the principal elements of the English sixteenth-century constitution were exported to the New World, took root there, and were given new life at precisely the time they were being abandoned in the home country. These Tudor institutions were still partially medieval in character. The Tudor century saw some steps toward modernization in English politics, particularly the establishment of the supremacy of the state over the church, a heightened sense of national identity and consciousness, and a significant increase in the power of the Crown and the executive establishment. Nonetheless, even in Elizabethan government, the first point of importance is "the fundamental factor of continuity with the Middle Ages."[4] The sixteenth century saw, as Chrimes says, "The Zenith of the Medieval Constitution." The changes introduced by the Tudor monarchs did not have "the effect of breaking down the essential principles of the medieval Constitution, nor even its structure."[5] Among these principles and structures were the idea of the organic union of society and government, the harmony of authorities within government, the subordination of government to fundamental law, the intermingling of the

---

[3]Carl J. Friedrich, *The Age of the Baroque: 1610-1660* (New York 1952), pp. 215-216.

[4]A. L. Rowse, *The England of Elizabeth* (New York 1951), p. 262.

[5]S. B. Chrimes, *English Constitutional History*, 2nd ed. (London 1953), pp. 121-123. See also W. S. Holdsworth, *A History of English Law*, 3rd ed. (London 1945), vol. IV, p. 209 ff.

legal and political realms, the balance of power between Crown and Parliament, the complementary representative roles of these two institutions, the vitality of local governmental authorities, and reliance on local forces for the defense of the realm.

The English colonists took these late medieval and Tudor political ideas, practices, and institutions across the Atlantic with them during the great migrations in the first half of the seventeenth century. The patterns of thought and behavior established in the New World developed and grew but did not substantially change during the century and a half of colonihood. The English generation of 1603-1630, Notestein remarks, was "one in which medieval ideas and practices were by no means forgotten and in which new conceptions and new ways of doing things were coming in. The American tradition, or that part derived from England, was at least in some degree established by the early colonists. The English who came over later must have found the English Americans somewhat settled in their ways."[6] The conflict between the colonists and the British government in the middle of the eighteenth century served only to reinforce the colonists' adherence to their traditional patterns. In the words of our greatest constitutional historian, "The colonists retained to a marked and unusual degree the traditions of Tudor England. In all our study of American institutions, colonial and contemporary, institutions of both public law and private law, this fact must be reckoned with. The breach between colonies and mother country was largely a mutual misunderstanding based, in great part, on the fact of this retention of older ideas in the colonies after parliamentary sovereignty had driven them out in the mother country."[7] In the constitutional debates before the American Revolution, the colonists in effect argued the case of the old English constitution against the merits of the new British constitution which had come into existence during the century after they had left the mother country. "Their theory," as Pollard says, "was essentially medieval."[8]

These ancient practices and ideas were embodied in the state constitutions drafted after independence and in the Federal Constitution of 1787. Not only is the American Constitution the oldest written national constitution in the world, but it is also a constitution which in large part simply codified and formalized on the national level practices and institutions that had long existed on the colonial level. The institutional framework established in 1787 has, in turn, changed remarkably little in 175 years.

---

[6]Wallace Notestein, *The English People on the Eve of Colonization: 1603-1630* (New York 1954), p. xiv. See also Edward S. Corwin, *The "Higher Law" Background of American Constitutional Law* (Ithaca 1955), p. 74.

[7]Charles Howard McIlwain, *The High Court of Parliament and Its Supremacy* (New Haven 1910), p. 386.

[8]A. F. Pollard, *Factors in American History* (New York 1925), p. 39.

Hence, the American system "can be properly understood, in its origin, development, workings, and spirit, only in the light of precedents and traditions which run back to the England of the civil wars and the period before the civil wars."[9] The American political system of the twentieth century still bears a closer approximation to the Tudor polity of the sixteenth century than does the British political system of the twentieth century. "Americanisms in politics, like Americanisms in speech," as Henry Jones Ford put it, "are apt to be Anglicisms which died out in England but survived in the new world."[10] The British broke their traditional political patterns in the seventeenth century. The Americans did not do so then and have only partially done so since then. Political modernization in America has thus been strangely attenuated and incomplete. In institutional terms, the American polity has never been underdeveloped, but it has also never been wholly modern.[11] In an age of rationalized authority, functional specialization, mass democracy, and totalitarian dictatorship, the American political system remains a curious anachronism. In today's world, the American political system is unique, if only because it is so antique.

II. THE RATIONALIZATION OF AUTHORITY

In seventeenth-century Europe the state replaced fundamental law as the source of political authority, and within each state a single authority replaced the many that had previously existed. America, on the other hand, continued to adhere to fundamental law as both a source of authority for human actions and an authoritative restraint on human behavior. In addition, in America, human authority or sovereignty was never concentrated in a single institution or individual but instead remained dispersed throughout society as a whole and among many organs of the body politic. Traditional patterns of authority were thus decisively broken and replaced in Europe; in America they were reshaped and supplemented but not fundamentally altered. The continued supremacy of law was mated to the decisive rejection of sovereignty.

Undoubtedly the most significant difference between modern man and traditional man is in their outlook on man in relation to his environment. In traditional society man accepts his natural and social environment as given. What is ever will be: it is or must be divinely sanctioned; and to attempt to change the permanent and unchanging order of the universe and of society is

---

[9]McIlwain, *High Court*, p. 388.

[10]*The Rise and Growth of American Politics* (New York 1900), p. 5. See also James Bryce, *The American Commonwealth* (London 1891), vol. II, p. 658.

[11]See the distinction between modernization and political development in Huntington, "Political Development and Political Decay" [reprinted above].

both blasphemous and impossible. Change is absent or imperceptible in traditional society because men cannot conceive of its existence. Modernity begins when men develop a sense of their own competence, when they begin to think that they can understand nature and society and can then control and change nature and society for their own purposes. Above all, modernization means the rejection of external restraints on men, the Promethean liberation of man from control by gods, fate, and destiny.

This fundamental shift from acceptance to activism manifests itself in many fields. Among the more important is law. For traditional man, law is an external prescription or restraint over which he has little control. Man discovers law but he does not make law. At most he may make supplementary emendations of an unchanging basic law to apply it to specific circumstances. In late medieval Europe, law was variously defined in terms of divine law, natural law, the law of reason, common law, and custom. In all these manifestations it was viewed as a relatively unchanging external authority for and restraint on human action. Particularly in England, the dominant concept was "the characteristic medieval idea of all authority as deriving from the law." As Bracton put it, "Law makes the King." These ideas remained dominant through the Tudor years and were in one form or another at the basis of the writings of Fortescue, St. Germain, Sir Thomas Smith, Hooker, and Coke. Even after the Act of Supremacy, Parliament was still viewed as a law-declaring body, not a law-making body. Even during the first phases of the constitutional struggles of the seventeenth century, Prynne argued that "the Principal Liberties, Customs, Laws" of the kingdom, particularly those in the "great Charters," were "FUNDAMENTAL, PERPETUAL, & UNALTERABLE."

The obverse of fundamental law is, of course, the rejection of determinate human sovereignty. For the men of 1600, as Figgis observes, "law is the true sovereign, and they are not under the necessity of considering whether King or Lords or Commons or all three together are the ultimate authority in the state."[12] The sovereignty of law permitted a multiplicity of human authorities, since no single human authority was the sole source of law. Man owed obedience to authority, but authority existed in many institutions: king, Parliament, courts, common law, custom, church, people. Sovereignty, indeed, was an alien concept to the Tudor Constitution. No "lawyer or statesman of the Tudor period," as Holdsworth says, "could have given an answer to the question as to the whereabouts of the sovereign power in the English state."[13] Society and government, Crown and people, existed together in harmony in a "single body politic." The Tudor regime, says Chrimes, "was essentially the culmination of the medieval ideals of monarchical government, in alliance with the assent of parliament for

[12]John Neville Figgis, *The Divine Right of Kings* (Cambridge 1922), p. 230.
[13]Holdsworth, p. 208.

certain purposes, and acknowledging the supremacy of the common law where appropriate. No one was concerned about the location of sovereignty within the State."[14] This indifference to sovereignty made the "whole standpoint" of the most notable expounder of the Elizabethan constitution, Sir Thomas Smith, "nearer that of Bracton than that of Bodin."

Fundamental law and the diffusion of authority were incompatible with political modernization. Modernization requires authority for change. Fundamental changes in society and politics come from the purposeful actions of men. Hence authority must reside in men, not in unchanging law. In addition, men must have the power to effect change, and hence authority must be concentrated in some determinate individual or group of men. Fundamental and unchanging law may serve to diffuse authority throughout society and thus to preserve the existing social order. But it cannot serve as authority for change except for lesser changes which can be passed off as restoration. The modernization that began in the sixteenth century on the Continent and in the seventeenth century in England required new concepts of authority, the most significant of which was the simple idea of sovereignty itself, the idea that there is, in the words of Bodin, a "supreme power over citizens and subjects, unrestrained by law." One formulation of this idea was the new theory, which developed in Europe in the late sixteenth century, of the divine right of kings. Here, in effect, religious and, in that sense, traditional forms were used for modern purposes. "The Divine Right of Kings on its political side was little more than the popular form of expression for the theory of sovereignty."[15] The doctrine became dominant in France after 1594 and was introduced into England by James I. It admirably served the purposes of the modernizing monarchs of the seventeenth century by giving the sanction of the Almighty to the purposes of the mighty. It was a necessary "transition stage between medieval and modern politics."[16]

In addition, of course, other political theorists responded to the needs of the time by furnishing more "rational" justifications of absolute sovereignty based on the nature of man and the nature of society. On the Continent, Bodin and the Politiques looked to the creation of a supreme royal power which would maintain order and constitute a centralized public authority above parties, sects, and groups, all of which were to exist only on its sufferance. Bodin's *Republic* was published in 1576; Hobbe's *Leviathan*, with its more extreme doctrine of sovereignty, appeared in 1651. Closely linked with the idea of absolute sovereignty was the concept of the state as an entity apart from individual, family, and dynasty. Twentieth-century modernizing Marxists justify their efforts by the needs of the party; seventeenth-century modernizing monarchs justified their actions by

[14]Chrimes, pp. 122-123.
[15]Figgis, *Divine Right*, p. 237.
[16]*Ibid.*, p. 258.

"reason of state." The phrase was first popularized by Botero in *Della Ragion di Stato* in 1589. Its essence was briefly defined by another Italian writer in 1614 when he declared, "The reason of state is a necessary violation of the common law for the end of public utility." One by one the European monarchs took to legitimizing themselves and their actions by reference to the state.

In both its religious and its secular versions, in Filmer as well as in Hobbes, the import of the new doctrine of sovereignty was the subject's absolute duty to obey his king. Both versions helped political modernization by legitimizing the concentration of authority and the breakdown of the medieval pluralistic political order. They were the seventeenth-century counterparts of the theories of party supremacy and national sovereignty, which are today employed to break down the authority of traditional local, tribal, and religious bodies. In the seventeenth century, mass participation in politics still lay in the future; hence rationalization of authority meant concentration of power in the absolute monarch. In the twentieth century, the broadening of participation and the rationalization of authority occur simultaneously, and hence authority must be concentrated in either a political party or a popular charismatic leader, both of which are capable of arousing the masses as well as challenging traditional sources of authority. In terms of modernization, the seventeenth century's absolute monarch was the functional equivalent of the twentieth century's monolithic party.

On the Continent in the seventeenth century the medieval diffusion of authority among the estates rapidly gave way to the centralization of authority in the monarch. At the beginning of the century, "every country of western Christendom, from Portugal to Finland, and from Ireland to Hungary, had its assemblies of estates."[17] By the end of the century most of these assemblies had been eliminated or greatly reduced in power. In France the last Estates General until the Revolution met in 1615, and the provincial estates, except in Brittany and Languedoc, did not meet after 1650. By the seventeenth century only six of the original twenty-two Spanish kingdoms retained their *cortes*. The *cortes* in Castile was already suppressed; those in Aragon were put down by Philip II; Olivares subdued Catalonia after a long bloody war. In Portugal the *cortes* met for the last time in 1697. In the kingdom of Naples parliamentary proceedings ended in 1642. The Great Elector put down the estates in Brandenburg and Prussia. The estates of Carniola, Styria, and Carinthia had already lost their powers to the Hapsburgs, who were also able during the early part of the century to curtail the powers of the estates in Bohemia, Moravia, and Silesia. The Danish crown became hereditary in 1665; that of Hungary in 1687. Toward the end of the century, Charles XI reestablished absolute rule in Sweden.[18] By 1700

---

[17]Clark, p. 83.
[18]See Clark's summary of constitutional trends, pp. 86-87.

the traditional diffusion of powers had been virtually eliminated from continental Europe. The modernizers and state-builders had triumphed. The tendencies toward the substitution of sovereignty for law and the centralization of authority also occurred in England. James I sundered the Crown from Parliament, challenged the traditional authority of the law and of the judges, advocated the divine right of kings. Kings, he said, "were the authors and makers of the laws and not the laws of the kings." James was simply attempting to modernize English government and to move it along the paths already well developed on the Continent. His efforts at political modernization were opposed by Coke and other conservatives who argued in terms of fundamental law and the traditional diffusion of authority. Their claims, however, were out-of-date in the face of the social and political changes taking place. "Coke, like most opponents of the King, had not really grasped the conception of sovereignty; he maintained a position, reasonable enough in the Middle Ages, but impossible in a developed unitary state."[19] Centralization was necessary and at times it seemed that England would follow the continental pattern. But in due course the claims for royal absolutism generated counterclaims for parliamentary supremacy. When James I, Filmer, and Hobbes put the king above law, they inevitably provoked Milton's argument that "the parliament is above all positive law, whether civil or common, makes or unmakes them both." The Long Parliament began the age of parliamentary supremacy. It was then that England saw "practically for the first time a legislative assembly of the modern type,—no longer a mere law-declaring, but a *law-making* machine."[20] Fundamental law suffered the same fate in England that it had on the Continent, but it was replaced by an omnipotent legislature rather than by an absolute monarchy.

American development was strikingly different from that in Europe. At the same time that the modernizing monarchs were suppressing the traditional estates, that men were asserting their power to make law, that Richelieu was building an absolute state in France and Hobbes was proclaiming one in England, the old patterns of fundamental law and diffused authority were transported to a new life in the New World. The traditional view of law continued in America in two forms. First, the idea that man could only declare law and not make law remained strong in America long after it had been supplanted by positive conceptions of law in Europe. In some respects, it persisted right into the twentieth century. Secondly, the old idea of a fundamental law beyond human control was given new authority by identifying it with a written constitution. A written constitution can, of course, be viewed as a contract, deriving its authority from conscious, positive human action. But it may also and even concurrently be

[19]Figgis, *Divine Right*, p. 232.
[20]McIlwain, *High Court*, pp. 93-96.

viewed as a codification of limitations already imposed upon government by custom and reason. It was in this latter sense that men accepted the idea of fundamental law in sixteenth- and seventeenth-century England and embodied it in their colonial charters and declarations of rights. The combination of both theories created a situation in which "higher law as with renewed youth, entered upon one of the great periods of its history. . . ."[21]

The persistence of fundamental-law doctrines went hand in hand with the rejection of sovereignty. The older ideas of the interplay of society and government and the harmonious balance of the elements of the constitution continued to dominate American political thought. In England, the ideas of the great Tudor political writers, Smith, Hooker, Coke, "were on the way to becoming anachronisms even as they were set down."[22] In America, on the other hand, their doctrines prospered, and Hobbes remained irrelevant. Neither the divine right of kings, nor absolute sovereignty, nor parliamentary supremacy had a place on the western shores of the Atlantic. "Americans may be defined," as Pollard has said, "as that part of the English-speaking world which instinctively revolted against the doctrine of the sovereignty of the State and has, not quite successfully, striven to maintain that attitude from the time of the Pilgrim Fathers to the present day." The eighteenth-century argument of the colonists with the home country was essentially an argument against the legislative sovereignty of Parliament.

> It is this denial of all sovereignty [continues Pollard] which gives its profound and permanent interest to the American Revolution. . . . These are American ideas, but they were English before they were American. They were part of that medieval panoply of thought with which, including the natural equality of man, the view of taxes as grants, the laws of nature and of God, the colonists combatted the sovereignty of Parliament. They had taken these ideas with them when they shook the dust of England off their feet; indeed they left their country in order that they might cleave to these convictions. And now they come back, bringing with them these and other sheaves, to reconvert us to the views which we have held long since but lost awhile.[23]

To the extent that sovereignty was accepted in America it was held to be lodged in "the people." Popular sovereignty, however, is as nebulous a concept as divine sovereignty. The voice of the people is as readily identified as is the voice of God. It is thus a latent, passive, and ultimate authority, not a positive and active one.

The difference between American and European development is also manifest in theories and practices of representation. In Europe, the elimina-

---

[21]Corwin, p. 89.
[22]George H. Sabine, *A History of Political Theory*, rev. ed. (New York 1950), p. 455.
[23]Pp. 31-33.

tion of the medieval representative bodies, the estates, was paralleled by a decline in the legitimacy accorded local interests. On the Continent the absolute monarch represented or embodied the state. Beginning with the French Revolution, he was supplanted by the national assembly which represented or embodied the nation. In both instances, the collective whole had authority and legitimacy: local interests, parochial interests, group interests, as Rousseau argued, lacked legitimacy and hence had no claim to representation in the central organs of the political system.

The rationalization of authority in Britain also produced changes in representation which stand in marked contrast to the continuing American adherence to the older traditional concepts. In sixteenth-century England both king and Parliament had representative functions. The king was "the representative head of the corporate community of the realm."[24] The members of Parliament still had their traditional medieval functions of representing local communities and special interests. In the late medieval Parliament, "the burgess is his town's attorney. His presence at parliament enables him to present petitions for confirmation of charters, the increase of local liberties, and redress of grievances, and to undertake private business in or near London for constituents."[25] Thus, the king represented the community as a whole, while the members of Parliament represented its component parts. The M.P. was responsible to his constituency. Indeed, an act passed during the reign of Henry V required members of Parliament to reside in their constituencies. In the late sixteenth century this legal requirement began to be avoided in practice, but local residence and local ties still remained qualifications for most M.P.'s. "The overwhelming localism of representation in Parliament is its dominant feature," writes Rowse of Elizabethan England, "and gives it vigor and reality. Everywhere the majority of members are local men, either gentry of the country or townsmen. The number of official members, privy councillors and such, is very small, and even they have their roots. . . . An analysis of the representation shows a very small proportion of outsiders, and still smaller of officials.[26] The members not only resided in their constituencies and represented the interests of those constituencies, but they were also paid by their constituencies for their services. Each constituency, moreover, was normally represented by two or three members of Parliament.

The constitutional revolution of the seventeenth century dealt the death blow to this "Old Tory" system of representation. It was replaced by what

---

[24]Samuel H. Beer, "The Representation of Interests in British Government: Historical Background," *American Political Science Review* 51 (Sept. 1957), p. 614.

[25]Faith Thompson, *A Short History of Parliament: 1295-1642* (Minneapolis 1953), p. 59.

[26]P. 306. Cf. Pollard, *The Evolution of Parliament,* 2nd ed., rev. (London 1926), p. 159, who argues that the nationalizing changes began in the late Tudor years.

Beer terms the "Old Whig" system, under which the king lost his active representative functions and the M.P. became "the representative of the whole community, as well as of its component interests." Parliament, as Burke phrased it in the classic statement of the Old Whig theory, is "*a deliberative* assembly of *one* nation, with *one* interest, that of the whole— where not local purposes, not local prejudices, ought to guide, but the general good, resulting from the general reason of the whole." Hence the M.P. should not be bound by authoritative instructions from his constituents and should rather subordinate their interests to the general interest of the entire society. With this new concept came a radical break with the old tradition of local residence and local payment. The last recorded instance of a constituency paying its representatives was in 1678. Increasingly during the seventeenth century, members no longer resided in their constituencies. The statute was "evaded by the admission of strangers to free burghership," and it was finally repealed in 1774.[27] At the same time, the number of multiple-member districts declined, with their complete elimination in 1885. All these developments made Parliament the collective representative of the nation rather than a collection of representatives of individual constituencies. Thus the theory and practice of British representation adjusted to the new fact of parliamentary supremacy.

In America, of course, the Old Tory system took on new life. The colonial representative systems reproduced Tudor practices, and subsequently these were established on a national scale in the Constitution of 1787. America, like Tudor England, had a dual system of representation: the President, like the Tudor king, represented the interests of the community as a whole; the individual members of the legislature owed their primary loyalties to their constituencies. The multimember constituencies which the British had in the sixteenth century were exported to the colonial legislatures in America, adapted to the upper house of the national legislature, and extended to the state legislatures where they remain in substantial number down to the present. Local residence, which had been a legal requirement and a political fact in Tudor England, became a political requirement and a political fact in America. It reflected "the intense localism . . . which persisted in America after it had been abandoned in the mother country." Many key British political figures in the nineteenth and twentieth centuries were able to stay in Parliament because they were able to change their constituencies. "What a difference it would have made to the course of English politics," as one commentator observed, "if Great Britain had not thrown off, centuries ago, the medieval practice which America still retains!"[28] Contrariwise, Americans may view with astonishment and disdain the gap that political modernization has created between the British M.P. and his constituents.

[27]Herbert W. Horwill, *The Usages of the American Constitution* (London 1925), p. 169.
[28]Horwill, p. 169-70.

III. DIFFERENTIATION OF STRUCTURE

In comparing European and American development, a distinction must be made between "functions" and "power." In this article, "power" (in the singular) means influence or control over the actions of others, and "function" refers to particular types of activity, which may be defined in various ways. "Powers" (in the plural) will not be used, since most authors use it to mean "functions." It is thus possible to speak with the Founding Fathers of legislative, executive, and judicial functions, and, with Bagehot, of dignified and efficient functions—and also to speak of legal and political functions, military and civil functions, domestic and foreign functions. Governmental institutions may be equal or unequal in power and specialized or overlapping in function.

In Europe the rationalization of authority and the centralization of power were accompanied by functional differentiation and the emergence of more specialized governmental institutions and bodies. These developments were, of course, a response to the growing complexity of society and the increasing demands upon government. Administrative, legal, judicial, and military institutions developed as semi-autonomous but subordinate bodies in one way or another responsible to the political bodies (monarch or parliament) which exercised sovereignty. The dispersion of functions among relatively specialized institutions, in turn, encouraged inequalities in power among the institutions. The legislative or law-making function carried with it more power than did the administrative or law-enforcement function.

In medieval government and in Tudor government the differentiation of functions was not very far advanced. A single institution often exercised many functions, and a single function was often dispersed among several institutions. This tended to equalize power among institutions. The government of Tudor England was a "government of *fused* power" (functions)— that is, Parliament, Crown, and other institutions each performed many functions. In the seventeenth and eighteenth centuries British government evolved toward a concentration of power and a differentiation of function. In Great Britain, as Pollard argues, "Executive, legislature, and judicature have been evolved from a common origin, and have adapted themselves to specific purposes, because without that specialization of functions English government would have remained rudimentary and inefficient. But there has been no division of sovereignty and no separation of powers." [29]

In America, in contrast, sovereignty was divided, power was separated, and functions were combined in many different institutions. This result was achieved despite rather than because of the theory of the separation of

[29]Pollard, *Evolution of Parliament.* p. 257.

powers (i.e., functions) which was prevalent in the eighteenth century. In its pure form, the assignment of legislative, executive, and judicial functions to separate institutions would give one institution a monopoly of the dominant law-making function and thus would centralize power. This was in part what Locke wanted and even more what Jefferson wanted. The theory was also, of course, found in Montesquieu, but Montesquieu recognized the inequality of power that would result from the strict separation of functions. The "judiciary," he said, "is in some measure next to nothing." Consequently, to obtain a real division of power, Montesquieu divided the legislative function among three institutions representing the three traditional estates of the realm. In practice in America, as in Tudor England, not only was power divided by dividing the legislative function but other functions were also shared among several institutions, thus creating a system of "checks and balances" which equalized power. "The constitutional convention of 1787," as Neustadt has said, "is supposed to have created a government of 'separated powers' [i.e., functions]. It did nothing of the sort. Rather, it created a government of separated institutions *sharing* powers [functions]."[30] Thus America perpetuated a fusion of functions and a division of power, while Europe developed a differentiation of functions and a centralization of power.

In medieval government no distinction existed between legislation and adjudication. On the Continent such institutions as the *Justiza* of Aragon and the French *parlements* exercised important political functions into the sixteenth century. In England, Parliament, an essentially political body, was viewed primarily as a court down to the seventeenth century. The courts of law, as Holdsworth observes, "were, in the days before the functions of government had become specialized, very much more than merely judicial tribunals. In England and elsewhere they were regarded as possessing functions which we may call political, to distinguish them from those purely judicial functions which nowadays are their exclusive functions on the continent, and their principal functions everywhere. That the courts continued to exercise these larger functions, even after departments of government had begun to be differentiated, was due to the continuance of that belief in the supremacy of the law which was the dominant characteristic of the political theory of the Middle Ages."[31]

In England, the supremacy of the law disappeared in the civil wars of the seventeenth century and with it disappeared the mixture of judicial and political functions. English judges followed Bacon rather than Coke and became "lions under the throne" who could not "check or oppose any points of sovereignty." In the eighteenth century, Blackstone could flatly state that

---

[30]Richard E. Neustadt, *Presidential Power: The Politics of Leadership* (New York 1960), p. 33.
[31]P. 169.

no court could declare invalid an act of Parliament, however unreasonable it might be. To admit such a power, he said, "were to set the judicial power above that of the legislature, which would be subversive of all government." Parliament had evolved from high court to supreme legislature.

In America, on the other hand, the mixture of judicial and political functions remained. The judicial power to declare what the law is became the mixed judicial-legislative power to tell the legislature what the law cannot be. The American doctrine and practice of judicial review were undoubtedly known only in very attenuated form in late sixteenth-century and early seventeenth-century England. Indeed, the whole concept of judicial review implies a distinction between legislative and judicial functions which was not explicitly recognized at that time. It is, nonetheless, clear that Tudor and early Stuart courts did use the common law to "controul" acts of Parliament at least to the point of redefining rather sweepingly the purposes of Parliament. These actions did not represent a conscious doctrine of judicial review so much as they represented the still "undifferentiated fusion of judicial and legislative functions." This fusion of legislative and judicial functions was retained by American courts and was eventually formulated into the doctrine and practice of judicial review. The legislative functions of courts in America, as McIlwain argues, are far greater than those in England, "because the like tendency was there checked by the growth in the seventeenth century of a new doctrine of parliamentary supremacy." Unlike English courts, "American courts still retain much of their Tudor indefiniteness, notwithstanding our separation of departments. They are guided to an extent unknown now in England by questions of policy and expediency." [32] Foreign observers since De Tocqueville have identified the "immense political influence" of the courts as one of the most astonishing and unique characteristics of American government.

The mixing of legal and political functions in American government can also be seen in the consistently prominent role of lawyers in American politics. In fourteenth- and fifteenth-century England lawyers played an important role in the development of parliamentary proceedings, and the alliance between Parliament and the law, in contrast to the separation between the Estates General and the French *parlement,* helped to sustain parliamentary authority. In Elizabethan England, lawyers played an increasingly important role in Parliament. In 1593, for instance, forty-three percent of the members of the House of Commons possessed a legal education. The Speaker and the other leading figures in the House were usually lawyers. Subsequently, the role of lawyers in the British Parliament declined in significance, reaching a low in the nineteenth century. In the twentieth century only about twenty percent of the M.P.'s have been lawyers. In America, on the other hand, in the colonial governments, in the state

[32]McIlwain, *High Court.* pp. ix, 385-386.

governments, and in the national government, the Tudor heritage of lawyer-legislators has continued, with lawyers usually being a majority of the members of American legislative bodies.[33]

Every political system, as Bagehot pointed out, must gain authority and then use authority. In the modern British system these functions are performed by the dignified and efficient parts of the constitution. The assignment of each function to separate institutions is one aspect of the functional differentiation that is part of modernization. It can be seen most clearly, of course, in the case of the so-called constitutional monarchies, but in some degree it is found in almost all modern governments.[34] The American political system, however, like the older European political systems, does not assign dignified and efficient functions to different institutions. All major institutions of the American government—President, Supreme Court, House, Senate, and their state counterparts—combine in varying degrees both types of functions. This combination is, of course, most notable in the Presidency. Almost every other modern political system from the so-called constitutional monarchies of Great Britain and Scandinavia to the parliamentary republics of Italy, Germany, and France before De Gaulle, to the Communist dictatorships of Eastern Europe separates the chief of state from the head of government. In the Soviet system, the differentiation is carried still further to distinguish chief of state from head of government from party chief. In the United States, however, the President unites all three functions, this combination being both a major source of his power and a major limitation on that power, since the requirements of one role often conflict with the demands of another. The combination of roles perpetuates ancient practice. The Presidency was created, as Jefferson declared in 1787, as an "elective monarchy"; the office was designed to embody much of the power of the British king; and the politics that surround it are court politics.[35]

The Presidency is, indeed, the only survival in the contemporary world of the constitutional monarchy once prevalent throughout medieval Europe.

[33]See J. E. Neale, *The Elizabethan House of Commons* (London 1949), pp. 290-295; Rowse, p. 307; Thompson, pp. 169-173; Donald R. Matthews, *The Social Background of Political Decision-Makers* (New York 1954), pp. 28-31.

[34]Walter Bagehot, *The English Constitution* (London 1949), p. 3-4. See also Francis X. Sutton, "Representation and the Nature of Political Systems," *Comparative Studies in Society and History* 2 (Oct. 1959), p. 7: ". . . the kind of distinction Bagehot made when he talked of the 'dignified' and 'efficient' parts of the English constitution is observed clearly in many states. . . . The discrimination of functions here rests, of course, on an analytical distinction relevant in any political system. It is that between symbolic representation and executive control."

[35]Thomas Jefferson, Letter to James Madison, December 20, 1787, *Writings* (Washington 1903-05), vol. VI, pp. 389-90; Ford, p. 293. For an elegant—and eloquent—essay on the President as king, see D. W. Brogan, "The Presidency," *Encounter* (Jan. 1964), pp. 3-7. I am in debt to Richard E. Neustadt for insights into the nature of the American monarchy and into the similarities between White House politics and palace politics.

In the sixteenth century a constitutional monarch was one who reigned and ruled, but who ruled under law ("non sub homine sed sub Deo et lege") with due regard to the rights and liberties of his subjects, the type of monarch that Fortescue had in mind when he distinguished *dominium politicum et regale* from *dominium regale*. In the seventeenth century this old-style constitutional monarch was supplanted by the new-style absolute monarch who placed himself above the law. Subsequently, the eighteenth and nineteenth centuries saw the emergence of a new so-called "constitutional monarchy" in which a "dignified" monarch reigned but did not rule. Like the absolute monarch he is a modern invention created in response to the need to fix supreme power in a single organ. The American Presidency, on the other hand, continues the original type of constitutional monarchy. In functions and power, American Presidents are Tudor kings. In institutional role, as well as in personality and talents, Lyndon Johnson far more closely resembles Elizabeth I than does Elizabeth II. Britain preserved the form of the old monarchy, but America preserved the substance. Today America still has a king, Britain only a Crown.

In most modern states the legislative function is in theory in the hands of a large representative assembly, parliament, or supreme soviet. In practice, however, it is performed by a relatively small body of men—a cabinet or presidium—which exercises its power in all fields of governmental activity. In America, however, the legislative function remains divided among three distinct institutions and their subdivisions, much as it was once divided among the different estates and other constituted bodies in late medieval Europe. On the national level this arrangement derives not from the ideas of any European theorist but rather from the "institutional history of the colonies between 1606 and 1776."[36] The relations among burgesses, councils, and governors in the colonies, in turn, reflected the relations among Crown, Lords, and Commons in the late sixteenth century.

In modern politics, the division of power between two bodies in a legislative assembly generally varies inversely with the effective power of the assembly as a whole. The Supreme Soviet has little power but is truly bicameral; the British Parliament has more power but is effectively unicameral. America, however, is unique in preserving a working bicameralism directly inherited from the sixteenth century. Only in Tudor times did the two houses of Parliament become formally and effectively distinguished, one from the other, on an institutional basis. "The century started with Parliament a unitary institution, truly bi-cameral only in prospect." When it ended, the growth in "the power, position, and prestige of the House of Commons" had made Parliament "a political force with which the Crown and government had to reckon."[37] The sixteenth century represented a peak

[36]Benjamin F. Wright, "The Origins of the Separation of Powers in America," *Economics* 13 (May 1933), p. 169 ff.

[37]Neale, *Elizabeth I and Her Parliaments* (New York 1958), vol. I, pp. 16-17.

of bicameralism in English parliamentary history. Each house often quashed bills that had passed the other house, and to resolve their differences the houses resorted to conference committees. Originally used as an "occasional procedure," in 1571 the conference committee was transformed into "a normal habit." In Elizabethan Parliaments, conferences were requested by one or the other house on most bills; the conference delegations were at times instructed not to yield on particular items; and when there were substantial differences between the versions approved by the two houses, the conference committee might substantially rewrite the entire bill, at times at the urging and with the advice of the Queen and her councillors. Although all this sounds very contemporary, it is, in fact, very Tudor, and it is this conference committee procedure that was carried over into the colonial legislatures and then extended to the national level. In Great Britain, however, the practice died out with the rise of cabinet responsibility to the Commons. The last real use of "Free Conferences," where discussion and hence politics were permitted, occurred about 1740.

The participation of two assemblies and the chief executive in the legislative process caused the continuation in America of many other legislative methods familiar to Tudor government. An assembly that legislates must delegate some of its work to subordinate bodies or committees. Committees made their appearance in the Tudor Parliament in the 1560's and 1570's. The practice of referring bills to committees soon became almost universal, and the committees, as they assumed more and more of the functions of the House, became larger and more often permanent. The committees were also frequently dominated by those with a special interest in the legislation that they considered. Bills concerned with local and regional problems went to committees composed of members from those regions and localities. By the turn of the century the larger committees had evolved into standing committees which considered all matters coming up within a general sphere of business. This procedure reflected the active role of the Commons in the legislative process. The procedure was, in turn, exported to the colonies in the early seventeenth century—particularly to the Virginia House of Burgesses—where it also met a real need, and 150 years later was duplicated in the early sessions of the national Congress. At the same time in England, however, the rise of the cabinet undermined the committee system that had earlier existed in Parliament; the old standing committees of the House of Commons became empty formalities, indistinguishable from Committees of the Whole House, long before they were officially discontinued in 1832.

The division of the legislative function imposed similar duties upon the Speaker in the Tudor House of Commons and in subsequent American legislatures. The Tudor Speaker was a political leader, with a dual allegiance to the Crown and to the House. His success in large measure depended upon how well he could balance and integrate these often conflicting responsibilities. He was the "manager of the King's business" in the House, but he was also the spokesman for the House to the Crown and the defender of its rights and privileges. He could exercise much influence in the House by his control, subject to veto by the House, over the order in which bills were called up for debate and by his influence on the "timing and framing of questions." The struggle between Crown and Parliament in the seventeenth century, however, made it impossible for the Speaker to continue his loyalties to both. His overriding duty was now to the House, and, in due course, the impartiality of Onslow in the eighteenth century (1727-1761) became the norm for Speakers in the nineteenth and twentieth centuries. Thus in Britain an office that had once been weighted with politics, efficient as well as dignified, radically changed its character and became that of a depoliticized, impartial presiding officer. In America, on the other hand, the political character of the Tudor Speakership was perpetuated in the colonial assemblies and eventually in the national House of Representatives.

The sharing of the legislative function among two assemblies and the chief executive gives a strikingly Tudor character to the contemporary American law-making process. In Elizabethan England, Rowse observes, the "relations between Crown and Parliament were more like those between President and Congress than those that subsist in England today."[38] The Tudor monarchs had to badger, wheedle, cajole, and persuade the Commons to give them the legislation they wanted. At times they were confronted by unruly Parliaments which pushed measures the monarch did not want, or debated issues the monarch wished to silence. Generally, of course, the monarch's "legislative program," consisting primarily of requests for funds, was approved. At other times, however, the Commons would rear up and the monarch would have to withdraw or reshape his demands. Burghley, who was in charge in Parliamentary relations for Elizabeth, "kept a close eye on proceedings and received from the Clerks during the session lists showing the stages of all bills in both Houses." Elizabeth regularly attempted to win support in the Commons for her proposals by sending messages and "rumours" to the House, by exhorting and instructing the Speaker on how to handle the business of the House, by "receiving or summoning deputations from the Houses to Whitehall and there rating them in person," and by "descending magnificently upon Parliament in her coach or open chariot and addressing them" personally or through the Lord Keeper.

Although the sovereign did not "lack means of blocking obnoxious bills during their progress through the two Houses," almost every session of Parliament passed some bills that the Crown did not want, and the royal veto was exercised. Although the veto was used more frequently against private bills than against public ones, important public measures might also be stopped by the Crown. During her reign Elizabeth I apparently approved 429

[38]P. 294.

bills and vetoed approximately 71. The veto, however, was not a weapon that the Crown could use without weighing costs and gains: ". . . politics—the art of the possible—were not entirely divorced from Tudor monarchy. Too drastic or ill-considered a use of the royal veto might have stirred up trouble." [39] The tactics of Henry VIII or Elizabeth I in relation to their Parliaments thus differed little from those of Kennedy or Johnson in relation to their Congresses. A similar distribution of power imposed similar patterns of executive-legislative behavior.

The differentiation of specialized administrative structures also took place much more rapidly in Europe than it did in America. The contrast can be strikingly seen in the case of military institutions. A modern military establishment consists of a standing army recruited voluntarily or through conscription and commanded by a professional officer corps. In Europe a professional officer corps emerged during the first half of the nineteenth century. By 1870 the major continental states had developed most of the principal institutions of professional officership. England, however, lagged behind the Continent in developing military professionalism, and the United States lagged behind Great Britain. Not until the turn of the century did the United States have many of the institutions of professional officership which the European states had acquired many decades earlier. The division of power among governmental institutions perpetuated the mixing of politics and military affairs, and enormously complicated the emergence of a modern system of objective civilian control. Even after World War II, many Americans still adhered to a "fusionist" approach to civil-military relations and believed that military leadership and military institutions should mirror the attitudes and characteristics of civil society. [40]

American reluctance to accept a standing army also contrasts with the much more rapid modernization in Europe. In the sixteenth century European military forces consisted of feudal levies, mercenaries, and local militia. In England the militia was an ancient institution, and the Tudors formally organized it on a county basis under the Lord Lieutenants to take the place of the private retinues of the feudal lords. This development was a step toward "domestic tranquility and military incompetence," and in 1600, "not a single western country had a standing army: the only one in Europe was that of the Turks." By the end of the century, however, all the major European powers had standing armies. Discipline was greatly improved,

[39]Neale, *House of Commons*, pp. 410-412, and *Elizabeth I and Her Parliaments*, *passim*. Until the eighteenth century, Privy Councillors, of course, functioned as advisers to the King much as cabinet members now do to the President. Perhaps reflecting both this similarity and the later drastic change that took place in the British cabinet is the fact that in the United States the executive leadership is still called "the Administration," as it was in eighteenth-century Britain, while in Britain itself, it is now termed "the Government."

[40]See, in general, Huntington, *The Soldier and the State* (Cambridge, Mass., 1957), *passim*.

uniforms introduced, regulations formalized, weapons standardized, and effective state control extended over the military forces. The French standing army dates from Richelieu; the Prussian from the actions of the Great Elector in 1655; the English from the Restoration of 1660. In England the county militia continued in existence after 1660, but steadily declined in importance.

In America, on the other hand, the militia became the crucial military force at the same time that it was decaying in Europe. It was the natural military system for societies whose needs were defensive rather than offensive and intermittent rather than constant. The seventeenth-century colonists continued, adapted, and improved upon the militia system that had existed in Tudor England. In the next century, they identified militia with popular government and standing armies with monarchical tyranny. "On the military side," as Vagts says, "the war of the American Revolution was in part a revolt against the British standing army. . . ."[41] But in terms of military institutions, it was a reactionary revolt. The standing armies of George III represented modernity; the colonial militias embodied traditionalism. The American commitment to this military traditionalism, however, became all the more complete as a result of the War of Independence. Hostility to standing armies and reliance on the militia as the first line of defense of a free people became popular dogma and constitutional doctrine, even though these were often departed from in practice. Fortunately, however, the threats to security in the nineteenth century were few, and hence the American people were able to go through that century with a happy confidence in an ineffective force protecting them from a nonexistent danger. The militia legacy, however, remained a continuing element in American military affairs far into the much more tumultuous twentieth century. It is concretely manifest today in the political influence and military strength of the National Guard. The idea that an expert military force is better than a citizen-soldier force has yet to win wholehearted acceptance on this side of the Atlantic.

IV. TUDOR POLITY AND MODERN SOCIETY

The rationalization of authority and the differentiation of structure were thus slower and less complete in America than they were in Europe. Such was not the case with the third aspect of political modernization: the broadening of political participation. Here, if anything, America led Europe, although the differences in timing in the expansion of participa-

---

[41] Alfred Vagts, *A History of Militarism*, rev. ed. (New York 1959), p. 92. See generally Louis Morton, "The Origins of American Military Policy," *Military Affairs* 22 (Summer 1958), pp. 75-82.

tion were less significant than the differences in the way in which that expansion took place. These contrasts in political evolution were directly related to the prevalence of foreign war and social conflict in Europe as contrasted with America.

On the Continent, the late sixteenth and the seventeenth centuries were periods of intense struggle and conflict. For only three years during the entire seventeenth century was there a complete absence of fighting on the European Continent. Several of the larger states were more often at war during the century than they were at peace. The wars were usually complex affairs involving many states tied together in dynastic and political alliances. War reached an intensity in the seventeenth century which it had never reached previously and which was exceeded later only in the twentieth century.[42] The prevalence of war directly promoted political modernization. Competition forced the monarchs to build their military strength. The creation of military strength required national unity, the suppression of regional and religious dissidents, the expansion of armies and bureaucracies, and a major increase in state revenues. "The most striking fact" in the history of seventeenth-century conflict, Clark observes, "is the great increase in the size of armies, in the scale of warfare. . . . Just as the modern state was needed to create the standing army, so the army created the modern state, for the influence of the two causes was reciprocal. . . . The growth of the administrative machine and of the arts of government was directed and conditioned by the desire to turn the national and human resources of the country into military power. The general development of European institutions was governed by the fact that the continent was becoming more military, or, we may say, more militaristic."[43] War was the great stimulus to state-building.

In recent years much has been written about "defensive modernization" by the ruling groups in non-Western societies, such as Egypt under Mohammed Ali, the eighteenth- and nineteenth-century Ottoman Empire, and Meiji Japan. In all these cases, intense early efforts at modernization occurred in the military field, and the attempts to adopt European weapons, tactics, and organization led to the modernization of other institutions in society. What was true of these societies was also true of seventeenth-century Europe. The need for security and the desire for expansion prompted the monarchs to develop their military establishments, and the achievement of this goal required them to centralize and to rationalize their political machinery.

Largely because of its insular position, Great Britain was a partial exception to this pattern of war and insecurity. Even so, one major impetus

---

[42]Clark, p. 98; Quincy Wright, *A Study of War* (Chicago 1942), vol. I, pp. 235-40. See also Clark, *War and Society in the Seventeenth Century* (Cambridge 1958), *passim.*
    [43]*Seventeenth Century*, pp. 99, 101-2.

to the centralization of authority in English government came from the efforts of the Stuart kings to collect more taxes to build and man more ships to compete with the French and other continental powers. If it were not for the English Channel, the Stuart centralization probably would have succeeded. In America in the seventeenth century, however, continuing threats came only from the Indians. The nature of this threat, plus the dispersion of the settlements, meant that the principal defense force had to be the settlers themselves organized into militia units. There was little incentive to develop European-type military forces and a European-type state to support and control them.

Civil harmony also contributed significantly to the preservation of Tudor political institutions in America. Those institutions reflected the relative unity and harmony of English society during the sixteenth century. English society, which had been racked by the Wars of the Roses in the fifteenth century, welcomed the opportunity for civil peace that the Tudors afforded. Social conflict was minor during the sixteenth century. The aristocracy had been almost eliminated during the civil wars of the previous century. England was not perhaps a middle-class society but the differences between social classes were less then than they had been earlier and much less than they were to become later. Individual mobility rather than class struggle was the keynote of the Tudor years. "The England of the Tudors was an 'organic state' to a degree unknown before Tudor times, and forgotten almost immediately afterward." Harmony and unity made it unnecessary to fix sovereignty in any particular institution; it could remain dispersed so long as social conflict was minimal.

The only major issue that disrupted the Tudor consensus was, of course, religion. Significantly, in sixteenth-century English history the Act of Supremacy meant the supremacy of the state over the church, not the supremacy of one governmental institution over another or one class over another. After the brief interlude of the Marian struggles, however, the shrewd politicking and popular appeal of Elizabeth restored a peace among religious groups which was virtually unique in Europe at that time. The balance between Crown and Parliament and the combination of an active monarchy and common law depended upon this social harmony. Meanwhile on the Continent, civil strife had already reached a new intensity before the end of the sixteenth century. France alone had eight civil wars during the thirty-six years between 1562 and 1598, a period roughly comprising the peaceful reign of Elizabeth in England. The following fifty years saw Richelieu's struggles with the Huguenots and the wars of the Fronde. Spain was racked by civil strife, particularly between 1640 and 1652 when Philip IV and Olivares attempted to subdue Catalonia. In Germany, princes and parliaments fought each other. Where, as frequently happened, estates and princes espoused different religions, the controversy over religion inevitably broke the medieval balance of powers between princes and parliaments.

English harmony ended with the sixteenth century. Whether the gentry were rising, falling, or doing both in seventeenth-century England, forces were at work in society disrupting Tudor social peace. The efforts to re-establish something like the Tudor balance broke down before the intensity of social and religious conflict. The brief period of Crown power between 1630 and 1640, for instance, gave way "to a short-lived restoration of something like the Tudor balance of powers during the first year of the Long Parliament (1641). This balance might perhaps have been sustained indefinitely, but for the rise of acute religious differences between the Crown and the militant Puritan party in the Commons."[44] In England, as in France, civil strife led to the demand for strong centralized power to reestablish public order. The breakdown of unity in society gave rise to irresistible forces to reestablish that unity through government.

Both Puritan and Cavalier emigrants to American escaped from English civil strife. The process of fragmentation, in turn, encouraged homogeneity, and homogeneity encouraged "a kind of immobility."[45] In America, environment reinforced heredity, as the common challenges of the frontier combined with the abundance of land to help perpetuate the egalitarian characteristics of Tudor society and the complexity of Tudor political institutions. And paradoxically, as Hartz has pointed out, the framers of the Constitution of 1787 reproduced these institutions on the federal level in the belief that the social divisions and conflict within American society made necessary a complex system of checks and balances. In reality, however, their Constitution was successful only because their view of American society was erroneous. So also, only the absence of significant social divisions permitted the continued transformation of political issues into legal ones through the peculiar institution of judicial review.[46] Divided societies cannot exist without centralized power; consensual societies cannot exist with it.

In continental Europe, as in most contemporary modernizing countries, rationalized authority and centralized power were necessary not only for unity but also for progress. The opposition to modernization came from traditional interests: religious, aristocratic, regional, and local. The centralization of power was necessary to smash the old order, break down the privileges and restraints of feudalism, and free the way for the rise of new social groups and the development of new economic activities. In some degree a coincidence of interest did exist between the absolute monarchs and the rising middle classes. Hence European liberals often viewed favorably the

---

[44]Chrimes, p. 138.

[45]Louis Hartz, *The Founding of New Societies* (New York 1964), pp. 3, 4, 6, 23. Hartz's theory of fragmentation furnishes an excellent general framework for the analysis of the atrophy of settlement colonies, while his concept of the American liberal consensus in large part explains the preservation of Tudor political institutions.

[46]Hartz, *The Liberal Tradition in America* (New York 1955), pp. 9-10, 45-46, 85-86, 133-134, 281-282.

concentration of authority in an absolute monarch, just as modernizers today frequently view favorably the concentration of authority in a single "mass" party.

In America, on the other hand, the absence of feudal social institutions made the centralization of power unnecessary. Since there was no aristocracy to dislodge, there was no need to call into existence a governmental power capable of dislodging it. This great European impetus to political modernization was missing. Society could develop and change without having to overcome the opposition of social classes with a vested interest in the social and economic status quo. The combination of an egalitarian social inheritance plus the plenitude of land and other resources enabled social and economic development to take place more or less spontaneously. Government often helped to promote economic development, but (apart from the abolition of slavery) it played only a minor role in changing social customs and social structure. In modernizing societies, the centralization of power varies directly with the resistance to social change. In the United States, where the resistance was little, so also was the centralization.

The differences in social consensus between Europe and America also account for the differences in the manner in which political participation expanded. In Europe this expansion was marked by discontinuities on two levels. On the institutional level, democratization meant the shift of power from monarchical ruler to popular assembly. This shift began in England in the seventeenth century, in France in the eighteenth century, and in Germany in the nineteenth century. On the electoral level, democratization meant the extension of the suffrage for this assembly from aristocracy to upper bourgeoisie, lower bourgeoisie, peasants, and urban workers. The process is clearly seen in the English reform acts of 1832, 1867, 1884, and 1918. In America, on the other hand, no such class differences existed as in England. Suffrage was already widespread in most colonies by independence, and universal white manhood suffrage was a fact in most states by 1830. The unity of society and the division of government meant that the latter was the principal focus of democratization. The American equivalent of the Reform Act of 1832 was the change in the nature of the Electoral College produced by the rise of political parties, and the resulting transformation of the Presidency from an indirectly elected, semi-oligarchical office to a popular one. The other major steps in the expansion of popular participation in the United States involved the extension of the electoral principle to all the state governors, to both houses of the state legislatures, to many state administrative offices and boards, to the judiciary in many states, and to the United States Senate. Thus, in Europe the broadening of participation meant the extension of the suffrage for one institution to all classes of society, while in America it meant the extension of the suffrage by the one class in society to all (or almost all) institutions of government.

In Europe the opposition to modernization within society forced the modernization of the political system. In America, the ease of modernization within society precluded the modernization of the political system. The United States thus combines the world's most modern society with one of the world's most antique polities. The American political experience is distinguished by frequent acts of creation but few, if any, of innovation. Since the Revolution, constitutions have been drafted for thirty-eight new political systems, but the same pattern of government has been repeated over and over again. The new constitutions of Alaska and Hawaii differ only in detail from the constitution of Massachusetts, originally drafted by John Adams in 1780. When else in history has such a unique series of opportunities for political experiment and innovation been so almost totally wasted?

This static quality of the political system constrasts with the prevalence of change elsewhere in American society. A distinguishing feature of American culture, Robin Williams has argued, is its positive orientation toward change. In a similar vein, two observers have noted, "In the United States change itself is valued. The new is good; the old is unsatisfactory. Americans gain prestige by being among the first to own next year's automobile; in England, much effort is devoted to keeping twenty-five-year-old cars in operating condition."[47] In three centuries, a few pitifully small and poor rural settlements strung along the Atlantic seaboard and populated in large part by religious exiles were transformed into a huge, urbanized, continental republic, the world's leading economic and military power. America has given the world its most modern and efficient economic organizations. It has pioneered social benefits for the masses: mass production, mass education, mass culture. Economically and socially, everything has been movement and change. Politically, however, the only significant institutional innovation has been federalism, and this, in itself, of course, was made possible only by the traditional hostility to the centralization of authority. Fundamental social and economic change has been combined with political stability and continuity. In a society dedicated to what is shiny new, the polity remains quaintly old.

Modernity is thus not all of a piece. The American experience demonstrates conclusively that some institutions and some aspects of a society may become highly modern while other institutions and other aspects retain much of their traditional form and substance. Indeed, this may be a natural state of affairs. In any system some sort of equilibrium or balance must be maintained between change and continuity. Change in some spheres renders unnecessary or impossible change in others. In America the continuity and stability of government has permitted the rapid change of

---

[47]Williams, *American Society*, 2nd ed., rev. (New York 1961), p. 571; Eli Ginzberg and Ewing W. Reilley, *Effecting Change in Large Organizations* (New York 1957), pp. 18-19.

society, and the rapid change in society has encouraged continuity and stability in government. The relation between polity and society may well be dialectical rather than complementary. In other societies, such as Latin America, a rigid social structure and the absence of social and economic change have been combined with political instability and the weakness of political institutions. A good case can be made, moreover, that the latter is the result of the former.[48]

This combination of modern society and Tudor polity explains much that is otherwise perplexing about political ideas in America. In Europe the conservative is the defender of traditional institutions and values, particularly those in society rather than in government. Conservatism is associated with the church, the aristocracy, social customs, the established social order. The attitude of conservatives toward government is ambivalent: Government is viewed as the guarantor of social order, but it also is viewed as the generator of social change. Society rather than government has been the principal conservative concern. European liberals, on the other hand, have had a much more positive attitude toward government. Like Turgot, Price, and Godwin, they have viewed the centralization of power as the precondition of social reform. They have supported the gathering of power into a single place—first the absolute monarch, then the sovereign assembly—where it can then be used to change society.

In America, on the other hand, these liberal and conservative attitudes have been thoroughly confused and partly reversed. Conservatism has seldom flourished because it has lacked social institutions to conserve. Society is changing and modern, while government, which the conservative views with suspicion, has been relatively unchanging and antique. With a few exceptions, such as a handful of colleges and churches, the oldest institutions in American society are governmental institutions. The absence of established social institutions, in turn, has made it unnecessary for American liberals to espouse the centralization of power as did European liberals. John Adams could combine Montesquieu's polity with Turgot's society much to the bafflement of Turgot. Nineteenth-century Europeans had every reason to be fascinated by America: It united a liberal society which they were yet to experience with a conservative politics which they had in large part forgotten.

V. TUDOR POLITY AND MODERNIZING SOCIETIES

Recently much has been made of the relevance to the currently modernizing countries of Asia, Africa, and Latin America of the earlier

---

[48]Merle Kling, "Toward a Theory of Power and Political Instability in Latin America," *Western Political Quarterly* 9 (Mar. 1956), pp. 21-31.

phases of modernization in the United States. It has been argued that the United States was and still should be a revolutionary power. The American Revolution, it has been said, "started a chain reaction" beginning with the French Revolution and leading on to the Russian Revolution which was "the American Revolution's child, though an unwanted and unacknowledged one."[49] But the effort to see connections and/or parallels between what happened in America in the eighteenth century and what is happening in Asia, Africa, and elsewhere in the twentieth century can only contribute to monstrous misunderstandings of both historical experiences. The American Revolution was not a social revolution like the French, Russian, Chinese, Mexican, or Cuban revolutions; it was a war of independence. Moreover, it was not a war of independence of natives against alien conquerors, like the struggles of the Indonesians against the Dutch, or of the Vietnamese or the Algerians against the French, but was instead a war of settlers against the home country. Any recent parallels are in the relation of the Algerian *colons* to the French Republic or of the Southern Rhodesians to the United Kingdom. It is in these cases, in the last of the European "fragments" to break their European ties, that the eighteenth-century experience of America may be duplicated. These, however, are not parallels of which American liberal intellectuals and statesmen like to be reminded.

The case for the relevance of the American experience to the contemporary modernizing countries has also been couched in terms of the United States as "The First New Nation." The United States, it has been argued, was the first nation "of any consequence to emerge from the colonial dominance of Western Europe as a sovereign state in its own right, and to that extent it shares something in common with the 'emerging nations' of today, no matter how different they may be in other respects."[50] The phrase "new nation," however, fails to distinguish between state and society, and hence misses crucial differences between the American experience and those of the contemporary modernizing countries. The latter are, for the most part, more accurately described by the title of another book: "Old Societies and New States."[51] America, on the other hand, was historically a new society but an old state. Hence the problems of government and political modernization that the contemporary modernizing states face differ fundamentally from those that confronted the United States.

In most countries of Asia, Africa, and Latin America, modernization faces tremendous social obstacles. The gaps between rich and poor, between modern elite and traditional mass, between the powerful and the weak—

[49] Arnold J. Toynbee, "If We Are To Be the Wave of the Future," *New York Times Magazine,* Nov. 13, 1960, p. 123.

[50] See Seymour Martin Lipset, *The First New Nation* (New York 1963), Part I; J. Leiper Freeman, "The Colonial Stage of Development: The American Case," unpublished paper, Comparative Administration Group, 1963, p. 4.

[51] See Clifford Geertz, ed., *Old Societies and New States: The Quest for Modernity in Asia and Africa* (New York 1963).

gaps that are the common lot of "old societies" trying to modernize today—contrast markedly with the "pleasing uniformity" of the "one estate" that existed in eighteenth-century America. As in seventeenth-century Europe these gaps can be overcome only by the creation of powerful, centralized authority in government. The United States never had to construct such authority in order to modernize its society, and hence its experience has little to offer modernizing countries today. America, De Tocqueville said, "arrived at a state of democracy without having to endure a democratic revolution" and "was born equal without having to become so." So also American society was born modern; and it hence was never necessary to construct a government powerful enough to make it so. An antique polity is compatible with a modern society but it is not compatible with the modernization of a traditional society.

The Latin American experience, for instance, is almost exactly the reverse of that of the United States. After independence the United States continued essentially the same political institutions it had had before independence, which were perfectly suited to its society. At independence the Latin American countries inherited and maintained an essentially feudal social structure. They attempted to superimpose on this social structure republican political institutions copied from the United States and revolutionary France. Such institutions had no meaning in a feudal society. These early efforts at republicanism left Latin America with weak governments which until the twentieth century lacked the authority and power to modernize the society. Liberal, pluralistic, democratic governments serve to perpetuate antiquated social structure. Thus in Latin America an inherent conflict exists between the political goals of the United States—elections, democracy, representative government, pluralism, constitutionalism—and its social goals—modernization, reform, social welfare, more equitable distribution of wealth, development of a middle class. In the North American experience these goals did not conflict. In Latin America, they often clash head on. The variations of the North American political system which North Americans would like to reproduce in Latin America are simply too weak, too diffuse, too dispersed to mobilize the political power necessary to bring about fundamental change. Such power can be mobilized by revolution, as it was in Mexico and Cuba, and a historical function of revolutions is to replace weak governments by strong governments capable of achieving social change. The question for Latin America and similarly situated countries is whether other ways short of violent revolution exist for generating the political power necessary to modernize traditional societies.

However it occurs, the accumulation of power necessary for modernization makes the future of democracy rather bleak. Countries, such as France and Prussia, which took the lead in political modernization in the seventeenth century have had difficulty in maintaining stable democracy in the twentieth century. Countries in which the seventeenth-century tendencies toward absolute monarchy were either defeated (England), stalemated (Sweden), or absent (America) later tended to develop more viable democratic institutions. The continued vitality of medieval estates and pluralistic assemblies is associated with subsequent democratic tendencies. "It is no accident, surely," Carsten observes, "that the liberal movement of the nineteenth century was strongest in those areas of Germany where the Estates survived the period of absolute government." Similarly, in seventeenth-century Spain, Catalonia was the principal locus of feudal opposition to the centralizing and rationalizing efforts of Olivares, but in the twentieth century it has been the principal locus of Spanish liberalism and constitutionalism. In eighteenth-century Europe also, the conflict between traditional liberties and modernizing reforms was a pervasive one, and the conservative and even reactionary efforts of the "constituted bodies" to maintain and to restore their privileges laid the basis for later, more popular, resistance against despotism.

If a parallel exists between seventeenth-century modernization and twentieth-century modernization, the implications of the former for the latter are clear. Despite arguments to the contrary, the countries where modernization requires the concentration of power in a single, monolithic, hierarchical, but "mass," party are not likely to be breeding grounds for democracy. Mass participation goes hand-in-hand with authoritarian control. As in Guinea and Ghana, it is the twentieth-century weapon of modernizing centralizers against traditional pluralism. Democracy, on the other hand, is more likely in those countries that preserve elements of traditional social and political pluralism. Its prospects are brightest where traditional pluralism is adapted to modern politics, as appears to be the case with the caste associations of India and as may be the case with tribal associations in some parts of Africa. So also, Lebanon, the most democratic Arab country—indeed, perhaps the only democratic Arab country—has a highly traditional politics of confessional pluralism. Like the states of seventeenth-century Europe, the non-Western countries of today can have political modernization or they can have democratic pluralism, but they cannot normally have both.

In each historical period one type of political system usually seems to its contemporaries to be particularly relevant to the needs and demands of the age. In the era of European state-building in the seventeenth century, the "pattern-state," to use Sir George Clark's phrase, was the Bourbon monarchy of France. Indeed, the new state that emerged in that century, as Clark argues, "may be called the French type of monarchy not only because it reached its strongest and most logical expression in France, but also because it was consciously and deliberately copied elsewhere from the Bourbon model."[52] This type of centralized, absolute monarchy met the

---

[52]*Seventeenth Century*, pp. 83, 90-91.

paramount needs of the time. In the late eighteenth and nineteenth centuries, the pattern-state was the British parliamentary system. The countries of Europe then faced the problems of democratization and the incorporation into the polity of the lower social orders. The British system furnished the model for this phase of modernization. Today, in much of Asia, Africa, and Latin America, political systems face simultaneously the needs to centralize authority, to differentiate structure, and to broaden participation. The system that seems most relevant to the simultaneous achievement of these goals is a one-party system. If Versailles set the standard for one century and Westminster for another, the Kremlin may well be the most relevant model for the modernizing countries of this century. The heads of minor German principalities aped Louis XIV; the heads of equally small and backward states today may ape Lenin and Mao. The primary need their countries face is the accumulation and concentration of power, not its dispersion, and it is in Moscow and Peking and not in Washington that this lesson is to be learned.

Nor should this irrelevance of the American polity come as a great surprise. Historically foreigners have always found American society more attractive than the American polity. Even in the seventeenth and eighteenth centuries, as Beloff observes, "the political appeal of the new country was less potent than the social one." De Tocqueville was far more impressed by the democracy of American society and customs than he was by its democratic institutions of government. In the last century Europeans have found much to emulate in American business organization and in American culture, but they have found little reason to copy American political institutions. Parliamentary democracies and one-party dictatorships abound throughout the world. But surely one of the striking features of world politics is the rarity of other political systems based on the American presidential model.

The irrelevance of the American polity to the rest of the world, however, must not be overdone. It is of little use to societies that must modernize a traditional order. But, as the American experience itself demonstrates, a Tudor polity is quite compatible with a modern society. Consequently it is possible, although far from necessary, that as other societies become more fully modern, as the need to disestablish old, traditional, feudal, and local elements declines, the need to maintain a political system capable of modernization may also disappear. Such a system will, of course, have the advantage of tradition and of association with successful social change, so the probabilities are that it will not change greatly. But at least the possibility exists that there may be some evolution toward an American-type system. The "end of ideology" in Western Europe, the mitigation of class conflict, the tendencies toward an "organic society," all suggest that the European countries could now tolerate more dispersed and relaxed political institutions. Some elements of the American system seem to be creeping back into Europe from which they were exported three centuries ago.[53] Judicial review has made a partial and timorous reappearance on the Continent. After De Gaulle, the constitution of the Fifth Republic might well shake down to something not too far removed from the constitution of the American Republic. Mr. Harold Wilson was accused, before and after coming to power, of acting like Mr. President. These are small straws in the wind. They may not mean anything. But if they do mean anything, they mean that the New Europe may eventually come to share some of the old institutions that the New World has preserved from an older Europe.

[53]See, e.g., Stephen Graubard, ed., *A New Europe?* (Boston 1964); Stanley Hoffmann, "Europe's Identity Crisis: Between the Past and America," *Daedalus* 93 (Fall 1964), pp. 1249, 1252-53. On the role of the courts see Taylor Cole, "Three Constitutional Courts: A Comparison," *American Political Science Review* 53 (Dec. 1959), pp. 963-984; and Gottfried Dietze, "America and Europe—Decline and Emergence of Judicial Review," *Virginia Law Review* 44 (Dec. 1958), pp. 1233-1272.

6

The French Experience
of Modernization

Bernard E. Brown

Few theorists today admit to a belief in the "idea of progress."
But, if the literature in comparative politics in the past several years is any
guide, virtually all political scientists now believe in the concept of
"modernization." Modernization theory is being invoked to compare
traditional and modern societies, to analyze the evolution of individual
political systems, and to appraise the effectiveness of political institutions in
one or several political systems. All of the problems and subjects of political
science are now being reexamined in terms of some concept of modernization.

It is generally argued that the enormous development of science and
technology since the early nineteenth century has brought about a
fundamental transformation of all political systems. Most recent studies
present a polar contrast between "traditional" and "modern" societies in
terms of four major elements of any social system: the economy, social
structure, political institutions, and the values that permeate the whole and
justify coercion. The kind of change that involves modernization of each of
these elements may be briefly summarized: (1) In traditional *economies* the
overwhelming mass of the population is engaged in various forms of
subsistence agriculture or husbandry. Modern economies are characterized
by the use of science and technology in the production of the means of
existence. (2) Traditional *social structures* are relatively simple. The family is
the dominant social unit, and face-to-face relations (through the tribe, clan,
or feudal order) characterize the entire society. Modern social structure is
complex, bureaucratized, and highly differentiated. An individual belongs to
any number of specialized associations, such as trade unions, business
groups, sporting societies, religious organizations, and the like. (3)

"The French Experience of Modernization" by Bernard E. Brown is reprinted by permission
from *World Politics* 21 (April 1969), pp. 366-391.

Traditional *states* resemble large families, while modern states resemble specialized associations. In modern states political functions, like social functions, are assigned to different categories of people. A civil service is created, with a logical structure, hierarchy of command, and power based on knowledge rather than on family connections. (4) Traditional *values* are those of the family, emphasizing personal and filial loyalty. Attempts to view and understand the universe are in terms of mysticism, religion, and unprovable speculation; these constitute useful myths that hold together the social system and bring about acceptance of its structures and rules. Modern values are those of science. Political rule is justified by rational principles, not by invocation of divine right or heredity.

Modernization implies a particular kind of change in at least one of the above factors, bringing about corresponding changes in the other categories. A social system has an internal logic in that its various parts bear a *necessary* relationship to one another. Thus, a society imbued with ancestor-spirit, and in which authoritative decisions are made by witch doctors, is not capable of sustaining a massive industrial economy. Conversely, once an advanced industrial economy comes into being, the habits of thought and of science and the discipline of the machine are incompatible with a feudal social structure. Such assertions are broad; as Thorstein Veblen pointed out in a seminal work rather neglected by students of modernization, changes in the level of technology do not immediately bring about corresponding social changes. New social classes emulate the values and life styles of their "betters," a propensity that introduces a note of dissonance.[1] Correlations among the economic, social, political, and cultural factors are loose, but they exist; if they did not there would be no point in discussing modernization as a process.

One problem is evident from any survey of the literature. In order to sharpen the contrast between the two types, the "traditional" model is made so primitive that it is relevant only to tribal societies and prehistoric Europe. The kind of traditional society that preceded the modern form in Western Europe and North America, for example, was quite complex by any standard, and probably closer to "modernity" than to the ideal type of traditionalism. These extreme typologies also blur the significant differences among traditional societies—the kind of differences so brilliantly illuminated by Alexis de Tocqueville in his works on France, England, and the United States. Ideal types based on polar contrasts may be analytically useful as a check-list for observers or as a means of directing attention to the

[1] *The Theory of the Leisure Class* (1899). Veblen's essay on the "discipline of the machine" in *The Theory of Business Enterprise* (1904) is an excellent statement of the influence of technology upon social and political values. One major exception to the general view that the above defined factors are correlated in any social system is Wilbert S. Moore, *Social Change* (Englewood Cliffs, N.J. 1963), in which the looseness of social structure is stressed.

relationships among factors in any social system. The disadvantage is that the typology may take on a life of its own. Instead of seeking to grasp the internal logic of a political system with the aid of typological schemes, the observer may spend all his energy working out the abstract logic of a typology that has no relation to reality.

Whatever the mathematical and logical beauty of typologies, political scientists presumably are interested in the payoff for research. Does modernization theory deepen our understanding of political life? What difference does it make in the organization of research and study? Does it have explanatory power? One way of answering these questions—perhaps the best way, in fact—is to apply modernization theory to an individual political system. In this paper we shall take as a case study the French political system. Surely no argument is needed to demonstrate the importance of France in the development of modern Europe, or the contribution of the French to the industrial and scientific revolutions of the nineteenth century. We shall first examine the specific application of modernization theory to France by three highly imaginative and skilled observers: C. E. Black, Samuel P. Huntington, and Stanley Hoffmann.[2] Taken together, their writings offer a comprehensive view of the French experience of modernization from nation-building through late industrialization. We shall then return to the larger question of the utility and relevance of modernization theory in comparative politics.

THREE VIEWS OF FRENCH MODERNIZATION

C. E. Black's *The Dynamics of Modernization* is probably the best single book on the subject yet to appear. Professor Black moves fluently and surely from theory to practice and back again. He identifies four stages of political modernization:

> (1) *the challenge of modernity*—the initial confrontation of a society, within its traditional framework of knowledge, with modern ideas and institutions, and the emergence of advocates of modernity; (2) *the consolidation of modernizing leadership*—the transfer of power from traditional to modernizing leaders in the course of a normally bitter revolutionary struggle often lasting several generations; (3) *economic and social transformation*—the development of

[2]C. E. Black, *The Dynamics of Modernization: A Study in Comparative History* (New York 1966); Samuel P. Huntington, "Political Modernization: America vs. Europe," *World Politics* 17 (Apr. 1966), pp. 378-414 [reprinted above]; and Stanley Hoffmann, "Paradoxes of the French Political Community," in Hoffmann, ed., *In Search of France* (Cambridge, Mass. 1963), pp. 1-117.

economic growth and social change to a point where a society is transformed from a predominantly rural and agrarian way of life to one predominantly urban and industrial; and (4) *the integration of society*—the phase in which economic and social transformation produces a fundamental reorganization of the social structure throughout the society.[3]

Black's typology of political modernization is based on the timing of the consolidation of modern political leadership (whether early or late in relation to other countries), the nature of the challenge of modernity to traditional institutions (whether internal or external), the continuity of territory and population in the modern era, the independent or dependent status of the nation, and the solidity of political institutions when the nation entered the modern era. The first of seven patterns that make up the typology is formed by the experience of Great Britain and France. In both countries the revolution that consolidated political leadership came early as compared to that of other countries (1649-1832 in Britain and 1789-1848 in France), the major challenge of modernity was primarily internal, there was an unusual continuity of both territory and population in the modern era, and the political institutions were fairly stable as the country entered the modern era. Professor Black then cites 1832-1945 as the period of economic and social transformation in Britain, 1848-1945 in France; and since 1945 as the phase of social integration in both countries.

In this analysis the similarities between British and French modernization are emphasized. The major differences between the two nations are thus the earlier rise to power of a modern leadership and the somewhat earlier industrialization in Britain. Black recognizes that the French never achieved the same degree of political consensus as did the British. But he suggests that the basis for orderly development in France was laid by the modern institutional framework established by the Napoleonic Code in 1802. In spite of the apparent political instability, he concludes that "France has nevertheless undergone at the administrative level a relatively gradual and stable transformation under many generations of skilled civil servants trained in the *grandes écoles*."[4]

Professor Black's typology of seven patterns is a stimulating way of comparing and evaluating the general process of political modernization in the world. But its specific application to France raises several questions. Was modern leadership in France first consolidated in 1789? The implication in Black's analysis is that this stage occurred in Britain more than a century earlier. No one would deny the importance of the English Civil War or the French Revolution as decisive turning points in British and French political history, especially as regards the shaping of political institutions and the

[3]Black, pp. 67-68.
[4]*Ibid.*, p. 109.

evolution of consensus. But that Britain and France, so closely related in all things, were a century apart in political modernization is implausible. Britain and France were both presented with the same kind of challenge in the course of the seventeenth century—basically the inability or unwillingness of the country as a whole to sustain the burden of a greatly expanded monarchical apparatus. The French monarchy proved somewhat more flexible and adaptable at the time; it was thus able to weather the storm. In spite of the political turmoil in seventeenth-century Britain, and the success of reformers in France, it would appear that similar developments were taking place in the two societies during the seventeenth and eighteenth centuries. De Tocqueville pointed out, for example, in his classic study, *The Old Regime and the French Revolution*, that the entire political, administrative, and social structure of the nation was being transformed well before the Revolution. In a famous passage, he wrote, "Chance played no part whatever in the outbreak of the Revolution; though it took the world by surprise, it was the inevitable outcome of a long period of gestation, the abrupt and violent conclusion of a process in which six generations had played an intermittent part. Even if it had not taken place, the old social structure would nonetheless have been shattered everywhere sooner or later."[5] Undoubtedly, a new political leadership emerged in 1789. But new social forces came to the fore, and began to participate in the political system, long before that date.

On the other hand, Professor Black may be overstating the similarities between Britain and France when he argues that in both countries there was "a relatively orderly and peaceful adaptation of traditional institutions to modern functions." In one sense this was certainly the case; France today is roughly as "modern" as Britain, and presumably her traditional institutions (at least those dating from the Revolution and the Napoleonic Code) have proved adaptable. But how useful is this approach for an understanding of French development? Modernization there has been, yes; but its pace, the way in which new social groups created by modernization have entered into the political system, and the role played by the State in furthering modernization have all been quite distinctive in France.

The contention that the *grandes corps* really run France, despite the political bickering on the surface, is a venerable thesis. Studies of decision-making suggest that in France, as in all complex parliamentary systems, the civil service is itself divided politically. Major interest groups develop special channels of access to the civil service as well as to parliament, thus creating "whirlpools" of influence and power throughout the political system. For example, with regard to the issue of state subsidies to beetgrowers and other producers of alcohol there is a split within the French civil service; the

⁵Alexis de Tocqueville, *The Old Regime and the French Revolution* (Garden City, N.Y. 1955), p. 20.

Ministry of Agriculture is generally in favor of subsidies and the Treasury is generally opposed. Alliances are thus formed that include civil servants, interest groups, deputies, and party leaders on both sides of issues. The French civil service has been fortunate in the past in recruiting exceptional talent; but it has not been a unified political force, nor has it been able to resolve the problem of political legitimacy. In this sense, the French experience provides us with a contrast to that of Britain and other nations where there is general agreement on fundamental political values and institutions.[6]

Our attention is directed especially to the period preceding the Revolution by Samuel P. Huntington, in his study of political modernization in America and Europe. He argues that modernization involves three things: rationalization of authority (replacement of traditional political authority by a single, secular, national authority), the development of specialized political structures to perform specialized functions, and mass participation in the political system. "On the Continent," comments Huntington, "the rationalization of authority and the differentiation of structures were the dominant trends of the seventeenth century," and he cites Richelieu, Mazarin, Louis XIV, Colbert, and Louvois as "great simplifiers, centralizers, and modernizers."[7] In addition, the seventeenth century saw the growth and rationalization of state bureaucracies and standing armies. Thus, in two important respects, the process of modernization took place on the Continent by 1700. A new political leadership rose to power in 1789; yet the way had been prepared over a long period of time.

It seems strange that divine right and hereditary monarchy should be considered forces for modernization. But Huntington explains that a prime requisite of modernization is the belief that men can act purposefully and effect change. Traditional society is permeated by a belief in unchanging custom and fundamental law. The modernization that began in the sixteenth century on the Continent required a new concept of authority, namely, that there was a sovereign who could make decisions. "One formulation of this idea was the new theory, which developed in Europe in the late sixteenth century, of the divine right of kings. Here, in effect, religious and, in that sense, traditional forms were used for modern purposes." Since mass participation in politics was a later phenomenon, modernization in the

---

[6]For example, Jean Meynaud describes the governmental universe in France as a system of power centers negotiating and bargaining with one another, *Nouvelles études sur les groupes de pression en France* (Paris 1962), pp. 249-50, 279. Among the case studies that point up the pluralistic nature of decision-making in France: Aline Coutrot, "La loi scolaire de décembre 1959," *Revue française de science politique* (June 1963), pp. 352-388; and Gaston Rimareix and Yves Tavernier, "L'élaboration et le vote de la loi complémentaire à la loi d'orientation agricole," *ibid.*, pp. 389-425. Also B. E. Brown, "France," in J. B. Christoph, ed., *Cases in Comparative Politics* (Boston 1965), pp. 129-206.

[7]Huntington, p. 379.

seventeenth century meant the rise of the absolute monarchy. "In terms of modernization, the seventeenth century's absolute monarch was the functional equivalent of the twentieth century's monolithic party."[8]

Huntington's analysis of Continental developments is a useful and necessary corrective. Most observers are fascinated by the Revolution, and have neglected the modernizing reforms of the Old Regime. But to consider monarchy the spearhead of modernization is an oversimplification of the situation in France. The absolute monarchy both furthered the trend to modernization and slowed it. It contributed to modernization by breaking the power of the local lords; it slowed modernization by glorifying irrational values, sustaining an archaic social structure, and imposing a terrible financial load upon the people. The modernizers in France before the Revolution also included the social critics, some who demanded parliamentary control of the executive, and some who greeted the American Revolution as the harbinger of a new era in history.

Nor were the advocates of fundamental law all opponents of modernization. It is true that some traditionalists invoked fundamental law to protect the privileges of the corporations. On the other hand, some modernizers tried to secure popular participation in the political system by appealing to fundamental law above the will of the monarch. In France as in colonial America, the doctrine of higher law was used for several political purposes, among which was the promulgation of rational principles of legitimacy.

Stanley Hoffmann deals with the later stages of modernization in France in his essay, "Paradoxes of the French Political Community." He begins with the two familiar models of feudal-agrarian society and industrial society, and then places France on the continuum. He suggests that a "Republican synthesis" gradually emerged in the century after the French Revolution and flourished in the period 1878-1914. The basis of the Republican synthesis was a unique mixture of the two models, neither one nor the other, but rather a "halfway house between the old rural society and industrialization." The French economy was both static and modern at the same time. Industrialization took place, but without an industrial revolution. The business class adopted many of the attitudes of the aristocracy that it had replaced, particularly that of emphasizing family continuity and social prominence rather than efficient production. The agricultural sector remained massive and largely traditional in orientation. Slow industrial growth in turn made it difficult to grant concessions to the working class, which was consigned to a "social ghetto." Comments Hoffmann, "For more than a century the political problem of France was to devise a political system adapted to the stalemate society."[9]

The basic solution to this problem under the Third Republic was the

[8]*Ibid.*, pp. 384, 386.
[9]Hoffmann, p. 12.

combination of a centralized and efficient bureaucracy with a strictly limited state. Politics became a kind of game in which a divided parliament prevented the formation of effective political executives. "But this game, played in isolation from the nation-at-large by a self-perpetuating political class, saw to it that the fundamental equilibrium of society would not be changed by the state."[10] However, the foundations of the Republican synthesis were undermined by the crises of the 1930's. The depression and the rise of Nazi Germany produced tensions in French society that the regime could not overcome. The assailants of the Republic converged and overwhelmed it. Writing in 1962, Hoffmann concluded that "the stalemate society is dead"—though many of the old tensions remained. It was killed by the transformation of French society during and after World War II—by the emergence of fully industrial attitudes, the more active role of the state in planning economic development, a reorientation of the French business class, and structural changes in the working class.

But the use of ideal types as literary devices makes French society appear to be far more static than was the case under the Third and Fourth Republics, and more dynamic than it actually was under the Fifth Republic. For example, there was a period of very rapid and impressive economic growth from 1896 to 1914, with important social and political consequences. The Third Republic created conditions in which the whole infrastructure of the modern economy was perfected—including the railroad network, canals, and modern communications. Its greatest contribution perhaps was to lay the foundation of a universal, free, and secular educational system. This may not be the most desirable way to bring about modernization, but it surely is one way to do so. The balance among social forces and economic sectors was shifting, more or less rapidly, under both the Third and Fourth Republics. French society was, and still is, a mix of traditional and modern elements; but this is hardly unique. All industrial societies are characterized by tension between traditional and modern sectors. Nor is the French political system the only one alleged by critics to be "incoherent." If there is a distinctive French experience of modernization it will be found in the timing of the crises of modernization and in the persistent alienation of large groups at all stages of modernization, up to and including the present.

Modernization theory obviously is not a magic wand that eliminates the need for research or produces universal agreement among observers. But it is a fruitful way of organizing study, and permits significant comparison among political systems. In order to further comparative study of modernization, we offer the following generalizations concerning the French experience.

1. The traditional phase in France that preceded modern society was feudalism. But feudal society in France was relatively advanced compared to,

---

[10]*Ibid.*, p. 16.

say, tribal societies. Feudalism contained important elements of "modernity." The process of modernization in France, therefore, has been long and complex, dating at least from the eleventh century, and perhaps from as far back as the Roman conquest.

2. In the century before the Revolution, the social structure of France was gradually transformed. A system in which privilege derived from heredity was at least partly replaced by a system based on wealth and individual effort. The Revolution was the culmination of a long period of social change, whose pace then was greatly accelerated.

3. The values justifying feudalism and absolute monarchy lost their popular base under the Old Regime. The trend toward rationalization of political authority, brought to a logical conclusion by the Revolution, was a development of centuries.

4. In spite of continuing political turmoil the economic and social foundations of modernity were laid during the nineteenth century. Far from being a stalemate society, France under both the Third and Fourth Republics took on the characteristics of all modern societies.

We shall now discuss each of these generalizations at length.

1. The Traditional Society

Feudalism was a highly personal political relationship between man and man, between subordinate and superior. As one historian has put it: "It is the possession of rights of government by feudal lords and the performance of most functions of government through feudal lords which clearly distinguishes feudalism from other types of organization."[11] Feudalism was a "model" traditional society in every respect. The mass of the population was engaged in subsistence agriculture or animal husbandry, the primary social unit was the family, the basic values of the society were those of personal loyalty, fealty, and courage, and the state (in so far as it continued to exist) was a larger version of family organization and power. The feudal system reposed on mutual duties and rights of people in a direct personal relationship, with the enjoyment of land rights as the foundation of the structure.

If typological analysis is a checklist of characteristics, the contrast between feudalism and contemporary society in France is virtually total. But historical processes are too complex to be reduced to these terms. When placed in the context of French historical development, it may be seen that

---

[11]Joseph R. Strayer, "Feudalism in Western Europe," in Rushton Coulborn, ed., *Feudalism in History* (Princeton 1956), p. 16. On feudalism in France see also Marc Bloch, *Feudal Society* (Chicago 1961); A. Tilley, ed., *Medieval France* (New York 1964); and for an excellent synthesis, J. Touchard *et al.*, *Histoire des idées politiques* (Paris 1959), vol. I, pp. 155-163.

feudalism departed from the traditional model in a number of ways. First, feudalism throughout Western Europe was a response to the decay of the highly organized Roman Empire. Until the tenth century, the Roman way of life prevailed in Gaul. Citizens owned land and slaves, subject to restrictions imposed upon them by the state. But the state then disintegrated. No central authority was able to protect the inhabitants of Western Europe from the incessant incursions of Saracens and Scandinavians. Under these new circumstances the Roman notion of a centralized state became obsolete. Defense and security inevitably became local responsibilities. Thus, feudalism was not comparable to primitive tribal societies; it rather should be viewed as a civilized society in decline or decay. The difference is important. Under feudalism the memory of the centralized authority of the past always remained alive. One leading French historian contends that in the Middle Ages in France there were, strictly speaking, no feudal institutions. Only the monarchy was legitimate; the functions of administering justice, raising armies, and levying taxes were generally recognized as attributes of monarchy, conceded to or usurped by feudal powers.[12] When conditions and the technology of warfare changed, it was possible for the Capetian kings to revive the spirit of social and national unity. The reconstruction of authority that has fallen into decay is quite different as a political process from the creation of central authority where none has ever existed.

Most important, the rise of feudalism in the eleventh century coincided with a resurgence of the cities, a development that eventually sapped the feudal system. The period in France that most closely approximates the model traditional economy was the five centuries that preceded feudalism, rather than feudalism itself. It was from the sixth through the eleventh centuries, apparently, that the Franks became an almost wholly rural people engaged in subsistence agriculture. Artisans during this period abandoned the towns and retired to the countryside. Commerce declined abruptly, the cities were largely deserted, and municipal administration ceased to exist. By the eleventh century the process of urbanization resumed. The renaissance of town life was the result of many factors: a deliberate desire to create the conditions of a peaceful and secure existence within the confines of a commune; technological innovations in transport and manufacturing that made it economically feasible for merchants and artisans to congregate in towns; and a general desire on the part of merchants to terminate their nomadic existence and degrading dependence upon the goodwill of the local lords.

[12]See the seminal work by Ferdinand Lot with the collaboration of Robert Fawtier, *Histoire des institutions françaises au moyen âge* (Paris 1957), vol. I, p. viii; and vol. II, p. 9 for the comment, "the only political regime France had in the Middle Ages was the monarchy." Vol. II is an extraordinarily complete analysis of the rise of the royal power.

Everywhere, the city people sought to free themselves from the domination of feudal lords. This became easier as the cities prospered and could afford to recruit mercenaries. Nobles then found it necessary, in some cases profitable, to grant special charters to the towns, in effect exempting them from feudal obligations. Many communes were based on a clearly modern rather than traditional theory of governance. They were created by "common oath" on the part of the inhabitants, that is, an agreement among equals rather than between a superior and his subordinates. The "consular cities" enjoyed complete municipal liberty, with citizens electing representative councils invested with large financial and executive powers.

The inhabitants of the *bourgs* (or bourgeois) did not fit into the feudal structure. Merchants and artisans worked on their own, handled money, had no obligations to the lords, and were receptive to new ideas. The bourgeois became likewise a firm support for the royal power, which alone could integrate the resources of large domains and provide adequate security for the towns. The medieval towns were breeding grounds of new values and ideologies that challenged the traditional notions of religion, cultivated skepticism concerning the established order, and glorified the qualities of intelligence, liberty, and work.[13]

There was no steady, ineluctable progression from traditional to modern. The balance among the rival forces shifted frequently—particularly during the period of economic stagnation in the fourteenth century which brought about a decline of the middle class and a corresponding increase in the power and prestige of the clergy and lords. The secular trend, however, was to transform military vassalage into nobility in the service of the crown, and to transfer the idea of contract to the level of people and monarch. In brief, the social structure, economy, political institutions, and cultural values of medieval France by the thirteenth century already contained major elements of "modernity."

2. The Breakup of the Traditional Society

The dramatic events of the Revolution have tended to draw the attention of observers away from the rapid pace of social change in the seventeenth and eighteenth centuries. In each of the social orders of the Old Regime—the clergy, aristocracy, and third estate—structural transforma-

---

[13]On urbanization in the Middle Ages: Roland Mousnier, *Les XVI et XVII siècles* (Paris 1965), especially chap. 3; H. Van Werveke, "The Rise of Towns," in *The Cambridge Economic History of Europe*, vol. III, edited by M. M. Postan, E. E. Rich, and E. Miller (Cambridge 1963), pp. 3-40; L. Halphen, "Industry and Commerce," in A. Tilley, ed., *Medieval France*, pp. 183-192; and J. Touchard and others, vol. I, pp. 169-179. On the bourgeois support for monarchy, Robert Fawtier, *The Capetian Kings of France* (London 1964), pp. 199-215.

tions took place that eventually undermined the whole delicate balance of feudal privilege.[14]

As is natural in any pre-industrial society, religious values permeated medieval France. The clergy propagated and popularized the values that sustained the feudal regime, and enjoyed a privileged position as the "first estate." Church revenue from the tithe and other levies amounted to about 13 percent of the gross national income, to which must be added income from vast church-held lands. The church performed a number of vital functions within the society, including the maintenance of a network of welfare and educational institutions.

Yet the clergy's grip on power was shaken. The priestly life was subjected to serious criticism and satire by the intellectuals. That respect so necessary to the maintenance of any priestly class began to evaporate, and concern became general over the waste and irrationality of a system of tithes. Furthermore, the clergy was itself divided sharply into a small group of high-living and wealthy archbishops, and a mass of impoverished priests. When the great explosion took place, a divided priestly class was unable to rally mass support for the old regime.

The position of the nobility likewise was transformed in the century preceding the Revolution. It, too, was affected by the process of modernization. The very composition of the nobility underwent a change. It was not a completely closed caste, since new elements were admitted to noble rank by a variety of methods. The king had the right of conferring nobility upon deserving commoners (usually men of great wealth, civil servants, and military officers). Whatever their origins, the nobles enjoyed extensive feudal privileges, which they sought desperately to maintain against pressures from the peasantry, the rising middle classes, and from the king. After 1750 the power of the aristocracy increased along with that of the middle classes. As Gordon Wright has put it: "The eighteenth century nobility was increasingly inclined to attack and destroy the *status quo*. The revolutionary goal of the discontented nobles was a return to a semi-mythical medieval system, to an unwritten constitution that had allegedly been torn up by the absolutist kings and their bourgeois ministers."[15]

All the rest of the population—some 98 percent—was the third estate. In the course of the eighteenth century the bourgeoisie rose in spectacular fashion within the social structure. Considerable fortunes were made in industry (by such entrepreneurs as Decretot, Van Robais, Oberkampf, Réveillon, and Dietrich), in trade (especially by the shipping interests of Havre, Bordeaux, and Marseilles) and in finance. Perhaps 10 percent of the

[14]For an excellent social and political analysis of this period, see Georges Dupeux, *La société française, 1789-1960* (Paris 1964), pp. 59-102, and Gordon Wright, *France in Modern Times* (Chicago 1960), chaps. 1 and 2.

[15]Gordon Wright, p. 18.

bourgeoisie was enabled, through investments and loans, to live entirely on dividends, without engaging in any kind of work. As the bourgeois acquired wealth, he tended to buy up land and cultivate it, thereby reestablishing a link between the middle class and agriculture. It has been estimated that perhaps 25 to 30 percent of all arable land in France by 1789 was in the hands of the bourgeoisie. Most of the *petite bourgeoisie* were engaged in trade or skilled work, and usually were organized in corporations.

There were stirrings within the peasantry, too. In 1779, serfdom was legally abolished in the last few places where it had survived. The peasants were juridically free, and altogether owned perhaps 40 to 45 percent of the land. However, the individual holdings were small, and relatively few peasants were well off. The number of landless peasants and seasonal workers in rural areas probably was greater than the number of individual landholders.[16]

The implications of these social trends were very great. First, they contradicted the assumption on which the old Regime was based—that society was a pyramid, with peasants and middle classes at the base, with aristocracy above them and a king above all. Says Cobban: "The division of the nation into *noblesse, noblesse de robe,* clergy, bourgeois and peasants was a simplification which concealed the real complexity of French society. Each class had in fact its own internal divisions, which prevented it from being a coherent unit." Basically, it was impossible for the old feudal political system to survive in this kind of society. The new standards of performance related to wealth, ability, talent, and occupational role; considerations of noble birth were less relevant, and in the long run, if taken seriously would have led to an impairment of the efficiency of the society. As R. R. Palmer has pointed out, "Western Europe in the eighteenth century was already a complicated society, with elaborate mechanisms operating in the fields of government, production, trade, finance, scientific research, church affairs, and education. The allocation of personnel to these enterprises on the basis of birth and social standing could not but hamper, and even pervert (one thinks of the established churches, some of the universities, and many branches of government), the achievement of the purposes for which such institutions were designed. The old feudal days were over. It was no longer enough for a lord to look locally after the needs of his people. The persistence and even the accentuation of an aristocratic outlook derived from earlier and simpler conditions presented problems for European society itself, as well as for the individuals and classes that made it up."[17]

The rise of the bourgeoisie did not have to mean a fight to the death

[16]Georges Dupeux, pp. 72-73.

[17]Citations are from Alfred Cobban, "The Decline of Divine Right Monarchy in France," *New Cambridge Modern History* (Cambridge 1957), vol. VII, p. 235, and R. R. Palmer, *The Age of the Democratic Revolution* (Princeton 1959), p. 68.

between the middle class and the nobility. Several different solutions were conceivable: The middle class could have disdained aristocratic values altogether, in which case the nobility might have ceased to be a political power; or the nobility could have opened its ranks to the newcomers and gradually absorbed its leading elements, thereby creating a greatly expanded new ruling class. But time ran out for peaceful solutions. Relations among aristocracy, bourgeoisie, and peasantry became increasingly bitter. The nobility resisted the pretensions of the middle classes and tried to block the development of embryonic capitalism. Eighteenth-century France had all the characteristics of a political system unsettled by the process of modernization.

3. Reason and Revolution

One of the basic assumptions of modernization theory is that as a society becomes more complex, the values serving to legitimize political authority become more rational. Or, rather than imply any causal relationship, rationalization of authority proceeds along with industrialization and increasing complexity of social structure. This assumption is borne out in a striking manner by the French experience, because of the great divide marked by the Revolution of 1789. The pattern of legitimacy clearly underwent a radical transformation, and took a form of greater rationality. But closer examination makes it apparent that the rationalization of authority was accentuated, not created, by the Revolution. It was part and parcel of the secular trend of modernization in all spheres of French society under the Old Regime.

Huntington has emphasized the modernizing role of the monarchy in breaking up feudal society. Hence, the theory of divine right of kings was more rational, or more modern, than feudalism itself. He comments, "The modernization that began in the sixteenth century on the Continent and in the seventeenth century in England required new concepts of authority, the most significant of which was the simple idea of a sovereignty itself, the idea that there is, in the words of Bodin, a 'supreme power over citizens and subjects, unrestrained by law.' One formulation of this idea was the new theory, which developed in Europe in the late sixteenth century, of the divine right of kings. Here, in effect, religious and, in that sense, traditional forms were used for modern purposes." [18]

Huntington's view is a useful reminder that ideal types make little sense outside historical context. The notion that a ruler receives a mandate from a divine source is characteristic of traditional societies; yet in the Europe of the

---

[18]Huntington, p. 384.

seventeenth century it was part of the breakthrough to modernity. But even here we must beware of historical oversimplification. Divine right of kings was not a new theory. The Franks, before the conquest, combined hereditary right with election; an Assembly of Warriors elected a king from among members of the Merovingian family, which presumably had divine connections. After the Frankish conquest, the Merovingians tried to free themselves of this dependence upon the assemblies, but were only partially successful. The rise of the Carolingian and Capetian dynasties brought a renewed emphasis upon election, since heredity could not be invoked as the overriding principle of legitimacy in an era of dynastic rivalries. Once their grip on power seemed secure, the Capetians sought to reestablish the principle of divine right, which gradually became accepted by the thirteenth century—though even in the fourteenth century there were several occasions when an Assembly of Barons played at least a subsidiary role in choosing a king. Divine right and religious consecration was the ancient theory of governance, was weakened under feudalism, and then revived as the centralizing forces in French society triumphed over feudalism. Under Louis XIV an absolute monarchy replaced a weak feudal monarchy; in a sense the monarchy reverted to the pre-feudal principle of divine right.[19]

The thesis that the absolute monarch was the agent of modernization can also be reversed, with perhaps even more validity. H. R. Trevor-Roper has argued cogently that the general European crisis of the seventeenth century had its origins in the rise of absolute monarchy. The Renaissance state, he contends, grew up in the sixteenth century at the expense of the cities. One by one, the great cities fell under the control of assorted princes and kings, whose military and administrative machines were irresistible. Monarchy helped bring about national unity, but once the Renaissance court was created, it became a wholly uneconomic and parasitic agency. The tested principles of commerce and industry were replaced by ostentation and deliberate waste. The burden of monarchy became too great to be borne; the sensible course was to eliminate the whole parasitic crew and return to the productive way of life that had made the medieval cities great. In England the royal power resisted and was swept away; in France the king, perhaps out of luck and apathy, allowed Richelieu to reduce royal expenses and enforce a mercantilist policy. The old regime was given a reprieve. According to Trevor-Roper, "By the seventeenth century the Renaissance courts had grown so great, had consumed so much in 'waste,' and had sent their multiplying suckers so deep in the body of society, that they could only flourish for a

---

[19]On the principle of election and religious consecration in the feudal period, see Ch. Petit Dutaillis, *The Feudal Monarchy in France and England* (London 1936), pp. 28;Robert Fawtier, *The Capetian Kings of France*, pp. 48-49; and Maurice Duverger, *Les constitutions de la France* (Paris 1950), pp. 11-17.

limited time, and in a time, too, of expanding general prosperity. When that prosperity failed, the monstrous parasite was bound to falter."[20]

This is not to deny the importance of the monarchy, and especially of the royal administrations, as a channel for innovative practices. But the medieval monarchy cannot be understood through the simple use of ideal types, nor can it be considered the sole agency of modernization. The rise of absolute monarchy in France coincided with the general modernization of French society, but so did the rise of opposition to absolutism.

It is also misleading to contrast divine right of kings with the concept of fundamental law, as if the latter characterized static traditional societies and the former embodied the principle of change. In France the situation was more confused. There were actually two different trends in theorizing about the fundamental laws of the kingdom. One view can properly be called "traditional," in that the fundamental laws were considered the creation of history and of God, beyond the competence even if the king to change. But a second view also developed, according to which fundamental laws were made by the people, and could be modified by the people through the Estates General. This conception, derived from the doctrine of social contract, was clearly more compatible with the process of modernization than were theories of divine right and hereditary monarchy. As Rushton Coulborn put it, the theory of divine right was a "clumsy idea," an "interim notion," and a "slogan, not an argument." And he concludes, "the return to serious thought about the relations between rulers and ruled is marked by the extraordinary doctrine of Original Compact, or Contract."[21]

The social contract is in one sense an extension of the doctrine of "fundamental laws" under the Old Regime. The political struggles of the eighteenth century revolved around the question of whether fundamental laws restrained the powers of the monarch. It was generally accepted under the Old Regime that the monarch could not change the rules concerning succession to the throne, or alienate the public domain, or be anything but a Catholic. An effort was made by a number of Estates General to establish the principle of parliamentary approval of all new taxes as a fundamental law, but the monarchy managed to defeat these efforts. This view of fundamental law led ultimately to the notion that the people originally possessed sovereign powers, and then delegated these powers to their governors.

[20]H. R. Trevor-Roper, "The General Crisis of the Seventeenth Century," in T. Aston, ed., *Crisis in Europe, 1560-1660* (New York 1965), p. 95. See also the dissent by Roland Mousnier, arguing that the monarchy was a progressive force, *ibid.*, 102. The thesis that modernization of French society took place through the crown is also presented by Barrington Moore, Jr., in *Social Origins of Dictatorship and Democracy* (Boston 1967). But note the strong statement by Alfred Cobban on the inherent incapacity of the French monarchy, as early as the reign of Louis XIV, to deal with changing conditions, in "The Decline of Divine Right Monarchy in France," p. 239.

[21]Rushton Coulborn, ed., pp. 311-312. On the fundamental laws under the Old Regime and social contract theory, see M. Duverger, pp. 31-37.

Once again it is necessary to emphasize the length and complexity of the process of modernization. By the eighteenth century the view was general that man was a creature of unlimited possibilities, that he was basically rational, and that the major purpose of political institutions was to permit him to develop his creative abilities to the fullest. As Gordon Wright has commented: "Enlightenment concepts were far more subversive than its proponents knew; they could scarcely be reconciled with the dominant ideas on which the old regime rested. The institutions of eighteenth-century France were still based on authority and tradition, not on any rational or utilitarian test; the old ideal of an organic society could not be harmonized with the new concept of an atomistic one made up of autonomous individuals." [22]

The ideas of the Enlightenment undermined the positions of both of the main contenders for power in the two decades that preceded the Revolution. The *Parlements* tried, with some success, to check the monarch, basically in the interest of the hereditary aristocracy. The king replied by affirming that full sovereignty resided in his person only. "Public order in its entirety," Louis XV proclaimed in the *séance de la flagellation,* in 1766, "emanates from me, and the rights and interests of the Nation, which some dare to set up as a body distinct from the Monarch, are necessarily joined with mine, and rest only in my hands." Neither the claims of absolute monarchy nor the proposals to restore aristocratic privilege were consonant with the intellectual mood of the time. By the standards of reason and the Enlightenment, the assertion that all sovereignty reposed in the king was absurd; and the contention that hereditary officeholders of the *Parlements* represented the nation only a little less so. When the showdown came, both protagonists found themselves without popular support. [23]

The new principles of political authority were rational in essence; they were compatible with either constitutional monarchy or a parliamentary republic, but marked an irrevocable break with both absolutism and feudalism. The Tennis Court Oath, the August decrees abolishing feudalism, and the Declaration of the Rights of Man and Citizen signalled the emergence of a wholly new principle of political legitimacy. Contrast, for example, Louis XV's pronouncement at the *séance de la flagellation,* the remonstrance of the *Parlement* of Paris in March, 1776, (glorifying the inequalities of feudalism) with the clear, forceful language of 1789. The Declaration was drawn up, in its own terms, "so that this Declaration, constantly present before all members of the social body, shall recall to them ever their rights and their duties; so that the acts of the legislative and

[22]Gordon Wright, p. 31.

[23]On the clash between the king and the Parlements, see Palmer, pp. 86-99, and René Rémond, *La vie politique en France, 1789-1848* (Paris 1965), pp. 31-40. On the Enlightenment, see notably Gordon Wright, pp. 28-39; and the fine synthesis in Jean Touchard and others, vol. II, pp. 383-449.

executive Powers, being compared at every instant with the goal of all political institutions, shall be more respected. . . . ." And the Constitution of 3 September, 1791, "abolishes universally the institutions that infringe upon liberty and the equality of rights—there is no longer any nobility, nor peerage, nor hereditary distinctions, nor distinctions among orders, nor feudal regime. . . . There is no longer, for any part of the Nation, nor for any individual, any privilege, nor any exception to the common law of all Frenchmen."

The revolutionary principle of political legitimacy was not accepted by conservatives, and the revolutionaries were themselves divided; the result was a long period of constitutional instability. Although France was converted almost overnight into a modern state as regards the official principle of legitimacy, it did not thereby achieve a large popular consensus on its basic institutions. The transformation of French society continued. But the way in which the successive crises of modernization were surmounted was drastically affected by endemic constitutional instability. In turn, the nature of controversy over the regime evolved in response to the pressures of modernization.

4. Modernization and Consensus

Science and technology shape the politics of all modern societies. The development of industry necessarily brings about a redistribution of the active population within the economy. The percentage of the population engaged in agriculture decreases, those remaining on farms are able greatly to expand production in spite of their reduced numbers, and the percentage of the population engaged in industry, services, and administration increases. New social groups form and make claims upon the political system. In terms of historical sequence, these groups are the capitalists and businessmen in general, the managerial class, and the working class. At a later stage of industrialization the scientists and intellectuals become so numerous and important in the society that they also become a distinct force. In France, as in all other nations that have gone or are going through the process of industrialization, the entry of each of these social groups into the political system has posed an acute problem.

The first task is to gain an overall view of the extent to which French society has been reshaped. In French census statistics the active population is classified on the basis of participation in three large sectors of the economy: the primary sector (agriculture, forestry, fishing), the secondary (industry, mining, construction, production of energy), and the tertiary (all other activities, including distribution, administration, and personal services). One century ago the agricultural sector was more important than the other two combined; there were slightly more than two farmers for one

worker and one person in the tertiary sector. In 1964 the agricultural sector
was the least important of the three; the number of persons engaged in
farming had been reduced by almost two-thirds, with corresponding
increases in the other two sectors. The following table summarizes these
trends.[24]

YEARS	1851	1881	1901	1921	1931	1936	1954	1962	1964
Primary sector (%)	53	48	42	43	37	37	28	21	18
Secondary sector (%)	25	27	31	29	33	30	36	38	42
Tertiary sector (%)	22	25	27	28	30	33	36	41	40

One striking feature of contemporary France is the swift pace of social
change. In the ten-year period from 1954 to 1964 the number of people
engaged in agriculture declined by almost 40 percent, while the number of
those in the secondary and tertiary sectors increased by about 15 percent.
The political implications of these trends are obvious. The peasantry is now
the smallest of the major social groups. Given their minority position, the
peasants must make their claims upon the political system mainly through
interest groups rather than through political parties seeking to form a
political majority. Although the industrial workers have become more
numerous, they still do not constitute a majority by themselves. Only through
alliance with either the peasantry or elements of the middle classes can they
form a majority. Not only are the middle classes—business, proprietary,
managerial, and professional groups—important because of the functions
they perform, they are also a massive political force, about as numerous as
all workers engaged in industrial production.

France now resembles the other industrial nations of the world, with
roughly the same kind of balance among the three major sectors of the
economy. In 1964 the number of people in the agricultural sector in France
amounted to 18 percent of the total—smaller than in Italy (25 percent), or
Japan (26 percent) or the Soviet Union (34 percent), but larger than in
Germany (12 percent), the United States (8 percent), or Britain (4 percent).
The number of people engaged in the tertiary sector in France was about 41
percent of the total, as compared to 58 percent in the United States, 48
percent in Britain, 42 percent in Japan, 38 percent in Germany, 33 percent in
Italy, and 32 percent in the Soviet Union.[25]

In all other respects as well, French society is displaying the general
characteristics of modernization. The movement of population toward urban
centers has been massive, as is normal. In 1846 the number of people living
in communes of two thousand inhabitants or more amounted to 24 percent

---

[24]Table based on Georges Dupeux, p. 33, and *Tableaux de l'économie française* (Paris 1966),
p. 48a; and *Atlas historique de la France contemporaine* (Paris 1966), p. 45.
[25]All figures are from *Tableaux*, p. 48a.

of the population, and those living in communes of five thousand inhabitants or more to about 17 percent; the comparable figures in 1962 were 62 percent and 55 percent. Particularly striking has been the growth of the Paris metropolitan area as an industrial and administrative center. Almost 20 percent of the nation's population now lives and works in the Paris region, as compared to only about 3 percent a century ago.[26]

Although the outlines of French social structure are like those of most other industrialized nations, the manner in which that social structure evolved was quite distinctive. Industrialization in France up to 1815 was slow, and generally a result of the application of English methods in the field of textile manufacture. The way to industrialization had been prepared by the Revolution, which eliminated feudal barriers and created a vast market. But French energies were then directed mainly toward defense of the Republic and the creation of the far-flung Napoleonic empire. The industrial revolution did not begin until about 1815, and even then development was sluggish.

Protected by high tariffs, French businessmen were more interested in financial speculation than in creating mass industries. Aristocratic values were amazingly resilient in France after the Revolution, when the successful bourgeois sought to adopt the life-style of the class that had been virtually wiped out as an economic force. David S. Landes has emphasized the contrast between the British and French entrepreneurial classes throughout the eighteenth century: "What distinguished the British economy . . . was an exceptional sensitivity and responsiveness to pecuniary opportunity. This was a people fascinated by wealth and commerce." The French business class was handicapped by its greater attentiveness to what was considered gracious living. Landes speaks of the development within the French body social of "psychological and institutional antibodies to the virus of modernization."[27]

French industrialization was delayed, not prevented. Production increased regularly in the period from 1815 to 1848. Coal production and pig iron output went up dramatically, and a start was made in the metallurgical and chemical industries and in the building of railways. In all spheres, economic development following the English pattern, but at a slower pace and less energetically.

Another phase of economic development began under the Second

[26]Figures on urbanization from Dupeux, pp. 20-21, 23-26.

[27]Citations from David S. Landes, "Technological Change and Development in Western Europe, 1750-1914," in H. J. Habakkuk and M. Postan, The Industrial Revolution and After, IV of The Cambridge Economic History of Europe, pp. 298, 463. On early industrialization in France, see J. H. Clapham, The Economic Development of France and Germany, 1815-1914 (Cambridge 1955); Georges Dupeux, pp. 35-48; and Gordon Wright, pp. 196-209, 343-353.

Empire, when industrial production roughly doubled between 1852 and 1870. The government of Louis Napoleon tried deliberately to create favorable conditions for capitalist development, and succeeded rather well. The banking system was adapted to the needs of an industrializing economy, providing a channel from the public and its savings to the entrepreneurs. This was also a period of adventurous experimentation by French businessmen, who introduced many innovations in the merchandising field (including the department store) and thoroughly modernized the metallurgical and textile industries. In addition, an extensive railway network was constructed. After a slow start, France seemed well on the way to catching up to and surpassing Great Britain. By 1870 France's industrial production exceeded the value of its agricultural production, and its economic growth in the preceding fifty years had been second only to that of Britain.

After the defeat by Prussia in 1870 and the establishment of the Third Republic, there was a period of relatively slow economic growth that lasted until the 1890's. In a sense this was an understandable consequence of losing the war. As J. H. Clapham has remarked, "But the war of 1870, even more the Parisian turmoil of 1871 and the long years of national gloom and self-distrust which followed, chilled the confident ardor without which no nation ever did great work—even in factory building. France was doubting the value of her government and her Republican institutions, and doubting of her own destiny, for the best part of a generation after 1870. Contrast the self-confident, not to say self-satisfied, frame of mind in the England of 1860, in the Germany of 1875, in the United States of always." [28]

There followed, from 1895 to World War I, a period of economic development comparable to that under the Second Empire. From 1870 to 1914 industrial production tripled and real wages went up by some 50 percent. The discovery and exploitation of vast iron ore deposits in Lorraine gave a new impetus to French industrialization. At the same time, a protectionist agricultural policy largely shielded the peasants from the challenge of competition. It was during this period that the contrast between the "two Frances"—one modern and dynamic and the other pre-industrial and static—become significantly sharp. From 1924 to 1930 there was a brief period of rapid economic growth, averaging about 4 percent a year, and then the general decline of the depression. After the destruction of World War II, it took several years simply to regain the pre-war level. But beginning in 1950 there began a new era of rapid growth—about 6 percent a year, far larger than in any other period of French history. Between 1949 and 1965, for example, annual production of steel increased from 9 million tons to 20 million; of automobiles from 286,000 to 1.6 million; of agricultural

[28]Clapham, p. 233.

tractors from 17,000 to 90,000; of housing units from 51,000 to 412,000. National revenue in this period more than doubled, and industrial production as a whole almost tripled.[29] From this brief survey, several points stand out. (1) Rapid economic growth took place from 1815 to 1848 (Restoration and July Monarchy), from 1851 to 1870 (Second Empire), from 1895 to 1914, from 1924 to 1930 (Third Republic), and from 1950 to the present (Fourth and Fifth Republics). There were thus periods of relative stagnation and of vitality under both monarchies and republics. (2) Until recently the size of the nonindustrial and even pre-industrial sector in the French economy was large compared to that of countries like Britain, Germany, and the United States. (3) Since 1950 there has been a real breakthrough in the attitude of businessmen and intellectuals toward modernization. The pre-industrial mentality glorified individuality and family enterprise ("mon verre est petit, mais je bois dans mon verre," etc.). This has largely given way to an affirmative view of science, technology, and industrial progress. But the political consequences of these developments are still obscure. The Fourth Republic was overthrown after eight years of impressive economic progress. The Fifth Republic has been beset periodically by grave crises, and its constitution has been under challenge by opposition parties from the day of its promulgation. Rapid modernization since 1950 has brought no discernible consensus concerning the basic values and institutions of the political system.

The French experience of modernization calls attention to the importance of the timing of crises, and the manner in which new social groups have entered upon the political scene. The brutal change of the Revolution produced a series of shock waves in public opinion that made it exceedingly difficult to establish solid political institutions. The aristocracy refused to accept the Republic, and the beneficiaries of the Revolution were restive under monarchy. Even after the establishment of a durable compromise in the form of the Third Republic, the rival forces continued to promulgate incompatible views concerning the way in which the Republic ought to be structured. In short, the French by an accident of timing had to confront the staggering problems of industrialization without the benefit of a stable political system. Industrialization took place anyway, and a series of regimes was able to help the process along.

Fitful industrialization created special problems for the leaders of the emergent social groups. In France, as elsewhere, the first great political crisis of modernization involved the relationship between the rising capitalist and

---

[29]On late industrialization in France, Gordon Wright, pp. 453-463, 548-567. Also, Charles P. Kindleberger, *Economic Growth in France and Britain* (Cambridge, Mass. 1964). Kindleberger identifies the periods of economic expansion as 1851-68, 1879-82, 1896-1913, 1919-29, and since 1949.

managerial classes on the one hand, and the landed aristocracy on the other. These relations were marked by hostility on the part of the aristocracy and lack of firm purpose on the part of the business elements. Instead of fusing, the two social groups tended to distrust one another, even though the middle class emulated the life-style of their social "betters." The same pattern was repeated in the second great political crisis of modernization—the relationship between the established business class and the increasingly articulate and politically conscious proletariat. Once again there was hostility on the one side and distrust on the other. There was established a tradition, then, of alienation rather than participation, of rejection rather than acceptance.[30]

France is now going through a period of rapid change comparable to that under the Second Empire and Third Republic. One novel aspect of this change is the spectacular rise of the intellectuals, managers, and highly skilled workers as a new kind of professional elite. Will the latest phase of modernization bring about a new spirit in politics, or will the rising social groups perpetuate the tradition of alienation, rejection, and hostility inherited from the earlier confrontations? It has long been the hope of Gaullists that politics would become more pragmatic and less ideological as modernization proceeds. But the Gaullist regime has not been able to provide for meaningful participation in the political system by the major social groups. Instead of being readily and willingly absorbed into the new industrial society, large numbers of university students and intellectuals have repudiated the regime, the educational system, and even the society itself. Modernization in France has always provoked movements of anarchistic and nihilistic protest. Like the Republic itself, modernization has enemies on both the Left and the Right. Whether a modern Republic can survive and advance in a divided society has been, and remains, the chief interest and potential tragedy of French politics.

The democratic or liberal prototype for modernization in Asia, Africa, and Latin America may prove to be France, rather than Britain or the United States. In most developing countries that aspire to parliamentary democracy today, as in France in the past, there is an absence of consensus over the basic institutions of the nation. At the same time there is a determination on the part of the political elites to modernize their nations as quickly as possible. But pre-industrial attitudes permeate the society; the business class is lacking in entrepreneurial vigor; the civil service and

[30]The entry of major social groups into the political system is dealt with by Gordon Wright, pp. 210-226, 354-365; and in especially suggestive fashion by Georges Dupeux, pp. 104-164, 171-218, 240-278. Shepard B. Clough stresses the importance of the timing of political and social conflict in "Social Structure, Social Values and Economic Growth," E. M. Acomb and M. L. Brown, Jr., eds., *French Society and Culture Since the Old Regime* (New York 1966), pp. 66-84.

military are relatively well organized and are disposed to direct national purposes, and strong Communist and other revolutionary movements signal alienation of workers and intellectuals from the national community. Industrialization is now taking place under conditions of bitter social antagonism and unstable parliamentary institutions in many countries of the "third world." For purposes of comparative analysis the most relevant model among the democratic industrial societies may well be the French experience of modernization.

7

Communism and Russian History

Richard Pipes

The question implied in the title of this paper arose almost the instant the Bolsheviks had assumed authority over Russia. Already in the summer of 1918 a group of scholars and publicists, mostly of a moderately conservative persuasion, brought out in Moscow a volume of essays devoted to this very problem.[1] But it was only after 1920, that is, after the Bolsheviks had firmly ensconced themselves, that the historical roots of Russian communism attracted the intense attention of both émigré and foreign observers. The vast literature on this subject produced in the 1920's and 1930's has not yet been adequately surveyed; indeed, serious scholars have shied away from it, because so much that has been written on the connections between communism and Russia consists of wild pseudo-historical philosophizing. Generalizations about the historiography of the problem must of necessity, therefore, be very tentative. It does appear, however, that the interpretations formulated in the inter-war period fall into two principal schools corresponding to intellectual trends familiar from pre-revolutionary Russian history: Slavophile (or, to be precise, neo-Slavophile) and Westerner.[2]

The Slavophile view, whose most articulate exponent was Nicholas Berdiaev, assumed the uniqueness of Russian culture, laying particular stress on the alleged religiosity of the Russian people, or its "soul." "In the

Reprinted by permission of the University of Washington Press from Donald W. Treadgold, ed., *Soviet and Chinese Communism: Similarities and Differences* (Seattle and London: 1967), pp. 3-23.

[1]*Iz glubiny* (Moscow, 1918). This book was put together on the initiative of Peter Struve, and included many contributors to the well-known symposia, *Problemy idealizma* (1902-3) and *Vekhi* (1909). The opening of the Red Terror in August 1918 prevented its publication. Later on, the stock was distributed by the printers, and at least two copies found their way abroad.

[2]I do not include, of course, theories concerning the Revolution of 1917 as such; nor theories which ascribe communism either to a plot (German, Jewish, etc.) or to historical inevitability.

Russian soul," Berdiaev wrote, "there is a sort of immensity, a vagueness, a predilection for the infinite, such as is suggested by the great plain of Russia."[3] These spiritual qualities attract the Russian toward all kinds of chiliastic movements. In modern times, Russian religiosity has chosen secular outlets: a transposition has taken place "of religious motives and religious psychology into a non-religious and anti-religious sphere, into the region of social problems, so that the spiritual energy of religion has come to flow into social channels, which thereby took on a religious character."[4] To Berdiaev, the Third International was merely a modern counterpart of the Third Rome, the two ideas sharing a common messianic and chiliastic spirit. Communism to him was, of course, an evil, but not an unmitigated one. The movement performed a moral cathartic function in that it liberated humanity from the illusions of a terrestrial paradise. A similar view was advanced by Fedor Stepun, who considered Bolshevism "a historically comprehensible aberration of the religious energy of the Russian people."[5]

The Westerner argument was most convincingly put forward by Peter Struve. Even in the 1890's, when still a Marxist, Struve felt that Russia needed most of all freedom, for only through freedom could she acquire internal stability and the means to develop her potential. He opposed the patriarchal political and agrarian system of autocratic Russia as preventing the emergence among the people of a sense of civic responsibility, respect for law and property, industriousness and thrift (what the Germans call *Tüchtigkeit*), and all the other qualities which he subsumed under "culture" and considered the cause of Europe's greatness. Struve attached particular importance in this connection to capitalism. Capitalism to him was not merely or even primarily an economic phenomenon. It was a cultural phenomenon performing a necessary civilizing function. Despite his (partly deserved) reputation for intellectual inconstancy, Struve remained loyal to this particular view throughout his life. He considered communism to be the consequence of the lack of economic and political freedom in prerevolutionary Russia and therefore of "culture" in the broadest sense of the word. For this he blamed mainly the Imperial government, and secondarily the intelligentsia.[6] The Russian Revolution, as Boris Nolde, a historian of views similar to Struve's, once put it, was the work not of "citizens" but of "subjects."[7]

---

[3]N. Berdyaev, *The Russian Idea* (New York, 1948), p. 2. Has any theory ever been formulated to ascribe "immensity, vagueness, and a predilection for the infinite" to the inhabitants of the plains of Nebraska?

[4]N. Berdyaev, *The Russian Revolution* (London, 1932), p. 10.

[5]F. Stepun, *The Russian Soul and the Revolution* (New York-London, 1935), p. 9.

[6]Among Struve's many scattered writings on the subject, the most important is *Razmyshleniia o Russkoi Revoliutsii*, originally delivered as a talk to officers and sympathizers of the Volunteer Army in Rostov on Don (Nov., 1919), and subsequently (1921) published in Sofia as a pamphlet.

[7]B. Nolde, *L'ancien régime et la Revolution russe* (Paris, 1928), p. viii. The views of P.

The two hypotheses rested on different premises. One held that Russia had turned Communist because she was inherently predisposed that way; the other explained communism by Russia's lack of opportunity to reach a sufficient level of westernization.

In the 1920's and 1930's, the Slavophile view enjoyed for good reasons greater acceptance of the two. To Russian émigrés, it held out the hope that the tragedy which they and their country had experienced had not been in vain; odious as it was, communism fulfilled a great historic task—it was Russia's contribution, her "word." To foreigners, it offered an equally comforting message to the effect that the rest of the world enjoyed immunity from communism since it was a peculiarly national, Russian disease. This argument gained added strength from an old predisposition of Westerners to regard Russia as special and exotic. The writings of Berdiaev on this subject, for all their looseness and confusion, enjoyed for a time great popularity and appeared in many translations.

But history has been unkind to the Slavophiles, and since the end of World War II their views have been steadily losing ground. The spread of communism outside Russia—its conquest of China, and penetration into southeast Asia, the Middle East, Africa, and Latin America—inevitably discredited a theory which treated communism as a by-product of Russian national character. In the late 1940's, one could still read prophecies that communism, as a specifically Russian movement, stood no chance in China, being incompatible with Chinese traditions and habits of thought. But after the Communists had established firm authority in Peking, Chinese traditions and habits of thought notwithstanding, such arguments lost force. For it would be certainly a hopeless task to seek common elements conducive to communism in the national tradition or national ethos of such different countries as Russia, China, and Cuba.

One consequence of this experience has been a shift of consensus from a neo-Slavophile to a modified Westerner position. The theory which may be said to enjoy widest support at present derives from the concept of "modernization," a rather vague term by which is meant the totality of phenomena attending the transition of a society from a traditional (i.e., pre-dominantly agrarian and rural) to a modern (i.e., industrial and urban) one. Some consider communism to be a natural and perhaps even inevitable by-product of this process of modernization; others treat communism as its aberration and the Communists as "scavengers" who take advantage of the upheavals attending it to seize power. This theory tends to minimize the national factor, and in this respect it differs from the customary Slavophile as well as Westerner views presented in the older Russian works, each of

Miliukov also belong to this school, although Miliukov was less philosophical in his interpretations, preferring to deal with concrete historical factors. See his *Rossiia na perelome* (Paris, 1927), vol. I, pp. 1-121.

which rested in its own way on a view of Russia's historic past. Insofar, however, as this theory, too, views communism as a product of specific and to some extent predictable historical factors, it may be regarded as a variant of the Westerner approach. Westerners like Struve and Nolde always denied that communism could or would remain confined to Russia.

We may begin our discussion by stating our acceptance of the concept of "modernization" in a qualified form to allow for national divergences. Like any major historic movement—feudalism, absolutism, liberalism, nationalism—"modernization" takes different forms in different countries, and in the long run the differences are as important as the similarities.

It is clear that since the outbreak of the French Revolution, forces have been set in motion which alter radically the quality of social life. A kind of dynamism has appeared which unsettles institutions, habits, and attitudes of considerable antiquity and wide acceptance. The virtue of the term "modernization" lies in the fact that for all its imprecision, it does suggest the dominant direction which modern life takes: against tradition, against everything that exists simply because it is and always has been. "Modernization" involves the application of some objective criteria to question the worth of institutions, customs, or values. No one has stated this outlook more succinctly than the leader of the Russian so-called nihilists, Dmitrii Pisarev, who in the 1860's advised his followers: "What can be broken should be broken; that which withstands the blow is worthwhile; that which shatters into smithereens is rubbish. In any event, strike right and left, for this cannot and will not cause any harm."

The dynamism implicit in "modernization" places society and state under severe strain. It is evident that some countries withstand this strain better than others. Japan industrialized quickly, westernized its population, waged and lost a major war, and yet managed to preserve its social stability and political continuity. Her neighbor, China, did not. The great powers of Western Europe have, on the whole, weathered the great transformations attending "modernization" surprisingly well, and managed in the nineteenth century—the century of revolutionary changes—to avoid revolution. This is even truer of the smaller states of western and northern Europe, such as the Low Countries and Scandinavia. On the other hand, the countries on the southern and eastern peripheries of Europe, such as Spain and Russia, have had a very difficult time of it.

Whether a given country will or will not go Communist (or, for that matter, Fascist) seems ultimately to depend on its capacity to absorb and assimilate the shocks engendered by "modernization"—in other words, on its viability. The critical question, therefore, is: what makes some political organisms more viable than others? Obviously, a question of such scope cannot be dealt with in this paper, and yet it cannot be altogether avoided, since it is central to the topic.

In premodern conditions, the viability of a political organism depended on factors very different from those that count today. What mattered then was the wealth of the reigning house, its dynastic connections, and its ability to administer. The well-ordered traditional state, that of a Louis XIV and a Frederick II, sought to attain stability through the exercise of control from above. How to achieve such control was one of the principal concerns of applied political science in the age of absolutism. This conception of politics, naturally, tended to deprecate the need for society's participation in affairs of state.

The French Revolution radically altered this traditional conception of the strong and efficient state. It did so less by the force of argument than by the argument of force: less by the cogency of its claims on behalf of the individual than by the effectiveness of its armies. Napoleon proved beyond doubt that a citizen army, organized by mass conscription, could beat the best trained professional regiments. The traditional monarchies of Europe were slow to draw the obvious consequences from this experience, but sooner or later learn they did. The reform movement of vom Stein and his Prussian colleagues, designed to bring the citizenry into more active participation in running the country, were particularly efficacious and laid the foundations of subsequent German hegemony on the continent. They were carried out, it must be noted, not as concessions to popular pressures, let alone to the abstract ideals of liberty and equality, but from considerations of power politics pure and simple.

The defeat of Napoleon and the triumph of old-style absolutism dampened for a while European enthusiasm for reform, but not for long. The revolutions of 1830 and especially those of 1848 paved the way, both in England and on much of the continent, for large-scale reform undertakings. The sixty or seventy years preceding the outbreak of World War I witnessed changes which transformed the mass of the Western population from passive subjects into active citizens. These reforms are generally depicted—and rightly—as "liberal" in the sense that they increased the voice of the ordinary man in public affairs. But it would be a mistake to interpret the increased participation of the citizenry in matters previously reserved for the ruling elite as resulting in a diminution in the power of the state. Quite on the contrary: liberal political and social reform everywhere *increased the power of the state both internally and externally;* and indeed, it was often deliberately undertaken for this purpose.

Space limitations prevent us from citing more than two examples illustrating this contention.

First as concerns the effects of political reform, that is, the introduction of representative government and the extension of the franchise. Already Napoleon I showed how the popular vote, skillfully exploited, could enhance the power of the sovereign: how to manipulate referenda to secure majorities of 99.99 per cent (the referendum on the Constitution of the year VIII held in 1799), and to structure representative institutions so that they became useful adjuncts of the administration. Napoleon III demonstrated even more impressively the authoritarian uses of "liberal" processes and institutions by employing all the then known paraphernalia of political liberalism to establish a personal dictatorship. This example was not lost on Bismarck, whose constitutional reforms, notably the extension of the suffrage to all male Germans—on the face of it, a measure so alien to his authoritarian temper—had been coldly calculated to strengthen the hand of the monarchy against its liberal and socialist opponents. (That his calculation did not quite work out is another matter.) Other European countries also gradually extended the franchise for similar reasons: either to forestall rebellion, or to gain mass support against internal and external enemies. The English Reform Bill of 1867 resulted from a political maneuver of the Conservatives to win public support against the Liberals. Wherever it was introduced, democratic franchise greatly enhanced the stability and power of a country, for it made possible the participation of the mass of citizens in activities, such as war, where it had become essential. It is unlikely that England, France, and Germany could have fought the First World War with quite the same suicidal determination had they been directed by governments of the old absolutist kind.

Education provides another example of the stabilizing consequences of liberalization. The notion that the state was obligated to furnish instruction to its citizenry may have been conceived by religious reformers and philosophers, but it was realized by politicians. The public school system, originated in Prussia and France and adopted by the 1870's in some measure by most European countries, owed its spread, at least in part, to an awareness that an educated citizenry was a source of national strength. Public education could and was used not only to provide the skills required by the modern economic and military establishments but also to imbue the citizenry with a sense of patriotism and respect for law. Through it, the modern state has been able to mold minds in a way that would have been entirely beyond the reach of the traditional absolutist state. By means of its school system, France stimulated a sense of national identity among its peasants and helped produce in 1870-71 popular resistance against the German invaders. The Ottoman government failed when it tried at the same time to promote the ideal of an all-embracing "Ottoman" nationality, for its schools were in the hands of religious groups opposed to modern nationalism.

Political reform and public education are only two forms out of the many that the process of political rejuvenation through liberalism took in the leading countries of Western Europe. One may also mention the establishment of universal military service, political parties, social legislation, labor unions, and consumer cooperatives. These, and similar devices, involved to an unprecedented degree the citizen of the advanced Western countries in the total life of society and state. To appreciate how radical these reforms were, one must abandon some rather prevalent conceptions of the pre-nineteenth-century West. As late as the eighteenth century, the vast majority of Westerners led in the rural areas lives of squalor and brutality, and had virtually no contact with the centers of "Western civilization" located in the cities and manors. How bad things were may be gathered from the fact that at the time of the Industrial Revolution hundreds of thousands of Englishmen preferred to move from the country into the city slums to put themselves at the disposal of a ruthless industrial machine. Bad as conditions were in the early industrial towns, they must have been preferable to those in the villages where the majority of the population resided.[8]

It is this silent, unspectacular upheaval, made possible by nineteenth-century wealth and peace, that saved Western Europe from the violent revolutions which Marx and Engels had prophesied in 1847-48. By 1895, even Engels had to concede that such revolutions were unlikely, and that the road to a better social order lay not by way of the barricade but the voting booth.[9] By pulling the citizenry into partnership, the liberalized European state averted revolution: for were he to destroy the state, the citizen of post-1870 Western Europe would in effect destroy himself.

The transformation of subjects into citizens did not altogether bypass Russia. But here (as in other countries outside the industrial West) the task was greater, the means smaller, and the will weaker; so that in 1914-17, when put to the ultimate test, Russia proved unequal to the challenge.

In the course of the sixteenth and seventeenth centuries, the Muscovite state had evolved a system of monarchial absolutism, which, given the responsibilities confronting the country and the paucity of the means at its disposal, worked surprisingly well. The system rested on the principle of universal service. In theory, and to a large extent in practice, every inhabitant of Muscovite Russia, from the highest to the basest, had to serve the state, either directly (the nobility and to some extent the merchants) or indirectly (the peasants). It was not only the peasant who was enserfed in the sixteenth and seventeenth centuries—it was all of society. According to the service system, the rights of Russian subjects were the function of their obligations: rights derived from duties and did not exist outside of them.[10]

---

[8]The older view that the mass migration of Englishmen into the cities in the late eighteenth and early nineteenth centuries resulted from the Enclosure Acts is no longer tenable in the light of modern research.

[9]Introduction to Marx's *Class Struggle in France,* in K. Marx and F. Engels' *Sochineniia,* vol. XVI, part 2 (Moscow, 1936), pp. 463-486.

[10]The only significant exception to this rule were monasteries.

Naturally, such a system could not tolerate "society" as a counterpart to state; society as a whole and in its parts constituted an element of the state machine. The social reforms of Peter the Great, notably his Table of Ranks, were from this point of view not innovations, but efforts to improve the operations of the traditional Muscovite manner of government.[11]

The main reason for this system of government must be sought probably in the immensity of the task confronting the Russian medieval monarchy. The Muscovite state was the largest empire in the world, the territory over which it claimed sovereignty being several times the size of all Europe. The administration of such a vast area would have taxed the resources of the richest government. Russia's means were quite inadequate for this purpose, the country being short of capital and civil servants. To collect taxes and to raise an army, the monarchy had to have recourse to a variety of drastic measures designed to keep the population in place and mutually responsible for the fulfillment of its state obligations. To make matters worse, the long eastern and southern frontiers of the empire were wide open to incursions of Turkic groups, some of which claimed title as successors to the Mongols and, as such, sovereigns of Russia. The Crimean Tatars time and again invaded the territory of Muscovite Rus', looting and burning it with impunity. Because of this vulnerable frontier, Muscovite Russia may be said to have been in a state of constant siege. The system of state service was evolved to meet these problems. It was generally accepted as indispensable. Even the so-called boyar opposition to autocracy did not clamor for exemption from service but merely for the right to be consulted.

The dissolution of this brand of absolutism may be said to have begun with the death of Peter the Great (1725). By this time the eastern and southern frontiers had become stabilized, the Turkic inhabitants no longer offering a serious threat to the modernized Russian army garrisoned in chains of fortress towns. At the same time, the monarchy weakened because Peter had abolished the law of succession, and thereby made the Russian throne a tool of guard regiments and court intriguers, often financed by interested foreign parties. The choice of these groups usually fell on children and women, neither of whom were likely to make full use of the enormous prerogatives vested in the Russian crown. As a result, from 1730 onward, Russian society underwent a process of "*raskreposhchenie*" or "emancipation" from state control. The process proceeded by fits and starts, the monarchy sometimes taking back what it had given, but its general course was unmistakable and irreversible.[12]

The first social group to win emancipation was the gentry. The gentry

---

[11]"Service" in this context is different from that familiar in feudalism, since it was an instrument of royal absolutism.

[12]This subject constitutes the major theme of V. Leontovitsch's provocative *Geschichte des Liberalismus in Russland* (Frankfurt am Main, 1957).

took advantage of every crisis in St. Petersburg, and especially those attending changes of monarchs, to win easements of their obligations. In 1762 they finally secured complete release from all compulsory service. Catherine the Great, being foreign and lacking a good claim to the crown, had special reason to please this group. Her Charter to the Nobility of 1785, confirming the gentry's freedom from service obligations as well as their ownership of land (originally given them on condition of service) and granting them new privileges (e.g., trial by peers, exemption from corporal punishment, freedom to travel abroad, etc.), created in Russia the first social group with rights independent of duties. The year 1762 and 1785 marked thus the beginning of Russian "society" as a counterpoise to the Russian state.

The process of social emancipation resumed in the 1860's in the guise of the so-called Great Reforms. The defeat in the Crimean War had persuaded the monarchy and some of its conservative officials that a state which accorded society no place was intrinsically weak. The reforms were intended to remedy this situation by creating for private citizens a narrow but well-defined sphere of public activity. In this sense, the reforms are rightly regarded as liberal. Had they been continued, imperial Russia might well have acquired the requisite stability and made a more or less peaceful transition to modern statehood.[13] But the fact is they were not continued. Indeed, the tendency in the last four decades of the nineteenth century was to limit even those rights which had been granted to society. In the end, the reforms of Alexander II did not bring society into partnership with the state or even develop in it a sense of genuine involvement in the state. Among the educated, having at first whetted appetites they produced frustration and resentment, while among the mass of inhabitants they failed to shake the traditional indifference to public affairs.

It is not my intention to belittle the reforms of Alexander II. The reforms fulfilled an important role if only because having done away with serfdom they made possible the emergence of a common Russian citizenship. In the *zemstva* and city councils, as well as in the courts, the ordinary citizen for the first time in Russian history received an opportunity of working for his country's benefit: earlier, the very demand for such an opportunity had been considered seditious. But surely the reforms did not go far enough to have been of significant political benefit.

.

It may be argued, of course, that the Hapsburg Empire did undergo liberalization in the second half of the nineteenth century, and yet it too in the end collapsed. But the Hapsburg Empire was intrinsically weaker than the Russian Empire because of the antagonisms among its nationalities. Russia's nationality problem was much less critical because the great Russians constituted some 45 per cent of the population, and with the kindred Ukrainians and Belorussians, 65 per cent of the population, whereas in the Austro-Hungarian Empire, the Germans constituted only 24 per cent. Moreover, Austria lost the war.

The liberation of the serfs in 1861 completed the process of *raskreposhchenie* of society begun ninety-nine years earlier with the gentry. An act of bold statesmanship, it contained, however, safeguards which vitiated its political value. The worst of these was the subordination of the peasant to the commune. The economic drawbacks of communal landholding are too familiar to require elaboration. But the political effects of this measure were no less debilitating. By denying the peasant the opportunity to own his land, the government deprived him also of the best school of political education. For the average citizen everywhere, the management of property, especially real estate, represents the main and sometimes only exercise in practical politics. It brings him in direct contact with legislatures and courts, local as well as central, and develops in him a sense of political pragmatism: a property owner may not like the authorities who tax him but he cannot help being concerned with their activities. Furthermore, by being tied to the commune, the peasant remained in an inferior social condition: he was still a peasant rather than a Russian. When the country entered World War I, a large proportion of its rural population lacked an elementary sense of citizenship or of national identity. Some peasants even wondered in August 1914 whether the declaration of war affected their own villages. The full consequences of this immaturity became apparent only after two and a half years of war when military discipline dissolved. At that time, Lenin, Trotsky, and Bolshevik agitators could persuade the peasant to desert the ranks and head back for the village, whereas those who appealed to his sense of patriotism with little success.

The organs of self-rule, the *zemstva* and city councils established in 1864, also proved inadequate to the task. These institutions had been introduced to secure society's assistance in carrying out responsibilities of local government for which St. Petersburg lacked the means. Although their competence was restricted to nonpolitical concerns, they might still have performed an important political function had they not been hamstrung in every possible way both in their original constitution and in subsequent performance. The mere fact that the leaders of the *zemstva* and city councils were forbidden to organize nationally indicated the mistrust the authorities felt toward them. In the 1880's and 1890's their sphere of competence, narrow to begin with, was further limited by the bureaucracy. The imperial government, instead of availing itself of the good will available in the provinces to bolster its position, constantly antagonized the organs of self-rule, and in the end transformed them into centers of resistance. It is only thanks to the innate moderation of the men who ran these institutions that the friction between the organs of self-rule and the bureaucracy did not break out in the open before 1904.

Even the judiciary reform, by all accounts the best of the reforms of Alexander II, was not allowed to become an effective instrument of civic education. Having tasted defeat before jury courts the government transferred trials involving the broad category of political crimes to the jurisdiction of administrative courts. As a result, Russian society was excluded from participating in judiciary proceedings involving the security of the state. Even more pernicious from this point of view was the practice introduced in 1892 of placing vast areas of the country under martial law as a means of suspending the normal operation of the courts.[14]

But the worst sin of the government lay in its adamant refusal to concede the country a constitution and a parliament. Its position on this issue was quite untenable. By the end of the nineteenth century all the European countries, including conservative Germany and Austria, operated under constitutional and parliamentary regimes. Even the Ottoman Empire, that synonym for backwardness and despotism, had made an attempt in this direction in 1876—a whole thirty years before Russia! The Russian government's commitment to autocratic monarchy went so far that it rejected out of hand even the innocuous Slavophile proposals for a consultative assembly to inform the tsar of the wishes of the "land." By this policy, the government punished itself much more than society. From 1874 on, it came under constant attack from a small but determined group of revolutionaries. Had Russia possessed a parliament of some kind, the government would have certainly enjoyed its support in the struggle against sedition of the overwhelming majority of the deputies. Instead, the government had to fight the revolution alone and unaided. Even if the public rejected the methods and aims of the revolutionaries, it did not feel affected, and perhaps derived some satisfaction from the discomfiture of the authorities.

All the political flaws of the Great Reforms—those of commission no less than those of omission—derived ultimately from a deep-seated mistrust of the population. Centuries of treating the country as a "command" and its inhabitants as servitors had accustomed the government to regard any sign of vitality on the part of its subjects as a threat to its existence. It was convinced the emancipated peasants would turn into bandits unless tied to the commune, that the *zemstva* and city councils would encroach on its sovereign authority unless strictly controlled, that juries would always decide in favor of the defendants, and that parliament would stand in permanent opposition. The government sensed the need for society's support, but did not really dare to invite it. The spectacle of social and political conflict in Western Europe reinforced this negative attitude.

The necessity of bringing the Russian state and society together is apparent not only by hindsight. In the second half of the nineteenth century a number of prominent Russian publicists realized it and constantly clamored for it. Among them was Iurii Samarin, a leading Slavophile, who pleaded for closer ties between the monarchy and the mass of the population,

[14]See Marc Szeftel, "Personal Inviolability in the Legislation of the Russian Absolute Monarchy," *American Slavic and East European Review,* Feb., 1958, pp. 1-24.

especially the peasantry. His philosophy of "revolutionary conservatism," derived in large measure from the German State Socialists, called for an authoritarian but dynamic monarchy committed to social reform. Another was Boris Chicherin. As a Right Hegelian, Chicherin believed in the strong state; but he also felt that a state could not be strong when it encroached upon spheres of activity best left to society and the individual citizen. But neither Samarin nor Chicherin was listened to. The former died in emigration an embittered man, while Chicherin suffered oblivion in his own lifetime (as well as since), being rejected by the conservatives for wanting to weaken the state, and by the liberals for wanting to strengthen it.

Had the imperial regime followed Leont'ev's advice and "frozen" itself, it might have succeeded for a long time with this policy. But the government felt itself committed to westernization, and allowed dynamic "modernizing" forces to penetrate and undermine its authority. Aspiring to the status of a major world power, it reformed its army, introduced public education, constructed railroads, and did many other things incompatible with its rigid and conservative political philosophy. It both westernized the country and refused to let westernization take its course.

The inconsistency of the imperial policy appeared most vividly in the realm of cultural policy. The government never made a serious effort to prevent the influx into Russia of Western ideas, including those of an unmistakably radical tendency. (It is common knowledge, for example, that the translation of Marx's *Capital* appeared in Russia with the imprimatur of the censorship, but it is perhaps less known that both the first [1872] and the second [1885] volumes were printed in the typography of the Imperial Ministry of Transport.) Utilitarianism, positivism, anarchism, socialism, social Darwinism, and other ideologies were freely allowed to penetrate into Russia; and being in stark contrast to the official policy of the regime, inevitably widened the cleavage between state and society.[15] On the one hand stood the regime with its officialdom, on the other that amorphous body of public-minded citizens known as the intelligentsia. The regime made no attempt to conciliate the intelligentsia by attracting it into positions of responsibility. Deprived of a chance to acquire a sense of political realism, the intelligentsia tended to become more and more estranged, and to view its relationship to the government as one of irreconcilable hostility. The irresponsibility of the educated combined with the anarchism of the uneducated created an obvious threat to national survival—a fact noted by the contributors to the celebrated symposium *Vekhi* in 1909.

---

[15] The frontiers of imperial Russia were open to travel, and many Russians took advantage of this fact to make extensive trips in foreign countries. In one decade (1872-81) three million Russian citizens went abroad; in the year 1900, 200,000 Russians traveled outside their country for an average of eighty days. See B. Ischchanian, *Die ausländischen Elemente in der russischen Volkswirtschaft* (Berlin, 1913), p. 5n. I am indebted to Mr. Robert C. Williams for calling my attention to this source.

The advent of industrialization compounded the problems created by the estrangement of the peasantry and the intelligentsia. In a single decade —1890-1900—the numbers of Russian industrial workers doubled. These workers were not the grey mass they are often assumed to be. In 1897, 58 per cent of Russian industrial workers could read; among the skilled workers, such as the St. Petersburg metallurgists, the percentage of literates reached 73 per cent.[16] (It may be noted that the ratio of literates among recruits entering the Russian army in 1913 exceeded 70 per cent.) These workers, especially the first generation, do not seem to have been interested in politics of any sort, let alone in revolution. But the restrictions under which they lived drove them inexorably into opposition. They were forbidden to organize trade unions or even to form circles for mutual assistance and self-education. By trying to keep workers in a condition similar to that of the peasants, the government in effect opened the doors of factories to socialists. Much as the workers distrusted the socialists, they had no other allies in their struggle for better wages and working conditions, and secondary education. Had Russian labor been given an opportunity to develop in the open, there is every reason to expect that it would have evolved in as moderate a fashion as its counterparts in England or Germany. The enormous success of the police-sponsored labor unions (*zubatovshchina*) provides adequate proof of the essentially pacific, apolitical trend of Russian labor.

We could compound such illustrations showing the conflict between the government's principles and attitudes on the one hand, and the practical consequences of its commitment to westernization on the other. They stood behind the tug-of-war between the regime and all elements of society that erupted after 1900 and culminated in the Revolution of 1905.

The Revolution of 1905 appeared to the government as a calamity and the end of Russia; but it could have well marked the salvation of the imperial government, as the revolutions of 1848 had saved Europe in the long run from greater upheavals. The Constitution of 1906, given as a concession to avoid the complete breakdown of authority, was a workable arrangement. For all its limitations, it was not a "sham," as has been claimed.[17] It gave society, through its elected representatives, a voice in domestic legislation, as well as a forum from which the government and its officials could be criticized without fear of reprisals. The Duma had no precedent in the Russian past, but the country took to it with enthusiasm. By giving in the first election in its history a majority to Constitutional-Democrats, the party of constitutional action *par excellence,* it demonstrated its acceptance of the system.

But the imperial government and the bureaucracy treated the Duma from the beginning as an affront, a living reminder of its humiliation in

[16]A. G. Rashin, *Formirovanie rabochego klassa Rosii* (Moscow, 1958), pp. 584, 591.

[17]Max Weber, *Russlands Übergang zum Scheinkonstitutionalismus, Beilage, Archiv für Sozialwissenschaft und Sozialpolitik,* vol. XXIII, No. 1 (1906).

October 1905. The premature dissolution of the first two Dumas, even if permitted by the fundamental laws, was a display of contempt for the nation's representatives. Even more so was the unconstitutional reform of the electoral law carried out in 1907 to assure the preponderance of conservative deputies. Such actions encouraged extreme groups, especially on the left, who from the start had maintained that the constitution was a fraud.

Already in 1906, when the government's bad faith became apparent farsighted Russians predicted dire consequences. The following passage, written by Struve in the spring of 1906, bears eloquent testimony of this fear:

> As before, the leading, most powerful, and immense revolutionary force is the government itself. In its stubborn refusal to concede authority to the only element still capable of reviving the country and establishing in it a stable order, the government broadcasts in the country sparks of indignation, decomposition, and anarchy. These people do not know the most important thing about the art of politics—to make decisions in time and with bold and direct *actions* to anticipate and regulate *events*. The leading party in the Duma [i.e., the Constitutional Democrats] still enjoys enough moral and political respect in the country to be able to furnish authority; it still—and this is important—believes in itself. Ignoring this unique constructive power in the country, the government aggravates anarchy, and in this anarchy may exhaust itself, burn out and perish that force which still has the capacity to organize the country and save the monarchy.
>
> The Constitutional Democratic Party may yet suffer in the course of the Russian Revolution the fate of the other, more moderate movement [i.e., landed conservatives]. Now it is too late to call to power Shipov. On January 9, 1905 it was still possible. Similarly, the moment has not yet come, but it may, or, more precisely, must come when it will be too late to call to power [the Constitutional-Democrats] Muromtsev, Petrunkevich, and Miliukov, when they, too, will be powerless to keep the stream of the revolution within the confines of normal development, when the future waves of an irrepressible anger of the masses, accumulated over the centuries, boiling and foaming, will inundate the ancient structures of the Russian monarchy.
>
> There is one additional dangerous symptom. Earlier, there had been blind faith in the political omnipotence of the Tsar; he could do anything. But this faith, if not entirely calm, was at least passive. It helped the people not to move mountains, but patiently to bear the misery of political and social oppression.
>
> It was a conservative faith and on it rested immovable autocratic Russia. Today, this passive, blind faith has been extinguished in the soul of the people; it has been replaced by another faith, also blind, but active. The people still believe in political miracles, but they do so not with the quiet, passive faith of a child, but with the active, violent faith of a youth, inflamed by passion. Yesterday, this youth believed, and perhaps even today he still believes, that the Duma can do everything; tomorrow, he will believe that he himself, or his creation, the Constituent Assembly, will accomplish miracles. One may contemptuously shrug one's shoulders at such a simple faith in the miraculous force of political institutions; one can and even must refute and fight it; but one cannot fail to see

in it a mighty destructive force capable of sweeping everything from its path. This destructive force can be fought only through the most rapid possible transition to political forms capable of giving the people in the shortest time the maximum of political education and self-education.[18]

If, despite this inherent weakness, Russia carried on the war as long as it did, the reason must be sought in the conciliatory attitude of the Duma and moderate public leaders. Carried away by patriotic zeal, they buried their disagreements with the imperial government, and threw their prestige behind it. The committees formed by the Duma in 1914-15 to organize production and supply proved essential to the war effort. Yet even now, in the midst of the war which had exposed the woeful inadequacy of its means, the government chose to snub the elected representatives of its citizenry. When, in the autumn of 1915, it prorogued the Duma, it sealed its own fate. The abdication of Nicholas II a year and a half later was, from the perspective of history, an inevitable consequence of the government's refusal to take the Duma into partnership in the conduct of war.

The tsar's abdication threw Russia into anarchy. Deprived of direction from above, the bureaucratic apparatus simply dissolved; there was no one to replace it, because the country had not been permitted to develop institutions capable of assuming responsibility for its administration in time of need. The peasantry, in and out of uniform, now gave vent to all its suppressed resentments. Its destructive fury in 1917-18 was directed not so much against the imperial regime, nobility, or church, as against all that had been created in Russia since the early eighteenth century: cities, industry, learning, manners—in a word, all that Western "culture" they had not been able to share. Memoirs of participants in the Revolution abound in incidents illustrating this mood. In late 1917, General Denikin, traveling in disguise to the Don to join the Volunteer Army, was astonished and terrified by it:

> First of all [I noticed] everywhere a flood of boundless hatred for people as well as ideas; for everything that was socially and intellectually above the mob, that carried the smallest trace of prosperity, even for inanimate objects that betokened some level of culture alien or inaccessible to the mob. In this feeling one could discern direct anger accumulated over the centuries, brutalization caused by three years of war, and hysteria stimulated by revolutionary leaders . . . The psychology of the mob gave no indication of striving to rise to a higher level of life; dominant was one desire: to grab or destroy.[19]

Awareness of this temper had a very discouraging effect on all those interested in re-establishing law and order. Had the mass revolt aspired to concrete aims, it might have been satisfied and soon stilled. But there was something

---

[18] P. Struve, "Skazka po belogo bychka," *Svoboda i kul'tura*, No. 8, May 31, 1906, pp. 606-7.

[19] A. Denikin, *Ocherki russkoi smuty* (Paris, 1922), vol. II, pp. 147-148.

elemental in this anti-Western, anti-modern explosion, and many felt that it had to spend itself before order could be reimposed.

There were in Russia in 1917-20 three potential contenders for power: the liberals (among them, moderate conservatives and socialists), the generals, and the Jacobin radicals. The *ancien régime*, it may be noted, never offered the slightest threat of a restoration. In 1917, its innumerable Grand Dukes simply retired from public life to their estates or to the West, and consistently spurned invitations to join the anti-Bolshevik struggle. The unconcern of the members of the imperial family for the fate of Russia is one of the more striking features of the Revolution.

The liberals tried to hold the authority which had devolved upon them with the abdication of the tsar, and failed. The story of the Provisional Government is familiar and requires no recapitulation. Ultimately, the liberals may be said to have lost out because they lacked the will to power: precisely because they wanted to hold power, not to exercise it. Russian liberals, like their counterparts in other authoritarian states, had been so accustomed to fighting the government that they failed to develop the political instincts necessary to run a country. The collapse of Russian liberalism in 1917 was not so different from that of German liberalism in the 1920's, or Spanish liberalism in the 1930's. Liberalism, as a theory of freedom, by its very nature operates best within a stable political environment; it is not well suited to the task of establishing political stability.

The generals seemed to have a better chance. Indeed, from the summer of 1917 onward, the country expected a "Bonapartist" coup. Russian intellectuals liked to believe in the "inexorable laws of history," and, being well versed in the story of the French Revolution, looked for a repetition of the 18th Brumaire. This historical miscalculation accounted in large measure for Kerensky's worst error: the alliance in late summer 1917 with the radicals against the so-called "danger from the right." But the anticipated coup never came (the Kornilov incident hardly deserves the name), and Bonapartism proved to have been largely an imaginary threat. The Russian generals turned out to be remarkably apolitical. The leaders of the White Armies displayed neither political acumen nor interest, being content to leave politics to the casual assortment of intellectuals, mostly liberal or liberal-socialist, who had gathered around them. Had there been an effective Russian conservative movement, the generals undoubtedly would have rallied behind it. They had neither the ability nor the ambition to create such a movement themselves.[20]

There is another factor to keep in mind in connection with the army. In dealing with the Russian Revolution, one concentrates so heavily on its

---

[20]It would be interesting to find what factors in the social background or professional training of Russian generals accounted for their disinterest in politics.

internal aspects that one forgets the preoccupation of the time with war. The officers were concerned not with Russia's political regime as such, but with fighting the Germans, Austrians, and Turks. When they first organized the Volunteer Army, it was with the intention of reactivating the front. (Later on, they joined the Red Army in droves for similar patriotic reasons to expel the Poles.) Their anti-German feeling was very strong, one may almost say obsessive. Now, in 1918, the Germans were the only force capable of dislodging the Bolsheviks. They were at the point of doing so (June-July, 1918) and even put out various feelers to army leaders and right-wing politicians. But these feelers were rejected out of hand, and the Germans had no choice but to continue backing, militarily and financially, the Bolshevik government in which they were losing confidence. The anti-German nationalism of the army at a time when alliance with the Germans offered the only hope of overthrowing the Soviet government was no mean factor in the ultimate outcome of the Revolution.

When we survey the political situation in 1917 and 1918, we find no one in Russia except Lenin willing to assume political responsibility. The moderates reigned but did not rule, preferring to entrust all decisions to a future Constituent Assembly. The generals wanted to continue the war at all costs, and left politics to the politicians. The imperial family withdrew, turning its back on Russia. The question was not so much who would succeed in the struggle for power, as who would engage in it—who would assume the authority that lay unclaimed and unwanted.[21] The celebrated incident in the early summer of 1917 when Lenin, hearing an orator assert that no party in Russia wanted to assume responsibility, shouted, "There is such a party!", illustrates better than any generalization the political vacuum of the time.

It is tempting to discover in Lenin deep Russian traits, but close analysis of his actions and thoughts reveals little that can be described as typically Russian. He had undoubtedly learned a great deal from the terrorists of the *Narodnaia volia*, and his loathing of compromise reveals a characteristic trait of the Russian intelligentsia. But he lacked the really fundamental qualities of a Russian *intelligent:* love for the "people," respect for learning (he detested "professors" most of all), belief in progress, kindness and generosity. His temperament and outlook had in them more of Wilhelmian Germany than imperial Russia. Of course, one can find in Russian revolutionary history individual forerunners of Lenin; but there are even more of them in the revolutionary history of nineteenth-century France.

[21]The absence of any formal "power seizure" in October 1917 is particularly stressed in S. Melgunov's excellent but paradoxically titled monograph, *Kak Bol'sheviki zakhvatili vlast'* ("How the Bolsheviks Seized Power"; Paris, 1953).

The question of the relationship of communism to Russian history contains really two questions: why did the imperial state collapse? and, why did the successor state assume the form that it did? To the first question one may formulate the following answer: The imperial government, having initiated for reasons of power and prestige technical, economic, and educational modernization, refused to soften the resultant shocks by allowing corresponding modernization of society and the political apparatus. To the second question it may be replied that when the imperial government collapsed, anarchy was inevitable, because the state had no political underpinnings to support it once the monarchy was gone; and that the only way out of anarchy in Russia, as elsewhere, was an authoritarian regime. The authoritarian regime inevitably, unconsciously slipped back into the habits and institutions which had prevailed in Muscovite Russia, its only available model. It reharnessed society back into the service of the state. Communism undid two centuries of slow emergence of Russian society as a counterpoise to the government. It is in this sense, it seems to me, and only in this sense that one can speak of the historic roots of Russian communism.

8

The New Germanies: Restoration, Revolution, Reconstruction

Ralf Dahrendorf

It is often taken for granted that the German history of the past hundred years is a sequence of discontinuities. To look for consistency in modern Germany's history, let alone a guiding principle, seems hopeless in view of the extreme changes in her political make-up. But it is always risky to confuse the letter of a Constitution with "legal reality," to confuse political institutions with the social structure on which they are based. For, on closer inspection, the changes in German *society* in the course of the last century—as against Germany's political institutions—do indeed reveal a consistent and recognisable principle. The history of German society since the mid-19th century can be understood as a painful—sometimes slow, sometimes more rapid—but persistent movement towards modernity and away from the traditional authoritarian structures of pre-Enlightenment and pre-industrial days. Kant's famous definition of the Enlightenment—"the German's escape from his self-caused backwardness"—might not be a bad description of German social development over the last century, were it not that a neat formula of this kind extenuates the suffering, the violence, and the terror that were involved.

To-day German social historians tend to agree with Thorstein Veblen's thesis (put forward as early as 1915) that modern German society must be understood in terms of the peculiar form the process of industrialisation assumed in Germany. Whereas in Britain and France the industrial revolution was accompanied, or even preceded, by a bourgeois revolution, Germany's famous "revolution from within" (as Heine was the first to call it)—*i.e.*, German Idealism—proved a poor substitute for the power-claims successfully advanced elsewhere by a self-confident bourgeoisie. Germany's rapid industrialization—in three waves during the 1850s, 1870s, and 1890s—did not lead to the social and political hegemony of a new

Reprinted by permission of the author and publisher from *Encounter*. XXII (April 1964). pp. 50-58.

enterpreneurial class. Instead, an older ruling class—largely Prussian, consisting of aristocratic civil servants, officers, diplomats and landowners—strengthened its position. There were economic reasons for this—e.g. the development of agricultural prices—but the causes of this surprising development were, above all, social. Members of the new entrepreneurial class were less interested in being represented in Parliament than in receiving the honorary title of *Leutnant* on their 60th birthdays—in being able to document, with a *"von"* before their name, that they had found recognition in the eyes of the old upper class. It is typical of this development that the science of Political Economy was transformed, in Germany, into something called *Nationalökonomie*, and that German liberals became known as National Liberals. If by "capitalism" we understand the social and political predominance of the private entrepreneur, industrial Germany in the late 19th century was not capitalist, but presented rather the paradox of a feudal-industrial society.

This odd combination of modernity in economic affairs and backwardness in social affairs—unique at the time—had important political effects. Representative government was the indispensable instrument for a bourgeoisie advancing a claim to power. Only by equal representation could it hope to make its voice heard. Equal representation, and the counterplay of government and opposition, were therefore the formal expression of its will-to-power. But the German bourgeoisie did not advance a claim to political power. Rather, it permitted the authoritarian state to survive industrialisation: a state resting on the assumption that certain individuals, by virtue of very special insight, and guided by the "well-understood interests" of their subjects, are called upon to make all the political decisions. Not without reason has this state been described as "paternalistic": as in the Wilhelminian family, the authority of the father, harsh in punishment but genuinely concerned with the welfare of his subjects, was all-pervading.

Still, whatever the merits of a sketch of this kind, it is bound to mislead. It misconstrues reality, partly by over-simplifying it, but even more because it reduces a dynamic historical process to a static picture. In point of fact, this strange combination of an industrial economy with feudal values and authoritarian structures did not go unchallenged even in Imperial Germany. But the process of dismantling this combination and replacing "traditional" by "rational" values, authoritarian by modern institutions, remained extremely slow. The attempt, in 1918-19, to catch up with the bourgeois revolution after the completion of industrialisation (and to combine it with the anticipated proletarian revolution) failed because the old ruling class and its values, though damaged, had been by no means destroyed by the "revolution of 1918." As soon as the Weimar Republic found itself in trouble—whether in the field of foreign affairs, economic policy, or internal order—there arose a call for the "proven" authoritarian leaders of the past. The Hindenburg elections, government by emergency decree, the coalition of Hitler's first cabinet—all bear witness to this tendency. It is a commonplace that Hitler, too, was carried to power on the waves of this prevailing anti-parliamentarianism.

But it was, and is, an error to identify anti-parliamentarianism with National Socialism. Hitler and his party did not represent the Prusso-German tradition of the authoritarian welfare state. National Socialism marks the entry into German history of "modern politics"—in its ugliest, totalitarian form. In their impact on German society, one might say, the Nazis were the executors of the German revolution that never took place. As so often, the horrors of revolution grew with belatedness. Still, National Socialism completed for Germany the break with those traditional authoritarian values, institutions, and leaders which had characterised German society throughout the period of industrialisation. The most obvious evidence of the revolutionary impact of the Nazi régime is the near-total destruction of the old Prusso-German upper class—through the rise of a party élite of "new men"; through the disappearance of Prussia as a political and administrative entity; through the death of almost an entire generation of young officers from old aristocratic families in the campaigns of the first years of the war; through the systematic liquidation of the old German upper class after the revolt of July 20th, 1944; and finally through the destruction of the economic basis of the old élite as a result of the division of Germany. All these events can be seen as stepping-stones in the painful journey of German society out of a traditional, authoritarian past into modern political reality.

The contradiction, then, between a modern industrial economy and a pre-industrial—or, at least, pre-capitalist—structure of society, dominated some seven decades of German history.

Not until 1945 was the contradiction fully resolved (if one can say this without cynicism), in the *tabula rasa* situation of a country whose economic capacity had fallen back to an almost pre-industrial state, at precisely the moment its traditional economic and social structure had lost its basis. Thus, German social development in the post-war era was fraught with several alternative possibilities—the only possibility that was ruled out was a reconstruction of that authoritarian tradition which, even in the Weimar Republic, was still the strength as well as the weakness of the country. One often hears to-day, in East and West Germany, references to "authoritarian" traits in politics and society. But if the term is used at all precisely, it can refer only to fast-vanishing remnants of a lost past. German social development in the postwar era is in no sense a "restoration": it is a road to new destinations.

For subsequent generations, the most important change may well seem one which has little to do with these social developments—I mean, of course, the division of Germany. And, beyond that, the fact that while both halves have turned away from the older traditions, they have turned in radically different directions. In a sense, of course, a unitary German society within set territorial boundaries is itself less than a century old. But the divergences in the recent development of East and West Germany are starker even than were the divergences between the German states before the creation of the Empire in 1871. Despite the official hostility, one cannot overlook a certain inner convergence of these German states in the 18th and 19th centuries. But to-day, official hostility is reflected in a real divergence of social development. Before 1871, there were several German states—but one German society. To-day we may still insist that there are not two German states. But even the most enthusiastic advocates of reunification would find it difficult to deny the existence of two German societies.

In 1945, both halves of Germany faced much the same challenge. The economy was in desperate straits; no able and self-confident group of leaders was in sight; all traditional rules of social and political behavior had lost their validity. Yet, from the first day of reconstruction, the response to the challenge differed radically in the two halves of Germany. There were, to be sure, differences between the Western zones of occupation as well—some of which are noticeable, even to-day, in the appearance of cities, in the peculiar features of institutions such as the press or local government. But these differences are as nothing compared to the profound contrast between the Eastern and the Western Zones. What started out as the influence of the occupying powers soon merged with more or less indigenous forces and traditions, as the Western Zones grew into the German Federal Republic, the Eastern Zone into the German Democratic Republic. Whatever one may think of the legitimacy of the two governments—and although no democrat will hesitate to choose the Federal Republic—it becomes ever harder to deny the reality of these two political entities and their social bases.

These are historical events of some consequence, concerning even those not directly involved in them. The question is: whether the texture of German society before 1945 has proved strong enough to impose its unifying tradition on a divided Germany, or whether external force can so determine the course of history that a society grown together over many decades can be torn apart within fifteen years. Nor can we shirk the question whether German reunification is not becoming an increasingly remote hope as the two halves stabilise their differences. Whatever the answers to these burning (and rarely discussed) questions, the fact remains that since 1945 the two halves of Germany have grown apart socially as well as politically. For both, Germany's authoritarian tradition came to an end with the Nationalist Socialist revolution. In the East, the resulting vacuum was filled by totalitarian institutions and the new social structure supporting them. Whereas the West, with its new social and political institutions, launched the first successful experiment in liberal representative government in German history.

Even before the Berlin Wall, it was not enough to judge East German developments merely from the fluctuating refugee statistics. Of course, these figures did register changes in political pressure, and pointed to the basic lack of legitimacy of the current political order. Nevertheless, the fact is that most of those whose home was in East Germany are still living there, and would still be living there even if they had a chance to leave. Obviously, people's unreadiness to leave does not necessarily imply recognition of a régime. But, at least in its consequences, the absence of active protest is a kind of acceptance. And in this sense—not to speak of the many whose career depends on the present political set-up in the East—the political and social development of East Germany since the war has a more than ephemeral reality.

The most important single feature of East German social development has been the emergence, or rather the systematic creation, of a new and homogeneous upper class. In amusing contrast with their ruling Marxist ideology, the Soviet occupation forces and their German satellites have reconstructed East German society from its "superstructure" rather than from its "real basis." For, however loath one is to explain historical events in conspiratorial terms, there can be little doubt that this process was the result of deliberate planning. As early as May, 1945, the Soviet authorities began to build up a new political and economic élite. The leaders of the four original parties (Communists—KPD, Social Democrats—SPD, Christian Democrats—CDU, Liberal Democrats—IDP) differed considerably in social background and political orientation. In the beginning there was, moreover, an administrative élite of experts; and many sections of society were not immediately affected by the changes at all. But within a year, in the spring of 1946, the second stage in the formation of a closed political élite had begun with the systematic exclusion of "difficult" groups and individuals. There were early indications of this trend in the so-called "Anti-fascist Front of Democratic Unity." There was the compulsory fusion of the Communist and Social Democratic parties into the Socialist Unity Party (SED) in 1946. A little later came the systematic subversion of the so-called bourgeois parties (CDU and LDP), as well as the creation of a number of satellite parties of the SED (the National Democratic Party, the Peasants' Union, etc.). Since about 1948, East Germany has possessed an increasingly homogeneous political class, fundamentally united in outlook, despite the surface appearance of organizational variety.

A similar process—if with a different intention—was very nearly brought about by the Nazis during the twelve years of their rule. What is new in East Germany, and perhaps of lasting importance, is the next step in the creation of a ruling class. Since 1948, if not earlier, there has been a clearly recognisable attempt to combine all the élite of society—politicians, the military, lawyers, professors, economic leaders, and artists (and, in the end, church leaders as well)—into a uniform "new class." This has not proved equally easy in all cases; even to-day the process is by no means complete. But we have to recognize that the creation of a homogeneous ruling class in East Germany has been largely realised. Nationalisation of all private firms has turned managers into state functionaries. In the reconstruction of the Army, the officer corps proper had almost no say (though here, too, certain traditions of the German army are likely to impede its complete *Gleichschaltung*). The abolition of most of the university faculties of law, and the invention of the "People's Judge," meant a break with one of the central institutions of German tradition (though the common historical background of the legal systems remains a unifying factor even to-day). The complete switch-over of education to a system of "polytechnical education," and the privileged position of real and so-called "workers and peasants," as well as the general indoctrination with Marxism-Leninism, has already made East and West German degrees and diplomas almost impossible to compare (though in some fields a common scholarly tradition remains alive). The only structure which has resisted many attempts at political domination, and has still not been completely subdued, is the Lutheran church.

It is perhaps necessary to emphasise that these trends are not superficial changes that can be reversed in a year or two. The man who has become a People's Judge by virtue of a diploma acquired from the new Academy of Administration; the Manager of the large State enterprise; the General of the People's Army; the Dean of the Workers' and Peasants' Faculty; these are not simply imposed office-holders, but new social dignitaries whose very existence is bound up with the new society. It is probably safe to assume that one-tenth of the population of East Germany is personally tied to the régime in this way. And it is clear that a homogeneous upper class of this kind, interchangeable in its membership, perpetually refreshed but not modified by planned social mobility, is a powerful basis for totalitarian political institutions and contributes to their stability.

There is much else to support the thesis that East German totalitarianism has acquired a social basis. All analysts of National Socialism have noted the connection between totalitarian institutions and efforts to cater for, and eventually win over, the youth of a country. Those who have reason to be worried about their legitimacy need to concern themselves, above all, with youth. For youth is not only "the future," it is (as we know from student risings in many countries, and specifically from the Hungarian revolution of 1956) also a potential threat. There are many indications of this concern of East Germany's leaders with youth—a concern which often takes the form of giving young people highly responsible positions in order to tie them to the existing order. Despite the high number of young people among the refugees from East Germany, not all of these measures are likely to have been unsuccessful.

Regarding this stabilisation of totalitarian political institutions, I should mention a further point. The ideology of Marxism-Leninism in itself is hardly more than a toy for certain party theoreticians. There is, however, a notion, widespread not only in East Germany but also among refugees in the West, according to which "the whole" is more important than its parts, and the welfare of "society" and "the state" takes precedence over the welfare of the individual. People who have turned their backs on the DDR in disgust and despair often remark after a few weeks in the West, "there is one point in favour of the East—there 'the whole' still means something! In the West everybody just follows his own wishes. . . ." Precisely because such remarks— unintentionally, to be sure—cast doubt on the very basis of Western freedom, they show the remarkable impact of certain value-patterns in the Communist East: value-patterns which are more in keeping with totalitarian institutions than many of their adherents realise. For the totalitarian state rests much of its authority on this permanent emphasis on the precedence of "the whole"—which in effect means the new ruling class—over the individual.

It is useless to indulge in speculation about how long the present régime in East Germany can survive. For years there have been indications of internal instability. The new ruling class may be homogeneous; but it is also very mediocre. Occasional waves of terror may succeed in maintaining totalitarian institutions; but they do not enhance the legitimacy of the régime. In any case, belief in the precedence of "the whole" loses much of its strength if Big Brother controls every aspect of life too noticeably. And yet, more has happened East of the Elbe since 1945 than the imposition of a rule of terror based on Soviet bayonets. To-day, East German political institutions have a social substructure which contributes to their main-tenance. Any liberalisation of East Germany would require not only the abolition of the régime, but also a fresh social revolution. The fact that there have been profound changes in East German society provides its rulers with their only reasonably reliable guarantee of stability. But it also presents Germans with an intractable problem where reunification is concerned.

A man from Mars, standing for half an hour in the city centers of Leipzig and Frankfurt-on-Main, would hardly guess that both cities were part of the same country less than twenty years before. In fact, of course, the most striking difference between the two cities—the grey austerity of Leipzig, and the conspicuous wealth of Frankfurt—is a significant pointer to West German development since the war. The most frequently repeated cliché about West Germany—the "economic miracle"—is indeed, properly under-stood, her most surprising and most characteristic feature.

In the first place, the mere extent of West Germany's economic develop-ment since the war is astonishing. Germany's economy (much like that of Britain and the United States) struggled desperately throughout the interwar period to return to the level of 1913. That level has been left behind. Indices of production are not always satisfactory measures of industrial development, but in this case the total index does hint at the truth. If we take the total industrial production of Germany in 1913 as 100, production had sunk to 38 by 1919. The temporary recovery up to 1929 (103) was soon undone during the Depression (1932: 60). It was not until 1939 that the level of 1913 was reached and surpassed (126). In so far as it is possible to produce an index for 1945-46, 40 per cent of 1913 seems too high rather than too low an estimate. West German industrial production to-day, on the other hand, with an index of considerably above 300 (1963), and still growing in volume, bears witness to an unprecedented economic explosion for the post-war years.

Germany has shared with other Western countries, of course, this transition to mass production and affluence. More important, in our context, is a second feature, an aspect of the economic miracle which is peculiar to Germany and which, in terms of German history, probably constitutes the real German miracle. I have referred to the peculiarities of industrialisation in Germany. Though largely based on private capital, industrialisation in Germany was "national-liberal," that is, national-conservative in character. But in 1945—or, more precisely, in 1948—after the cruel destruction of the old Prusso-German ruling group, Germany had the unique opportunity of repeating the process of industrialisation from its beginnings. And then something totally unexpected happened. This second industrialisation took place in a strictly liberal-capitalist spirit, so that (if this does not sound paradoxical) the economy and society of post-war Germany provide the first example of true capitalist organisation in all German history.

It is hard to recall, after 15 years, just how surprising this development was. Even now, one is tempted to say that the liberal experiment of 1948-9 went against all economic rationality. On the eve of the currency reform, laymen and experts were convinced that gradual, limited liberalisation was the only path away from rationing, economic controls, and planning to a more prosperous society. Yet they were quite wrong. Joseph Schumpeter had predicted for the economy—and Karl Mannheim for the whole of society—the inevitability of increasing state intervention. No wonder people in all political parties were convinced, in 1949, of the necessity of far-reaching economic planning. To-day, we are faced with the remarkable fact that public property, in the second half of the 20th century, is being turned back to private hands. There is no doubt that entrepreneurial success in post-war Germany was, to some extent, a result of the abstinence of the state, especially in tax matters—and is therefore not entirely due to the spontaneous initiative of the new middle class. Still, the fact remains that vigorous private initiative—or, what is merely another way of saying the same thing: an unbounded individual desire for gain—was the motive force of the economic recovery of Western Germany. Of course, there can no longer be, in our time, a "pure" capitalism, such as existed in the early period of English and American industrialisation. But, as far as Germany is concerned, she has never before come as close to capitalist patterns of social organization as in the years since 1948.

Many features of contemporary German society show the effects of this economic miracle. Like East Germany, West Germany had to develop a new class of leaders after the disappearance of the old upper class. It would be an exaggeration to say that this task had already been completed. Obviously, an unplanned social development proceeds somewhat more slowly than one which is conceived and controlled in detail. Here, one must agree with the recent comment of the Bonn correspondent of *The Times* that there are no real signs of the emergence of "Society" with a capital S in Bonn. But many holders of leading political and economic positions in the Federal Republic, and to a lesser extent in other spheres of society, *do* differ considerably from their predecessors. The most pronounced change is the much greater influence of economic leadership groups. The proportion of cabinet ministers and members of parliament who, by family or occupation, have connections with industry has risen very considerably. In the economic sphere itself, the urge to exert political pressure has grown stronger, now that even medium-scale entrepreneurs no longer have anybody "above them" to tell them what to do or not to do. Indeed, perhaps the very absence of "Society" is a sign of this change. A tendency towards *nouveau riche* behavior—a liking for medieval choir-stools in the dining room, for conspicuous consumption, a horrific lack of taste in matters of art and literature—is one of the unmistakable characteristics of this new society in West Germany.

These developments chiefly concern the top of the social structure. But a corresponding change in values can be observed throughout West German society. As against the heroic past, with its emphasis on *Gemeinschaft* and hard work, the whole of German society is to-day (to quote a phrase of Schumpeter's about capitalism) "bathed in an economic light." So striking is this new illumination that the foreign visitor, in search of the much-praised and much-abused "German national character" of the past, finds hardly a trace of it. The Germans of to-day are neither particularly industrious nor particularly enamoured of the military—neither particularly subservient nor particularly romantic. Probably the most crucial change in the social values of West Germans is the setting up of individual success and private pleasure as the twin guide-lines of behavior. What scornful critics denounce as "materialism" and "exaggerated individualism" is in fact a necessary correlate of any quasi-capitalist social order—the desire to increase individual happiness, coupled with a readiness to protest against any external intervention in one's own pattern of life (especially if it comes from the state).

The significance of these new developments is that they have reversed the historic trend of German society towards a monolithic type of social organisation. When a sample of people in the Federal Republic was asked recently which social groups they thought were "too powerful," opinion was almost equally divided between Industry, the Church, and the Military. This seems to indicate that there are several groups competing for influence, and that no single group is capable of assigning all others their place within the whole. The concept of "pluralism" has lost almost all its meaning by frequent and indiscriminate use. But if one means by it the existence of competing groups of more or less equal rank, West German society can be accurately described as "pluralistic." Pluralism is, of course, always precarious. At any given time, one or other competitor in a pluralistic system tends to have a slight advantage over the others. But what matters, and what is new in West Germany's development, is that no one social group holds the reins of power permanently in its hands. Society, therefore, remains sufficiently flexible to give everybody a chance to see his claims represented.

It is here that the political significance of the changes in the West German social structure becomes apparent. Now that quasi-capitalist patterns of social organisation have emerged, there is, for the first time in German history, hope that German society will provide a stable foundation for representative government. Representative institutions remain a dead letter if rigidities of the social structure effectively prevent any chance of a non-violent change. This was one of the main problems of the Weimar Republic. But the social changes since the war have undone many of these rigidities. An entrepreneurial ruling class is more likely to fight off state tutelage than a ruling class of civil servants, army officers, and landlords. The man who has grown accustomed to determining his own course of action, and who makes personal happiness the criterion of his actions, is not so easily persuaded to accept authoritarian or totalitarian rule. Where there is a plurality of groups competing for domination, each one has an interest in the maintenance of conditions of free and fair conflict. In this sense, the conclusion seems justified that the structural changes in West German society since the war hold out a better chance for representative government than ever before in German history.

It would be pleasant to conclude this analysis of some changes in the German social structure on an optimistic note. But this favourable prognosis for German democracy should be qualified by adding that it is intended in relative terms—that is, by comparison with earlier phases of German history. And since not even the most ardent admirer of Germany could describe our country as a natural breeding-ground of democracy, this conclusion may not amount to very much. Indeed, a number of reservations and threats to the development I have depicted are too clearly in evidence.

In the first place, the very combination of the quantitative and the qualitative economic miracle—the affluent society and liberal elements in the new Germany—raises serious questions. Are not these changes a mere consequence of economic prosperity? Are not the changes in West German society as superficial as those in East Germany? Might not a new economic crisis have consequences like those of the Depression of 1929? Although objections of this order are widespread (both inside and outside Germany), their basis in fact is by no means as certain as is often believed. Thus, the causal connection between the economic crisis and Hitler's rise to power is at best tenuous—especially in view of the fact that those most directly hit by the crisis, the unemployed, did *not* turn to the Nazis in significant numbers. Still, this cannot invalidate the objection that the real test for the stability of representative institutions in West Germany is yet to come, and that less favourable economic developments would be one of the conditions of this test.

Again, it is impossible to be dogmatic as to whether those elements in the German social structure, which in the past were such effective obstacles to democracy, have really been destroyed as effectively as my interpretation suggests. There are clearly many remnants of the past in German society: "compromised" individuals in prominent positions in politics, the army, the legal system and elsewhere. There are also extremist quasi-political groupings, especially in the wake of the refugee organizations—though these have mostly shrunk to mere cadres of functionaries. Perhaps more important, there are unchanged patterns in important fields such as education. No doubt, all these traces of Germany's authoritarian past are merely leftovers, and therefore less important than those who see West Germany only in their light so often assume. But one cannot deny that resistance to representative democratic government is present in many a dark corner of German society.

Conscious anti-democratic tendencies apart, the most profound resistance to the changes I have described is found in an attitude of mind the connection of which with political democracy may not be immediately evident. As against what Talmon has called "totalitarian democracy," representative government involves recognition of the necessary interplay of incompatible interests and ideas. Conflict, the antagonism of government and opposition—but also of interest groupings in all spheres of society—is the lifeblood of democracy. Those who reject conflict as such, therefore, go some way towards rejecting representative institutions. Yet this attitude is very common in Germany. In lieu of political parties fighting one another for power, people would prefer the seeming harmony of an all-party coalition. There is (at least among non-participants) a widespread desire to settle industrial strife by state intervention or by some utopian once-and-for-all solution. Similar reactions are to be found within the educational and legal communities, and within many private organisations. But nowhere is this *penchant* for settling problems "for good" by one decisive—and, in effect, authoritarian—decision so evident as in people's attitudes to social conflict.

I have said that pluralism—the full competition of large groupings and institutions—often rests on a precarious equilibrium. That is why it is difficult to allay fears that one of the competing institutions—industry, the church, the military—might become so powerful that it would use its predominance to destroy the competitive system itself. On the other hand, an attempt to analyse these fears more precisely ("the Federal Republic is a clerical state," "Big Business decides everything") tends to reveal that they are debating points rather than sober descriptions of social reality.

There is, however, one threat to the development of more liberal patterns in German society which might lead to the abolition of social pluralism and which ought not to be underestimated. This arises from the fact that social changes in East as well as West Germany have taken place in the context of a world conflict between East and West. It appears to be a general law that human groups react to external pressure by increased internal coherence. In the East-West conflict, each society finds itself in such a position of pressure from without. For totalitarian countries, this does not constitute any particular threat, since they are in any case based on a structure of total mobilisation. But external pressure may lead the liberal societies of the West to restrict internal liberties in the name of resistance to totalitarian pressure. There are some indications that both the United States and West Germany will be exposed to this danger if they refuse to recognise new political developments which are in fact reducing the pressure from without. Here is a new threat to liberal political and social structures, and one difficult to counter. The paradoxical possibility that democracy can be destroyed while it is being protected deserves the attention of all who are concerned for the survival of representative institutions.

There can be no doubt, of course, that the Federal Republic is superior to the German Democratic Republic in terms of the legitimacy of its political order. In West Germany, it is true, there could be a more active acceptance of the new political institutions—but then legitimacy is perhaps always a passive phenomenon of the absence of revolt. Nevertheless, it would be irresponsible of me to describe the changes in West German society as final, and representative institutions as secure. The two halves of Germany reacted in very different ways to the *tabula rasa* of 1945. With some exaggeration, one might say that the one half has chosen the totalitarian, the other the representative face of the Janus-head of modern politics as its model. This ambiguous fact points to the chance of a reunification in the foreseeable future. It points equally to the possibility—is it hope or danger?—of an internal, perhaps violent, breakdown of the régime in the East, as well as the threat of a renewed defeat of representative democracy in the West.

C

THE EMERGENCE OF MASS POLITICS

9

Parties, Elites, and Political Developments in Western Europe

Hans Daalder

This paper is in many ways an exercise in the impossible. It treats exceedingly complex social phenomena that are tacitly reduced to a common denominator by the use of deceptively simple concepts such as "party," "elite," and "political development." It threatens to fall victim to what someone once called the "propinquity fallacy": because Europe is one geographic area, it is supposed that its political experiences can be lumped together in one general treatment. This study deals, not with *one* political system at a *given* time, but with widely *different* systems *through* time—a somewhat strange exercise for one who is thoroughly sceptical of such over-general constructs as the "European continental political system," [1] or of the superficial assumption that European societies followed a similar political course. The addition of the *s* after "political development" in the title is therefore deliberate. It is my profound conviction that true analysis will pay detailed attention to variation in political developments between European states as well as within each of them.

Hans Daalder, "Parties, Elites, and Political Developments in Western Europe," from *Political Parties and Political Development*, eds. Joseph LaPalombara and Myron Weiner (Copyright © 1966 by Princeton University Press), Social Science Research Council; pp. 43-77. Reprinted by permission of Princeton University Press. Article and footnotes abridged. The author is grateful to the late Otto Kirchheimer, Val R. Lorwin, and Joseph LaPalombara, who criticized an earlier draft of this paper.

[1] Gabriel Almond's analysis in "Comparative Political Systems," *Journal of Politics* 18 (1956), is a considerable advance over earlier writings that ascribed "continental" politics to such institutional factors as proportional representation and assembly government. Even so, his statement: "The Scandinavian and Low Countries stand somewhere in between the Continental pattern and the Anglo-American," *ibid.*, still betrays a similar attitude. Why should France, Germany, and Italy be more "continental," than Holland, or Switzerland, or more "European" than Britain? One wonders whether the description of the smaller European democracies as "mixed" is not in fact an elegant way of saying that they apparently have some Anglo-Saxon virtues in addition to a number of "continental" vices.

At the same time, this recognition makes the task for a single political scientist well nigh hopeless. He has intimate knowledge of a few systems of government at the most, and is likely to read his own rather than true conclusions into those systems he does not know so well. What follows here consists therefore mainly of a series of eclectic remarks—usually termed hypotheses, but more honestly called impressions. At the outset of the journey I seek refuge in that excellent, if worn-out, defense that it is up to those who really know the individual political systems concerned to test, prove, or more likely to disprove, my generalizations.

The starting point of this paper is the proposition that European states fall *prima facie* into at least three distinct groups: (1) countries which developed slowly from oligarchies into consistently stable democracies: e.g. Britain, the Scandinavian countries, The Netherlands, Belgium, and Switzerland; (2) countries which have undergone serious reversals in political regime, whereby democratic constitutions have given way to autocratic or even totalitarian systems of government: e.g. France, Germany, Austria, and Italy; and (3) countries which continue to have authoritarian regimes of a somewhat traditional nature, and in which democratic groups tend to form at most an underground or exiled opposition: i.e. Spain and Portugal.[2]

It is much easier to say what factors are *not* responsible for these differences in political development than to indicate their actual causes. Obviously there is no immediate relationship to differences in stages of economic development. In the group of stable democracies there are countries that underwent the industrial revolution relatively early (Britain, Belgium) and countries which entered the modern industrial era late (e.g. Norway and The Netherlands). Similarly, German industrial development came relatively early and in full force; yet here the lapse into totalitarian dictatorship was the most gruesome ever. Moreover rapid economic development did not save the French Fourth Republic, nor does it stabilize political conditions in Italy.

Consequently it will be necessary to probe deeper and to seek for other factors that are often of an historical nature. The main variables on which this paper will center are: (1) the importance of the earlier elite setting; (2) the degree of coincidence or disparity between political and economic developments; (3) the "reach" or "permeation" of (democratic) parties as against other power holders in various European societies; and (4) the cleavage lines of the party system itself.

It it not suggested that these factors are sufficient to give a satisfactory explanation of the very complex and diverse processes of development which European countries underwent, whether generally or individually. They have

---

[2]As the main focus of this paper is on problems of political development, I shall not deal further with the latter group in the pages that follow.

been selected primarily because of their interest for comparative purposes in accordance with the terms of reference set for the papers in this volume.

I. THE IMPORTANCE OF THE EARLIER ELITE SETTING

Differences in Political Development before the Nineteenth Century

The great complexity of the relationships among various social classes and status groups in European society, as that between state and society generally, has tended to be confused by the cliché assumption (found typically in college textbooks as well as the *Communist Manifesto*) that there was a "natural" evolution in Europe from feudalism through absolutism and bourgeois revolution toward modern democracy. This view is an egregious simplification for a variety of reasons.

First, it pays far too little attention to the fact that the term "feudalism" is used to describe fundamentally different structures in medieval Europe. The political relationships among king, aristocracy, clergy, cities, and peasantry as well as the economic relationships among landowners, burghers, artisans, peasants, and serfs showed great variation. If the starting point differs how can one expect linear or even parallel developments afterwards?

Second, present-day European states originated in very different ways. Roughly speaking, one can divide these states, according to the manner in which political unification came about, into four groups: (1) those in which effective centralization came early and with relatively little tension (e.g. Britain, Sweden); (2) those in which centralization came early but against considerable resistance (e.g. France); (3) those in which centralization came late but fairly gradually (e.g. The Netherlands, Switzerland); and finally (4) those in which central political power was established only as a consequence of considerable political violence in the nineteenth century (Germany, Italy).

Of these four groups, (1) and (3) had eventually rather similar characteristics. There was at no time a violent clash between political and social realities. Central power enmeshed itself gradually into the social system, and both regional and social groupings in turn achieved a growing influence on the center, thus making for a society which was both truly integrated and fairly pluralistic in nature. Things were different in France, Germany, and Italy. There central control tended to be imposed by military and bureaucratic power. Hence the state came to some degree to hover above the society; the ruled came to feel themselves subjects rather than citizens, and to regard authority with a mixture of deference and distrust rather than as a responsive and responsible agency in which they had a share.[3]

Third, differences in the manner of social and economic development, even before the nineteenth century, tended to strengthen this contrast. In Britain and The Netherlands economic development ever since the middle ages was relatively free from state intervention. Autonomous economic development tended to make the newly rising bourgeoisie a much more powerful challenger of the powers that were than equivalent groupings could be in, say, Colbertist France or Cameralist Prussia. In the latter countries the state took a much more active hand in economic development, and in the process bureaucrats tended to become more managerial while the bourgeoisie tended to become more officialized than was true in Britain or the Low Countries. In the latter case, civil freedoms and a measure of responsible government preceded the establishment of a powerful central bureaucracy; in France the new social forces were eventually powerful enough to revolt, but in the process they succeeded only in building up safe-guards against the bureaucracy rather than absorbing it or making it fully accountable; in the German Reich, finally, liberal groups failed to seize power and fell prey to the stronger hold of the *Polizei-* or *Beamtenstaat*.

Finally, European societies experienced different effects from the religious wars and their aftermath. In some countries the religious composition of the population remained homogeneous (whether Roman Catholic or Lutheran). There the church often remained for long an appendage of the upper classes; if this assisted them in their bid for the support of more traditionally oriented lower-class elements, it also tended eventually to provoke both fundamentalist and anticlerical protest. In other countries (notably in Switzerland, The Netherlands, Britain, and parts of Germany) various religious groups contested with one another until they finally reached some measure of tolerance or accommodation. In this way religious pluralism[4] and religious dissent often provided the spearhead of political resistance against entrenched elites, ultimately forcing a recognition of the limits of state power and of the justice of individual and corporate rights.

[3] In Germany most political forces submitted fairly rapidly to the existence of the new *Reich*, in contrast to the situation in Italy, where Church resistance and regional opposition continued for a much longer time. This made the existence of the new Italian state for a long time more precarious but may, on the other hand, have provided a safety valve that prevented nationalist unifiers from going to the extremes experienced in Germany. [Cf. article by Groth reprinted below in this volume—Eds.]

[4] The fact of religious pluralism seems more important than the particular religion in question. Whereas the Catholic Church in the Latin countries identified closely with vested social interests and alienated large sections of the population in the process, Dutch Catholics turned into a distinct protest group that pleaded for a separation of church and state, represented a considerable challenge of the outs against the dominant Liberal bourgeoisie, and maintained an effective hold on lower-class groups. Similarly, Lutheranism tended to be much

The Transition to Modern Democratic Politics

Through such factors (and others such as the incidents of geography and war)[5] some political systems in Europe had hardened along autocratic lines by the eighteenth century, while others had maintained or even strengthened a pluralist setting that, however oligarchical, allowed a measure of political influence to a variety of political and social groups. This vital difference was to affect the establishment of political parties during the nineteenth century in at least two respects: in the ease with which they became a recognized part of the political system, and in the role which they came to assume within it.

In Britain, the Low Countries, Switzerland, and Sweden, conciliar forms of government, whether in cities or in the center, had a long and honorable tradition. The style of politics tended to be one of careful adjustment, of shared responsibility, of due respect for ancient privileges. Attempts at absolute kingship eventually broke on the concerted strength of particularist interests, whether corporative, regional, or social. As the political order was in a very real sense built upon parts, the idea that men could reasonably be partisans found ready recognition even before the age of formalized party politics. There never was a "monochromatic, unicentric world," in Sartori's sense, to form an obstacle to the formation of parties.[6]

In these countries the view that government was somehow a trust toward the governed had old roots, however elitist actual systems tended to be until late in the nineteenth century. Intra-elite competition, being a recognized and even institutionalized phenomenon, made it easier to weather what the editors have called the crisis of participation. Conflicts between towns, between town and country, or among various religious groups created certain links between clashing oligarchies and sub-political groups below them. Competing elites sometimes sought lower-class support to strengthen their

---

more an instrument of vested authority in Germany than in Switzerland, while in Scandinavia it played the dual role of both maintaining an official religion and inspiring fundamentalist protest against a too modernist sphere in the central cities. Calvinism too was in practice much more nonconformist in some societies than in others, depending on whether its hold was strongest on existing elites or on lower-class elements.

[5]Geographical factors made certain European societies more secure from foreign attack than others: the insular position of England, the mountains of Switzerland, the rivers and canals of The Netherlands made these countries to a large extent immune against invasion on land. Consequently there was no urgent need for them to develop large standing armies. This had profound consequences for domestic political and administrative structures. In Lord Esher's telling phrase, the Navy often proved "a constitutional force," while an army was more readily "a royal force" (*Journals and Letters of Reginald, Viscount Esher,* London, 1934, vol. I, p. 269). Similarly, the early development of a citizen-militia in Switzerland was a great deal removed from the compulsory militarization of Prussian *Untertanen.*

[6]Giovanni Sartori, *Parties and Party Systems* (New York: Harper & Row, forthcoming).

position, thus granting the lesser orders a political title and whetting their political appetites. Conversely, new claimants could exercise some influence on an oligarchical system simply by the threat of potential support to one or other side within it. Once some social groups were granted a measure of influence, this tended to provoke further demands from those yet further down until, finally, the burden of proof in the suffrage debate came to rest on those who defended restriction rather than on those who advocated extension of suffrage. Some upper-class groups came to doubt their own title, while most came to realize that fighting democracy might be more dangerous to their social position than democracy itself. Thus both pressures from competing elites downward and concomitant pressures from sub-elites upward made for a competitive gradual extension of democratic rights.

This process was facilitated by the circumstance that it came about in slow, evolutionary ways. Neither in political theory nor in actual behavior was there an abrupt transition from elite politics to mass politicization. Political newcomers were slowly accommodated. At any one time they tended to be given at most only part-power—enough to give them a sense of involvement and political efficacy but not enough to completely overthrow the evolving society. Older political styles that had been developed to guarantee the rights of aristocrats or *hauts bourgeois* were thus more easily transferred. The "political domain," to use Neumann's term,[7] expanded only slowly. Since at any one time the political stakes were relatively modest, the upper classes were less afraid and the lower classes less threatening. Older and newer elites were thus held more easily within the bounds of one constitutional, if changing, political system that neither alienated the one into reactionary nor the other into revolutionary onslaughts on it. In time, however, the over-all political order could thus become more truly responsive to the demands of a wide variety of political groups within it. In 1867 Bagehot thought "dignified parts of government" necessary to keep the masses from interfering with the "efficient government" of the few; a century later the many were efficiently using those very same "dignified parts of government" to secure substantial concessions to themselves.[8]

Developments were very different in those societies where power was heavily concentrated by the end of the eighteenth century. In France royal absolutism provoked truly revolutionary resistance of a much more drastic and upsetting character than appeared in the English Civil War of the seventeenth century, let alone in the Glorious Revolution of 1688. If the king called on the *droit divin* to claim absolute power, so did liberal thinkers of

---

[7] Sigmund Neumann, *Modern Political Parties* (Chicago: University of Chicago Press, 1956), p. 404.

[8] Walter Bagehot, *The English Constitution*. London, 1867, World's Classics ed., Oxford, 1952, pp. 4 ff. The fact that most of the countries here treated have remained monarchies would seem to have been a consequence more than a cause of these developments.

the Enlightenment on the basis of the nation or the people. From the outset a leading strand of French democratic thought became therefore "totalitarian" in Talmon's sense,[9] becoming highly suspicious, for instance, of *corps intermédiaires* between the individual and the state. If in the countries described earlier pluralism seemed the natural corollary of liberty, in the latter it was often regarded as the prolongation of inequality and privilege. The traumas of the French Revolution created lasting and bitter divisions in French society. Articulate political groups continued to harbor fears and suspicions of one another, doubting one another's intentions and having different views of the legitimacy of past regimes and present institutions. Paradoxically, in that European country where popular sovereignty was proclaimed first and most explicitly no governmental system ever rested on a universal basis of popular support and respect. Traditionalist groups continued to be politically strong, and the newer bourgeoisie and the rising working classes came to be divided in their respective allegiances. Democratic regimes met with a continuous threat from the right. Democratic groups suspected the state even when they were nominally in control of it. This in turn made it more difficult for successive regimes to achieve their goals or to capitalize on their positive achievements and to gain legitimacy and lasting adherence throughout the nation.

In Prussia, and later in the German *Reich,* the bureaucratization and militarization of the society had gone much further than in France before the existing power division was challenged. In France democratizing forces generally triumphed, however precariously. In Germany the Kaiser-*Junker-*Army-Bureaucracy[10] complex was for a long time strong enough to manipulate the new social forces rather than to have to adjust to them. From the outset large sections of the new industrial capitalist classes were drawn into the existing power cluster; this left the fate of German liberalism to the faltering hands of mainly professional and intellectual groups rather than to a strongly unified economic class. In most European countries bourgeois elements had triumphed sufficiently to occupy key positions in the political system before the real onslaught of the working classes was felt. In Germany, on the other hand, the existing power groups were powerful enough to maintain themselves against both, even offsetting bourgeois demands for responsible parliamentary government with a careful weaning and manipulation of the new working classes. Typically, a democratic breakthrough came not of its own strength but only in the aftermath of lost wars. The

---

[9] J. L. Talmon, *The Origins of Totalitarian Democracy* (London 1952), *passim.*

[10] For a sophisticated analysis of the way in which the Prussian *Junkers* maintained their social position and lost their political independence by their submission to the "new social factor . . . the state power" see Joseph Schumpeter, "Social Classes in an Ethnically Homogeneous Environment," in *Imperialism and Social Classes,* Meridian Books ed., 1960, pp. 144 ff.

explicit democratic articles of the Weimar Constitution were to become the hallmark of success of democratic forms on paper at the expense of social substance.

The Different Role of Parties

The role of parties in European countries varied considerably with such substantial differences in actual political development.

In countries where modern mass democracy evolved slowly from a preexisting pluralist society various regional, social and ideological groupings tended to form what might be called "proto-parties" at a rather early stage. Consisting of informal groupings seeking to obtain preferential treatment for themselves and the definite interests which they represented, they tended to fill certain functions of the modern political party (such as interest aggregation and to a lesser extent political recruitment), but not others (such as political socialization and political mobilization). As the increasing power of parliamentary assemblies tended to bring such groupings nearer to the effective decision-making centers, organization came to be at a premium. Similarly, when new social claimants came to exert pressure for representation, organization outside the parliament became not only profitable but essential for political survival. The process of party formation tended to spread therefore from existing competing elites downwards, but this very process also facilitated a reciprocal movement. Party organization itself created many new elite-posts even if only at sub-parliamentary levels. Second-rung leaders who provided an essential link with important elements in the expanding electorate had to be accommodated, and some in time fought their way to the top. Party competition for various groups in the electorate made some existing parties more responsive to new demands, while new social groupings came to imitate and expand existing forms of party organization.

In countries where autocratic regimes prevailed longer the development of parties showed different characteristics.

Autocracy in its more explicit forms was incompatible with free party organization. Instead factionalism and a limited measure of interest representation tended to predominate. Democratic stirrings could take form only in intellectual protest movements or outright conspiratorial activity. Thus even some of the earlier democratizing movements, both on the liberal and on the socialist side, showed strong influences of secret societies.

In the more limited autocracies that the constitutional lawyers of another day used to call constitutional monarchies (as distinct from parliamentary monarchies) a measure of party organization could come about more easily. Even traditionalist political forces had eventually to resort to at least nominal electoral processes; but in their case parties were not so much the cause as a symptom of effective political power. Certain bourgeois and professional groups sought to use the parliamentary benches for a measure of oppositional politics that was often ineffective for lack of courage and organization. Further to the left, certain *Weltanschauungsparteien* showed tighter organizational forms and ideological programs; their verbal fervor tended to be symptomatic, however, of their weak position in the present. They made up for their lack of current influence with the vista of an utopian future, and could be "wholistic" in their ideological claims precisely because they had little chance ever to be confronted with the compromises that partial power entails; only a more basic political and social revolution could change their role in a fundamental fashion.

Finally, under conditions of more democratic rule the political role of parties became more important. But often past divorce from active political power continued to hinder them in the exercise of their nominal functions, while at the same time their somewhat timid hold on governmental power was endangered by the hidden sabotage or open competition from anti-democratic groups. We shall return to this point in section III, when we shall discuss the "reach" or "permeation" of democratic party systems.

II. COINCIDENCE OR DISPARITY BETWEEN POLITICAL AND SOCIO-ECONOMIC DEVELOPMENT

The complex processes which we have come to denote in shorthand as the Industrial Revolution exercised a massive influence on political developments throughout Western Europe. Everywhere the self-contained political life of separate small communities was broken up, a development which freed the individual from older political bonds and allowed for the growth of wider, if often less compendious, political loyalties. Social and economic changes created considerable turmoil, which furnished the raw material for new political alignments. State and society grew more closely together as the scope of central power expanded, while simultaneously many new social forces came to exercise strong pressures for specific government action. In the process many new links were forged between the state and its citizens through the expansion of administration and the establishment of a great number of new political groups. The modern political party itself can be described with little exaggeration as the child of the Industrial Revolution.

It would be a mistake, however, to draw conclusions too easily about specific causal determination, for in practice socio-economic changes differed greatly from one country to another and within different regions of a single country. Furthermore the political effects of seemingly similar socio-economic changes varied according to the specific political settings in which they made themselves felt. It seems useful therefore to consider the effects of economic development according to at least three criteria. When did economic development start? How fast did it come? What political effects did it have on various social strata?

Time and Tempo of Socio-economic Development

The criteria of time and tempo give four logical possibilities according to the following scheme:

Figure 1. Modes of socio-economic development

Timing

		Early	Late
Tempo {	Gradual	I	III
	Rapid	II	IV

Of these four possibilities, II is not a real one; early European economic development germinated slowly. I is more representative for European experience. Without further proof it may generally be postulated that political strains were comparatively easy to cope with in this case: the very slowness of the process of socio-economic change gave the political system considerable leeway in meeting social and economic changes and in adjusting itself to them; these changes themselves were at any one moment also less drastic, hence less upsetting.

Somewhat similar considerations apply to III, but here a new factor enters. While in I social, economic, and political changes tended to move concurrently, a certain disparity between political and socio-economic changes could arise in countries in which economic change came late. Once new political ideas, new institutions, and new political techniques had developed in certain countries (like the United States or Great Britain), they could not but influence similar groupings in economically less developed societies as well. Political factors could therefore acquire a much greater autonomous momentum in the latter case. Thus the attempt was made to transfer certain institutional devices long before social realities showed corresponding changes. Ruling elites might deliberately concede the forms rather than the substance of democratic institutions to divert political unrest and maintain their own positions virtually intact. An elected parliament might be allowed, but not responsible government. Or a wide franchise might be granted, but only after adequate care was taken that this conveyed little power—the weighting of votes, the refusal of the private ballot, and slated apportionment of seats being particularly useful expedients in this respect. Rather than providing an effective lever in the hands of the masses, such "democratic" reforms could paradoxically develop into a measure of plebiscitary control over them. This could result in an enduring alienation of sizable sections of the population rather than in their permanent integration in an effectively responsive political system.

France provides the classic case in Western Europe of such a disparity between political and socio-economic changes. At a very early moment the country was caught in the whirlpool of mass politics. The principle of popular sovereignty was recognized long before a politically articulate people could make its will felt. Hence almost a century after the French Revolution the country could still live up to Laboulaye's description of France as "a tranquil people with agitated legislators." Agitation in the *Carrousel de Paris*, not being very meaningful in terms of a large number of social and economic variables in France, could not but prematurely disillusion French citizens with politics as such. To quote Philip Williams' description of the situation that prevailed in France until quite recently, "her atomized, small-scale structure promotes political individualism, strong local loyalties, and a political psychology more adapted to resistance than to positive construction. It reinforces the old tendency to 'incivisme,' the lack of civic consciousness which makes so many Frenchmen regard the state as an enemy personified in the tax-collector and the recruiting sergeant."[11] But this in turn meant also a lack of sufficient incentive for political change. To quote Williams again, "It was because there was no majority for action in the country that there was no pressure strong enough to overcome the resistance which found so many points of advantage in the constitutional framework."[12] When finally massive social and economic changes did come, these were consequently not easily channeled along earlier established institutional and political lines.

Finally, IV, in which economic changes are both fast and late, offers the greatest political difficulties of all; all the problems of III are repeated and compounded by the state of insecurity and flux which is inherent in rapid social and economic development itself. In Europe such conditions are found only in certain regions and usually within the bounds of a more comprehensive, stable, articulated political system. Not so in the developing countries, where politicization far outstrips socio-economic changes, and where these social and economic changes themselves, if forthcoming at all, only add to the discomfort of a body politic already weakened in other ways.

[11] Philip Williams, *Politics in Post-War France*, 2nd ed. (London 1958), p. 3.
[12] *Ibid.*, p. 8.

Social Classes and Economic Development

What were the political consequences of economic development (or the lack of it) for the various social classes in Europe? Obviously such a question can in the context of this paper be answered only in the most general, that is, misleading, terms. Even the concepts we use, such as *aristocracy, bourgeoisie, peasantry, middle classes, working classes,* are not really satisfactory; they are indefensible (but necessary) simplifications of social categories and social divisions that are in reality very complex. The following discussion contains therefore, only a very rough sketch, and a highly impressionistic one at that.

First then, the effect of economic development on the nobility: In certain countries (e.g. The Netherlands[13] and Switzerland) the position of the nobility as against that of burghers and independent peasants tended always to be weak and to grow weaker as capitalism expanded. In other countries, notably in Britain, and to a more limited extent Germany, old aristocracies adapted themselves relatively successfully to the new facts of industrialization. This assisted them in their bid for continued political influence (even though other factors made for different attitudes toward democracy). A positive stance in favor of economic development and a paternalistic rejection of the extremes of Manchester Liberalism by both Tory squires and Prussian *Junkers* made it easier for the conservatives of both countries to maintain a measure of liaison with a significant section of the rising working classes (as well as to retain considerable rural support), which in turn facilitated the establishment of conservative mass movements in both countries.

In contrast, French and Italian aristocracies did not excel in economic initiatives and so tended to be anachronistic, their remaining political power resting more exclusively on traditional resources like their hold on the church, the land, the military, or administration. The gap between them and the rising bourgeoisie tended to grow wider than in either England or Germany. Or, to be more precise, the continued influence of the aristocracy divided the new bourgeoisie into those who adjusted themselves to the style of living of their continuing "betters"[14] and another section that sought to

[13] In the Province of Holland the Estates consisted in the seventeenth century of 19 members: one representative of the nobility, and 18 delegations of cities, manned by burghers.

[14] In Prussia the same phenomenon occurred, much to the distress of Max Weber, who was angered by the tendency of "an amalgamation between a landed aristocracy corrupted by money-making and a capitalist middle-class corrupted by aristocratic pretensions." See Reinhard Bendix, *Max Weber—an Intellectual Portrait* (New York: Anchor Books ed., 1962), p. 40. The greater political and economic prestige of the German upper classes presumably lessened revolutionary resistance to them, contrary to the situation in France and Italy, where

fight such influences. The bourgeoisie as a whole was therefore less easily credited with political ability or economic skills than were their Dutch or Swiss or English counterparts.

This fact influenced the political reactions of other groups in the population. For one thing, it helps to explain the large influence of professional and intellectual groups in these societies (considered by some observers to have been the outstanding characteristic of the politics of the French Third Republic)[15] which could not but strengthen the tendency toward the highly ideologized politics that seems typical of political societies in which political claims outstrip underlying socio-economic realities.

It also had an unfavorable effect on the relations between bourgeois and worker. In the Latin countries the patriarchal family firm long remained the characteristic form of economic enterprise. The *Patron* was a far cry from the revolutionary bourgeois of the *Communist Manifesto*. A low esteem for his economic qualities reinforced the defeatist outlook of the proletariat,[16] already skeptical of politics for reasons which we discussed earlier. A vast gap tended to develop not only between employer and worker but also between the professional socialist politicians who took part in the parliamentary game and the generally syndicalist masses who rejected all party action. This weakened both. It eventually assisted the Communist *encadrement* of the French and Italian working classes; and it goes far to explain the checkered results of both democratic institutions and social reform policies in France and Italy.

The evolution of working-class politics in most other European countries stands in considerable contrast. There the industrial revolution generally developed more thoroughly and effectively. At the earlier stages, social dislocations tended to produce a "hump of radicalism." But the rapid growth of large-scale industries and urbanization soon laid the foundation for well-organized trade unionism and concurrent social-democratic action, quickly shifting from empty revolutionary phraseology to more immediate short-term goals within the existing socio-economic systems. If this strengthened democracy in systems which were already democratizing themselves, it weakened the incipient stirrings of democracy in those societies in which modernization took place largely under continued autocratic auspices (as in Germany).

Somewhat similar factors influenced the political position of the

revolutionary sentiment may have been fanned by the low prestige accorded to traditionalist political and economic elites.

[15]Cf. T. B. Bottomore, *Elites and Society* (London 1964), pp. 64 ff.

[16]See Val Lorwin's already classic "Working Class Politics and Economic Development in Western Europe," *American Historical Review* 63 (1958), pp. 338-351; and S. M. Lipset, "The Changing Class Structure of Contemporary European Politics" [reprinted below].

peasantry. In all European countries the relative importance of the agricultural sector declined as economic development proceeded; but whereas in some countries this process caused relatively little political tension, in others it provoked violent conflict. In some countries strong protectionist policies both symbolized and maintained the power of certain agricultural groups; whether these were large landowners (as the Prussian Junkers) or a large mass of generally inefficient small farmers (as in France) depended on earlier developments in land tenure and social organization generally. In other countries the reduction of the agricultural sector went on at a much faster pace. But simultaneously foreign competition, self-help, and government policies facilitated modernization. Thus Danish and Dutch farmers managed well. Typically, Scandinavian agrarians often cooperated with socialist parties, in contrast to France, where sizable blocs of peasant votes turned to rightist or Communist extremists; their mood was mainly one of apolitical malaise instead of one of definite expectation of positive action.

Speaking more generally, economic development has caused the decline of some groups and the rise of others. The specific nature of the complex underlying processes has often been confused by the facile use of the hazy notion of the "middle classes." One should at least distinguish between more traditional elements, like the *artisanat*, the retail traders, and small-scale employers who form the residue of social and economic developments, and the "new" middle classes of technical, managerial, administrative, and professional people, who are rather their result. Political attitudes have tended to differ correspondingly. While in France, for instance, Poujadism tended to find its main support among the earlier groups, Gaullism has tended to appeal more strongly to the "new" middle class. The rise of the latter has tended to make for a new dimension in the political controversy between right and left also in other countries, forcing both traditional socialists and traditional conservatives to take note. Otto Kirchheimer deals brilliantly elsewhere in this volume with the far-going political transformations that seem to result from this situation in European politics.

III. THE "REACH" OR "PERMEATION" OF THE PARTY SYSTEM

Partly as a consequence of historical factors European parties have differed greatly in the extent to which they have permeated and enveloped other political elites. In some countries the role of parties has become all-pervasive; in others the parties have penetrated far less successfully to the mainsprings of political power. Substantial differences are also encountered in the extent to which parties have become true integrating agencies between political elites on the national and on the local scene. In this section the "reach" of a party system is briefly analyzed along the following three dimensions: the extent of involvement of traditional political elites in the party system; the measure of absorption of new political claimants; and the degree of "homogenization" which parties provide between national and local political elites.

Party Systems and Traditional Elites

In European societies the relationship of traditionally powerful political elites and the party system seems to have taken one of three forms: they have participated from the outset, slowly learning to share power with newer groups; they have participated in the party system but only half-heartedly and with reactionary intentions; or they have stayed outside altogether, seeking to maintain their influence through other power structures (notably the military, the bureaucracy, business, or the church). The precise developments depended greatly on the way parties originated and the specific nature and extent of the democratizing process.

As we have noted, some European parties were in many ways the outcome of earlier institutionalized conflict on the elite level; factions hardened increasingly into substantial political organizations as these conflicts spread from the elites downward into an ever widening circle of political actors. Though older elites were eventually confronted with new parties outside their control, they never came in immediate conflict with the party system. This facilitated the transition from oligarchical to polyarchical forms of government.

In other European countries parties were first established in opposition to autocratic regimes that forbade or at least restricted the scope of party conflict. Eventually in these countries too older elites found it necessary to participate in electoral processes. But parties established under their auspices tended to remain little more than outward appearances, democratic figleaves, so to speak, for entrenched power positions that had their real basis elsewhere. Consequently right-wing parties in various European countries came to assume basically different attitudes toward the rules of the game of democratic party politics. The acceptance of the substance of democratic ideals and practices is still the clearest criterion with which to distinguish Scandinavian or British Conservatives from, say, the right in France, Weimar Germany, or present-day Italy. In the latter the constant presence of potentially or actually anti-democratic parties within the party system has hindered the effective working of democratic politics; it has narrowed the range of democratic rule; it has caused disillusionment to spread to other potentially more democratic groups; and it finally eroded the very existence of democratic regimes.

The "reach" of the party system over against other traditional political elites is revealed most clearly in its relation to the permanent bureaucracy. Bureaucracies have been far more responsive to the party system in some countries than in others. Much has depended on historical relations and the specific characteristics of the ensuing party system. Thus it was of profound significance whether an articulated party system developed before, after, or concurrently with the rise of a bureaucracy. In France and Germany powerful bureaucracies were built up as social control-mechanisms long before non-bureaucratic social groups had learned to use the weapon of political organization to secure influence. Ever since, parties have had difficulty in obtaining full control, and to this day bureaucracies have tended to enjoy a distinct political existence. In Britain, on the other hand, the build-up of a modern civil service occurred after non-official social groups were securely in political control; ever since, the civil service has loyally accepted control by party ministers. Many other European countries would seem to fall between these two cases. State bureaucracies developed earlier than in Britain, but non-state groups were strong enough to make their weight felt simultaneously, and ultimately to prevent them from becoming uncontrollable elements in the body politics. To use a somewhat simple metaphor, the British Civil Service was from the outset below party; the French and German bureaucracies were to a very real extent above it; in other cases parties and bureaucracies tended to be on one line. In systems where certain parties tended for long to have a hegemonic position they often staffed the bureaucracies after their own image; thus Liberal dominance made the Dutch bureaucracy long a Liberal perquisite, and in somewhat similar fashion the *Democrazia Cristiana* is at present heavily represented in the Italian bureaucracy. Alternation between parties could lead to an attempt to take the bureaucracy out of politics (as in Britain), but also to competitive politicization by rival parties. Coalition politics has often led to a careful distribution of administrative "fiefs" to rival parties, as in present-day Austria and Belgium, or to balanced appointments of rival partisans not only at the ministerial level but also in *cabinets du ministre,* or even in established administrative posts.[17] Generally speaking, bureaucratic traditions, fortified by political and legal doctrines, have prevented such devices from degenerating into the full excesses of the American nineteenth-century spoils system. Contrary to traditional belief, they have worked not too badly in those systems in which the party system itself was reasonably cohesive and effective. In a segmented society like the Netherlands, carefully balanced political appointments would even seem to have smoothed the relations among the parties and between politicians and bureaucrats. They have given parties the certainty that their views were taken into consideration at the beginnings of policy formation and in the details of policy execution;

[17]See Val R. Lorwin, *The Politicization of the Bureaucracy in Belgium* (Stanford: Center for Advanced Study in the Behavioral Sciences, 1962).

they have provided officials with a new avenue by which to obtain political support for administrative concerns; they have thus acted as brokers between officials and politicians and between various parties, softening political conflict in the process.

The Party System and New Claimants

As in their relation toward older elites, party systems have differed in their responsiveness to the claims of new groups seeking political representation. In European history the outs at the lower end of the scale have been either lower-class groups (notably the working classes and the peasantry) or religious protesters (e.g. Dutch Calvinists and Catholics, English Non-Conformists, the Norwegian Left). Again, the relation between these new claimants and the party system took any of three forms: their absorption into a pre-existing party system which gradually came to widen its appeal; the formation of special parties; or their continued exclusion from the party system.

Robert Dahl[18] has suggested in the case of the United States that the non-appearance of a special working-class party was due to a considerable extent to the fact that representative government and a wide franchise were introduced before an urbanized proletariat came to exert new demands on the system. Hence parties and political techniques suitable to the operation of parties were evolved in time to grapple with this new challenge and to accommodate labor in the existing system. In contrast, in Britain representative government came early, the urban proletariat next, and general suffrage only at the end. While developments were such as to keep new rising groups within the constitutional order, the existing parties were not elastic enough to accommodate the rising demands of the working classes. In Germany, urbanization and the general suffrage preceded representative government, thus sterilizing political party activity into necessarily ineffective attitudes. With somewhat similar ideas in mind, Stein Rokkan has asked for further study of the interesting relationship between franchise extension, special electoral arrangements (such as weighting of votes, privatization of electoral preferences, proportional representation versus other electoral systems), and the mobilization of new groups into the political system.[19] These studies must then be further related, I suggest, to such factors as the earlier elite-setting, and the extent of disparity between political and social and economic development (also in their regional varia-

---

[18]See Robert A. Dahl, ed., *Political Opposition in Western Democracies* (New Haven 1966), chap. 13.

[19]See his "Mass Suffrage, Secret Voting and Political Participation," *European Journal of Sociology* 2 (1961), pp. 132-152.

tions) to account for the measure of actual involvement of the out-groups in one political framework.

Generally speaking, then, not the establishment of special parties representative of the lesser groups of society but only their psychological identification with the political order and the responsiveness of that order, in turn, to new demands can serve as the true measure of the relation between the party system and new claimants. A responsive political order may ensure an effective political participation of new claimants without the establishment of special parties. Special parties, on the other hand, can both integrate and isolate according to the reaction of other parts of a party system. Thus Dutch Calvinists and Catholics established highly segmented political and social organizations but jointly rose to power and in the process ensured the integration of their clienteles into the political system, actually making it more integrated, responsive, and democratized.[20] The same cannot be said, it seems to me, of the Norwegian Christians or of various parties composed of nationality interests in the Austrian-Hungarian Empire. The uncritical use of the term "fragmentation," thus, does not bring the analysis much further if attention is not paid at the same time to the question whether a division of a political system into a number of quite distinct spiritual and political groups ultimately means the break-up of one society, or rather the growing of roots of very different groupings in one constitutional order. To use Sartori's terms, seemingly fragmented systems can in practice be centrifugal or centripetal,[21] and only exact sociological analysis can reveal which is ultimately the case.

Just as older elites in certain cases stayed outside (if not above) the party system, so various groups of society remained outside or below it even after the general franchise was introduced. As suggested earlier, one cause may have been a disparity between a strong politicization of the working classes and the granting to them of the means of effective political action. In the Latin countries anarchism and syndicalism were strengthened by the acute feeling that party and parliamentary activity could achieve little in practice. Vested interests may so continue to dominate the parliamentary scene that even their nominal voters may feel manipulated rather than active participants. This has been for long true of Italy, for instance, and still is to a lesser extent of most European countries.

If we combine the first and the second paragraph of this section, the "reach" of a party system in relation to various groups in the society might be visualized as follows. Most removed (though not necessarily antagonistic)

---

[20]See H. Daalder, "The Netherlands: Opposition in a Segmented Society," in Dahl, *op. cit.*, chap. 6.

[21]Giovanni Sartori, *op. cit.*, and "European Political Parties: The Case of Polarized Pluralism," in Joseph LaPalombara and Myron Weiner, eds., *Political Parties and Political Development* (Princeton 1966), chap. 5.

would be those political groups which are outside or below the system altogether; by definition they are politically unorganized. Following them are conscious anti-system groups that reject the existing political order but have some measure of group identification (e.g. the syndicalists, even though they rejected party organization and put their trust in spontaneous rather than institutional leaders). A somewhat closer participation is found among those who organize in political anti-system parties but with the deliberate aim of participating in order to destroy; in practice, however, the very act of participation tends to create certain vested interests in the system (cf. Robert de Jouvenel's famous *dictum* that there is more in common between two deputies one of whom is a revolutionary than between two revolutionaries one of whom is a deputy). Anti-system parties may therefore show a wide range between outright rejection and near-acceptance, and their influence may become so great that their presence becomes a significant variable within the system. Somewhat further on the road to involvement are those isolationist parties that have no chance to gain even part-power but continue to organize definite subcultural groups that wish their voices to be heard (even if with little chance of their being taken into account). Next in the scale would come opposition parties that effectively compete for office, proximity to power being the criterion with which to measure real involvement. Here again there is considerable scope for variation; whereas some are natural "outs," others are semi-government supporters. Finally come governing parties, tied most closely to the existing system, the extent of their dominance being the measure of their effective control. A simplified representation of this scheme is given in Figure 2.

Party Systems: The Center and Local Realities

The central-local axis provides yet another dimension by which to measure the permeation of party systems. Increased interaction between the center and the localities greatly affected the formation and organization of parties. Generally speaking, a two-way process took place: political forces in the center sought to extend their political bases by mobilizing political support over wider geographic areas, while political groups in the periphery organized to promote regional interests with the center.

This two-way movement resulted in very different situations. In some cases, a fundamental nationalization of politics led to a far-reaching "homogenization" between politics at the center and in regional areas; such a movement was facilitated by the absence of strong economic or cultural regional cleavages, by good communications, and by the entry of issues that helped to nationalize politics (e.g. class). In other cases ethnic, linguistic, religious, or geographic barriers prevented such an osmosis from taking place. Politicization tended to strengthen centrifugal rather than centripetal

Figure 2.

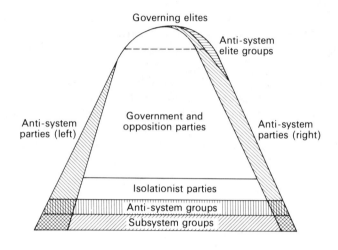

Governing elites

Anti-system elite groups

Anti-system parties (left)

Government and opposition parties

Anti-system parties (right)

Isolationist parties

Anti-system groups

Subsystem groups

——————— Non-participation ———————   ——— Participation ———
Boycott and indifference   Opposition of principle   Democratic parties

Subsystem groups   Anti-system parties (left)   Government parties

Anti-system elite groups   Anti-system parties (right)   Loyal opposition parties

Anti-system groups below the elite   Isolationist parties

The area of effective democratic party government is restricted to that of the Government and loyal opposition parties—hence the "reach" of a democratic party system is measured by its total proportion of the political pyramid. This proportion is very different in various European societies: while in some it is nearly coterminous with the whole (England, Sweden) in others it occupies only a relatively small area (present-day Italy, Weimar Germany, French Fourth Republic). Proportions are far from stable moreover. On the one hand, isolationist and anti-system parties may gradually be domesticated into the system (e.g. the Nenni Socialists). On the other hand, increasing opposition to the system (as measured by a proportionate increase in the strength of anti-system groups and anti-system parties), and mounting indifference (as apparent in an increase of subsystem groups) may narrow the area of democratic politics. Anti-system parties may seek deliberate involvement to discredit democratic politics and thus to increase both anti-system and subsystem groups. This is the reasoning behind traditional Communist tactics and seems to reflect fairly accurately the situation in France before 1958, when anti-system parties, anti-system groups, and political malaise made the area of democratic politics shrink to such an extent as to make it practically ineffective.

tendencies (separatist political movements like that of the Irish in nine-teenth-century Britain, or of nationality groupings in the Austrian-Hungarian Empire, forming their logical extreme). In yet different cases politics at the center and in the localities tended to remain highly differentiated spheres, with only minimal linkages between them. Although this did not threaten national existence, it complicated national politics. Again, a comparison between Britain and France offers an instructive contrast.

In Britain leaders and labels penetrated relatively early from the center into the constituencies, thus drawing national and local elites into one reasonably unified system. Although certain regional sentiments and interests continued to have some importance, to this day providing British parties with distinct pockets of regional strength, they were not such as to fragment the decision-making process at the center. The essence of British politics is therefore national politics, and British parties are above all national political organizations. In France, on the other hand, local concerns long continued to dominate the choice of national parliamentary personnel. This caused a curious paradox: provided the local representative showed due respect for local sensitivities and interests, he was, on the national scene, as far as his constituents were concerned to a considerable extent a free agent. The French Chamber became therefore very much *"La Maison sans Fenêtres,"* a meeting place of local interests and individual personalities rather than of cohesive, integrated national political parties. Nationalization of politics occurred therefore more easily on the level of ideological debate than of political will, of political oratory rather than of effective national political organization. For the rest, the French Chamber tended to be more highly sensitive to interest groups (pressuring M.P.'s in their local base) than to issues of more national importance. This accentuated the cleavage between the French bureaucracy (feeling itself the self-appointed guardian of France in a truly Parisian way) and the Chamber, stronger in resisting the executive than in dominating it, more ready to veto than to formulate national policies.

The "homogenization" of politics between the center and the localities is therefore an important factor in the politics of both. An effective linkage helps to legitimize the national political order. Where links are absent, alienation is likely to ensue. The character of the party system is an important variable in this process. Parties can be agencies of both integration and disintegration. They assist national integration if they serve as genuine brokers between disparate regional or social interests (without losing their national existence in the process). They are likely to strengthen centrifugal forces, on the other hand, if they become the passive tools of sectional interests. Paradoxically, synthetic unifiers who seek to identify their own sectional interests with that of the one and indivisible nation can contribute as much to such disintegrating tendencies as those who deny the existence of one political community from over-particularistic concerns.

IV. THE CLEAVAGE LINES OF THE PARTY SYSTEM

European countries reveal considerable differences according to the character and the intensity of the cleavage lines that form the basis for political conflict and political organization. These differences are partly due to objective differences in social structure; certain social cleavages did exist in some countries but not in others (e.g. ethnic diversity). They depend further on the circumstance of whether and to what extent particular cleavages were effectively politicized; factors such as religion or class have been much more exploited in some political systems than in others. Finally, considerable variations also exist in the persistence of cleavage lines in the party system. Whereas some issues have been of only passing importance and have subsequently fallen out of the political domain, others have remained characteristic dividing lines long after their original *raisons d'être* has been forgotten. In this way the particular history of past political controversy has continued to exercise a substantial influence on political loyalties and on the way in which new issues are focused and processed. Therefore only careful historical, sociological, and political analysis can do full justice to the distinct qualities of any given political system. It follows that it is much easier to categorize a number of cleavages that seem to have been historically important in European political development than to evaluate their importance for political stability or effective decision-making.

In early days David Hume considered "factions from interest" and "factions from affection" as the most normal cases, proclaiming, unlike Burke, the rise of a new category of "factions from principle": "the most extraordinary and unaccountable phenomenon that has yet appeared in human affairs." Generally speaking, the most important dividing lines in Europe have tended to be: class or sectional interest (the landed versus the moneyed interests; parties representative of sections of industry or commerce, labor, or agriculture); religion (Modernists versus Fundamentalists, Catholics versus Protestants, Clericals versus Anticlericals, Anglicans versus Non-Conformists); geographic conflict (town versus country, center versus periphery); nationality or nationalism (ethnic minority parties, extreme-nationalist movements, and parties having their real allegiance to another national state, etc.); and regime (status quo parties versus reform parties, revolutionary, or counterrevolutionary parties).

The difficulty of qualitative analysis of the importance of cleavage structures comes out in the exaggerated attention paid to quasi-mechanical factors, such as the number of cleavages, or whether they run parallel to or cut across one another. Both English and American literature seem to be based often on the *a priori* notion that the political universe is by nature dualistic, so that two-party systems are the self-evident political norm. This view is reinforced by Duverger's analysis, which attempts to reduce the explanation also of multiparty systems to a "superposition of dualisms," [22] to the non-coincidence of dividing lines in the body politic. While "bargaining parties" in a dualist system are likely to ensure both stability and the orderly solution of successive issues, so the standard argument goes, a multiparty system leads perforce to fragmentation and *immobilisme*.

This view is based on a slender empirical basis. Britain and the United States have two parties, their politics are apparently satisfactory to the theorist, *ergo* a two-party system is good. In contrast, France, Weimar-Germany, and Italy had many parties, their politics were unsatisfactory, hence a multiparty system is a lesser if not an outright degenerated form. This type of reasoning then leads to the curious term of "working multiparty systems" [23]—phenomena that are apparently somewhat akin to "the boneless wonder" of Barnum's Circus. Such a view testifies to an insufficient awareness of the political experience of a host of smaller European countries (such as Belgium, The Netherlands, Denmark, or Switzerland) that have successfully governed themselves for generations under complex multiparty systems. Would it not be possible on the basis of the politics of these countries as confidently (but equally subjectively) to assert that the best political system is one in which all important social groupings have occasion to have themselves politically represented in separate parties, which can then use the forum of parliament and coalition government to reach the politics of compromise?

The confusion is clearly revealed by our tendency to hold two conflicting theories with equal conviction. On the one hand, we argue that politics is best served by a constant dualistic regrouping of political forces in distinct majority-minority positions. On the other hand, we hold with equal conviction that a political system can quickly be brought to the breaking-point if a number of cleavages come to run parallel to one another—for instance, if conflicts about religion, nationality, and class each make for the same division of society. Whereas we point at one time to the crisscrossing of cleavage lines as the main source of political inefficiency, we assert at another moment that only adequate cross-pressures, which offset tendencies toward increased polarization, can make for a working political community. It is to this variable that we look to explain why Flemish and Walloons, why Capital and Labor, why Clericals and Anticlericals can continue to cooperate in feasible political systems. I suggest that this paradox cannot be explained unless new variables are also taken into account.

Of crucial importance are not only the severity and incidence of

[22]M. Duverger, *Political Parties* (London 1954), pp. 229 ff.

[23]Cf. Gabriel A. Almond, in *The Politics of the Developing Areas* (Princeton: Princeton University Press, 1960), and Dankwart Rustow, "Scandinavia: Working Multiparty Systems," in Sigmund Neumann, *op. cit.*, pp. 169ff.

conflicts but also the attitudes political elites take toward the need to solve them by compromise rather than combat. Such attitudes are deeply rooted in political culture, itself the product of complex historical factors that differ greatly from one country to another. Traditional leadership styles, the traumatic memory of past conflicts (which may either perpetuate conflict, or cause parties to draw together), a realistic sense of what can be reached through political action and what not, the presence of substantial or imaginary common interests, the extent to which party leaders are more tolerant than their followers and are yet able to carry them along—all are important. Unfortunately they are evasive of systematic analysis except in a specific context. . . .

10

The Structuring of Mass Politics
in the Smaller European Democracies:
A Developmental Typology

Stein Rokkan

There is a curious awkwardness about discussions of "types" in comparative politics. Aristotle and Montesquieu taught us to proceed by classifications of regimes, and the current generation of computer enthusiasts have offered us more and more powerful tools for the handling of wide ranges of attributes of political entities and for the establishment of complex multi-dimensional typologies. Yet as soon as we are confronted with a concrete table of alternative types and look over the lists of cases assigned to each cell, our first reaction is almost immediately to add further distinctions, to reject the imposition of similarities across historically distinct units. The student of politics is torn between two sets of super-ego demands: he feels an obligation to reduce the welter of empirical facts to a body of parsimoniously organized general propositions but he also feels under pressure to treat each case *sui generis,* as a unique configuration worthy of an effort of understanding all on its own. This is of course a dilemma common to all social sciences but is particularly difficult to handle in the study of such highly visible, amply documented macro-units as historical polities. . . . It is probably significant that the great "leap forward" in comparative politics came with the mushrooming of new macro-units on the world arena in the 'fifties: the increase in numbers and the decrease in the average level of familiarity made it psychologically easier to treat the units as if they were the anonymous subjects of a census or a survey rather than multi-faceted, multi-layered historical configurations. It is probably no less significant that the early enthusiasm for global generalization has been on the wane in the

Reprinted by permission of author and Cambridge University Press from *Comparative Studies in Society and History,* X (January 1968), 173-197. Article and footnotes abridged.

last two or three years: the massive inflow of scattered information has caught up with the theory-builders and the greater familiarity with configurational details has increased the resistance to the simplifying typologies of the pioneers.

Hopefully, this does not mean that the discipline has come full circle: that we are back to the production of idiosyncratic monographs on unique constellations of institutions and processes. The phase of global generalization-mongering has taught us to look for the significant communalities in the operation of political systems and to concentrate on a series of critical choice-points in their historical development. What we have to learn is to develop *multi-dimensional typologies for configurational complexes:* typologies which tap significant elements of each historical-political context and yet allow wide-ranging comparative analysis dimension by dimension. . . .

This paper explores one possible line of progress in this direction: it represents an effort to formulate a model for the generation of one set of such configurational typologies.

The model I shall propose focuses on a limited range of institutions within a limited range of politics: it represents an effort to arrive at a parsimonious description of *the critical steps in the development and structuring of competitive mass politics* in the countries of Western Europe.

This concentration on one set of institutions and one set of countries does not imply an outright rejection of the efforts made to construct universal models of political development: some elements of the region-specific model I shall propose may be built into models for other regions of the world but the basic structure of the model reflects a uniquely European experience.

The model grows out of work on the comparative sociology of elections and electoral behavior: in fact, the first version was worked out in response to the call for a broader theoretical framework for a series of cross-national analyses of socio-cultural factors affecting the behaviour of voters.[1]

Countless tables have been prepared for country after country for the electoral choices of the two sexes, for the different age groups, for the various occupational strata, denominations, ethnic and linguistic divisions. There are well-known difficulties of comparison on the side of the *independent* variables in such analyses but these are vastly easier to handle than the difficulties on the *dependent* side: the variations in the actual political choices of the different citizenries. The twin processes of urbanization and industrialization have tended to increase the comparability of occupational structures across the nations but have not produced anything approaching uniformity

---

[1]S. M. Lipset and S. Rokkan, "Cleavage Structures, Party Systems and Voter Alignments: an Introduction," in S. M. Lipset and S. Rokkan (eds.), *Party Systems and Voter Alignments* (New York: Free Press, 1967), pp. 1-64.

in the *structures of political alternatives* confronting the citizens of the different polities. . . .

There are many ways of proceeding in such comparative analyses of the choices before different national electorates.

One can proceed *synchronically* and map out the differences among the electoral alternatives country by country during a given period of time, e.g., the years since World War II:

— one possibility is to start at the *micro* level of the voter and inquire into the sources of variations in the *subjective rank ordering of the different parties* on different dimensions of identification, ideology, candidate characteristics or policy expectations;[2]

— another is to focus on the *candidates presented* and work out indices of distinctiveness among the parties;[3]

— a third is to look at the themes of the campaigns, the programmes and the public expressions of party ideologies and identify the dimensions of differentiation;[4]

— and a fourth is to check the *legislative behaviour* of the party representatives, their votes and their stands on electorally significant issues.[5]

One can also proceed *diachronically* and try to pin down the crucial differences from country to country in *the sequences in the establishment of the rules of the electoral game and in the formation of party alternatives:* this is the historical-developmental approach chosen in this paper.

In future work it will be essential to link up such diachronic approaches with the several synchronic procedures: in fact it will not be possible to check through all the predictions from the developmental model without a sequence of such synchronic analyses at a number of time points before and after the "freezing" of each national system of alternatives.

The developmental model to be explored posits clear-cut time limits to its operation:

— its *terminus a quo* is the conflict over the cultural-religious identity of the emerging nation-state in the sixteenth century;

— its *terminus ad quem* is the establishment of universal and equal

---

[2]A pioneering effort along these lines is Philip Converse, "The Problem of Party Distances in Models of Voting Change," in Kent Jennings and Harmon Zeigler (eds.), *The Electoral Process* (Englewood Cliffs, N.J.: Prentice-Hall, 1966), pp. 175-207.

[3]Data archives for parliamentary personnel are under development in a number of countries and will soon allow detailed comparisons of variations in the socio-economic distinctiveness of the parties at this level, see e.g., Henry Valen, "The Recruitment of Parliamentary Nominees in Norway," *Scandinavian Political Studies* 1 (1966), pp. 121-166.

[4]For an example of a possible approach see Olavi Borg, "Basic Dimensions of Finnish Party Ideologies," *Scandinavian Political Studies* 1 (1966), pp. 94-120.

[5]Here again a number of national studies of party cohesion and party distinctiveness will offer possibilities of cross-country comparisons, see e.g., Mogens N. Pedersen, "Consensus and Conflict in the Danish Folketing 1945-65," *Scandinavian Political Studies* 2 (1967), pp. 143-166.

electoral democracy and the "freezing" of party alternatives, in most countries during the 1920's.

This limitation in time span obviously also defines the geographical focus of the model: it only applies to the territories and the polities which were immediately affected by the clashes between the Reformers and the Roman Church and the consequent strains between secular and religious powers.

In fact, this paper will limit its focus even further: it will be essentially concerned to fit evidence for the *smaller* of the polities within this orbit into the over-all model.[6]

The eleven "smaller European democracies" to be dealt with in this paper[7] are the five Nordic countries, the three Benelux countries, the Irish Republic, the Swiss Confederation, and Austria.

All these countries can point to long histories of competitive parliamentary politics. By the early 1920's they all had *extended the rights of political citizenship to all adults:* in Switzerland exclusively to the men, in Belgium to only a few war-qualified women (mothers and widows of fallen soldiers) in addition to the men, in the other nine countries, and from 1949 onwards also in Belgium, to women on a par with men. There were also important similarities in the character of electoral competition in the eleven countries: the conflicts over representation had been increasingly nationalized through the development of mass parties and the stakes of the struggle had been fundamentally changed through the introduction of some form of *Proportional Representation.* This is indeed a highly significant common denominator across the eleven countries: they had all left the plurality principle, some of the Swiss cantons already in the early 1890's, Belgium in 1899, Finland in 1906, Sweden in 1909, the other countries from 1915 to 1922. (Interestingly Iceland did not go all the way when the electoral law was changed in 1920: the traditional system was kept up in the rural districts and was not replaced by PR until 1959). This is perhaps the one characteristic which sets the clearest contrast between the political structures of the smaller and the larger polities in Western Europe. Britain stuck steadfastly to the plurality system, France suffered only brief lapses into proportionalism while Germany and Italy experienced protracted difficulties and controversies over their electoral arrangements ever since PR was introduced in the wake of World War I. There was obviously a great deal of discussion of the pros and cons of electoral systems in the smaller countries

[6] For further discussion of the "fit" for Britain, Prussia/Germany, France, Italy, and Spain, see S. M. Lipset and S. Rokkan, *op. cit.,* pp. 38-50.

[7] The paper in fact represents an early report on one facet of the work carried out within the collaborative international project "The Politics of the Smaller European Democracies." This project is supported by the Ford Foundation and is directed by four "editors": Hans Daalder, Robert Dahl, Val Lorwin, and Stein Rokkan.

as well but once the party systems had accommodated themselves to the new rules of the game there were hardly any serious, sustained campaigns for a return to plurality-type elections: there was a great deal of debate over the threshold levels and districting, but very little over the principle of proportionality as such.[8] This contrast between the larger and the smaller polities is doubly significant in the light of the analyses offered in the polemical literature against PR. Again and again we come across attempts to reconcile the theorizing with the empirical evidence by emphasizing the differences in the consequences of electoral decisions for the smaller as against the larger countries: PR is tolerable in the smaller units because they face lesser loads of decision-making, it is disastrous for the larger countries because of their burdens of responsibility.

These elements add up to a good prima facie case for a comparative analysis of the structuring of mass politics just in these countries: the similarities of the electoral institutions make it easier to pin down the effects of differences in historical circumstances and socio-cultural structure. Indeed, the very fact that these are the PR countries par excellence invites such attempts at comparison: PR helps to "freeze" the early structures of articulation and aggregation and for that very reason makes it easier to pinpoint variations in the socio-cultural basis of support for the different political alternatives.[9]

With all the similarities they developed in their formal institutions these eleven countries do indeed offer an extraordinary range of variations in the structuring of their political life: not only did they proceed along very different paths towards their present systems of competitive mass democracy but they still offer strikingly different electoral alternatives to their citizenries. To understand the similarities and the differences in the behaviours of the voters in these eleven countries we shall clearly have to go back into history and consider the steps in the setting of these widely differing alternatives for electoral choice: we shall have to resort to developmental analysis to pin down the sources of variations in the "macro" conditions for "micro" behaviours.[10]

Through an intriguing process of dialectics this "return to history" has been strongly stimulated by the programmatically ahistorical analyses of

[8]For details on PR thresholds see Stein Rokkan, "Electoral Systems," *International Encyclopedia of the Social Sciences*, 1968.

[9]This point has been brought out with great force in Giovanni Sartori's analysis of the aggregating effects of "strong" electoral systems such as the single-member plurality, the absolute majority run-off or the high-threshold, small-constituency PR as against "weak" systems such as the low-threshold, large-constituency PR: see *Parties and Party Systems* (New York: Harper & Row, forthcoming), chap. 21.

[10]For a first attempt at a clarification of the issues of "macro"-"micro" logic see S. Rokkan, "The Comparative Analysis of Political Participation," in A. Ranney (ed.), *Essays on the Behavioral Study of Politics* (Urbana: Univ. of Illinois Press, 1962), pp. 47-90.

the psychology of partisanship pursued with such vigour by the great team of electoral analysts at the University of Michigan:[11] the concentration on variations in the intensity of identifications with such historically given entities as political parties must of necessity arouse curiosity about the origins, the age and the continuity of these objects in the political landscape.

Parties do not simply present themselves *de novo* to the citizen at each election: they each have a history and so have the constellations of alternatives they present to the electorate. In single-nation studies we need not always take this history into account in analyzing current alignments: we assume that the parties are equally visible "givens" to all the citizens within the nation. But as soon as we move into comparative analysis we have to add a historical dimension: we simply cannot make sense of variations in current alignments without detailed data on differences in the sequences of party formation and in the character of the alternatives presented to the electorates before and after the extension of the suffrage. We have to carry out our comparative analyses in several steps: we first have to consider the initial developments toward competitive politics and the institutionalization of mass elections, we next have to disentangle the constellation of cleavages and oppositions which produced the national system of mass organizations for electoral action, and then, and only then, can we make headway toward some understanding of the forces producing the current alignments of voters behind the historically given alternatives. In our Western democracies the voters are only rarely called upon to express their stands on single issues: they are faced with choices among historically given "packages" of programmes, commitments, outlooks, and sometimes, *Weltanschauungen,* and we cannot understand their current behaviours without some knowledge of the sequences of events and the combinations of forces which produced these "packages". Our task is to develop realistic models to explain the formation of different systems of such "packages" under different conditions of national politics and socio-economic development and to fit information on these variations in the character of the alternatives into our schemes for the analysis of current electoral behaviour.[12]

This is a task I shall try to tackle for the eleven smaller polities in this paper: I shall suggest, in crude outline, a model for the explanation of variations in the sequences of democratization and in the structuring of the party systems in these countries, and shall discuss, by way of conclusion, some of the implications for comparative research on electoral behaviour. . . .

[11] The original designs were heavily influenced by Lewinian field psychology, see especially the theoretical introduction to Angus Campbell *et al., The American Voter* (New York: Wiley, 1960). The Michigan analysts were themselves among the leaders in the movement to develop the historical dimensions of electoral analysis and have pioneered the organization of a large-scale computer archive for time series data for elections and censuses: see A. Campbell *et al., Elections and the Political Order* (New York: Wiley, 1966).

[12] S. M. Lipset and S. Rokkan, "Cleavage Structures, Party Systems and Voter Alignments: an Introduction," *op. cit.,* pp. 2-3.

The Four Institutional Thresholds

Sir Lewis Namier once likened elections to locks in a canal: they allow the rising socio-cultural forces to flow further through the established channels of the system but also make it possible to stem the tide, to keep back the flood. This simile is possibly even more appropriate in describing the typical sequences in processes of democratization and mass mobilization: any rising political movement has to pass through a series of locks on its way inwards towards the core of the political system, upwards towards the central arena of decision-making.

In our current attempt to pin down sources of variations among our eleven countries we have focussed on four such critical points: we might have stuck to the hydraulic imagery and called them "locks", but we prefer the statistically more appealing term *threshold*.

The first is the threshold of *legitimation:* from which point in the history of state formation and nation-building was there effective recognition of the right of petition, criticism, demonstration against the regime? from which year or decade will historians judge that there was regular protection of the rights of assembly, expression and publication, and within what limits?

The second is the threshold of *incorporation:* how long did it take before the potential supporters of rising movements of opposition were given formal rights of participation in the choice of representatives on a par with the established strata?

The third is the threshold of *representation:* how high were the original barriers against the representation of new movements and when and in what ways were the barriers lowered to make it easier to gain seats in the legislature?

And the fourth is the threshold of *executive power:* how immune were the executive organs against legislative pressures and how long did it take before parliamentary strength could be translated into direct influence on executive decision-making, whether under some form of *Proporz* rule of access for minority parties or through the institutionalization of cabinet responsibility to legislative majorities?

The two first thresholds control the development of competitive mass politics. Once the threshold of legitimation is lowered there is a significant change in the character of politics: conspiratorial elite conflicts and repressive measures against dissidents tend to give way to public debate and open competition for support. Once the suffrage threshold is lowered the potential audience for such debate and the potential market for such competitive efforts increase by leaps and bounds; the result will almost invariably be a rush to develop organizations for the recruitment of support and for the consolidation of political identities.

Empirically, changes in the one threshold sooner or later generated pressures for change in the other but the timing of such decisions varied significantly from polity to polity.

To gain some understanding of the sources of such variations we clearly have to analyze the sequences of state formation and institution-building in each polity. The starting points for the processes of democratization varied markedly from case to case: to take only two extremes within the range of our eleven smaller democracies, the Swiss could build further on well-established traditions of representative city government and even of direct popular consultations in some rural cantons, while the Danes had lived under absolute monarchic rule from 1660 to 1831.

Four dimensions of variation seem particularly important in accounting for the timing of decisions on the two first thresholds:

First, the extent of territorial consolidation during the Middle Ages—the early national dynasties *vs.* the loosely federated provinces and cities within the successive Continental empires.

Second, the continuity in the operation of the medieval organs of representation—the countries maintaining some form of representation by territory and/or estates throughout the period from the Reformation to the French Revolution *vs.* the countries subjected to protracted periods of absolutist rule.

Third, the differentiation between old-established and newly-independent polities after the French Revolution—the older polities established up to 1648 *vs.* the newer ones generated through territorial separation and secession from 1814 onwards.

And fourth, the size and strength of the dominant polity before secession—the British-Irish case *vs.* the Danish-Norwegian.

These four criteria generate a typology for the ordering of the current West European polities by the initial conditions of democratic development. This is set out in Table 1.

The consequences of these marked differences can be traced from one point to the other in the process of democratization. Four generalizations about such effects seem worthy of detailed consideration:

First, the stronger the inherited traditions of representative rule, whether within estates, territorial assemblies or city councils, the greater the chances of early legitimation of opposition.

Second, the higher the international status of the dominant country the higher the barrier of legitimation in the dependent territory, the greater, consequently, the risk of violence in the internal politics of the seceding nation-state.

Thirdly, the stronger the inherited traditions of representative rule, the slower, and the less likely to be reversed, the process of enfranchisement and equalization.

And fourth, whatever the traditions of representation, the greater the threat to the aspirations of national independence the fewer the steps in the process of democratization.

Table 1. A developmental typology of conditions for the growth of mass democracy in Europe

Medieval consolidation	Continuity of representative organs	Status in international system		Polities in given category
		Seniority	Power rating: for old-established units its *own* rating; for later units the rating of the *territorial centre*	
1. Separate dynasty	11. High: minimal periods of absolute rule	111. Old-established	1111. Major 1112. Lesser	Britain Sweden
		112. Late independence	1121. Major	Ireland (under Britain to 1922)
			1122. Lesser	Finland (under Sweden to 1809, Russia to 1917)
	12. Low: protracted periods of absolute rule	121. Old-established	1211. Major	Spain France Prussia Austria: Empire
			1212. Lesser	Denmark
		122. Late independence	1221. Major 1222. Lesser	Austria: Rep. Norway (under Denmark to 1814, Sweden to 1905) Iceland (Denmark to 1940)
2. Cities, principalities and provinces within successive Continental Empires	21. Minor external disruptions: strong traditions of local democracy, minimal efforts of centralization	211. Old-established	2111. Major 2112. Lesser	No case Switzerland
		212. Late independence		No case
	22. Strong traditions of estate representation but brief periods of near-absolutist centralization	221. Old-established	2211. Major 2112. Lesser	No case Netherlands
		222. Late independence	2221. Major	Belgium (under Austria to 1794, France to 1815, Netherlands to 1831)
			2222. Lesser	Luxembourg (Netherlands, 1815-1839, part of German *Bund* to 1866)
	23. Oligarchic-absolutist heritage: violent centralization	232. Late independence	2321. Major	Italy (unified 1860-1870)

There are no simple ways of testing the two first hypotheses: there are few incontrovertible measures of the severity of sanctions against opponents and competitors. It is certainly possible to pin down the sequences of legislative and ministerial decisions on the freedom of expression and the right of association, but it is much more difficult to map the regularity of enforcement. Statistics of political violence, illegal demonstrations, secret organizations may be obtainable for a number of countries, but so far no serious attempts have been made at comparative analysis. Whatever the difficulties of precise measurement there is no dearth of qualitative evidence of the importance of the factors singled out in the two first hypotheses. There is little doubt that the absolutist heritage tended to keep the barrier of legitimation at a high level: the checkered record of censorship, repression and alienation in Spain, France, Prussia, Austria and Italy cannot easily be matched in the other countries of Western Europe. But the size of the polity and its experiences in acquiring independence will temper this generalization. . . . Three of the new European nation-states of the twentieth century have had particularly unhappy histories of civil strife: Finland, Ireland and Austria. It is tempting to look for common features in their location in the international system: in all the three cases a small national unit was divided under the impact of the presence of a dominant and threatening neighbor. . . . It is tempting to try out the generalization that the weaker or the more evenly equilibrated the pressures from the international environment, the greater the drive to legitimize oppositions within the body politic and the more persistent the efforts to accommodate conflicting forces within an overarching system of pluralist decision-making.[13]

The two hypotheses about the process of enfranchisement and equalization are easier to test: the succession of electoral laws can be coded on the different dimensions without great violence and the accelerating production of electoral statistics allows detailed quantitative controls for levels of participation and rates of mobilization.[14]

Table 2 allows quick inspection of the characteristic variations in sequences of democratization. The sequences for the eleven smaller countries have been located between two extremes: the English model of slow, step-by-step enfranchisement without reversals but with long periods of

[13]This argument has been elaborated in further detail by Gerhard Lehmbruch in *Proporzdemokratie: Politisches System und politische Kultur in der Schweiz und in Österreich* (Tübingen: Mohr, 1967): he stresses the functions of pluralist segmentation and *Proporz* executives for the stabilization of the national polity against disruptive pressures from the international environment; his main examples are Switzerland, Austria, the Lebanon and Cyprus.

[14]Cf. S. Rokkan, "Electoral Mobilization, Party Competition and National Integration," J. LaPalombara and M. Weiner, eds., *Political Parties and Political Development* (Princeton: Princeton University Press, 1966), pp. 241-265, and S. Rokkan and J. Meyriat, eds., *International Guide to Electoral Statistics* (Paris: Mouton, 1968).

formal recognition of inequalities; the French model of early and sudden universalization and equalization of political citizenship but with frequent reversals and with tendencies towards plebiscitarian exploitation of mass support.

Of the polities with strong traditions of representative government, Sweden, the Netherlands, Belgium, Luxembourg came closest to the English: Ireland, of course, followed willy-nilly under British rule. The exceptions fall at each extreme of the series. The Swiss cantons, the units with the longest experience of democratic or representative rule, followed the French model and agreed to introduce universal manhood suffrage as early as 1848. What is important in their case, however, is that there were no reversals and that the process was not pushed further to the ultimate goal of suffrage for women as well as men. At the other extreme, the Finns had the most explosive of all histories of democratization: the country moved in one single step from estate representation to universal suffrage for women and men in 1906.

Of the polities with histories of absolutist rule, Denmark came closest to the French model: sudden universalization and equalization (1849) but reversal to oligarchic control of the Upper House (1866). The development in Norway differed on one important point: the wide suffrage introduced as early as in 1814 was extended in three steps from 1884 to 1913 without any of the transitional inequalities characteristic of the English model, but there were *no reversals*. The two remaining countries do not fit any of these patterns. The multi-national Hapsburg Empire was caught in a difficult dilemma: democratization was functional for the mobilization of support within the Cisleithian German territory but potentially explosive within the subject territories. The result was a complex series of compromises from 1848 to 1907. At the other extreme, the smallest of the pluralist polities at the periphery of Europe could look back on a strong if disrupted tradition of democratic rule and was not driven by external pressures to mobilize its population to a maximum: as a result, the Icelanders did not rush into full democracy after the re-establishment of the Althing but moved cautiously step by step, in fact almost *pari passu* with the very gradual process of liberation from the Danes.

The two first thresholds set the stage for the emergence of competitive mass politics: once a system has moved across these two first barriers, it enters the era of mass electioneering and mass organization. But this does not necessarily make for any uniformity in the structure of electoral politics: the stakes of the game will vary with the rules of representation and the rules of access to executive power.

The *threshold of representation* came under heavy pressure once the rights of political participation had been extended to most or all male citizens: the rising parties of the hitherto disfranchised protested against the numerical injustices of the plurality systems; the smaller of the already

Table 2. Variations in extensions of suffrage in Europe by type of inherited tradition of rule

Type of State Formation:	Medieval Dynasties:				Territories within Continental Empires:	
Inherited Style of Rule	Continuous Organs of Representation				City Oligarchies and Provincial Estates	
Older Nation-states	Britain		Sweden		Netherlands	
Newer "Secession States"		Ireland		Finland		Belgium
Initial Organ of Representation	House of Commons	Grattan's Parliament to 1801	Four-Estate Riksdag	Four-Estate Diet 1809	Estates-General: Two Houses 1815	Provincial Estates
Major Post-Revolutionary Reorganization		British Parliament 1801-1918 Dail 1918-	Two-Chamber Riksdag 1866	Unicameral Diet 1906	Direct Elections 1848	Parliament 1831
Percent of Population Enfranchised under Old Rules	1830: 2.3%	1830: 0.5% (?)	1865: 4.8% 1866: 5.7%		1851: 2.4%	1831: 1%
First Extension: Lower houses only	1832	1832	1909		1887	1848
Later Extensions	1867 1884	1867 1885			1896	1893
Formally Instituted Electoral Inequalities Character	Business, University votes	Business, University votes	Weighted tax vote			Plural votes
Terminated	1948	1923	1920			1919
Manhood Suffrage Minor Qualifications Removed	1918	1918				1919
Universal Suffrage: Women as well as Men	1929	1923	1920	1906	1917	1949

Table 2 (contd.)

Type of State Formation: Inherited Style of Rule	Territories within Continental Empires: City Oligarchies and Provincial Estates		Medieval Dynasties: Protracted Absolutist Rule				
Older Nation-states Newer "Secession States"	Luxemburg	Switzerland	Austria: Empire Republic	Iceland	Norway	Denmark	France
Initial Organ of Representation	Estate Assembly 1841	City Councils, Cantonal Assemblies	Provincial Estates, Indirectly elected Reichsrat 1861	Althing: Consultative 1843-1874	Storting 1814-	Provincial Estates 1831-1849	Estates-General 1789
Major Post-Revolutionary Reorganization	Direct Elections 1848, 1868 Reversal 1856	Nationalrat 1848	Four-Curiae Reichsrat 1873	Legislature 1874-		Two-Chamber Parliament 1849	National Assembly 1789 Convention 1792, etc.
Percent of Population Enfranchised under Old Rules	1848: 2%		1873: 6%	1903: 9.8%	1814: 10%	1849: 14-15%	1815: 0.25%
First Extension: Lower houses only	1848		1882	1903	1885	Reversal 1866 (Upper House only)	Reversals 1795, 1814, 1852
Later Extensions	1868, 1892 1901		1897 Fifth Curiae	1915			Extension 1830
Formally Instituted Electoral Inequalities Character			Marked Inter-Curia Inequality 1907				
Terminated		↓		↓	↓	↓	↓
Manhood Suffrage Minor Qualifications		1848 Cantonal Citizenship	1907	1920 Paupers	1898 Paupers	1849 (30 years) Servants, etc.	1793, 1848, 1875
Removed				1934	1913-19	1915	
Universal Suffrage: Women as well as Men	1919		1919	1920	1915	1915	1945

entrenched *regime censitaire* parties feared for their survival and found it easier to lower the barrier than to merge with the dominant party in defense against the new claimants for power.

This is a fascinating field of comparative analysis: what were the socio-cultural conditions and the organizational constellations that made decisions in one direction more likely than decisions in the other? what considerations of alternative pay-offs and costs produced enough consensus to maintain the barriers or to yield to the pressure for some form of PR? Unfortunately, much of the scholarly literature on electoral systems has been bogged down in questions of morality and long-term functionality for the survival of each regime: this has led to a great deal of speculation about hypothetical developments but very little concrete analysis of decision-making situations.

The eleven smaller European democracies offer an interesting array of cases for comparison: they all yielded to the pressures for a lowering of the threshold but at different times and for very different reasons. The ethnically and religiously most divided of the polities were the first to break with the old tradition of "winner-take-all" representation: Denmark as early as the 1850's to accommodate the Schleswig minority, five of the Swiss cantons in the early 1890's, Belgium in 1899, Finland in 1906. In the other countries the rapid growth of the working-class parties immediately before or in the wake of the extension of the suffrage threatened the survival of at least one of the older parties and produced constellations where PR was the "saddle-point" solution in the game of opposition forces. This was true for Belgium in 1899, for Sweden in 1909, for the Danish Lower House in 1915, for the Nether-lands, Luxembourg, Norway, Austria and the entire Swiss Confederation at the end of or just after World War I. Only one of the eleven countries lagged behind in this movement: Iceland introduced PR in its economically and politically differentiated capital in 1920 but kept up the plurality system in the rural districts all the way up to 1959.

In most of the smaller countries the pressures for a lowering of the threshold took longer to make themselves felt in the rural peripheries than in the centers of economic and administrative development; but once the pressures mounted in the centers, there was little over-all resistance to the PR solution. In the larger countries of Europe the extension of the suffrage and the continuing processes of urbanization and industrialization generated heavy pressures for a lowering of the traditional thresholds. But the central establishments could muster greater resources against these movements and did not yield as easily: the English survived even the 1931 crisis without succumbing to the lures of PR or the alternative vote; the French gave in only for brief periods after each World War and the Germans after the collapse in 1918.

It is tempting to generalize from these contrasts:

(1) The pressures for PR will increase with the ethnic and/or religious

heterogeneity of the citizenry and, even in ethnically/religiously homogeneous electorates, with the increased economic differentiation generated through urbanization and the monetization of transactions;

(2) PR is more likely to prove the line of least resistance in differentiated democracies with smaller governmental resources, while plurality systems are more likely to be effectively defended in larger polities with stronger governmental establishments.

There is a great deal of evidence for the effects of urbanization and economic growth on partisan competition and mobilization.[15] The lower the density, the smaller the communities, the less developed and differentiated the economy, the more personal and territorial the style of representation and the less developed the organizations for local electoral competition. This has been shown across a number of countries in studies of partisanship at the *local* level,[16] but there can be little doubt that similar processes are at work at higher-level units of government. In Switzerland five cantons and two half-cantons still retain the traditional style of plurality voting: these are among the geographically most isolated and economically most backward within the Confederation. . . .

It is much more difficult to fit the second of the two empirical generalizations into any body of established social science theorizing: why should the smaller democracies on the whole tend to yield so much more readily, and with much less regret, to the pressures for PR than the larger ones? Clearly not just because there were deeper cleavages and more parties to accommodate already and therefore greater concern at the outset to protect the stakes of each of the established organizations. This fits many of the cases but only raises further questions about differences in the conditions for cross-cleavage aggregation in smaller versus larger systems. To put it in abstract game-theoretical terms: is it theoretically plausible to assume that party leaders in smaller polities are more likely to depart from the zero-sum model of political competition than their opposite numbers in larger systems?

Coalition theorists such as William Riker admit that zero-sum reasoning tends to break down in small groups.[17] The strict principle of

[15]See S. Rokkan, "Electoral Mobilization," *op. cit.*

[16]For France see M. Kesselman, "French Local Government: a Statistical Examination of Grass Roots Consensus," *American Political Science Review* 60 (Dec. 1966), pp. 963-973. For details on Norway see S. Rokkan and H. Valen, "The Mobilization of the Periphery," in S. Rokkan, ed., *Approaches to the Study of Political Participation* (Bergen: Michelsen Inst., 1962), pp. 111-158, and T. Hjellum, "The Politicization of Local Government in Norway," *Scandinavian Political Studies* 2 (1967), pp. 69-93.

[17]"Especially in small groups making genuine decisions rather than playing what they know is a game, considerations of maintaining the solidarity of the group and the loyalty of members to it probably dominate considerations of maximum victory on particular decisions." W. H. Riker, *The Theory of Political Coalitions* (New Haven: Yale University Press, 1962), p. 51.

coalition up to the "majority + 1" point but no further simply will not work in collectivities below given sizes. The difficulty is that there is hardly a trace of systematic research on the effects of variations in size above the typical small-group level: will there still be meaningful differences at the 100 vs. 200 level, the 200 vs. 400? All we can do at this stage is to suggest a few hypotheses for further evaluation and, whenever possible, empirical testing:

The greater ease of communication in the smaller system: the smaller the total number of legislators the greater the frequency of interaction among party leaders and the greater their reluctance to force one set of established bargaining partners to merge with one larger set through the maintenance of a polarizing plurality system.

The smaller resources for side-payments for prospective coalition partners: the smaller the democratic polity, the more limited the resources to be gained through straight majority victories, the less the total amount of "side payments" available and the greater the cost of bargains with prospective coalition partners; the greater, consequently, the temptation to leave such potential coalition partners to their electoral fates under some form of PR.[18]

The greater dependence on the stability of the international system: the smaller the polity, the less the leeway for independent action and the greater the concern to maintain national unity across party lines; the greater the pressure to maintain solidarity, the less the emphasis on zero-sum plurality competition and the greater, therefore, the tendency to accept PR as a safeguard against the uncertainties of a polarized "all-or-none" constellation.[19]

In line with Giovanni Sartori's classification of electoral systems the option for PR may be characterized as a "strategy of the weak": the leaders of the smaller democracies were so much more willing to yield to the pressures for a lowering of the threshold of representation because they tended to prefer the safety of their established positions of control in minority parties to the uncertainties of mergers and "winner-take-all" plurality elections. This is a point of critical importance in the comparative study of party systems. The introduction of PR in the final phase of mass mobilization helped to stabilize, if not to ossify, the structure of partisan

[18] For a classification of such coalition costs, see Riker, *op. cit.*, "The Cost and Value of Side-Payments," pp. 115-120.

[19] Similar arguments have been advanced for the Netherlands by Arend Lijphart in *The Politics of Accommodation: Pluralism and Democracy in the Netherlands* (Berkeley: University of California Press, 1967) and in his paper, "Typologies of Democratic Systems," Seventh World Congress of Political Science, Brussels, 1967. All the eleven smaller democracies are markedly more dependent on international trade than any of the larger ones. See B. Russett *et al.*, *World Handbook of Political and Social Indicators* (New Haven: Yale University Press, 1964), Table 46 and the further analysis in Robert A. Dahl and Edward R. Tufte, "Size and Democracy," paper, Center for Advanced Study in the Behavioral Sciences, Stanford, 1967.

alternatives in the central, more differentiated regions of each country. The party systems of the 1960's still

> . . . *reflect, with few but significant exceptions, the cleavage structures of the 1920s.* This is a crucial characteristic of Western competitive politics in the age of "high mass consumption": *the party alternatives, and in remarkably many cases the party organizations are older than the majorities of the national electorates.* To most of the citizens of the West the currently active parties have been part of the political landscape since their childhood or at least since they were first faced with the choice between alternative 'packages' on election day.[20]

This "organizational lag" has rarely been given the attention it deserves in comparative work on contemporary electoral data: to understand the current trends in each country and in each type of locality we have to bring in information not only about processes of socio-economic change but also about the *age and stability* of the *party alternatives.*

> This joining of diachronic and synchronic analysis strategies is of particular importance for an understanding of the mass politics of the organizationally saturated "high mass consumption" societies of the sixties: decades of structural change and economic growth have made the old-established alternatives increasingly irrelevant but the high level of organizational mobilization of most sectors of the community has left very little leeway for a decisive breakthrough of new party alternatives. It is not an accident that situations of this type generate a great deal of frustration, alienation and protestation within the organizationally least committed sections of the community: the *young* and, quite particularly the *students.*[21]

Nor, it would seem, is it an accident that these waves of disaffection with the established party alternatives started out in the central areas and the cities: in many of the rural peripheries the old parties are still eagerly mobilizing further support and have not reached the same degree of structural ossification as at the centres.

Such variations in the lag between the process of socio-economic change and the process of political development cannot be studied without detailed consideration of the role of the parties in *executive decision-making:* the *fourth* and the final threshold in our abstract model.

Let us, to rub in the structure of our argument, again follow the fate of our typical movement of opposition to established privileges, whether based on Orthodox Protestant rejection of the State Church, Catholic protest against secular control of education, or working-class claims against owners and employers.

It has crossed the *first* threshold: it is given the right to communicate its views, to organize, to take part in elections. It has also crossed the *second*

---

[20]S. M. Lipset and S. Rokkan, "Cleavage Structures," *op. cit.,* p. 50.
[21]*Ibid.,* p. 54.

threshold: it is not only free to recruit support but each supporter is given rights to influence the choice of representatives on a par with the supporters of the established regime. It has even crossed the *third* threshold: it has not only collected votes but had them translated into seats in the legislature at the same rate as any of the earlier, and possibly larger, parties. This leaves the *final* threshold, the threshold of executive power: how many votes, how many seats are needed before the party is given a chance to exert effective influence on central decisions for the polity? . . .

Our eleven European polities varied significantly in the timing of decisions on the threshold of executive power: some of them followed the British example and introduced the principle of Cabinet responsibility to Parliamentary majorities well before the decisive extensions of the suffrage, some lowered the two thresholds roughly at the same time, while others stuck to the separation-of-powers doctrine for decades after the broadening of the suffrage. Belgium and the Netherlands came closest to the English model of *régime censitaire* parliamentarism. The Belgians introduced responsible government from the very beginning in 1831; the Dutch from 1848 onwards. Norway reached the same stage later but the victory of Parliament over the Executive was a result of a major wave of partisan mobilization and was soon to lead on to full manhood suffrage. Denmark, Sweden and the Austrian Empire came close to what we might call the German model: manhood suffrage came before the introduction of Parliamentary rule. The lag was particularly marked in Denmark: the wide suffrage introduced in 1849 had allowed the anti-establishment movements to mobilize broad support and gain a parliamentary majority long before the Executive finally gave way in 1901. The lag was not that critical in Sweden: manhood suffrage came in 1909 and the final victory over the Executive came in 1920. In Austria, as in Germany, the threshold fell with the military defeat of the old regime in 1918. In the three youngest of our eleven polities, Finland, and Ireland, the power of Parliament was tempered by the authority of the President. Both Finland and Ireland experienced great difficulties in establishing a balance between the elected representatives and the Executive in the early phase of independent government, but the *principle* of Cabinet responsibility to the majority of the elected representatives was never seriously challenged.

In all these cases the threshold of executive power was formally lowered to the 50 per cent point only: a party or a block could only gain access to Cabinet positions by securing majority support in the Legislature. The Swiss went one step further: they gave minority parties regular access to the cantonal and the federal executives and established the principle of *Proporz* representation not only at the level of the elected assemblies, but even in the designation of members of the Cabinet. This system of "two-tier PR" was approximated in other deeply segmented polities in Europe: the long series of coalition governments in the Netherlands allowed parties in the 10-15 percent range frequent if not automatic access to the Executive and the three-cornered struggles among the *familles spirituelles* in Belgium and Luxembourg and the *Lager* in Austria often lowered the threshold of executive power well below the 50 percent mark. In general, the likelihood of minority participation in the Executive appears to increase (a) with the distance of the largest party from the majority point, (b) with the closeness and "bargainability" of the policy alternatives represented by the potential coalition partners, (c) with the severity of the pressures from the international environment. Our eleven countries have differed markedly on each of these scores, both over time, from phase to phase since the introduction of parliamentary rule, and among each other. Any attempt to account for the variations in electoral behavior across all these countries must take this into account: in some countries elections have had the character of an effective choice among alternative teams of governors, in others they have simply served to express segmental loyalties and to ensure the right of each segment to *some* representation, even if only a single portfolio, in a coalition cabinet.

The salient differences in the structure of electoral alternatives can be brought out through a crude classification by type of contest: this is attempted in Table 3.

None of our eleven democracies has experienced extended periods of straight alternation between two major parties: the typical "ins-outs" politics characteristic of Britain, the United States and some of the white Commonwealth countries. Austria and Ireland, and during some periods Belgium, have come closest to what German commentators have called the two-and-a-half party system: two large parties running neck and neck for the majority point but generally thwarted in their endeavors by the persistence of one small above-threshold party. This was the situation in Austria practically from the first republican election: the Nationalist camp was just strong enough to prevent one of the two large parties from gaining a safe majority. The Irish party system came close to this model in the late 'twenties but the Republican *Fianna Fail* party was soon to take the lead and left the pro-treaty *Fine Gael* well behind in election after election. In fact, the Irish constellations of the 'fifties and 'sixties are almost halfway between the German-Austrian system and the Scandinavian: one large party near the majority point and several middle-sized parties competing for the next places. Belgium enjoyed a two-party system during the *régime censitaire* but has since oscillated between the Austrian-Irish constellation and what we shall call the "segmented pluralism" model.

In Sweden, Denmark and Norway the first elections after the introduction of PR produced very even distributions among three to four parties, but the Social Democrats soon moved up to the majority point and left the other contenders competing for the other half of the votes. This process went furthest in Sweden and in Norway: the Swedish Social Democrats entered the Executive as early as in 1917 and have managed to stay in power on majorities or near-majorities for over thirty years; the Norwegian Labour

Table 3.   A classification of the party systems of the smaller European democracies after World War I: By the likelihood of single-party majorities and the distribution of minority party strengths

Country	Period	Total seats (Lower house)	Largest party: Distance from Majority Point — Min.	Max.	Two next parties: Seats Below First Party — Second party Min.	Max.	Third party Min.	Max.	Other parties: Total Seats Min.	Max.
I. The British-German "1 vs. 1" System										
Austria	I. Rep.	159-183	−1	−11	45	67	2	16	0	3
Ireland	II. Rep.	165	+2	−9	60	(none)	1	11	0	5
	1922-32	128, 153	−5	−30	25	65	3	23	17	40
	1933-44	153, 138	+8	−2	50	68	21	46	7	24
	1944-65	147, 144	+4	−9	46	66	15	38	3	34
II. The Scandinavian "1 vs. 3-4" System										
Sweden	1921-32	230	−11	−25	58	76	17	46	28	39
	1936-44	230	+19	−3	76	106	68	92	26	41
	1948-64	230, 233	−2	−10	64	82	48	74	25	45
Denmark	1920-29	139, 148	−13	−23	20	37	3	18	19	22
	1932-57	148, 175	−6	−26	22	44	8	40	21	36
	1960-66	175	−12	−19	35	44	34	38	25	37
Norway	1921-30	150	−16	−28	14	30	6	29	27	38
	1933-57	150	+10	−6	45	64	34	62	21	31
	1961-65	150	−1	−7	50	58	37	45	31	33
III. Even Multiparty Systems: "1 vs. 1+2-3"										
1. Scandinavian "Split Working Class" systems										
Finland	1919-39	200	−15	−47	18	62	1	38	33	67
	1945-66	200	−44	−50	1	18	1	6	50	62
Iceland	1923-37	42, 49	+2	−6	10	19	2	8	0	5
	1942-63	49, 60	−5	−7	14	15	1	7	6	9
2. "Segmented Pluralism"										
Netherlands	1918-37	100	−18	−22	18	18	6	12	29	36
	1946-56	100	−16	−20		24		5	23	28
	1959-67	150	+25	−33	25	35	0	7	34	54
Belgium	1919-39	186, 202	−15	−31	39	55	1	9	9	48
	1946-65	202, 212	+2	−29	29	88	9	39	3	23
Luxembourg	1945-59	51, 52	0	−5	10	20	2	14	3	6
Switzerland	1919-39	187-198	−37	−44	8	17	2	17	42	53
	1943-63	194-200	−41	−47	3	13	0	9	46	50

party had its first taste of ministerial Socialism in 1927 and stayed in power for thirty years from 1935 to 1965. The Danish Social Democrats never reached clear majorities: they have enjoyed long periods of Cabinet power but have either relied on *ad hoc* aggregations of support in Parliament or entered into coalition with minor partners. With the spectacular gain of the Left Socialists in 1966, the Danish system has in fact moved closer to the other Scandinavian model: the type of structure produced in Finland and Iceland through the split between Communists and Social Democrats.

The Finnish constellation was quite similar to the Danish until the Second World War: one large Social Democrat party, one middle-sized Agrarian party, and a couple of parties (Finland: three, Denmark: two) in the 10-15 percent range. With the legalization of the Communist party in 1944 the working class Left was split down the middle: the result was a "1 *vs.* 1 *vs.* 1 + 3" system doomed to some form of coalition government or, when coalitions could not be kept together, transitional admixtures of technocrats or even direct trade union representatives. There was a similar development in Iceland: before the war a period of majorities or near-majorities for the Conservative-liberal Independence party, later an even split among 3 to 4 parties.

This, of course, had been the typical constellation in the religiously and ethnically split countries along the Protestant-Catholic border belt across the Continent. In the Netherlands and in Switzerland no party was ever within shooting range of the majority point after the end of World War I. In Belgium the situation was very similar before World War II, but changed for a couple of periods after World War II. From 1949 to 1954 and again in 1958 the Catholics hovered close to the majority point and the system approached the "1 vs. 1 + 1" constellation we identified as Austrian-Irish: this, of course, came to an abrupt end with the politicization of the linguistic cleavages in the 1960's and the resurgence of the Liberals and the Flemish Nationalists.

This typology of party constellations is purely numerical: the decisive criteria of differentiation are the proximity to the majority point and the evenness of the contests for the top position.

In our comments on the table we have slipped into concrete interpretations of particular national cleavage structures, but the thrust of our argument is that the abstract numerical constellation is of critical importance in the comparative study of electoral behavior: there is good reason to believe that it makes a difference, both in the style of party activity and in the behavior of potential supporters, how close the system is to straight majority dominance and how much responsibility each competing party has had for central executive decision-making. This is an important field for detailed research across countries and across parties. There has been a great deal of excited speculation about the "domestication" effects of proximity to national power[22] but no one has as yet tried to assemble even very simple arrays of information on party structure, party personnel and party ideology across countries differing in their sequences of decisions on the fourth and final threshold. To make any headway in this direction it would be essential to seek out socio-culturally similar parties at roughly the same levels of national strength and study their structures and their ideological out-pourings at three distinct stages of development: as a force of pure opposition outside and/or inside the Legislature, as a partner in a coalition, as the sole governing party. But the effects of such changes in proximity to the national power resources cannot be studied *in abstracto:* the institutional rules of the game set a variety of constraints on the actions of party personnel and party representatives once they approach power, but their actual options within these limits can only be understood against the history of cleavage articulation and interest aggregation in each country. . . .

[22]See e.g., S. Rokkan, "Norway: Numerical Democracy and Corporate Pluralism," in R. A. Dahl, ed., *Political Oppositions in Western Democracies* (New Haven: Yale University Press, 1966), pp. 89-105.

11

Trade Unions, Benefit Systems, and Party Mobilization Styles

Arnold J. Heidenheimer

The conditions under which the British Labour party and the German Social Democrats presently exercise power are probably the reverse of what an informed observer in the year 1912 might have forecast. It then appeared highly probable that the recently founded Labour party could for many decades hope to enter governments as no more than a junior coalition partner. By contrast, the rate of electoral progress of the Social Democrats, who won 36 percent of the vote in the elections of 1912, seemed to indicate that their goal of achieving power legally by becoming a majority party in the Reichstag might not be more than a decade or so away, given a certain optimism about imminent changes in the German constitutional system, such as the full introduction of the rules of parliamentary government. The literature relevant to an explanation of why such expectations were not borne out constitutes one of the most extensive bodies of scholarship in the social sciences. This article ventures to add to it by seeking to analyze the "horizontal" shaping of party mobilization traditions by organizational and benefit-extension techniques that were developed by British and German trade unions and contemporary workers' insurance systems during the 1890-1914 period.

The inquiry is built upon the consideration that the bulk of both parties' members, and during this period also a majority of their voters, had experienced their first organizational socialization through their member-

Reprinted by permission of the author and journal from "Trade Unions, Benefit Systems, and Party Mobilization Styles: 'Horizontal' Influences on the British Labour and German Social Democratic Parties," *Comparative Politics* 1 (Apr. 1969), pp. 313-342. Article and footnotes abridged and most tables deleted. An earlier version was presented to the 1968 Annual Meeting of The American Political Science Association. The author would like to acknowledge the very valuable research assistance of Miss Charlene Awenius and Mrs. Audrey Wells.

ship in labor unions and/or mutual insurance organizations such as Friendly Societies and Sickness Funds. Within these organizations leaders and officials extracted dues support from the membership, the proceeds from which were allocated to different categories of goal-related expenditures in ways about which a body of governmental and union statistics provides extensive evidence. Union income and expenditure patterns are analyzed with reference to what they indicate about the channeling of union resources into methods that writers like the Webbs and Franz Neumann have considered the three basic alternative techniques of goal achievement widely utilized by trade unionists—the methods of (1) *mutual insurance,* (2) *collective bargaining,* and (3) *legislative enactment.*[1] The activities of Friendly Societies and Sickness Funds (which we shall label primary insurance systems) were of course overtly relevant to union employment of the first technique, but, as will be shown, their roles could also be extremely relevant to questions of whether and how unions conditioned their membership in utilizing and supporting the other two techniques.

In the first section of this article, I shall examine how the pre-1890 sequence of union, insurance benefit program, and political party foundings conditioned goal orientations and shaped and influenced modal tendencies within both movements with regard to "investment" options. In the second section, I shall analyze the rates at which both union movements channeled their resources and induced their membership to maintain or increase their level of dues support. The units of analysis throughout are "union memberships." For Britain, the data here refer particularly to the "100 Principal Unions," a representative body of the larger British unions about whom statistical information is better than average; for Germany, the information is based on the *Zentralverbände* affiliated to the "Free Trade Unions," whose number varied between forty and sixty-five over the twenty-four-year period. Most of the third section is devoted to ascertaining the differences between Britain and Germany in the degree to which commitment to specific union goals, such as sickness benefit extension or buildup of union treasuries, were related to rates of political mobilization. Information here is based upon samples of twenty-six large British unions and twenty-three German unions with large Berlin memberships.

In the fourth section, I shall point out how union influences may explain some of the great differences in organization and mobilization style that have distinguished the two parties for the past two generations. There I shall also pose and attempt to answer more general questions relating to the advantages and liabilities of subculture alliances for parties which start as "parties of the movement" and are in transition to making themselves acceptable as potential "parties of government."

[1]Sidney and Beatrice Webb, *Industrial Democracy* (London 1898), Part II; Franz Neumann, *European Trade Unionism and Politics* (New York 1936), pp. 11-12.

I. DEVELOPMENT SEQUENCES AND UNION OPTIONS DURING THE PERIOD 1890-1914

After the Chartist interlude, most British workers joined nineteenth-century working-class organizations primarily in response to appeals to their individual and exclusive group interests. It was only very gradually, during the second half of the century, that goals applicable to larger collectivities, such as those of class and national community, began to appear more relevant. For the vast bulk of British skilled workers, membership in Friendly (Mutual Insurance) Societies came first; this was followed by the founding and growth of trade unions that were more explicitly oriented toward collective bargaining functions; and last came the right to vote and to participate meaningfully in political action. In Germany the sequence was rather the reverse. Both Bismarck and Bebel taught the working class to think in terms of public or inclusive collective benefits, which would be extended to them as Germans or as members of the working class. In Germany, too, the opportunity to derive basic sickness and invalidity benefits through a state-sponsored compulsory insurance system largely preceded opportunities for deriving similar benefits through the trade unions. The Social Democratic party (SPD) antedated, and for decades dominated, the nascent union movement, and the opportunity to vote came earlier for most workers than did the opportunity to organize effectively for purposes of collective bargaining at the factory or industry level.

Thus, in Britain many more British workers were members of Friendly Societies (1872 membership, about four million), which utilized mutual-help techniques for the satisfaction of individual welfare goals, than were members of the trade unions of the 1870's (1872 membership, about one million), which sought to utilize the same techniques to achieve exclusive goods for their members. In turn, the primarily craft-based unions achieved respectable mass memberships before very many of their members were enfranchised by the electoral reforms of 1867 and 1884, and several decades were to pass until, from 1906 on, Labour candidates gave many an opportunity to vote for a political party that specifically espoused working-class goals. The goals that British workers sought to achieve by legislative enactment before 1890 were often exclusive collective goals; thus, there were instances of successful agitation by alliances of unions in the mining and cotton industries for legislative regulation of the length of the working day and other matters related to their particular industries. Because of this tendency the Trades Union Congress (TUC) actually declined in significance once it had secured the broad goal of legal recognition of the unions' right to strike through the Trade Union Acts of 1871-1875. To the extent that particular unions became politically active in local policies, or in supporting or sponsoring candidates for Parliament, they did so largely with reference to their own sectional interests. In the short run, these commitments greatly impeded the emergence of a class-based party.

In Germany, by contrast, many workers assumed the role of SPD voters, even under the anti-Socialist laws, long before they took out union memberships. Many in Germany believed in the 1890's that the country was not fertile ground for union growth, partly because of the dominant position of political parties, but mainly because of the existence of public insurance schemes. The latter were implemented on the basis of the Sickness, Invalidity, and Accident Insurance bills which Bismarck pushed through the Reichstag from 1883 to 1885. Between 1885 and 1906 these schemes paid 1.7 million accident claims and 1.9 million invalidity pensions. But the insurance system which affected the most workers was that based on the Sickness Funds, which made seventy million sickness reimbursement payments during the same period.[2] By 1892, some seven million German wage earners were members of the Sickness Funds, and by 1907 their number had grown to twelve million; in the same years the membership of the Free Trade unions numbered 237,000 and 1.8 million, respectively.

The years 1890-1914 may be viewed as the molding-period during which the unions and parties shaped most of the traditions that they have maintained ever since. Moreover, in terms of size, environmental conditions, and options regarding the employment of alternative techniques, the unions of the two countries were as comparable as they ever were, until perhaps the mid-1950's. During this period, the rise of the New Unionism diluted the craft character of British unions, while in Germany the repeal of the anti-Socialist laws (1890) and the revision of the Associational laws (1899) removed some of the more overt obstacles to union development in a variety of industries. Options regarding political activation also gradually became more comparable. In Britain franchise extension, the founding of the Independent Labour party (ILP), and the proliferation of other labor political groups that culminated in the 1900 founding of the Labour party created conditions which rapidly became similar to those which developed in Germany after 1890. It is widely known that the two situations remained vastly different, not only in regard to the distribution of prevailing ideologies

---

[2]There were several varieties of Sickness Funds operating within the framework of the compulsory public program. The great majority of manual workers were insured by the *Ortskrankenkassen* (OKK), which in 1908 numbered 4,768 and had 6.3 million members. There were also five other categories of Sickness Funds, but their combined membership was lower than that of the OKK, whose share of insured workers increased to 70 percent by 1928. In the subsequent discussion of Free Trade Union-Sickness Fund relations, reference is usually to the OKK. While it is not claimed that the Sickness Funds are "typical" of the complex panoply of public welfare-distribution agencies, they are here treated as surrogates for the process of benefit collectivization.

but also in regard to the policies taken toward union growth and political mobilization by such institutions as churches, state bureaucracies, and employers. But, insofar as they wanted to employ one or more of the Webbian techniques, unions in both countries were, within broad limits, free to do so. In the following section I shall briefly characterize the dominant national trends in terms of whether, how, and when they did utilize these tactics.

Organizational Model Options

Option 1: To subordinate membership and organizational growth in favor of greater exclusive goods for the existing membership, through benefit distribution, as well as through increased leverage in collective bargaining. Whereas this option was taken in Germany by a few well-established unions such as those in the printing industry, in Britain this pattern was followed by most of the powerful craft unions, few of whom were very active in organizing large new potential memberships during the 1890's. In Germany the strong Socialist commitments of most of the union leaders inhibited frank avowal of such objectives, as did the unions' weaker bargaining positions.

Option 2: To pursue decentralized growth with minimal emphasis on inter-union coordination and maximal emphasis on adaptation to local and industry conditions. This certainly was the option chosen by the bulk of the British unions. One indication of this trend is that there were 1,233 separate unions in 1890 and that their number actually increased to 1,269 in 1910. Another indicator was the characteristic reluctance of the local and regional components of British unions that did achieve nominal national membership to delegate power and funds to the union executives. The lack of central coordination in British trade unionism was bemoaned by the Webbs[3] in 1887, and twenty-five years later G. D. H. Cole complained that "the Trade Union movement, *as a whole,* has no brains. . . . The statistical departments of English Trade Unionism do not exist; there is no idea at the centre what is happening anywhere else. . . . There is no Trade Union literature and there is no staff capable of writing it. . . . Great Britain cannot go lagging behind the rest of the world, allowing the most backward nations to pass her in methods of organization, and doing nothing to catch them up. This very question of Trade Union structure is the very worst of all instances of our incompetence."[4]

Option 3: To emphasize centralized growth with close coordination of mobilization efforts through strong national union federations and their

---

[3]Webb, pp. 265ff.
[4]G. D. H. Cole, *The World of Labour* (London 1913), p. 246.

full-time officials. This option was initially chosen by the German unions when they coordinated themselves within the Generalkommission in 1891, and it was relentlessly pursued in the subsequent decade. Throughout the period, the Free Trade Union membership (which covered some 80 percent to 90 percent of unionized workers, the remainder being attached to much smaller Liberal and Christian federations) was encompassed in some forty to sixty national unions. The independence of the union locals was continuously undermined, while the numbers of full-time union officers responsible mainly to national headquarters increased faster than did membership.

Policy Options toward Primary Insurance Systems

Option 1: To accept the prevailing distribution of benefit responsibility between primary insurance systems and unions and to make no attempt to alter the balance. It was easier for British unions to adopt this option, as most did, because the Friendly Societies did not constitute the deterrent to union mobilization that the officially-sponsored Sickness Funds did in Germany. By 1890 most of the older British unions had well-established benefit programs that encouraged maintenance of membership. Closely linked in their genealogy and supervised in a rather parallel, permissive manner by the Registrar of Friendly Societies, the two groups of organizations complemented each other so well that they left remarkably little evidence of conflicts or acrimony.

Option 2: To rival primary insurance systems by greatly increasing union benefit programs. Although membership in German Sickness Funds was compulsory for most industrial workers, as opposed to voluntary membership in the Friendly Societies, it was Germany that developed the more competitive situation. The unions started out by concentrating on such benefits as unemployment insurance which the state-sponsored program deliberately excluded, but later, in order to attract and hold members, they began to offer other benefits that supplemented those included in the Sickness Funds.

Option 3: To infiltrate the primary insurance systems. The lack of coordination between branches of different British unions would have handicapped a systematic attempt to capture control of Friendly Societies in the same localities. There is no evidence that the goal was seriously entertained anywhere, although there are some instances of the reverse taking place.[5] In Germany, however, the Sickness Fund law provided that local Funds be administered by boards elected by the contributors. Since two-thirds of the contributions were paid by the workers and only one-third by the employers,

---

[5]John Corbett, *The Birmingham Trades Council, 1866-1966* (London 1966), p. 168.

the workers could, if they were well organized, win control of local Sickness Funds. The Free Trade Unions soon recognized this opportunity, with the consequence that the "strong union organization linking workers of the same trade naturally became take-off points for the organization of elections to the insurance boards."[6]

Political Mobilization Options

Option 1: To maintain an official policy of union neutrality but to encourage uniform political activation of members as voters and party members. The German Associational laws[7] forced the Free Trade Unions to remain officially neutral even though virtually all their leaders were enrolled as Social Democrats. In Britain political neutrality remained convenient for most unions, since their leaders included Socialists, Liberals, and even Conservatives. In Germany the pre-existing and well-organized Social Democratic party encouraged the unions to act as its "recruitment agencies." With time, however, the union leaders found this appellation obnoxious and claimed "equality" with the party. After achieving equal recognition at the Mannheim SPD Congress of 1906, their rate of converting union members into "union-and-party members" became still more impressive, so that by 1912 probably well over 25 percent of unionists were also enrolled in the party.

Option 2: To politicize union membership incrementally through a variety of limited campaigns in circumscribed geographic areas and/or time periods involving limited demands in terms of material sacrifices, changes in party identification, and so forth. The linking of most unions to the Labour party can be perceived as the culmination of a long process that began with union petitions to MP's, developed into local alliances and the sponsorship of Liberal-Labour candidates by individual unions, and later encompassed the founding of the ILP and the Labour Representation Committee (LRC), whose slowly expanding activities were backed by a gradually increasing number of unions. In this sense, British unions were literally drifting into the Labour party, as legislative enactment proved a worthwhile method and as it

[6]Paul Kampffmeyer, "Die Entwicklung der deutschen Gewerkschaften," *Annalen für soziale Politik und Gesetzgebung* 1 (Berlin 1912), p. 118.

[7]Until the adoption of the Reich Associational Law of 1908, different regulations applied in various Länder, and there were also different penalties attached to being constituted as a "political association." In Prussia and elsewhere political associations were required to submit membership lists to the police, and were barred from enrolling women, apprentices, and youths. There were continuous prosecutions through which the police attempted to impose these obligations on various unions.

became possible gradually to surmount the obstacles to effective political mobilization.

Option 3: To enter into a corporate commitment through which union efforts were unreservedly placed at the disposal of a chosen political party which regards itself as an instrument of a labor movement. As legislative enactment proved an effective technique, the British unions were encouraged to make heavier investments in political activity and to forge enduring corporate ties to the Labour party. The party's acceptance of a socialist platform coincided with the replacement of demands for exclusive, sectional goods by demands for inclusive-collective, or public, goods.

II. GROWTH RATES IN SUPPORT EXTENSION AND INVESTMENT

In the course of the 1890's, the German Free Trade Unions slowly built up their membership and very gradually narrowed the gap between their membership and that of the "100 Principal Unions" whose characteristics will be examined here as representative of British trends.[8] At the beginning of the decade German membership (1892: 237,000) was about one-quarter that of the British (1892: 905,000), but the gap slowly narrowed until toward the end of the 1890's German membership (1899: 580,000) was nearly half as large as the British (1899: 1,164,000). During the same period, however, the German unions made very slow progress in reducing the tremendous difference between their income and accumulated funds figures and those of the British unions. In 1892 the total German union funds amounted to only 2 percent of British union funds, and by 1899 the proportion had risen to only about 8 percent. As regards income, the German unions collected about 7 percent as much as the British unions did in 1892, and by 1899 they were collecting about 21 percent of the British figures.

Benefit and Dues Extraction Increases

The reasons that the German unions extracted comparatively little from their members lie less in wage, strike, and employment patterns

---

[8] I have not discovered any passages in the publications of the Board of Trade and the Registrar of Friendly Societies which clearly explain the selection of the "100 Principal Unions." But the selection appears to have been made on the basis of both representativeness and size. Thus, the list generally includes those larger unions which in the various industrial sectors represented close to two-thirds of unionized workers.

than in the fact that most of them long remained hostile on ideological grounds to the introduction of the type of union benefit programs to which the average British union was devoting three-fifths of its expenditures.

After close to a decade of difficulties in enrolling and retaining new members, the German unions in the course of a few years radically revised their attitudes and practices toward the inclusion of benefits in union programs and the desirable level of dues. . . .

As Table 1 indicates, the reorientation of the German unions in the late 1890's resulted in dramatic differences between their rate of increasing per capita dues and that of the British unions. Whereas in the 1890's the average

Table 1. **Indices of growth of income and funds, 100 British unions and German free trade unions** *(British union income and funds for 1892= 100)*

	Income				Funds			
	British		German		British		German	
Year	Amount (000's of £)	Index	Amount (000's of marks)	Index	Amount (000's of £)	Index	Amount (000's of marks)	Index
1891 ...			1,117	4			426	1
1892 ...	1,477	100	2,032	7	1,620	100	646	2
1893 ...	1,625	110	2,246	8	1,382	85	801	2
1894 ...	1,634	111	2,686	9	1,579	97	1,319	4
1895 ...	1,560	106	3,037	10	1,748	108	1,640	5
1896 ...	1,676	113	3,616	12	2,188	135	2,324	7
1897 ...	1,982	134	4,084	14	2,272	140	2,951	9
1898 ...	1,902	129	5,509	19	2,644	163	4,373	13
1899 ...	1,835	124	7,687	26	3,226	199	5,578	17
1900 ...	1,950	132	9,454	32	3,733	230	7,746	24
1901 ...	2,050	139	9,723	33	4,139	255	8,798	27
1902 ...	2,094	142	11,098	38	4,426	273	10,254	32
1903 ...	2,109	143	16,420	56	4,612	285	12,974	40
1904 ...	2,124	144	20,191	68	4,680	289	16,110	50
1905 ...	2,228	151	27,812	94	4,830	298	19,636	61
1906 ...	2,364	160	41,603	141	5,222	322	25,313	78
1907 ...	2,518	170	51,397	174	5,668	350	33,243	103
1908 ...	2,767	187	48,544	164	5,201	321	40,840	126
1909 ...	2,585	175	50,529	171	5,079	314	43,481	134
1910 ...	2,716	184	64,372	218	5,153	318	52,576	162
1911 ...	2,952	200	72,172	244	5,595	345	62,106	192
1912 ...	3,230	219	80,376	272	5,002	309	80,798	249
1913 ...	4,132	280	82,177	278	5,700	352	88,069	272

per capita dues of German union members were little more than one-quarter of those in British unions, within scarcely two decades the difference between the average dues levels was almost completely erased. As striking as the rate of German dues increases is the static level of the British dues. Because the rapidly growing unions of unskilled workers had low dues levels, the average of British union dues actually declined after 1911, and in 1912 the average of German union dues was at a higher absolute level in Germany than in Britain.

Whereas it took the British unions twenty years to double their total dues income above the level of 1892, the German unions covered the same absolute distance in a five-year period between 1905 and 1910. It proved more difficult, however, to approach the much higher level of funds which the British unions had accumulated mainly as the result of their longer existence and more fully developed benefit programs. By 1907 the German Free Trade Union membership was larger than that of the British groups, but it was only in that year that the funds of the German unions were as large as those of the British group fifteen years earlier. Yet here, too, the Germans came very close to bridging the gap, and by 1912 the eighty million Reichmark in German union treasuries were equivalent to 80 percent of the five million pounds held by the British union group. . . .

Table 2.   Average annual dues income per capita of British (100 principal) and German ("free") trade unions *(in shillings and marks)* *

Period	British Unions	German Unions
1892-1898	33.50	10.8
1899-1907	34.33	20.54
1908-1914	33.67	30.82

*Throughout the 1890-1914 period, 1 mark = 1 shilling.

Intra-movement Ranges and Configurations

Since highly aggregated indicators, such as those utilized in the previous section, may camouflage intra-movement differences of great significance, Table 3 provides information about the range of union dues within the two movements. It is based on the average level of dues within each of the hundred British unions in 1904 and the sixty-four German unions in 1906; therefore, it does not take account of intra-union differences in dues levels. These data indicate that, at a time when total union membership was in both countries close to two million, inter-union diversity in regard to dues levels was immensely greater in Britain than in Germany. In Germany, the deviation from the norm of average union dues levels ranging from fifteen to thirty marks a year was very limited, with only 15 percent of the total union membership enrolled in unions whose average dues were outside these limits. In Britain, only 44 percent of the membership was in unions whose average dues were within the same range; 30 percent of the membership paid more than fifty shillings a year, while 15 percent of the members were in unions whose average dues were below fifteen shillings.

Table 3. **Distribution of 100 British and 64 German trade unions and their memberships regarding average annual dues**

Britain (1904)								Average Annual Dues in Marks/Shillings	Germany (1906)					
N	% of U.M.	N	% of U.M.	N	% of U.M.	N	% of U.M.		N	% of U.M.	N	% of U.M.	N	% of U.M.
				25	15.3			0 to 15	6	1.7				
						38	44.1	15 to 30	50	85.3				
				15	11.1			30 to 40			3	9.2		
		18	19.1					50 to 70					5	3.8
4	10.4							over 70						

Source: Computations on the basis of official British and Generalkommission statistics cited in Hans Fehlinger, "Gewerkschaftsfinanzen in Deutschland und England," *Sozialistische Monatshefte*, XIV (?) (1908), 619-628.

One can deduce from these data that in Germany the labor movement not only had a fairly consistent ideological coloration, but it also exhibited strong modal organizational and mobilization tendencies that long remained underdeveloped or entirely lacking within British trade unionism. The diversity-homogeneity dichotomization extended to all levels of union organization in the two countries during this period. Local British union branches jealously maintained great autonomy against their own union executives, and they also retained the lion's share of dues income in their own treasuries. In many craft unions of the 1890's, the executive had little power and was, for economy's sake, recruited entirely from members who lived in the city where headquarters was located; many among even the larger unions did not create representative national executives until after 1900.[9] In Germany the unions quickly moved to centralize decision-making powers in their executives to the point where most union statutes provided that elections to branch executives were subject to the approval of the national executive. Whereas in Britain the union executive was long "confined to that of a center of communication between practically autonomous branches," in many German unions the local branches even lost their names, as a vocabulary based on constitutive concepts was changed to one based on

[9]Webb, p. 46; H. A. Clegg, Alan Fox, and A. F. Thompson, *A History of British Trade Unions Since 1887* (Oxford 1964), vol. I, pp. 476-477.

an administrative model. Thus, in many statutes, the term *"Ortsverein"* was replaced by terms like *"Zahlstellen"* and *"Filialen,"* which were under the supervision of *"Bezirksleiter"* and *"Gauleiter"* whose position was explicitly likened to that of *"Ober-präsidenten"* within the Prussian administration.

This process of administrative development and concentration[10] was made possible by the higher level of dues support infusion, and it served also to impose prevailing trends fairly uniformly throughout the movement. The figures in Table 4 indicate how swiftly the initiative to increase dues was imposed upon the majority of the unions. Whereas in 1898 two-thirds of the unions had dues levels of less than twenty pfennig a week, and only three had dues of more than forty pfennig, by 1907 almost two-thirds had dues levels of more than forty pfennig, and only two unions retained the lower dues levels which had been modal nine years earlier.

Table 4.   Percent of German unions levying various average dues, 1892-1907

Year	Total No. of Unions	%Weekly Dues		
		Less than 20 Pf.	21 to 40 Pf.	41 Pf. or more
1892.	39	82.0	10.3	7.7
1898.	55	67.2	27.3	5.4
1907.	61	1.6	36.1	62.3

Source: Correspondenzblatt, XVIII (Statistical Supplement), 189.

Modal Patterns in Union Expenditures

One great advantage in utilizing unspent dues income to build up respectable fund balances in union treasuries was that the unions could meet changing opportunities and conditions by channeling these resources in any desired mix toward such alternative goals as the support of strikes, the

---

[10]The much greater uniformity prevailing within the German union movement is borne out not only with respect to the much greater powers which the Generalkommission exercised in comparison to the evanescent Trades Union Congress, but also with regard to the geographical concentration of union headquarters and leaders. One of the Webbs' great complaints was that British trade unionism lacked a capital city, so that the small number of permanent officials was dispersed between London, Manchester, Newcastle, Glasgow, Aberdeen, Liverpool, and Leicester, as well as numerous other local centers of industry. This situation changed only very gradually, with union headquarters and leaders remaining spread throughout the country. In Germany, by contrast, it changed very quickly after 1902, when the Generalkommission moved from Hamburg to Berlin, and by 1914 three-fifths of its constituent unions—thirty-two out of forty-nine—maintained headquarters in Berlin. Since most of their executive members were full-time officials, this meant that the overwhelming majority of the movement's key leaders were close to each other and to the Socialist party executive and Reichstag groups.

increase of union benefits, administrative expansion, and (marginally) various forms of political activity. The German unions exhibited a quite different pattern of expenditure from the unimodal pattern of the British unions; throughout the period the British group deviated little from the standard practice under which 60 to 70 percent of union expenditures went toward benefits payable directly to members and comparatively little was devoted to administrative and strike-connected expenses. In Germany the pattern tended to be bi- or tri-modal; during periods of industrial strife, administration, benefits, and strike expenditures each consumed close to a third of typical union budgets, while at other times expenditures tended to be predominantly and equally distributed between administration and benefits.

In Germany the expansion of benefit programs and the growth of the bureaucracy reinforced each other more strongly than was the case in Britain. As the number of officials expanded, so did the variety of benefits that were offered to attract and hold new members. In 1892, only about one-fifth of German unions were paying sickness insurance, but by 1904 the proportion (60 percent) paying sickness benefits was almost as large in Germany, which had a compulsory primary benefit system, as it was in Britain, which did not. Indeed, by 1914 all but two of the forty-eight unions then affiliated to the Generalkommission were extending sickness benefits to their members, and forty were also offering unemployment insurance.

The share of German union expenditures devoted to administration did not decline after the unions became established and expanded their benefit programs; it remained at a consistently high level of 35 to 40 percent of total expenditures, or about twice the level that prevailed in Britain.[11] In return for this expenditure the German union members received a larger number of services provided by a far greater number of full-time paid union officials. Reliance on paid full-time officials became one of the hallmarks distinguishing the German union—and later also the party—organizations. Thus, by 1914 the German Metal Workers' union had about as many full-time officials (739) for its half-million members as the Webbs had estimated in 1892 for the *entire* British union movement with its membership of 1.5 million.[12] Whereas the British unions maintained fairly consistently a low ratio of three to five officials per ten thousand workers, the Germans

---

[11] Union procedures in classifying expenditures are obviously subject to a considerable amount of ambiguity, but all sources consistently bear out the relationships noted here. Thus, the *1914 Statistisches Jahrbuch der Gewerkschaften,* pp. 104-105, lists British administrative expenditures as 18.39 percent of total expenditures for 1912 and those for Germany at 41.88 percent. The German figures are approached only by those of the Austrian unions and by some smaller movements (like the Dutch) which were still at an earlier stage of development. When calculated as a percentage of 1912 union expenditures, German administrative costs were higher than those in all other listed countries except Sweden.

[12] Beatrice and Sidney Webb, *The History of Trade Unionism,* rev. ed. (London 1920), p. 577.

simultaneously built up a pattern under which the norm became eleven to twelve full-time officials per ten thousand members.[13] This characteristic difference between the two union movements has survived strikingly into the present era.

The growth patterns of the inter-union organs of coordination also differed greatly. Most significant at the national level were the peak federations or congresses; at the local level, the trades councils sought to coordinate some of the activities of various union branches in a particular city. At both levels the British institutions had the longer history, but the German ones rapidly grew more influential in the 1890-1914 period. Though the Trades Union Congress had been established in 1872, it changed little after becoming, in the 1890's, an "annual gathering of Trade Union officials in which they delivered, with placid unanimity, their views on labour legislation and politics."[14] The unanimity lessened later on, but the Webbs judged that "as an institution it can hardly be said to have shown, between 1890 and 1917 at least, any development at all."[15] Whereas the Generalkommission employed some thirty-four full-time officials by 1914, the TUC as late as 1902 had only one employee. . . ."[16]

III. INSURANCE BENEFIT ORIENTATIONS AND POLITICAL MOBILIZATION

After about 1900, most larger British and German Free Trade unions simultaneously employed the Webbian technique of "mutual insurance," as exemplified by union welfare benefit programs, and the technique of "legislative enactment," as exemplified by corporate or individual affiliation of portions of their membership to the Labour and Social Democratic parties. Moreover, the relative investment in these techniques can be measured by careful analysis of certain indicators which we shall examine for samples of twenty-six British and twenty-three German unions, with special reference to the period 1906-1907. We shall be particularly interested in discovering any difference between the two groups in the degree to which political mobilization correlated with such indicators of "exclusive-collective" benefit orientation as size of average sickness benefits, per capita union funds, and "high payout" policies. The relationship between insurance orientation and political mobilization will be examined also with reference to the unions' attitude toward the primary insurance systems,

[13]Gerhard A. Ritter, *Die Arbeiterbewegung im wilhelminischen Reich* (Berlin 1963), p. 170; Webb, *History*, pp. 465-586.

[14]Webb, *History*, p. 360.

[15]*Ibid.*, p. 563.

[16]H. A. Clegg, Alan Fox, and A. F. Thompson, p. 251.

which became more directly comparable after the National Insurance Act of 1911 established a compulsory British health insurance system that was somewhat similar to the one which had prevailed in Germany since 1885.

Sickness Insurance Emphasis and Political Mobilization

The data . . . may be examined in light of the expectation that those unions which paid lower sickness benefits would also exhibit higher rates of political mobilization because of their greater emphasis on achieving collective benefits through legislation. For Britain, the literature has stressed the key role played in the founding of the Labour party by some of the "new unions" of unskilled workers and others, whose leaders placed political action above the traditional "mutual insurance" goals. Our data bear out this impression in showing that, of the thirteen unions which were paying below-median sickness benefits in 1907, eleven had joined the Labour group (LRC) in the two years that followed its founding in February 1900. By contrast, among the thirteen unions that paid above-median sickness benefits, seven required the spur of the ominous Taff Vale decision of 1901 to join the party. The German data, however, do not show a correlation between the two indicators utilized there—sickness benefits payments and the proportion of Berlin unions members who were also enrolled in the SPD. The unions paying below-median benefits were not represented disproportionately among the high-party membership group, nor were the high-benefit unions significantly overrepresented among the low-mobilization group.

The size of the benefits paid by the British unions in 1907 also served as a predictor of how the union memberships would vote later, in 1913, on the question of authorizing their unions to establish political funds. Of the thirteen "below-average-benefit paying" British unions, eight were to vote for political action by ratios of better than two to one, whereas among the thirteen "above-average-benefit paying" unions, only three did the same.

Dues Payout Policies and Political Mobilization

In order to relate "income-and-payout" characteristics of British and German unions to the degree to which their memberships become politically mobilized, we created a fourfold union-finance typology composed of (1) "poor unions" (those with below-average funds and income), (2) "low-payout unions" (those with below-average income but with above-average funds), (3) "well-off unions" (those with above-average funds and income), and (4) "high-payout unions" (those with below-average funds despite above-average incomes). In regard to mobilization typologies, we utilized for Germany a trichotomized category developed from the party membership ratios of Berlin unions and for Britain an index which combines information about the union's affiliation behavior in 1900-1905 with its membership vote on political action in 1913-1916. From our alternative emphasis assumptions, we expected that:

> *Hypothesis A:* The "poor" unions would be the most highly politically mobilized, with the "low-payout" unions next in line, and the "well-off" and "high-payout" unions ranking near the bottom.
>
> *Hypothesis B:* This distribution pattern would be more pronounced in Germany than in Britain, since the more socialist program and ideological style of the SPD should have attracted the poorer, more public-goods oriented union memberships in greater numbers than did the Labour party in Britain.

However, . . . Hypothesis A is borne out only for the British unions, while Hypothesis B is disproved by our data. The step pattern indicated for the British unions shows a remarkably good fit to the interrelationship suggested by Hypothesis A. Even more surprising, however, is the fact that the German unions show not only less good fit than the British, but that, indeed, they tend to show almost a reversal of the expected order. . . .

The British pattern can be perceived as being congruent with a stronger commitment to Socialism. The Socialist methods of achieving inclusive collective goods through legislative enactment appealed to union memberships who had lesser stakes in exclusive benefit systems. But if the pattern discerned in Berlin can be found to hold true for SPD membership on a national basis, it would suggest a considerable incongruence in the German situation. What the orthodox Marxist party leaders hoped to gain from the union alliance was the infusion of union resources and funds in confrontations with the employers; what they actually got in their membership was primarily workers who had been attracted by the unions' mutual benefit role and who tended to perceive Socialism largely in terms of the strengthening of exclusive welfare programs. In seeking to reconcile programmatic strategy with mobilizational tactics, the leaders may well have been conditioned by the attachments that developed among the party-union rank and file. Since those unions which were most heavily overrepresented within the party membership were also the ones most highly committed to "exclusive" methods of achieving welfare goods, it is easy to understand how the rank and file's ambiguous attitude perpetuated the lack of clarity regarding priorities among the leadership.

Sickness Funds as the Third Pillar of the Labor Movement?

Once the German unions had become strongly committed to running their own welfare benefit programs in order to attract and hold members, the idea of presenting slates of candidates who might also control the primary insurance systems developed very quickly. In Britain, the view had prevailed that the best method of checking fraudulent claims was to keep Friendly Societies small, so that a member's claims could be checked through the voluntary services of his peers and neighbors. By contrast, both mobilizational and patronage incentives induced the Free Trade Unions to organize slates for the Sickness Fund elections. The 1902 Congress empowered the Generalkommission to represent the interests of insured workers before the Reich Insurance Bureau and to arrange slates for the elections of local Sickness Society executives. With majority control of the local boards, the union representatives could influence the selection of full-time employees (whose number grew to 2,900 by 1912) and thereby open up white-collar jobs for Social Democrats. Thus, according to a Socialist writer, "the trade union elite moved into the insurance institutes, the Sickness societies, the Land insurance institutes, the insurance courts, etc.," and in so doing "this elite assumed wholly new responsibilities."[17] The Sickness Society officialdom became a main portal to the practical administrative and conservative side of social democracy. ...[18]

In Great Britain, Lloyd George's National Insurance Act of 1911 gave the British unions a good opportunity to stake out claims to a portion of the new compulsory Primary Insurance System. The striking contrast to Germany lies in how completely they bungled the chance. The Act provided that a variety of organizations—Friendly Societies, trade unions, and commercial companies—could qualify as Approved Societies with which workers could take out health insurance. Pressure from the commercial companies, which threatened to politicize their army of collectors, undermined the hopes of the Friendly Societies which had expected to be chosen to implement the legislation.[19] But it was the unions which ended up hindmost in recruiting members to join their own Approved Societies. As a member of the Railway Servants recalled: "We established an Approved Society under the Act. Unfortunately, many of our members—some of them the most prominent—for minor concessions in contributions, benefits, and pensions, succumbed to the blandishments of the companies, and did not see the value of Trade

---

[17]Kampffmeyer, p. 118.

[18]Carl Schorske, *German Social Democracy, 1905-1917* (Cambridge, Mass., 1955), p. 206.

[19]Bentley B. Gilbert, *The Evolution of National Insurance in Great Britain* (London 1966).

Unionism over all."[20] Lacking skilled officials, the Railway Servants' General Secretary hired some of his union's unemployed members to handle the clerical work engendered by the scheme, but they later became embroiled in bitter rows over questions of productivity and pay. Although implementation of the Act helped union recruitment in the 1912-1913 period, a subsequent TUC survey showed that by the early 1920's only about one-quarter of union members carried their health insurance with the Approved Societies of the unions. Later, the enrollment in both Friendly Societies and Trade Union Societies declined as the share of the commercial companies increased: by 1938, the trade unions were carrying health insurance for about 8 percent of the eighteen million insured workers, the Friendly Societies insured about 16 percent, and the remaining 75 percent were enrolled by the large commercial companies.[21]

IV. THE INFLUENCE OF UNION AND BENEFIT SYSTEM ORGANIZATIONAL TECHNIQUES ON PARTY MOBILIZATION STYLES: ANALYSES AND PROJECTIONS

The Analysis of Contrasting Behavior Patterns

Bases of voter mobilization The differences between the organizational options selected by the German and British unions may be compared to those between a field army in war time and a Quartermaster Corps in time of peace. The British unions had their annual musters, but the rest of the time their resources remained scattered in multiple depots, with supports extended grudgingly upon repeated demand. Whereas in Berlin the Generalkommission had at its instant command the services of a highly coordinated network of officials and detailed knowledge about the numbers of books loaned out or speeches made in a provincial substation, the TUC was probably hard put to ascertain whether some of its component unions were alive or dead. Moreover, the uniformity of organization support extraction and discipline which was imposed on almost all member German unions after 1900 provided the Socialist contraculture with an organizational backbone that remained completely absent in Britain. German trade union writers even equated Socialism with organization. Replying in 1912 to "well-meaning people outside our ranks . . . who cannot understand our restless striving for improved organizations," Adolf Braun wrote: "To this

[20]G. W. Alcock, *Fifty Years of Railway Trade Unionism* (London 1922), pp. 419-421.
[21]Gilbert, p. 428.

one must reply that the striving for the better organization is something which is peculiar to Socialism. This restless striving for organizational improvement, for the best expression of the collective will, the search for the organic, *this regard for organization as an end in itself, all this is something specifically Socialist"* (my emphasis).[22]

This coincidence of tactical and ideological priorities caused theoreticians like Kautsky to join mundane party secretaries in urging a maximization of campaign mobilization efforts. By 1912, voter mobilization became almost an obsession.[23] The SPD not only put up candidates in even the most hopeless districts but, moreover, it unleashed an agitation campaign that utilized leaflets which, according to a careful observer of campaign literature, were both much more "effective" and much more "spiteful" than those put out by the other parties.[24] The SPD surpassed the other parties in the use of graphic, centrally distributed campaign materials. These efforts were supported both by Revisionists, who hoped that the party would gain greater influence within the existing parliamentary system, and by the dominant party center, which expected that "the mere growth of isolated Social Democracy would subjectively and objectively cause such havoc in the opposing camp that society would disintegrate and Social Democracy be able to step into its place."[25] If this goal was virtually the obverse of that propounded by the Fabian articulators of Labour party strategy, so were the mobilization tactics which the two parties employed.

Bases of party membership   The culmination of the SPD's development into a mass membership party occurred during a decade (1900-1912) which recorded a peak in the rate of increase in union members' dues payments and their participation as voters in union, Sick Fund, and other elections. An unusually large proportion of the workers responded to ideological appeals by assuming the additional responsibilities of party membership, which increased more rapidly than union membership. The more activist workers appear to have spent about 7 percent of their incomes on union and party dues, activities, and contributions. At no time during either the pre-1914 or post-1918 period (with the possible exception of 1911-1914) did the British working-class movement sustain feats of similar intensity and magnitude that might have reinforced appeals for individual membership sacrifices from large proportions of Labour supporters. Thus, even if British union leaders had been willing to relinquish the bargain-rate political leverage

[22]Adolf Braun, "Organisations probleme," *Die Neue Zeit* 31 (1912), Part II, p. 916.

[23]Peter Nettl, "The German Social Democratic Party, 1890-1914, as a Political Model," *Past and Present.* No. 30 (April 1965), p. 83.

[24]Ludwig Bergstraesser, "Zur Geschichte der parteipolitischen Agitation und Organisation in Deutschland," *Vergangenheit und Gegenwart* 2 (1912), pp. 250-252.

[25]Nettl, p. 82.

which the collective affiliation system accorded them, it is unlikely that a transition from a collective to an individual membership system would have been successful among the less highly mobilized British workers.

Recruitment of party officials   In both countries, the unions were instrumental in molding the organizational structures adopted by the parties. The Labour Representation Committee followed closely the model of the TUC, which had for decades afforded itself only a one-man secretariat. Because local unions run by part-time officers were scarcely willing to support full-time party employees, by 1914 the Labour party still had only a handful of agents. In Germany, however, the unions had highly developed administrative staffs even before 1905, when the SPD finally adopted a national organizational statute. (Earlier adoption of the statute had been prevented by the Reich Associational laws.) At that point the party employed only sixteen regional organizers, with the result that "the party bureaucracy was far less integrated and influential than the trade union bureaucracy."[26] At the 1905 SPD Congress, the South Germans wanted to create smaller party districts that would be relevant to local elections and Land politics, but they were outvoted by the Prussian and trade union delegates who adopted the large Reichstag districts that would focus on politics at the national level. One supporting argument made by the party executive was that "the development of the centralized trade unions proves that the tautly centralized form of organization is the one that most appeals to the workers."[27] Thereafter, the number of full-time regional and district party secretaries mushroomed (to 157 in 1914), as did the number of writers, editors, and other employees in party-controlled enterprises.[28] As a route of upward mobility within the party hierarchy, however, the party bureaucracy remained a very much secondary channel. Thus, of the Social Democratic officeholders in the Hamburg *Bürgerschaft* of 1919, "59 percent . . . had achieved their leadership positions as the product of diligent work in one of the labour bureaucracies" but only about 5 percent had worked their way up through the bureaucracy of the party itself.[29]

The relatively good salary and status perquisites of both party and union officials had a perverse effect after 1918, when the party was notoriously unable to produce enough qualified candidates to replace reactionary intermediate-level civil servants. Recent research has shown that

[26]Wolfgang Hirsch-Weber, *Gewerkschaften in der Politik* (Berlin 1959), p. 13.

[27]Wilhelm Schroeder, *Handbuch der sozialdemokratischen Parteitage von 1863 bis 1909* (Munich 1910), p. 181.

[28]Dieter Fricke, *Zur Organisation und Tätigkeit der deutschen Arbeiterbewegung 1890-1914* (Leipzig 1962), p. 51.

[29]Richard Comfort, "Free Trade Unions and Council Government in Hamburg," *International Review of Social History* 9 (1964), Part 1, p. 62.

numerous experienced party and union officials turned down offers of civil service positions because the salaries attached to them were effectively no higher, or even lower, then those they were receiving in well-cushioned party-union positions.[30]

Projection: The Utility of Subculture Alliances for Potential Parties of Government in Welfare Societies

Welfare collectivization and party interest group relationships It is very likely that differences in the sequence by which welfare benefits were collectivized, as well as variations between the major determinants of status in the two societies, brought greater electoral advantage to the Labour party than they did to the SPD. The Labour party benefited both from the relatively late introduction of collective welfare programs and from the fact that "successive legislation . . . proceeded by a series of almost haphazard precedents."[31] This sequence encouraged the "slow underground social upheaval, moving independently of leaders or organization"[32] that, according to Beatrice Webb, characterized the growth of the Labour party.

The SPD, by contrast, never quite overcame the attitudes and expectation patterns created by the timing and manner in which Bismarck had introduced social insurance in Germany. Although he failed in his immediate objective of immunizing workers against Socialism, Bismarck succeeded in the long term as the vested interests which developed in the social security system served to limit the support which the SPD could attract by advocating further steps in welfare collectivization. The German unions were unwitting instruments in this chain of effects in ways that the British unions obviously were not. . . .

Organizational inputs and the channeling of class hostility Perhaps no set of commitments resulted in more quixotic long-term consequences than those related to the question of organizational development: Should it be a primary, or merely a concommitant, goal? The German unions emphasized centralized growth and close coordination of mobilization efforts, and they bequeathed that emphasis to the SPD. But the German movement, which was innovative and consistent in its aim of enrolling its mass membership in decision-making processes, came to be identified with "the iron rule of oligarchy" or, at least, with the impersonal *Apparat*. The British unions pursued decentralized growth, mainly because of parochial jealousies and

---

[30]Wolfgang Runge, *Politik und Beamtentum* (Stuttgart 1965), pp. 54-55.

[31]W. G. Runciman, *Relative Deprivation and Social Justice: a Study of Attitudes to Social Inequality in Twentieth-Century England* (London 1966), p. 69.

[32]*Ibid.*, p. 138.

lack of organizational dedication. Nevertheless, the Labour party, whose organization was largely molded in the union image, somehow developed a reputation for party-building which long was a model throughout the Western world.

This anomaly may be partially explained in terms of differences both in the objective inequalities characteristic of the British and German class systems and the way in which at various periods these inequalities were perceived as relative deprivations by members of the different classes. For a very long time in Britain, existing inequalities were not fully recognized as relative deprivations by the working class, because the more privileged classes on the other side of the deep manual-nonmanual barrier were so removed that they did not constitute reference groups. In the German setting ideology served as a substitute for direct social contacts (which may anyway have been more frequent), with the result that the magnitude and frequency of relative deprivations tended fully to reflect, and very probably to magnify, objective class inequalities. Clearly, the different organizations and functions of unions and parties were important variables in the situation.

Hobsbawm is probably fairly correct in holding that, although in Britain Socialism constituted "a potential program of modernization for trade unions," the post-1889 New Unionism "did not achieve its object." On the contrary, it tended to tie the trade union movement more to nineteenth-rather than twentieth-century industrial Britain.[33] During periods of labor surplus, a fragmented and skeletal trade union structure largely prevented the working class from appreciating the full extent of class inequalities. By examining the evidence of relative class deprivation in the interwar period, Runciman found that "there remained wider inequalities of class than manual workers and their families appeared to realize and resent."[34] Such a finding would surely not hold for interwar Germany, where the pattern of competition among both unions and parties tended to nurture and magnify class grievances. But in Britain the membership growth of trade unions did not in itself threaten the middle class, which tolerantly continued to perceive the unions as the spokesmen for the underdog.

In Germany, however, party and union functionaries were lumped together as objects of the hostility engendered by the relative class deprivation that was felt by large sections of the middle class. There is scarcely a British equivalent to the universal German middle-class hostility to *"Funktionäre,"* by which is usually meant union and party officials rather than government bureaucrats. Indeed, it may be that in Germany today latent hostility toward the larger and more pervasive official bureaucracy has been redirected

[33]E. J. Hobsbawm, "Trade Union History," *Economic History Review* 20 (Aug. 1967), pp. 362-363.
[34]Runciman, p. 73.

toward low-status union and party officials.[35] Hostility has certainly remained high in the postwar period of labor scarcity, when the centralized union organizations (their exemplary "no-strike" policy notwithstanding) continued to provide a ready target for the relative class deprivation felt by portions of the middle class.

During the postwar period of full employment and labor scarcity, the emphasis on decentralization in British trade union structure tended to become even more accentuated, despite an increased membership concentration in the larger unions. Union dues fell far below their "real" equivalent in previous eras. Moreover, with approximately one full-time official for every three thousand members, the union structure was characterized by "the lowest ratio of any movement of comparable size in the world."[36] The demand for leadership at the plant level led to the unparalleled rise in influence of the shop stewards—part-time officials who came to perform functions that were not always provided for in union rule books. The shop stewards were able to "take advantage of local differences in union strength, the demand for labor . . . and the desire of employers to settle inside the works" in order to obtain benefits far greater than those achieved by the national unions in industry-wide bargaining. When pressed to investigate the increase in unofficial strikes, the TUC admitted in 1960 that a minority of stewards were apt to "misuse their position" and had led "needless" strikes that were "contrary to policy."[37]

If equivalent unofficial strikes had impeded German economic stability, voters would surely have expressed their animosity against the SPD; in Britain, however, neither ideology nor organization was strong enough to provide a psychological link between occurrences in the plant and in parliament. The lack of connection has been borne out by the fact that the economic policies of Labour governments have been undercut as severely by non-authorized strikes as were those of Conservative governments. A British writer, comparing the two union movements in 1967, even called for public subsidies to help British unions bring their educational and other efforts up to a level equal to that of the Germans.[38] Whereas in Germany trade union organizational techniques have helped maintain class hostility and have retarded the SPD's attractiveness as a potential majority government party, in Britain it has been more characteristic that static or declining union organizational efforts severely undercut the policy goals of Labour governments *after* they had succeeded in winning power.

[35]Bruno Seidel, "Functionaer," *Handworterbuch der Staatswissenschaften* 4 (Goettingen 1965), p. 190-197.

[36]W. E. J. McCarthy, "The Challenge Facing British Unions," *Annals*. No. 350 (Nov. 1963), p. 131.

[37]*Ibid.*, p. 133.

[38]John Huddleston, "Trade Unions in the German Federal Republic," *Political Quarterly* 38 (Apr. 1967), p. 176.

Union Goal Achievement Methods and Legislative Outputs

Interaction with radically different political regimes and varied economic systems has led the German unions to develop techniques of goal achievement which in the present era can no longer be adequately classified within the three Webbian categories. Legislative enactment, collective bargaining, and mutual insurance as techniques have been inextricably intertwined, and the new mutations have become institutionalized in the form of Labor Courts, codetermination structures, and other decision-making bodies to which the unions send representatives. By providing a greater variety of services and opportunities for participation, the unions have maintained a higher level of identification and activation among their members, who have become so tightly integrated into the *Parteienstaat* that oppositional elements have been almost encouraged to defect to the "extra-parliamentary" opposition. The tensions between unions and the Labour party in Britain are due almost to an inverse set of factors. The manner in which welfare benefits were collectivized in Britain caused mutual insurance to atrophy as a trade union technique, whereas collective bargaining and legislative enactment came to be pursued in their traditional modes in different locales by almost completely distinct structures and personnel.

It is evident from the identity of union representatives delegated into Labour party and parliamentary positions, as well as from their activity there,[39] that legislative output has been both a defensive and a secondary concern for British union leaders during the postwar period: "What exactly does the T.U.C. Establishment expect the Labour party to give it? The only real answer to this question is—security. . . . What they ask of the Labour party is, first, that it should protect them from anti-union legislation . . . that it should ensure full employment and a reasonable level of welfare. . . . It will be seen that this is essentially a defensive attitude."[40] The undernourishment of the TUC and related central structures has resulted in limiting the consensus overlap among the demands of diverse unions essentially to the maintenance of traditional demands which have been hallowed for several generations.

The most notable defensive achievement of the British union leadership has been the warding off for half a century of all infringements on the unique legal immunities—which, in contrast to general practice elsewhere, block effective legal sanctions for breach of contract—that were achieved through legislative enactment from 1870 to 1913. During this period the unions in

---

[39]William D. Muller, "The Parliamentary Activity of Trade Union MP's, 1959-1964" (unpub. Ph.D. diss., University of Florida, 1966).

[40]Michael Shanks, "Politics and the Trade Unionist," *Political Quarterly* 30 (Jan. 1949), p. 46.

some respects had a stronger strategic position than they have had since the alliance with the Labour party becamed institutionalized. The defensive stance of contemporary union leaders is thus not irrational—especially as they do not have to engage in demonstrative offensive actions in order to compensate a feeling of power deprivation among their followers. According to Runciman, the "relative power deprivation felt by the manual stratum tended to decline as the Labour movement appeared to grow steadily more powerful." [41] The maintenance of a reasonably high level of mobilization was thus relatively simple as long as the unions' bargaining position was unimpaired and as long as the activity of the Labour party added to, rather than detracted from, the subjective power consciousness of the bulk of the working class.[42]

The contrasting pattern in Germany, as identified by Popitz and his associates in their study of Ruhr workers in the 1950's, was marked by feelings of "individual powerlessness as against the modern superstructures" that they attributed to a generational pessimism that was far more profound than in earlier periods.[43] The unions of the post-1945 period ("who one day suddenly were there again") for some time were unable to compensate the workers' pronounced feelings of relative power deprivation, for, unlike their predecessors of the pre-1914 era, they were not the product of the workers' own endeavours and sacrifices.

This syndrome probably helps explain why the German unions' self-assigned political roles, as well as their demands and expectations toward the SPD, have been both markedly broader in range of policies and more offensive in nature than has been true for British unions. Thus their direct involvement in such controversial issues as rearmament and the Emergency Laws may in part be attributed to the unions' perceived need to restore the German workers' sense of confidence in union power. In this context it was not possible for unions to delegate functions of political articulation wholly to the SPD or to the parliamentary system, although from other perspectives it might have been expedient to do so.

Clearly, an adequate understanding of why organizations choose particular options among alternative means of goal-achievement seems to require full consideration of the record of prior experiences with such techniques. Their decisions are not necessarily directly shaped by the dominant values of their national political culture, but they are influenced by organizational and subculture traditions of considerable strength and persistence. Without consideration of such variables, it might well appear anomalous that the

---

[41]Runciman, p. 135.

[42]Ominous threats on both scores may have contributed to the sensational losses inflicted on the Labour party in the 1967-1968 local elections.

[43]Heinrich Popitz, Hans Paul Bahrdt, et al., *Das Gesellschaftsbild des Arbeiters* (Tübingen 1957), pp. 174-175.

prime legislative concern of unions in the British "participant" political culture has remained the fending off of statutory regulation, whereas in the German "subject" political culture unions have continued to give top priority to demands for increased participation in decision-making processes through extension of the "codetermination" laws.

12

The "Isms" in Totalitarianism

Alexander J. Groth

A major theme in political literature since the nineteen fifties has been a "unitotalitarian" approach to the study of modern dictatorships. The principal totalitarian "isms"—Fascism, Nazism and Communism— have been viewed as examples of one common species, containing no doubt some variations and differences; but practically, or operationally, the divergencies have been thought considerably less important than the similarities.[1] The emphasis has been heavily on the structure and methods underlying the exercise of political control by the "Leader" and the "Party." In what is undoubtedly the outstanding modern study of the subject, Friedrich and Brzezinski have attempted to extrapolate predictive hypotheses from the common pattern of totalitarian dictatorship expressed in a familiar syndrome of six interrelated characteristics.

In 1956 they wrote:[2]

> The Fascist and Communist systems . . . have shown a continuous, though inter- mittent, tendency to become more 'totalitarian'. . . . If one extrapolates from the past course of evolution, it seems most likely that the totalitarian dictatorships will continue to become more total, even though the rate of intensification may slow down.

If the prophecy has remained visibly unfulfilled in the case of Soviet Russia, may we not attribute its failure to the method underlying the prediction?

Reprinted by permission from the *American Political Science Review*, LVIII (December 1964), 888-901. Footnotes abridged by permission of the author.

[1]Carl J. Friedrich and Zbigniew Brzezinski, *Totalitarian Dictatorship and Autocracy* (Cambridge: Harvard University Press, 1959), p. 7: ". . . it is very important to explain [that] the totalitarian dictatorships, Communist and Fascist, are *basically alike*." Cf. William Ebenstein, "The Study of Totalitarianism," *World Politics* 10, No. 2 (Jan. 1958), pp. 274-288, and Daniel Bell, "Ten Theories in Search of Reality: The Prediction of Soviet Behavior in the Social Sciences," *ibid.*, No. 3 (Apr. 1958), pp. 327-356.

[2]Friedrich and Brzezinski, *op. cit.*, p. 6 and *ibid.*, p. 300.

I

The unitotalitarian approach has undoubtedly served a valuable purpose. It has focused attention upon a common range of means employed by modern dictatorships with justified emphasis upon what totalitarians do rather than what they ideologically or propagandistically profess. It has shifted the inquiry from a deceptive point of maximum apparent divergence to one of closest apparent identity. On the other hand, "unitotalitarianism" has had some serious disadvantages.

Preoccupied with structural and outward uniformities it has been less sensitive to the differences, particularly among the respective socio-economic contents of the "isms." It is argued here that a common theoretical framework of totalitarianism for the analysis of systems widely divergent in other respects (social, economic and cultural) is likely to be misleading if the uniformities are construed too broadly and their significance is over-emphasized. The problem is in a sense analogous to the development of a political model for such widely differing entities as for example Great Britain, Ceylon, United States, India, and Venezuela on the basis of shared political traits: absence of official ideologies; economies combining private enterprise with government controls; popularly elected legislatures and elective executives; freedom of the press, religion, petition and assembly; the existence of law courts, theoretically and constitutionally independent of the executive; multiplicity of political parties, trade unions and interest groups, etc. It is clear that, though having much in common, the political process in each of these societies is sufficiently distinct and molded by such diverse traditional, cultural, social, economic and religious influences as to render reliance on a single common denominator very dubious. That is, the reliance is dubious if one expects to be able to predict the future course of these entities from the common model, or to understand each through the traits common to all. Such insight would naturally require at least equivalent attention to the underlying differences.

The problem of "totalitarianism" is analogous in this sense. The common traits attributed to Italy and Germany on the one hand and Soviet Russia on the other have been in varying degrees and at various times characteristic of all three: official ideology, mass party and leader, terror, monopolistic propaganda, centralized control of the armed forces and the economy, etc. If these regimes—and any others—have in fact shared such characteristics one may certainly be justified in giving them a common classification and in assuming that comparable "inputs," other things being equal, have produced comparable "outputs"—that terror, *e.g.*, has produced widespread fear and thus rendered the given societies in some respects the "same" or "similar."

On the other hand, it goes beyond mere logical deduction or plain reading of the evidence to conclude that what is similar in some respects is similar in all, or that the "similarities" rather than the "differences" offer the best key to the understanding of the working of all these regimes.

While alike in many ways, the regimes of Fascist Italy and Nazi Germany may actually offer us few, if any, clues to the future development of Communist states. This will certainly be the case if the "differences" between these regimes are more important operationally than the similarities, particularly with respect to that admittedly very elusive term: "change."

The purpose of this essay is not to explore all the characteristics which differentiate the several "totalitarian" systems. It is rather to focus attention on the socio-economic aspect of the subject, an aspect which is particularly neglected in the "unitotalitarian" interpretation, and one which is certainly crucial to an understanding of the Fascist, Nazi and Soviet states.

Even if one assumes that the political scientist is interested in a very narrowly defined conception of the political process—with a bare minimum of concern for the impact of "politics" for such areas as culture, religion and the economy, and assumes also that political phenomena are "significant" only to the degree that they are manifested in outward behavior, he must nevertheless concern himself not merely with *what* is being done, and *how*, but also with the problem of *"who* does it to *whom."* If we grant that actions have consequences, political techniques must be viewed as inevitably reacting upon their users, and upon the entire political process of which both the "techniques" and the "technicians" are a part. Political techniques, after all, may be used to produce changes which alter the whole group basis of politics. Such changes may ultimately affect the identity of the "rulers" themselves and thereby (if not for other reasons) also the nature of the methods employed as well as a host of other factors. In different contexts similar, even identical, political techniques could very well produce divergent results—and *vice versa.* Hence, the question of context, certainly the problem of the identity of the power holders and the particular distribution of rewards and punishments by them, are no less important than the techniques.

It is not argued here in Marxist fashion that the political structure is either solely or predominantly determined by the socio-economic "sub-structure." An important reciprocal influence, nevertheless, seems obvious. Friedrich and Brzezinski say, however:[3]

> Such questions as who holds formal title to property, how 'profits,' that is to say, rewards, are determined, and whether former owners and decision makers continue to hold positions, provided they conform to the regime's commands are of relatively minor significance. What is decisive is the overpowering reality of totalitarian control by the dictator and his party.

Ibid., p. 211.

One might be justified in asking of "minor significance" to whom? The business elite, 'for example? If the matter is not, after all, of "minor significance" to business, might it not have consequences which the political scientist should find "significant?" The question of *what* is being done is no doubt important but so is the matter of *who* does it. To illustrate, business communities anywhere could not be indifferent to the matter of whether they are to be "in" or "out." There is some evidence that in the past this has influenced their behavior and might under some conditions do so again. On the other hand, was it not of importance to Hitler that the leaders of the armed forces who were similarly under the "overpowering reality of totalitarian control by the dictator and his party" were not, by and large, party men themselves? (Even if allegedly he alone decided whom the armed forces would fight, when they would fight and under what conditions.)

We need to know the group physiognomy of the regime, its impact upon the group structure of the society it rules, and what sorts of changes capable of influencing the social structure the regime sponsors or fosters.[4] Nothing less can give us an understanding of the potentialities for change inherent in any system, notwithstanding the difficulties in gathering evidence.

The drawback of the unitotalitarian approach is that it is implicitly indifferent to empirical research on the nature of the "isms" from the standpoint of their differential socio-economic consequences.

The studies of the 'thirties and 'forties, by scholars like Franz Neumann, Gaetano Salvemini, R. A. Brady, C. T. Schmidt, Welk, Sweezy and others (even if sometimes marred by a Marxist bias) could undoubtedly be augmented, enriched and modified from available postwar sources on the Nazi and Fascist dictatorships.[5] They could also be significantly correlated with continually accumulating data on the Soviet and Communist states. Pending further research, however, there is considerable evidence already available for the view that in important respects the Fascist, Nazi and Communist regimes are basically different and that these differences are likely to result in divergent paths of development for Communist as compared with the defunct Fascist and Nazi states.

II

The Communists, wherever they have succeeded in capturing power, have generally undertaken measures directly and indirectly uprooting

[4]Cf. David Apter, "A Comparative Method for the Study of Politics," *American Journal of Sociology* 64, No. 3 (Nov. 1958), pp. 221-237, for a general model concerned with "mobility opportunities."

[5]See Arthur Schweitzer, *Big Business in the Third Reich* (Bloomington: Indiana University Press, 1964), for an excellent postwar reappraisal.

existing socio-economic elites: the landed nobility, business, large sections of the middle class and the peasantry, as well as the bureaucratic elites, the military, the civil service, the judiciary and the diplomatic corps. They have done this through mass expropriation, expulsion, persecution and, as in the case of Soviet Russia, even through mass slaughter. In the case of the forty-six year old Russian dictatorship it would not be an exaggeration to say that the bureaucratic elites of pre-1917 society had been virtually exterminated by the mid-1930s.[6] In the places of political, economic, administrative and military managers of Russian society before the October Revolution, new personnel had appeared: new both in terms of their physical as well as largely their social identity.

Second, in every instance of Communist seizure of power there has been a significant ideological-propagandistic commitment toward a proletarian or workers' state, particularly to the worker-peasant concept of the ruling Party.[7] This commitment, however tarnished and compromised in everyday practice, has been accompanied by opportunities for upward social mobility for the economically lowest classes, in terms of education and employment, which invariably have considerably exceeded the opportunities available under previous regimes. Finally, in every case the Communists have attempted to change basically the character of the economic systems which fell under their sway, typically from an agrarian to an industrial economy.[3]

In this threefold sense, Communist regimes, particularly that of Russia, have been revolutionary. They have been revolutionary not merely to the extent of the changes they effected upon seizure of power but revolutionary also in terms of their long-term social goals and consequences. The "New Soviet Man" emerged from a society rendered, by any standard, vastly more industrialized, urbanized and literate.

Fascism (both in the German and Italian versions) to the extent that it can be judged by its performance in power, was socio-economically a counter-revolutionary movement. Assuming control in periods of social crisis it certainly did not dispossess or annihilate existent socio-economic elites, however thoroughly it tamed them. Quite the contrary.[9] Fascism did not arrest the trend toward monopolistic private concentrations in business but

[6]See, e.g., C. E. Black (ed.), *The Transformation of Russian Society* (Cambridge: Harvard University Press, 1960), pp. 235-350.

[7]Cf. Leonard Schapiro, *The Communist Party of the Soviet Union* (New York 1960), pp. 435-437, 522-526.

[8]See, e.g., Nicolas Spulber, *The Economics of Communist Europe* (New York 1957), particularly pp. 340, 343.

[9]A large body of literature testifying to this point appeared during the 1930s and the Second World War. Outstanding examples were Gaetano Salvemini, *Under the Axe of Fascism* (London: Victor Gollancz, 1936); Franz Neumann, *Behemoth* (New York: Oxford University Press, 1942); R. A. Brady, *The Spirit and Structure of German Fascism* (New York, 1937); Maxine Y. Sweezy, *The Structure of the Nazi Economy* (Cambridge: Harvard University Press, 1941); and Carl T. Schmidt, *The Plough and the Sword* (New York: Columbia University Press,

instead augmented this tendency. Fascism did not secure a radical change in the division of national income.[10] On the whole, the status and relative affluence of the small business man, the worker and the poorer farmer *vis à vis* the more privileged social groups could only be described as either stationary or declining.[11]

The Fascists did not undertake the wholesale destruction of the existing bureaucracies controlling the apparatus of the state. They required submission and outward conformity to their policies. Undoubtedly, they treated the civil service as a "spoils plum" and, while disposing of "unreliable elements," they added to the existent structures from among their Party supporters. But Conservative and "quietist" elements in the civil service were frequently absorbed into the New Order, both in Italy and in Germany, sometimes by merely formal acceptance of party status.[12] Hence, much of the pre-Fascist apparatus survived Fascist rule.

Persistently, and not surprisingly, the Fascists have been regarded as the militant allies and defenders of besieged reactionary and capitalist interests. In power, the Nazis and the Fascists did not preach egalitarianism nor did they undertake large scale programs which might increase the mobility prospects and opportunities of the lower social strata. On the whole, they followed *status quo* and even retrogressive social policies. The Fascists did not attempt a basic reorientation of the national economy in Italy and in Germany they did so only when, and insofar as, it promoted rearmament, mainly from 1935 onwards.

Fascism preserved the economic basis of traditional elites in business and agriculture by maintaining both private profit and the right of inheritance. Whatever the nature of the regimentation and controls which the Fascist regimes imposed upon property and property owners, these controls did not spell confiscation and class extinction. Postwar evidence does not indicate, as some thought during and before the Second World War, that the Fascists "cancelled" real profits through such devices as forced loans, bribes and blackmail.

Fascism also preserved an important political role for the old elite groups, in both official and socio-economic senses of the word. The repre-

---

1938). Whatever their Marxist biases and predilections, these works presented a considerable body of factual evidence showing that the social and economic consequences of Fascism were advantageous to the affluent and either relatively or absolutely disadvantageous to workers, small business, and other lower-income groups.

[10]See Max Ascoli and Arthur Feiler, *Fascism for Whom?* (New York 1938), p. 255.

[11]Cf., e.g., Salvemini, *op. cit.,* pp. 182-189; Neumann, *op. cit.,* pp. 434-436; Schmidt, *op. cit.,* pp. 159-175.

[12]See, e.g., Karl W. Deutsch and L. J. Edinger, *Germany Rejoins the Powers* (Stanford, California: Stanford University Press, 1959), particularly pp. 80-86. Cf. Herman Finer, *Mussolini's Italy* (New York 1935), pp. 270-271; Max Ascoli (ed.), *The Fall of Mussolini* (New York 1948), pp. 22-23.

sentatives of the "established interests" participated both in the shaping and the implementation of political and military policies of the Fascist and Nazi regimes—a far cry from mere regimented subservience and the simple one-way "order-taking" sometimes alleged.

In Germany, Hitler clearly was not anybody's "mere puppet" before or during World War II; but obviously he did not make or implement all of the decisions of the Third Reich either. Nor must we assume that if non-Party influences were subordinated to the Party and the Leader, they were therefore nil.

Despite voluminous evidence to the contrary, a persistent myth, and one of the underlying assumptions of unitotalitarianism has been the notion of overwhelming, one-sided direction and control of the Fascist, and particularly the Nazi, system by the Leader and his Party. The fact that pre-Fascist elites both *could* and *did* play highly important political roles in the Fascist and Nazi regimes is often either denied or completely minimized. The question is certainly one of crucial significance and it cannot be simplified to the query: (a) was Hitler a puppet of the industrialists and the military, or (b) was he an "absolute ruler"? Political processes are not so simple. Friedrich and Brzezinski assert that:

> While the dictatorships of Mussolini and Hitler as well as that of Stalin were intact, there existed no scientifically reliable way of resolving this question, since the testimony of one observer stood flatly opposed to that of another. We are now in a more fortunate position. The documentary evidence clearly shows that Mussolini and Hitler were the actual rulers of their respective countries. Their views were decisive and the power they wielded was "absolute" in a degree perhaps more complete than ever before (*op. cit.,* p. 17).

It would not be inconsistent with any of the postwar accounts of the Fascist systems to argue that Hitler and Mussolini were by far the most important individual decision makers in their respective regimes, but the absolute, all-embracing power of the leaders, whether exercised directly or through their party followers, is mythical. The July 20, 1944 conspiracy in Germany would have been unthinkable and the successful removal of Mussolini in July 1943 likewise impossible, had totalitarian control been monolithic. In 1940 Mussolini did not bother to consult his Fascist Grand Council on Italy's entry into the War but he did consult the King, and the King seriously considered stopping him.[13] Ultimately, as Charles F. Delzell has written:[14]

> The Duce fell chiefly because of his own disastrous foreign policy, for when it became clear that Italy had lost the war, he forfeited the support of the powerful forces (Crown, capital, clergy, army and bureaucracy) which in the past had generally welcomed and benefited from his dictatorship.

[13]Charles F. Delzell, *Mussolini's Enemies* (Princeton, N.J.: Princeton University Press, 1961), p. 182. Cf. L. Villari, *The Liberation of Italy* (Appleton, Wisconsin: C. C. Nelson, 1959), p. 14.
[14]Delzell, *op. cit.,* p. 223.

Writing of the political role of the German Army, John W. Wheeler-Bennett has said:[15]

> Up to 1938 the Army had been the final arbiter of the political destinies of the Reich. They had first supported, and then condoned the overthrow of, the Republic and had made a major contribution to Hitler's coming to power. They had entered into a pact with the Party in order to preserve their privileged status and influence and had, as a result been guilty of complicity in the Blood Purge of June 20, 1934. Well knowing what they did, they had accepted Hitler as Chief of State and had pledged their loyalty to him personally as their Supreme Commander, always with the reservation that at their own good pleasure they could unmake the Caesar they had made.

Whatever the specific merits of each of these assessments, it is clear that the German Army was not a cipher and that its influence after 1933 in Germany finds no parallel in Soviet experience after 1917, or for that matter in *any* of the Communist states. If the armed forces have been a factor in Soviet politics, they certainly were not the Tsarist armed forces.[16] Such illustrations could be multiplied. Postwar Allied inquiry into German economic organization confirmed at least a co-partnership role for leaders of large business firms in the planning and policy-making functions of the German economy. Discussing the pre-war record of Nazism, Arthur Schweitzer writes:[17]

> The party dominated the political and ideological—the main informational and educational—lines of action but was forced to stay out of the military and most of the economic ministries of the state and had to tolerate the military and economic ideals and policies of its allies. The SS controlled the regular and secret police and the instruments of terror but had to abstain from military intelligence and refrain from acting within the spheres of power belonging to the military and to big business. Whereas in fundamental conflicts there prevailed a close partnership between the party and the SS, or between the generals and big business, in daily policy decisions and administrative matters the lines of authority and influence were clearly drawn.

However subordinated to the dictators, the old elites were neither extinguished nor impotent. A significant decision-making role involving a considerable measure of influence, discretion, or delegated authority, and in some instances blunt bargaining power, rested with representatives of elites which were not creatures of the Nazi regime and whose status, influence and

[15] *The Nemesis of Power* (London: Macmillan, 1953), p. 694.

[16] In Russia 71.9 percent of the divisional commanders and 100 percent of the corps commanders were Communists in 1928. Merle Fainsod, *How Russia is Ruled* (Cambridge: Harvard University Press, 1958), p. 401. Cf. I. deSola Pool *et al.. Satellite Generals* (Stanford, California: Stanford University Press, 1955), p. 4.

[17] Schweitzer, *op. cit..* p. 505. Cf. also pp. 5-6 and 506-507 for the author's conclusions on these points. Summarizing the experience of the thirties, the author says: "Whether in terms of power or functions, the top Nazi leaders were only occasionally able to influence, and could not lay down, the economic and military policies of the regime," p. 507.

outlook owed nothing to the Nazis. The same was true of Italy. The old elites, both bureaucratic and socio-economic, typically looked down upon the Fascist politicians as crude upstarts who may have been useful, or perhaps even indispensable once, but who were certainly not directly identified with the old elites themselves—their "pedigree," their traditions, their values, etc. To these elites, the Fascists were part of a passing scene.

III

In this "coexistence" between the Fascist and pre-Fascist elites lay at once the strength and the weakness of the Hitler and Mussolini brands of totalitarianism. If the Fascist and Nazi managers, party chieftains and administrators represented a new stratum, it was nevertheless a stratum superimposed upon and commingled with the upper layers of an established socio-economic order. The "revolutions" of 1922 and 1933 were as easy as any in history. But the price of power shared with the "pre-revolutionary" elements spelled drastic vulnerability to the Fascists. The displeasure and opposition of some of the old elites endangered the very existence of the Fascist regimes—and the lives of their leaders—when subjected to the ordeal of defeat in war. Certainly the "plots" against Hitler and Mussolini are highly revealing on this point. It was not simply that some of the well established pre-Fascist elements became the sources of anti-Fascist conspiracy. Above all, they had both the *access* to the leaders and the *capability* of wielding the apparatus of the state wherewith to dispose of their dictators. Where the German military narrowly failed (and most accounts agree that their ultimate failure was due not to the simple preponderance of Nazi power confronting them but to lack of group resolution within)[18] the Italian King and his coterie of military and royal supporters succeeded.

In the history of the Soviet regime, despite many well-nigh staggering strains and defeats, no genuine attempt at Stalin's power was ever launched "from the inside."[19] Could it be that the Communist revolution in Russia, more difficult to achieve, had acquired some characteristics of greater durability? In the long run, the answer is probably yes, on grounds analogous to those once advanced by Machiavelli: he who would rule absolutely must remould the society over which he rules. Absolute claims to

[18]Cf. Gerhart Ritter, *The German Resistance* (New York 1958), pp. 152-155; Constantine Fitzgibbon, *20 July* (New York 1956), pp. 186-194; see also George K. Romoser, "The Politics of Uncertainty: The German Resistance Movement," *Social Research* 31, No. 1 (Spring 1964), pp. 73-93.

[19]It is assumed here that the "Doctors' Plot" of 1948 was a figment of Stalin's—and MVD's—imagination.

power cannot be made good without correspondingly absolute sources at one's command. Veto-groups cannot be long tolerated:[20]

> . . . he who proposes to set up a despotism, or what writers call a tyranny, must renovate everything . . . organize everything in that state afresh; *e.g.*, in its cities to appoint new governors, with new titles and a new authority, the governors themselves being new men; to make the rich poor and the poor rich.

In the upshot of Fascist rule for twelve years in Germany and 22 in Italy the group structures of their respective societies endured remarkably stable and relatively unchanged. None of the traditional economic elite groups had been eliminated or significantly diminished. The have-nots made very few inroads upon the haves.

IV

These facts have great political significance: they provide some elements for a rational understanding of group behavior as well as predictive implications for the respective "isms."

Both internally and externally, Fascism, Nazism and Communism have addressed themselves to, and relied upon, different "clienteles."[21] If we wish to understand what groups and social strata are both potentially and actually providing support for these movements, we must understand something of their image: a compendium of their policies, their ideologies and their propaganda themes. If these movements are "basically alike" why do they appeal to different, rather than to similar or even identical, clienteles?[22] Is it politically "significant" that Communism has actively courted non-white races while Fascism rejected and attacked them? Is it "significant" that Communism has found widespread following among urban workers in several Western European countries, whereas Nazism and Fascism have appealed heavily to the middle and lower-middle classes?

On the other hand, the reciprocal relationships are important also. If the nature of the clientele is largely determined by the nature (or image) of the "ism," it is reasonable to assume that the clientele, in turn, exerts an influence upon the whole framework of institutional, ideological and policy expressions of a given "ism." Clearly the roles of totalitarian leaders cannot

---

[20] *The Discourses of Niccolo Machiavelli*, trans. L. J. Walker (New Haven: Yale University Press, 1950), vol. 1, p. 233. Hitler apparently perceived the problem of "unassimilated" and politically significant groups as being a "brake" on his dictatorship. What, if anything, he might have done about this "after the war" is another matter. Cf. *The Goebbels Diaries*, ed. and trans. Louis P. Lochner (Garden City, New York: Doubleday, 1948), pp. 287, 515.

[21] Cf. Daniel Lerner *et al.*, *The Nazi Elite* (Stanford, California: Stanford University Press, 1951), pp. 69-72, 84; Finer, *op. cit.*, pp. 364-376.

[22] Cf. Seymour Martin Lipset, *Political Man* (Garden City, New York: Doubleday, 1960), pp. 131-176.

be understood apart from the claims and expectations of their followers and the flexibility of leadership, however authoritarian, must always be discounted to some extent by this factor.

Both internal and external constituencies must be taken into account in appraising the nature of a particular "ism." Thus, the "isms" differ not merely in the "facts" which give rise to their being differently perceived. They also differ because of these divergent perceptions themselves, which in turn give rise to different kinds of expectations and claims upon the behavior of the particular regimes. The role of the external constituency may vary widely but it would not be unjustifiable to apply Neustadt's concept of the President's external constituency in an ever greater degree to Krushchev or Mao than to the President of the United States.[23]

A movement's reputation for being "rightist" may in itself alienate traditionally "leftist" sources of support and *vice versa*. Under certain conditions some groups may be more likely than others to support or oppose the movement; an ordinarily unwelcome choice between "two great evils" may nevertheless be made far more coherently than the possibilities of random selection would indicate. Similarly, the difficult decision to oppose an entrenched regime is also likely to reflect the impact of the regime's policy upon diverse groups and social strata. Before the totalitarian seizure of power in Germany and Italy business and landed interests were on the whole much more favorable to the Nazis and Fascists than toward the Communists.[24] After 1938 in Germany, the military elites provided more anti-Nazi resistance than did the business interests.[25] According to evidence which can be similarly related to regime policies, Soviet peasants oppose the Communist system more strongly than do industrial workers, who in turn are less attached to the system than the new Soviet intelligentsia.

Political loyalties, elite recruitment, group demands on the decision makers and, indeed, the choice and shape of political policies themselves are bound to be seriously influenced by the social and economic characteristics of a society and the socio-economic policies pursued by its rulers. The reorganization of the whole social structure—or its absence—is likely to have far-reaching political consequences for the development of a regime. Stated in terms of an ideal, rather than actual, polarity, the implications of socio-

[23]Richard E. Neustadt, *Presidential Power* (New York 1960), p. 7.

[24]This relative and contingent (crisis-born) preference does not seem to be subject to any serious dispute although the question of precisely how effective and important was the support of business interests, in bringing the Fascist regimes to power, continues controversial and unresolved. Works often cited on both sides of the issue are far from conclusive: L. P. Lochner, *Tycoons and Tyrant* (Chicago 1954), pp. 115-117; Fritz Thyssen, *I Paid Hitler* (New York 1941), p. xv. Cf. Lipset, *op. cit.*, pp. 148-149.

[25]Cf. Deutsch and Edinger, *op. cit.*, pp. 100-103 for some comparisons of the anti-Nazi resistance records of business, trade union, and S.P.D. and C.D.U. elites. Cf. Gabriel A. Almond and W. H. Kraus, "The Social Composition of the German Resistance," *The Struggle for Democracy in Germany*, ed. G. A. Almond (Chapel Hill: University of North Carolina Press, 1949), pp. 64-107.

economic development for the totalitarian regimes might be stated as follows:

If "Fascism" or "Nazism" does not basically change the social structure over which it rules, if it does not remake it in a common image, then indeed it has no alternative to the cycle: serious crisis—unrest—insecurity of the regime—increased use of violence and repression—or capitulation.

If "Communism" does change the underlying social structure in the direction of a desired homogeneity, it may in time dispense with the political tool of mass violence, and, even in periods of crisis, rule with the use of subtler methods, closer to persuasion than to physical compulsion.

It is not argued here that the actual, historic differences between Fascism and Nazism on the one hand and Communism on the other have been quite so great. The Russian Communists did not change everything in sight nor did the Fascists and Nazis leave all things as they found them. But, so far as the record of history serves us, the gap or divergence in the socio-economic characteristics of these regimes has been very considerable. Such divergence, even if it be in many respects one of degree (in the area of social mobility, *e.g.*) suggests not "similar" but "different" tendencies of development and therefore, also, "different" rather than "similar" political implications.

If political attitude and behavior are the resultants of a variety of factors of which propaganda, education, coercion, status, religion and income are examples, then a regime which effectively manipulates the greater number of such factors is more "totalitarian" than one which manipulates fewer, and the difference of degree may be ultimately as significant as one between '"medicine" and "poison." All other things being equal, the regime with the greater range of means at its command should be able to exercise more effective control and enjoy more flexibility in policy.

If Fascism and Nazism do not basically restructure the societies over which they rule, and if, because of clientele considerations they are really unable to do so, then despite the framework of terror, propaganda and indoctrination of the Hitler-Jugend and Balilla variety, the "isms" can operate effectively *only* by not making demands which would outrage the class and caste interests, and attitudes, of elites inherited from previous regimes. Where demands for total obedience are pressed upon a highly heterogenous political clientele, violence may indeed prove a frequent and indispensable tool of enforcement for the totalitarian regimes. Where vital interests of the old elites and the new regimes clash, a relapse into a conservative neo-constitutionalism of the Franco variety is highly likely. This could occur either through the more or less voluntary accommodation by the dictator, as in Franco's case after 1940, or through a *coup d'etat* as in Italy in 1943.

Understandably, mass violence and social upheaval were far less characteristic of Fascism and Nazism at the outset of their existence than of Communism, since these regimes did not attempt to modify seriously the socio-economic *status quo;* they were more characteristic of Russian Communism precisely because it sought to change so much. Conversely, however, Fascism never rid itself of the resort to crude violence because it did not sufficiently mold its political clientele. To the end of their existence, both Fascism and Nazism relied heavily on the personnel of the pre-revolutionary elites whose identification with the totalitarian regimes was always conditional. These elites served Hitler and Mussolini only because and insofar as the Nazi or Fascist policies appeared to them useful and unavoidable for the realization of particular objectives: defeat of Communism, maintenance of their own perquisites, the realization of a "Greater Germany," and so on.

It is widely agreed, and there is certainly substantial evidence, that the great majority of these elites in Germany continued to adhere to Hitler's cause, out of conviction or despair, until his defeat. But so long as they shared the political, military and economic apparatus of the German state and remained a pillar of the Nazi movement, they constituted a potentially dangerous element for the dictatorship, a threat requiring constant maintenance of surveillance, terror and repression.

V

Time and war cut short the existence of the totalitarian regimes of Italy and Germany, so that today we could not compare some forty-odd years of development for all three "isms." Would the Nazi and Fascist States have grown more or less "total" had they survived? Would they have tended to approximate more closely or diverge more widely from the older, more "mature" Soviet totalitarianism?

The unitotalitarian approach necessarily suggests that, driven by the common pursuit of power, all three dictatorships were in fact, proceeding in the same direction.

The unitotalitarian scheme interprets the divergent socio-economic policies of the totalitarian regimes as derivative from one pattern, permeated by the same purposes and different mainly, if not exclusively, in terms of their time-table. In comparing the policies of the Communists and Fascists, we find Brzezinski asserting somewhat cryptically that: "Very specific circumstantial factors prevented the Fascist and Nazi regimes from launching similarly large-scale schemes of social reconstruction."[26] An analogy is implied between, on the one hand, the entire period of Fascist rule in Italy from 1922 to 1944, and in Germany from 1933 to 1945, and the

---

[26]Z. Brzezinski, "Totalitarianism and Rationality," *The American Political Science Review* 50 (Sept. 1956), p. 757.

1921-1928 NEP period in Russia on the other. The implication of the analogy is that all totalitarians wish to "change everything" but the revolutionary process requires some tactical pauses for a "consolidation of forces."

The evidence for this proposition rests most heavily, and most plausibly, on the experience of the Second World War. Few authorities would maintain that up to 1939, for example, Soviet Russia and Fascist Italy were equally "totalitarian" even in terms of merely the six specific criteria employed in the Friedrich and Brzezinski study. Yet, as of 1939 only about five years separated the Communist from the Fascist tenure of office. At most, twenty-two years of "Communism" confronted seventeen years of "Fascism"; if, with greater realism, the periods of power are considered from the assumption of effective control over the whole of the respective countries, they are about equal. In terms of displacement of the traditional, pre-revolutionary elites, the comparison of Italy and Russia in the 1930s shows far greater divergences. During all these years it is quite impossible to discover the evidence of Fascism's "dangerous designs on the bastions of wealth and privilege" from its actual accomplishments. And it would require extraordinary artfulness to deduce a menacing attitude toward the socio-economic *status quo* from the official, publicly disseminated Fascist pronouncements during this period. Mussolini's *The Doctrine of Fascism* could hardly be confused with Lenin's *State and Revolution* on this score.

In the case of Germany, the period of pre-war Nazi control, 1933-1939, is somewhat more plausible in comparison with Russian Communist rule for several reasons. First, the Nazi record in terror and brutality quickly appeared to outdo Mussolini's "best efforts." Second, capitalizing on German military traditions and the more sophisticated manipulative apparatus of a highly industrialized state, the Nazi regime presented to the world a much more plausible image of totalitarian unity, cohesion and might. Third, and foremost, the entire period was sufficiently short so that Hitler could always be credited, by the credulous, with not having had enough time to carry through even "further reforms."

In this interpretation, the Roehm Purge was a tactical maneuver analogous to Lenin's tactical repudiation of the Left extremists in the Communist Party of 1921. The Roehm Purge, however, was not preceded by mass expropriation of landlords and *entrepreneurs* in Germany as was NEP in Russia. Nor was it ever followed by such expropriation. And what of Hitler's actual policies with respect to the established elites and elite recruit-ment? Up until 1938 the Army Generals enjoyed a position of relative autonomy and privilege within the Nazi regime. And the 1938 shift in command was a far cry from the "proletarization," "communization" and "politicization" which the Soviet regime was intensively applying to the Red Army from its inception. Nor was the treatment of the Army Generals an isolated case. The pre-1933 leaders of industry, commerce and agriculture were no clcser to either personal or financial liquidation in 1939 than in 1933.

Was the Nazi social revolution to be planned and implemented by the aristocratic, and middle class elites which had patronized the Nationalist Party and other conservative causes? Clearly, these elements would not have favored, let alone spurred, such a revolution. Did Hitler himself advocate a social upheaval? In *Mein Kampf* he was vague and cynical about the Party's "unalterable" 1920 program; but on the other hand, he specifically courted and praised such established interests as the Army and the bureaucracy, and even had some kind words for the Monarchy. If anything, Hitler's own pronouncements after 1925 on such subjects as property and class warfare tended toward increasing socio-economic conservatism, not radicalism. The last major remnants of the Nazi nucleus of social radicalism had, in fact, been purged with Ernst Roehm in 1934. The extirpation of the Jews was genocide, not class warfare.

Admittedly, the Second World War brought about a great intensification of totalitarian controls and terror within the Fascist and Nazi systems, particularly after the July 1944 conspiracy against Hitler. Yet, the conclusion that somehow this increase in totalitarian activity was equivalent to, or even a forerunner of, a social and economic revolution falls far short of available evidence. Unlike the Soviet precedent, Hitler's terror at home was aimed not at whole social classes but at suspected individuals.

The intensification of Party control in the apparatus of the State— political, economic, military—did not have any really new social and economic orientation. The criterion of Nazi attitudes toward actual and potential opposition was loyalty to the Party and to the Fuehrer. But the concept of Party in Nazi Germany, unlike Russia, had no specific class content and orientation. Hence, for all the punitive and "radical" measures taken by the Hitler regime during the war and particularly after 1944, none —except as against Jews—included significant expropriation of landed or major industrial properties, wholesale expulsion of the members of the old nobility or the Junker class from government service, nor even large scale expulsion of non-Party members from important positions in the armed services, provided their loyalties to Hitler were not in any doubt. On the "positive side" there was no attempt during the war to attract the following of the lower class strata by the kind of Party recruitment drives which periodically recur in the Communist movement. There were no tangible, widely publicized legislative and fiscal concessions to the social and economic interests of these classes at the expense of, or even to the apparent disadvantage of, the upper strata.

Until the very last days of his regime, Hitler did not undertake any measures changing the hitherto existing balance between the "haves" and "have-nots" of Germany. In this sense, his totalitarianism did not deeply plough the ground of German society. The record does not support an easily accomplishable "bolshevik about-face" by either of the Axis chiefs; Mussolini's belated, personal attempt at "social radicalism" was one of utter failure and frustration.[27]

Both Hitler and Mussolini obviously attempted to make themselves thoroughly invulnerable and durable through such devices as terror, propaganda and educational indoctrination of the youth. But, hampered by the very constellation of forces which helped them to seize and maintain power, they, unlike the Communists, did not supplement these totalitarian devices with socio-economic measures of equal radicalism (or "totalitarianism"). Hitler effectively outlawed the political organizations of the non-Nazi Right but he did not destroy its social and economic base. Until the very last he was served and surrounded by the Right's former supporters and sympathizers in the General Staff, the bureaucracy, the diplomatic corps and the economy. To move with them involved little risk. To move against them could have been literally fatal as the events of July 1944 very nearly proved.

When the fortunes of war turned against the Fuehrer, neither the Hitler Jugend nor the Gestapo could undo the consequences of Nazism's compromising affiliations—the ominous presence of Colonel Claus von Stauffenberg and others like him in high places. This presence was no accident. Such vulnerability was an intrinsic part of the basic socio-economic design of Fascism and Nazism.

Both regimes failed to carry through the social and economic revolutions which alone could have given them a monopoly on the production of new elites and the suppression of the old. The outward appearance of mastery was compromised by the reality of interdependence and partnership between an old and a new order. Fascism and Nazism alike failed to deal with the economic bases of class antagonism and class differentiation inherited from previous regimes. Each regime imposed the gloss of political and police controls upon societies which, from the standpoint of the distribution of wealth, with all its implications, reflected an inherited old order, not a new one. Without a socio-economic revolution, the Fascist and Nazi dictators could never free themselves of their Rightist associations with all the implicit vulnerability; without it they could not meet most of the traditional demands of the working class and of the clientele of the political Left. In consequence of this failure to revolutionize, the Fascist and Nazi regimes were rendered "brittle," precarious and vulnerable from many quarters. Above all, however, the disaffection of the inherited Rightist elements always represented the most immediate danger to the dictators since these elements were in the best positions of access in the bureaucratic-military apparatus of the two regimes.

[27] Cf. *ibid.*

VI

It is frequently asserted and implied that the Nazi and Fascist dictatorships could somehow escape the perils of their domestic vulnerability by means of externally directed violence. Might not conquest, and the preparation for conquest abroad, stabilize these regimes internally? Could the pursuit of warfare silence and eliminate domestic conflicts, thus making it unnecessary for the dictators to employ violence at home? Undoubtedly, the policies of the Fascist and Nazi regimes were oriented in this direction. War could produce beneficial, however shortlived, economic consequences at home in terms of increasing employment, wages and profits. It could also mobilize considerable loyalties of national patriotism toward the support of the respective regimes. It likewise provided a more or less "natural" opportunity for these regimes to extend and tighten administrative and police controls. Yet war-making, no less than other enterprises, was bound to involve problems and consequences peculiar to itself. If the war effort were to be accompanied by widespread material and moral deprivations at home, and if it appeared to be doomed to failure, the stresses and strains in the social fabric which the war sought to prevent would be likely to reappear. The elites which were convinced of Hitler's genius in 1940 were unlikely to display equal fervor and conviction in 1943 or 1944. The "monolith" was doomed to show its hidden fissures just as it did in the case of Mussolini's Italy where the war, ironically mocking the dictator's design, proved to be his undoing, not his salvation. The resort to violence became actually more, not less, necessary. Only a very successful and unlikely "Orwellian war of indefinite duration" could have averted such consequences for Fascism and Nazism.

On the other hand, the conclusion that the successful termination of war (which in 1940 certainly seemed plausible for the Axis) would have enabled Fascism and Nazism to expand indefinitely war trends and war policies is highly suspect. It does not make allowance for the actual disappearance of the war stimulus, and it assumes (but does not prove) the complete passivity, docility and unimportance of Fascism's, and Nazism's, elite allies. Considerable evidence is to be found for the opposite point of view.[28]

Granted that both dictators realized the difficulty of their position, it is not enough to show that they personally, from time to time, wished for changes. Like all politicians, they faced environmental limitations which

---

[28]F. W. Deakin explores, very instructively, the problem of what *did* happen to Mussolini when he attempted some "social radicalism" in 1944. *The Brutal Friendship* (New York 1963). See especially pp. 670-671.

circumscribed their ability to act, and these limitations were, in turn, characteristic of the very nature of the movements they both led. If they had won, it would have been far easier for Hitler and Mussolini to maintain, like Franco, an impeccable, albeit authoritarian conservatism than to embark on schemes of radical social upheaval, even if they personally desired such an upheaval. Postwar efforts by either dictator to carry out policies fundamentally hostile to the basic values of the bureaucratic and socio-economic elites upon which both regimes had always depended might well have dislodged the Fascist and Nazi Parties from power. It is not without significance that by Hitler's own choice the last chieftain of the Third Reich was Grand Admiral Doenitz, a representative of the pre-1933 bureaucratic military establishment. The "establishment" proved more durable than the Party and survived the Party.[29]

The assumption that ultimately Italy and Germany would have proved as "reformist" as Russia is based on scant evidence such as face-value acceptance of private remarks made by the embittered Fascist leaders on the verge of defeat and in part on acts and decrees which they issued when both victory and effective control were being irretrievably lost. Given their past performance, their ideological-propagandistic commitments and the constellation of forces supporting them, within and without the Fascist parties, it is difficult to believe that military victory could have made successful social reformers out of Hitler and Mussolini.

On the other hand, the "social engineering" of the Russian communist regime has conferred a remarkable degree of invulnerability upon it. Probably since the 1920s, and certainly since the 1930s, Stalin was beyond the physical reach of any but his own party creatures. In all the later succession conflicts, including the grim Beria episode, the issue has never been "Communism, yes or no;" instead it has been a question of the identity of the leadership and of the nuances of policy. The issues in Germany in 1944 and Italy in 1943 were much more critical than that. In one case, after a rule of 21 years, the Party was ousted from power by the *coup* against the dictator; in the other case it would have been ousted, had the *coup* succeeded.

Thus it would appear that in response to external or internal pressures, the Fascist and Nazi systems were likely to revert through a *coup d'etat* to a more traditional, or *status quo ante* order of society.

Using Soviet Russia as a model of Communism it is obvious, however, that reversion to a *status quo ante* is, and for a very long time has been, precluded: unless the dead be, virtually, recalled. The physical liquidation of one leadership group by another remains a constant, though today probably greatly diminished, possibility; the Communist facade of the regime is far less vulnerable. The key decision makers—military, economic and

---

[29]Cf. Arthur Schweitzer's conclusion, p. 555.

political—are overwhelmingly Communist themselves, reared in a single political tradition over a span of two generations and on the whole far more homogenous than the Fascists or Nazis in their social background. Formal renunciation of "Communism" would be tantamount to a gratuitous self-repudiation for the members of these elites;[30] this was Khrushchev's difficulty in renouncing Stalinism. It is not suggested here that the development of Russian Communism must necessarily be one toward "more and more freedom" or something akin to a parliamentary democracy on a western model as is sometimes believed.[31] On the contrary, elements indigenous to Russian history, tradition and culture could very well impede such tendencies. What is implied is a transition from overt violence to conditioned, voluntary compliance. Communism, having largely uprooted the old order of society and substituted new elite groups may in time pass on to less overt methods of pressure and manipulation. The Khrushchev regime in Russia was fosterer of this transition.

A note of caution however, is in order. The socio-economic variable, though highly important, is obviously not the only one and its time-table is problematical. Communism in Russia, and internationally, may well fail in the solution of tasks other than the creation of new socio-economically homogeneous elites. It may prove unable, for instance, to establish a homogeneity of national interests and attitudes; national conflicts, as in the Sino-Soviet case, may impede and thwart the processes of socio-economic transformation within the various Communist states, perhaps ultimately even defeating the grand design of Communist "social engineering." Such contingencies, however, should not invalidate or preclude the identification of any important trends evident so far.

On socio-economic grounds alone, the future development of the other Communist states is not really accounted for by the Soviet experience. Important differences must be recognized. Most of the Eastern European nations in 1944 possessed larger upper and middle classes in relation to the rest of their populations than did Russia in 1917. And in no case were the former elite groups subjected to such an intensive process of physical liquidation as happened in the U.S.S.R. in its Revolution, Civil War and collectivization drives. Nor was the process of material expropriation as drastic and swift in all cases as it had been in Russia. Thus Poland today retains a far greater measure of private ownership in both land and industry, 19 years after 1945, than did Russia at the corresponding period in 1936. The Communist parties of all the satellite nations are still largely "pre-

---

[30]Cf. Fainsod, *op. cit.*, p. 484: "The members of the elite in the final analysis have a vested interest in the perpetuation of the Soviet System."

[31]In 1953 Isaac Deutscher saw three alternatives for future Soviet developments: relapse into Stalinism; military dictatorship, and the most likely: "socialist democracy." *Russia: What Next?* (New York: Oxford University Press), p. 208.

revolutionary" in their derivation and have "coopted" many members from the old middle classes and from other political movements.[32] All these factors combine to give them a vulnerability which is still comparable to that of the Fascist regimes, and which could only be removed or minimized by the successful implementation of radical Communist policies over a prolonged period of time. Yet, the stimulus and support for such policies could well depend on the Soviet attitude which has been undergoing profound changes of erosion and relaxation from the Stalinist demand for conformity and militancy among the satellites.

In any event, the "totalitarian" similarities among Fascist Italy, Nazi Germany and Soviet Russia have not been such as to warrant predictions of the future development of each from a pattern common to all. The characteristics of totalitarianism commonly emphasized during the 1950s are certainly valid and important descriptions so far as they go, at least of Nazi Germany and of Soviet Russia. But the entire construct is too static, narrow and substructurally insensitive to support significant predictions on the future of the presently surviving totalitarian regimes.

[32]Brzezinski, *op. cit.*, p. 374. Cf. Richard F. Staar, *The Communist Party Leadership in Poland* (Washington: Georgetown University, 1961).

D

SOCIAL CLEAVAGES, PARTY
COMPETITION, AND GROUP INTERESTS
IN THE WELFARE STATE

13

The Changing Class Structure and Contemporary European Politics

Seymour M. Lipset

During the 1950's commentators on both sides of the Atlantic began to depict Western society by terms such as "The End of Ideology," "the post-industrial society," and the "post-bourgeois society."[1] While emphasizing different themes, these commentators agreed that the growth of bureaucracy and "affluence" in Western industrial democratic society has made possible a social system in which class conflict is minimized. True, an

This article originally appeared in *Daedalus* 93 (Winter 1964), pp. 271-303. The text reprinted here is a revised version which appeared as "The Modernization of Contemporary European Politics" in Seymour M. Lipset, *Revolution and Counterrevolution: Change and Persistence in Social Structures*, rev. ed. (Garden City: Anchor Books, 1970), pp. 267-304. Reprinted by permission of the author and *Daedalus*, Journal of the American Academy of Arts and Sciences, Boston, Mass.

[1]It is difficult to establish credit for the origin of this concept. Raymond Aron certainly deserves recognition for having presented it in the form which was widely followed by other writers in the West. See Raymond Aron, "Fin de l'age ideologique?" in Theodore W. Adorno and Walter Dirks (eds.), *Sociologica* (Frankfurt: Europaische Verlaganstalt, 1955), pp. 219-233, and *L'Opium des intellectuels* (Paris: Calmann-Levy, 1955), pp. 315-334. However, it should be noted that two major European scholars, T. H. Marshall and Herbert Tingsten, enunciated the same basic thesis without using the term in the late 1940's and early 1950's. Tingsten's early writings on the subject were presented in various articles in the Stockholm newspaper, *Dagens Nyheter*, while Marshall elaborated on the theme in his now almost classic essay, "Citizenship and Social Class," first presented in 1949 and recently reprinted in his volume *Sociology at the Crossroads* (London: Heinemann, 1963), pp. 67-127. See also Edward Shils, "The End of Ideology?" *Encounter* 5 (November, 1955), pp. 52-58; Herbert Tingsten, "Stability and Vitality in Swedish Democracy," *The Political Quarterly* 26 (1955), pp. 140-151; S. M. Lipset, "The State of Democratic Politics," *Canadian Forum* 35 (1955), pp. 170-171; Otto Brunner, "Der Zeitalter der Ideologien," in *Neue Wege der Sozialgeschichte* (Gottingen: Van den Hoeck und Ruprecht, 1956), pp. 194-219; Lewis Feuer, *Psychoanalysis and Ethics* (Springfield: Charles C. Thomas, 1955), pp. 126-130; Otto Kirchheimer, "The Waning of Opposition in Parliamentary Regimes," *Social Research* 24 (1957), pp. 127-156; Stein Rokkan, *Sammenlignende*

argument does remain as to the relative income at any given moment of the rural sector, of different groups of workers, of private corporations, and so forth. But each group accepts the others' right to legitimate representation within the structure of representation and discussion.

The linkage between level of industrial development and other political and social institutions is obviously not a simple one.[2] Greater economic productivity is associated with a more equitable distribution of consumption goods and education—factors contributing to a reduction of intra-societal tension.[3] As the wealth of a nation increases, the status gap inherent in poor countries, where the rich perceive the poor as vulgar outcasts, is reduced. As differences in style of life are reduced, so are the tensions of stratification. And increased education enhances the propensity of different groups to "tolerate" each other, to accept the complex idea that truth and error are not necessarily on one side. All of these consequences occur even though the relative distribution of *wealth does not* become less equal:

An explanation for the reduction in the appeal of total ideologies (*Weltanschauungen*) as simply derivative from the social concomitants inherent in increasing economic productivity is clearly oversimplified. T. H. Marshall has suggested that such extreme ideologies initially emerged with the rise of new strata, such as the bourgeoisie or the working class, as they sought the rights of citizenship, that is, the right fully to participate socially and politically. As long as they were denied such rights sizable segments of these strata endorsed revolutionary ideologies. In turn, older strata and institutions seeking to preserve their ancient monopolies of power and status fostered conservative extremist doctrines.

The history of changes in political ideologies in democratic countries, from this point of view, can be written in terms of the emergence of new strata, and their eventual integration in society and polity. The struggle for

Politisksosilogi (Bergen: Chr. Michelsens Institutt, 1958); Daniel Bell, *The End of Ideology* (Glencoe: The Free Press, 1960), esp. pp. 369-375; and S. M. Lipset, *Political Man* (Garden City, N. Y.: Doubleday, 1960), esp. pp. 403-417. Daniel Bell has written of the "post-industrial society." See his "The Post Industrial Society" (mimeographed, 1962). Ralf Dahrendorf describes comparable phenomena as the "post-capitalist society." See his *Class and Class Conflict in Industrial Society* (Stanford: Stanford University Press, 1959), esp. pp. 241-318, and Gunnar Myrdal, *Beyond the Welfare State* (New Haven: Yale University Press, 1960). George Lichtheim has commented on many of these ideas under the heading of the "post-bourgeois" society. See his *The New Europe* (New York: Frederick A. Praeger, 1963), esp. pp. 175-215; see p. 194. For an effort to sum up the empirical findings on the subject see M. Rejai, *et al.*, "Political Ideology: Empirical Relevance of the Hypothesis of Decline," *Ethics,* 78 (July 1968), pp. 303-312.

[2]For an excellent article on this subject see Val Lorwin, "Working Class Politics and Economic Development in Western Europe," *American Historical Review* 63 (1958), pp. 338-351.

[3]See Simon Kuznets, "Economic Growth and Income Inequality," *American Economic Review* 45 (1955), p. 4.

such integration took the form of defining the place in the polity of the old preindustrial upper classes, the church, the business strata, and the working class. The variation in the intensity of "class conflict" in many European nations has been in large measure a function of the extent to which the enduring economic struggle among the classes overlapped with the issues concerning the place of religion and the traditional status structure. Such controversies usually were perceived in "moral" terms involving basic concepts of right versus wrong, and hence they were much more likely than economic issues to result in sharp ideological cleavage and even civil war. The continuance of extremist movements in nations such as Germany and the Latin countries of southern Europe may be traced to the force of moral sentiments inherent in concerns for traditional status or religious privileges. Where such issues were resolved without becoming identified with the economic class struggle, then, as Marshall suggests, intense ideological controversy declined almost as soon as the new strata gained full citizenship rights. But it should be noted that ethnic, racial or religious groups, like American blacks or Ulster Catholics, who are still deprived in citizenship terms will continue to find uses for extreme tactics and occasionally ideologies.

Still a third factor related to the general decline in ideological bitterness has been the acceptance of scientific thought and professionalism in matters which have been at the center of political controversy. Insofar as most organized participants in the political struggle accept the authority of experts in economics, military affairs, interpretations of the behavior of foreign nations and the like, it becomes increasingly difficult to challenge the views of opponents in moralistic "either/or" terms. Where there is some consensus among the scientific experts on specific issues, these tend to be removed as possible sources of intense controversy. As the ideology of "scientism" becomes accepted, the ideologies of the extreme left and right lose much of their impact. Ironically, however, opposition to "scientism" has become particularly intense among left-wing student activists and their adult intellectual supporters. These groups correctly perceive "scientism" as a support for political gradualism.

But whatever the long-run sources of the reduction of the appeal of total ideologies (and there are short-run factors as well, such as the impact of wars both hot and cold), the fact remains that there has been a reduction in the intensity of class-linked political struggles in most of Europe. This chapter surveys developments in the economies, social structures, and political parties of European societies which are relevant to an analysis of such trends. Within the context of a broad comparative analysis it also deals with the sources of deviations from these trends. The analysis thus seeks to define the elements in the changing structures which make for a lessening or persistence of class ideologies in different parts of Europe.

CLASS AND POLITICAL CONSENSUS AFTER 1945

The "miracle" of the postwar economic growth of Europe has been well documented. A combination of circumstances—the depression crises, prolonged experience with state economic intervention and planning under fascism or wartime regimes, the sharp increase in approval of socialist or welfare state concepts during and immediately following the war and the need for some years after the conflict to plan for and even furnish the capital for capital investment—resulted in a far greater amount of planning and government involvement in spurring economic growth than had existed in any democratic state before 1939.[4] The nationalization of businesses in France under the first De Gaulle regime surpassed the most grandiose ambitions of Third Republic Socialists, and systematic planning emerged in the early 1950's.[5] The Austrian economy is characterized by large-scale government ownership. Italy retained and even expanded the considerable government economic sector developed under Fascism. In Germany, the numerous dependent war victims and the presence of refugees from the East, comprising more than one-quarter of the population of West Germany, involved the state in welfare and other expenditures that took a large share of the gross national product for many years.[6] And in Britain, the Labour government undertook an elaborate program of nationalization and welfare expenditures which have basically not been challenged by their Conservative successors.

In almost all of these nations, therefore, two general events of considerable significance for class behavior have occurred. On the one hand, many of the political-economic issues that occasioned deep conflict between representatives of the left and of the right were resolved in ways compatible with social-democratic ideology. On the other hand, the dominant strata, business and other, discovered that they could prosper through economic reforms that they regarded a decade earlier as the rankest socialist measures. The socialists and trade unionists found that their formal structural

---

[4]For systematic data on government ownership generally in Europe, see John O. Coppock, "Government Expenditures and Operations," in J. Frederick Dewhurst, John O. Coppock, P. Lamartine Yates, and associates, *Europe's Needs and Resources. Trends and Prospects in Eighteen Countries* (New York: Twentieth Century Fund, 1961), pp. 436-442. See also Massimo Salvadori, "Capitalism in Postwar Europe," in *ibid.*, pp. 746-758.

[5]On the nature and extent of planning in postwar France see Pierre Bauchet, *La planification française. Quinze ans d'expérience* (Paris: Editions du Seuil, 1962).

[6]In "Germany in 1952, something like 37 per cent of the stock of industry was State-owned." Roy Lewis and Rosemary Stewart, *The Managers: A New Examination of the English, German, and American Executives* (New York: Mentor Books, 1961), p. 233. The figure is probably lower now.

objectives, in many cases, had been accomplished with the cooperation of their political rivals. The need for government planning for economic growth and full employment was generally accepted; the obligation of the state to provide welfare services for the ill, the aged, and other dependent groups was viewed as proper by all parties; and the right of the trade union and political representatives of the workers to participate in decisions affecting industry and politics also was increasingly coming to be accepted. Domestic politics in most of these societies became reduced to the "politics of collective bargaining," that is, to the issue of which groups should secure a little more or less of the pie.

The transformation in class attitudes as reflected in political and interest group behavior is most noticeable in northern non-Latin Europe and among the socialist and Roman Catholic political parties. Large-scale extremist or avowedly authoritarian parties have almost completely disappeared north of France and Italy, with the exception of Finland and Iceland. The Norwegian and Austrian socialists who subscribed to a relatively left-wing Marxist view before World War II are now clearly moderate social-democratic parties.[7] The latter took part for twenty years in a stable coalition regime with the bourgeois People's party. The German Social Democratic party ruled its country for some years in alliance with the Christian Democrats and now governs in coalition with the liberal Free Democrats. The parties of the three German-speaking nations, Switzerland, Austria, and Germany, have given up any adherence to Marxism or class-war doctrines and are little concerned with any further expansion of the area of state ownership of industry.[8] The 1959 Godesberg Program of the German party explicitly revoked the traditional policy of public ownership of the means of production.[9] An indication of the mood of European socialism may be found in a description of an international socialist conference:

> In July, 1958, the socialist international held a congress in Hamburg. The name of Karl Marx was mentioned exactly once. The old slogans of the class struggle

[7] See Hubert Ferraton, *Syndicalisme ouvrier et social-democratie en Norvège* (Paris: Armand Colin, 1960) for a detailed analysis of the transformation of the Norwegian Labor party from a radical oppositionist to a moderate governmental party. For a detailed account of the general changes in Norway see Ulf Torgensen, "The Trend Towards Political Consensus: The Case of Norway," *Acta Sociologica* 6, Nos. 1-2 (1962), pp. 159-172. For analysis of the changes in the Austrian parties, see Alexander Vodopivec, *Wer regiert in Österreich?* (Vienna: Verlag für Geschichte und Politik, 1961).

[8] For a detailed account of the changes in the approach of the Swiss Socialist party, a movement rarely discussed in social-science political analysis, see François Masmata, "Le parti socialiste suisse" (thesis for the Doctor of Research degree, École Politique, mimeographed, Paris: Foundation Nationale des Sciences Politiques, Cycle Superieur d'Études Politiques, 1963).

[9] See Jossleyn Hennessy, "Productive Unrest in Germany," *New Society* 1, No. 15 (Jan. 10, 1963), pp. 21-23. For the text of the new program which favors competition, see *Die Zeit* 22 (June 7, 1963), p. 14.

and exploitation had disappeared. But the words "liberty," "democracy," "human dignity" came up again and again. . . . The principal theoretical speech was made by Oscar Pollack [famed theoretician of prewar Austro-Marxism]. His theme was, "Why is it that we cannot get the working classes excited about socialism any longer?" The answer that Pollack gave is that their lot is so improved, in a way which would have been incredible to nineteenth-century Socialists of any variety, that they are no longer easily moved by the slogans of class struggle and socialism.[10]

On the right, one finds that those parties which still defend traditional European liberalism (*laissez-faire*) or conservatism (social hierarchy) are extremely weak. The Scandinavian Liberals and Agrarians now accept much of the welfare state. Many Scandinavian bourgeois politicians, in fact, propose that their countries adopt Swiss political practice, a permanent coalition of all parties in which collective-bargaining issues are fought out and compromised within the cabinet.[11] The Roman Catholic parties, on the whole, have accepted the welfare state and economic planning, and have even supported increases in government ownership. They willingly participate in coalitions with socialist parties in many countries. Roman Catholic trade unions, once the bitter rivals of the so-called free or socialist unions in most Roman Catholic countries, either participate in the same unions as the socialists, as in Germany and Austria, or cooperate closely with the socialist unions, as in the Benelux nations. Issues concerning the relationship of church and state, particularly as they affect education and family legislation, still separate the left wing of the Roman Catholic parties from the socialists, but these are not of grave moment as compared to their agreement on economic and class matters. In Germany the traditional base of the opposition to a democratic regime, the regions beyond the Elbe, the homeland of the Junkers and feudal social relationships, is no longer part of the nation.[12] West Germany today is physically and socially largely comprised of regions and classes which historically have shown a willingness to sustain modern socioeconomic and political systems. Although once playing a major role in politics, the civil service and the army, the old aristocracy today participate little in these institutions.

Reactionary parties in postwar Europe have tended on the whole to be peripheral movements based on the outlying regions and strata which have not shared in the rapid economic growth, which find themselves increasingly outside of the new cosmopolitanism and which have lost out in the relative struggle for influence and status. Thus in Norway the Christian party,

---

[10]Bertram D. Wolfe, "A Century of Marx and Marxism," in Henry L. Plaine (ed.), *Darwin, Marx, and Wagner* (Columbus: Ohio State University Press, 1962), pp. 106-107.

[11]See Dankwart A. Rustow, *The Politics of Compromise* (Princeton: Princeton University Press, 1955), pp. 219-223.

[12]Theodore Schieder, *The State and Society in Our Times* (London: Thomas Nelson and Sons, 1962), p. 121.

which seeks to further traditional values, is clearly a provincial party based on the lower middle classes of the rural and provincial communities.[13] Poujadism was the classic case of a movement appealing to the *resentments* of declining strata; its base was the backward parts of France which had been losing population, and the petit bourgeoisie whose relative position in French economy and society had worsened with the growth of the metropolis and large business and government. In Italy, the Monarchists and Neo-Fascists have recruited strength from roughly comparable groups, a pattern that has also characterized the support of the Austrian Freedom and the German National Democratic parties.[14]

Not unexpectedly, studies of the attitudes and behavior of the entrepreneurial strata in various parts of Europe suggest that the managerial groups in the traditionally less developed countries of Europe, such as France and Italy, have been the most resistant to yielding their historic autocratic and paternalistic view of the role of management, a point elaborated in the previous chapter. "In general, France and Italy have been characterized by a large number of small enterprises, looked on by the family as a source of personal security and conducted in an atmosphere of widespread absence of trust."[15] The resistance to accepting trade unions as a legitimate part of the industrial system has been greater in these nations than anywhere else in democratic western Europe. And consequently, the presence of extreme views of class and industrial relations among leaders of workers and management has contributed to resisting the pressures inherent in industrialization to stabilize such relationships. The available evidence would suggest that Italian industrialists may be more resistant to accepting a *modus vivendi* with trade unions and the planning-welfare state than are the French, although, as shall be noted, the relative situation is reversed among the worker-based Communist parties of these countries.[16] It is difficult to account for these variations other than to suggest that fascism as practiced in Italy for two decades conditioned many Italian businessmen to a pattern of labor-management relations that they still long for. Conversely, however, fascism spared the Italian Communists the experience of having repeatedly

[13]On Norway, see Stein Rokkan and Henry Valen, "The Mobilization of the Periphery," *Acta Sociologica*, 6, Nos. 1-2 (1962), 111-141.

[14]On France and Italy, see Mattei Dogan, "Political Cleavage and Social Stratification in France and Italy," in S. M. Lipset and S. Rokkan (eds.), *Party Systems and Voter Alignments* (New York: Basic Books, 1967), pp. 129-195.

[15]See the various studies reported in Frederick Harbison and Charles A. Myers, *Management in the Industrial World. An International Analysis* (New York: McGraw-Hill, 1959). On Italy see also Joseph La Palombara "La Confindustria e la politica in Italia," *Tempi Moderni* 4 (Oct.-Dec., 1961), pp. 3-16; on France see François Bourricaud, "Le 'Jeune Patron' tel qu'il se voit et tel qu'il voudrait être," *Revue Économique* 6 (1958), pp. 896-911; Lewis and Stewart, *op. cit.*, esp. pp. 165-187; Harbison and Myers, *op. cit.*, p. 123.

[16]See La Palombara, *op. cit.*, and Bourricaud, *op. cit.*, pp. 901, 903.

to purge the various levels of leadership of a mass party. The party could emerge after World War II with close intellectual links to its pre-fascist, and more significantly pre-Stalinist, past and with a secondary leadership and rank and file whose major formative political experience was the Resistance rather than the Comintern.

Class conflict ideologies have become less significant components of the political movements supported by the middle classes in Germany, Italy, and France. In Germany and in Italy, the Christian Democratic type parties, with their efforts to retain the support of a large segment of the unionized working classes, have made a trans-class appeal in favor of moderate changes. As compared to pre-fascist days, they have gained considerably at the expense of older, more class-oriented, more conservative parties. The classically liberal Free Democratic and Liberal parties receive about 7 per cent of the vote in each country. In France, the Christian Democrats (MRP) were not able to retain the massive upper- and middle-class conservative vote which the party inherited in the first elections of the Fourth Republic, as a result of the traditional right's being discredited by its involvement with Vichy. Large-scale anti-labor and anti-welfare state parties arose in the late 1940's and 1950's. The Gaullism of the Fifth Republic, however, has replaced such parties in the affections of the conservative and business part of the electorate. Gaullism is oriented to a trans-class appeal designed to integrate the lower strata into the polity, and it supports economic and social reforms which foster economic growth and reduce class barriers.

Looking at the policies of business toward workers and their unions, it would appear that Germany first, and much more slowly and reluctantly, France and Italy, in that order, have been accepting the set of managerial ideologies characteristic of the more stable welfare democracies of northern and western Europe.[17] Curiously, the one country in which research data exist which bear on the relationship between degrees of modernization and bureaucratization of industry and the attitudes of industrial managers is contemporary Spain. A study of the Spanish businessman by Juan Linz indicates clearly that the larger and more modern a factory, the more likely is its manager to believe in, or accept, modern personnel policies with their denigration of the particularistic rights of *patrons* and their assumptions concerning universalistic treatment of subordinates. It is interesting to note that whether a manager is an owner or not seems to have little bearing on his attitudes on such issues. If the Spanish pattern occurs in the other Latin

---

[17] Stanley Hoffman, "Paradoxes of the French Political Community," in Hoffman, *et al., In Search of France* (Cambridge: Harvard University Press, 1963), pp. 61-62; see also Laurence Wylie, "Social Change at the Grass Roots," in *ibid.,* p. 184. For a detailed analysis of the problems of analyzing the complexity of French economic life see Raymond Aron, *France Steadfast and Changing* (Cambridge: Harvard University Press, 1960), "Myths and Realities of the French Economy," pp. 45-77.

countries as well, it would suggest that those who argue that significant changes are occurring among managers in France and Italy are correct. As yet, however, few systematic comparative data exist on the subject, and many of the available analyses rely heavily on published statements of, or interviews with, the officials, that is, ideologues, of business associations. The latter tend to mouth, and probably even believe, the traditional *laissez-faire* and anti-labor ideologies which many of their members no longer follow in practice.

THE INTEGRATION OF THE WORKING CLASS

But if the evidence drawn from developments in various parts of the continent suggests that the secular trends press for political moderation, for the politics of collective bargaining, it is also important to note that these trends do not imply a loss of electoral strength for working-class-based parties. In fact, in all European countries varying majorities of the manual workers vote for parties which represent different shades of socialism. As the workers have become integrated into the body politic, they have not shifted from voting socialist to backing bourgeois parties. If anything, the opposite seems to have occurred. In the Scandinavian nations, for example, "all evidence indicates that social class explains more of the variation in voting and particularly more of the working-class voting than some decades ago. This has occurred simultaneously with the disappearance of traditional class barriers. As equality has increased the working class voters have been more apt to vote for the worker's own parties than before."[18]

A comparative look at the pattern of working-class voting in contemporary Europe reveals that with the exception of Holland and Germany, the leftist parties secure about two-thirds or more of the working-class vote, a much higher percentage than during the depression of the 1930's.[19] The two exceptions are largely a by-product of the Roman Catholic-Protestant cleavage in their countries. The traditionally minority German and Dutch Roman Catholics have considerable group solidarity, and the Christian Democratic and Roman Catholic parties in these countries secure a larger working-class vote than occurs anywhere else on the continent. Close to 70 per cent of German Protestant workers vote Socialist, as do "humanist" and moderate Calvinist Dutch workers, as opposed to the conservative Dutch Calvinists, who are more like the Roman Catholics. The

---

[18]Erik Allardt, "Traditional and Emerging Radicalism" (mimeographed paper), p. 5.
[19]See Mattei Dogan, "Le Vote ouvrièr en Europe occidentale," *Revue française de sociologie* 1 (1960) pp. 25-44.

leftist working-class-oriented parties have increased their strength in much of Europe during the 1960's. It is clear, therefore, that the easy assumption made by many, concerning American as well as European politics, that greater national affluence would mean a weakening of the electoral support for the left is simply wrong. Regardless of how wealthy a nation may be compared to its past, all democratic countries, from the lands of the Mediterranean basin to Sweden, Australia, or the United States, remain highly stratified societies in which access to education, economic opportunity, culture, and consumption goods is grossly unequal. The nature of such inequalities varies greatly; in general the poorer a country, the greater the gap in the standard of consumption between the classes. However, in all countries the more deprived strata, in income and status terms, continue to express their resentments against the stratification system or perhaps simply their desire to be represented by politicians who will seek further to redistribute the goods of the society, by voting for parties which stand for an increase in welfare state measures and for state intervention in the economy to prevent unemployment and increase their income *vis-à-vis* the more privileged strata.

Greater national wealth and consequent lower visible class differentials, therefore, do not weaken the voting strength of the left as compared with the right; rather, their effects become most evident in the decline of ideological differences, in changes in the policies advocated by different parties. The leftist parties have become more moderate, less radical, in the economic reforms which they espouse. A look at the political history of Europe indicates that no mass lower class-based political party, with the single exception of the German Communists, has ever disappeared or significantly declined through losing the bulk of its votes to a party on its right.[20]

The loyalties once created for a *mass* left-wing party are rarely lost. The most striking testimony to this has been the ability of the Finnish Communist party to retain mass support and even to grow since World War II, in spite of the Russian invasion of the country in 1940, the subsequent war of 1941-1945, and the Russian annexation of Karelia. The Communists are able to secure a quarter of the vote even though 10 per cent of the population are refugees from the Russian-annexed territory. The support for the Communist party goes back to the Finnish Civil War, which followed the Russian revolution, when the Social Democratic party, the largest party under Czarist rule, divided into two roughly equal groups in reacting to Bolshevism. And although the Communist party was illegal for much of the period between the wars, it seemingly lost little backing. In recent years, it

---

[20]Although the German Communists secured about 16 per cent of the vote in 1932, they were never so large as the Social Democrats. The latter always retained their status as the predominant party of the workers. Hence even the German case is not a real exception.

has grown somewhat during a period of rapid economic development and a sharply rising standard of living.

But if workers have remained loyal to the parties of their class on election day, they show much less commitment to these parties the rest of the year. All over Europe, both socialist and Communist parties have complained about losses in membership, in attendance at party meetings, and in the reading of party newspapers. Such changes attest to the growth of what French intellectuals are increasingly coming to describe as the problem of *dépolitisation*.[21] Another phenomenon illustrating these trends is the growing tendency of all the working-class organizations to place less emphasis on traditional *political* doctrines and to put more stress on representation of concrete interests. Roman Catholic trade unions are also increasingly reluctant to intervene directly in politics.

In discussing the implications of changes such as these, a number of French political analysts have argued that what is occurring in France, and presumably in some other countries as well, is not so much a decline in political interest (*dépolitisation*), as of ideology (*déidéologisation*). Thus René Rémond, in introducing a general symposium on these issues, points out that while political parties have suffered a considerable decline in membership, this has not been true of other French associations; that in fact there has been a considerable increase in the number of voluntary associations in France. Such groups, while nonpartisan, play important roles in politics in representing the specific interests of their members. André Philip has even suggested that contemporary France finally is developing the social infrastructure recommended by Tocqueville as a condition for stable democracy, widespread support for secondary associations. He suggested that this is another consequence of modernization, since the pattern of commitment to one group which represents the individual totally is a characteristic of the early phase of development. In a modernized society, any given group or party will report a relatively low level of direct participation by their members or supporters since the segmentalized individual involved in many roles must support diverse groups, and hence seemingly takes on the role of spectator in most of them.[22]

It would seem as if much of France, radical intellectuals and students apart, has taken the plunge of finally dropping its historic commitments to total *Weltanschauungen* and seeing the problem of progressive social change as a pragmatic and gradual one. And insofar as Frenchmen are able to see some of the changes and policies which they advocate being adopted, even by

[21]See especially the various articles in Georges Vedel (ed.), *La Dépolitisation, mythe ou réalité?* (Paris: Armand Colin, 1962).

[22]Colloque "France Forum," *La Démocratie à refaire* (Paris: Editions Ouvrières, 1963), "La Dépolitisation de l'opinion publique," pp. 15-74. The relevant comments of Rémond are on pp. 26-27; Philip's statements are on pp. 38-39.

a government which many of them distrust, their motivation to continue to participate in such pragmatic parapolitical activity continues.

There are many ways in which the more pragmatic orientation of Europeans manifests itself, but the changes in trade-union behavior are most noticeable. As already noted, in a number of countries socialist and Roman Catholic unionists are cooperating as they never did before World War II. The fact of such cooperation reflects the extent to which both have moved away from ideological or political unionism toward pragmatic or even, in the American sense of the term, "business unionism." In Italy and France, the trend toward a *syndicalisme de controle* is furthered by the emerging patterns of plant unions and supplementary factory contracts.[23] Such organization and negotiation for the first time involve the unions in dealing with the concrete problems of the factory environment such as job evaluation, rates, productivity, and welfare.[24] The pressures in this direction have come primarily from the non-Communist unions, although the Communist unions have also increasingly come to accept such institutions, more in Italy than in France.[25] The increase in economic strikes as distinct from political ones, though often resulting in an over-all increase of the strike rate, has been interpreted by some observers as reflecting the integration of the workers into the industrial system; an economic strike is part of a normal bargaining relationship with one's employer. Some suggested that the Italian strike wave of 1961 and 1962 was perhaps the first of this type since the war in that country.[26]

Other major strikes in the 1960's were also notable for the extent to which they increasingly resemble a typical American strike flowing from a breakdown in collective bargaining. Most strikes usually ended by a negotiated settlement in which the unions secure more than they had been offered initially. Few turned into political strikes, although the governments were directly involved in the negotiations. Essentially there was increasing recognition on both sides that the strike is a normal part of the collective-bargaining process, although De Gaulle showed some initial reluctance to concur, while he was President. In France the Communist-controlled CGT

[23]See Jean Maynaud, "Apatia e responsibilita dei cittadini," *Tempi Moderni.* New Series 5, No. 9 (Apr.-June 1962), pp. 30-38.

[24]See Arthur M. Ross, "Prosperity and Labor Relations in Western Europe: Italy and France," *Industrial and Labor Relations Review* 16 (1962), pp. 63-85; see also Vera Lutz, *Italy. A Study in Economic Development* (London: Oxford University Press, 1962), pp. 222-223; and Joseph A. Raffaele, *Labor Leadership in Italy and Denmark* (Madison: University of Wisconsin Press, 1962), pp. 291-293.

[25]See Serge Moscovici, *Reconversion industrielle et changements sociaux* (Paris: Armand Colin, 1961), pp. 127-128.

[26]E. A. Bayne, "Italy's Seeds of Peril, Part IV," *American Universities Field Staff Reports Service.* Southeast Europe Series 10, No. 4 (July 1962).

did occasionally call for protest strikes, while the much less politicized unions affiliated to the Socialist Force Ouvrière and the Roman Catholic CFTC generally called trade-union strikes. The Communists were forced to change their tactics, to shift from political protest to economic strikes. The great French strikes of May and June 1968 were ended by a typical wages and hours agreement. The CGT strongly opposed the demands by students that the strikers adopt political objectives. The German New Left SDS students were so dismayed by the lack of political support from workers and the unions that they dissolved their national organization in the spring of 1970. These strikes in Italy, Germany, and France may signify the beginning of a new era in labor relations—one in which strikes are recognized as part of the normal bargaining relationship rather than an embryonic civil war the outbreak of which is threatening to leadership on both sides.[27]

The relative weakness of traditional leftist ideology in western and southern Europe is suggested also by various attitude surveys taken since the 1950's. These studies indicate that the actual sentiment favoring a "socialist solution" to economic or social problems is much lower than the Socialist or Communist vote. It again demonstrates that people will vote for such parties without commitment to the once basic ideological values of these parties.

In Britain public opinion polls taken before Labour regained office in 1965 indicated that only 18 per cent of the electorate favored more nationalization. Among Labour party voters 39 per cent supported increased nationalization, 46 per cent would have left things as they were, and 15 per cent actually favored some denationalization. Conversely, only 43 per cent of the Conservatives advocated denationalization.[28]

A comparative analysis of attitudes toward ownership of industry in seven European countries based on interviews in the spring of 1958 reported strong sentiment favoring public ownership of industry only in Italy, the nation which has the largest support for radical ideologies in the form of large Communist and left-Socialist parties.[29]

In France, where about half the workers have voted Communist in most postwar elections, with another 20 per cent going to the Socialists, and a large majority voting for the Communist-controlled CGT trade-union federation in Social Security Board elections, opinion data suggest that the workers are not so hostile to the existing institutions as this record might

---

[27]See Club Jean Moulin, *L'État et le citoyen* (Paris: Editions du Seuil, 1961), "Vers le syndicalisme d'enterprise," pp. 271-279, for an analysis of the structural pressures changing the nature of French unionism.

[28]*Gallup Political Index*, Report No. 38, March 1963, p. 34.

[29]See studies completed by Affiliates of International Research Associates and reported in DIVO Institut, *Umfragen: Ereignisse und Probleme der Zeit im Urteil der Bevölkerung* (Frankfurt: Europaische Verlangsanstalt, 1959), p. 77.

imply. As early as 1956 a detailed survey of French workers reported that
53 per cent thought there was "confidence" in the relations between employees and management, as contrasted to 27 per cent who said there was
"distrust." More than four-fifths believed their employer was doing his job
well; nine-tenths thought the quality of the work done at their plant was
good; only 13 per cent thought there was a great deal of waste in their firm;
57 per cent stated that they had a chance for a promotion at their work; and
86 per cent reported they liked their jobs. Although the Communists had
secured the vote of a majority of French workers shortly before this survey,
only 12 per cent of those interviewed stated they were very much interested in
politics, about the same percentage as that which reported strong interest in
trade-union activities.[30] And when asked in which country "the workers are
best off," 54 per cent said the United States as compared with 14 per cent
who answered the Soviet Union.[31]

How many of the French Communist voters actually adhere to a
class-war perspective and a generally Communist view of politics is a
question that is impossible to answer. French experts who have examined the
available evidence from studies of workers' attitudes differ in their
interpretations. Thus Raymond Aron suggests that the polls indicate that
about two-thirds of French Communist supporters are "convinced Communists," while Mattei Dogan believes that less than half of them think of
political action and the class struggle in the Marxist sense of the term.[32]
During the strikes in May and June 1968 the Communist party strongly
opposed the revolutionary objectives of the student radicals. The only party
supporting them, in part, the Unified Socialist party (PSU), secured 3 per
cent of the vote in the June 1968 elections. In the 1969 presidential election,
the PSU candidate received 3.5 per cent.

The weakness of a sharp class-conflict view of politics in Germany is
borne out by an opinion study which asked a sample of the electorate their
opinions concerning class solidarity and party voting. Less than one-fifth
took a purely class view of voting behavior, that is, that workers should
always vote for the Socialists, and middle-class people always for the non-socialist parties. The majority agreed with the statement that workers or

---

[30]"The French Worker: Who he is, how he lives, what he thinks, what he wants," *Réalités* 65
(April 1956), pp. 8-18.
[31]The findings of a study conducted for *Réalités* by IFOP, the French Gallup Poll; see also
Charles Micaud, *Communism and the French Left* (New York: Frederick A. Praeger, 1963), pp.
138-139.
[32]Aron, *France Steadfast and Changing*, pp. 39-40; Mattei Dogan, "Il compartamento
politico degli operai francesi," *Tempi Moderni* 9 (Apr. 1962), pp. 26-27. Dogan reports that in
1952 the majority of workers supporting the Communists told interviewers that "the doctrine of
this party was not the main reason for their vote" (*op. cit.*, p. 25). See also Micaud, *op. cit.*, pp.
140-141.

middle-class people might vote for either tendency, depending on the political situation and the issues involved. More than three-fifths of those in middle-class occupations, although predominantly non-socialist in their voting habits, agreed with the opinion that the division between the bourgeoisie and the workers was no longer strong and that a doctor or a professor might vote either Christian Democratic or Social Democratic, depending on the particular issues of a campaign. Conversely, only 30 per cent of the workers thought that a worker must always vote for the Social Democrats, while half of the worker respondents agreed with the statement that a worker should choose between the parties according to the issues.[33] As in France, the New Left ideological groups secured little adult support. In the September 1969 elections, the radical left ADP (Action for Democratic Progress) received 0.6 per cent of the national vote.

The ideology of the "open society" in which competent individuals can succeed seems to have permeated much of Europe, a phenomenon which may also contribute to a reduction of class tension. Thus surveys in a number of countries which inquired as to the chances of capable individuals rising socially in their country found large majorities which reported their belief that the chances were good. The percentages of respondents saying that chances were good were 90 in Norway, 88 in England, 72 in West Germany, and 70 in Belgium. The one European country covered in this study in which the proportion of those who were optimistic about mobility was less than half was Austria, but even there the positive answers outweighed the pessimistic ones, 49 per cent to 34 per cent. Italy and France were not covered in this comparative study. However, another set of surveys which inquired as to careers one would recommend to a young man found that the Italians ranked second only to the English in suggesting high-status professional occupations (62 per cent). The strongest French preference seemed to be for careers in the civil service, an orientation which distinguished them from all other European nations except the Belgian. It should be noted also that the Italians and the French were least likely among the citizens of eleven

[33]Viggo Graf Blucher, *Der Prozess der Meinungsbildung dargestellt am Beispiel der Bundestagswahl 1961* (Bielefeld: Emnid Institut, 1962), pp. 73-75. See also Heinrich Popitz, Hans Paul Bahrdt, Ernst August Jures, and Hanno Kesting, *Das Gesellschaftsbild des Arbeiters* (Tübingen: Mohr-Siebeck, 1957), p. 233. Similar findings are reported in Alfred Willener, *Images de la société et classes sociales* (Berne: Stämpfli, 1957), pp. 153, 206. See also Ralf Dahrendorf, "Burger und Proletarier: Die Klassen und ihr Schicksal," in his *Gesellschaft und Freiheit* (Munich: Pieper, 1961), pp. 133-162, esp. p. 175; Rainer M. Lepsius, "Zum Wandel der Gesellschaftsbilder in der Gegenwart," *Koelner Zeitschrift für Soziologie,* 14 (1962), 450; Hansjurgen Daheim, "Die Vorstellungen vom Mittelstand," *ibid.,* 12 (1960), 252; and Renate Mayntz, *Soziale Schichtung und Soziale Wandel in einer Industriegemeinde* (Stuttgart: Ferdinand Emke, 1958), p. 103. For a poll of workers, see Institut für Demoskopie, *Jahrbuch der Öffentlichen Meinung, 1947-1955* (Allensbach: Verlag für Demoskopie, 1956), pp. 265, 267.

European countries to recommend a career as a skilled worker or artisan to a young man.[34]

There is some direct evidence that modernization results in a positive attitude by workers toward their occupational situation. A French study of the consequences of modernization in textile factories in northern France brings this out clearly. The author notes that the workers view the effects of technological innovation as a "good thing," that they see it as resulting in an increase in employment, greater possibilities for social mobility, and increased earnings.[35] The findings of French factory surveys with respect to worker reaction to modernization are paralleled in a report on the comparative strength of the Communist party in five large Italian factories which varied in their degree of modernization. The less modernized the plants the larger the proportion of workers who belonged to the Communist party, holding size of plant constant.[36]

But if workers react positively to working in modernized, more bureaucratic work environments, if they see these as offering greater opportunity for higher earnings and mobility, if job satisfaction is actually higher in many of these, the fact remains that when one looks at the sources of left-wing strength, either in voting or in union membership, and in the extent to which men agree with "anti-capitalist" attitudes, such strength is to be found disproportionately in the larger factories and the larger cities.[37] This seeming contradiction reveals an interesting relation between the variables linked to the over-all characteristics of a national political class culture and the same variables operating within a given society. As noted above, nations with a high level of industrialization and urbanization tend to have a low level of ideological conflict. But within nations, whatever the level of intensity of political controversy, larger factories and cities tend to be the strongholds of the left politics dominant in the country, Communist, Socialist, or Democratic.[38] Trade unions also are generally stronger in large factories in large cities. It would seem that while greater industrialization and urbanization with consequent greater national wealth make for a more

[34]DIVO Institut, op. cit., pp. 120, 124.

[35]Claude Durand, "Positions syndicales et attitudes ouvrières à l'égard du progrès technique," Sociologie du travail 4 (1960), p. 351.

[36]Mario Einaudi, J. Domenach, and A. Garoschi, Communism in Western Europe (Ithaca: Cornell University Press, 1951), pp. 43-44.

[37]Dogan, op. cit., p. 26. For reports of opinion data on characteristics of working-class vote, data on traits of union members and their attitudes drawn from a secondary analysis of the IBM cards of a survey of French workers completed by the French Institute of Public Opinion (IFOP) in 1956, see Richard Hamilton, Affluence and the French Worker in the Fourth Republic (Princeton: Princeton University Press, 1967).

[38]See Lipset, Political Man, pp. 263-267.

stable polity, *within* any system these social factors are conducive to fostering working-class political and trade-union strength.

How might we account for this? In part it may be related to the fact that the large factory environment sustains fewer informal relations between members of different classes, reducing the possibility that the members of the lower class will be influenced personally by the more conservative and more prestigeful members of middle and higher classes such as owners, managers, and supervisors. And the more concentrated the members of a lower class are in a social environment, the easier it is for common class attitudes to spread among them and for representatives of class-oriented parties or other organizations to reach them and activate their anti-elitist sympathies.[39]

But although the emergence of large social environments that are class homogeneous facilitates the spread of lower class-based movements, the same factors operating in the social structure as a whole become linked with other tendencies operating to reduce class friction. On the working-class level these involve a rise in standards of living, educational levels, and opportunity for upward social mobility within industry. In all countries with large Communist movements (Italy, France, and Finland), within any given structural environment, the better-paid workers are more moderate in their political views than the poorer ones. Modernization reduces the sources of worker hostility to management by altering the sources of managerial behavior. These trends involve a decline in the family-owned corporation and in the domination of the economy by the *patron* type who sees himself as all powerful, and the rise within the management strata of a corporate leadership characterized by a division of labor and by the requisite of formal higher education. Accompanying the growth in large systems is a consequent increased emphasis on universalistic and achievement values, on judging individuals on the basis of their specific roles as worker or manager. As management's resistance to formalizing the labor-management relationship gradually declines, union labor's commitment to an ideological view of unionism, as distinct from a business or pragmatic view, is also reduced.

---

[39]German data indicate that the larger the plant a man works in the more likely he is to discuss politics with his fellow workers in the factory. Wolfgang Hartenstein and Gunther Schubert, *Mitlaufen oder Mitbestimmen* (Frankfurt: Europaische Verlanganstalt, 1961), p. 25. Conversely, the larger the size of the work unit, the fewer the workers who report that they chat informally with a higher up. See Juan Linz, "Cleavage and Consensus in West German Politics: The Early Fifties," in Lipset and Rokkan (eds.), pp. 293-294; Lipset, *Political Man*, p. 251; Hamilton, *op. cit.*, pp. 206-208; which report correlations of size of plant and radicalism. However, Eric Nordlinger, *The Working-Class Tories* (Berkeley: University of California Press, 1967), reports contrary findings for England.

THE NEW MIDDLE CLASS—THE BASE FOR EMPLOYEE POLITICS

The emergence of the new middle class—the increasingly large layer of clerks, salesmen, technicians, middle management, civil servants—has served to introduce as a major factor in the European polity a group which itself is so exposed to conflicting pressures from the left and the right that it can contribute to stabilizing class tensions. A broad middle class has a mitigating position because it can give political rewards to moderate parties and penalize extreme parties on both sides—right and left. Its members wish to obtain more for themselves and their offspring; they advocate universalistic equality in the educational and other aspects of the status-allocating mechanisms; they often uphold the extension of the welfare state. Yet their position among the relatively privileged in status and possession terms makes them supporters of political and social stability, of the politics of collective bargaining. And the larger a proportion of the electorate and the labor force formed by the new middle class, the more both the left and the right must take this group into account in determining their own policies. The political and trade-union influence of the new middle class is largely thrown on the side of pressing for greater opportunity, not greater social equality. The unions of the middle class are interested in maintaining, or even extending, the income gap existing between themselves and the manual workers. They often abstain from affiliating to the same central federation as the manual unions, and many of them are led by men who back "liberal" rather than labor parties. In some countries of Europe, and in Israel in recent years, there have been strikes by unions of salaried professionals in order to widen the gap between themselves and manual workers.[40] However,

---

[40]On the behavior of white-collar workers in various countries see R. M. Blackburn, *Union Character and Social Class* (London: Batsford, 1967); Adolf Sturmthal (ed.), *White Collar Unions: Contemporary Developments in Industrialized Societies* (Urbana: University of Illinois Press, 1966). See also S. M. Lipset, "White Collar Workers and Professionals—Their Attitudes and Behavior Towards Unions," in William A. Faunce (ed.), *Industrial Sociology* (New York: Appleton-Century-Crofts, 1967), pp. 525-548; Michel Crozier, "Les attitudes politiques des employés et des petits fonctionnaires," in M. Duverger (ed.), *Partis politiques et classes sociales en France* (Paris: Armand Colin, 1955), pp. 85-99; *Petits fonctionnaires au travail* (Paris: Centre National de la recherche scientifique, 1955); "L'ambiguité de la conscience de classe chez les employés et les petits fonctionnaires," *Cahiers Internationaux de sociologie* 28 (1955), pp. 78-97; "Les relations de pouvoir dans un système d'organisation bureaucratique," *Sociologie du Travail* 1 (1960), pp. 61-75; "Classes sans conscience ou préfiguration de la société sans classes," *European Journal of Sociology* 1 (1960), pp. 233-245; "Le rôle des employés et des petits fonctionnaires dans la structure française contemporaine," *Transactions of the Third*

interest in income differences apart, these rapidly growing new middle classes press the political system toward consensus because as employees they favor many of the same statist policies that were long pressed by the representatives of the manual workers. Otto Kirchheimer in fact has argued that it is the very growth of these strata, who form the mass base of the "bourgeois" parties, that is largely responsible for the decline of ideology.[41]

It is important to recognize that the bourgeois parties are no longer bourgeois in the classic sense of the term. That is, the proportion of those who are self-employed, or who have close ties to the self-employed on the land or in the town, is an increasingly small part of the electorate. Most large parties now represent employees, manual or nonmanual. And while these strata differ in their orientations to many issues, they are also united on many welfare concerns. Swedish political history is an apt illustration of this point. The dominant Social Democrats were experiencing a secular decline in support, largely, according to survey analyses, because the white-collar segment of the population was growing relative to the manual sector. The party introduced a major reform, an old-age pension of 65 per cent of salary, in large part because their electoral researches had suggested such a proposal would be popular not only with their traditional manual supporters but with many white-collar workers. The proposal was ultimately carried in a referendum, and the party increased its national vote substantially. Even more significant, perhaps, is the fact that the Liberal party, which accepted the general principle of the enlarged pension, gained enormously at the expense of the Conservatives, who took a traditional position against high taxes and against increases in the functions of the state. This suggests that the political struggles of the future will increasingly take place between parties representing the status concerns and economic interests of the two employee strata, and that the parties drawing heavily from the self-employed will continue to lose influence.[42]

World Congress of Sociology (Amsterdam: International Sociological Association, 1956), III, pp. 311-319; Roger Girod, *Études sociologiques sur les couches salariées* (Paris: Marcel Rivière, 1961); Fritz Croner, *Die Angestellten in der modernen Gesellschaft* (Frankfurt: Humbolt, 1954); John Bonham, *The Middle Class Vote* (London: Faber and Faber, 1954); David Lockwood, *The Blackcoated Worker* (London: Allen and Unwin, 1958); E. Dahlstrom, *Tjanstemännen, Naringlivet och sämhallet* (Stockholm: Studieförbundet näringsliv och Samhälle, 1954). See also S. M. Lipset and Mildred Schwartz, "The Politics of Professionals," in H. M. Vollmer and D. L. Mills (eds.), *Professionalization* (Englewood Cliffs, Prentice-Hall, 1966), pp. 299-310.

[41] Kirchheimer, *op. cit.*, p. 148.

[42] It is interesting to note that a similar pattern has emerged within the United States. See Herbert J. McClosky, Paul J. Hoffman, and Rosemary O'Hara, "Issue Conflict and Consensus among Party Leaders and Followers," *American Political Science Review* 54 (June 1960), pp. 406-427.

COMMUNISM RESISTS THE TREND

The dominant structural trend in Europe involves the final triumph of the values of industrial society, the end of rigid status classes derivative from a preindustrial world, and increasing emphasis on achievement rather than ascription, on universalism rather than particularism, and on interaction among individuals in terms of the specific roles played by each rather than in terms of their diffuse generalized statuses. The heightening standard of living of the masses gives them greater market power and enables them to affect much of culture and societal taste. All these changes imply the emergence of a somewhat similar social and political culture, one which increasingly resembles the first advanced industrial society to function without institutions and values derivative from a feudal past, the United States. And as has been indicated earlier, this should mean the end of class-linked severely ideological politics.

Yet there is one major force which in a number of countries has rejected this view of European social change and which has done its best to block these trends—the Communist party. It is clear that the very existence of powerful Communist movements in countries such as France and Italy has been a major force perpetuating the institutions and values of the old society. In countries in which the Communists are the largest working-class party, in which they secure around a quarter of all votes, it has been difficult to elect a progressive government to office. If governments must secure a majority from the non-Communist three-quarters of the population, they have to rely in large part on the conservative and traditionalist elements. The fact that one-quarter of the electorate, constituting one-half or more of the social base of the "left," have been outside of the political game inevitably gives a considerable advantage to the conservatives. In effect, by voting Communist, French and Italian workers have disfranchised themselves. Thus not only does a mass Communist party serve to fossilize the ideological orientations characteristic of a preindustrial society among the working class, it contributes to preserving premodern orientations on the right.

A series of political developments—the revival of French Communist support recouping most of the electoral losses it suffered between 1956 and 1958 as a result of the Hungarian revolution and the Gaullist coup, the continued massive strength of Finnish Communism and the fairly continuous slow growth in the vote of the Italian Communists—each of which has occurred during long periods of prosperity and economic growth—would seem to contradict the thesis that economic growth and an improvement in social conditions enhance the prospects for political stability.[43] In these countries economic modernization has seemingly not been followed by a reduction in ideological tensions.

The countries with large Communist parties, however, remain among the less modernized of the big nations; their industry tends to be less centralized in large plants. Thus in the mid-1950's the proportion of German employees in plants with more than 1,000 workers was twice as high (38.9 per cent) as it was in France (17.6 per cent), while only 12 per cent of the employed Germans were in plants with fewer than 50 workers, in contrast to 37 per cent of the French.[44] The European countries in which communism is strongest are among those with a relatively small proportion of their total population living in metropolitan areas.[45] The rank-order correlation between the proportion of Communist votes in a nation and urbanization is minus .61, while the comparable correlation between left extremist voting and an index of industrialization is minus .76.[46] Insofar as the general pattern of politics, class relations, and other social attitudes is affected by the degree of bureaucratization of industrial and community life, it is clear that the nations with large Communist movements are on the whole among the less developed in these respects of the nations of Europe.

The comparative analysis of the consequences of economic growth on class relationships in relatively industrialized societies is further complicated by the fact that processes endemic in such improvement affect those workers who are accustomed to the industrial system differently from those who are drawn into it. For the former, increased bureaucratization of industry should make for improvement in income and the conditions of work, and thus should serve to moderate their propensity toward extremist politics. For the latter, the experiences of dislocation inherent in social and geographical mobility, particularly the shift from rural or small-town background to crowded urban slums, and from the pace and discipline of rural work to that of the factory, may increase their potential for support of political radi-

[43]E. A. Bayne. "Italy's Seeds of Peril," I, *American Universities Field Staff Reports Service.* Southest Europe Series 10, No. 1 (June 1962), p. 7, and "Unions on the March Again," *The Economist.* April 13, 1963, p. 137.

[44]For Germany see the *Statistisches Jahrbuch,* 1959, p. 179, and for France in 1954 see Institut national de la statistique et des études economiques, *Mouvement Economique en France de 1944 à 1957* (Paris: Presses Universitaires, 1958), p. 42.

[45]See Jack P. Gibbs and Kingsley Davis, "Conventional Versus Metropolitan Data in the International Study of Urbanization," in Jack P. Gibbs (ed.), *Urban Research Methods* (Princeton: Van Nostrand, 1961), pp. 422-424.

[46]William Kornhauser, *The Politics of Mass Society* (Glencoe: The Free Press, 1959), pp. 143, 150. The degree of urbanization was measured by the proportion of the population living in cities with more than 20,000 population, while industrialization was measured by the proportion of the labor force in nonagricultural occupations.

calism.[47] The need to adjust quickly to new social conditions and cultural norms makes individuals receptive to new values and ideologies which explain the sources of their discontent in revolutionary terms.[48] It should also be noted that the decline in the number of the chronically unemployed —from 2.5 million in 1950-1951 to well under a million in the early 1960's—in Italy may have increased rather than decreased the vote available to the extreme left. There are two empirical generalizations about the political behavior of the jobless and the formerly unemployed that hold true in a number of countries. First, the unemployed are much more likely than those regularly employed to be uninformed and apathetic about politics. Their insecurity would seem to reduce their availability for any "outside" interest, including the act of voting. Second, employed individuals who report a past experience of unemployment, or areas which were once centers of high rates of unemployment, are much more likely to exhibit leftist voting propensities than those with more fortunate economic histories.[49]

The most comprehensive analysis of the sources of, and changes in, the support of a mass European Communist party, that of Erik Allardt in Finland, strongly suggests that economic growth in the less industrialized regions of a rapidly developing nation heightens the possibilities for extremist class-conscious politics. He points out that the characteristics of Communist strength in regions in which communism has gained greatly since World War II, the north and east, are quite different from those in the areas in which it has always been strong, the south and west. The latter are the original industrialized sections of the country. His detailed statistical analyses point to the conclusion that *"increase in Communist strength in all areas is related to changes which in one way or another are likely to uproot individuals."*[50] Ecological analysis indicates that increases in the per-capita income of the poorer regions are correlated highly with gains in Communist support. Allardt's analysis also suggests some of the factors underlying the continuation of Communist strength once attained. Stable Communist

[47]The change in the Italian occupational structure has been dramatic. See Bayne, "Italy's Seeds of Peril," II, No. 2 (June 1960), p. 6.

[48]See Edvard Bull, Jr., *Arbeidermilje under det industrielle gjennombrudd. Tre norske industristrok* (Oslo: 1958), as cited in Stein Rokkan and Henry Valen, "Parties, Elections and Political Behaviour in the Northern Countries: A Review of Recent Research," in Otto Stammer (ed.), *Politische Forschung* (Koln: Westdeutscher Verlag, 1960), pp. 107-108, 110; Lipset, *Political Man*, pp. 68-71. See also John C. Leggett, "Uprootedness and Working-Class Consciousness," *American Journal of Sociology*, 68 (1963), pp. 682-692. Leggett also cites various historical studies which point to the link between "uprootedness" and radicalism.

[49]Lipset, *Political Man*, pp. 187, 198, 236; see also S. M. Lipset, *Agrarian Socialism* (Berkeley: University of California Press, 1950), pp. 176-177.

[50]Allardt, "Traditional and Emerging Radicalism," p. 21. In an earlier study Allardt has demonstrated that areas with the highest proportions of unemployed during the depression gave the highest support to the Communists in 1951-1954. See Erik Allardt, *Social Struktur och Politisk Aktivitet* (Helsingfors: Söderstrom, 1956), p. 84.

strength, that is, little fluctuations up or down, is associated with the older industrial areas in which the party has been strong since the Russian Revolution and which also give strong support to the Social Democrats. In such regions the Communists have erected an elaborate network of party-linked voluntary associations and leisure activities, so that, as in parts of France and Italy, one almost has a functioning Communist subculture unaffected by political events.

As already noted, it is doubtful that structural changes alone will result in the decline of a mass Communist party.[51] Where the party is strong, it endeavors, as in Finland, to isolate its base from serious influence by non-Communist sources. There are plenty of social strains inherent in the situation of the worker or poor peasant to reinforce acceptance of leftist doctrine, and a mass movement can claim that any improvements are the result of its agitation. The Communist sector of the electorate will join the democratic political game in the foreseeable future only if their party, as a party, does it. There is little doubt that if the various European Communist parties had been genuine national parties—that is, if their behavior had been largely determined by experiences within their own countries—they would have evolved in much the same way as the European socialist parties. And consequently, it is necessary to recognize that any predictions about their future behavior must be part of an analysis of developments within the Communist-controlled nations. The break between the Soviet Union and China permits genuine autonomy for all national Communist parties, so that the pattern of independence from Russian control emerging in Italy has occurred elsewhere as well.

The doctrinal base for such a change in the role of Communist parties has been advanced by various Yugoslav and Italian Communists.[52] The former have argued that there is a worldwide pressure for socialist innovations which is inherent in the nature of large-scale capitalist economic institutions. They accept the proposition that Communist movements and ideologies as they emerged in eastern Europe and Russia are appropriate for underdeveloped countries which have not had the experience of large and legally instituted labor, political, and union movements nor the experience of political freedom.[53] The more developed nations not only can avoid the experiences of the less developed Communist societies, but they can and are

[51]Greece may be an exception to this generalization. See Marcello Dell' Omodarme, "Greece Moves toward Dictatorship," *Atlas* 3 (1962), pp. 301-305 (translated from *Communitá*, December 1961).

[52]An analysis of the similarities in the approaches of the Yugoslav and Italian Communists may be found in François Fejto, "Le parti communiste français et le 'polycentrisme,' " *Arguments* 6 (1962), pp. 69-70.

[53]See Walter Z. Laqueur, "The End of the Monolith: World Communism in 1962," *Foreign Affairs* 40 (1962), p. 362.

moving toward socialism while preserving political freedom. It has even been suggested that in the United States, socialist adjustments and institutions exist even though Americans refuse to accept the term socialism to describe the changes occurring within their society. Coexistence is possible, say these Yugoslavs, not only because major war is impossible in an atomic age, but because there is no basic cleavage between the Communist and the capitalist world, since the latter is ceasing to be capitalist in any traditional meaning of the term. Hence Communists in the developed countries will not have to make a revolution or come to power in their own right. By collaborating with other "progressive forces," they can hasten the emergence of socialist institutions.

The Italian Communist party has gradually modified its ideology so that some sophisticated observers would now describe it as a left social-democratic rather than a Communist party. Like the Yugoslav party, it no longer sees a fundamental dichotomy between capitalism and socialism, but rather argues that "there exists in the capitalist world today an urge towards structural reforms and to reforms of a socialist nature, which is related to economic progress and the new expansion of the productive forces."[54] And its late leader, Palmiro Togliatti, went on to argue the need to "correct" Lenin's position that "bourgeois state apparatus cannot be used for building a socialist society," in the light of "the changes which have taken place and which are still in the process of being realized in the world."[55] It denies the need for one-party dictatorship in Italy, and it has accepted Italian membership in the Common Market. Communist municipal office-holders work closely with business groups in fostering the interests of their cities, and party-controlled labor unions play a somewhat more responsible role in collective bargaining and Italian life generally than has been true for Communist unions in the past.[56] The Chinese Communists correctly point to the Italian party as the foremost example of reformist heresies among the nongovernmental parties. If the Italian electorate has not turned away from

---

[54]Quoted in the Editorial Department of Hongqi, *More on the Differences Between Comrade Togliatti and Us* (Peking: Foreign Languages Press, 1963), p. 13.

[55]Togliatti's report, *op. cit.*, p. 130 (emphasis mine). For a discussion of some of the issues underlying the question of Marx and Engels' original position, the influence of the Paris Commune on them, and Communist revisionism, see S. M. Lipset, "The Sociology of Marxism," *Dissent* 10 (1963), pp. 59-69. This is a review article on George Lichtheim, *Marxism: An Historical and Critical Study* (New York: Frederick A. Praeger, 1961). This book must also be read in this context. Lichtheim argues that Marxism as a revolutionary doctrine is appropriate only to countries in the period of early industrialization.

[56]In Italy see Giorgio Galli, "Italy," in Walter Laqueur and Leopold Labedz (eds.), *Polycentrism: The New Factor in International Communism* (New York: Frederick A. Praeger, 1962), pp. 127-140; and Giorgio Galli, "Italy: The Choice for the Left," in Leopold Labedz (ed.), *Revisionism* (New York: Frederick A. Praeger, 1962), pp. 324-336.

the Communists, the Communists have moved to the right. Thus the effect of a reduction in social strains among sections of the Italian workers may be reflected in the changed behavior of their party and unions.[57]

But if the experiences and the behavior of the Italian party suggest an adaptation to the emergence of stable political institutions and economic modernization in Italy, the French Communist party simply has adjusted more slowly and its policies until very recently seemingly challenged the underlying interpretation here.[58] The French party also had to react to the end of Soviet domination of party life and to economic modernization in France. But where the Italian party and its union federation, the CGIL, modified their programs and explicitly decided to cooperate "with what they termed the representatives of neo-capitalism," during the late 1950's, the French party in large part refused and remains in 1970 the most "conservative" communist party in Western Europe. It continued to insist that capitalism could not reform itself, that the workers could not make long-term improvements in their social situation, and that the unions must remain primarily political instruments. The Italian party decided to join forces with modernization, the French party continues to resist it.[59] The reasons for the differences in tempo of the parties are complex and I cannot detail them here.[60] Briefly, they would seem to relate to the fact that the French party was Stalinized and proletarianized in its leadership and membership during the 1930's and 1940's, while Fascism enabled the Italian party to escape some of these consequences; after 1944 it recruited and retained many non-Stalinist intellectuals in its organizations. Palmiro Togliatti, the leader of the Italian party until his death in 1964, though an official of the Comintern during the 1930's, more closely resembled the pre-Stalin leaders of Communism than his French equivalent Maurice Thorez, who won and maintained leadership as a result of following Stalin's every turn.[61] The variations in the Italian and French political systems have meant that elected local

---

[57]For an indication of the diversity of opinion and level of open debate which exists among the leadership of the Italian Communist party, see the translations of the report published in *L'Unità*, the organ of the party, of a two-day debate within the central committee. Perry Anderson, "Debate of the Central Committee of the Italian Communist Party on the 22nd Congress of the C.P.S.U.," *New Left Review*, Nos. 13-14 (January-April, 1962), pp. 151-192. For the history of open debate within the Italian party, see Guglielmo Negri and Paolo Ungari, "La vita dei partito," in Alberto Spreafico and Joseph La Palombara (eds.), *Elezioni e comportamento politico in Italia* (Cremona: Edizioni di Communitá, 1963), pp. 175-180.

[58]But for a different interpretation, see Lichtheim, *op. cit.*, p. 180.

[59]See Pierre Fougeyrollas, "France," in Laqueur and Labedz, *op. cit.*, pp. 141-151.

[60]An excellent analysis of the differences between the Italian and French parties may be found in Fejto, *op. cit.*, pp. 66-72. A similar point is made by Laqueur, *op. cit.*, p. 369.

[61]See Ignazio Silone's essay in R. Crossman (ed.), *The God That Failed* (New York: Harper, 1949), pp. 106-112, and Antonio Gambino, "Togliatti's Balancing Act," *Atlas* 3 (1962), pp. 126-127 (translated from *L'Espresso*, Dec. 31, 1961).

Communists have had more real power and involvement in running munici-
palities and other institutions in Italy than in France.[62] The Italian Socialists, in part because of their long Fascist experience, have been much less
hostile to the Communists than have been the French Socialists. Hence the
Italian party has never been so isolated from non-Communists as the French.
These differences between the French and Italian Communist parties may be
related to the facts that the Italian party has lost fewer members than the
French (both parties have lost a considerable portion of their membership as
compared with their postwar high point), and that the Italian party has done
better at the polls during the 1960's.[63]

Communist parties without a Moscow-centered world party would be
like national Roman Catholic churches without a pope, without the need to
follow a dogma decreed from a single source. And many observers predict
that the individual parties will follow the road of Protestantism, of deviation,
of variation, of adjustment to particular national conditions, much as the
Social Democrats did half a century or more earlier. Those parties which
operate within democratic societies will be under constant pressure to modify
their totalitarian structures, as in fact the Italian party seems to be beginning
to do.[64]

Given the history of the Communist movement, the training which its
leaders have received in totalitarian methods, and the use of conscious
deception, the acceptance (even though now critical) of the experiences of
one-party regimes as a positive model, no one who cares about freedom can
accept a Communist party as an equal player in a parliamentary game. On
the other hand, the possibility that changes in the Communist world are
permitting sufficient independence and variations among Communist
parties to allow some of them to react to the forces which press them to act as
regular participants within political democracies should not be ignored. The
more positively involved are Communists and their *followers* in a political
system which in fact is paying off socially and economically, the more
difficult it will be for a given Communist party to renew an alienated stance
among its supporters should the leadership decide to do so. Hence the
possibility may be held out that the vicious circle of Communist-reactionary
resistance to modernization in Latin Europe may be breaking down, not only
as a result of the decline of the reactionary groups, but because of changes

---

[62]See Michel Crozier, "La France, terre de commandement," *Esprit* 25 (1957), pp. 790-792.
[63]See Hamilton, *op. cit.*, pp. 27-28. See also Crozier, "La France, terre de commandement."
[64]Richard Lowenthal, "The Rise and Decline of International Communism," *Problems of*
Communism 12 (Mar.-Apr. 1963); see also Laqueur, *op. cit.*, pp. 371-373.

within Communism. Even Communism may be yielding to the pressures making for a decline of ideology and of class war.

CONTINUING SOURCES OF STRAIN

There are many sources of political strain within stable democratic societies. The stratification systems of all inherently involve a grossly inegalitarian distribution of status, income, and power. Even the very "affluent" United States contains a large minority living in poverty by its own standards.[65] A look at consumption standards for Europe finds that very large minorities or majorities in different European countries still lack many items which are available to all but a few in the United States.[66] Status inequality would seem to be experienced as punitive by the lower classes in all systems. But while all societies present some ideological justification for enduring consumption and status inequalities, the concept of mass citizenship that arose with the Industrial Revolution undermines the stability of class systems because it implies, as T. H. Marshall put it, that "all are equal with respect to the rights and duties with which the status is endowed."[67] Hence he argues that modern democratic industrial society is historically unique in seeking to sustain a system of contradictory stratification values. All previous societies had class systems that assumed inequality, but they also denied citizenship to all except a small elite. Once full and equal political (manhood suffrage) and economic (trade-union organization) citizenship was established, the egalitarian emphasis inherent in the concept sustains a successful and continuing attack on many aspects of inequality. Much of democratic politics involves the efforts of the lower strata to equalize the conditions of existence and opportunity.

The tension between equality and inequality is endemic in modern industrial democratic society. The dominant strata will continue the attempt to institutionalize their privileges, to find means to pass on to their kin and offspring the privileges they have gained. This conflict, however, does not

---

[65]See S. M. Lipset, *The First New Nation* (New York: Basic Books, 1963), pp. 321-335 for an earlier discussion.

[66]A quick glance at any statistical table reporting on income or consumption standards in Europe suggests the extent to which European affluence is considerably below that of the United States. See J. Frederick Dewhurst, "Consumption Levels and Patterns," in Dewhurst *et al., op. cit.,* pp. 146-147, 161-162; P. Lamartine Yates, "Household Operations," in Dewhurst *et al., op. cit.,* pp. 266, 267, 1005; Report of DOXA, 15, No. 16 (Aug. 1961), p. 2; and "Tableau général de la consommation des français de 1950 à 1960," *Consommation* 8 (July-Dec. 1961), pp. 5-174.

[67]Marshall, *op. cit.,* p. 87.

mean that one or the other tendency must triumph, or that the strain will destroy or even necessarily weaken the social fabric. The predominant character of modern industrial democracy, as a free and evolving society, is in part a result of the chronic tensions between the inherent pressures toward inequality and the endemic emphasis in democracy on equality.

The wave of writings in the 1950's that somehow saw in the growth of affluence in the Western world the emergence of a peaceful social utopia— which would not require continued political struggle between representatives of the haves and of the have-nots—ignored the extent to which the content of these very concepts changes as society evolves. As Marshall has pointed out, ever since the beginning of the Industrial Revolution almost every generation proclaimed a social revolution to elevate the lower strata. "From the 1880's to the 1940's people were constantly expressing amazement at the social transformation witnessed in their lifetime, oblivious of the fact that, in this series of outbursts of self-congratulation, the glorious achievements of the past became the squalid heritage of the present."[68]

But in spite of the progress leading one generation to proclaim the significance of recent social improvements, only a few years later others are arguing that the present conditions of the poor, of the lowly, are intolerable, that they cannot possibly be tolerated by free men who believe in equality.[69] And as Marshall indicates, such phenomena do not "mean that the progress which men thought they made was illusory. It means that the standards by which that progress was assessed were constantly rising, and that ever deeper probing into the social situation kept revealing new horrors which had previously been concealed from view."[70] The large literature dealing with poverty in the 1960's provided a new demonstration of Marshall's thesis.

The problem of the lower strata is now seen not only as a consequence of limited resources, but of "cultural deprivation" as well. It is clear that in all countries, variation in participation in the intellectual culture serves to negate the dream of equal opportunity for all to mount the educational ladder; consequently, access to the summits of the occupational structure is still grossly restricted. In Sweden, for example, in spite of thirty-five years of Social Democratic government providing free access to universities together with state bursaries, the proportion of working-class children taking advantage of such opportunities has hardly risen. Few commodities are distributed as unequally in Europe as high-school and university education. The simple improvement in economic standards of living, at least at its present pace, does little to reduce the considerable advantages held by the culturally

---

[68]*Ibid.*, p. 268.

[69]See Howe, *op. cit.*, pp. 325-326. See also John Goldthorpe and David Lockwood, "Not So Bourgeois After All," *New Society* 1, No. 3 (Oct. 18, 1962), p. 19.

[70]Marshall, *op. cit.*, pp. 269-270.

privileged strata to perpetuate their families in an equally advantaged position.[71] And socialist parties in a number of countries are beginning to look for ways to enhance the educational and cultural aspirations of lower-class youth. Here, then, is the most recent example of the conflict between the principles of equality inherent in citizenship and the forces endemic to complex stratified society that serve to maintain or erect cultural barriers between the classes. The latter operate as a consequence of the differential distributions of rewards and access to culture, and must be combated continually if they are not to dominate.[72]

In conclusion, this survey of economic and social developments accompanying the modernization of European society has shown compelling evidence for the moderation of ideological differences in Europe as a consequence of the increasing affluence of European nations, the attainment of economic as well as political citizenship by the workers, the gradual absorption and assimilation of the remnants of European society still living in feudal or otherwise underdeveloped economic and social conditions. The changes in parties of the left, especially Communist parties, to a more moderate orientation toward capitalist society and class conflict have been shown to be also related to broad changes in the international Communist world, as exemplified by the thesis of polycentrism and the reinterpretation of Marxism concerning the possibility of a rapprochment with capitalism. But it has also been pointed out that industrialization does not remove sources of tension. These sources are endemic to an industrial society which permits a relatively open struggle for the fruits of individual effort and which does not automatically give access to opportunity for individual advancement to those on the lower rungs of the status ladder. Finally, it has been argued that much of the anachronistic ideological politics of the "Poujadist" left and right is a response to anachronistic orientations and forms of industrial organization still present in some sectors of European society, as among some peasants and small businessmen in France, or as a result of the preservation of outmoded forms of production and extraction, as in Britain and Belgium.

It should be clear, however, that not only do class conflicts over issues related to division of the total economic pie, influence over various institutions, symbolic status and opportunity, continue in the absence of *Weitanschauungen*, but that the decline of such total ideologies does *not*

---

[71]See H. Bouterline Young, "Detection and Encouragement of the Talented in Italian Schools," *The British Yearbook of Education, 1962* (London: Evans Brothers, 1962), pp. 275-280. See also Christiane Peyre, "L'Origine sociale des élèves de l'enseignement secondaire en France," in Jean Floud et al., *Ecole et société* (Paris: Marcel Rivière, 1959), p. 10.

[72]See Mark Abrams, "Social Class and Political Values" (paper presented to the British Sociological Association, Scottish Branch, Conference in Edinburgh, May 3-4, 1963), pp. 13-14.

mean the end of ideology. Clearly, commitment to the politics of pragmatism, to the rules of the game of collective bargaining, to gradual change whether in the direction favored by the left or the right, to opposition both to an all-powerful central state and to *laissez-faire* constitutes the component parts of an ideology. The "agreement on fundamentals," the political consensus of Western society, now increasingly has come to include a position on matters which once sharply separated the left from the right. And this ideological agreement, which might best be described as "conservative socialism," has become *the* ideology of the major parties in the developed states of Europe and America. As such it leaves its advocates in sharp disagreement with the relatively small groups of radical rightists and leftists at home, particularly the students among the latter, and at a disadvantage in efforts to foster different variants of this doctrine in the less affluent parts of the world.[73]

[73]I have discussed the source of student activism, the main remaining mass base for total ideological politics in articles published elsewhere. See especially my articles in S. M. Lipset (ed.), *Student Politics* (New York: Basic Books, 1967); S. M. Lipset and Philip Altbach (eds.), *Students in Revolt* (Boston: Houghton Mifflin, 1969).

14

The New Group Politics

Samuel H. Beer

By the early 1950's Labourites and Conservatives seemed well on the way toward executing a classic movement of a two-party system. From positions widely separating them on issues of substantial, even fundamental, importance, they had moved markedly toward one another. Within the Labour Party, as we have seen, powerful forces resisted this movement; and one could never say that British Socialism had quite deserted its ancient ideological orthodoxies. Yet on the scale of Left and Right, as defined in British politics, each party was shifting toward the center, as the party of the Left extended its appeal to groups on its Right and the party of the Right extended its appeal to groups on its Left. Class and ideological contours faded, while interest groups appeared as more prominent features of the political scene. It was against the background of these developments that R. T. McKenzie concluded in 1958 that "pressure groups, taken together, are a far more important channel of communication than parties for the transmission of political ideas from the mass of the citizenry to their rulers."[1]

We will examine the role of interest groups in the formation of Conservative social and economic policy in the 1950's and how it compared with the role of party. But before we turn directly to this question, it will be helpful to sketch the general outlines of group politics in the postwar period. From our previous account the two main features have emerged: the "realities of governing" that led Governments and parties to bargain with organized producers and the "realities of winning power" that led them to bid for the support of groups of consumers among the voters.

From BRITISH POLITICS IN THE COLLECTIVIST AGE, by Samuel H. Beer. Copyright ©1965 by Samuel H. Beer. Reprinted by permission of Alfred A. Knopf, Inc. Reprinted by permission of Faber and Faber Ltd. from *Modern British Politics*. Footnotes are renumbered.

[1] R. T. McKenzie, *British Political Parties* (London: Heinemann, 1958).

These two features were not separate parts of the political system. They were rather two different sets of relationships among the same entities. In one set of relationships, for instance, the groups were "producers," in the other, "consumers," but obviously most producers were also consumers and vice versa. It was primarily because government attempted to control or manage the economy that producer groups acquired power to influence policy. On the other hand, it was mainly because programs of the Welfare State appealed to groups as consumers that Governments and parties were incited to appeal for their support by means of these programs.

Yet the Managed Economy and the Welfare State were not two separate and distinct activities of the pattern of policy. Action to maintain full employment comes under both headings. A change in direct taxation is both a measure of economic policy (affecting prices, imports, saving, and incentives) and a measure of social policy (affecting the distribution of disposable income among various social strata). Depending, however, on how the political situation is viewed—from the perspective of the Managed Economy or that of the Welfare State—the flow of influence is seen to come, respectively, from producers or from consumers.

Moreover, the modes and channels of influence varied between the two sets of political relationships. Producers influenced policy largely through direct contact with the executive in what may be called a system of functional representation. The power of consumers was especially expressed through the system of parliamentary representation, in which party government was the dominating feature.

In sum, then, the two perspectives on the flow of power direct attention to the following relationships: 1) controlled economy : producer groups : functional representation : bargaining for cooperation and 2) welfare state : consumer groups : party government : bidding for votes.

PRODUCER GROUPS AND THE MANAGED ECONOMY

Viewed from Whitehall, the most powerful forces confronting (not to say arrayed against) a Government in this time were the organized bodies of producers representing the main sectors of the economy: trade unions, trade associations, and professional organizations. Pressure groups were nothing new in British politics, but in the twentieth century they had assumed a distinctively new form. In social base, structure, purpose, political tactics, relations with government, and the foundations of their political power they greatly differed from the transient, voluntary associations of like-minded reformers that sought to win Victorian Parliaments over to their schemes of legislation. We have already gained some idea of what these "Collectivist" pressure groups were and how they operated when we examined the bargain of 1948 struck between government, labor, and business. I will not try to call the roll nor to describe in detail their modes of organization and operation, all of which has been ably done by other writers.[2] I will, however, consider in general terms three questions: What were the bases of their political power? How was this power mobilized? Through what channels was it brought to bear on policy-making?

Bases of Power

We begin from the fact that these groups were based on a productive function. Typically, their members consisted of wage-earning or salaried employees with the same or related occupations; of business enterprises concerned with a common product, process, or activity; of professional people with similar training and *expertise*. To say that performance of a productive function endows persons or groups with political power is to call up the shades of syndicalism—and rightly so. For in spite of its exaggerations and utopianism, the syndicalist analysis has great relevance to the structure of power in the modern state. According to that analysis, the political power of the producer group rests on its ability to refuse to perform its function in the economy. In Britain the extreme use of this power in the "general strike" had been attempted only once, and then only halfheartedly, and after 1926 the syndicalist prescriptions rapidly lost their appeal.

These prescriptions, to be sure, presumed that government, if not entirely laissez faire, would not be deeply engaged in regulating, planning, or managing the economy. The syndicalist, therefore, was obliged to suppose that producer groups could influence government only indirectly by coercing the whole community. But the syndicalist analysis is also relevant, and certainly more realistic, in the era of the mixed economy. For insofar as government has committed itself to intervention in the economy, it must have access to or control over instrumentalities that are in the command of producers. In a totalitarian system this dependence on the cooperation of producers can be minimized, though not entirely eliminated. But in a free country, as government extends its powers over the economy, it must at the

---

[2]See Allen Potter, *Organized Groups in British National Politics* (London 1961), J. D. Stewart, *British Pressure Groups: Their Role in Relation to the House of Commons* (London 1958); Samual E. Finer, *Anonymous Empire: A Study of the Lobby in Great Britain* (London 1958); Harry Eckstein, *Pressure Group Politics: The Case of the British Medical Association* (London 1960); Graham Wootton, *The Politics of Influence: British Ex-Servicemen, Cabinet Decisions and Cultural Change, 1917-1957* (London 1963); Peter Self and Herbert J. Storing, *The State and The Farmer* (London 1962).

same time so act as to win a substantial degree of consent and cooperation from the groups being regulated. "The greater the degree of detailed and technical control the government seeks to exert over industrial and commercial interests," E. P. Herring wrote more than a generation ago, "the greater must be their degree of consent and active participation."[3]

Legal theory may tell us that the state is sovereign, particularly in Britain where the authority of Parliament is unlimited by constitutional restraints. Hence, when Parliament commands, all persons and groups must obey and, if control over a certain sector of the economy is authorized by law, the producers in that sector, whether organized or unorganized, must in theory comply. In this light, the extension of government intervention appears as a one-sided growth in state power. But there is also a flow of power in the other direction.

Advice.   The most obvious instrumentality which producers command and which government needs is advice. Advice includes sheer information: for instance, the statistical data without which neither the regulation of a particular trade nor management of the economy as a whole would be possible. But the advice that government seeks from producers consists also of their technical knowledge and judgment. Obviously no ministry engaged in economic control can have staff large and specialized enough to enable it to make policy and administer it without the advice of the producers in the sector concerned. "The form and functioning of British Government," Professor S. E. Finer has written, "are predicated upon the assumption that it will be advised, helped and criticised by the specialist knowledge of interested parties."[4]

When, for instance, the Poisons Board considered modifications of the Poisons List and Rules, it sought the advice of the trade and had, therefore, since 1930 maintained close relations with the Association of British Chemical Manufacturers. For similar reasons, when the Ministry of Food was drafting the hygiene regulations of a new Food and Drugs bill it consulted with the relevant trade association, the Cake and Biscuit Alliance, as a result of whose representations various amendments were made to the original proposals.[5] Again, when the Minister of Transport, acting under wide delegated powers, revised the regulations on construction and use of motor vehicles, he regularly sought and received the advice of the Society of Motor Manufacturers and Traders.[6] Even in the case of the most important of the "peak" organizations of British industry, the Federation of British

---

[3]*Public Administration and the Public Interest* (New York 1936), p. 192.

[4]S. E. Finer, "The Political Power of Private Capital," Part II, *Sociological Review*, new ser., vol. IV, No. I (July 1956), p. 14.

[5]*Industrial Trade Associations: Activities and Organization* (London 1957), pp. 77, 82.

[6]See the Society's annual reports, *passim;* for example, *Fifty-First Annual Report and Accounts* (1952), p. 13.

Industry, most of its relations with departments were concerned with questions on which it could bring to bear the technical knowledge at the command of its staff and members. As Professor Finer reported after a study —"based on file after file of dusty minutes"—of the Federation's relations with government, "overwhelmingly its persuasion is concerned with technical and administrative minutiae," rather than questions of general public policy.[7]

The need of departments for such technical advice and criticism is of long standing and has typically resulted from the piecemeal intervention characteristic of Radical politics. But the technical "know-how" of producers has also been indispensable to that kind of economic planning which depends on physical programming and direct control. This was a major reason for the fact that during the war the general type of control in the Ministry of Supply was a converted trade association. Knowledge of the technical aspects of a trade or occupation, however, shades off into knowledge of economic conditions and relationships. Producer groups are sources of what Allen Potter has called "market intelligence," "facts and opinions about what is happening and is likely to happen" in their sector of production and its relations with other sectors.[8] Hence, even as the government relaxed its methods of control over the economy as a whole and turned toward the methods of economic management, it continued to need access to this broader "economic knowledge" possessed by producers.

The strategy of economic management is "situational" in the sense that its essential technique is to obtain a desired result not by direct command or request, but indirectly by manipulating the economic situation confronting producers and consumers. A remark that one of Britain's planners made to me in the early 1950's illustrates the difference. "We are rather disillusioned with physical programming," he said. "We prefer to get results not by commanding what must be done, but by putting out a piece of cheese and trusting that some particular mouse will go after it." National income analysis provides the basic framework for such "situational" control. A certain change in direct taxation, which changes the disposable income of consumers, will presumably have some roughly calculable effect upon imports, private saving, and incentives. Similarly, a change in interest rates will have an effect upon the flow of capital to and from Britain, a movement in wage rates upon prices, an expansion or contraction of government current expenditure upon the level of employment, certain tax remissions upon investment by firms and so ultimately upon productivity. On such matters, government can learn a great deal from its professional economists. But often ministers and officials have also found it necessary to seek the judgment of representatives of the productive sectors involved.

[7]"The Federation of British Industries," *Political Studies* 4, No. 1 (Feb. 1956), p. 67.
[8]*Op. cit.*, p. 193.

Immediately after the war, for instance, a principal element in the Labour Government's economic policy was the export drive. One possible source of greater exports was the motor car industry; and the question of what action the government might take to encourage the export of motor cars was an urgent subject of discussion in the advisory committee established by the Ministry of Supply to provide a means of regular consultation between the government and the industry.[9] According to the industry representatives, British purchasers of cars were discouraged from buying larger models because the annual tax on use was based on engine size. As a result, the British industry was geared to the production of a smaller car that did not compete well in foreign markets with the larger American car. Therefore, they advised that if the annual tax were put on a flat-rate basis, demand would shift toward a larger car and the industry would accordingly direct its production toward a product with better sales possibilities abroad. Indeed, the main producers on the committee, while they made no promises, indicated that if the Government made such a change in taxation they would "include in their forward plans provision for the development and quantity production of a larger model."[10] The committee was persuaded and ultimately so also was the Chancellor of the Exchequer, who in 1947 changed the annual tax to a flat-rate basis, apparently with beneficial results for British exports.

Planning based on direct physical control faces the problem of winning the acquiescence of the controlled to the scheme of behavior imposed on them. "Situational" planning avoids this problem by allowing the controlled to follow their normal market behavior. Since, however, such planning also seeks to guide that behavior, it confronts the new problem of foreseeing how controlled sectors will respond to manipulated changes in the situation. To ask the advice of producers about such questions may seem to invite replies that are less than impartial. Both sides, Government and producers, are acutely aware of the dangers of the temptation to "bluff." A Director-General of the F.B.I., for instance, characterizing the advisory work of the organization as an exercise in "the art of persuasion," declared that the first essential was to create and maintain "confidence on the part of the Government in one's *bona fides*."[11] Such consultation is, to be sure, rather like asking the mice just how much cheese it would take to get them to run in a different direction. But after all, who would know better?

[9]For composition and terms of reference of this committee, see below, p. 376.

[10]*National Advisory Committee for the Motor Manufacturing Industry: Report on Proceedings* (London: Ministry of Supply, H.M.S.O., 1947), p. 14. For this example generally, see the *Report, passim;* also the *Annual Report* for 1947 of the Society of Motor Manufacturers and Traders, p. 7, and P.E.P.'s *Industrial Trade Associations,* p. 50.

[11]Sir Norman Kipping, *The Federation of British Industries* (London 1954), pp. 4-5.

Acquiescence. In seeking to control the economy government needs not only the advice of producers, but also in many instances their active co-operation in carrying out a program or policy. The producers may be brought directly into administration, as trade associations were during the war. Or they may be employed individually in carrying out a program, as in the case with doctors under the National Health Service. Or again, even when producers in a sector are not directly engaged as agents of government, a program may require their wholehearted acceptance if it is to be effective, as the system of price control during and after the war needed to have from businessmen something more than mere grudging consent to "the law." And referring generally to the effectiveness of direct controls, the authors of the Radcliffe Report observed that

> it is necessary in this context to remember that the post-war controls themselves depended much on voluntarism. If it can be shown that there are good and sufficient reasons in the public interest why controls should be imposed, they can be effective for a short time without an elaborate administrative structure.[12]

The relations of the Labour Government and the iron and steel industry will illustrate how the refusal of such cooperation, as well as of advice, may be used by a producer in resisting government policy. In 1947, Hugh Dalton recalls, the Government "began to negotiate" with the companies over its plans for nationalization of the industry. In response the steelmasters "threatened that if we nationalized the industry, they would retain Steel House, its staff and its records, and so make the work of a new Public Board almost impossible."[13] In their approaches to Attlee, according to Dalton, "they seemed to have some success," Attlee charging Morrison with looking into the possibility of measures less than nationalization.[14] When in 1948, after much chopping and changing, the Government finally announced its intention to nationalize, the representatives of the steel companies withdrew in protest from the Iron and Steel Board, which had been set up as a controlling body for the industry.

Whether or not these reprisals by the industry affected the form in which Labour nationalized the industry, they did not, at any rate, prevent its being taken into public ownership under the Act of 1949. At this juncture, the industry intensified its policy of noncooperation. The leaders of the steel industry boycotted the public corporation established to own and control the industry, refusing to serve on it and dissuading all important figures from serving. Moreover, the industry's trade association, the British Iron and Steel

---

[12]Committee on the Working of the Monetary System, *Report* Cmd. 827 (London 1959), para. 184 (Radcliffe Report).

[13]*High Tide and After: Memoirs 1945-1960* (London 1962), pp. 248-9.

[14]*Ibid:* p. 249, and *Herbert Morrison, An Autobiography* (London 1960), p. 296.

Federation, refused to permit representatives of the public corporation to sit on its Council, on its committees, or even on the two trading companies of the Federation that respectively controlled imports and exports and disposed of surplus steel.[15]

What would have been the ultimate outcome of this "strike action" by the industry against nationalization we cannot know, since shortly thereafter the Conservatives returned to power and the industry was denationalized. For our present analysis, however, the important fact is that these sanctions of noncooperation by the industry had come close to paralyzing the public corporation's "control over the policy and operations of the publicly-owned companies" and its ability to "discharge [its] duties under the Act." In its first report the public corporation said:

> It was clear to the Corporation that to secure adequate control over the policy and operations of the publicly-owned companies and to enable the Corporation to discharge their duties under the Act they would require either to create an organisation independent of, but in part similar and parallel to, that of the Federation, or alternatively to come to some arrangement with the Federation which would afford the Corporation the benefit of the services and advice of the Federation and control of its policies in the public sector.[16]

This example illustrates the great difficulties in which noncooperation by an organized group can sometimes put government. Usually, neither government nor organized producers will push matters to a showdown. Anticipation of what might well happen, however, will affect their negotiations. Indeed, it is the anticipation by government of the need for such cooperation that makes it often accurate to refer to its relations with producers groups as "negotiation" and not merely "consultation."[17] In 1948, for instance, the Government could have contrived some means of imposing on business by law its proposals for reduction of profits, perhaps on the lines of the statutory limitation of dividends developed by Gaitskell in 1951. It preferred, however, a voluntary arrangement, even though this achieved only "restraint" on dividends and not reduction of profits. Similarly, in its relations with the unions at the same time, the Government was quite aware that, even if it had been able to hold its parliamentary majority behind a legally imposed policy, it would have had to have a substantial degree of voluntary cooperation from unions and workers if any policy regarding wages were to be effective.

---

[15]For an account of these events, see Finer, "The Political Power of Private Capital," pp. 16-19.

[16]Iron and Steel Corporation of Great Britain, *Report and Statement of Accounts for the Period Ending 30th September, 1951,* para. 45.

[17]On the distinction between "negotiation" and "consultation" in British practice see Harry Eckstein, *op. cit.,* pp. 22-5.

In these instances the difficulties of an imposed solution were no doubt vividly before the minds of officials and ministers. But government may develop relations of cooperation with a key producers group in which there is such a gentlemanly give and take that no mention and little thought of sanctions are occasioned. The Conservative Government's relations with the City were of this character. In the years 1955-57, for instance, the Government from time to time called on the banks for help in carrying out its anti-inflationary policy by tightening credit.[18] In bringing about a restriction of bank loans, the Government could have invoked its legal powers under the Bank of England Act and given the banks unequivocal instructions. But it preferred the method of "jollying along," or what D. H. Robertson has called "ear-stroking"—that is, the use of "encouragements which are not quite promises, frowns which are not quite prohibitions, understandings which are not quite agreements."[19] The method is brought out in a minute from Prime Minister Eden to the Chancellor of the Exchequer, Harold Macmillan, in December 1955:

> As to this question of imports, I should be most reluctant to contemplate any return to licensing and Government control as I am sure you would be. Is it not, however, possible to get something of the same results by other methods? Cannot the banks, for instance, be given some indication from time to time that such and such materials are those for the import of which we should be most reluctant to see money advanced? If something of this kind were practicable I should much prefer it to import control.[20]

The banks were highly responsive—indeed, according to the Governor of the Bank of England, through whom the Government and banks formally communicated with one another, the British banking system was "the most responsive of any large banking system [in the world] to indications of official policy."[21] In turn the Government showed itself ready on some points to accommodate its wishes to the advantage and convenience of the banks. According to one authority on the history of monetary policy in this period, the methods of "ear-stroking" were successful, partly because bankers knew that the Government had powers of coercion in reserve, but also because "the bankers have received a considerable reward for cooperation in the form of higher interest rates."[22]

---

[18] See Peter B. Kenen, *British Monetary Policy and the Balance of Payments, 1951-1957,* (Cambridge, Mass. 1960), chap. III, "The New Monetary Policy." See also *Radcliffe Report,* pp. 118-9, 142-50, 161-3, and 188.

[19] Quoted in Kenen, *op. cit.,* p. 200.

[20] Anthony Eden, *The Memoirs of Anthony Eden: Full Circle* (Boston 1960), p. 358.

[21] *The Banker* (Nov. 1956), p. 715. Report of speech at Mansion House on October 9th, 1956.

[22] Kenen, *op. cit.,* p. 200. See also Harry G. Johnson, "The Revival of Monetary Policy in Britain," *Three Banks Review* (June 1956). He writes: "The intimate small-group relationship

Similarly, the Chancellor could be responsive when his requests might cause the banks administrative difficulties. In the fall of 1957, for instance, while tightening the squeeze on credit, the Chancellor asked the banks to promise an all-round cut of 5 per cent in their loans. The execution of this scheme would rest with the banks, as each would have to decide which requests from its customers were to be refused or reduced. Anticipating much friction from such a task the bankers demurred. In the end the Chancellor settled for an agreement that bank advances simply would be frozen at their 1957 level.[23]

Approval. How much bargaining power a producers group will have and how far it will try to use this power in its relations with Government will, of course, be affected by other factors than those we have been considering. Our concern has been to isolate those particular factors based on the productive function performed by a group that give it a bargaining potential. Broadly, they are the government's need for advice and for acquiescence. But there is also a third factor which is also specifically related to the performance of a productive function and which further helps account for that extreme hesitation of departments and Governments—commented on by many students of British pressure politics—to confront an open and public break with producers groups. It is the attitude (one detects it not only among officials and ministers, but also among M.P.'s and members of the general public) that such organized groups have a "right" to take part in making policy related to their sector of activity; indeed, that their approval of a relevant policy or program is a substantial reason for public confidence in it and conversely that their disapproval is cause for public uneasiness. It is in short an attitude reflecting the widespread acceptance of functional representation in British political culture. It coexists, of course, with a general adherence to standard constitutional doctrines asserting the

---

between the members of the banking system, and the dominant position of the Bank of England, raise the question as to how far the revival of monetary policy can be accurately described as a return to control of the financial system by anonymous and impersonal market forces" (p. 10). And later, "A cynic might well argue that the return to flexibility is merely a facade, designed to improve the appearance and the public relations potential of an oligopolistic agreement, and to hide the fact that what has really been achieved has been to bribe the banks, by means of higher interest earnings, into enforcing directives which, in the less profitable days of cheap money, they were inclined to disregard as much as they decently could" (p. 11).

[23]Andrew Shonfield, *British Economic Policy Since the War,* rev. ed. (London 1959), pp. 254-5. "On the industrial side, the banks on the whole managed to avoid positive reductions of existing advances, though they had to be discouraging to applications for new advances." Hence, "the blow fell not on projects already in train but on capital projects in their earliest planning stages. . . . It was not, that is to say, the current level of demand that was affected; rather, action was upon the possible prolongation and development of the boom." *Radcliffe Report,* pp. 162-3, para. 460.

sovereignty of Parliament and the exclusive right of ministers to make final decisions, subject to Parliament. If forced into a sharp and systematic formulation, that attitude would be in conflict with these doctrines—as indeed the actual practice of negotiation modifies in fact the sovereignty of Parliament. Yet as a current of opinion it is nevertheless a real force, restraining the hand of Government and strengthening the hand of organized producers.

Such an attitude, for instance, helps account for a peculiar "convention" that emerged in the relations of the Government and the National Farmers Union after the war. From the beginning of the annual price review, Professor Self has observed, "the Government emphasized that the final decision over agricultural guarantees was exclusively its own, as constitutionally it was bound to be." At the same time, "a convention soon emerged whereby the Union gave a formal endorsement of some kind to the final settlement," a confirmation which the Government, whether Labour or Conservative, was able to win each year throughout the postwar years until 1956.[24] The interesting point is that ministers, far from finding this endorsement a political liability (suggesting, as it might to an old-time Radical, that a "sinister interest" had triumphed over the common good) welcomed and used it when publicly defending their agricultural policy, a practice which, as Professor Self notes, itself further strengthened the understanding that Government ought to secure such endorsement.

A similar and perhaps even stronger attitude, according to Professor Harry Eckstein, has affected the relations of the Ministry of Health and the British Medical Association. In analyzing why these relations have so often consisted not in mere consultation, but in negotiation, he has found two attitudes of particular importance. One is "the widespread belief . . . that technical experts (practitioners) have some singular competence even in regard to social policies and administrative forms that touch upon their fields of practice." The other is the "persistent corporatism" of British political culture, which results today in the fact that "functional representation . . . is not only tolerated, but even insisted upon." From these two broad attitudes springs that "frequent normative insistence on negotiations between government and 'voluntary' associations on matters of policy" which has been particularly pronounced in the relations of government and organized medicine.[25]

In postwar Britain the cooperation that government needed from producer groups took various forms. I have identified them broadly as advice, acquiescence, and approval. To identify them and illustrate their use do not tell us what in general their role has been in British government. But

---

[24]Self and Storing, *op. cit.*, p. 63 and *passim*.
[25]*Op. cit.*, p. 24.

our analysis does, I think, show quite clearly that producer groups have a power to affect policy-making that is quite separate from their position in the system of parliamentary representation and party government. We may prefer to call some relationships influence rather than power. When, for instance, a producers organization by rational argument persuades a department to take a new line, we may wish to call this influence, since the group has not won its way by use of a sanction. But what I have been particularly concerned to show is that producer groups do have sanctions—the denial (in various degrees) of advice, acquiescence, and approval—which can cause, to put it mildly, "administrative difficulties" and which, by anticipation, endow the group with bargaining power in its relations with government.

The source of this power is not the fact that the group or its members has a role—for instance, as voters or contributors to party funds—in the system of parliamentary representation, but derives from the group's performance of a productive function. Should such power, therefore, be called "economic power"? That would have been the appropriate term to characterize the sanctions which inhered in producers according to the old syndicalist analysis. In essence those consisted in the power to coerce government indirectly by depriving the economy of an important service. The sanctions of producer groups in the Managed Economy do not take that form. They arise from the fact that Government has taken over functions once performed by the economic system, in particular, by its market mechanisms. We can say that governmental action has become part of the economic process; or that elements of the economic process have been taken over by Government. From their position in the "mixed economy" resulting from this interpretation of polity and economy, producer groups derive their new powers.

Mobilization of Power

If producers are to use these new powers to influence Government and, indeed, if Government is to obtain the cooperation necessary for the Managed Economy, producer groups must be organized. Very large firms, it is true, have usually maintained regular contacts with departments independently of the representational efforts of the trade associations to which they belonged. As our examples have shown, however, the relations of Government with producers were normally with a nation-wide organization. By means of such organization the group achieved a capacity for unified decision-making and action. How far it has such capacity for unified behavior, how far it has mobilized its power as a producer group—we may call its degree of concentration.

Concentration cannot be measured on a single coordinate. One dimension is "density,"[26] that is, the per cent of eligibles, such as individuals or firms, that have been organized. Thus it is possible to calculate for a certain category of producers at a certain time an index of density (for example, in 1953 42 per cent of the total working population of Britain belonged to trade unions) and make comparisons with an earlier period or another country. A high degree of density, however, is compatible with a situation in which there is a low degree of unity because the organized are divided into many separate bodies. A second dimension of concentration, therefore, is amalgamation, taking this to mean how far the organized have been brought together in one body, whether by outright merger, federation, or other similar arrangements. Although amalgamation can be high when density is low and vice versa, in fact, over time the trend among producer groups in Britain has been toward an increase of concentration on both co-ordinates. It is possible, of course, for an organization scoring perfectly in indices of density and amalgamation to be a clumsy and distracted giant. Still, the measurable aspects of concentration serve to mark out the long-run trends.

Trade associations. Trade associations, as we have observed, already existed in mid-Victorian times. Then, as later, their purposes were only in part political, including such functions as the collection and dissemination of information among members, the coordination of steps to mitigate competition, and the representation of employers in relations with trade unions, as well as the advocacy of the interests of a branch of industry or commerce before government. They did not appear in any number until the latter years of the nineteenth century, but from that time the trend toward concentration had been continuous, paralleling the rise of big government, big business, and big unions.

Unlike British labor, British business did not produce a single "peak" organization. On the whole, commerce was organized separately from industry. By the 1950's, the Association of British Chambers of Commerce, founded in 1860, had grown to include some 100 constituent chambers including 60,000 members, some of which, incidentally, were manufacturers. Retail merchants not embraced by the A.B.C.C. had local bodies federated nationally in the National Chamber of Trade. In industry there were three "peak" organizations, the Federation of British Industries, the National Union of Manufacturers, and, for dealing with labor matters, the British Employers Confederation, whose 270 affiliates negotiated with 70 per cent of the employed population.

---

[26] I am indebted to Professor S. E. Finer for the notion of density as a dimension of concentration.

In the industrial sector, at which we will look more closely, concentration had gone very far. By the 1950's trade associations were virtually all-embracing in their membership: 90 per cent of the larger firms and 76 per cent of the smaller belonged to one or more of the 1,300 industrial trade associations.[27] Along with this increase in density had gone a strong trend toward amalgamation. Inter-industry organization achieved its first solid success during World War I with the formation of the Federation of British Industries and the National Union of Manufacturers. Tending to represent the larger firms, the F.B.I., by the end of its first year, included 62 trade associations and 350 individual firms; by 1925, 195 associations and 2,100 firms; and by 1957, 283 associations and 7,533 firms. By the latter date most manufacturing firms were directly or indirectly affiliated with the organization, which now represented some six-sevenths of all industrial concerns employing more than ten workers.[28]

Particularly important in the world of industrial trade associations were some thirty or forty larger associations, each of which covered a complete industry. Leading examples, some of which we have encountered in previous pages, were: the Society of British Aircraft Contractors; the British Man-Made Fibres Federation; the Association of British Chemical Manufacturers; the Federation of Master Cotton Spinners Associations; the British Engineers Association; the British Iron and Steel Confederation; the Society of Motor Manufacturers and Traders; the British Non-Ferrous Metals Federation; the Cake and Biscuit Alliance; and the British Plastics Federation. A principal purpose of these organizations was to achieve cohesion in the relations of their respective industries with Government and in their memoranda or constitutions most mentioned the need to "speak with one voice" when consulting or negotiating with departments. Their success in reconciling intra-industry differences of opinion, however, was variable. Where the industry consisted of many small firms there was likely to be difficulty. On the other hand, a high degree of economic concentration, as in the motor car industry, iron and steel, and chemicals, enhanced the group's capacity for unified action.

In general, cohesion was promoted by the tendency of larger firms to have a preponderant voice in the affairs of their respective associations. This resulted not so much from provisions of formal organization, which might or might not give greater voting power to larger firms, but rather, as Professor Finer has observed, from "the businessman's general attitude that the bigger the firm, the bigger its stake and therefore its entitlement to 'the big say.' "[29] In the F.B.I., for instance, as he has shown, while the organization could not be said to be dominated by "a small clique of large firms," the big concerns

---

[27]Computed from data in *Industrial Trade Associations.*

[28]Finer, *Anonymous Empire,* p. 9, and "The Federation of British Industries," p. 62.

[29]"The Federation of British Industries," p. 71.

clearly carried a great deal of weight. Their activity was particularly marked in the standing committees, "the true centres of policy-making." [30] In 1955, for instance, of the eighteen standing committees of the F.B.I., the chairmen almost without exception came from giant concerns, such as General Electric, the Steel Company of Wales, Courtaulds, Associated Electrical Industries, Imperial Chemicals, and Richard, Thomas and Baldwins, with Unilever alone accounting for four. [31] Thanks at least in part to such leadership, the F.B.I. was able to say that its "statements or representations carry the backing or acceptance of all important sections of industry." Sometimes a substantial divergence of opinion did emerge, in which case the F.B.I. would not attempt to "speak with one voice." The issues on which unanimity was not reached, however, arose "surprisingly rarely." [32]

Trade unions.   Trade unions had shown a similar trend toward concentration. From late Victorian days, when they had embraced only a modest part of the working population, their membership had grown immensely. While this increase was by no means steady, over the whole period from 1892 to 1953 membership in all trade unions rose from 1,576,000 to 9,524,000, these figures representing an increase from 11 per cent to 42 per cent of the total occupied population. At the same time, amalgamation, which set in strongly after World War I, reduced the number of separate unions and produced the huge organizations of recent decades. By the 1950's, for instance, seventeen unions included 6,500,000 members, some two-thirds of all union membership. This aspect of concentration was even more marked among the unions affiliated with the T.U.C., of which the six largest in 1952 included fully 50 per cent of the total affiliated membership. [33]

"The whole trend of union development," Professor B. C. Roberts has written, "seems to be towards the consolidation of union membership in a relatively small number of unions, each of which is gradually obtaining exclusive jurisdiction over a particular area of employment." Moreover, within the individual unions authority has tended away from the local and toward the national level, the general secretaries in particular benefiting from this centralization. Only by the creation of such "a dominating driving force" have some of the big unions, which include widely diverse elements, been cemented into cohesive groupings. [34]

[30] *Ibid.,* p. 70.

[31] *Ibid.,* pp. 83-4.

[32] Kipping, *op. cit.,* p. 4.

[33] Transport and General Workers Union; Amalgamated Engineering Union; National Union of Mine Workers; General and Municipal Workers; National Union of Railwaymen; Shop, Distributive and Allied Workers. See T.U.C. *Report 1953,* pp. 14-61.

[34] B. C. Roberts, *Trade Union Government and Administration in Great Britain* (Cambridge, Mass. 1956), pp. 53, 114, 463.

Labour's peak organization, the T.U.C., had not had a serious rival since its foundation in 1868 and had weathered the various surges in union growth without disruptive splits such as that between the A.F. of L. and the C.I.O. in the United States. From 1894, when its affiliated membership, standing at 1,000,000, represented 65 per cent of all unionists, the T.U.C., with some ups and downs, increased that proportion until in 1953, with membership at 8,094,000, it reached 85 per cent.

Like the larger firms in the world of organized industry, the larger unions exercised great influence within the trade union movement. Within each of the nineteen groups from which members were chosen for the General Council, it was usually, although not invariably, the largest that were regarded as "most representative" and won seats on the Council. Moreover, in contrast with other unions represented on the Council, the very largest had more than one member. In 1952-53, for instance, the Transport Workers and the General and Municipal Workers each had three and the Mineworkers and the Amalgamated Engineers each had two.[35] These were still the days, it will be recalled, of the Deakin-Williamson-Lawther triumvirate. In general, as Roberts has observed, the long-run trend has been toward growing authority on the part of the T.U.C. over its affiliated organizations.[36]

The long-run trend is undeniable. But this is not to say that the capacity for unified decision-making among both workers and employers is adequate to the tasks of Britain's present-day economy. The powers of the T.U.C. over its affiliates are not extensive. It has no power to intervene in the wage policies of individual unions; and its ability to bring about changes in union structure or to intervene in disputes between its affiliates is severely limited. As we have seen in an instance involving a major question of public policy, the wage restraint bargain of 1948-50, the unions as a whole were able to concert their action sufficiently to make an agreement and to keep it with good faith. The General Council, however, could not by its own influence and authority make this agreement and was obliged to call on a meeting of the union executives. Many of those who believe that a wages policy, and not mere wage restraint, must be a regular part of economic management have concluded that far greater centralization of power is necessary, in particular, a strengthening of the General Council.[37]

[35] T.U.C. *Report* 1953, p. 3.
[36] *Op. cit.,* p. 436.
[37] See, for instance, the analysis and proposals of Michael Shanks, *The Stagnant Society* (London 1961), esp. chap. IV, "Trade Unions in Trouble," and chap. V, "A Radical Labour Movement"; and Andrew Shonfield, *op. cit.,* chap. XI, "A Way Forward."

Channels of Influence

In the British political system one may distinguish four main structural elements, corresponding to four main phases of policy-making, on which a group might seek to exert influence: the electorate, the legislature, the party, and the executive. It is a commonplace of any study of British pressure groups that on the whole they focus most attention on the executive, meaning by this both civil servants and ministers. The exceptions are important. The most obvious is the way the trade unions have used the Labour Party and their own sponsored M.P.'s to promote both the "interests of labour" and the ideals of Socialism. Yet the unions individually and through the T.U.C. have, especially since winning full governmental "recognition" during World War II, maintained close and continuous contacts with the executive. Along with other producers organizations, they are represented in a vast, untidy system of functional representation that has grown up alongside the older system of parliamentary representation. It is mainly through this system that the powers of advice, acquiescence, and approval are brought to bear on public policy.

The principal conditions that created and have maintained this system are two: on the one hand, those powers related specifically to the productive function performed by the members of the organizations and, on the other hand, the extension of government control over the economy. I find it impossible to give causal primacy to one or the other condition. Such organizations have used their producers power to bring about extensions of government control. Yet the extension of government control has itself elicited the bargaining potential of producers, endowing them with the ability to influence the manner and purposes of that control.

Consider, for instance, the growth of trade associations. Again and again in their history it has been a development in government policy that has stimulated their concentration. In the 1920's government encouraged them as a means of promoting "rationalisation." Later the tariff system created by the adoption of "the great policy" led to further growth and still closer contacts. Only associations, not individual firms, could negotiate with the Import Duties Advisory Committee, and the Committee, as we have seen, might require a *quid pro quo*—such as reorganization of the industry under the supervision of a strengthened association—as a condition for recommending protection. In both world wars, trade associations, sometimes formed at the instigation of government, performed important functions, being called on to provide expert advice and to serve as instruments of control. After 1945, particularly where government was carrying out programs involving direct regulation and control, it used trade associations for similar purposes, encouraging industrial producers in their efforts to "speak with one voice."

The principal formal channel through which producers organizations gained representation was the advisory committee—of which there were some 850 in 1958, according to a reply to a Parliamentary Question.[38] Not all these committees had such representatives nor, even when a producers group was in effect represented on a committee, were the representatives formally nominated by the relevant producer organization. The number of committees on which producer groups were in actuality represented, however, was formidable. In the 1950's these committees ranged from such high-level bodies as the Economic Planning Board, the National Joint Advisory Council of the Ministry of Labour, and the National Production Advisory Council on Industry (on which the relevant peak organizations —the T.U.C., B.E.C., and F.B.I.—were represented) to the multitude of committees attached to the main economic departments. The latter were connected with the system of "sponsoring" departments which grew up during World War II, and which meant that every industry and every branch of it, no matter how small, had a sponsoring department or section of one somewhere in the government machine.

To illustrate the composition and duties of one of these departmental advisory committees, we may take a brief look at the National Advisory Council for the Motor Manufacturing Industry, a body whose operations we have already had occasion to observe. Established in 1946, this committee was in 1955 moved to the Board of Trade, whose permanent secretary was its chairman. In addition to him, there were three government representatives from the Board of Trade, Ministry of Transport, and Ministry of Supply, respectively. The seven employers representatives, appointed on the recommendation of the Society of Motor Manufacturers and Traders, consisted of two from the "Big Six" among motor car manufacturers, one from the specialist producers, two from the makers of heavy commercial vehicles, one from the manufacturers of accessories and components, and one from the body builders, all these being either chairmen or managing directors of their firms. On the industry side there were also two officials of the Society of Motor Manufacturers and Traders, ex officio. The four trade union representatives were nominated by and came from the Amalgamated Engineering Union (one), the National Union of Vehicle Builders (one), and the Confederation of Shipbuilding and Engineering Unions (two). There was also one "independent" member.

The committee's terms of reference, which it will be noted excluded labor questions, were:

> To provide a means of regular consultation between the Government and the motor manufacturers on such matters as the location of industry, exports, imports, research, design and progress of the industry.[39]

[38]*Advisory Committees in British Government* (London 1960), p. 11.

[39]*National Advisory Council for the Motor Manufacturing Industry: Report on Proceedings* (1947), p. 5.

The subjects discussed in the committee would in part depend upon the shape of government policy. As we have seen, the export drive led to the discussion of a different basis for the annual use tax on motor cars. When scarce materials were being allocated, the industry might find itself obliged to defend its use of a scarce material such as copper or nickel. A topic that industry representatives felt strongly about was the heavy purchase tax on cars and, although this was a Treasury matter, they might bring it up in the committee in the hope of enlisting the support of the Board of Trade in their efforts to persuade the Chancellor of the need for reduction. Then there were questions of regulation, such as the rules governing the construction and use of cars, which the minister drew up and revised, acting under wide delegated powers and relying heavily upon the technical knowledge of the industry. Again, when the Government was about to engage in negotiating trade agreements with other countries, the industry might find the committee a convenient place to urge that an attempt be made to open larger markets for British motor cars.

While these committees, which brought together the sponsoring department and the producer organization, had practical value to both sides (and, moreover, by the symbolism of formal status enhanced the position of the consulted groups), they did not constitute the sole means of contact. Apart from such committees, although often around them, a great mass of daily, informal consultation had grown up. Private and public bureaucrats continually called one another on the telephone and discussed a problem on a first-name basis. As for luncheon, in the dining room of the Athenaeum, according to an official of one of Britain's largest corporations, "you can hardly hear yourself for the grinding of axes."

CONSUMER GROUPS AND THE WELFARE STATE

We get a rather different view of group politics in postwar Britain if we look at the political arena not from the perspective of producer groups and the Managed Economy, but from that of consumer groups and the Welfare State. The main elements and relationships revealed by this view are easy to grasp. We can readily imagine them if we take the view of the embattled political leader as he considers the realities of winning or keeping power, and his responsibility for leading his party to victory. Tensely aware of the narrow electoral balance between the parties, sincerely concerned to protect the public interest against the dangers represented by the other party, he ponders the differential response among voters to the benefits and burdens of the Welfare State and considers how a change, or promise of change, would affect the electoral allegiance of this group or that.

But we need not merely imagine these thoughts. Sir Anthony Eden has left us a candid record of them. "I wanted to feel that I had the country's support for the work I wished to do," he wrote when recalling his approach to the general election of 1955. "Nothing but the verdict of the nation at the polls could really give me that." Yet he was aware that "the margin was pretty narrow: a small percentage either way would decide." Favoring the Conservatives' "political case" were "three years of achievement by the Government" and "the prosperous condition of the country"—"in 1955 employment was at a very high level." Moreover, he states, "I knew that if we were to improve our position I must in particular get my message to the better skilled industrial worker, who could be expected to benefit from the kind of society we wanted to create." Against this background, Sir Anthony devoted "four-fifths of the space" of his election address to home politics, summing up what had been done "at home" as follows:

"Earnings are higher;
Savings are much higher;
Taxes are lower;
Pensions and social benefits have been increased;
A million new homes have been built;
Rationing is a thing of the past;
There is variety and abundance in the shops.
There is more hope, more choice, more freedom for all."[40]

Bidding for the Pensioners' Vote

It will be helpful to take one item from Eden's summing up and look more closely at its relation to the electoral problem.

A favorite object of the *Economist*'s scorn in the 1950's was what it called "the present habit of bidding for pensioners' votes before every general election." Recalling that in 1951 Labour had raised pensions only three weeks before polling day, in 1954 it found that again as an election approached, both parties were engaged in this competition. Labour, it held, had started the "Dutch auction," but the Conservatives had not failed "to raise the bidding in turn."[41]

That the *Economist* should explain these party decisions as "bidding for votes" does not prove the point. When, like the *Economist* in this instance, one is urgently, indeed furiously, pressing one's own views on a government, it is tempting to accuse ministers of yielding to pressure when they fail to follow one's advice. Yet given the narrow electoral balance between the parties (as late as April 1955, the Gallup Poll showed the Conservatives ahead by only one percentage point[42]) it would have been a wonder if there were not something of a "scramble for votes." Moreover, the elderly were a

---

[40]*Op. cit.*, pp. 299, 309-10.
[41]*Economist*, July 24, 1954, pp. 261-2; Nov. 20, 1954, p. 627; Dec. 11, 1954, pp. 883-7.
[42]*Ibid.* May 7, 1955, p. 452.

large and growing proportion of the population, some 4.6 million men and women being in receipt of retirement benefits under National Insurance. It would be callous to claim that the pensions were generous; in addition, their purchasing power was being continually eroded by inflation. Among these millions, in short, there was a large group to whom an increase would be a significant benefit.

The sequence and timing of party moves with regard to old age pensions as the election approached make it hard to believe that electoral considerations were not a major factor in the decisions of party leaders. The Conservative conference of 1953, to be sure, far from favoring greater benefits, viewed with concern the growing burden of old age pensions on the national finances and urged that steps be taken to make continued employment more attractive to the elderly.[43] Labour, however, made a strong move in the course of drawing up its new policy statement, *Challenge to Britain*, which was drafted by the N.E.C. and approved by conference in 1953. Debated and adopted under an unusual procedure, which enabled conference to amend particular sections and not merely to accept or reject the document as a whole, the draft submitted by the N.E.C. was altered on a number of significant points. One of these items, which concerned old age pensioners, underwent a gentle process of escalation that is worth tracing.

The original draft of *Challenge* had pledged that a Labour Government would make an annual review of the cost of living and on that basis restore the real value of old age pensions and other benefits under National Insurance.[44] On the agenda for the conference of 1953 were thirty-four resolutions and amendments dealing with this question, most of them giving special emphasis to the problem of old age pensioners and all but one asking for an increase in benefits.[45] The composite resolution based on them asked for an "immediate" increase and the establishment of a minimum "related to the cost of living."[46] In the debate, the supporters of the amendment based their case mainly on the claims of social justice and Socialist principle, e.g., "to each according to his need, from each according to his ability."[47] One speaker, however, an organizer for the National Federation of Old Age Pensions Associations, also delicately noted that "millions" of old age pensioners would be "listening in" on the radio report of the decision of conference on this matter. Starting from an acknowledgement of that fact, the N.E.C. spokesman, Edith Summerskill, observed that "what I am going to say now is of importance to every low-paid worker and to every beneficiary under the National Insurance scheme."[48] Dr. Summerskill then accepted the

[43] 1953 CPCR, pp. 91-4.

[44] *Challenge to Britain* (June 1953), p. 23.

[45] *Agenda*. 1953 Labour Party Conference, pp. 52-4 and 112-3.

[46] *Composite Resolutions and Amendments*. 1953 Labour Party Conference, No. 39.

[47] 1953 LPCR, p. 189.

[48] *Ibid*. p. 192.

demand for an increase, which would be immediate and not dependent on an annual review, although, as she pointed out, this committed "our future Chancellor of the Exchequer to a very big expenditure of money, maybe in the region of £140 million."

The final version of *Challenge,* as revised by the N.E.C. in the light of the amendments made by conference, and published in December 1953, included the pledge of an immediate increase, but also, echoing the demand of at least one of the resolutions submitted to conference, went on to promise that benefits would be restored to the purchasing power they commanded "when the National Insurance scheme was introduced."[49] This statement left open the question whether the base year was to be 1946, when the Act was passed, or 1948, when payments under it began. Labour's pledge took final form when, questioned on this matter, the party declared that the base year was to be 1946.[50]

The Conservative response to this pledge was for a time delayed. The Government had excellent grounds: it claimed to be waiting on the reports from two inquiries, including that of a committee (under Sir Thomas Phillips) set up to review the problems arising from Britain's position as an aging nation. Presumably, therefore, its scheme could not be formulated until these reports were in. Yet as early as a pensions debate in July, and long before either report was available, the Conservatives had virtually met Labour's bid by indicating that they intended to make good to "old pensioners, the war disabled, the sick, and the unemployed the whole of the injury and loss they suffered in six years of Socialist administration."[51]

At the Labour conference in the fall, Dr. Summerskill, again mentioning the "millions of old age pensioners sitting around their radios" to hear the report on the conference, took the opportunity to "refresh" their memories with a restatement of what Labour had promised and then gladly accepted a resolution repeating that pledge.[52] Similarly, the Conservative conference, now that the lead had been given by the party chiefs in Parliament, asked for an immediate increase in old age pensions. Welcoming the motion, the Minister of Pensions and National Insurance again declared that the Government's plan, when announced, would enable Conservatives to claim that "we have made good to the war disabled, the sick, the unemployed and the old age pensioners the whole of the loss and damage which they suffered under the Socialists in the years from 1946 to 1951."[53]

In December the Phillips committee report was published, and in the

---

[49]*Challenge to Britain* (Dec. 1953), p. 25.
[50]1954 LPCR, p. 118.
[51]Osbert Peake, Minister of Pensions, in the debate of July 21, 1954. 530 *H.C. Deb.* 1393.
[52]1954 LPCR, pp. 113-9.
[53]1954 CPCR, p. 51.

same week the Government's scheme was introduced in Parliament.[54] This may hardly seem to have given time for serious consideration of the committee's findings. The Government, said the *Economist*, "harried by the Opposition," had "hustled" the committee into finishing its report, "so that it could be published in the same week as the Minister announced the increases in pensions. But this was an empty form. The Phillips report has not been considered by the Government and probably will not be."[55] In any case, the Conservative scheme carried out the commitment to give a flat rate-increase in old age pensions and other benefits, which fully restored their purchasing power to their original post-war level. Opportunely, the new scales came into effect shortly before the general election of 1955. In the campaign, 71 per cent of Conservative election addresses referred proudly to the Conservative record on pensions, while 63 per cent of the Labour addresses looked forward to what pensions would be under a Labour Government.[56]

Consumer Groups and Government Policy

In speaking of "consumer groups," I am not using the term "consumer" in a technical economic sense, although I am thinking of persons interested in consumption. By a consumer group I mean a number of voters whose material well-being is affected in the same way by some measure of government action, actual or prospective. The main immediate source of a person's material well-being is his income from work or ownership. But in the Welfare State income is supplemented by benefits and reduced by burdens. The supplements—the "social dividend," if you like—may take the form of direct payments to the individual or of subsidies to community services, such as housing or education. Nor in identifying such groups should one confine one's attention to benefits conventionally regarded as constituting the Welfare State, although in the postwar years these have been by far the most important politically. An improvement in the road system, for instance, is a benefit to auto users, and the agitation of automobile associations for such benefits will be a political factor to be considered by party managers. In short, the groups benefiting or expecting to benefit from the "social dividend" constitute a complex of pressures supporting the vast pattern of expenditure of the Welfare State. The Government would like to reduce taxation, Enoch Powell, the Financial Secretary to the Treasury, told the 1957 Conservative conference. But to do that they must be able first to reduce expenditure and the "minority whom a

---

[54]See 535 *H.C. Deb.* 146-148 (Dec. 1, 1954) and Cmd. 9338 for the increases and the timetable of their coming into effect.

[55]*Economist*, Dec. 11, 1954, p. 883.

[56]David E. Butler, *The British General Election of 1955* (London 1955), pp. 32-3.

limitation of expenditure affects, is always more vocal than the majority who will ultimately benefit."[57]

Then, in addition to benefits, government action also involves burdens on the material well-being of voters and their families. The Welfare State consists not only of programs of services but also programs of taxation accomplishing some redistribution of income among persons and between objects of expenditure. Thus, for instance, those who pay income tax at the standard rate constitute a group to whose electoral behavior party leaders may be responsive. From the point of view of the economist, income tax is a powerful weapon of fiscal policy, and in a time of overexpansion an increase in income tax would seem to be one of the most effective ways of reducing the general level of demand. During the 1950's, however, Governments did not use income tax in this way, one reason being their anticipation of the negative political reaction of groups affected. "The most serious handicap of fiscal measures, as a method of operating on the level of demand," commented the Radcliffe Report, "is that individual tax changes, as distinct from the budget total, have to overcome opposition on varied grounds having nothing to do with the general economic situation" (para. 517, pp. 184-5). Or as Michael Shanks put it: "Political pressures on Governments to reduce income tax, or at least not to raise it, are apt to be very strong indeed—especially before an election."[58]

But the Government action that is relevant to the existence and activity of such groups does not consist only in separate measures. For instance, both full employment and the inflation that occurs when employment is overfull have an uneven incidence on the material well-being of voters and, depending upon this incidence, different groups of voters will hold Governments and parties responsible for the corresponding benefit or burden. Indeed, within the same household husband and wife may evaluate the same government action differently, the one as wage earner applauding the rise in wages resulting from an expansionary policy, the other as housewife deploring the rise in prices. The general point, however, is that when a government has taken intervention to the point reached in Britain, voters hold it responsible not only for additions to and subtractions from other income, but also for the trend of that "other income" as well. The programs of the Managed Economy will be the ground for electoral reaction not only among the producer groups they directly affect, but also among the consumer groups incidentally affected by economic policy.

In this view of consumer groups as actors in the political system, there are several points that are important. First, the behavior of these groups is a function of the interaction of polity and economy. By this I mean that one

---

[57] 1957 CPCR, p. 44.
[58] *Op. cit.,* p. 189.

cannot understand their activity by trying to attribute it solely to conditions arising outside of and independently of the political system. On the contrary, this activity was shaped by programs that already existed and by the competition of parties in proposing developments of those programs.

Perhaps when discussing the early days of Radical social reform, one might need to change this emphasis and account for the demands of groups mainly on the basis of their experience in a newly industrialized economy. Even then, however, when explaining why certain demands were brought forward in the political arena and accounting for the form they were given, one would be obliged also to consider the political culture of the time.[59] At any rate, once the Welfare State had begun its rise, and certainly once its basic code of policy had been established, its programs did much to define the further demands made upon government and the boundaries of the groups making them. As benefits, these programs created a clientele which might well demand "more." As burdens, they created a clientele which might well demand "less." In one way or the other they provided foci around which the interests of the consumer groups affected could crystallize. Just as producer groups were often stimulated to organize and were given a role and a footing in the new system of functional representation by the extension of the Managed Economy, so also consumer groups were brought to political awareness and activity by the Welfare State.

Moreover, these programs were the subjects of a continuous and ardent party battle. The immediate experience of consumers told them where their wishes were not being met by existing policies: the newly married couple seeking in vain to find housing they could afford; the old age pensioner noticing his retirement benefit buying less and less each year; the surtax payer reflecting that rates were hardly less progressive under the Conservatives than under Labour. But immediate experience had to be interpreted before it could become the basis of a political response. Some could do this for themselves. Those who belonged to a producer organization, whose members, as consumers, were similarly affected by Government actions, might find it providing such interpretation, pointing out which program or policy was to blame, proposing a specific remedy, and justifying the demand in terms of some view of the common good. But foremost in offering these interpretations were the political parties. Problems of housing, pensions, educational opportunity for youth, the cost of living, full employment, and heavy taxation provided major themes of their discussions of domestic affairs in Parliament and at elections. By pointing out where the material welfare of certain groups had been affected, showing what the causes had been, and proposing remedies, the parties' interpretations of these problems clarified and sharpened the demands of consumers groups among the electorate.

[59]See Samuel H. Beer *et al.*, *Patterns of Government: The Major Political Systems of Europe,* rev. ed. (New York 1962), pp. 56-7.

These demands, in short, did not arise autonomously from the immediate experience of consumers, but very largely from the interaction of that experience with interpretations offered by organizations, especially the political parties.

The role of party in shaping public opinion has often been noted. It has been said, for instance, that a principal function of a major party is to aggregate the demands of a large number of groups in the electorate. Where party government is as highly developed as in Britain—I wish to emphasize —the role of party is much greater. Party does not merely aggregate the opinions of groups, it goes a long way toward creating these opinions by fixing the framework of public thinking about policy and the voters' sense of the alternatives and the possibilities. In turn, of course, the party may find itself under pressure from such opinion. And when in its competition for votes it responds to this pressure, the flow of influence seems to be in only one direction, from voters to party. But by taking a wider view we will see that the parties themselves, backed by research staffs, equipped with nation-wide organizations, and enjoying the continuous attention of the mass media, have themselves in great part framed and elicited the very demands to which they then respond.

Since the 1940's, for instance, British parties have been subject to a demand among certain sections of public opinion, particularly among wage earners, that they commit themselves to keeping down unemployment to a level of 1 or 2 per cent. This demand of "vulgar Keynesianism" arose from various sources. But obviously a principal one has been the propaganda (and, when in power, the action) of the parties themselves. Similarly, the demand that the cost of living be stabilized—particularly strong among groups with fixed incomes—has been sharpened and strengthened by the claims of both parties that the Government, as inflation continued from the late forties into the fifties, had the duty and the means to halt the price rise. Hence, when ministers and officials find their efforts to manage the economy hemmed in by pressure from these two blocs of public opinion, they are confronting what is in no small part a consequence of the intense party competition of the past decade or two.

The parallel with the effect of mass advertising upon the demands of consumers in the economy is irresistible. One is tempted to say that as great retailing organizations manipulate the opinion of their markets, creating the demands of which in economic theory they are supposed to be the servants,[60] so also the massive party organizations of Collectivist politics create the

---

[60]"As a society becomes increasingly affluent," writes J. K. Galbraith, "Wants are increasingly created by the process by which they are satisfied. . . . Increases in consumption, the counterpart of increases in production, act by suggestion or emulation to create wants. Or producers may proceed actively to create wants through advertising and salesmanship." *The Affluent Society* (Boston 1958), p. 158. Galbraith calls this the "dependence effect."

opinion which in democratic theory they are supposed merely to reflect. Thus the popular sovereignty of democratic theory is undermined by the same means as is the "consumers sovereignty" of liberal economics.[61] But this gloomy view of Collectivist politics neglects various factors, not least the role of producers organizations in eliciting, and in protecting against party manipulation, the political demands of their members. In any case, some degree of manipulation of opinion by parties may be the price paid for a representation of consumer interests. The power of organized producers in a modern democracy is readily seen and widely recognized. Indeed, many fear that, overshadowed by these giants of the Collectivist economy, the consumer group, only poorly organized, or perhaps not organized at all, will be unable to bring its interests forcefully to the attention of Government. But this view neglects the function of the tightly knit, competitive political party. Keenly on the scent of votes and pressed sharply by its rival in the chase, it probes every neglected thicket in the political landscape for its quarry.

However one may assess the merits, the fact is that not only political parties, but indeed the whole vast apparatus of modern government and politics has a role in forming the opinion by which it is supposed to be governed. In this respect the mixed economy is paralleled by the mixed polity. In the era of Collectivist policy, we cannot separate the sphere of government from that of the production of material goods and services. Neither can we in the era of Collectivist politics separate the sphere of government from that of the formation of public opinion—the sphere of "ideal production." As government policy has deeply penetrated the economic market place, so also have the massive concentrations of contemporary politics invaded the market place of ideas.

PARTY GOVERNMENT AND GROUP POLITICS

It is common enough in democratic political systems for competing parties to try to broaden their electoral support by appeals to consumer groups. But the process of "bidding" that one finds in Britain's postwar politics depended on a rather special combination of conditions. Among these conditions were the decline of class antagonism; the wide

[61]Nigel Nicolson, a Conservative M.P. who was denied renomination by his constituency party because of his opposition to the Suez action, expresses great alarm over this tendency. Party managers and candidates, he declares, "use all modern means of mass-communication to create a mass mind which does not require to think and therefore ceases to discriminate," while the mass media and general education, rather than "discovering, instructing and expressing the public's point-of-view . . . have merely served to stamp it out from two huge rounded moulds." *People and Parliament* (London 1958), p. 50.

acceptance of the basic framework of the Welfare State and Managed Economy; and the narrow electoral balance between the parties that became noticeable as the Conservatives regained popular support in the late forties and was manifest in the results of elections and public opinion surveys during the fifties and into the sixties. These conditions set the stage for a competition between the two major parties focusing on group appeals. Insofar as a principal aim of a party is to win power, such a tactic in such a situation was highly rational. But before a party can act rationally in this sense, it must have, in a high degree, the capacity for unified decision-making. It must have some system for considering the situation, deciding and stating authoritatively what its promises will be, and effectively carrying them out if it wins power in the state. Like the producer group that possesses a strong potential for bargaining, the party must mobilize and unify its resources for bidding. And in the Collectivist period of British politics, just as one can trace the rise of concentration among producers groups, so also one can find a similar tendency to concentration in British parties.

One result has been the "mass party," embracing in its membership millions of persons; Labour in 1952 meticulously reported a total of 5,849,002 as compared with the Conservative rounded estimate of 2,750,000. While the number of dues-paying members of the two major parties amounted to over one third of the total vote cast in the general election of 1955, the huge majority of these numbers were inactive, except to pay the modest dues solicited from them and presumably to vote for their party at elections. But even if there were on each side thousands rather than millions of party activists,[62] they and the extra-parliamentary parties to which they belonged constituted vast and elaborate organizations extending into virtually every constituency.

Yet these mass parties had managed in a remarkable degree to "speak with one voice." To an Attlee harassed by Bevanite rebels on the back-benches, in the constituencies, and among the unions, or to a Macmillan assaulted by Suez rebels under the leadership of a Cecil, this assertion may seem painfully laughable. It is when we look at the situation in the light of what once prevailed—or what prevails in other parties such as those of the United States—that we properly appreciate the degree of cohesion achieved. The rise of party unity in parliamentary divisions is the most striking exhibit. From the mid-nineteenth century, when it had fallen to American levels, party cohesion in Britain had steadily risen until in recent decades it was so

---

[62]R. T. McKenzie has suggested that the total "active" membership of the Labour Party is less than 130,000. "Policy Decision in Opposition: A Rejoinder," *Political Studies* 5, No. 2 (June 1957), p. 182n. Elsewhere he has estimated the "politically active" as "a hundred thousand or so in each party." "Parties, Pressure Groups and the British Political Process," *Political Quarterly* 29, No. 1 (Jan.-Mar. 1958), p. 10.

close to 100 per cent that there was no longer any point in measuring it.[63] In the House of Commons were two bodies of freedom-loving Britons, chosen in more than six hundred constituencies and subject to influences that ran back to an electorate that was numbered in the millions and divided by the complex interests and aspirations of an advanced modern society. Yet day after day with a Prussian discipline they trooped into the division lobbies at the signals of their Whips and in the service of the authoritative decisions of their parliamentary parties. We are so familiar with this fact that we are in danger of losing our sense of wonder over them.

Writing of American parties, Stephen Bailey asks: "On matters of national policy, what individual or group speaks with authority for each of the national parties?"[64] In Britain, on the other hand, although the processes differed as greatly between the two parties as do the conceptions of Tory and Socialist Democracy, each party had means for deciding what it stood for and acting accordingly. Nor was this cohesion in utterance and act confined to Parliament. At general elections the party manifesto was accepted and supported by all candidates. Labour imposed this obligation by strict rule; the Conservatives were less explicit, but no less demanding. And in general the election addresses of candidates faithfully reflected the agreed party views, just as the votes of M.P.'s reflected the decisions of their parties and the actions of Governments bore out their election pledges.

These were in short "strong" parties. What were the consequences for the role of groups in politics? Sometimes it is argued that "strong" parties mean "weak" pressure groups and that party government in the British style is the enemy of group politics. And, to be sure, one can easily see how the ability of a party to make a decision binding on its M.P.'s could enable it to hold its majority against some group demand. But if a "strong" party can in this way more effectively resist group demands, so also can it more effectively yield to them. The more cohesive the party is in utterance and action, the more effectively it can bid for group support. It can control what promises will be made in its name and, once having made them, it can deliver the legislative votes needed to honor them. The mere structural fact of "strong" parties does not tell us what the role of groups will be. Indeed, given other suitable conditions, party government in the British style can be highly favorable to the rise of a politics in which "bidding" for the support of consumer groups by highly competitive parties is a major feature.

---

[63]See above, chap. VI, pp. 184-185, chap. IX, pp. 257, 262.

[64]*The Condition of Our National Political Parties.* Fund for the Republic Occasional Paper (New York 1959), p. 8.

15

The Transformation of the Western European Party Systems

Otto Kirchheimer

I. LOAD CONCEPT AND PARTY FAILURES

I have been intrigued enough by the LaPalombara-Weiner concept of the load to use it as a point of departure for inquiring into the successes and failures of major European political parties as transmission belts between the population at large and the governmental structure.

The British case has a pristine beauty: national unity brought about in the sixteenth century consolidation of the establishment, followed by a seventeenth century constitutional and social settlement allowing for the osmosis between aristocracy and bourgeoisie. The settlement happened early enough to weather the horrors and concomitant political assaults of early nineteenth century industrialism. The fairly smooth and gradual integration of the working classes was completed late enough so that the unnerving cleavage between the political promise and the social effectiveness of democracy (LaPalombara and Weiner's "distribution crisis") lasted only a couple of MacDonald-Baldwin decades. Thus once we omit the 1910-1914 interlude, Great Britain offers a case where problems could be handled as single loads. The time factor thus merges into and coincides with the load factor. The impact of constitutionalism slowly unfolds in the eighteenth century, then follows the acceleration of middle-class and the beginning of working-class integration during the nineteenth century, and the tempestuous combination of the consequences of full political democratization with the demands of a distributionist society after the First World War.

From Otto Kirchheimer, "The Transformation of the Western European Party Systems," in *Political Parties and Political Development,* eds. Joseph LaPalombara and Myron Weiner (copyright ©1966 by Princeton University Press; Princeton Paperback, 1969), Social Science Research Council, pp. 177 through 200. Reprinted by permission of Princeton University Press.

Where do we get if we apply the single-load concept to the French case? If there was a French problem of national identity, it was almost oversettled by 1793, with the revolution only intensifying results in principle reached by 1590. Universal suffrage, that is, political democracy as the constitutional basis of the French state, has been almost continuously on the program since 1848 and was definitely achieved in the early 1870's. Whatever the subsequent upheavals in executive-legislative relations, the popular basis of the French regime has not been contested except for the short-lived Pétainist period. But why did political integration, the business of transforming the state apparatus of the bourgeois society into a cooperative enterprise of all social classes, stop so short of success? Why is it that this goal has been reached only now, to some extent at least, as a simple byproduct of increased material well-being and ensuing lessening of social antagonism in the French species of industrial society? How is it that the political parties contributed so little to the end result?

There are reasons why French society in spite of, or because of, the early introduction of universal suffrage could force its working class to accept a position of stepchildren. They were a minority in a society not particularly favoring disruption of the existing social equilibrium by accentuated industrialization. Yet without such industrialization there was little chance of creating a unified party system. Instead there was a dichotomy between parties of individual representation (with their double basis in the local parish pump and the operations of the parliamentary faction) and the incipient mass party of the working class, the Socialist party of the first decade of the century. Most bourgeois parties remained restricted electioneering organizations with loose connections to still looser parliamentary factions having little radius of action beyond the parliamentary scene (Duverger-LaPalombara-Weiner's internally created parties).[1]

Through the courtesy of Alain[2] these parties were equipped with an ultra-democratic theory of eternal vigilance to be exercised by the proverbial small man over his intermediaries in party and parliament. But the reality was far different. Behind the façade of democratic vigilance political fragmentation excluded the party from advancing from the stage of *ad hoc* parliamentary combinations to permanently organized transmission belts between population and government. Party organizations and party conventions were over-sized *Cafe de Commerce* confabulations of *raisonneurs* without effective mandate.[3] Thus the bourgeois parties and the parliamentary

---

[1] The internal-external creation dichotomy has to be viewed in the light of presence or absence of a supporting framework of religious or class-motivated parallel organizations. The local committee of the internally created bourgeois party and its financial backers can never serve as such a fool-proof prop of electoral success as can the network of parallel organizations typical of external parties.

[2] Alain, *Éléments d'une doctrine radicale* (Paris 1925).

[3] For a study of the working of the most characteristic of these parties see Daniel Bardonnet, *Évolution de la Structure du Parti Radical* (Paris 1960).

government they carried saw themselves at every turn of events disowned as mere bubbles blown up by the *pays légal* to be confronted with the *pays réel* discovered from the confluence of thousands of discordant voices. Yet neither the *raisonneurs* nor the more or less benevolent intermediaries of the *Comité Mascuraud* watching over the parliamentary performance of rival political clans in the interest of the commercial and industrial community could substitute for the people at large.[4]

As these parties had to face less of a challenge from class-based integration parties than did their German neighbors, they could afford to become inoperative in semi-crisis periods. In such periods they were, as office-holding combinations, bailed out in the 1920's and early 1930's by proconsul saviors, Poincaré and his cheap imitator Doumergue. Yet as opinion-transmitting conveyor belts they had more and more to contend with the welter of anti-democratic organizations.

The last democratically legitimized attempt of the Third Republic to integrate the working class into the political system was Léon Blum's *Front Populaire*. Its failure was in part a failure of the parties, in part a consequence of international events. With its failure the Third Republic, with its juxtaposition of bourgeois parliamentary clans and class-based integration parties, was near its end.

How did it happen that the Fourth Republic failed to integrate the Communist party into its political system and allowed both the SFIO (French Section of Workers' International or Social Democratic party) and the MRP (Popular Republican Movement, or Christian Democratic party) to slip into the habits of the bourgeois parties of the previous periods? Should we single out two load factors: the supervening, mutually exclusive international policy commitments of the majority of the French political parties and the Communists, and the crisis of decolonization? Yet the end of tripartism in 1947 need not have arrested the transformation of French parties into organizations able to integrate major social groups into the political system and able to work in coalition—collaboration or in alternative shifts. There is no reason why the challenge of *personalismo* in the form of Gaullism and the challenge of the Communist working class opposition of principle had to lead to an atavistic return to the party system of the 1920's. Decolonization was a challenge which the parties might have faced with clear-cut policy propositions. Working-class integration and decolonization, the former on the agenda for virtually half a century, the latter a limited

---

[4]*Ibid.* Pp. 251-256 contain details about the *Comité Mascuraud* (named after a Senator of the Seine Department), officially called the *Comité Républicain de Commerce et de l'Industrie,* the major agency for distributing commercial and industrial funds to bourgeois parties. For the *Comité Mascuraud* and other channels, more important later, see also Henry W. Ehrmann, *Organized Business in France* (Princeton: Princeton University Press, 1957), pp. 219ff.

problem, were burdens which an operative party system could have mastered.

Yet the majority of the French political parties had never progressed beyond the stage of local-interest messengers and parliamentary clubs with or without ideological overtones. They were equally unable to make commitments in the name of their voters or to obtain legitimacy through transforming the voters' opinions and attitudes into impulses converted into governmental action. They therefore had little to do with the continuity of the state, which remained the business of the bureaucracy. Major sociopolitical options were avoided, or, if and when they had to be faced, they became the work of individual politicians temporarily supported by strong elements in the community. It is doubtful whether even such a combination as that of Caillaux and Jaurès, which appeared likely in the spring of 1914, would have been able to establish the party as an effective transmission belt between population and government and a basis for policymaking. It might have failed because of the bourgeois distaste for devices which would transmit and thereby increase popular pressure on political action. In the single-load job of integrating the *couches populaires* into the French polity the performance of the political party remained unimpressive.

The rise of Italian and German political organizations in the middle of the nineteenth century cannot be separated from the history of belated unification. Unification was a competitive effort between the political endeavors of Cavour and Garibaldi and his adherents in Italy and between Bismarck and the Liberals in Germany. The respective statesmen's timing and actions cannot be understood without the urgency of these competitive pressures. But did the more nimble hand of Cavour provide the party system greater chances than the staccato fist of Bismarck?[5] What did Cavour's and Bismarck's styles of unification mean in terms of party loads and chances?

Could the Italian Left, the *Partito d'Azione,* have tried to find contact with the southern peasant masses?[6] Could it by such contact have established a basis for national loyalty transcending class and region? Or was it inevitable that it had to become part witness, part victim, of a *trasformismo* which remained an essentially commercial operation rather than an instrument of national integration? The possibilities may have been slight, but at any rate the attempt was never even made. In Germany, on the other hand, even the lateness and the Little Germany formula involved in the founding of Bismarck's Reich did not prevent that creation from soon

---

[5] A German author has recently put the case as follows: "Bismarck's policy to the Liberals was unfair in that he achieved what the Liberals wanted to have achieved, but he gave them neither the chance nor the means to do it on their own." E. Pikart, "Die Rolle der Deutschen Parteien im Deutschen Konstitutionellen System," in *Zeitschrift für Politik* (1962), pp. 12-15.

[6] The point is discussed in some detail in Antonio Gramsci, *Il Risorgimento, Opere di Antonio Gramsci,* vol. 4 (1949), pp. 100-104.

becoming a socially and economically viable unit. All political forces, whether friendly or hostile to the Founding Father, accepted his Reich as a basis of operation. But in terms of the chances of the political parties the outcome was not much different. Italy had found a fictitious solution of its national identity problems, workable in constitutional but not in socio-political terms. Bismarck's heirs, the combined forces of bureaucracy, army, industrialists, and agrarians, upheld for about the same time both in Prussia and in the Empire a constitutional setup which prevented any approach to effective working-class participation in the government. In both Italy and Germany the mismanagement of the crises of national identity and of participation increased the problem load which the nation had to face at the end of the First World War. However, it would be difficult to evaluate the differential impact of these load factors as compared, for example, with France. Here, without any crisis of national identity and without constitutional barriers to working-class participation, the long smoldering participation crisis came fully into the open in the mid-thirties. I would argue that the extent of the 1940 breakdown is clearly related to this crisis of participation.

Is the load concept helpful, then, in analyzing the failure of the continental parties to assume their appropriate roles in the 1920's? May we, for example, argue that the belatedness in accepting a constitutional regime which would have allowed political democracy to become fully effective mili-tated against successful political integration of the working classes into the German political system in the 1920's? The acceptance of this argument hinges on some further differentiation. By "political integration" we mean here the capacity of a political system to make groups and their members previously outside the official political fold full-fledged participants in the political process. Many a mass party, however, was neither capable of nor interested in integrating its members into the existing political community. The party might even want rather to integrate its followers into its own ranks *against* the official state apparatus.

II. THE ANTEBELLUM MASS INTEGRATION PARTY

Socialist parties around the turn of the century exercised an important socializing function in regard to their members. They facilitated the transition from agrarian to industrial society in many ways. They subjected a considerable number of people hitherto living only as isolated individuals to voluntarily accepted discipline operating in close connection with expectations of a future total transformation of society. But this discipline had its roots in the alienation of these parties from the pre-World

War I political system whose demise they wanted to guarantee and speed up by impressing the population as a whole with their exemplary attitudes.[7]

During and soon after the First World War the other participants in the political game showed that they were not yet willing to honor the claims of the working-class mass parties—claims based on the formal rules of democracy. This discovery was one of the primary reasons why the social integration into the industrial system through the working-class organizations did not advance to the state of a comparable political integration. Participation in the war, the long quarrels over the financial incidence of war burdens, the ravages of inflation, the rise of Bolshevist parties and a Soviet system actively competing for mass loyalty with the existing political mass organizations in most European countries, and finally the effect of the depression setting in at the end of the decade—all these were much more effective agents in the politicization of the masses than their participation in occasional elections, their fight for the extension of suffrage (Belgium, Britain, Germany), or even their *encadrement* in political parties and trade union organizations. But politicization is not tantamount to political integration; integration presupposes a general willingness by a society to offer and accept full-fledged political partnership of all citizens without reservations. The consequences of integration into the class-mass party depended on the responses of other forces in the existing political system; in some cases those responses were so negative as to lead to delayed integration into the political system or to make for its disintegration.

Now we come to the other side of this failure to progress from integration into the proletarian mass party and industrial society at large[8] to integration into the political system proper. This is the failure of bourgeois parties to advance from parties of individual representation to parties of integration, a failure already noted in France. The two tendencies, the failure of the integration of proletarian mass parties into the official political system and the failure of the bourgeois parties to advance to the stage of integration

---

[7]The German end of this story and Bebel's emergence as commander-in-chief of a well-disciplined counter-army have often been commented upon. It has recently been discussed in Guenther Roth, *The Social Democrats in Imperial Germany* (Ottawa 1963). Similar observations on the social integration function of socialism are equally valid for Italy. As essentially hostile an observer as Benedetto Croce notes these factors in his *History of Italy, 1870-1915* (New York 1963); Robert Michels in his *Sozialismus in Italien* (Karlsruhe 1925), p. 270 *et seq.* provides ample documentary proof.

[8]Integration into industrial society: while the worker has accepted some aspects, such as urbanization and the need for regularity and the corresponding advantages of a mass consumer society, powerlessness as an individual and the eternal dependence on directives by superiors make for strong escapist attitudes. The problems are discussed in detail in André Andrieux and Jean Lignon, *L'Ouvrier d'aujourd'hui* (Paris 1960). The ambiguous consequences to be drawn from these facts and their largely negative impact on the political image of the workers are studied in detail in H. Popitz, *et al., Das Gesellschaftsbild des Arbeiters* (Tuebingen 1957).

parties, condition each other. An exception, if only a partial one, is that of denominational parties such as the German Center or Don Sturzo's *Partito Popolare*.[9] These parties to a certain extent fulfilled both functions: social integration into industrial society and political integration within the existing political system. Yet their denominational nature gave such parties a fortress-type character seriously restricting their growth potential.[10]

With these partial exceptions, bourgeois parties showed no capacity to change from clubs for parliamentary representation into agencies for mass politics able to bargain with the integration-type mass parties according to the laws of the political market. There was only a limited incentive for intensive bourgeois party organization. Access to the favors of the state, even after formal democratization, remained reserved via educational and other class privileges. What the bourgeoisie lacked in numbers it could make good by strategic relations with the army and the bureaucracy.

Gustav Stresemann is the politician who stood at the crossroads of this era, operating with a threefold and incompatible set of parties: the class and the denominational democratic mass integration parties; the opposition-of-principle parties integrating masses into their own fold against the existing order; and the older parties of individual representation. Forever on the lookout for viable compromises among democratic mass parties, old-style bourgeois parties of individual representation, and the powerholders outside the formal political party structure, Stresemann failed. For the party of individual representation from which he came could not give him a broad enough basis for his policies.[11]

Not all bourgeois groups accepted the need for transformation to integration parties. As long as such groups had other means of access to the state apparatus they might find it convenient to delay setting up counterparts to existing mass parties while still using the state apparatus for keeping mass integration parties from becoming fully effective in the political market. Yet after the second World War the acceptance of the law of the political market became inevitable in the major Western European countries. This change in turn found its echo in the changing structure of political parties.

[9]For the typology of the denominational party, see Hans Maier, *Revolution und Kirche* (Freiburg 1959).

[10]Another exception was that of parties such as the German Nationalist party of the 1920's, whose conservative predecessor in the days before World War I had already profited from the ability of the agrarian interest representation (Landbund) to funnel enough steady support to its companion organization in the political market. See in general: Thomas Nipperdey, *Die Organisation der deutschen Parteien vor 1918* (Dusseldorf 1961), vols. V and VI.

[11]See the conclusions of Wolfgang Hartenstein, *Die Anfänge der Deutschen Volkspartei* (Dusseldorf 1962), and H. A. Turner, *Stresemann and the Politics of the Weimar Republic* (Princeton: Princeton University Press, 1963).

III. THE POSTWAR CATCH-ALL PARTY

Following the Second World War, the old-style bourgeois party of individual representation became the exception. While some of the species continue to survive, they do not determine the nature of the party system any longer. By the same token, the mass integration party, product of an age with harder class lines and more sharply protruding denominational structures, is transforming itself into a catch-all "people's" party. Abandoning attempts at the intellectual and moral *encadrement* of the masses, it is turning more fully to the electoral scene, trying to exchange effectiveness in depth for a wider audience and more immediate electoral success. The narrower political task and the immediate electoral goal differ sharply from the former all-embracing concerns; today the latter are seen as counter-productive since they deter segments of a potential nationwide clientele.

For the class-mass parties we may roughly distinguish three stages in this process of transformation. There is first the period of gathering strength lasting to the beginning of the First World War; then comes their first governmental experience in the 1920's and 1930's (MacDonald, Weimar Republic, *Front Populaire*), unsatisfactory if measured both against the expectations of the class-mass party followers or leaders and suggesting the need for a broader basis of consensus in the political system. This period is followed by the present more or less advanced stages in the catch-all grouping, with some of the parties still trying to hold their special working-class clientele and at the same time embracing a variety of other clienteles.

Can we find some rules according to which this transformation is taking place, singling out factors which advance or delay or arrest it? We might think of the current rate of economic development as the most important determinant; but if it were so important, France would certainly be ahead of Great Britain and, for that matter, also of the United States, still the classical example of an all-pervasive catch-all party system. What about the impact of the continuity or discontinuity of the political system? If this were so important, Germany and Great Britain would appear at opposite ends of the spectrum rather than showing a similar speed of transformation. We must then be satisfied to make some comments on the general trend and to note special limiting factors.

In some instances the catch-all performance meets definite limits in the traditional framework of society. The all-pervasive denominational background of the Italian *Democrazia Cristiana* means from the outset that the party cannot successfully appeal to the anticlerical elements of the population. Otherwise nothing prevents the party from phrasing its appeals so as to maximize its chances of catching more of those numerous elements which are not disturbed by the party's clerical ties. The solidary element of its doctrinal core has long been successfully employed to attract a socially diversified clientele.

Or take the case of two other major European parties, the German SPD (Social Democratic party) and the British Labour party. It is unlikely that either of them is able to make any concession to the specific desires of real estate interests or independent operators of agricultural properties while at the same time maintaining credibility with the masses of the urban population. Fortunately, however, there is enough community of interest between wage-and-salary earning urban or suburban white- and blue-collar workers and civil servants to designate them all as strategic objects of simultaneous appeals. Thus tradition and the pattern of social and professional stratification may set limits and offer potential audiences to the party's appeal.

If the party cannot hope to catch all categories of voters, it may have a reasonable expectation of catching more voters in all those categories whose interests do not adamantly conflict. Minor differences between group claims, such as between white-collar and manual labor groups, might be smoothed over by vigorous emphasis on programs which benefit both sections alike, for example, some cushioning against the shocks of automation.

Even more important is the heavy concentration on issues which are scarcely liable to meet resistance in the community. National societal goals transcending group interests offer the best sales prospect for a party intent on establishing or enlarging an appeal previously limited to specific sections of the population. The party which propagates most aggressively, for example, enlarged educational facilities may hear faint rumblings over the excessive cost or the danger to the quality of education from elites previously enjoying educational privileges. Yet the party's stock with any other family may be influenced only by how much more quickly and aggressively it took up the new national priority than its major competitor and how well its propaganda linked the individual family's future with the enlarged educational structures. To that extent its potential clientele is almost limitless. The catch-all of a given category performance turns virtually into an unlimited catch-all performance.

The last remark already transcends the group-interest confines. On the one hand, in such developed societies as I am dealing with, thanks to general levels of economic well-being and security and to existing welfare schemes universalized by the state or enshrined in collective bargaining, many individuals no longer need such protection as they once sought from the state. On the other hand, many have become aware of the number and complexity of the general factors on which their future well-being depends. This change of priorities and preoccupation may lead them to examine political offerings less under the aspect of their own particular claims than under that of the political leader's ability to meet general future contingencies. Among the major present-day parties, it is the French UNR (National Republican Union) a latecomer, that speculates most clearly on the possibility of its channeling such less specialized needs to which its patron saint De Gaulle constantly appeals into its own version of the catch-all party. Its assumed asset would rest in a doctrine of national purpose and unity vague and flexible enough to allow the most variegated interpretation and yet—at least as long as the General continues to function—attractive enough to serve as a convenient rallying point for many groups and isolated individuals.[12]

While the UNR thus manipulates ideology for maximum general appeal, we have noted that ideology in the case of the *Democrazia Cristiana* is a slightly limiting factor. The UNR ideology in principle excludes no one. The Christian Democratic ideology by definition excludes the non-believer, or at least the seriously non-believing voter. It pays for the ties of religious solidarity and the advantages of supporting organizations by repelling some millions of voters. The catch-all parties in Europe appear at a time of de-ideologization which has substantially contributed to their rise and spread. De-ideologization in the political field involves the transfer of ideology from partnership in a clearly visible political goal structure into one of many sufficient but by no means necessary motivational forces operative in the voters' choice. The German and Austrian Social Democratic parties in the last two decades most clearly exhibit the politics of de-ideologization. The example of the German Christian Democratic Union (CDU) is less clear only because there was less to de-ideologize. In the CDU, ideology was from the outset only a general background atmosphere, both all-embracing and conveniently vague enough to allow recruiting among Catholic and Protestant denominations.

As a rule, only major parties can become successful catch-all parties. Neither a small, strictly regional party such as the South Tyrolian Peoples' party nor a party built around the espousal of harsh and limited ideological claims, like the Dutch Calvinists; or transitory group claims, such as the German Refugees; or a specific professional category's claims, such as the Swedish Agrarians; or a limited-action program, such as the Danish single-tax Justice party can aspire to a catch-all performance. Its *raison d'être* is the defense of a specific clientele or the lobbying for a limited reform clearly delineated to allow for a restricted appeal, perhaps intense, but excluding a

---

[12]The difficulties of a party in which the dynamics of personalization substitute completely for agreed-upon goals as well as the style of operations fitting the personal loyalty variant of the catch-all party become readily apparent from the description of the Third UNR Party Congress by Jean Charlot, "Les Troisièmes Assises Nationales de L'U.N.R.—U.D.T.," in *Revue Française de Science Politique* 14 (Feb. 1964), pp. 86-94.

wider impact or—once the original job is terminated—excluding a life-saving transformation.

Nor is the catch-all performance in vogue or even sought among the majority of the larger parties in small democracies. Securely entrenched, often enjoying majority status for decades—as the Norwegian and Swedish Social Democratic parties—and accustomed to a large amount of interparty cooperation,[13] such parties have no incentive to change their form of recruitment or their appeal to well-defined social groups. With fewer factors intervening and therefore more clearly foreseeable results of political actions and decisions, it seems easier to stabilize political relations on the basis of strictly circumscribed competition (Switzerland, for instance) than to change over to the more aleatory form of catch-all competition.

Conversion to catch-all parties constitutes a competitive phenomenon. A party is apt to accommodate to its competitor's successful style because of hope of benefits or fear of losses on election day. Conversely, the more a party convinces itself that a competitor's favorable results were due only to some non-repetitive circumstances, and that the competitor's capacity of overcoming internal dissension is a temporary phenomenon, the smaller the over-all conversion chance and the greater the inclination to hold fast to a loyal—though limited—clientele.

To evaluate the impact of these changes I have found it useful to list the functions which European parties exercised during earlier decades (late in the nineteenth and early in the twentieth centuries) and to compare them with the present situation. Parties have functioned as channels for integrating individuals and groups into the existing political order, or as instruments for modifying or altogether replacing that order (integration-disintegration). Parties have attempted to determine political-action preferences and influence other participants in the political process into accepting them. Parties have nominated public officeholders and presented them to the public at large for confirmation.

The so-called "expressive function"[14] of the party, if not belonging to a category by itself, nevertheless warrants a special word. Its high tide belongs to the era of the nineteenth-century constitutionalism when a more clear-cut separation existed between opinion formation-and-expression and the

[13]Ulf Torgersen, "The Trend Towards Political Consensus: The Case of Norway," in Stein Rokkan, ed., *Approaches to the Study of Political Participation* (Bergen 1962); and Stein Rokkan and Henry Valen, "Regional Contrasts in Norwegian Politics" (1963, mimeographed), esp. p. 29. For both weighty historical and contemporary reasons the Austrian Social-Democratic party forms a partial exception to the rule of less clear-cut transformation tendencies among major class-mass parties in smaller countries. It is becoming an eager and rather successful member of the catch-all club. For the most adequate treatment see K. L. Shell, *The Transformation of Austrian Socialism* (New York 1962).

[14]Cf. Sartori's paper, "European Political Parties: The Case of Polarized Pluralism," chap. 5, above. Cf. Sartori, *Parties and Party Systems* (New York, Harper & Row, forthcoming).

business of government. At that time the internally created parliamentary parties expressed opinions and criticism widely shared among the educated minority of the population. They pressed these opinions on their governments. But as the governments largely rested on an independent social and constitutional basis, they could if necessary hold out against the promptings of parliamentary factions and clubs. Full democratization merged the opinion-expressing and the governmental business in the same political parties and put them in the seat either of government or an alternative government. But it has left the expressive function of the party in a more ambiguous state. For electoral reasons, the democratic catch-all party, intent on spreading as wide as possible a net over a potential clientele, must continue to express widely felt popular concerns. Yet, bent on continuing in power or moving into governmental power, it performs this expressive function subject to manifold restrictions and changing tactical considerations. The party would atrophy if it were no longer able to function as a relay between the population and governmental structure, taking up grievances, ideas, and problems developed in a more searching and systematic fashion elsewhere in the body politic. Yet the caution it must give its present or prospective governmental role requires modulation and restraint. The very nature of today's catch-all party forbids an option between these two performances. It requires a constant shift between the party's critical role and its role as establishment support, a shift hard to perform but still harder to avoid.

In order to leave a maximum imprint on the polity a party has to exercise all of the first three functions. Without the ability to integrate people into the community the party could not compel other powerholders to listen to its clarions. The party influences other power centers to the extent that people are willing to follow its leadership. Conversely, people are willing to listen to the party because the party is the carrier of messages—here called action preferences—that are at least partially in accord with the images, desires, hopes, and fears of the electorate. Nominations for public office serve to tie together all these purposes; they may further the realization of action preferences if they elicit positive response from voters or from other powerholders. The nominations concretize the party's image with the public at large, on whose confidence the party's effective functioning depends.

Now we can discuss the presence or absence of these three functions in Western society today. Under present conditions of spreading secular and mass consumer-goods orientation, with shifting and less obtrusive class lines, the former class-mass parties and denominational mass parties are both under pressure to become catch-all peoples' parties. The same applies to those few remnants of former bourgeois parties of individual representation which aspire to a secure future as political organizations independent of the vagaries of electoral laws and the tactical moves of their mass-party competitors.[15] This change involves: a) Drastic reduction of the party's ideological baggage. In France's SFIO, for example, ideological remnants serve at best as scant cover for what has become known as *"Molletisme,"* the absolute reign of short-term tactical considerations. b) Further strengthening of top leadership groups, whose actions and omissions are now judged from the viewpoint of their contribution to the efficiency of the entire social system rather than identification with the goals of their particular organization. c) Downgrading of the role of the individual party member, a role considered a historical relic which may obscure the newly built-up catch-all party image.[16] d) De-emphasis of the *classe gardée,* specific social-class or denominational clientele, in favor of recruiting voters among the population at large. e) Securing access to a variety of interest groups. The financial reasons are obvious, but they are not the most important where official financing is available, as in Germany, or where access to the most important media of communication is fairly open, as in England and Germany. The chief reason is to secure electoral support via interest-group intercession.

From this fairly universal development the sometimes considerable remnants of two old class-mass parties, the French and the Italian Communist parties, are excluding themselves. These parties are in part ossified, in part solidified by a combination of official rejection and legitimate sectional grievances. In this situation the ceremonial invocation of the rapidly fading background of a remote and inapplicable revolutionary experience has not yet been completely abandoned as a part of political strategy. What is the position of such opposition parties of the older class-mass type, which still jealously try to hold an exclusive loyalty of their members, while not admitted nor fully ready to share in the hostile state power? Such parties face the same difficulties in recruiting and holding intensity of membership interest as other political organizations. Yet, in contrast to their competitors working within the confines of the existing political order, they cannot make a virtue out of necessity and adapt themselves fully to the new style of catch-all peoples' party.[17] This

[15]Liberal parties without sharply profiled program or clientele may, however, make such conversion attempts. Val Lorwin draws my attention to the excellent example of a former bourgeois party, the Belgian Liberal party, which became in 1961 the "Party of Liberty and Progress," deemphasizing anticlericalism and appealing to the right wing of the Social Christian party, worried about this party's governmental alliance with the Socialists.

[16]Ample material to points b) and c) may be found in the interesting study by a practicing German politician: Ulrich Lohmar, *Innerparteiliche Demokratie* (Stuttgart 1963), esp. pp. 35-47 and 117-124. See also, A. Pizzorno, "The Individualistic Mobilization of Europe," in *Daedalus* (Winter 1964), pp. 199, 217.

[17]However, even in France—not to speak of Italy—Communist policies are under pressure to accommodate to the new style. For a concrete recent example see W. G. Andrews, "Evreux 1962: Referendum and Elections in a Norman Constituency," in *Political Studies* 2 (Oct. 1963), pp. 308-326. Most recently, Maurice Duverger, "L'Eternel Marais Essai sur le Centrisme Français," in *Revue Française de Science Politique* 14 (Feb. 1964), pp. 33, 49.

conservatism does not cost them the confidence of their regular corps of voters. On the other hand, the continued renewal of confidence on election day does not involve an intimate enough bond to utilize as a basis for major political operations.

The attitudes of regular voters—in contrast to those of members and activists—attest to the extent of incongruency between full-fledged participation in the social processes of a consumer-goods oriented society and the old political style which rested on the primordial need for sweeping political change. The latter option has gone out of fashion in Western countries and has been carefully eliminated from the expectations, calculations, and symbols of the catch-all mass party. The incongruency may rest on the total absence of any connection between general social-cultural behavior and political style.[18] In this sense electoral choice may rest on family tradition or empathy with the political underdog without thereby becoming part of a coherent personality structure. Or the choice may be made in the expectation that it will have no influence on the course of political development; it is then an act of either adjusting to or, as the case may be, signing out of the existing political system rather than a manifestation of signing up somewhere else.

IV. THE CATCH-ALL PARTY, THE INTEREST GROUP, AND THE VOTER: LIMITED INTEGRATION

The integration potential of the catch-all mass party rests on a combination of factors whose visible end result is attraction of the maximum number of voters on election day. For that result the catch-all party must have entered into millions of minds as a familiar object fulfilling in politics a role analogous to that of a major brand in the marketing of a universally needed and highly standardized article of mass consumption. Whatever the particularities of the line to which a party leader owes his intraparty success, he must, once he is selected for leadership, rapidly suit his behavior to standard requirements. There is need for enough brand differentiation to make the article plainly recognizable, but the degree of differentiation must never be so great as to make the potential customer fear he will be out on a limb.

Like the brand whose name has become a household word, the catch-all mass party that has presided over the fortunes of a country for some time, and whose leaders the voter has therefore come to know on his television set

---

[18]This hypothesis is discussed in more detail in George Lavau, "Les aspects socio-culturels de la dépolitisation," in Georges Vedel, ed., *La Dépolitisation: Mythe ou Réalité?* (1962), esp. p. 198. For some other explanations see Seymour Martin Lipset, "The Changing Class Structure and Contemporary European Politics," in *Daedalus* (Winter 1964), pp. 271-303.

and in his newspaper columns, enjoys a great advantage. But only up to a certain point. Through circumstances possibly outside the control of the party or even of the opposition—a scandal in the ranks of government, an economic slump—officeholding may suddenly turn into a negative symbol encouraging the voter to switch to another party as a consumer switches to a competitive brand.

The rules deciding the outcome of catch-all mass party competition are extremely complex and extremely aleatory. When a party has or seeks an almost nationwide potential constituency, its majority composed of individuals whose relation to politics is both tangential and discontinuous, the factors which may decide the eventual electoral outcome are almost infinite in number and often quite unrelated to the party's performance. The style and looks of the leader, the impact of a recent event entirely dictated from without, vacation schedules, the weather as it affects crops—factors such as these all enter into the results.

The very catch-all character of the party makes membership loyalty far more difficult to expect and at best never sufficient to swing results. The outcome of a television contest is dubious, or the contest itself may constitute too fleeting an exposure to make an impression that will last into the election. Thus the catch-all mass party too is driven back to look out for a more permanent clientele. Only the interest group, whether ideological or economic in nature or a combination of the two, can provide mass reservoirs of readily accessible voters. It has a more constant line of communication and higher acceptance for its messages than the catch-all party, which is removed from direct contact with the public except for the comparatively small number intensively concerned about the brand of politics a party has to offer these days—or about their own careers in or through the party.

All the same, the climate of relations between catch-all party and interest groups has definitely changed since the heyday of the class-mass or denominational integration party. Both party and interest group have gained a greater independence from each other. Whether they are still joined in the same organization (like British Labour and the TUC [Trades Union Congress]) or formally enjoy complete independence from each other (like the German SPD and the DGB [Workers' Federation]), what matters most is the change of roles.[19] Instead of a joint strategy toward a common goal there appears an appreciation of limited if still mutually helpful services to be rendered.

The party bent on attracting a maximum of voters must modulate its interest-group relations in such a way so as not to discourage potential voters who identify themselves with other interests. The interest group, in its turn, must never put all its eggs in one basket. That might offend the sensibilities of some members with different political connections. More important, the

---

[19]See the conclusions of Martin Harrison, *Trade Unions and the Labour Party Since 1945* (London 1960).

interest group would not want to stifle feelings of hope in another catch-all party that some moves in its direction might bring electoral rewards. Both party and interest group modulate their behavior, acting as if the possible contingency has already arrived, namely that the party has captured the government—or an important share in it—and has moved from the position of friend or counsellor to that of umpire or arbitrator. Suddenly entrusted with the confidence of the community as a whole, the government-party arbitrator does best when able to redefine the whole problem and discover solutions which would work, at least in the long run, in the favor of all interest claimants concerned.

Here there emerges a crucial question: What then is the proper role of the catch-all party in the arbitration of interest conflicts? Does not every government try to achieve best tactical position for exercising an effective arbitration between contending group claims? Is the catch-all party even needed in this connection? Or—from the interest viewpoint—can a society dispense with parties' services, as France now does?

A party is more than a collector of interest-group claims. It functions at the same time as advocate, protector, or at least as addressee of the demands of all those who are not able to make their voices felt as effectively as those represented by well organized interest groups: those who do not yet have positions in the process of production or those who no longer hold such positions, the too young and the too old, and those whose family status aligns them with consumer rather than producer interests.

Can we explain this phenomenon simply as another facet of the party's aggregative function? But functionalist phraseology restates rather than explains. The unorganized and often unorganizable make their appearance only on election day or in suddenly sprouting pre-election committees and party activities arranged for their benefit. Will the party be able and willing to take their interests into its own hands? Will it be able, playing on their availability in electoral terms, not only to check the more extreme demands of organized groups but also to transcend the present level of intergroup relations and by political reforms redefining the whole political situation? No easy formula will tell us what leader's skill, what amount of pressure from objective situations has to intervene to produce such a change in the political configuration.

In this job of transcending group interests and creating general confidence the catch-all party enjoys advantages, but by the same token it suffers from an infirmity. Steering clear of sectarianism enhances its recruiting chances in electoral terms but inevitably limits the intensity of commitment it may expect. The party's transformation from an organization combining the defense of social position, the quality of spiritual shelter, and the vision of things to come into that of a vehicle for short-range and interstitial political choice exposes the party to the hazards of all purveyors of nondurable consumer goods: competition with a more attractively packaged brand of a nearly identical merchandise.

V. LIMITED PARTICIPATION IN ACTION PREFERENCE

This brings us to the determination of action preferences and their chances of realization. In Anthony Downs's well-known model action preference simply results from the party's interest in the proximate goal, the winning of the next election. In consequence the party will arrange its policies in such a way that the benefits accruing to the individual members of the community are greater than the losses resulting from its policy.[20] Downs's illustrations are frequently, though not exclusively, taken from fields such as taxation where the cash equation of political action is feasible. Yet Downs himself has occasionally noted that psychological satisfactions or dissatisfactions, fears or hopes, are elements in voters' decisions as frequently as calculations of immediate short-term benefits or deprivations. Were it different, the long-lasting loyalty of huge blocks of voters to class-mass integration parties in the absence of any immediate benefits from such affiliation could scarcely be explained. But can it be said that such short-term calculations correspond much more closely to the attitudes connected with the present-day catch-all mass party with its widely ranging clientele? Can the short-term benefit approach, for example, be utilized in military or foreign-policy issues?

In some countries in the last decade it has become the rule for catch-all parties out of office simply to lay the most recent shortcomings or apparent deterioration of the country's military or international position at the doorstep of the incumbent government, especially during election campaigns: thus in the United States the Republican party in 1952 with regard to the long-lasting indecisive Korean War, or in Germany more recently the Social Democrats with regard to Adenauer's apparent passivity in the face of the Berlin Wall. In other instances, however, the opposition plays down foreign or military issues or treats them in generalities vague enough to evoke the image of itself as a competitor who will be able to handle them as well as the incumbent government.

To the extent that the party system still includes "unreformed" or—as in the case of the Italian Socialist party—only "half-reformed" class-mass type integration parties, foreign or military issues enter election campaigns as policy differences. Yet even here the major interest has shifted away from areas where the electorate could exercise only an illusory choice. The electorate senses that in the concrete situation, based in considerable part on

---

[20]"It always organizes its action so as to focus on a single quantity: its vote margin over the opposition in the test at the end of the current election period." In A. Downs, *An Economic Theory of Democracy* (1957), p. 174.

geography and history, the international bloc affiliation of the country rather than any policy preference will form the basis of decision. It senses too that such decisions rest only partially, or at times nominally, with the political leadership. Even if the impact of the political leader on the decision may have been decisive, more often than not election timetables in democracies are such that the decision, once carried out, is no longer contested or even relevant to voter choices. As likely as not, new events crowd it out of the focus of voters' attention. Few voters still thought of Mendès-France's 1954 "abandonment" of Indo-China when Edgar Faure suddenly dissolved the Assembly in December 1955. While a party may benefit from its adversary's unpopular decisions, such benefits are more often an accidental byproduct than the outcome of a government-opposition duel with clearly distributed roles and decisions.

A party may put up reasonably coherent, even if vague, foreign or military policies for election purposes. It may criticize the inept handling of such problems by the government of the day, and more and more intensively as it gets closer to election day. But in neither case is there a guarantee of the party's ability to act as a coherent body in parliament when specific action preferences are to be determined. Illustrative of this dilemma are the history of EDC in the French Parliament and the more recent battles within the British parties in regard to entrance into the Common Market (although the latter case remains inconclusive because of De Gaulle's settling the issue in his own way, for the time being). Fortuitous election timetables and the hopes, fears, and expectations of the public do not intermesh sufficiently with the parliamentary representatives' disjointed action on concrete issues before them to add up to the elaboration of clear-cut party action preference.

The catch-all party contributes general programs in the elaboration of domestic action preferences. These programs may be of a prognostic variety, informing the public about likely specific developments and general trends. Yet prognostics and desirability blur into each other in this type of futurology, in which rosy glasses offer previews of happy days for all and sundry among the party's prospective customers. These programs may lead to or be joined with action proposals in various stages of concretization. Concrete proposals, however, always risk implying promises which may be too specific. Concretizations must remain general enough so that they cannot be turned from electoral weapons to engines of assault against the party which first mounted them.

This indeterminacy allows the catch-all party to function as a meeting ground for the elaboration of concrete action for a multiplicity of interest groups. All the party may require from those who obtain its services is that they make a maximal attempt to arrive at compromises within the framework of the party and that they avoid coalescing with forces hostile to the party. The compromises thus elaborated must be acceptable to major interest groups even if these groups, for historical or traditional reasons, happen not to be represented in the governing party. Marginal differences may be submitted to the voter at elections or, as older class-mass parties do on occasion, via referenda (Switzerland and Sweden). But expected policy mutations are in the nature of increments rather than major changes in intergroup relations.

It is here that the difference between the catch-all and the older form of integration party becomes most clearly visible. The catch-all party will do its utmost to establish consensus to avoid party realignment. The integration party may count on majority political mechanisms to implement its programs only to find that hostile interests frustrate the majority decision by the economic and social mechanisms at their disposal. They may call strikes (by labor or farmers or storekeepers or investors), they may withdraw capital to safe haven outside the country, they may undermine that often hypocritically invoked but real factor known as the "confidence of the business community."

VI. INTEGRATION THROUGH PARTICIPATION IN LEADERSHIP SELECTION—THE FUTURE OF THE POLITICAL PARTY

What then remains the real share of the catch-all party in the elaboration of action preferences? Its foremost contribution lies in the mobilization of the voters for whatever concrete action preferences leaders are able to establish rather than *a priori* selections of their own. It is for this reason that the catch-all party prefers to visualize action in the light of the contingencies, threats, and promises of concrete historical situations rather than of general social goals. It is the hoped-for or already established role in the dynamics of action, in which the voters' vicarious participation is invited, that is most in evidence. Therefore the attention of both party and public at large focuses most clearly on problems of leadership selection.

Nomination means the prospect of political office. Political office involves a chance to make an impact via official action. The competition between those striving to influence official action puts into evidence the political advantage of those in a position to act before their political adversaries can do so. The privilege of first action is all the more precious in a new and non-repetitive situation where the political actor can avoid getting enmeshed in directives deriving from party action preferences. Much as the actor welcomes party support on the basis of revered (but elastic) principles, he shuns specific direction and supervision. In this respect the catch-all party furnishes an ideal background for political action. Where obtaining office becomes an almost exclusive preoccupation of a party, issues of personnel are reduced to search for the simplest effective means to put up winning combinations. The search is especially effective wherever the party becomes a channel by which representatives of hitherto excluded or neglected minorities may join the existing political elite.

The nomination of candidates for popular legitimation as office-holders thus emerges as the most important function of the present-day catch-all party. Concentration on the selection of candidates for office is in line with an increasing role differentiation in industrial society. Once certain levels of education and material welfare are reached, both intellectual and material needs are taken care of by specialized purveyors of communications and economic products. Likewise the party, which in less advanced societies or in those intent on rapid change directly interferes with the performance of societal jobs, remains in Western industrial society twice removed—through government and bureaucracy—from the field of direct action. To this state of affairs correspond now prevailing popular images and expectations in regard to the reduced role of the party.[21] Expectations previously set on the performance of a political organization are now flowing into different channels.[22]

At the same time, the role of the political party as a factor in the continued integration of the individual into the national life now has to be visualized in a different light. Compared to his connection with interest organizations and voluntary associations of a non-political nature and to his frequent encounters with the state bureaucracy, the citizen's relations with the political party are becoming more intermittent and of more limited scope.

To the older party of integration the citizen, if he so desired, could be closer. Then it was a less differentiated organization, part channel of protest, part source of protection, part purveyor of visions of the future. Now, in its linear descendant in a transfigured world, the catch-all party, the citizen finds a relatively remote, at time quasi-official and alien structure. Democratic society assumes that the citizen is finally an integral and conscious participant in the affairs of both the polity and the economy; it further assumes that as such he will work through the party as one of the many interrelated structures by which he achieves a rational participation in his surrounding world.

Should he ever live up to these assumptions, the individual and society may indeed find the catch-all party—non-utopian, non-opressive, and ever so flexible—an ingenious and useful political instrument.

[21]See the discussion of political attitudes in Habermas, *et al., Student und Politik* (Neuwied 1961), and the German preference scale quoted in R. Mayntz, "Loisirs, participation sociale et activité politique," in *Revue Internationale des Sciences Sociales* (1960), pp. 608-622.

[22]See the contribution of S. Mallet, "L'Audience politique des syndicats," in Léo Hamon, ed., *Les nouveaux comportements politiques de la class ouvrière* (Paris 1962), esp. pp. 241-244.

What about the attitude toward the modern catch-all party of functional powerholders in army, bureaucracy, industry, and labor? Released from their previous unnecessary fears as to the ideological propensities and future intentions of the class-mass party, functional power-holders have come to recognize the catch-all party's role as consensus purveyor. In exchange for its ability to provide a clear-cut basis of legitimacy, functional powerholders are, up to a point, willing to recognize the political leadership claims of the party. They expect it to exercise certain arbitration functions in intergroup relations and to initiate limited political innovations. The less clear-cut electoral basis of the party's leadership claim and the closer the next election date, the smaller the credit which functional power-holders will extend to unsolicited and non-routine activities of the political powerholders impinging on their own positions. This lack of credit then sets the stage for conflicts between functional and political leadership groups. How does the catch-all party in governmental positions treat such conflicts? Will it be satisfied to exercise pressure via the mass media, or will it try to re-create a militant mass basis beyond the evanescent electoral and publicity levels? But the very structure of the catch-all party, the looseness of its clientele, may from the outset exclude such more far-reaching action. To that extent the political party's role in Western industrial society today is more limited than would appear from its position of formal preeminence. Via its governmental role it functions as coordinator of and arbitrator between functional power groups. Via its electoral role it produces that limited amount of popular participation and integration required from the popular masses for the functioning of official political institutions.

Will this limited participation which the catch-all party offers the population at large, this call to rational and dispassionate participation in the political process via officially sanctioned channels, work?

The instrument, the catch-all party, cannot be much more rational than its nominal master, the individual voter. No longer subject to the discipline of the party of integration—or, as in the United States, never subject to this discipline—the voters may, by their shifting moods and their apathy, transform the sensitive instrument of the catch-all party into something too blunt to serve as a link with the functional powerholders of society.[23] Then we may yet come to regret the passing—even if it was inevitable—of the class-mass party and the denominational party, as we already regret the passing of other features in yesterday's stage of Western civilization.

---

[23]For some recent strictures on slavish party dependence on the results of polls, see Ulrich Lohmar, *op. cit.*, pp. 106-108.

16

Ideology and the Organization of Conflict

Samuel H. Barnes

Ideology is one of the most frequently cited and inadequately understood subjects of empirical political inquiry. It easily lends itself to diverse and conflicting usages and, with a few notable exceptions, research on it has been inconclusive and non-cumulative. If the theorist of ideology consequently faces many pitfalls, he also thereby gains considerable freedom of interpretation. I will take advantage of this freedom in order to criticize the utility of most usages of ideology and to suggest an alternative approach.

I assume that the most important problems facing the student of ideology are empirical; that is, they do not involve the analysis of the merits and shortcomings of particular ideologies or the historical origins of contemporary ideological disagreements, though these important topics also merit attention. Rather, the most pressing problems concern how ideologies affect the structure of political conflict on the macro level and individual action on the micro level. They involve the relationship between political thought and behavior, and this relationship is primarily a problem of linkage. I maintain that this linkage takes place largely in the organizations in which elites and masses come together for political action, and that political organization is consequently the most promising focus for research on ideology.

There is mounting evidence that mass publics do not react in ideological terms. It seems equally true that much contemporary political conflict has an ideological dimension. This paper seeks to contribute towards the resolution of this seeming contradiction: It is presented not as a solution but as a

Reprinted by permission of the author and journal from *Journal of Politics,* 28 (August 1966), 513-30. An earlier version of this article was presented at the Annual Meeting of the American Political Science Association, Washington, D.C., September 8-11, 1965.

beginning. In it. I (1) suggest a restricted usage of the term ideology; (2) review and criticize methods of operationalizing and measuring ideology and its dispersion; (3) propose political organization as the most promising focus for research on ideology; and (4) discuss how ideology relates to the organization of political conflict.

I. THE MEANING OF IDEOLOGY

Most difficulties in the operationalization of the concept of ideology can be traced to the meaning of the term adopted by the researcher. David Minar has reviewed these various usages and I do not want to retrace the field that he covered so well.[1] I agree with Minar that we need a definition "that reaches beyond mere attitudes, reasons stemming from the considerations of utility or suggestiveness, of historical identity, and communicability"; and we further agree on the need for a denotation that combines some of these elements with "a political theory of ideology that casts it as a sort of ideational background of politics, that conditions behavior and accounts for some of the basic continuities in political society."[2]

In this paper I will make a distinction between political belief systems and political ideologies. I will retain belief system as an open term referring to the set of political attitudes held by an individual, whether exhibiting constraint or not.[3] An ideology is a belief system that is internally consistent *and* consciously held. This approach rejects formulations that view ideology as a mere collection of political attitudes or policy preferences. Constraint must exist among components of an ideology; knowing one belief must increase the probability of guessing another correctly; components must "hang together." Most constrained belief systems undoubtedly relate directly or indirectly to one of the major traditions of political thought—the great isms—such as, for example, liberalism, communism, fascism, social Catholicism, or the several varieties of socialism. For the great isms are, among other things, attempts to work out the logical ramifications of some basic insight or insights; hence, at least originally and in their philosophical

---

[1] David Minar, "Ideology and Political Behavior," *Midwest Journal of Political Science* 5 (Nov.1961), pp. 317-331.

[2] *Ibid.*, p. 326.

[3] For a discussion of belief systems see Philip Converse, "The Nature of Belief Systems in Mass Publics," in David Apter (ed.), *Ideology and Discontent* (New York: The Free Press, 1964), pp. 206-261. My distinction between belief system and ideology is similar in many respects to Robert E. Lane's latent and forensic ideologies. See *Political Ideology* (New York: The Free Press, 1962).

formulations, they are highly constrained systems of thought. But not everyone who claims to adhere to a particular ism necessarily accepts all of the logical consequences of his act of faith. Consequently, the degree of constraint in a belief system is an empirical question; it must be demonstrated, not assumed, and only constrained and consciously held belief systems will be labeled ideologies.

To adopt a broader view of ideology would make it virtually synonymous with political attitudes. Actually, a particular political system may contain a wide range of political attitudes, many of which may be compatible with several ideologies. Recognition of the distinction between political attitudes and political ideology might clarify much of the present debate over the decline of ideology. Even if political attitudes become increasingly similar, their divergent ideological bases need not disappear.

To adopt a broader view of ideology would also complicate any discussion of the relationship between the great isms and the belief systems of mass publics. Although ideas do have consequences for the behavior of a small portion of the population, evidence is accumulating that ideologies as consciously held, internally constrained systems of thought do not form part of the mental equipment of mass publics anywhere. Retaining the limited view of ideology resolves the problem of whether the beliefs of mass publics should be considered ideological or not by converting the problem into an empirical one. This is not to suggest that the belief systems of mass publics are unrelated to traditional ideological concerns. They often have ideological ramifications, but these are more likely to be superimposed by the analyst than consciously held by the subjects. Kaplan's warning that we not confuse an act with an action is pertinent here: The meaning attached by the observer to action should not be attributed to the actor.[4]

Nor does this formulation imply an absence of constraint in the belief systems of mass publics. Socialization may give rise to coherent belief systems without involving the consciousness of the subject. For example, socialization in a closed society with a high consensus can cause mere traditionalists to appear as ideologues.[5] And political organization can provide the functional equivalent of ideology, or "ideology by proxy."[6] While these give rise to constraints in belief systems, their significance for ideology is vastly different. And it is these differences that we need to investigate. But we must first examine some methodological problems in the study of ideology.

---

[4]Abraham Kaplan, *The Conduct of Inquiry* (San Francisco: Chandler Publishing Company, 1964), p. 122.

[5]For example, Mattei Dogan notes that Italian Christian Democratic women are traditionalists, not conservatives: "Le donne italiane tra il cattolicesimo e il marxismo," in Joseph LaPalombara and Alberto Spreafico (eds.), *Elezioni e comportamento politico in Italia* (Milan: Edizioni di Comunita, 1963), pp. 406-474.

[6]See Angus Campbell, *et al., The American Voter* (New York: John Wiley and Sons, 1960), p. 220; for the reconstructed logic of this process, see Anthony Downs, *An Economic Theory of Democracy* (New York: Harper, 1957).

II. APPROACHES TO THE MEASUREMENT OF IDEOLOGY

Measurement is the handmaiden of science. It may not be the sole path to scientific significance, but it is certainly the principal route to greater precision. Without a concern for measurement it is difficult to make a meaningful statement about mass publics. And an examination of the ways in which ideology has been measured reveals that much work remains to be done. In the following discussion, examples are chosen as illustrative of emerging problems; I make no pretense at a thorough coverage. The measurement of ideology has two principal dimensions—the measure of individual ideology and the measure of its distribution within a population. Several approaches to the measure of individual ideology deserve mention here.

One approach involves the utilization of open-ended questions to construct a scale of ideological sensitivity, in which those "whose comments imply the kinds of conception of politics assumed by ideological interpretations of political behavior and political change" are separated out.[7] This method revealed that less than 12% of the American electorate exhibited any substantial ideological sophistication; it also demonstrated the importance of education, as almost one-third of the college educated were classified as ideologues or near ideologues. Comparable results are reported for the French electorate,[8] and for members of an Italian Socialist Federation.[9] It seems unlikely that the level of ideological sophistication, as measured in this manner, is very high among mass publics anywhere.

The above measure tells us something about ideological sophistication but nothing about the substance of the ideology. One way to get at substance is through depth interviews that probe into aspects of belief systems difficult to tap with more standardized tests. This was the method employed by Lane in his study of fifteen inhabitants of an Eastport housing development.[10] While this study sacrificed considerations of quantification and sampling in return for depth, it identified several significant features of American belief systems that should facilitate the design of larger projects in the future.

Another approach utilized in particular by social psychologists equates ideology with general attitude structure and deduces ideological patterns

[7]Campbell, et al., op. cit., p. 227. See this chapter for a complete discussion of this approach, pp. 216-265.

[8]Philip Converse and Georges Dupeux, "The Politicization of the Electorate in France and the United States," Public Opinion Quarterly 26, (Spring 1962), pp. 1-23.

[9]Samuel H. Barnes, "Participation, Education, and Political Competence: Evidence from a Sample of Italian Socialists," American Political Science Review 60 (June 1966), pp. 348-354.

[10]Lane, op. cit.

from responses to questions probing specific attitudes toward criminals, alcoholism, governmental intervention, authority, religion, etc.[11] This approach has several basic weaknesses from my point of view. The first is that it often barely touches on *political* ideology, the relationship between a factor such as tendermindedness, for example, and political behavior is not always clear. Secondly, this approach makes it difficult or even impossible to distinguish values (i.e., normative judgments) and opinions, whether salient, intensively held, or rationally examined, from ideologies. Finally, as will be clarified below, this approach evades what I consider to be a crucial question —whether or not there is a functional relationship between such specific attitudes and ideology.

An approach to the study of ideology that has the virtues of simplicity of operationalization and availability of data extracts ideology from the speeches and publications of individuals and organizations. This too involves several obvious pitfalls. If the writings largely concern proposals for public policy one is inferring ideology from policy; this is similar to inferring thought from action, or at least proposed action. Unless great care is devoted to sampling problems, which is rare, it is also difficult to avoid bias in the selection of "typical" statements. Through careful selection of sources and statements one can often show a group or an individual to be for or against almost anything at one time or another. And one can learn nothing in this way about the attitudes and beliefs of the inarticulate rank and file. Writing about the Christian Anti-Communist Crusade, Wolfinger et al conclude: "Failure to distinguish between the pronouncements of political leaders and the opinions of their supporters involves some grave risks in attempting to explain the appeal of the radical right."[12] This warning is relevant for most individuals or groups deeply involved in political struggles. Finally, this approach is especially prone to assuming commitments on the part of the writer that may not be warranted. In politics, argument is often exaggerated for dramatic effect, advantages in bargaining, and other reasons, and one cannot assume that public pronouncements actually reflect the underlying belief system of an organization or individual.[13]

Especially suited to the study of conflict is an approach that utilizes responses to batteries of attitudinal questions to study consistency among the responses of individuals (constraint) and among members of a particular

[11]For an example of this usage and a discussion of its origins, see Paavo Koli, "Ideology Patterns and Ideology Cleavages," *Transactions of the Westermarck Society* 4 (1959), pp. 75-143.

[12]Raymond E. Wolfinger, Barbara Kaye Wolfinger, Kenneth Prewitt and Sheilah Rosenhack, "America's Radical Right: Politics and Ideology," in Apter (ed.), *op. cit.,* p. 275.

[13]An otherwise useful work that exhibits all three of these weaknesses is Joseph Monsen, Jr., and Mark W. Cannon, *The Makers of Public Policy: American Power Groups and Their Ideologies* (New York: McGraw-Hill, 1965).

group (consensus). These attitudinal questions may involve public policy issues or they may probe more basic attitudes, but the pattern of responses is utilized as a measure of ideology.[14] Some researchers are aware of the many pitfalls involved in this method. Thus the authors of *The American Voter* write:[15]

> At the very best, judgment on the presence or absence of a functional relationship between two or more attitudes demands some degree of inference on the part of the investigator. In most attitude studies, functional relationships are presumed to exist where it is found that knowledge of a person's belief on one issue helps to predict his belief on some other issue. It is important to recognize than an individual may hold attitudes that appear congruent from the point of view of the analyst when there is in fact no functional contact between them.

What seems significant about these approaches is their assumptions concerning the ideological origins of constraint. This approach tends to assume what needs to be demonstrated—the existence within mass publics of stable underlying patterns of attitudes toward political objects.

Yet, convincing evidence is accumulating that they do not exist. Using panel survey data, Philip Converse was able to confront the problem directly. He concluded that changes in attitudes over time towards a number of policy questions could not be adequately explained as resulting from genuine conversions; rather, individuals must have responded at random.[16] As a consequence, they exhibited little more constraint in their belief systems than would be expected by chance alone. Elites, on the other hand, exhibited far more constraint. It must be emphasized that these questions concerned major contemporary issues. Had the individual respondents possessed stable underlying mechanisms for ordering their attitudes they would have exhibited greater constraint.

The measurement of the content of belief systems has not progressed very far. But it seems likely that mass publics are low in ideological sophistication and largely devoid of genuine constraints in their belief systems stemming from ideological considerations. And it is even more likely that mass publics do not exhibit constraints stemming from commitment to the isms of traditional political thought. As will be indicated below, it is likely

---

[14]For example, Herbert McCloskey, "Conservatism and Personality," *American Political Science Review* 52 (March 1958), pp. 27-45; McCloskey, *et al.,* "Issue Conflict and Consensus Among Party Leaders and Followers," *American Political Science Review* 54 (June 1960), pp. 406-27; McCloskey, "Consensus and Ideology in American Politics," *American Political Science Review* 58 (June 1964), pp. 361-382; Campbell, *et al., op. cit.,* pp. 188-215; Samuel J. Eldersveld, *Political Parties: A Behavioral Analysis* (Chicago: Rand McNally, 1964), pp. 183-219.

[15]Campbell, *et al., op. cit.,* p. 191.

[16]Apter (ed.), *op. cit.,* p. 242.

that organizational ties are as important as ideology in the development of individual constraints within mass publics.

The second major dimension in the measure of ideology concerns its distribution within a population. This is primarily a sampling problem, but statistical sampling theory can resolve it only in part. However, careful attention to sampling in research design can eliminate the purely formal problems. National samples make possible reasonably accurate mapping of the distribution of belief systems within a population. This is especially important in democracies for the study of elections, for example, where elections determine the general orientation of public policy; and the distribution of opinion is an important subject in all polities. But the relationship between the national distribution of belief systems and the policy process is less clear as the election period recedes and new issues arise. The relationship is even more confusing in those polities, democratic or not, where the relationship between elections and the formation of a government is complex or even problematical, as in the French Fourth Republic. And this will probably prove even more obviously to be the case in developing countries where elite belief systems can be expected to diverge markedly from those of the mass.

These considerations suggest the need for a supplementary purposive sample designed to capture in greater detail the structure of the beliefs of "strategic elites."[17] In all polities these should include party, executive, legislative, bureaucratic, associational, and economic elites. The inclusion of others, the weight assigned to each, the degree of penetration into middle and lower strata (regional and local elites, for example), the amount of geographical spread desired, and the level of ideological sensitivity assumed —these will depend upon the structure of political conflict in the polity, the resources available to the researcher, and his judgment as to the payoff potential of various designs. It is necessary that we recognize that individual belief systems are not of equal importance in politics, and that the nonrandom aspect of sampling must be consciously confronted. Indeed, it may turn out that the best sampling unit is not the individual at all, whether within the elite or mass, but organizations, with a subsample of individuals that pays particular attention to their roles within the organization.

It is clear that any empirical approach to the study of ideology must deal with the measurement problem, for no generalizations about ideology and conflict can be better than the measurement techniques on which they are based. While many useful methods exist for measuring ideology and its dispersion, all have weaknesses, and considerable impovement is both desirable and possible.

[17]As developed by Suzanne Keller, *Beyond the Ruling Class: Strategic Elites in Modern Society* (New York: Random House, 1963).

III. IDEOLOGY AND ORGANIZATION

Tough-minded analysts of society and politics have tended to view ideologies as mere cloaks masking interests. For Marx, ideologies were rationalizations of class interest. For Bentley, they were "spooks." But for some, on the other hand, ideology is elevated to a leading position, guiding the actions of individuals and polities alike.

Most contemporary analysts of conflict take an intermediate position. Thus Dahrendorf writes, "Ideologies understood as articulated and codified manifest interests are again but a technical condition of organization. Ideologies do not create conflict groups or cause conflict groups to emerge. Yet, they are indispensable as obstetricians of conflict groups, and in this sense [act] as an intervening variable."[18] Dahl likewise views "patterns of attitudes and opinions" as intervening factors helping to account for variations in conflict and consensus.[19] Boulding, too, seems to take an intermediate position, though this must be inferred from scattered comments: "The extent to which ideological differences result in overt conflict depends mainly on the extent to which these differences are embodied in organizations designed for conflict," and "The conflict of ideologies . . . is partly ecological and partly organizational."[20] In addition, Coser, following Simmel, seems to view ideology, if not as an independent force, at least as a device for objectifying conflict so that individuals fight "not for self but only for ideals of the groups they represent."[21] And Mannheim sees a mutual interplay between ideology and interest in the role of intellectuals, who serve as apologists for interests but "in return for their collaboration with parties and classes" leave an ideological imprint on them.[22]

This middle position does indeed seem to be the only sensible one to assume. It would be absurd to argue, for example, that ideological considerations do not enter into the motivations of a communist intellectual; it would be equally foolish to assume that all peasant communists are ideologically motivated. The following general finding may serve to illustrate this point: Studies of communist movements in many countries, using a variety of research techniques, suggest that hard core ideologues are primarily

[18]Ralf Dahrendorf, *Class and Class Conflict in Industrial Society* (Stanford: Stanford University Press, 1959), p. 186.

[19]Robert Dahl (ed.), *Oppositions in Western Democracies* (New Haven: Yale University Press, 1966), chap. 13.

[20]Kenneth Boulding, *Conflict and Defense: A General Theory* (New York: Harper & Row, 1962), p. 278.

[21]Lewis Coser, *The Functions of Social Conflict* (New York: The Free Press, 1956), p. 118.

[22]Karl Mannheim, *Ideology and Utopia* (New York: Harcourt, Brace, 1946), p. 142.

middle-class professionals and intellectuals, few in number, who were attracted primarily by the ideological appeal of Marx; lower-class communists seem litle affected by ideology.[23]

"The inevitable," Lenin is reported to have said, "requires a lot of hard work." No idea has ever made much headway without an organization behind it. And no organization has ever made much headway without satisfying the needs of substantial numbers of people. While small organizations and movements may have thrived on the ideological enthusiasm of their members alone, it is difficult to make a big impact without organizing large numbers of people.[24]

It was pointed out above that the belief systems of mass publics seldom exhibit constraints among elements, and that elites are the hosts of ideologies. It is through organization that the ideologies of elites become politically relevent. The important question, What is the impact of the ideological preferences of elites on the goals of their political organizations? is often asked. But this is only half of the relationship. The opposite but related question is of at least equal significance: What is the impact of political organization on the ideologies of the elites? Numerous scholars have remarked upon the degeneration of charismatic and ideological movements into bureaucratic entities. This is perhaps an almost inevitable consequence of the necessities of organization, and it has profound consequences for the study of ideology. While ideological considerations relate largely to goals, organizations tend to develop internal dynamics of their own that include a multiplicity of goals. For participants they are instrumental organizations as well, often providing income and status in addition to the achievement of the organizational goal; in fact, organizational and individual goals may conflict. Moreover, organizations must come to terms with the belief systems of participants and clients, and ideological goals may become displaced in the process. Lenin and others have noted several advantages of small elite structures over mass organizations. His brilliant solution to the problem of the impact of organization on ideology was an elite party devoted to goal achievement working through other, primarily instrumental, organizations.

---

[23]See, for example, Gabriel Almond, *The Appeals of Communism* (Princeton: Princeton University Press, 1956); Hadley Cantril, *The Politics of Despair* (New York: Basic Books, Inc., 1958); R. V. Burks, *The Dynamics of Communism in Eastern Europe* (Princeton: Princeton University Press, 1961), esp. chap. 2; Gene D. Overstreet and Marshall Windmiller, *Communism in India* (Berkeley: University of California Press, 1959); Arnold C. Brackman, *Indonesian Communism* (New York: Frederick A. Praeger, 1963).

[24]For a recent statement of the reconstructed logic of the distinction between the motivations of members of large and small groups see Mancur Olson, Jr., *The Logic of Collective Action* (Cambridge: Harvard University Press, 1965). For an evaluation of the utility of Mansur's theory for empirical research see Samuel H. Barnes, "Party Democracy and the Logic of Collective Action," in William J. Crotty (ed.), *Approaches to the Study of Party Organization* (Boston: Allyn & Bacon, 1968).

This seems to have arrested but not prevented the disintegration of ideology in this case.[25]

Wherever ideologies seem to be important in politics they have a firm organizational basis. This seems to be true even in the United States where those who score high on ideological sensitivity and constraint also score high on party identification, and the least sophisticated ideologically flit from party to party if they vote at all.[26] And there is considerable evidence that American party elites are more ideological and also more extreme in their attitudes than the rank and file; these latter are, in fact, rather similar. Herbert McCloskey concludes the following:[27]

> Partisan differences are greater between the informed than between the un-informed, between the upper-class supporters of the two parties than between the lower-class supporters, between the 'intellectuals' in both parties than be-tween those who rank low on 'intellectuality.'

And it equally seems likely that it is largely the elites dominating American political organizations, especially professional people, who are most strongly committed to the tenets of liberal democracy, the dominant American ideology.[28]

Countries such as France, Italy, the Netherlands, and Belgium—which are conventionally viewed as exhibiting great ideological cleavages—likewise feature extensive organizational underpinnings for their ideological debates. In these polities individuals are often socialized into subcultures rigidly separate from one another, and may belong solely to organizations reflecting the belief system of that particular subculture. It is probable that organizational ties to parties, trade unions, and other associations are more important than ideology in imposing constraints on mass belief systems. Much evidence suggests that organized Catholics in the Netherlands, Belgium, France, or Italy, or communists in the latter two countries, for example, are much more strongly influenced by their organizational ties and face to face relationships than by considerations of ideology. Simmel and Coser have noted the association between extensive face to face relationships and intense conflict.[29] These ties and relationships, rather than ideology as

---

[25]See Richard Lowenthal, *World Communism: The Disintegration of a Secular Faith* (New York: Oxford, 1964); Philip Selznick, *The Organizational Weapon* (New York: McGraw-Hill, 1952).

[26]Campbell, *et al., op. cit.,* pp. 263-265.

[27]McCloskey, "Consensus and Ideology in American Politics," *op. cit.,* p. 372. But Eldersveld casts some doubt on these conclusions (*op cit.,* p. 188), and Edmond Constantini presents data that contradict them completely ("Intra-party Attitude Conflict: Democratic Party Leadership in California," *Western Political Quarterly* 16 (Dec. 1963), pp. 956-972.

[28]See Robert E. Lane, "The Fear of Equality," *American Political Science Review* 53 (March 1959), pp. 35-51.

[29]Coser, *op. cit.,* p. 62.

such, may account for the seeming ferocity of "ideological" conflict in such countries.

These nonideological origins of constraint may turn out to be very important indeed, and especially so in polities characterized by deep cleavages, low education, and high levels of politicization. In such polities individuals may exhibit considerable constraint in their belief systems without being ideologically sophisticated.

IV. IDEOLOGY AND POLITICAL CONFLICT

I have indicated that it is through organizations that the ideologies of elites affect the belief systems of mass publics. I have also suggested that organizations respond to many types of motivation, of which ideology is only one. I will now examine some of the ramifications of this view of ideology for the structure of political conflict of a polity.

A discussion of ideology and conflict requires a basic distinction between levels of analysis. The discussion of polities as wholes entails macro analysis; the study of individual behavior involves micro analysis.[30] The functional role of an ideology or organization for the polity may be quite different from its role for individuals, and any linkage between the macro and micro levels must be demonstrated, not assumed.

At a given time, any particular polity possesses a given structure of conflict and a particular political culture or cultures (as used, for example, in the works of Gabriel Almond). As components of culture, political belief systems are learned through socialization. A polity may have one or several significant belief systems; in the latter case we say that its political culture is fragmented. Generally when we refer at the macro level to an ism such as Soviet communism or Austrian socialism or Italian social Catholicism, we are utilizing a form of shorthand to identify a particular political culture or subculture that is conventionally identified with a particular ideology.

But if this shorthand leads us to make assumptions about the belief systems of individuals within the subculture we may be misled completely. For example, Gabriel Almond and Sidney Verba have demonstrated that in Italy the present constitutional parties (especially the Christian Democrats) are "supported in large part by traditional-clerical elements who are not democratic at all, and not even political in a specialized sense of the term," while the anti-constitutional left wing (mainly Communists) "at least in part and at the rank and file voter level rather than among the party elite, manifests a form of open partisanship that is consistent with a democratic

---

[30]See Gabriel Almond and Sidney Verba, *The Civic Culture* (Princeton: Princeton University Press, 1963), pp. 32-36; V. O. Key, *Public Opinion and American Democracy* (New York: Knopf, 1961), chap. 16ff.

system."[31] And to take a less dramatic example, the Netherlands is divided into Catholic, Protestant, Socialist, and Liberal subcultures, each with its own ideology, associational network, party or parties, and means of mass communications. Yet on many dimensions there seem to be few differences between the substantive political attitudes of working class members of these subcultures, though they vote for different parties and live in separate subcultures. Examples can be multiplied almost at will. I doubt that knowledge of macro- or micro-politics is furthered by the analysis of ideology independent of its organizational context.

While it may not be useful to speak of ideologies as wholes, analysis that makes use of ideological dimensions may be quite helpful. As Converse has noted, mass beliefs are formed in clusters.[32] This is probably especially true in democracies, for total ideologies require total commitments that are difficult to maintain amidst the conflicting pressures of pluralist societies. But one can meaningfully speak of a liberal-conservative economic dimension in studying American attitudes, or of the clerical-anti-clerical dimensions in French and Italian politics.[33] Yet it must be noted that attitudes toward these dimensions at the micro level may be formed by non-ideological considerations. And it is likewise true that any particular position on any single dimension may be compatible with several ideologies. Thus one can be an economic conservative for Burkean reasons, or because of a commitment to laissez-faire economics or to social Darwinism, or out of pure economic self interest, or for nationalistic reasons, or from irrational contempt for the poor, or any number of other reasons.

The discontinuity between the positions of individuals on different dimensions has often been noted. Many Burkean conservatives support civil rights and medicare, and always vote Democratic. In other words, individuals may possess seemingly inconsistent belief systems. While this may be a source of discomfort for intellectuals, most people seem unconcerned except when circumstances publicize the inconsistencies, as in the present confrontation between racism and the American creed. Even in this case some people do not admit their incompatibility, though it has become difficult to defend intellectually their inclusion in a single belief system.

---

[31]Almond and Verba, *op. cit.,* p. 160.

[32]In Apter (ed.)., *op. cit.,* p. 211.

[33]Spatial models of party competition assume unidimensionality, whereas this is seldom the case, at least as the parties are perceived by mass publics. See Donald Stokes' criticism of spatial models: "Spatial Models of Party Competition," *American Political Science Review* 57 (June 1963), pp. 368-377. On the other hand, the greater ideological sophistication of elites combined with the unequal saliency of ideological dimensions at the macro level should cause us to pause before discarding spatial models altogether. Where dimensions—for example, economic liberalism-conservatism, clericalism-anticlericalism—tend to reinforce one another, as in Italy, spatial models may be quite useful at least at the macro level. Whether they are ever meaningful at the micro level remains to be seen.

Most people acquire the belief systems of those around them. Intellectuals are to some extent free of this determinism, for they are able to escape the limitations imposed on the imagination by time and place. But intellectuals can make contact with mass publics only with difficulty, and then only by working through organizations that have a largely instrumental character, such as schools, trade unions, and political parties. The degree to which ideological considerations intrude on instrumental ones varies greatly, of course, but it is probably not very high anywhere most of the time.

In Western society in general, and perhaps in Russian also, instrumental considerations have come to dominate. This is perhaps the consequence, if not always of democracy, at least of the importance of mass publics. For the belief systems of mass publics everywhere are increasingly similar; and in all cultures that have been touched by modernization, mass belief systems include a demand for greater material well-being. When mass publics are involved, ideologies of asceticism and self-denial do not do well in competition with those that promise more. An organization must adapt its ideology in order to enhance its chances of survival, whether it be the Communist Party of the Soviet Union, the Republican Party, or the Catholic Church.

The historical experiences of the Catholic Church serve to illustrate this contention. It has been noted that the instrumental needs of an organization have a tendency to dominate over ideological ones. The organizational structure of Catholicism and the instrumental functions the Church performed in a preindustrial society made it difficult for Catholicism to adapt quickly to the changed status of mass publics following the Industrial Revolution. As a result, new organizations espousing ideologies such as liberalism and socialism emerged to threaten its organizational survival. But the Church gradually adapted, and today in many countries has a full array of organizations for all social groups. Thus it has organized or sponsored trade unions, businessmen's clubs, democratic political parties, youth groups, and associations for almost every conceivable category of persons. It likewise has modified its ideology as reflected in Papal Encyclicals to accommodate to the belief systems of mass publics. Few organizations willingly disband. The continuity of the Catholic Church through numerous changes in social and political ideologies attests to the primacy of organization over political ideology, as does the prudence of Pope Pius XII during the Second World War.

In some countries, the necessity of coming to terms with the belief systems of mass publics has profoundly modified the ideologies of all political organizations so that they are quite similar on many dimensions, especially on the importance of the economic well-being of the masses. Marxist, Catholic, Protestant, and Liberal ideologies are generally compatible with most mass beliefs on this point. It is perhaps within this context that references are made to "the end of ideology." While there is growing consensus in Western countries, this is the result of convergence on some of the principal dimensions of political conflict, not of agreement on ideology. And other significant marginal differences become more important as organizational elites accentuate them to justify their survival. Note, for example, the importance of marginal differences between Democrats and Republicans in the United States, or Christian Democrats and Socialists in West Germany today. Differences on other dimensions may retain their significance despite convergence on the economic dimension. Thus in contemporary France attitudes towards clericalism, rather than economic or other outlooks, are still the best predictor of party allegiances.[34] And in the Netherlands, where subcultural and ideological differences coincide, the organizational networks developed within subcultures seem to guarantee the persistence of each, despite growing convergence in attitudes toward public policy on the part of two or three of the subcultures. With a complete structure of organizations to serve him, often combined with sanctions for nonparticipation, the individual today may be functionally isolated from deviant beliefs. Here, socialization into different political subcultures and organizational networks is as important as ideology as a basis for continuing cleavages in the polity.

These examples suggest that conflict that seems to be ideological is facilitated by the presence of structural discontinuities in the polity that encourage the maintenance of separate political and other organizations. Regional, linguistic, religious, ethnic, and economic seem to be the most important of these structural lines of division. These often coincide with one another, and the more they do so, the more likely are differences to be accompanied by elaborate ideologies. Economic development tends to reduce the importance of these differences because it tends to make for similar patterns throughout the polity, especially in the economic sphere. But development does not affect all areas equally, and some regions may lag behind others, as in the American South, Quebec, Southern Italy, and parts of France. Furthermore, development may merely add the dimension of industrial warfare to existing discontinuities in the political culture, though the circumstances under which this takes place remain somewhat obscure. Thus development may itself be a source of conflict. And there is increasing evidence that older lines of cleavage and conflict have an unexpected tenacity despite economic development; they may, in fact, be accentuated by it, as in Canada, Belgium, and the Netherlands. But in the absence of deep religious, linguistic, and regional cleavages, development does seem to contribute to the waning of the intensity of conflict, perhaps because of the growing similarity of ideologies on the subject of material well-being.

But, as pointed out above, organizations tend to persist. Despite growing convergence on many ideological dimensions, differences remain on

[34]Converse, in Apter (ed.), *op. cit.*, p. 248.

others, and ideological debate among elites may continue. Mass publics may not be greatly affected by it, but their loyalties to primary and secondary groups and hence directly or indirectly to organizations persist. As a result, political conflict may retain an ideological dimension long after ideology has ceased to be of much significance for policy making or for mass publics.

This discussion of the importance of organization points up the crucial ideological role of the most important organization of all—government. For most political conflict focuses sooner or later on the institutions of government; governmental organizations are crucial, and, like others, they have their own goals, elites, belief systems. Organizations such as legislatures, bureaucracies, commissions, etc., may or may not be broadly reflective of mass beliefs. The constitutional structure of the polity, and especially the electoral system, can facilitate or hinder the expression of particular ideological views. The relationship between mass beliefs and those of the governmental elites is thus crucial in understanding the actual role of ideology in politics. The distribution of mass beliefs may be only partially reflected in the formal organizations of the state. The electoral system may result in a legislature that does not adequately represent significant segments of the polity; the formation of the government may involve the exclusion of representatives of organizations and belief systems of great numerical importance within the polity. In this sense, too, belief systems are not of equal importance. While it is true that in the long run a polity can hardly ignore belief systems with strong organizational bases, the long run may be very long indeed. Thus the study of ideology and conflict must cope with the differential accessibility of the system to various ideologies.

The institutional structure of the polity is crucial not only for an understanding of the relationship between ideology and the outputs of the political system; it is also critical for the survival of particular ideologies. In ideologically well integrated polities the elites who dominate political organizations share most components of a common belief system; in other words, there is high consensus. These elites find it not only profitable but also possible to exclude proponents of deviant belief systems from important positions in the polity. Lacking visibility and legitimacy, the spread of deviant beliefs is greatly hindered. Political structure therefore greatly affects ideology. It makes a considerable difference whether the most influential organizations of the polity are accessible to or insulated from holders of deviant views. The differences between the United States and the Fourth French Republic are instructive on this point. Even partial success in capturing key positions greatly facilitates the growth of ideologically deviant organizations; this is exhibited by the parliamentary success of Communist parties in Italy and France. And the sharing of governmental positions seems to guarantee the perpetuation of the organizational bases of conflicting belief systems, as in Austria, Belgium, and the Netherlands.

Many unanswered questions remain in relation to ideology and the organization of conflict. How a particular structure of conflict arose is one of these. The dynamics of the formation and change of belief systems and ideologies at both the micro and macro levels is another. The role of ideology within a political organization is likewise poorly understood. But the importance of organization in mediating between ideology and behavior seems firmly established. Mass belief systems are part of the raw material of politics; they are a limiting factor but not a determining one. They condition elite behavior but do not determine it. Ideologies, on the other hand, require organization to render them politically significant, and organizations work profound transformations on ideologically motivated goals. Consequently, the best focus for the study of the relationship between political thought and behavior is the study of political organization.

17

Political Change in a Stalemated Society: Segmented Pluralism and Consociational Democracy in Austria

Rodney P. Stiefbold

I. INTRODUCTION

Throughout the era of mass politics—first as the cockpit of the Habsburg Empire, then as its German-speaking republican remnant with a palpable longing for Anschluss with Germany, then as a nascent nation determined to rebuild on the ashes of military defeat under the watchful and suspicious eyes of military occupying powers—the tiny Alpine country of Austria has been characterized by what Val Lorwin describes as "segmented pluralism." Under segmented pluralism social, cultural, and political activities are organized along the lines of ideological blocs or "segments" (subcultures). Within each segment individuals carry on most of their meaningful communications, social relations, and group memberships;

This article is comprised of substantial portions reprinted from "Segmented Pluralism and Consociational Democracy in Austria: Problems of Political Stability and Change," in *Politics in Europe: Structures and Processes in Some Postindustrial Democracies* by Martin O. Heisler, © 1974 David McKay Co., Inc. It is based on my earlier papers, "Elite-Mass Opinion Structure and Communication Flow in a Consociational Democracy (Austria)," presented at the Annual Meeting of the American Political Science Association, Washington, D.C., 1968; and "Parties, Groups and Chambers in the Political Bargaining Process: Pluralist Democracy in Austria," presented at the Annual Meeting of the American Political Science Association, Chicago, 1967.

I am grateful to a number of friends and colleagues for critical readings and written commentaries on earlier drafts of this article, including G. Bingham Powell, Jr., Giuseppe Di Palma, Arend Lijphart, Eric A. Nordlinger, Duncan MacRae, Jr., Gerhard Lehmbruch, Mark

although there is a high degree of communication and interaction within segments, there is relatively little movement across subcultural or segment boundaries.[1]

The hypothesis that there is a direct link between a nation's political culture and the performance of its political system is well established in contemporary political science. In accord with this hypothesis, empirical democratic theory has long ascribed several basic weaknesses to political systems characterized by "segmented pluralism," that is, by "mutually reinforcing" or "superimposed" social, organizational, and attitudinal cleavages. The first weakness is decisional ineffectiveness, or immobilism, which undermines a regime's legitimacy; and this, in turn, sets the stage for potentially destabilizing political movements or coups d'etats.[2]

Furthermore, countries fragmented into political sub-cultures lack what are said to be essential moderating influences promoting homogeneous political cultures and hence stable and viable political systems. These influences are psychological cross-pressures, which act at both the mass and the elite levels. At the mass level, there are no overlapping individual memberships in organizations having competing outlooks and making divergent claims on individual loyalties. At the elite level (in the absence of overlapping memberships by individual citizens), organizational leaders are not faced with the task of having to accommodate widely divergent views of heterogeneous members. Instead, influences such as family, church, interest groups, and political parties all tend to reinforce one another, leading, under hypothetically extreme conditions, to what Sidney Verba had described succinctly as

Kesselman, Kenneth P. Erickson, and my fellow co-editor of this book, Norman Vig. Several colleagues in the International Study of the Politics of the Smaller European Democracies provided useful critiques of some of the major theses presented here during meetings of the Smaller European Democracies group at Bellagio, Italy in 1966 and at Leiden, The Netherlands, in 1967. I am especially grateful to Val Lorwin and Stein Rokkan in this regard. Three fellow investigators of Austrian politics during the late Coalition period, Kurt Steiner, Frederick C. Engelmann, and William T. Bluhm, also provided me with useful comments. Financial support at various stages of my research has been provided through the Ford Foundation, the Rockefeller Foundation, the National Science Foundation, and the Foreign Area Fellowship Program administered by a Joint Committee of the Social Science Research Council and the American Council of Learned Societies.

[1]Val Lorwin, *Segmented Pluralism* (draft manuscript, mimeo), Center for Advanced Study in the Behavioral Sciences, Stanford, Calif. (1967); revised version published in *Comparative Politics* 3 No. 2 (Jan. 1971), pp. 141-175. Table 1 places Austria in the context of other Western democratic systems, using Lorwin's categorizations. I gratefully acknowledge the assistance of IFES-Vienna, which permitted me access to its classified data on organizational density and extent of membership, and which provided me (through Karl Blecha and Ernst Gehmacher) with help in classifying Austria and some other countries with respect to the schema in Table 1.

[2]Gabriel Almond, "Comparative Political Systems," *Journal of Politics* 18, No. 3 (Aug. 1956), pp. 391-409, esp. p. 408.

Table 1.   Extent of segmented pluralism, Western Democracies, 1905-1965

(a) Patterns and Density of Voluntary Organizations

Pattern of Organization	Density of Organization		
	Low	Medium	High
General or pragmatic		Ireland United States	Norway, Denmark, Sweden, Iceland, Britain
Partial segmented pluralism		France, Italy	Finland, West Germany
Segmented pluralism			**Austria,** Belgium, Luxembourg, Netherlands Switzerland

(b) Overall Extent of Segmented Pluralism in Various Spheres of Activity, 1950s

Major Spheres of Activity	Principal Segmented Pluralist Countries			
	Austria	Belgium	Netherlands	Switzerland
EDUCATION				
Primary	—	H*	H	M
Secondary	M	H	H	M
Higher	M	H	M	L
MASS MEDIA				
Press	H	M	M	M
Electronic	M		H	—
SOCIO-ECONOMIC ORGANIZATION				
Labor	H	H	H	H
Farmers	H	H	H	M
Small Business	M	H	H	—
Employers	M	L	M	L
Liberal Professions	M	M	M	—
Health Care	M	H	H	H
Consumers	H	H	—	L
LEISURE ACTIVITIES	H	H	M	M
POLITICS AND GOVERNMENT				
Religion-Party ties	H	H	H	M
Bureaucracy	H	H	—	H

*Legend: Degree of Segmented Pluralism. H= High (over 50% of facilities or organizations may be so characterized); M= Medium (10-50%); L= Low (under 10%).

a political system made up of two closed camps with no overlapping of membership. The only channels of communication between the two camps would be at the highest level. . . . Politics comes to resemble negotiations between rival states; and war or a breakdown of negotiations is always possible.[3]

Interwar Austria—the so-called First Austrian Republic, born of the destroyed Habsburg Empire and supplanted, after a brief civil war between Catholics and Socialists in 1934, by an indigenous clerical-fascist dictatorship, which was itself absorbed by Nazi Germany in 1938—corresponded closely not only to the classic fragmentation model, but even to the extreme situation hypothesized by Verba. Val Lorwin succinctly describes that interwar setting as follows:

> From the three "camps" or Lager of prewar days society and politics became polarized when the smallest and least widely organized of the three, the German Natiönals, threw much of their support to the "Blacks" against the "Reds." Class and geographical alignments deepened those of religion and ideology: Catholic businessmen, artisans, and farmers versus Socialist workers; rural areas versus industrial cities; the Black hinterland versus the Red capital.[4]

In addition moderate leaders of both the clerical-conservative Lager and the anti-clerical Socialist Lager lacked either the autonomy or security of position which might have permitted a bridging at the elite level of divisive conflicts of interest deeply rooted in the subcultures. Mass loyalties ran to the ideological blocs and their parties, whose flags, anthems, and private armies accurately reflected the reality of an Austrian state totally lacking in national unity or identity.

---

[3]Sidney Verba. "Organizational Membership and Democratic Consensus," *Journal of Politics* 27 (Aug. 1965), p. 470. See also Gabriel Almond and Sidney Verba, *The Civic Culture: Political Attitudes and Democracy in Five Nations* (Princeton: Princeton University Press, 1963), pp. 133-134.

[4]Lorwin, *op. cit.*, p. 4. "Lager" is the Austrian word for "camp" or "armed camp" (in connotation). On the organizational and ideological development of the Lager, see Adam Wandruszka, "Oesterreichs politische Struktur: die Entwicklung der Parteien und politischen Bewegungen," in *Geschichte der Republik Oesterreich*, ed. Heinrich Benedikt (Vienna Verlag fuer Geschichte und Politik, 1954), who is generally credited with establishing the Lager frame of reference for the analysis of Austrian politics. See also: Rudolf Schlesinger's comparative analysis of *Central European Democracy and Its Background: Economic and Political Group Organization* (London: Routledge & Kegan Paul Ltd., 1953). Peter Pulzer, "The Legitimizing Role of Political Parties: The Second Austrian Republic," *Government and Opposition* 4 (1969), pp. 324-344 applies the SSRC Committee on Comparative Politics model of successive crises in the course of political development, while Stein Rokkan sets the Austrian case in broad comparative perspective in his "The Structuring of Mass Politics in the Smaller European Democracies," *Comparative Studies in Society and History* 10, No. 2 (Jan. 1968), pp. 173-210. For an empirical study using statistical time series of major parties' development, with special attention to urban-rural and regional cleavages, see R. Stiefbold and T. P. Koppel, "The Three 'Lager' in Austrian Electoral History . . .," paper presented at International Political Science Association, Seventh World Congress, Brussels, Sept. 18-23, 1967, Specialist Meeting on Electoral Research.

In the face of this gloomy history of instability and decisional ineffectiveness, however, the Second Austrian Republic offers the social scientist a challenging deviant case. It is neither immobilist nor unstable, despite its historical legacy and its still fragmented political culture, in seeming defiance of political theorists who would have it so.

In terms of the highly original four-fold typology of democratic political systems recently proposed by Arend Lijphart, Austria is a near-perfect example of "consociational democracy."[5] The central characteristic of this type lies not in any specific institutional arrangements, but rather in elite attitudes and behavior when confronted with the condition of a fragmented political culture. Its defining feature is "overarching cooperation at the elite level with the deliberate aim of counteracting disintegrative tendencies in the system." Thus the consociational democracy is a paradoxical form of government in terms of older empirical theory: despite the burden of being a "conflict society" characterized by social, organizational, and attitudinal fragmentation, it is both stable and decisionally effective. Lijphart posits a number of preconditions and facilitating conditions for the success of consociational democracy (i.e., for its persistence and decisional effectiveness), which we shall discuss more fully in Section III below. For the moment we are concerned with simply the basic definition: the possibility that elite collaboration at the top of the system *can*, by rational choice and through development of supportive decision-making procedures, negate the hypothesized direct link from fragmented political culture (or "conflict society"[6]) to poor system performance.

[5]Lijphart, "Typologies of Democratic Systems," *Comparative Political Studies* 1, No. 1 (Apr. 1968), pp. 3-44 *passim.* Lijphart differentiates chiefly among three types of democratic systems, the centrifugal (competitive elite behavior, fragmented political culture, as in Italy); the centripetal (competitive elite behavior, homogeneous political culture, as in the Anglo-American countries); and consociational (coalescent elite behavior, fragmented political culture, as in the Netherlands, Austria, Belgium and Switzerland), pp. 30-31. He later adds a fourth type, depoliticized democracy (coalescent elite behavior, cultural homogeneity, as in the emerging "model democracy of the New Europe"), pp. 37-39. The specific theoretical work of Arend Lijphart used in this brief summary includes his *The Politics of Accommodation: Pluralism and Democracy in the Netherlands* (Berkeley and Los Angeles: University of California Press, 1968), esp. chaps. 7-10; his "Typologies" and his "Consociational Democracy," *World Politics* 21, No. 2 (Jan. 1969), *passim.* pp. 207-225. There is considerable overlap in these three works.

[6]In an article on "The Study of French Political Socialization," Fred I. Greenstein and Sidney G. Tarrow have recently summarized the propositions associated with the notion of "conflict society" as follows: "(1) attitudes are widely held, sharply crystallized, and intensely felt in the mass public; (2) individuals hold internally consistent attitudes (i.e., revolutionary or reactionary attitudes on issue 'a' will be matched by parallel attitudes on issue 'b'); (3) attitudinal disagreement is high and cumulative (i.e., disagreement on one issue is bolstered by disagreement on the next); and (4) agencies of socialization and membership inculcate and reinforce these attitudinal patterns." (*World Politics* 22, No. 1, Oct. 1969, p. 115). Thus the conflict society model juxtaposes segmented pluralist political organization and sociological distinctiveness with polarized public policy preferences which are rooted in ideological differences and characterized by intense involvement and great partisan hostility.

The Institutionalization of Consociational Democracy in Post-War Austria

Our primary focus in this paper is on Second Republic Austria during the period from 1945 to 1966 when the Catholic-Conservative People's Party (OeVP) and the Socialist Party (SPOe) joined in a carefully circumscribed contractual agreement to form a Great Coalition to govern Austria.[7] Many of our observations also characterize Austria under the single-party Conservative government which was formed after the elections of 1966 and the single-party Socialist government which replaced it after those of 1970; but a thorough investigation of elements of continuity and discontinuity between the two regimes—dissolution of the Great Coalition in 1966 amounted to a change not merely of governments but, to a great extent, also of regimes—deserves separate treatment exceeding the scope of this paper.[8]

Despite its historical legacy of intensely ideological class, ethnic, and confessional cleavages which have contributed internationally to the country's engagement in two world wars, and domestically to sporadic outbreaks of physical violence between the Lager terminating in a brief but fratricidal civil war in 1934, Second Republic Austria proved to be durable, capable of significant decision-making, and apparently legitimate in the eyes of its population. Stated differently, instead of instability, Austria under Great Coalition recorded an enviable record of dynamic political stability characterized by a remarkable capacity for gradual peaceful change. Instead of immobilism, it demonstrated decisional effectiveness. It proved capable of resolving—or at least defusing by subjecting to incremental adjustment through collective bargaining—many basic issues, some invested with high current or previous ideological content, that were contentious between the major subcultures or Lager. Among these were: mutually acceptable wage-

---

[7] On Austrian politics, see R. Stiefbold et al. (eds.), Wahlen und Parteien in Oesterreich (Vienna: Oesterr. Bundesverlag, 1966; 3 vols.); F. C. Engelmann, "Austria: The Pooling of Opposition," Political Oppositions in Western Democracies, ed. Robert A. Dahl (New Haven: Yale University Press, 1966); U. Kitzinger, "The Austrian Election of 1959," Political Studies 9, No. 2 (1961), pp. 119-140; O. Kirchheimer, "The Waning of Opposition in Parliamentary Regimes" (1957), now in Kirchheimer, Politics, Law and Social Change (New York: Columbia University Press, 1969), pp. 292-318; Kurt Steiner, Politics in Austria (Boston: Little Brown, 1972); and Gerhard Lehmbruch, Proporzdemokratie (Tuebingen: Mohr, 1966). The specific notion of rational contract as the basis of the Coalition regime has been particularly emphasized by Kirchheimer. The somewhat awkward phrase "contractarianism' is used by political theorist William T. Bluhm to underscore the same point. See his fine essay, "Nation-Building: The Case of Austria," Polity 1, No. 2 (Dec. 1968), esp. pp. 153 ff.

[8] For a comprehensive study of the Austrian political system, see Rodney Stiefbold et al., The Government and Politics of Austria (Stanford University Press, forthcoming), a volume in the cross-national research project on The Politics of the Smaller European Democracies, under the editorial direction of Stein Rokkan, Robert Dahl, Val Lorwin, and Hans Daalder. See also the literature cited in footnote 7.

price regulation and control; fiscal policies which successfully counterpointed both socialist and conservative concerns; agreement on both the extent and method of operation of Austria's large complex of nationalized industries; and renegotiation of the 1934 Concordat with the Vatican.

Several factors helped to establish and sustain a Great Coalition government between the two major Lager a scant twelve years after their civil war confrontation at the barricades: (1) the Soviet occupation after World War II and the threat to Austria's independence; (2) the need to pool resources in a common effort to oppose and finally to free Austria from all the occupation powers; (3) the demands of postwar reconstruction (applying the energies of both Lager to the solution of concrete common problems); (4) the influence of the United States and the Marshall Plan on the planning and policies for economic growth; (5) shared experiences by many of the elites as concentration camp cell mates; (6) a previous, although brief, First Republic experience in joint coalition; and (7) the desire to avoid doing anything which might plunge Austria again into civil war.

Two other closely interrelated factors were perhaps even more important for stabilization. The first was the purposive depoliticization of the decision-making environment through creation of a new set of procedural rules designed to minimize inter-elite rancorousness and avoid conflict over basic values (which in many cases remained highly divergent but generally latent). The second was the creation of new institutional resources designed to increase the capacity of the SPOe-OeVP coalition regime to cope with problems whose mere existence had overburdened the fragile First Republic:

—The former clerical-conservative Christian Social Party was recast as a federated "People's Party" (see Table 2) appealing to a somewhat more diverse theological and sociological clientele. Modeled on post-war Christian Democratic parties throughout Western Europe, it provided a flexible, adaptive organization capable of accommodating an increasingly representative cross-section of the Austrian electorate.

—A single Trade Union Congress was created, and a system of corporatist chambers of interest group representation was devised. Endowed by Austrian constitutional law with both administrative and advisory functions, the Black (clerical) Chambers of Commerce and Agriculture and the Red (Socialist) Chamber of Labor and TUC provided for a uniquely stabilizing mixture of both "multipolar" and "bipolar" interest aggregation and decision-making. These chambers functioned as a Para-Coalition of the interest groups, paralleling the related government ministries which "belonged" to each of the member parties in the coalition.

—An extra-constitutional body, called the Coalition Committee, was instituted for the purpose of bringing together the top leaders of both the Para-Coalition and the cabinet ministries, i.e., the top socio-economic and political elites of both Lager.

Table 2. Parties, groups, chambers and the Government Ministries: Principal actors in Austrian political and social-economic bargaining

	1. The Major *Lager* ("subcultures" or "segments")	2. Political Party Organizations	3. Major Interest Groups (voluntary orgs.)	4. The Chambers (*Kammern*)	5. Corresponding government ministries which were dominated by a single party during Great Coalition period' (to 1966)
CONSERVATIVE		*OeVP*. Austrian People's Party: actually a federation of 3 interest group peak assns.:	*OeBB*. Agrarian League	dominates Chamber of Agriculture	Agriculture
			OeAAB. (Catholic) Workers' and Employees' League	*Fraktion* in Chamber of Labor	Education
			OeWB. Business League	together, these dominate the Chamber of Commerce	Finance, Commerce (portfolios connected with business, agriculture, or religion)
			VOel. Union of Austrian Industrialists		
SOCIALIST		*SPOe*. Socialist Party of Austria. (Also has its own component organization parts, but they are not so explicitly based on or recognizable as "economic interests" as in the OeVP)	*OeGB*. Austrian Trade Union Federation	dominates Chamber of Labor	Social Welfare
					Interior
					Justice
					Transport (portfolios connected with labor and the internal protection of the Republic)

Source: R. Stiefbold, "Parties, Groups and Chambers in the Political Bargaining Process: Pluralist Democracy in Austria," paper presented at the annual meeting of the American Political Science Association, Chicago, 1967.

Thus the Austrian political system artfully bifurcated "political" and "socio-economic" interest aggregation and decision-making into a "Coalition" and a "Para-Coalition" then reunited them in an extra-constitutional body whose primary purpose was to mitigate potential, incipient, or actual party or group conflict.[9]

Under this unique governmental arrangement the two major political parties totally monopolized, along with their client interest groups and party-related ancillary organizations, the political life of the Austrian state. The two parties not only divided between themselves governmental posts such as cabinet ministries, as indicated in Table 2; they also parceled out among their adherents most of the significant administrative posts in the civil service and in the nationalized banks, industries, and communications network.

Parliament, as one might expect, was virtually emasculated as a separate decision-making site. Legislation took place only by mutual consent between the Coalition partners; legislative drafts might be elaborated in the interest groups and party organizations, or chambers, or Government ministries, or combinations of all of these, as in any other political system. But before the Nationalrat, the Lower House of Parliament, could act on a prospective bill, that bill had to be approved by the extra-constitutional Coalition Committee. Thereafter it was binding under the terms of the parties' "Coalition Contract" upon the members of both the Cabinet and the respective parliamentary fractions of the two parties. Members of the two coalition parties could exercise their normal parliamentary functions only with the permission of the partner party, permission which rested in each particular case on an agreement between the party leaders. Essentially, therefore, the entire system amounted to the elimination of major political opposition through government by party cartel, but within a system which allowed for the expression of limited opposition through new channels. Each coalition partner was simultaneously Government and Opposition.

The critical question concerning the balance of power between the two coalition partners turned on the ratio by which principal governmental and administrative posts were shared: that ratio was determined by the relative electoral and parliamentary strength of the two parties. Thus, despite the fact that the Austrian electorate was—in effect—not called upon to choose between rival potential governments, the electoral process retained a clear-cut meaning: the shift of votes between the two parties decided the conditions of their collaboration. It furnished a revised index of strength between the opposing coalition partners, and therefore heavily influenced

[9]On the Austrian "para-Coalition" see Rodney Stiefbold, "Parties, Groups and Chambers in the Political Bargaining Process: Pluralist Democracy in Austria," paper presented at the Annual Meeting of the American Political Science Association, 1967; and Herbert P. Secher, "Representative Democracy or 'Chamber State': The Ambiguous Role of Interest Groups in Austrian Politics," *Western Political Quarterly*, 13 (1960), pp. 890-909.

the resolution of the administrative and legislative issues which were controversial between them.

The two coalition parties normally divided close to 90% of the popular vote almost evenly between themselves; hence the slightest change was noted emphatically on either side, and sometimes led to significant revision of the formal coalition pact. In 1959, for example, the Socialist Party (SPOe) increased its percentage share of the popular vote by 1.29% to 41.8%, and gained three additional seats in the Nationalrat, the lower house of the national legislature [still one seat short of the People's Party (OeVP) parliamentary plurality]. By the rules of coalition politics, the election amounted to a "decisive" victory for the Socialists, and resulted in transfer of the Ministry of Foreign Affairs, the nationalized industries, and wage and price policy-making from control by the OeVP or bipartisan commissions to control by the SPOe.

The waning of ideology: the Austrian case.   Virtually every authoritative scholarly source, most politicians, most of the mass media elite, and most of the lay public would agree that substantial deideologisation has taken place in Austria, as throughout Western Europe, since World War II.

There are several relevant dimensions along which these changes have occurred as both a planned and a natural outgrowth of the Great Coalition experiment. One can speak of a progressive ideological dilution of the conflicts of interest between the major Lager, in the sense of ideological convergence on some previously contested issues (e.g., the Austrian state and nation); in the sense of growing functional dissociation of political ideology and practical politics; and, finally, in the sense of a decreasing impact of traditional ideology as a guide to political action.[10] (This last development was facilitated by the withdrawal of the Catholic Church from partisan politics in 1945, and by the adoption of a new Socialist party program in 1958 specifically renouncing anticlericalism and sharply reducing the salience of traditional Austro-Marxist phraseology.)

But this general picture of an Austrian political culture bedevilled by segmented pluralism, yet able to generate and support a political system that was somehow stable and viable and characterized by a substantial reduction

---

[10]Our differentiation of these aspects of *deideologisation* is based on Ulf Himmelstrand's provocative essay, "A Theoretical and Empirical Approach to Depoliticization and Political Involvement," *Acta Sociologica* 6, Fasc. 1-2, 1962, pp. 83-110, esp. p. 87. The often successful effort by Austrian political elites to play down differences in values in the interests of solving common problems according to commonly accepted procedural rules was, of course, self-reinforcing: as the behavior gained results, the results reinforced the motivation to continue to subsume, insofar as possible, conflicting values to a "partisan mutual adjustment" scheme of decision-making. Relevant here is the book by Charles E. Lindblom, *The Intelligence of Democracy: Decision-Making through Mutual Adjustment* (New York: The Free Press, 1965), esp. chap. 15. See also Verba's thoughtful article, "Some Dilemmas in Comparative Research," *World Politics* 20, No. 1 (Oct. 1967), pp. 111-127, esp. his remarks on p. 127.

in its ideological baggage, is at least partially misleading. Despite all these developments, "the two major subcultures remain separated socially and psychologically; *Lagermentalitaet* (Lager feeling and identification) persists. It has lost much of its philosophical basis, but retains its psychological reality; having lost much in ideology, it yet remains as mentality."[11] Thus did one of the most astute observers of Austrian politics (Engelmann) summarize the situation in 1965. And indeed, numerous indicators of continued psychological apartness, of the tendency to perceive Austrian politics in terms of still hostile camps sharing coalition out of mutual mistrust, could (and can still) be found.

In short, there are two quite different and equally valid perspectives from which one can view the Second Austrian Republic. Thus, one set of scholarly studies has emphasized the caricature-like nature of Austria's Para-Coalition which amounted in Austria to the institutionalization of the politics of corporatist interest group bargaining several years before it became fashionable for scholars to applaud and analyze similar decision-making trends in the rest of Europe. In this literature writers have usually emphasized the rational, pragmatic bargaining among interest group and chamber elites, which led frequently to concrete, mutually acceptable and beneficial results in socioeconomic policy questions during the period of rebuilding the post-war Austrian economy and state.

The second genre of scholarly literature, of course, has tended to emphasize a seemingly incongruous opposite situation related to the nexus which connects political parties, electoral politics, parliament, and governmental decision-making, where political life was dominated by a highly "expressive" or "ideological" verbal style. In that part of the political spectrum, according to this branch of the scholarly literature, decisional effectiveness and even political stability depended almost exclusively on practice of the "politics of accommodation" by a cartel of top subcultural elites. In this second view, Austria was pictured as a still highly politicized and hostile society divided along subcultural lines, densely organized, and ruled from above by enlightened elites who perceived their society as conflictual, and who therefore benevolently imposed a kind of "mechanical solidarity" upon their beleaguered countrymen—from the top down, but ostensibly in everybody's best interests. Bargaining behavior in which participants each give a little in order to reach compromise decisions was only intermittent and, in any case, limited to a handful of top party leaders. It certainly was not characteristic of the politics of middle- and lower-level party functionaries.

Elections, ideology, and consociational democracy. Particularly at election time, the Austrian political system seemed to reveal itself in what many authorities considered to be its true light—as not only *organizationally*

---

[11]Engelmann, "Austria: The Pooling of Opposition," *op. cit.,* pp. 267-268; cf. p. 276.

segmented, but also as *highly polarized and politicized* from top to bottom at all levels of elite and mass. As Robert Dahl has pointed out, conflicts involving politically distinct subcultures are frequently too explosive to be managed by such devices as ordinary parliamentary opposition or election campaigning or winning elections. Thus it is hardly surprising that Arend Lijphart, in discussing various conflict avoidance strategies available to consociational elites, specifically contemplates the possibility that elites will try to neutralize latent public anxieties and hostilities by eliminating or obscuring from public view political processes which are inherently rancorous: indeed, Lijphart argues, "the desire to avoid political competition may be so strong that the cartel of elites may decide to extend the consociational principle to the electoral level in order to prevent the passions aroused by elections from upsetting the carefully constructed and possibly fragile, system of cooperation," as they have occasionally done in consociational democracies such as Lebanon, Colombia, the Netherlands, or Belgium.[12]

But in Austria, as we noted above, such a solution was impossible: election returns provided the principal objective standard by which the two major Austrian political parties periodically reallocated spheres of political power, patronage, and influence between themselves within their Great Coalition. Hence a certain incompatibility between the requirements and practices of "electoral" democracy and those of "Consociational" democracy existed in Austria throughout the Great Coalition period. For it is clear that if a society were so divided it required consociational rule, it could hardly afford devisive elections; and that if a society were not so divided, it would not need consociational rule. Indeed exacerbative elections might so deeply politicize and mobilize the mass public as to pose a threat to government by elite cartel. Conversely, "integrative" or "catch-all" electoral tactics of the type which the literature on post-war European trends posits as increasingly "normal," involving "centrist" (as opposed to "right" or "left") appeals by each major political party to a cross-section of the entire electorate (as opposed to a homogeneous segment of it) would undermine segmented pluralism, promote the development of a more homogeneous political culture, and ultimately lead to transformation of crisis-based consociational rule into either a consensual coalition or alternating government-and-opposition political formula.

It is important to underscore both the pervasiveness of the stereotype of Austrian mass political culture that lies at the heart of Engelmann's observation concerning "Lagermentality," and the point that this stereotype condition was most clearly visible under electoral conditions. It is precisely the interaction of elites with non-elites in the electoral arena, and the

---

[12]Lijphart, "Consociational Democracy," p. 214; cf. his "Typologies," p.22. The points made by Robert A. Dahl are advanced in the latter's (ed.) *Political Oppositions in Western Democracies* (New Haven: Yale University Press, 1966), p. 358.

contrast with elite-mass interaction at other times, which structured the balance between costs and benefits in Austria's version of consociational democracy. This interaction necessarily turned on the question of whether or not Austria was a "conflict society"—polarized, ideological, politicized, partisan—and on the degree to which mass attitudes and elite perceptions of mass attitudes were congruent. The next sections (II-IV) deal with elite and mass opinion structure under both electoral and non-electoral circumstances and with elite-mass interaction in each case. By extrapolating from the case study of postwar Austria we are then able to raise important questions in Section IV about the conditions which facilitate or impede political change in consociational democracy in general, and hence to reflect on certain types of developmental problems which exist not only in Austria but in other industrially advanced societies as well.

II. MASS OPINION STRUCTURE

This section examines several dimensions of mass political culture in Austria, in an effort to ascertain to what extent Austria does or does not correspond to the model of a "conflict society," and to what extent Austrian political culture (or more simply, the structure of Austrian public opinion) might or might not affect elite electoral conduct or outcomes, or otherwise contribute to the systemic consequences of the democratic election process in Austria. We also want to adumbrate the important question considered in the next section, whether elite electoral behavior is influenced more by objective realities of the mass political culture or by elite perceptions of those realities, and how congruent these two things might be.

Unfortunately, our data are limited and we cannot provide real tests of all facets of the so-called conflict society model, but we can, by using less direct evidence, arrive at a reasonably complex understanding of our subject. Despite the relatively crude nature of available survey research and related data, we are able to marshall evidence which seems, at first glance, somewhat startling and unexpected. Thus our data do not betray a "conflict society"—polarized, ideological, politicized, partisan—in the Austrian setting; quite the contrary, in most respects. They suggest instead the following summary propositions about Austrian political culture—about mass opinion structure in the electoral arena:

—The majority of the electorate may be characterized as partially *depolarized,* endorsing the existing party system and the consociational political regime, in basic agreement on the legitimate ends of governmental endeavor, and "pragmatically" oriented to what are essentially bargainable bread-and-butter issues (rather than to traditional ideological and/or symbolic issues contentious between the Lager);

—as relatively *depoliticized,* exhibiting moderate (neither especially high nor low by international standards) levels of political interest and information, and moderate frequencies of political discussion; and finally,

—as also reflecting relatively *limited* inter-group *partisan hostility* in the sense that there appears to be a relatively low level of emotional commitment on the part of most citizens to the partisan Lager organizations, coupled with an apparently minimal impact of political partisanship on individuals in their "non-political" roles or spheres of activity.[13]

In short, while we cannot confront directly the thesis that the Austrian mass public exhibits continued attitudinal fragmentation corresponding to the great, sociologically and organizationally distinct, Lager—that the masses' orientations to substantive solutions of public issues are widely held, sharply crystallized, and intensely felt or that these are internally consistent from one issue to the next in harmony with the catechisms of the principal Lager—we can present a variety of evidence which suggests that the Austrian mass public, taken as a whole, exhibits limited polarity, considerable pragmatism, a relatively low political temperature, and certainly a much lesser degree of partisan hostility or concern than authorities on Austrian politics assert or imply.

Nonetheless, there are some indications of continued psychological apartness and distrust between the major camps; and perhaps capitalizing on these factors, national elections have tended to repolarize the electorate as they intensify mass political involvement, and increase public awareness of, attention to, and concern for the great ideological (symbolic) issues contentious between the Lager. At the same time, the political parties' campaign appeals have usually raised the spectre of fundamental change in the political regime (or at least in its modalities). As a result of all of these, elections tended to underline the "necessity" (or at least the elite's perception of necessity) of continuing existing consociational practices between the major political parties qua Lager through the mechanisms of Great Coalition and Para-Coalition.

[13] While individual scholars may quarrel with my usage of such terms as relatively, basically, partially, etc., all who are familiar with the body of writings on Austrian politics would no doubt agree that the traditional picture of Austria—albeit usually without much empirical supportive evidence—was one of a people which is highly polarized, ideological instead of pragmatic in issue delineation and problem-solving orientation, highly politicized, and severely partisan; in short, it is a picture of a country which would rank at or near the bottom of any group of democratic systems compared on these terms. This kind of interpretation was especially prevalent in scholarly writings of the 1950s and 1960s. A primary example, which both reflected and continued the prevailing analytical tone was the first major effort by a political scientist to analyze the Coalition political system: Herbert P. Secher, "Coalition Government: The Case of the Second Austrian Republic," *American Political Science Review* 52, No. 3 (Sept. 1958), pp. 791-808.

Basic Consensus

Basic consensus, in the sense used by Easton and Hess, means the congruence of basic value and attitudinal orientations, not necessarily at the level of the government, but at the level of the regime and/or the political community.[14] Such consensus existed in Austria under Great Coalition, at least in two crucial respects, covering not only the regime itself, but also—to a surprising extent—the designation and degree of urgency of the jobs to which that regime was expected to devote itself.

Public support for the Austrian party-coalition system. In Republican Austria the political parties have been traditionally and popularly perceived as tantamount to the State itself. The literature of Austrian politics abounds with references to the unique role that parties have played—institutionally and organizationally—in structuring Austrian political life.[15] Hence the public's view of the party system and the modes of interparty collaboration becomes a crucial indicator of the support it accords the political regime. As Jack Dennis has pointed out in his persuasive article on "Support for the Party System by the Mass Public," one can approach the question of mass support for public institutions at two rather different levels: public support may be construed and measured in terms of the observable "specific" returns (e.g., "the economic security of patronage, the pleasures of association with like-minded people, or perhaps the symbolic pursuit of preferred policy programs and leadership") which the supporters obtain from it; or it can be "diffuse," that is, "endorsement of the party system as a whole and of the general norm that partisan spirit and activity is allowable in political life." Specific support is exchanged for gratification of immediate demands, while diffuse support constitutes a reservoir of favorable attitudes or goodwill toward existing forms of political authority; it is thus relatively independent of the effects of daily system outputs.[16]

While the extraordinarily high Austrian ratio of members to voters in both the SPOe and the OeVP suggests a high degree of party system support in return for specific benefits, what seems to be a more remarkable finding is the traditional widespread support for *the existing party system,* despite (or perhaps because of?) the persistence of the Lager as mutually exclusive

---

[14]David Easton and Robert D. Hess, "Youth and the Political System," in S. M. Lipset and R. Lowenthal, eds., *Culture and Social Character* (Glencoe, Ill.: The Free Press, 1961), pp. 229-237.

[15]See Secher, "The Problem of the Austrian State: The Post World War II Experience" (unpublished doctoral dissertation, University of Wisconsin, 1953), and the literature cited in this study.

[16]Jack Dennis, "Support for the Party System by the Mass Public," *American Political Science Review* 60, No. 3 (Sept. 1966), pp. 600-601.

segments of political society. This was indicated by a 1956 finding that four-fifths of Austrian men and two-thirds of Austrian women supported the notion of a multiparty system, and by a 1962 disclosure that more than four-fifths of both men and women favored the then existing party system ("no additional parties").[17] The "no additional parties" answer is not exactly a "democratic" response in quite the same sense as is support for a multi-party system, of course; rather it may suggest approval of the black-red political balance, coupled with a desire not to see that precious balance compromised by the addition of more parties (see below).

Clearly, these findings indicate that—whether for positive or negative reasons—a wide measure of diffuse support existed for the party system and the Austrian political regime as then constituted. We already know, from previous analysis of Austria as a "segmented pluralist" society, that a high level of specific support exists for political parties within each of the major subcultures. But diffuse support can apparently coexist with a high level of segmentation. This does not necessarily imply that organic solidarity, based on growing functional interdependence across blocs, was developing within the bosom of the mechanical, normative solidarity imposed on Austria by the Great Coalition. On the contrary, as we have previously noted in the context of a paper on cross-national patterns of political socialization,[18] it is important to point out that diffuse support of political pluralism may mean something much different for the life and perspectives of the citizen of a high consensus society, such as Britain, than it does where dissensus is ingrained in socially reinforced subcultures, as in Austria. The citizen of the latter system may well tolerate and even support a multiplicity of parties because he knows realistically that such must exist to represent divergent interests—and to protect groups and individuals from their political adversaries. Such diffuse support may also be a reaction to previous unhappy experiences under authoritarian regimes (Dollfuss, Nazis) that violated the political and legal rights of some individuals and groups.

There is no intrinsic or logical reason why a functioning democratic regime cannot be built, as was perhaps true in the postwar Austrian case, on suspicion, distrust, and organizational apartness, as long as there are sufficient institutional arenas for bargaining, and a sufficient range and number of important issue areas that require and obtain minimal consulta-tion or even cooperative decision-making across subcultural lines. Perhaps sophisticated enough to recognize this need, along with the probability that

[17]Computed from data supplied by the Austrian Gallup-Institut, Vienna, and collected as part of Survey No. 960, a representative quota sample of 2500 Austrian men and women 18 years of age and over, interviewed in December, 1962. (Hereafter cited as "Nachwahlstudie 1962.")

[18]Jack Dennis, Leon Lindberg, Donald McCrone, and Rodney Stiefbold, "Political Socializa-tion to Democratic Orientations in Four Western Systems," Comparative Political Studies 1, No. 1 (Apr. 1968), pp. 82, 87, 96.

such intercultural contact occurs with least friction and most promise of success at the "top" of the political system, between corresponding elites, the public may come to support—consciously or not—the particular institutional arrangements which make this possible. New members of the political system, obviously less intimately aware of the political conditions that led to or necessitated such developments, may well internalize the same norms, without, however, being as consciously wedded to them. Thus the norms may persist, at least for a while, even after whatever objective needs gave rise to them have disappeared. Taken together, these various factors may help account for the widespread "diffuse support" accorded the party system and the Great Coalition regime by the Austrian electorate through the middle of the 1960s.

Issues and the jobs of government.   Although survey data on the issue orientation of the Austrian public leave much to be desired, in that they do not normally tap the respondents' feelings concerning what makes a given issue important or how it ought to be resolved, there *are* data concerning what Austrians perceive as the "jobs" or "issues" or "problems" most requiring governmental attention. From an examination of the frequency with which partisans of one party of the other spontaneously enumerate specific issues, or with which they single out specific issues from lists of potential issues submitted to them, it is at least possible (1) to establish that there is substantial inter-Lager and inter-party consensus at the level of the electorate as to what the issues are, and (2) to tentatively characterize mass issue orientation as essentially pragmatic and cautious, in that public attention is directed primarily to bread-and-butter (rather than to traditional, symbolic, or ideological) issues.

Thus, for example, when asked to select from a list of tasks facing the new government after the 1962 election those they regarded as most important, more than half of the respondents in a national sample chose "Stable Currency"; more than a third each checked "Stable Prices" and "Neutrality"; and about one-fifth, made cognizant by the election campaign of the increasing extent to which Austria's future prosperity might hinge on the modalities of the proposed association with the Common Market, checked that option. Issues such as the operative rules of the Great Coalition or South Tyrol interested no more than one in ten of those who had voted SPOe or OeVP in the preceding election. Moreover, except for a single issue —higher wages and salaries—the big party supporters were in substantial agreement both on the rank-ordering and on their levels of endorsement of particular issues.[19]

---

[19]"Nachwahlstudie 1962," *op. cit.* Obviously agreement on what are the issues is not tantamount to agreement on what the solution should be or even on how to go about reaching it. There is no substantive or procedural consensus with respect to solutions implied by consensus

But perhaps of greatest significance, from the point of view of this paper, is the fact that some of the issues found to be most salient and to discriminate most sharply between the political elites of the two chief Lager (see below)—such as the Habsburg question, educational reform, organization of the mass media, planning and nationalization, worker co-determination, influence of the Church, the contemporary significance of Austria's Austro-Marxist, clerical-fascist and Nazi pasts—rated little or no measurable spontaneous enumeration by the public while other issues salient at the elite level—neutrality and the questions of trade with Eastern Europe and association with the Common Market—are evoked at the mass level only in response to direct questions.

Intensity of Political Involvement

Not only does the Austrian mass public exhibit diffuse support for its political regime, and considerable consensus on the centrality of the specific problems that happen to have proved most amenable to resolution by consociational practices; by exhibiting a healthy measure of apathy towards day-to-day political affairs, it also provides the regime with substantial operational freedom, which is important for the reduction of day-to-day stress on the political system.

Political interest, information, and discussion.   There are few extant data bearing directly on the level of day-to-day political interest in the Austrian population. When asked directly, "Are you interested in politics?" a recent national sample divided as follows: one-fourth designated themselves as "very" interested, one-half as "somewhat" interested, and the rest as "not at all" interested. Pollsters scoff at the relevance of such direct questions, noting that "to be Austrian is to be political" and that more than two out of every ten Austrians are card-carrying members of political parties, and that media attention to political matters as well as frequency of political discussion suggest political interest is substantial.[20]

---

in defining the relevant problems. What I am arguing is that those problems on which the elites have been most capable of establishing decisionmaking machinery and finding middle-range, pragmatic "solutions" are also precisely those issues defined by the masses as the most important tasks of government. I do not mean to infer substantive consensus or policy outcomes or precise procedures among the masses, but I do infer—based chiefly on elite interview responses—that agreement on the essential tasks of government at the mass level was a powerful constraint on top elites to get results that would reinforce mass level support for the Coalition regime.

   [20]Interviews with the directors of the three most important commercial polling institutes, and with the director of the Social Science Study Group, "SWS," which is a semi-independent, Socialist and trade union oriented volunteer organization conducting periodic national surveys of differential technical quality. Vienna, 1965-1966.

Yet national survey data which tap the "information" dimension of political interest paint a more ambiguous picture of political intensity: although newspaper readership is high, the proportion of the population that reads political material regularly is relatively low—even in Vienna, where the political process is close at hand and where the population is consistently more attentive to political news. One-third of the national population watch the news daily on television, and about one-half listen to the news on the radio, but most of these cannot recall specific news items.[21] Finally, when asked such questions as "Who makes the laws?"—even in the days following an election campaign, when the salience of politics and the institutions of "Nationalrat" and "Government" can be assumed to be at their peak—one-fifth of the respondents confess total ignorance. In the judgment of Frank Pinner, expert observer of Austrian affairs and analyst of Austrian survey data, "public opinion polls attempting to probe voter attitudes and information reveal a condition rather common in the Western world: most voters are singularly uninformed and unmotivated"; moreover, "the voter's knowledge of issues, events, and personalities is in general so low that it is not possible to attribute to him a system of political beliefs."[22]

Pinner has somewhat overstated his case to make his point; having "a system of political beliefs," at least at a very general level, seems perfectly compatible with depoliticization and with having relatively little precise knowledge of issues, events, or personalities. This is an empirical question, of course. However, following Samuel H. Barnes' insightful argument in his "Ideology and the Organization of Conflict: On the Relationship between Political Thought and Behavior,"[23] I prefer to use the term *belief system* as an open term referring to the set of political attitudes held by an individual whether or not these attitudes exhibit "constraint," while reserving the term *ideology* to "a belief system that is internally consistent *and* consciously held" (p. 410). As Barnes points out, this formulation does not necessarily imply an absence of constraint in the belief systems of mass publics; in fragmented polities, individuals "are often socialized into subcultures rigidly separate from one another, and may belong solely to organizations reflecting the belief systems of that particular subculture" (p. 418). Under such circumstances the individual citizen "may be functionally isolated from

[21]Based on survey data made available to me by Karl Blecha, director of IFES, whose time and generosity I greatly appreciate. Blecha has pioneered in the empirical analysis of the relationship between politics and the mass media in Austria, and he has several forthcoming publications based wholly or partly on the extensive IFES and SWS data files on the mass media during the 1960s. One of Blecha's collaborators, Rupert Gmoser, has analyzed some of these data in "Herr und Frau Oesterreicher vor der Entscheidung: Die Nationalratswahlen 1966 im Spiegel der Meinungsforschung," *Die Zukunft* 7 (Apr. 1966) pp. 11-15.

[22]Frank A. Pinner, "On the Structure of Organizations and Beliefs: *Lagerdenken* in Austria," paper presented at the Annual Meeting of the American Political Science Association, 1967, p. 8.

[23]*Journal of Politics* 28 (June 1966), pp. 513-530 [reprinted above; page numbers in parentheses refer to this book].

deviant beliefs" (p. 422). Or political organization, especially when it is as salient a feature of the political landscape as in Austria, may "provide the functional equivalent of ideology, or 'ideology by proxy' " (p. 411).

The analytical point, in the Austrian case, may be this: if organizational segmentation persists, interelection political apathy among the mass public may be more apparent than real; mass apathy may be rather easily translated into intense mass electoral engagement by elites who capitalize on the organizational weapons and traditional ideologies at their command. The high electoral turnout—between 94% and 97% of the electorate in the Second Republic—may reflect, in part, the confluence of these factors.

However, on another indicator of politicization, the frequency of engaging in political discussion, Austrians show a higher aggregate level of political participation than, say, West Germans or Italians.[24] If we compare data from the 1961 West German *Wahlstudie* with what is probably the most detailed Austrian study to date (IFES, 1965), we find substantial differences in the levels of face-to-face political communication in the two countries. Thus 28% of Austrians, and one-third of those declaring a party preference, admit to multiple weekly discussions of politics, while in Germany only about 15% of both party and nonparty respondents could meet the much less rigorous requirement of discussing politics merely once a week. Talking politics in Austria may, of course, amount to little more than a kind of "expressive efficacy" on the part of individuals who find release for civic tensions (or merely behave according to long-standing cultural habits) in political gossip, without desiring personal responsibility and without perceiving themselves as being any more "relevant" to actual political decision-making than individuals who rarely talk politics. Nonetheless, knowledge of such patterns of communication about politics does afford some insight into the potential effect of campaign propaganda: the masses are depoliticized, but with a high, if latent, mobilization potential. The saliency of politics may be "low" on a daily basis, but, since communications patterns are organizationally fixed and non-overlapping, particularly among those major sectors of the electorate who support the OeVP or the SPOe, the saliency of politics can rather quickly bubble to the surface under extraordinary (for example, electoral) circumstances.

Pervasiveness of political partisanship. It is widely assumed and argued in the literature on Austrian politics and society that political partisanship— the self-conscious identification of an individual with a particular Lager, coupled with individual commitment to and concern for the integrity of that relationship—pervades nearly every nook and cranny of Austrian society. As

---

[24]See Almond and Verba, *The Civic Culture, op. cit.,* p. 116, for comparable data on Germany and Italy which suggest that Austria actually falls between Germany, where 39% never talk politics and 60% do so sometimes, and Italy, where 66% never talk politics and only 32% do so sometimes.

evidence one usually cites not only the organizational segmentation of Austrian society, but also the highly negative images said to be held about one party by supporters of the other party, as well as the high stability of voting patterns. Responsibility for the alleged continuing pervasiveness and intensity of the traditional Lager is attributed to highly homogeneous and intensely partisan patterns of political socialization supposedly prevalent in the Austrian family.

Two pieces of evidence derived from a recent post-Coalition survey of the Austrian electorate (which we use in the absence of data from the Coalition era, although we are aware that there may have been relatively significant changes in the patterns and/or intensity of political partisanship after two years of a working non-coalition government) tend to cast some doubt on both the pervasiveness and the intensity of political partisanship.[25] They suggest instead that both are much lower than has been widely assumed before, that, while the Lager are not yet mere "shells" psychologically speaking, it is primarily the organizational components that make the Lager such formidable factors in Austrian politics (e.g., under electoral conditions, when the Lager organizations become powerful instruments of mass political mobilization).

Tables 3 and 4 show the data for two indicators of the impact of politics on individuals' personal lives: respondents' degree of concern about the political like-mindedness of their associates in different social contexts, and their feelings regarding the hypothetical situation of the marriage of a daughter across party lines. In the first case (Table 3) it seems a striking commentary on the alleged level of politicization and partisanship in the Austrian family that a mere one-third of the respondents exhibit any concern at all if members of their own families hold political orientations different from their own, or that 60% report themselves as experiencing no displeasure whatsoever in that event. It is also interesting that 70% do not care at all about their friends' political persuasion; and that over half the respondents do not care if their work colleagues or superiors hold different views (with another one-quarter to one-third having "no answer," perhaps because they have not had occasion or felt the necessity to consider the matter).

Table 4 is also somewhat refutative of the notion of finely honed, highly manifest political partisanship extending even into the personal lives of average Austrian citizens: large percentages of either major party's supporters would view the marriage of their daughter to someone from the opposite party's ranks with indifference. The point is not that there is no evidence of the cumulative impact of group affiliations (e.g., family, religion or occupation, or party); there is. But in Austria today, as in West Germany, concern over the partisan affiliation of one's future son-in-law "is more frequently expressed positively as pleasure over marriage *within* the party

[25]I am greatly indebted to Professors Mildred Schwartz and Frederick C. Engelmann for use of the data discussed in the next few paragraphs.

Table 3.   Degree of concern by respondents in the event that their associates in various milieux would have a political orientation different from the respondents' own, in percentages of total sample (1968)

Type of associates	Degree of concern *					
	High	Sub-stantial	Some	None	Don't know	No answer
Family members	14%	5%	15%	59%	2%	4%
Good friends	5	4	16	69	2	4
Work colleagues	2	2	8	57	3	28
Work supervisors	1	1	5	57	5	31
Sales people	1	1	5	79	6	8
Sports, conversation	1	2	7	77	5	9
Churchgoers	1	1	4	75	6	14

Source: Engelmann-Schwartz Survey. Sample was multistage random probability of 1741 Austrian men and women over 20 years old, April 1968, carried out by the Institut fuer empirische Sozialforschung (IFES, Vienna; Director Karl Blecha).
*Due to rounding, percentages do not always add across rows to 100%.

rather than displeasure over marriage *out* of the party."[26] Only in the case of a Communist entering the family is there a striking variation on the general patterns; whereas three-quarters of the total sample indicate indifference regarding marriage of a daughter to someone supporting the OeVP, SPOe, or FPOe, 40% would experience displeasure and fewer than half, indifference. Perhaps the very contrast between concern over Communists and concern over others illustrates the extent to which the two dominant Lager (at least at the level of public opinion) now *accept* each other *within* the Austrian political system.[27]

[26]Almond and Verba, *The Civic Culture, op. cit.*, p. 137; see more generally pp. 132-139 for a discussion of marriage within and across party lines as an indicator of psychological distance between parties.
    There is a difference between the OeVP and the SPOe; my statement in the text, quoting Almond and Verba on Germany, applies to both Austrian parties but in particular to the OeVP. The Austrian Socialists, on the other hand, come closer to the Italian counterparts who are less often indifferent and more often express displeasure. The Socialist data are quite interesting: as compared with the OeVP data, I would interpret them as reflecting the slower pace of modernization and the still greater prevalence and tenacity of *Lagermentalitaet* to be found on the Austrian Left through the 1960s, most likely as a result of the more comprehensive and more tightly articulated organizational infra-structure of the Socialist Lager (with its greater cumulative "political socialization" impact).
    [27]Anti-communism, despite the tendency of the OeVP's campaign managers and functionaries—whom we shall designate as "middle-level political elites" later on in this analysis—to try "red scare" electoral tactics (by evoking the Popular Front or Austro-Marxist spooks), has been a cornerstone of Austria's limited inter-Lager consensus since World War II. Hence it is not

Table 4. How supporters of major parties would view marriage of daughter within or across party lines in Austria (1968)

Percentage who would feel:	OeVP toward OeVP marriage	OeVP toward SPOe marriage	SPOe toward OeVP marriage	SPOe toward SPOe marriage
Pleased	53%	2%	0%	36%
Displeased	1	19	14	0
Indifferent	43	72	81	62
Other, Don't know, No answer	3	7	5	2
Total Percentage	100%	100%	100%	100%
Total Number	372	372	567	567

Source: Engelmann-Schwartz Survey, as Table 3.

Political attitudes of youth. Austrian youth attitudes merit our special attention: they best reveal the trends in the attitudinal bases of the Lager, and help delineate more sharply the profile of the changing popular arena in which elite-mass electoral campaign interaction unfolds. What is of particular interest, of course, is the degree of concordance between youth and adult attitudes, given the potential significance of any differences for the timing and direction of political change.

Study of both published and unpublished data suggests that basic political orientations and levels of political involvement among Austrian youth differ substantially from those among adults.[28] Thus the younger Austrian is less deeply attached to the given political system and its principal actors. He may agree that Coalition was necessary and extremely useful in the rebuilding of the Austrian state, but he is less certain of its utility for the

---

surprising that 63% of the OeVP supporters would feel displeasure over the prospect of a Communist son-in-law (compared to 19% in the event of a Socialist entering the family), or that 36% of SPOe supporters would feel displeasure at a Communist marriage (compared to 14% at an OeVP marriage).

[28]Highly suggestive data on youth orientations toward the political system have been collected by Karl Blecha; they are partially reported in a series of internal IFES studies, notably "Jugend und Demokratie" (3 parts), 1967, and "Die Jungwaehler des Jahrganges 1945," 1966. Another important but unpublished study is the Austrian Gallup Institute's Survey No. 608 (February and March, 1959). There are several published studies relevant to an understanding of the various kinds of specific and diffuse support accorded the Austrian political system by its younger citizens: see, e.g., Karl Blecha, "Wo steht Oesterreichs Jugend politisch?" *Sozialistische Erzichung* (Oct. 10, 1965), pp. 226-234; Leopold Rosenmayr, *Familienbeziehungen und Freizeitgewohnheiten jugendlicher Arbeiter* (Vienna: Verlag fuer Geschichte und Politik, 1963).

future. He has less knowledge than older persons of the origins of the party system, a weaker image of the current party competitors, and is more attracted to personalities than to programs. If he is a party member, it is likely to be out of pragmatic considerations—it is good insurance "if you want to get ahead in Austria" or if you want an apartment in Vienna.[29]

The younger Austrian is also less intensely involved in political life than are his elders. In an IFES survey conducted just prior to the 1966 parliamentary election, from one-half to three-quarters of first-time voters in four election districts considered themselves less interested in politics than their parents. Only a small proportion of those interviewed reported frequent political discussion.[30] Supportive data have been reported by several commentators; for example, when a representative cross-section of the Austrian population was asked in 1962 (before the parliamentary elections) whether they read newspaper articles dealing with the election, a mere 23% of the youngest voters and just over one-third of those aged 22 to 30 years old said yes, whereas about half of all those over 30 reported reading such articles.[31] And in 1966 the national polling institutes found that indifference to the election outcome was considerably greater among first-time young voters than among any other age group.[32] Earlier data (1956 and 1959[33]) had indicated greater political involvement by youth: for example, it was found that an overwhelming majority considered the right to vote important, and, moreover, that less than half of those under 25 were prepared to state that the mere act of voting fulfilled one's obligation to participate in politics. Obviously, one must be cautious in drawing inferences from such disparate evidence, but scrutiny of unpublished Gallup Poll data suggests a similar waning of political involvement and electoral concern among youth in recent years.[34]

All of the data reported or cited above indicate that the level of politicization may be quite unrelated to continuing segmentation. The former acquires electoral significance when its embers are reignited by ideological fear-evoking election propaganda of party organization cadres and managers who intentionally utilize the organizational bases of segmented pluralism to reinforce partisanship, in order to crystallize, solidify, and mobilize their party's traditional ghetto bloc of voters in the perpetual quest for the 1% to 3% swing that would spell victory and bring appropriate spoils. Otherwise, among broad sectors of the electorate, political involvement (in

[29]Blecha, "Die Jungwaehler," op. cit., pp. 17-21, 38-40.

[30]Ibid., pp. 10-13.

[31]Blecha, "Wo steht Oesterreichs Jugend politisch?" p. 230.

[32]Gmoser, "Herr und Frau Oesterreicher," op. cit., p. 13; Blecha, "Die Jungwaehler," pp. 14-16.

[33]Austrian Gallup Institute (1959) and Dr. Fessel Institute (1956), both op. cit., note 28.

[34]I am indebted to Dr. Fritz Karmasin for the opportunity to review these data at length, and for cooperation in performing various computations at Gallup's Vienna headquarters.

terms of the pervasiveness of partisanship, and in the sense of having political interest, being informed, or talking politics) seems relatively low and is generally decreasing. Politics, in short, seems to have become less salient to the average Austrian.

Indicators of continuing political relevance of the Austrian Lager.   On the other hand, these findings should not obscure the central fact that abundant evidence exists to support the proposition that the Lager remained throughout the Coalition era (and for several years beyond, for most people) the central structural, social, and "cultural" realities affecting the style and patterns of elite-mass political interaction. We have already indicated in the Introduction to this paper, and will demonstrate empirically in Section IV, that the relevance of the Lager "mentality" tenaciously persisted among certain *elites* of both parties. From the perspective of *mass* political culture, there is abundant unpublished data confirming not merely the continuing social and organizational distinctiveness of the Lager, but also pointing to a hard *residuum* of strong subcultural (not merely party) identification coupled with feelings of distrust and apartness between adherents of different Lager.

Based on my familiarity with both published and unpublished survey data for the Coalition period, I would identify at least the following elements as part of the general atmosphere, in the 1960s, of perceiving political affairs in Lager terms.[35] I am *not* arguing that these are analytically part of a Lager psychosis or even necessarily part of what Engelmann called a Lager "mentality." I am, however, reporting, on the basis of considerable field research, that elite *and* mass respondents to interviews themselves identified these features of Austrian politics (in field interviews conducted in 1965-1966 before the collapse of Great Coalition in April 1966) as being—in the words of the last Chancellor of Austria under Great Coalition—"various aspects of a traditional Lager-centered framework for viewing the political world." These features, then, include:

—the widespread tendency to view the SPOe or the OeVP as distinctly class parties, sociologically and ideologically reflective of, and bound to, their own particular ghettos of mutually exclusive support;
—the high degree of organizational membership in both the Socialist and

[35]For an annotated list of political surveys, together with a short sketch of the contents of standard interview schedules and identification of principal sponsors (parties, pressure groups, governmental agencies, individuals), see my "Politische Meinungsforschung in Oesterreich, 1954-1965," in Peter Gerlich, Georg Ress, and Rodney Stiefbold, eds., *Nationalratswahl 1966* (Vienna: Verlag f. Jugend u. Volk/Oesterr. Bundesverlag, 1968), pp. 249-251. I am indebted to the directors of the major polling organizations—and to the clients, the sponsoring organizations—for permitting me at least limited access to many of these data. The directors are Dr. Fritz Karmasin (Gallup-Institut), Dr. Walther Fessel (Fessel-Institut), and Karl Blecha (Institut fuer empirische Socialforschung, IFES), all of Vienna.

Conservative (Catholic) subcultures, the relatively slight electoral fluctuation among social groups or between the major camps, and a level of voting participation which is consistently high even by European standards;

—the long-prevalent notion of so-called equilibrium voters (those voters who, trusting neither side waited to see which party seemed likely to win, then voted for the other in a conscious effort to maintain Black-Red parity), a thesis claiming considerable support by leading authorities on Austrian politics[36] and with some, if inconclusive, empirical underpinning;

—the complaints of Austrian survey research organizations, especially a few years ago, that political distrust and alienation from political life (even among some party members) resulted in high percentages of refusals to state party preference, or to report past party voting;[37]

—and finally, some evidence of political insecurity, in the form of pessimism concerning the outlook for Austria in the event of dissolution of the Great Coalition between OeVP and SPOe.

Summary of findings and implications.   Generally speaking, our analysis of some of the contours of mass opinion in Austria has suggested that the public's broad day-to-day political dispositions are characterized by regime support, considerable pragmatic agreement concerning the jobs of government, political apathy, and a low impact of political partisanship on the individual in his nonpolitical roles—but that Austria's continuing organizational segmentation into Catholic-Conservative and Socialist subcultures is complemented by lingering elements of psychological distrust and apartness. What makes these "lingering elements" significant is the political organizational component of Austrian life: segmented pluralist organizations are a formidable potential instrument of mass political mobilization—particularly, one would suspect, in a relatively unintegrated polity under conditions of an ideological campaign in a close election.

Still, the Austrian electorate in the Coalition era possessed essentially the same political dispositions as "electoral cultures" in much of the rest of Western Europe. Austrians appeared to have a vested interest in the existing system; they did not exhibit a high level of ideological commitment or political interest or involvement, but were concerned chiefly with bread-and-

---

[36] See, e.g., F. C. Engelmann, "Haggling for the Equilibrium: The Renegotiation of the Austrian Coalition, 1959" *American Political Science Review* 56, No. 3 (1962), pp. 657, 662, 653; Kitzinger, *op. cit.*, note 7, p. 120.

[37] This is a general phenomenon, confirmed repeatedly in my interviews of personnel in major and minor survey research institutes, and their clients, throughout Austria. In fact, this was one reason why the OeVP, in frustration over the fact that many of their eventual voters would not describe themselves in surveys as party identifiers, thus complicating party efforts to explore the political culture and policy preferences of its clientele, decided in 1966 to reduce its expenditures for survey research and to rely more extensively on a party and interest group-based organization similar to the SWS on the Socialist side. (Interview, Vienna, June 1966.)

butter issues. No doubt the diffuse support for the status quo and the apparent resistance to open-minded experimentation and innovation restricted the possibilities of change, the extent of disintegration, the magnitude of fluctuation, and the depth of post-election disaffection that might be induced by inflammatory campaign rhetoric; and it condemned splinter parties to insignificance.

III. THE CONDUCT AND CONSEQUENCES OF ELECTION CAMPAIGNS

According to Janowitz and Marvick[38] a truly democratic election ought to promote attitudes of political compromise and further social consensus; this apparently is based on the assumption, shared by Downs,[39] that under conditions of two-party competition, the votes at the center of the political spectrum are decisive in the struggle for power, forcing each of the major contestants to focus its appeals on the uncommitted votes in the middle, halfway between either pole in the system.

But in Austria under Great Coalition, despite some half-hearted steps in the direction of catch-all appeals by parties mindful of changing socio-economic conditions, election campaigns operated somewhat differently.[40] They were not primarily catch-all in character, nor did they contribute to the development of a catch-all national political style. For several reasons—the tiny size of any genuinely "floating" vote, the narrow margin needed to "win" an election, and with it important concessions by the opposing coalition partner, the extremely high level of voter turnout, and the continued perception by campaign elites of Austrian political parties as components of monolithic Lager—election campaigns Austrian-style turned into "scare" exercises in extremist political propaganda and organizational mobilization of the voters. Hence the villains of each successive campaign were Dollfus and clerical-fascism, Austro-Marxism and the hoax of a Communist-Socialist Popular Front, the threatened return of the Habsburgs, and the allegedly invidious intention of the other party to change the rules of Coalition conduct and thus sabotage Coalition work as it was accused of having tried to do in the past.

---

[38]Morris Janowitz and Dwaine Marvick, "Competitive Pressure and Democratic Consent," *Public Opinion Quarterly* 19, (Winter 1955-1956), pp. 381-400.

[39]Anthony Downs, *An Economic Theory of Democracy* (New York: Harper & Row, 1957).

[40]For an analysis, see my forthcoming study of Austrian electoral politics entitled *Segmented Pluralism, Consociational Democracy, and Austrian Electoral Politics: A Theoretical and Empirical Case Study of Austria under Great Coalition, 1945-1966*, esp. chap. 3. My generalizations in these and following paragraphs are based on interviews with campaign elites in Vienna and provincial capitals, 1965-1966, and descriptions of past campaigns in the popular press, on numerous internal memos of the campaign units of the national political party organizations, and on the available scholarly literature.

This "blatant evocation of historical fear,"[41] intended to drive home the urgent necessity for Great Coalition in the fragile Austrian setting—coupled with a sinister warning that electoral victory by the other party could wreck that Coalition—was, of course, designed less to attract floaters or detach and convert potential switchers than it was to mobilize each party's "ghetto vote" —that is, to awaken Lager sentiments and to evoke Lager reflexes among each bloc's apathetic partisans, to eliminate any possibility of dissidence and defection among bloc militants and ideologues, and to get both these groups to the polls on election day.

The impact of elections in a democracy is felt at both mass and elite levels. With respect to the mass level in Austria under Great Coalition, there do exist some (still classified) survey data which suggest that the *effect* of election campaigns corresponded closely to campaign elites' *intent* of recrystallizing and reinforcing distinct lines of social, organizational, and attitudinal cleavages between the "red" SPOe and the black" OeVP subcultures. But most of the extant published materials (and most of the still classified data) point to little more than a kind of "pulsation" of the system of social cleavages as a result of campaign stimuli, i.e., to the normal but temporary increase in intergroup awareness and apartness which one probably finds in any electoral democracy;[42] there is no evidence that these pulsation effects had deleterious long-term consequences at the mass level.

On the other hand, elite *perceptions* of the mass-level impact of elections contrast sharply with the above picture. Detailed interviews which my associates and I conducted with 131 Nationalrat deputies elected in 1966, and with public opinion pollsters, campaign staffs, and campaign managers of both major political parties, indicate clearly that—at least in the opinion of these elites—(1) the campaign exacerbated Austria's subcultural cleavages; and (2) these cleavages were in any case "durable constants on the Austrian political scene." In short, Austria still remained, in the eyes of her electoral elites, very much a conflict society," polarized, politicized, partisan, and ideological at the non-elite level. My interviews suggest further that the reason for this apparent misperception of mass political culture is to be found in the interlocking of three factors: First, the slide-rule faithfulness with which election outcomes were translated into periodic revisions of the inter-Lager balance of Coalition power placed a high premium on achieving incremental gains and avoiding incremental losses. Second, the easiest and safest way of accomplishing these ends (given the small number of potential "floating voters") was to be more efficient in mobilizing "your" Lager adherents than your opponent was in mobilizing "his" Lager adherents. Third, the "conflict society" perceptions harbored by those elites who were

---

[41]Kitzinger, *op. cit.*, note 7, *passim.*
[42]See Bernard Berelson *et al.*, *Voting* (Chicago: University of Chicago Press, 1954), p. 144, for a classic statement.

responsible for the conduct of election campaigns were nurtured by self-serving public opinion pollsters who emphasized in their written (and especially in their oral) briefings of these elites throughout the campaign *those data which indicated that the more highly politicized components of the electorate were reacting to the campaign with increasing feelings of insecurity, apprehension, and subcultural distinctiveness.* Thus the chain of electoral interaction seems clear: deliberate elite politicization of the masses, selective perception by the elite that such is the true state of the masses, and consequently reinforcement of the elites' previous views and "validation" of its previous efforts. At this point in our analysis therefore it appears plausible to argue that the electoral process under Great Coalition may have served basically to reinforce traditional features of Austrian politics; and that misperceptions by elites, or some elites, may have artificially prolonged the life of crisis-consociational rule beyond any "objective" necessity (in the sense that the data we have presented do not support the notion that Austria was really a "conflict society" in need of crisis-consociational rule; at most these data suggest a certain cultural and organizational hangover from an earlier era).

Italian political scientist Giovanni Sartori has argued, in a persuasive line of reasoning followed by such other contemporary scholars as Samuel Barnes and Giuseppe Di Palma, that mass political beliefs are part of the basic raw material of political democracy, a limiting or constraining factor but not a determinant one in structuring the behavior of political elites.[43] Both published and unpublished Austrian data from the Coalition era, some of them reviewed above, appear to underscore the limited explanatory power of mass political beliefs in describing or predicting political outcomes in the Austrian variant of Western industrial society. In fact, one might argue, they carry us a step further, suggesting that it is elites' *perceptions* of mass belief systems—rather than the mass belief systems themselves—that are ultimately most important in determining whatever influence mass publics have in policy formulation, review, or control via electoral and other political processes. Thus, in a peaceful and affluent context, which we might expect would encourage the competing political parties to devote their efforts to catch-all electoral tactics, we find instead that campaigning has as virulent an "ideological" edge as can be found in contemporary Europe. Furthermore, despite apparent public satisfaction with the Coalition regime, a survey of electoral outcomes during the Coalition era would show that substantial costs were exacted at the elite level by the electoral process, often including long post-election periods of decisional ineffectiveness while laborious efforts were made to recreate a minimal pool of interelite trust,

[43]Giovanni Sartori, *Democratic Theory* (New York: Frederick A. Praeger, 1965), pp. 78-79 and chaps. V and VI, *passim;* Barnes, "Ideology and the Organization of Conflict," *op. cit..* p. 530; and especially Giuseppe Di Palma, *Apathy and Participation: Mass Politics in Western Societies* (New York: Free Press, 1970), *passim.*

renegotiate the Coalition, and find a common set of programmatic goals which might allow a new Government to get moving forward again.

Obviously we have not resolved these seeming paradoxes in the Austrian case by examining political culture and public opinion data at the mass level. While that examination does now provide us with some clues as to why the Austrian system survived the change of regime from Coalition to Government-and-Opposition in 1966 with little or no mass-level disruption, it is still not at all clear why crisis-consociational rule *persisted so long* but was then *transformed so easily* at the elite level. What prevented a growth of mutual trust and confidence between the Lager in political spheres, when those commodities seemed abundantly available in arenas dominated by interest groups and chambers? Why was the original, 1945-based crisis-consociational rule not "self-devouring" under conditions of peace, prosperity, and prolonged political stability?

In the next section we shall seek answers to these questions. However, we shall first review some of the principal features of the mildly authoritarian and elitist model of "consociational" democracy proposed by Arend Lijphart as a viable alternative in divided societies to prevailing competitive and pluralistic models of democratic politics and government. Then we shall turn to an examination of pertinent Austrian data on elite opinion structure, role differentiation, and both inter- and intra-Lager communication patterns. Armed with the information and insights thus provided, and having appraised their consequences, we can then focus on the complicated problem of persistence and change in consociational democracy, and in so doing raise some broader questions of political development theory as well.

IV. ELITE OPINION STRUCTURE

The keystone in Lijphart's analysis of consociational democracy is the role played by political elites in the face of fragmented political cultures in trying to neutralize whatever immobilist or destabilizing tendencies might exist. For Lijphart, the elites cannot afford to behave ideologically, or at least not toward each other. Instead, consociational elites must be able to recognize the dangers inherent in a fragmented system, must be committed personally to the system's maintenance, must be able to transcend the divisive subcultural cleavages at the elite level, and must be able to forge appropriate solutions for the demands of the subcultures (by developing institutional arrangements and specific rules of the game for the accommodation of differences). If the leaders of the rival subcultures lack any one of these four "behavioral" attributes the system will not work: they are the prerequisites for consociational democracy.[44]

---

[44]Lijphart's summary of these propositions is found in "Typologies of Democratic Systems," *op. cit.*, pp. 24-25, and "Consociational Democracy," *op. cit.*, p. 216.

If the first brick in the structure of consociational democracy is interelite behavior at the top of the political system across subcultures, the second is the relationship between elites and masses within the same subculture. Thus, subcultures must remain as mutually exclusive as possible: there must be distinct lines of cleavage (sociologically and organizationally) between subcultures, which will be further enhanced if masses are psychologically committed to their subcultures, if they evince high partisanship.[45]

The success of the consociational venture will ultimately depend not only on the establishment of fruitful interelite cooperation, but also on the retention of the support and loyalty of the separate subcultures; elites must be more tolerant than followers, yet able to carry them along. Thus while the key features of consociational democracy are conciliatory intentions, attitudes, and behavior of subcultural elites, Lijphart does not discard the premise of direct linkage between political culture and system performance: for the politics of accommodation to work effectively, subcultural elites must be secure in their positions of leadership and relatively unencumbered by intraparty directives. And this combination of elite security and autonomy depends in turn on a particular admixture of mass-level attributes—namely, on the sociological distinctiveness, firm partisan attachment, and organizational mobilizability of separate groups of followers, or subcultures, combined with intrasubcultural attitudes of deference toward incumbent leaders and substantial diffuse support by all non-elites of the regime of government by elite cartel.[46] The detailed model is summarized in Table 5.

The Lijphart model is an intriguing explanation for the apparent success that such divided societies as Austria or The Netherlands have had in achieving and maintaining stable, effective, and legitimate political regimes under consociational elite rule. Nonetheless, several troublesome problems remain unresolved in Lijphart's model. Two of these are particularly thorny, yet vitally important: the dynamics of elite-mass interaction in consociational democracies, and how, once established, consociational

---

[45]*Ibid.*, pp. 26-27; cf. pp. 36-37. The question of degree of partisanship is somewhat unclear, since Lijphart apparently uses "fragmentation" at various points in his essay to apply to at least four distinct possible features of segmented pluralist societies: the social distinctiveness of subcultures and patterns of organizational affiliation, levels of intensity or politization, and degree of divergence of ideological positions. This is also a slight ambiguity: are followers "masses" in the sense of all supporters of a given Lager, or are they more highly politicized components of it, or are they a very particular organized component of it?

[46]Strictly speaking, Lijphart differentiates between the previously enumerated "behavioral" characteristics of elites, which he calls "essential," and the mass-level attributes and elite-level consequences just enumerated, which in his various analyses are labeled "facilitating conditions." It takes little effort to realize that the "essential" conditions can be met only when the mass-level attributes discussed here are also present. For a critical theoretical discussion and elaboration of these points, see my book, *Elites and Elections in a Fragmented Political System* (forthcoming), especially chap. 4 and 5; and Stiefbold, *Austrian Electoral Politics . . . , op cit.* [in footnote 40], esp. chaps. 1, 5, 6, and 7.

Table 5. The consociational democracy model: a clarification of the basic propositions and relationships

---

I. REQUIRED CONDITIONS FOR THE ESTABLISHMENT AND PERSISTENCE
OF THE REGIME OF CONSOCIATIONAL DEMOCRACY

   A. ELITE- and REGIME-Level Conditions

      1. Ability of subcultural elites to recognize the potential dangers of political fragmentation (because of prior personal experience or by having a capacity to learn from history).

      2. General conflict-avoidance role culture ("operational code"), based on elites' conciliatory political intentions and attitudes and on their commitment to maintenance of the system.

      3. Top subcultural elites' autonomy and security—i.e., their structured dominance and virtual impregnability within their subcultures. These two attributes are themselves dependent on the presence of four mass-level attributes: subcultural distinctiveness and mobilizability, intra-bloc deference to elite authority, and cross-bloc diffuse support of the regime.

      4. A level of "institutionalization" sufficient to maintain a favorable balance between system capabilities and system loads. By institutionalization in this context is meant: (a) new decision-making arenas (sites); (b) specific new procedural rules of the game; (c) the development of inter-elite and elite-mass interaction norms which stress purposive depoliticization and restrained partisanship; and (d) growing convergence between those behavioral norms and elites' actual political style. The latter means minimizing non-institutionalized RCB [rancorous conflictual behavior], i.e., avoiding public ideological posturing between subcultural elites, or vis-a-vis the mass publics.

      5. Successful conflict regulation in some problem- or issue-area, in order to achieve the benefits of the "demonstration effect," that is, reinforcement of elite motives and incentives to continue the behavior which achieved the success, and reinforcement of popular approbation and support.

   B. MASS-Level Conditions

      1. *Subcultural distinctiveness.* There are two dimensions here: (a) high degree of social distinctiveness of political groups, and (b) high political cohesion of social groups.

      2. *Organizational encadrement and mobilizability.* "Segmented pluralist" pattern of vertically structured secondary organization *(verzuiling)*, characterized by: (a) high organizational density in multiple spheres of activity (social, economic, cultural, political); (b) high overall rates of individual memberships in secondary organizations; (c) the cumulative patterning (i.e., superimposed, not crosscutting) of these individual group affiliations; and (d) the oligarchical dominance of secondary organizations by their elites and the pyramiding of these elites' authority to—and through— the extended organizational apparatus of a mass political party astride their subculture.

      3. *Deference.* Acceptance by nonelites of a highly subordinate and essentially inefficacious political position within their partisan elite-dominated subculture. This deference is conditioned by (a) generally acquiescent attitudes to political authority; (b) substantial depoliticization (including a low level of spontaneous political interest or participation, and low emotional intensity); (c) a clear and durable sense of partisan self-identity with one's "own" subculture; (d) a relatively low level of residual (but generally latent) inter-bloc partisan hostility.

      4. *Diffuse support* of the consociational political regime, i.e., a high level of non-particularized and non-output-oriented mass support, regardless of subcultural affiliation or identification, for regime values, norms, and structures. (This depolarization vis-a-vis the regime itself does not necessarily imply a diminution of inter-bloc conflicts-of-interest in terms of preferred policy outcomes on specific public issues; issue cleavages may persist, but there is "basic consensus" or "agreement on fundamentals.")

II. FACILITATING CONDITIONS FOR ESTABLISHMENT AND PERSISTENCE
OF THE REGIME OF CONSOCIATIONAL DEMOCRACY

   A. There should be *multipolarity* (a multiple balance of power among the subcultures).

   B. There should be an *external threat* to the existence or nature of the political system.

   C. There should be *moderate nationalism,* i.e., at least a minimum level of cultural integration.

   D. There should be a relatively *low total load* on the system.

---

regimes are sustained, modified, or transformed. High partisanship, reinforced by ideological posturing of elites within their subcultures,[47] is apparently useful at the intrasubcultural level to help maintain the organizational and sociological distinctiveness and cohesion of separated subcultures; but the elite cartel system of decision-making depends also on substantial mass support and avoidance of destabilizing mass involvement which ideological posturing by elites might produce.[48] Do elites in consociational democracies behave both ways? at different times? for different purposes? No answers are supplied.

Just as Lijphart does not concern himself with the precise linking mechanisms which operate between the level of individuals and groups and the level of elite behavior and system performance, he likewise leaves unresolved the question of how crisis-consociational regimes evolve, although he is quite explicit about the probable outcomes of such evolution in Europe. Lijphart apparently believes that prevailing Western European conditions of prosperity, peace, and the growth of public planning at national and pan-European levels will lead increasingly toward an altogether different type of democratic regime: the "depoliticized democracy," in which consociational practices will reflect consensus rather than cleavage. He foresees a direct and linear evolution in which growing, Europe-wide "depoliticization" and "deideologisation" of mass publics will reduce fragmentation, which in turn will reduce the need for resorting to elite-imposed "crisis"-consociational practices. At the same time these changes at the mass level will allow development of "natural" consociational practices based on the growth of functional interdependence of groups in society and on a correspondingly increased reliance on "normal" patterns of industrial society decision-making which emphasize the interaction of bureaucratic and interest-group elites.[49] But we still do not know how—by what linking mechanism or process—a politics of stable suspicion among a cartel of

---

[47]Lijphart, *The Politics of Accommodation, op. cit.,* p. 144; p. 141.

[48]*Ibid.,* chap. VII, "The Rules of the Game." See also my discussion in Part I above on "Elections, Ideology, and Consociational Democracy," and the references there to Lijphart's articles (cited in footnote 5).

[49]Lijphart, "Typologies," *op. cit.,* pp. 27, 28, 32, and 35 ff. The assumption here, of course, is that all advanced industrial societies, at least democratic ones, manifest increased consociationalism as a result of their increased reliance on patterns of decision-making which emphasize the interaction of bureaucratic and interest-group elites. Focusing on Western Europe as a whole Di Palma and Stiefbold have provisionally identified the more important general "rules of the game," which hold for consociational democracies as well: see our "Conflict and Elites in Western Industrial Societies: A Theoretical Reassessment and a Proposal," unpublished paper (Berkeley: Department of Political Science, and Faculty Committee for the Study of Industrial Societies, 1969), and Di Palma's Project Description: Political Conflict and Conflict Regulation in Western European Societies" (Berkeley: Department of Political Science, 1968, mimeo).

subcultural elites gets transformed into a politics of trust among those same elites; nor, conversely, do we know, from Lijphart's analysis, by what mechanisms such evolution is prevented. Again, if we are to go beyond mere description, beyond a mere snapshot of political regimes at one point in time and at a later point in time, we must focus on the dynamics of elite and mass interaction which facilitate or impede change in the locus and pattern of decision-making.

Empirical data suggest that elite-mass interaction in many countries, particularly under electoral circumstances, is characterized by considerable acerbity and ideologism. Moreover, an accumulating body of empirical evidence suggests "that the belief systems of mass publics seldom exhibit constraints among elements, and that elites are the hosts of ideologies," as Barnes observes.[50] Thus, McClosky et al. found that "whereas leaders of the two (American) parties diverge strongly, their followers differ only moderately in their attitudes toward issues"; that it is more accurate to assert "that the natural cleavages between the leaders are largely ignored by their followers"; and that leaders (compared to the great mass of their supporters) are more articulate, informed, and highly partisan.[51] And the data reported by Converse and Dupeux[52] for the French electorate and by Duncan MacRae, Jr.[53] for French legislators also support the primary notion that polarization of political opinion is more pronounced at the elite level, as well as the concomitant notion that polarization of public opinion seems to be, to a considerable degree, an elite-induced phenomenon. In stable and legitimate political systems, this may not pose a problem to system stability, since these elites are also likely to be highly committed to the given regime and more tolerant and more accepting of democratic norms than those whom they lead.[54] But in a subculturally divided society, political elites, according to Gabriel Almond, tend to exhibit a "general alienation from the political market. . . . The political actors come to the market not to exchange, compromise, and adapt, but to preach, exhort, convert, and transform the political system. . . ."[55]

In short, neither traditional empirical democratic theory of the Almond

---

[50] Barnes, "Ideology and the Organization of Conflict," *op. cit.*, p. 522 [p. 417 in this book]. See also Philip Converse's superb article, "The Nature of Belief Systems in Mass Publics," in *Ideology and Discontent*, ed. David Apter (New York: The Free Press, 1964), pp. 206-261.

[51] Herbert McClosky *et al.*, "Issue Conflict and Consensus among Party Leaders and Followers," *American Political Science Review* 58 (June 1964), pp. 372-373.

[52] Philip E. Converse and Georges Dupeux, "Politicization of the Electorate in France and the United States," *Public Opinion Quarterly* 26 (Spring 1962), reprinted in Angus Campbell *et al.*, *Elections and the Political Order* (New York: Wiley, 1966), pp. 269-291.

[53] Duncan MacRae, Jr., *Parliament, Parties, and Society in France 1946-1958* (New York: St. Martin's Press, 1967), *passim*, and pp. 326ff. and 333ff. especially.

[54] See, e.g., Almond and Verba, *The Civic Culture, op. cit.*, pp. 486-487.

[55] Almond, "Comparative Political Systems," *op. cit.*, p. 407.

variety, nor the leaders-followers data that can be adduced from various empirical studies make credible Lijphart's depoliticized, pragmatic, and cooperative "consociational" elites, especially in fragmented societies. But Lijphart's examples of functioning consociational democracies also refute the claim that polities with fragmented political cultures are inherently immobilist and unstable at least in part because of the recruitment and socialization experiences, and consequent political behavior, of subcultural elites. Particularly baffling is the case of Austria—which Engelmann specifically identifies as an example of the kind of "Continental European" system that Almond was ostensibly describing[56]—where the observer can find ample evidence of both ideological behavior by elites, with polarizing and destabilizing consequences, and of consociational behavior with its stabilizing and integrating consequences.

The difficulties of meshing the two possible interpretations of subcultural elites as assets or obstacles to political stability would appear to lie in the specific *level* of elites that we are talking about. It is at this point that an important insight from Karl Deutsch concerning "the decisive 'middle level' of communication and decision" becomes relevant:

> The strategic "middle level" . . . is that level of communication and command that is "vertically" close enough to the large mass of . . . citizens . . . to forestall any continuing and effective direct communication between them and the "highest echelons": and it must be far enough above the level of the large numbers of the rank and file to permit effective "horizontal" communication and organization . . . on its own level.[57]

In Deutsch's words, these are persons who "usually received very little publicity." They are the "men behind the scenes" in the sense that they are the "men who do the work of making, permitting, and executing the largest number of strategic decisions" (p. 156). Admittedly, the concept of middle-level elites is difficult to operationalize. Deutsch himself quickly decides that the group he is really concerned with—in the government, parties, mass media, armed forces, and pressure groups—is best characterized as *"upper middle level"* (p. 155; italics mine). Obviously, middle or upper middle level in these various contexts encompasses a very broad range of levels and types of elite roles which for theoretical clarity and empirical utility need to be rigorously distinguished from each other.

Unfortunately, there is not a very systematic, empirically based literature on middle-level elites or on intra-elite relationships. As Dwaine Marvick has pointed out, in modern theory about political systems, two components—top elites and mass publics—receive most of the attention; what is

---

[56] Engelmann, "Haggling for the Equilibrium," *op. cit.,* p. 662.

[57] Karl W. Deutsch, *The Nerves of Government: Models of Political Communication and Control* (New York: The Free Press, 1963), p. 154 and more generally pp. 154-157.

largely missing is behavioral evidence of how the interstitial components, the cadres, or middlemen of politics, do function, why, and with what consequences.[58] Hence, much of the real process and motivation of political and socioeconomic decision-making still remains relatively obscure for most political systems. Nonetheless, there is a sufficient core of studies to suggest, as Marvick does in his excellent summary of the available literature, that cadres, or middle-level elites, are key units in explaining top elite behavior, for a number of reasons:

> Top elites depend upon, often derive from, and not infrequently are coerced by those who may be called middlemen, or cadres; top elite deliberation is routinely shaped by cadres; top elite survival and success are commonly dependent upon cadres.[59]

Thus we might hypothesize, for example, that in any given political system elite acceptance and practice of the "new" politics of collective bargaining and pragmatic adjustment in decision-making,[60] or of "catch-all" electoral strategies, will depend on the type of elite role differentiation, the nature of elite recruitment and role socialization, and the communications and other relevant linkages among roles which obtain in that society.

In keeping with the Deutsch-Marvick thesis concerning the decisive significance of middlemen in communication and decision structures— and with a frequently observed distinction, as for example in Haas' formulation, between elites whose aims and behavioral style are "dramatic-political" and those whose aims and style Haas characterizes as "incremental-economic" (pragmatic, oriented to bargaining over largely technical economic issues)[61]—we posit a trio of principal elite roles which will be found in all national political systems. These are: (1) *top elites* who share major responsibility for overall system stability and regime performance and in whom is vested major decision-making authority; (2) party organization cadres, or *"partisans,"* whose tasks include making daily partisan

---

[58]Dwaine Marvick, "The Middlemen of Politics," *Approaches to the Study of Party Organization,* ed. William Crotty (Boston: Allyn and Bacon, 1968), p. 341.

[59]*Ibid.,* pp. 343-44. Marvick summarizes also the various meanings of such terms as "elite" and "cadre," and identifies a number of key research areas for both inter- and intra-elite analysis. For a similar effort to map what we know of top elites, see Lewis J. Edinger, "Political Science and Political Biography: Reflections on the Study of Leadership," *Journal of Politics* 26 (1964), pp. 648-675, and the "Introduction" to his edited volume, *Political Leadership in Industrialized Societies: Studies in Comparative Analysis* (New York: Wiley, 1967).

[60]See Robert A. Dahl's description, "Epilogue" to his *Political Oppositions in Western Democracies, op. cit.* Cf. also Di Palma and Stiefbold, "Conflict and Elites," *op. cit. passim.* The next few paragraphs draw on Di Palma's and my formulations in this paper, and on the discussions in the graduate seminar on conflict regulation in Western Europe which we jointly taught at Berkely in the Spring Quarter, 1969.

[61]Ernst B. Haas, "The 'Uniting of Europe' and the Uniting of Latin America," *Journal of Common Market Studies* 5 (June 1967), pp. 328-329. Obviously not all real life political or

propaganda and conducting election campaigns and whose deep ideological or philosophical commitment leads them to issue threats, demands, and emotional appeals on behalf of their party and its programs; and (3) interest group, chamber, media, and bureaucratic elites, or *"technocrats,"* who are responsible for day-to-day operation of major socioeconomic, governmental, and cultural institutions, and who practice the politics of "distributive bargaining," rendering decisions by the process of incremental adjustment, by engaging in pragmatic give-and-take with their counterparts in related organizational-elite roles.

In general terms, the principal hypothesis relating system or regime performance to elite role structure is simply this: the more partisan elites place constraints on the personal values, organizational role definitions, and decisional autonomy of top political and governmental elites, and on their communications with nonpartisan technocratic elites pursuing "incremental-economic" goals, the greater will be the strains upon accommodationist and bargaining politics, and hence the greater the total "load" on the political regime.

Linked to this master hypothesis are a number of subsidiary assumptions and hypotheses. Thus, for example, we should expect to find that accommodationist attitudes and bargaining behavior will be most widespread at the upper level of elites (i.e., among the consociational top elites in a country like Austria). The organizational roles of these individuals are likely to expose them to the interests of diverse groups within the society, and their constituencies (clienteles) are more likely to be heterogeneous than those of lower-level elite members. We also hypothesize that partisan elites are less likely than governmental or technocratic elites to embrace the politics of accommodation and sacrifice traditional ideological views. Party leaders have an organization to maintain, and ideological appeals are likely to solidify the support of rank-and-file party activists. In addition, party leaders below the top level are more likely to interact with like-minded individuals. Their environment is probably politically homogeneous and the communicative stimuli to which they are exposed therefore reinforce ideological attitudes. Because top elites require the allegiance of the party organizations in order to mobilize support for policies or at election time, the impact of partisan elites on top elite attitudes and behavior may occa-

---

economic actors can be so neatly classified, since in any given issue area the dramatic-political and incremental-economic distinction may well be ranged along a continuum in the same plane. Nonetheless, I would maintain that if measurement problems are properly and carefully dealt with, most real life actors could be classified as more nearly corresponding to the one or the other of these analytical distinctions. Finally, on the politics of "distributive bargaining" see Richard E. Walton and Robert B. McKersie, *A Behavioral Theory of Labor Negotiations: An Analysis of a Social Interaction System* (New York: McGraw-Hill, 1965), especially chap. II.

sionally be severe, leading under some circumstances to a possible reduction in consensus at this higher level—especially among those upper-level elites whose early careers had exposed them chiefly to party organization needs which socialized them to perceive the world through a systematically distorted partisan lens.[62]

The hypotheses advanced in this brief discussion become particularly problematic in "segmented pluralist" societies where rigid patterns of elite and activist recruitment and socialization through mutually exclusive organizational and associational channels may impose great *de facto* burdens on the day-to-day operational freedom of top decision-making elites. Despite commitment of these top elites to consociational politics, the historically derived structures of cleavage and access to the political market retain their relevance.[63]

Even if objective cleavages and inequalities decline and policy differences become attenuated, partisan organizations preserve many of their subcultural features; hence the significance of Barnes' argument for researching ideology in its organizational context. He writes: "The important question, What is the impact of the ideological preferences of elites on the goals of their political organizations? is often asked. But this is only half of the relationship. The opposite but related question is of at least equal significance: What is the impact of political organization on the ideologies of the elites?"[64] Almond and Verba make a corrolary point concerning the significance of different elite "role cultures" to the operation of democracy. They argue that "elite attitudes may be characterized by cultural heterogeneity, and thus 'seriously affect the performance of political systems,' if 'the elites are recruited from particular subcultures' or if 'the process of induction and socialization into these roles produces different values, skills, loyalties, and cognitive maps.' "[65]

---

[62]These functions of party organizations are stressed by many writers, few so forcefully as Barnes, "Ideology and the Organization of Conflict," *op. cit.,* esp. pp. 521-524 [pp. 416-419 in this book]; see also the literature cited there. Dwaine Marvick has written persuasively on these matters in "Communications in Political Parties," *Handbook of Communication,* ed. W. Schramm, I. Pool, *et al.,* esp. pp. 341-357. The "distorted partisan lens" idea is also treated in Murray Edelman's insightful essay "Myths, Metaphors and Political Conformity," *Psychiatry* (Aug. 1967), pp. 217-228.

[63]Among scores of studies which emphasize the points in this paragraph, see *inter alia:* William A. Gamson, *Power and Discontent* (Homewood, Ill.,: The Dorsey Press, 1968); G. Bingham Powell, Jr., *Social Fragmentation and Political Hostility: An Austrian Case Study.* (Stanford: Stanford University Press, 1971); Leon N. Lindberg, *Europe as a Political System: Measuring Political Integration* (unpublished manuscript, Center for International Affairs, Harvard University, April 1967); Walton and McKersie, *A Behavioral Theory of Labor Negotiations, op. cit.,* and Samuel P. Huntington, *Political Order in Changing Societies* (New Haven: Yale University Press, 1968).

[64]Barnes, "Ideology and the Organization of Conflict," *op. cit.,* p. 520 [p. 417 in this book].

[65]Lijphart, "Typologies," *op. cit.,* p. 32, quoting Almond and Verba, *The Civic Culture, op. cit.,* pp. 29-30.

If the top elites are recruited through socioeconomic organizations (e.g., major interest groups and chambers), they may already be socialized to a type of elite "role culture" which combines emphasis on a set of strict procedural rules with a set of general conflict-avoidance orientations by rival parties to a bargaining situation. They are used to practicing a politics of incremental adjustment of divergent policy positions, a process which allows decision-makers to proceed as soon as they agree on *what* needs to be done, even if they do not fully agree on *why* it needs to be done or on what specific *outcomes* are being sought.[66] On the other hand, if top elites are recruited from political party organization jobs in the political subcultures, they are likely to continue to share with middle-level partisan elites similar attitudes and perceptions and to respond with special attention to cues emanating from them, especially under circumstances (e.g., elections) which emphasize "political" as opposed to "technocratic" goals. But both the professional role and life-style situation of such medium-level party officials is one of substantial partisan isolation, coupled with distrust and distorted perception of the opposition parties. As Frank Pinner suggests, explicitly partisan organizations can thus become "powerful blockages to the free flow of information" from elite to mass and mass to elite; and under highly politicized circumstances, medium-level party officials may come to have extraordinary influence. "They may prevent or fail to transmit unorthodox thought at the organization's base," and they may give top elites "the impression that, in order to keep the confidence" of their rank and file membership, "they must at all cost avoid too close an association with their opposite numbers in the other party" or subculture.[67]

To paraphrase a remarkable recent study of hostile behavior among foreign-policy decision-makers,[68] a world perceived as hostile and threatening could urge a decision-maker to opt for an aggressive move in the face of a political crisis; he might be led by his perception, as filtered through middle-level elites, to believe that he must strike before being struck—that he must engage in publically dramatic rancorous or even disruptive political behavior, lest such prior behavior by elites of the other side place him at a disadvantage. In short, an important, perhaps critical area for research must be the perceptual framework of the strategic elites in divided societies. The opportunities afforded by election processes for mass political mobilization, and the dependence for political stability in countries like

[66]For data and theory on the pragmatic decision-making process in western democracies, see Lindblom, *The Intelligence of Democracy, op. cit.;* Walton and McKersie, *A Behavioral Theory of Labor Negotiations, op. cit.;* David Braybrooke and Charles E. Lindblom, *A Strategy of Decision* (Glencoe: The Free Press, 1963); and Ralf Dahrendorf, *Class and Class Conflict in Industrial Society* (Stanford: Stanford University Press, 1959), chap. 6.

[67]Pinner, "On the Structure of Organizations and Beliefs," *op. cit.,* pp. 20 ff.

[68]Dina A. Zinnes, "A Comparison of Hostile Behavior of Decision-Makers in Simulate and Historical Data," *World Politics* 18 (1966), pp. 474-499, esp. p. 474.

Austria on complex patterns of elite behavior, make the nexus between elite perceptions and behavior under electoral circumstances a critical one for students of political life in divided societies.

Just how useful these insights are in helping us to achieve a more multivariate (and more accurate) understanding of elite opinion structure and elite-mass interaction in a consociational democracy becomes clear when we consider Lijphart's formulations in the light of our empirical case study of Austrian national elites.

Data on Austrian Elites

The data reported below were collected in conjunction with the author's study of electoral politics and the dynamics of elite and mass compromise and dissent in postwar Austria, and in conjunction with the Smaller European Democracies Austria Project directed by the author.[69] The interview data discussed here or reported in tabular form all derive from an original elite sample of 450 persons chosen as respondents on the basis of their reputational and positional characteristics with respect to national political or social and economic policy-making. (Some local and provincial elites were included on the basis of their national decision-making relevance and influence, as judged by fellow decision-makers and or by established scholars and experts on Austrian politics.)

The three hundred persons who were eventually interviewed—most of the 150 who were not interviewed explicitly refused—include 112 members of the Austrian Nationalrat (Lower House of Parliament), 50 officials of the two major parties, 40 officials of the chambers and chief interest groups, 15 high-ranking federal civil servants, 40 officials of local and provincial governments, 20 academic personnel or other "outside consultants" serving as political advisors to one of the two major political parties at the time of the interview, and 23 important personal staff assistants serving higher officials in governmental, party, and chamber or interest group positions. Many of these individuals, who were first interviewed in 1965-1966 just prior to the universally unanticipated collapse of Great Coalition in April 1966 following

[69]My primary debt in structuring this research is to my former mentor and friend at Columbia, the late Otto Kirchheimer, under whose direction I began the "electoral politics/ elite/mass" project, and with whom I was collaborating on the Smaller European Democracies—Austria project. I am also indebted to Professor Dwaine Marvick of UCLA for many suggestions and for intellectual support during the period in which I was directing the Survey of Austrian National Elites (frequently cited by the acronym S.A.N.E.). The following is only a very brief description of the composition of the elite respondents in the S.A.N.E. interviews. The research design, procedures, and various methodological considerations are thoroughly discussed in my study Austrian Electoral Politics (see note 40). Only a small fraction of the data are reported or discussed in this paper.

Table 6.   Some distributions of "pragmatism" and "ideologism" among middle-level elites in divergent organizational milieux, by selected issue areas (SANE Interviews, 1965-1966)

Issue Area	Social-Economic Elites (chambers int. gps.) n = 90			Political Elites (party organiz.) n=75		
	Responses to questions concerning issue area in column at left were predominantly [a]:					
	I	E	P	I	E	P
1. Social-Economic[b]		+	+ +	+ +	+	
2. Political style and Performance[c]	+ +	+		+	+ +	
3. Foreign Policy[d]		+	+ +	+ +	+	
4. Social-Cultural and Symbolic[e]	+ +	+		+ +	+	

Source: The patterns reported in this table are based on data derived from depth interviews with 90 middle-level decision-makers in the major social-economic organizations (the three chambers, the Union of Austrian Industrialists and the Trade Union Federation), and 75 in the two major political parties (Socialist, SPOe; Conservative, OeVP). See text for discussion of original sample components. We arrived at these "middle-elite" subsamples by eliminating from the total SANE sample (N=300) the 30 respondents ascribed to the "top elite" category; 22 of the 112 Nationalrat deputies interviewed by us and identified by us as not owing primary occupational allegiance to a political party, interest group, or chamber; the 40 nationally prominent "local and provincial" elites interviewed by us; the 20 special consultants and the 23 special assistants to other SANE respondents.

Notes:

[a] These coding categories—I, ideological; E, eclectic; P, pragmatic—are derived from Ulf Himmelstrand, "A Theoretical and Empirical Approach to Depoliticization and Political Involvement, *Acta Sociologica* 6, Fasc. 1-2 (1962, Special issue on "Approaches to the Study of Political Participation," ed. Stein Rokkan), pp. 83-110. A single plus sign (+) means at least one-third of the responses in the total sample (including both Lager) fell into that cell of the table. A double plus sign (++) means that from one-half to two-thirds of the responses were allocated to that cell by the interviewers. Interviewer scoring was on the basis of Austrian phrases and words used most frequently to define the opposing party's position on an issue or to contrast the two parties' positions.

[b] *Social-Economic Issues:* (1) Wage-price problems. (2) Fiscal problems. (3) Housing problems. (4) Collectivism (e.g., operation of the nationalized industries complex).

[c] *Political Issues:* (1) Necessity for coalition. (2) Internal coalition strains and evaluation of coalition performance. (3) Questions of leadership succession and intra-Lager leadership conflicts. (4) Current or past public scandals.

[d] *Foreign Policy Issues:* (1) EEC association. (2) Closer E. Europe ties. (3) "Neutrality." (4) South Tyrol.

[e] *Cultural and Symbolic Issues:* (1) Mass media organization. (2) The Past: Habsburg, Nazism. (3) Church-State relations. (4) Educational reform.

Table 7. Relative rankings of three elite "role" groups by average frequency of "pragmatic" responses to questions concerning various dimensions of the political culture attributes of "polarity" and "politicization" (SANE, 1965-1966)

Attribute	Top Elites (N= 30)	Middle Level Socio-economic, or "Techno-crats" (N= 90)	Middle Level Political, or "Partisans" (N= 75)
Polarity			
1. Re. the consociational coalition regime itself	2nd	1st	3rd
2. Re. Issue Areas:			
—Social-Economic Issues	2nd	1st	3rd
—Political Issues	3rd	1st	2nd
—Foreign Policy Issues	2nd	1st	3rd
—Cultural and Symbolic Issues	(2nd)	(2nd)	3rd
Politicization			
1. Basic approach to politics and decision-making	2nd	1st	3rd
2. Cross-*Lager* marriage of daughter or son	2nd	1st	3rd
3. Concern over friends' political affiliations	2nd	1st	3rd

Source: Same as Table 6. "1st" is a group rank for that category of elites compared to the group ranks of either of the other elite role categories; the rank is dictated by the average of all individual scores on that item.

the OeVP's majority victory over the SPOe in the March 1966 parliamentary elections, were also reinterviewed in 1967 and 1968.

Elite Role Structure and Communication Patterns: Principal Findings and Implications

Alerted by previous studies contrasting Austria's unique system of functional representation with its regular political structures, and by Deutsch's hypothesis concerning the significance of the middlemen in a communication system, we sought to overcome the tangle of overlapping jobs in Austria's parties, groups, chambers, and government ministries and probe for differentiated "pragmatic" and "political" roles among elites. What we discovered was striking in its significance for at least the Austrian version on consociational democracy. The principal points are these:

—There is not one, single group of elites: rather, there are three functionally distinct groups. The smallest of these, comprising no more than 25 or 30 persons, is responsible for the overall pattern of consociational politics. These "top" elites provide the system with a steady guiding hand on a day-to-day basis, guaranteeing operational freedom to the middle-level socioeconomic elites, generally agreeing with them on issues, and inclined to support them in policy disagreements with middle-level political elites of the same Lager under all but electoral conditions.

—These top elites are highly pragmatic in their approach to politics, tend to see all but political (Coalition style) issues as bargainable. Inter-Lager contacts at this level are often more cordial than relations between top elites and partisan middle-level political elites in the same Lager. They exhibit surprisingly little role conflict—except at election time, when they become the "captives" of their own political elites.

—Under the duress of elections, there is thus substantial distortion of normal intra-Lager (and interelite) communication flow; the top elites tend to perceive mass opinion as both politicized and polarized, thus complicating the subsequent (post-election) capacity of top elites to "get back together," and further inculcating the Lager mentality whose pervasiveness at the mass level they overestimate in the first place.

—As Tables 6 and 7 make clear, the really significant cleavage (and this remains true even with party controlled!) in Austrian politics is between the socioeconomic elites of both parties and the political elites of both parties.

—Only on certain symbolic issues is there some erosion in the essentially "centripetal" tendencies of the socioeconomic elites. These elites deserve major credit for systemic viability, as well as for its ability to weather electoral battles—and perhaps most important of all, for the fact that the system was reasonably prepared for, and withstood a change of regime in April 1966.

Political socialization and recruitment processes served to guarantee the continued "integrity" of this trifurcated national elite role structure. New elites internalized the norms of their predecessors, especially in the sharply diverging middle-level roles, thus sustaining the duality of types of conflict and accommodation, cleavage and integration which characterized the Coalition and Para-Coalition subsystems, and which so strongly affected the manner in which political conflict in post-World War II Austria arose at various decision-making sites and was then resolved through accommodation or avoidance.

Top elites were "role-socialized" into the key "consociational" jobs transcending either the "technocratic" or "partisan" organizations from which these various elites had been recruited. Given the conditions of normal daily politics, top-level elites recruited from middle-level political roles generally assumed the much more accommodating and cooperative norms of their new "consociational" roles, while relinquishing much of the hardness and partisan rancorousness associated with their previous roles. Top elites recruited from middle-level "technocratic" jobs in the interest groups or chambers were already, by previous career training, socialized to norms of civility and depoliticization in interpersonal relations, and to the practices of collective bargaining politics with compromise outcomes. They were relatively "isolated" structurally and were psychologically detached from the expressively ideological styles of behavior which characterized more partisan political milieux. On the other hand, those top-level elites who had previously been party "cadres," that is, middle-level political men in the political party organizations, were prone to lapse back to bitterly partisan behavior during "crisis" circumstances—for example, at election time.

Ulf Himmelstrand has drawn attention to, and expressed concern about, the problematic consequences of an elite which is depoliticizing faster than and is more genuinely depoliticized than an electorate which retains organizationally reinforced ideological components and which might be mobilized to the detriment of the system on a periodic basis.[70] We would suggest that in the Austrian case (throughout the period of Great Coalition from 1945 to 1966) the elites were those who remained most problematic, not the mass electorate. Particularly at election time the middle-level political and repoliticized "top" or "consociational" elites perceived "issues" (often unperceived by the masses) and "hostilities" (often not felt by the masses) and acted according to these in ideologically relevant fashion, thereby repolarizing the political system and reducing its conflict-regulating capabilities.[71]

IV. SUMMARY AND CONCLUSIONS

At the outset of this study, we set ourselves two principal objectives. The first was the task of resolving the "Austrian paradox" (by

---

[70]Himmelstrand, "A Theoretical and Empirical Approach to Depoliticization and Political Involvement," op. cit., p. 119.

[71]Cf. on these points Lehmbruch's insightful speculations in Proporzdemokratie, op. cit., pp. 30-31. Fragmentary data from a case study of Viennese party officials support my general line of argument (see Pinner, "On the Structure of Organizations and Beliefs," op. cit., esp. pp. 19 ff.) Many of the arguments advanced here are also supported by G. Bingham Powell's careful study of the western Austrian community of Hallein: Social Fragmentation and Political Hostility: An Austrian Case Study, see esp. chaps. 4, 5, and 8.

explicating how stable, democratic, and decisionally effective government could be combined with a highly polarized, politicized, and organizationally fragmented political culture). The second was the task of elaborating, on the basis of the Austrian case, the hypothetically prerequisite and ⁄ or supportive conditions favoring the long-term maintenance of what Arend Lijphart has recently described as "consociational democracies." In both cases we addressed ourselves to the relationship we posited as most crucial: that between elites and the mass public. In so doing we have taken care to focus on mass opinion structure and political culture; on elite role and opinion structure, and related patterns of inter- and intra-elite political communications and patterns of decision-making behavior; and on the interaction of elites and masses under "crisis," i.e., electoral conditions. In general, we may summarize our principal findings, which help to resolve the reasons for the peculiar simultaneous existence of an "ideological Austria" and a "pragmatic Austria," and to explain their problematic interactions, as follows:

1. *Public Opinion.* Survey data reveal the Austrian mass public as highly supportive of the established consociational political regime and its authorities, and as being in basic interparty agreement concerning the centrality of the specific problems to which governmental endeavor should be directed. Moreover, both major party phalanxes exhibit a sufficiently low level of intensity of political involvement (on such indicators as interest, information, frequency of discussion) so that the political authorities are left with substantial day-to-day operational freedom. Finally, two indicators of the pervasiveness of political partisanship indicate that the impact of political considerations on the individual in his nonpolitical roles is much lower than has been widely assumed heretofore. And yet—some indications of psychological distrust and apartness remain, and despite the surprising homogeneity of day-to-day views on the issue-objectives of government policy, at election time the traditional ideological "camps" or Lager seem to reappear in more sharply delineated form.

2. *Elite Opinion.* With similar probing, elite interview data reveal sharply dichotomized elite opinion structures, with three principal sets of actors: *"top" elites,* whose cooperation and accommodation made the Great Coalition between mutually antagonistic subcultures work; *middle-level "socioeconomic"* elites, who made the para-coalition system of chambers, wage-price mechanisms, and the like work also; and *middle-level "political"* elites, whose die-hard ideological orientations and *Lagermentalitaet* (or *Lagerdenken*) mortgaged the political system to strains to which it eventually succumbed. To these latter political elites were entrusted most day-to-day political speech-making, nearly all of the important party organizational work, much of the electoral effort, and even the public definition of many principal issues.

3. *Interaction of elites.* While top elites communicate politically relevant signals to and receive them from both middle groups, they are generally more attuned to the middle-level socioeconomic elites, or "technocrats," whose role culture (oriented to pragmatic decision-making, with low salience of ideologically divisive issues) they share. Their principal interaction with the middle-level political elites, or "partisans," is under the duress of elections campaigning, at which times the top elites (particularly those recruited from among the partisans) may lapse back into ideological style, with much higher intensity of partisanship and hence great polarization on issues affecting the work and decisional effectiveness of even the highest level of consociational politics, the Coalition Committee.

4. *Stability of consociational democracy.* Thus in the Austrian variant of consociational democracy whatever developments there were toward a rapprochment, toward pan-Lager organic solidarity, suffered periodic setbacks; and the political system did not tend, in its basic features, to evolve toward a centripetal democracy. Given the periodic electoral opportunity to emphasize their outmoded concepts of political reality (perception of interparty goals as incompatible, of policy disagreements as fundamental Lager cleavages), the partisans forced both the mass public and the top elites back into the consociational stance, while effectively, and for a long post-election period, neutralizing the technocratic elites. The latter continued to communicate with each other and hence to make the system operate, but the scale of their meaningful interaction with top elites was severely reduced.

If we were to construct from the above findings and analysis a hypothetical model of relevant political communication in Austria's version of fragmented but consociational democracy, it could be schematically portrayed as in Figure 1.

Consociational Democracy and The Austrian Case.   Lijphart's analysis of the elite-mass relationship most supportive of consociational democracy as well as his model of political change, may be restated in terms of four principal propositions or groups of propositions:

(1) There must be distinct lines of cleavage between subcultures, accompanied by high density of subcultural organization, high partisanship (identification), and high mass support for elite-level consociational forms and practices.

(2) There must be overarching elite commitment, cooperation, and demonstrated ability to resolve contentious issues often and well.

(3) Overarching elite accommodation becomes and remains institutionally and behaviorally possible *because* of the mass-level attributes situation postulated in (1).

Figure 1. The relationship between elite structure and inter-Lager political communication under normal and electoral conditions

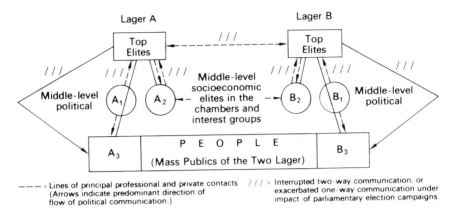

─ ─ ─ = Lines of principal professional and private contacts   / / / = Interrupted two-way communication, or
(Arrows indicate predominant direction of   exacerbated one-way communication under
flow of political communication.)   impact of parliamentary election campaigns.

(4) Decrease of both organization and psychological distinctiveness may lead, over time, to a distinctly different type of democratic political system, the depoliticized democracy. In that case consociational practices would result from consensus and the convergence of ideologies, not as a deliberate response to the tensions of a fragmented society. Moreover, there would be a change in the locus of principal decision-making from the highest actors (party leaders) to lower levels (where interest group representatives and bureaucrats predominate).

If we refine this analysis somewhat on the basis of the Austrian case we might restate the conditions that may be supportive of (contribute to the maintenance of) consociational democracy as follows:

(1) is the same as Lijphart, with one important caveat. While significant levels of partisanship must be present, the political stability and vitality of consociational systems are served best if that partisanship remains *potentially* mobilizable but *generally* latent, and if it is combined with a high degree of depoliticization sufficiently extensive to permit top elites and technocrats day-to-day bargaining flexibility. Thus centrifugal tendencies in the system are subverted at the same time that enough subcultural divisiveness is preserved to allow electoral subversion of whatever centripetal tendencies may exist.

(2) is also basically the same as Lijphart as far as the "top elites" are concerned; but our analysis of the Austrian case indicates the existence and functional utility of a *trio* of elite types and roles in consociational political systems.

Thus (3), elite accommodation at the top of the system, is possible not only because of the mass-level situation posited in (1), but also because of the *division* of elites noted in (2). Specifically, in a country in which the principal competing groups are entrenched in economy, society, and polity in such a way that electoral victory by one side would not represent a *de facto* physical threat to the loser, it is possible that the trichotimization of elite roles as described in this article is a prerequisite of continued consociational democracy —that without such a division the political system would evolve willy-nilly toward the centripetal or centrifugal type.

To restate the gist of the argument: our discovery of dual-track communication channels and specialized elites at the middle ranges provides us with an empirical explanation for why consociational democracy is not, under such deceptively docile conditions, self-devouring: One set of subsidiary elites (the partisans) "defends" consociational democracy against the "threat" of centripetal democracy, in that it seizes on the latent Lager bases of the political system and mobilizes them under the aegis of electoral necessity, creating the psychological conditions that led the top elites (supported by the mass electorate) into consociational democracy in the first place.

Meanwhile, another set of elites (the technocrats) "defends" the system against the "threat " of centrifugal evolution, in that it carries on efficiently and effectively the pragmatic, day-to-day business of socioeconomic decision-making (with prior political ratification by the top elites where that is necessary).[72]

[72]It is important to draw attention to some other critical features of the Austrian constellation, which were discussed tangentially in the first section of this essay: I mean in particular Austria's unique blend of political-administrative and "sociological" federalism, which served as intervening variables tending to support the preservation of status quo consociational forms and practices. To elaborate briefly: The firm entrenchment of the separate Lager in "their" particular federal ministries or (frequently) city or provincial administrations—"political" federalism in various governmental and administrative institutions and at various levels of the political system—was a significant feature of postwar stability, reducing the "load" on the central governmental and political apparatus of the country.

The term "sociological federalism" stems from Robert Dahl, as quoted in Verba, "Some Dilemmas in Comparative Research," *op. cit.*, note 10, p. 126. The point is this: divided political suzerainty over the various administrative sectors of the state by sociologically distinct units (the Lager *qua* parties) has the effect of reducing the all-or-nothing implications of electoral victory or defeat; as one Lager gets entrenched at other relevant sites in the system, including some not related to electoral outcomes and others which mitigate the unfavorable effects of an electoral defeat, the incentive to continue political-consociational forms of government may be increased because of simple comfort and inertia.

Eventually, of course, one of the secondary elites may gain the upper hand and retain it, particularly if intervening factors such as those mentioned above reduce the effectiveness of one of the sets of middle-level elites. In the Austrian case, "federalism" and prosperity and stability may have combined with the considerable machinery of the paracoalition technocratic elites to render less credible, over a period of a decade and a half, the recurrent politicizing efforts of the partisan political elites.

However, it must be emphasized that the perception that this might be true, and that the public would support a non-coalition experiment such as that which developed after the upset majority victory of the OeVP in 1966, is strictly an elite, or top elite, phenomenon.

As far as (4) is concerned, the Austrian case offers two important insights of potential cross-national relevance. First, it is not clear why both types of depoliticization ("natural" and "imposed") cannot coexist in the same system; nor is it clear that one of the types necessarily precedes or leads to the other. Austria's Coalition and Para-Coalition provided both types simultaneously.[73] Second, given the long history of functional representation (and especially the significance of the Para-Coalition institutions and practices) and given further, the bipolar nature of government ministries, we would argue that interest-group representatives and bureaucrats made their share of the principal decisions *throughout* the period of Great Coalition: depoliticization of elite and mass opinion did not alter the loci of various types of principal decision-making.

Elections and Political Development: The Problem of Institutionalization. Not only does the empirical Austrian case help clarify and elaborate the consociational democracy model, and help resolve some unsettled problems associated with that model; it also raises some interesting and broader questions of political development theory and allows us to reflect profitably on certain types of developmental problems which exist not only in Austria but in many other industrially advanced societies as well. In doing so, we may draw usefully on the work of a number of contemporary theorists of political change, such as Huntington, Rustow, Rokkan and others. Let us first look at Austrian political development in the post-war period in broad general perspective, then zero in on several specific hypotheses which appear particularly useful in explicating patterns of political change in Austria, and which, conversely, are thrown into bolder theoretical relief by the Austrian example.

General Developmental Trends

In the space of two brief decades, this small Alpine democracy —a bitterly and deeply divided country without so much as an agreed national identity, and with precious little democratic inclination or experience—was converted by deliberate elite design to democratic attitudes, expectations, and practices, in close approximation to the developmental scenario described by Dankwart Rustow in his perceptive article on

---

[73]Thus one finds, in the Austrian context, that there coexisted during much of the postwar Coalition period a genuinely organic solidarity and "natural" depoliticization resulting from successful collective bargaining in the para-Coalition institutions among the socioeconomic partners; and a more manufactured solidarity imposed by elites in more politicized arenas; plus a combination of both at the mass level. One reason both types may exist simultaneously and develop unevenly, is that the organizational bases of each (and their attendant role structures) tend to persist over time. Cf. Barnes' insightful discussion on pp. 528-29 of "Ideology and the Organization of Conflict," *op. cit.* [pp. 422-23 in this book].

"Transitions to Democracy."[74] A two-party system in "form" was converted to what Sartori would call a two-party system in "substance."[75] And a mildly authoritarian government by elite cartel imposed on the populace in 1945 became a British-type open regime of alternating Government and Opposition by 1966!

Yet, most remarkable of all, these objective realities remained unappreciated and even unperceived by the country's leadership until the almost incidental failure to successfully renegotiate the Coalition Pact after the OeVP electoral victory of 1966 stripped the Emperor of all his clothes. A quick, cold shower disabused the nation's elite with startling suddenness of its twenty-year mortgage to *Lagerdenken*. Since 1966 Austria has enjoyed uninterrupted single-party rule, first by the OeVP, then by the SPOe; and *Bereichskoalition* has replaced *Bereichsopposition* as Austria's own variety of what Lowi has called "interest group liberalism."[76]

Two Hypotheses: Explaining What Happened in Post-War Austria

As Table 8, which summarizes Austrian political develop-ment, suggests, there are numerous ways in which to relate the confluence of segmented pluralism, consociational democracy, and electoral politics in Austria to more general problems of political change in Western Europe. Two of these—organizational lag and behavioral lag—we shall explore briefly, in order to suggest some of the more fruitful directions in which

[74]*Comparative Politics* 2, No. 3 (Apr. 1970), pp. 337-363, esp. pp. 350 ff.

[75]"The Typology of Party Systems—Proposals for Improvement," in *Mass Politics: Studies in Political Sociology*, ed. E. Allardt and S. Rokkan (New York: The Free Press, 1970), pp. 331ff., 336 ff., 345 ff., 385 ff.

[76]T. Lowi, "The Public Philosophy: Interest-Group Liberalism," *The American Political Science Review* 60 (Mar. 1967), pp. 5-24, is the source of the phrase. The point made for Austria is derived from Stiefbold, S.A.N.E. Interviews, 1968, and runs throughout the interview protocols. The scope of and utter breathlessness with which these developments occurred are difficult to appreciate for anyone who did not experience the virulent partisan hostility of the late Coalition period, or did not witness its system costs. For documentation of these systemic loads and costs, see, *inter alia*, Vodopivec, *Die Balkanisierung Oesterreichs, passim;* Vodopivec, *Der verspielte Ballhausplatz* (Vienna: Molden, 1970), entire; Anton Pelinka and Manfred Welan, *Demokratie und Verfassung in Oesterreich* (Vienna: Europa Verlag, 1970), entire; the concluding chapters of Steiner, *Politics in Austria, op. cit.*, and R. Stiefbold, *Austrian Electoral Politics, op. cit.*, and William T. Bluhm, "Political Integration, Cultural Integration, and Economic Development: Their Relationship in the Nation-Building Experience of Republican Austria, paper presented to the Eighth World Congress of the International Political Science Association, Munich, 1970. For analyses of the mutual mistrust that persisted till the very last minute, see Nasmacher, *op. cit.*, and an incisive account by Carlo Moetteli, "Austria Between Yesterday and Tomorrow," *Swiss Review of World Affairs* (Apr. 1966), pp. 10-11

Table 8. Segmented pluralism, consociational democracy, and electoral politics: Some dimensions of political change in Austria, 1945-1966

Principal Development Problem	Regime Solution and Effects	Type of Solidarity or Integration	Major Functions of Parlia. Elections	Type of Partisan Competition Related to "Objective", Socioeconomic Conditions
(1945) Stabilization in face of perceived "conflict society"; need for Rustow's conscious elite decision, Huntington's institutionalization, Wriggins' aggregation of power.	Great Red-Black Coalition, with Coalition Committee (extra-legal) as center of political power: Lijphart's Consociational Democracy, guaranteed by firm segmented pluralist base (Lorwin). Para-Coalition of "social partners."	Mechanical solidarity, normative, based on procedural rules and centralized power imposed on mass public by top elites in perceived absence of value consensus or shared national identity.	Impart formal legitimacy by masses to rulers; provide for recurrent inter-Lager adjustment, a modicum of flexibility in otherwise inflexible system.	Firm social and organizational infra-structure of Lager and underdeveloped and destroyed economy provide no socioeconomic basis for recasting of partisan competition on basis of catch-all umbrella-type political parties.
(1966) Kesselman's "over-institutionalization and political constraint"; in Lorwin's terms, failure of *ontzuiling* to occur; put differently, in Barnes' terms, simple organizational persistence disguising real substructural changes and containing them. Subcultures, which facilitated elite security and autonomy, and regime stability and efficacy, now have become obstacle to development.	Coalition Committee no longer essential buckle on the system; now hindering developmental impetus provided by Para-Coalition. Conclusion, April 1966: no more Coalition. After brief "cold shower" an unbelievably smooth transition to a working Government-and-Opposition model.	Organic solidarity, though not at first recognized by elites with organizational blinkers hindering their perception of new realities. New solidarity or integration based solidly on shared national identity and increased value consensus, and resulting esp. from great increase in functional inter-dependence of the Lager or their subunits in all spheres.	In early 1960s elections serving extremely "conservative" functions, i.e., sustaining "crisis"-consociational rule and impeding development of "organic" solidarity and its counterpart, i.e., "natural" consociational rule.	New socioeconomic base now exists for recasting of partisan competition on basis of catch-all appeals. However, in initial phase it is combined with traditional ghetto mobilization, becoming ironic additional source of strain on regime, until after successful switch from Coalition to Government-and-Opposition formula. Thereafter we find decreasing ghetto mobilization and increasing catch-all appeals to the multiple attachment voters.

475

future research on problems of political development in advanced nations might be concentrated.[77]

1. *The thesis of organizational lag.* Between 1945 and 1966 the political-governmental problem facing Austria changed from what Huntington would call the challenge of "institutionalization" and the threat of political "decay" to what Mark Kesselman has recently and brilliantly analyzed in the French context as "overinstitutionalization and political constraint." What is involved here is the point that segmented pluralism, including the early "freezing" of partisan electoral alternatives as a result of the introduction of proportional representation electoral formulae in divided societies, has played a major role in stabilizing and rendering predictable the daily politics of low-consensus, deep-cleavage societies. As Lorwin suggests, it has been a valuable handmaiden of political modernization and social mobilization in a number of smaller European countries, including Austria. But as Kesselman and Urwin have illustrated, such thoroughgoing institutionalization, originally useful in controlling the potential volatility of divided societies, may eventually become inflexible itself, contributing to an ossification of the system as a whole and, by thus reducing its capacity to respond to new demands, ultimately weakening it. This is precisely what happened in Austria, where elites, especially in the Coalition subsystem, were simply too isolated, in partisan terms, to perceive what change was taking place and hence to respond to it.

2. *The thesis of behavioral lag.* Lewis J. Edinger, drawing on another facet of the Huntington concept of "institutionalization," suggests that the institutionalization of a regime depends chiefly on a growth of congruence

[77]The brief analysis which follows draws on the following studies: Samuel P. Huntington, *Political Order in Changing Societies* (New Haven: Yale University Press, 1968); Mark Kesselman, "Overinstitutionalization and Political Constraint: The Case of France," *Comparative Politics* 3, No. 1 (Oct. 1970) pp. 21-44; Derek Urwin, "Social Cleavages and Political Parties in Belgium: Problems of Political Institutionalization," *Political Studies* 18, No. 3 (Sept. 1970), pp. 320-40; Richard Rose and Derek Urwin, "Social Cohesion, Political Parties and Strains in Regimes," *Comparative Political Studies* 2, No. 1 (Apr. 1969), pp. 7-67; Lorwin, "Segmented Pluralism"; Rokkan, "The Structuring of Mass Politics"; Otto Kirchheimer, "The Transformation of the Western European Party Systems," in *Political Parties and Political Development* ed. J. LaPalombara and M. Weiner (Princeton: Princeton University Press, 1966), pp. 177-200; Samuel H. Barnes, "Ideology and the Organization of Conflict: On the Relationship Between Political Thought and Behavior," *Journal of Politics* 28 (June 1966), pp. 513-30; Lewis J. Edinger, "Political Change in Germany," *Comparative Politics* 2, No. 4 (July 1970); Murray Edelman, "Myths, Metaphors, and Political Conformity," *Psychiatry* 30, No. 3 (Aug. 1967); and G. B. Powell, Jr. and R. P. Stiefbold, *Social Structure and Political Conflict in Austrian Community Systems: A Preliminary Report* (Paper presented to the Eighth World Congress of the International Political Science Association, Munich, 1970). The articles by Rokkan, Kirchheimer, and Barnes are included in this book as Selections 10, 15, and 16, respectively.

between regime norms and political style. As we have noted several different times in this study, the consociational democracy model posits that elites will try to minimize public ideologism, or rancorous interelite behavior, lest it get out of hand and mushroom into a load the system cannot tolerate. And while Powell and I have suggested that rancorous behavior itself can become a norm under certain conditions, we have also demonstrated empirically that when great conflicts of interest over preferred policy outcomes exist among competing groups of elites, there is a much greater likelihood of successfully avoiding disruptive political conflict which might be destabilizing for the political system if the contending elites practice assiduously the so called norm of restrained partisanship, in their dealing with each other.

However, as this study has demonstrated, Austrian politics in the Coalition era was characterized by a highly expressive political style; and not only do many elites, as revealed by the SANE interview data, believe the semantics anyway, but also, as Edelmann warns, language forms create shared expectations and continuous reliance on a hortatory public speaking style incurs the risk that elites (and if not they, then their followers) will eventually come to believe what they hear, if they do not already. This incongruence between the regime norm of nonrancorous public behavior and a style which in fact relied on rancorous behavior thus led to precisely the opposite effect (underinstitutionalization) than that produced by organizations which "refused to die" after having outlived their usefulness. It was this combination of "under" institutionalization and "over" institutionalization, and especially the fateful interaction of the two recurrently triggered by national parliamentary election compaigns, that eventually undermined and destroyed the Austrian experiment in consociational democracy.

18

Group Influence and the Policy Process in the Soviet Union

Joel J. Schwartz and William R. Keech

It has become widely recognized that Soviet officials do not formulate public policy in a vacuum, and that, indeed, their deliberations take into account in some fashion the needs and demands of various elements of the society. Further, it has been observed that social groups of various types play a noticeable, if only rudimentary role in articulating interests to the top of the hierarchy. In fact one author has gone so far as to assert that communist policy-making results from a "parallelogram of conflicting forces and interests."[1] While such viewpoints are now far more widely accepted than in the early fifties, relatively little effort has been devoted to illustrating or illuminating how Soviet public policy in general or even a given Soviet policy can be importantly affected by group activity.

We propose here to make a contribution in that direction. Using the Educational Reform Act of 1958 as an exemplary case, we intend to show how and through what process groups can affect policy outcomes, and by identifying circumstances under which this takes place to generate some hypotheses about when such influence is most likely to recur. In their excellent analysis of Soviet policy formation, Professors Brzezinski and Huntington identify what they call "policy groups," which come closest of any nongovernmental groups to participating in policy formation. These groups, such as the military, industrial managers, agricultural experts and state bureaucrats,

Reprinted by permission of the authors and publisher from *American Political Science Review,* LXII (September 1968), 840-851. Footnotes are abridged by permission of the authors. The authors wish to express their appreciation to the University of North Carolina Research Council for supporting the research on this subject.

[1]H. Gordon Skilling, "Interest Groups and Communist Politics," *World Politics* 18 (Apr. 1966), p. 449.

whose scope of activity is directly dependent on the allocation of national resources and which are directly affected by any shift in the institutional distribution of power, . . . advocate to the political leadership certain courses of action; they have their own professional or specialized newspapers which, at times and subject to over-all Party control, can become important vehicles for expressing specific points of view.[2]

In this article we will investigate an instance wherein such groups seemed to influence policy with the result of virtually scuttling one of Khrushchev's own major proposals.

We do not mean to challenge the view that ultimate power in the U.S.S.R. resides at the top of the Communist Party hierarchy. Neither do we mean to infer that the top party leadership was forced by a "policy group" to act against its will. We do not suggest that the instance we cite is modal. Indeed it is the best example we are aware of. We hope that the major payoff in this paper will be in showing why things happened as they did. This is the first step in finding out whether and how often to expect them again.

The first major section of the paper will describe the situation we use as a basis for our speculative analysis about the Soviet decision making process. The second will attempt to explain why things happened as they did, and the third will report some hypotheses about when such phenomena are likely to recur.

I. DEBATE OVER THE 1958 ACT

A prominent feature of post-Stalin Russia has been the nationwide discussion of certain legislative proposals. This does not constitute a totally new innovation in the Soviet Union. During the preceding period such important laws as the constitution of 1936 received nationwide discussion before enactment. A few differences, however, deserve mention. First, the frequency of these discussions has substantially increased. Second and more important, the impact of these discussions on the proposed legislation has in some instances been far more than peripheral. This especially applies to the debate which surrounded the Educational Reform Act of 1958. A closer look at this debate will afford us an opportunity to consider how the opinion of various "publics" can influence the policy process.

There can be little doubt about whose initiative lay behind the proposed reform. At the thirteenth Komsomol Congress in April of 1958, First Party Secretary Khrushchev severely criticized the existing school system and

---

[2]Zbigniew Brzezinski and Samuel P. Huntington, *Political Power: U.S.A. U.S.S.R.* (New York 1963), p. 196.

demanded fundamental changes. This attack seems to have been motivated by three problems facing Soviet society in the mid-fifties, the cause of which Khrushchev linked to the existing school system.

First, the Soviet press had unceasingly criticized the denigrative attitudes of the younger generation toward physical labor. In the opinion of the First Secretary, the undue emphasis upon classical academic training and the neglect of the polytechnical side of education were largely responsible for this attitude.

Second, competition for admission to higher education had reached an excessive degree and this likewise had caused great concern among political leaders. The competition itself has largely been a by-product of changes in the economic and educational systems.

Prior to 1950 the rapid growth of the economy and the underdeveloped secondary educational facilities maintained the demand for skilled technical cadres at a higher level than the supply. Throughout this period the number of available places in higher education exceeded the number of secondary school graduates. The post war years, however, witnessed a remarkable acceleration of secondary school facilities and enrollment. In 1949, out of a total enrollment of thirty-three million pupils only about one million were in grades eight to ten. Four years later the number of pupils in secondary education had risen to four and one half million.[3] Now the annual supply of secondary school graduates greatly exceeded the number of vacancies in higher education. Since the Soviet regime, for reasons of its own, was unwilling to widen the availability of higher education, the gates of universities were closed to millions of youth regardless of their educational attainment.

An inevitable consequence has been the intensification of competition for the available number of places. The pressures for admission became abnormally high because of the widespread notion that a college degree represents the key to individual advancement and entrance into the new class of Soviet intelligentsia. Consequently, those high school graduates initially denied admission refused to accept their fate. Instead of entering the labor force, many of them became perennial college candidates. Very often they applied to schools whose area of specialization was of no genuine interest to them. But in the absence of alternatives they would often enter an agricultural institute just to be able "to study somewhere." Here again Khrushchev charged that the educational system had bred such attitudes. By allowing students to continue their education uninterruptedly and by stressing almost exclusively academic material, the schools naturally generated the expectation that the path to life lay solely through higher education.

[3]Nicholas DeWitt, *Education and Professional Employment in the USSR* (Washington 1961), p. 140.

The third problem involved the increasing stratification of Soviet society. The notion that higher education was the key to membership in the "new class" had a firm basis in fact. Yet these educational channels for upward social and political mobility were being drastically constricted as a consequence of their preemption by the incumbent political and bureaucratic elites. Khrushchev himself admitted that in the competition for admission to college the influence of parents often proved more important than the merit of the candidates. He further stated that only thirty to forty per cent of the enrolled students in higher education institutions came from worker and peasant backgrounds. The differential access to a prime source of mobility gravely concerned the First Secretary. Both the content and tenor of his statements clearly indicate that Krushchev sought to eliminate privilege and inequality from the Soviet educational system.

Finally we should mention an additional factor which *may* have influenced the reform movement. At the time of the debate some western scholars argued that the specifics of Khrushchev's proposals owed much to the serious labor shortage the Soviet economy was about to experience. The argument may be briefly summarized as follows. Because of severe war losses and a declining birth rate in the post war period the Soviet Union would have one-third fewer people entering the labor force during the late fifties and early sixties than normally would have been the case. Consequently the ambitious economic growth program could be achieved only if the vast majority of young people were channelled into the active labor force instead of higher education. It is important to note, however, that the Soviet press never cited a labor deficit as cause for the reform. Other evidence also casts doubt upon the validity of this thesis.

While there is room for disagreement as to what problems motivated the reform, there is no ambiguity regarding Khrushchev's proposals for dealing with them. In September of 1958, the party secretary published his "thesis" on school reorganization.[4] He suggested that continuous academic education be abolished and that all students be required to combine work with study. In effect this meant phasing out the ten year school which at that time constituted a completed secondary education. After finishing a seven or eight year primary school, said Khrushchev, every young person should enter the labor force. Those who wished to prepare themselves for higher education could continue their studies in evening and correspondence schools. Successful students would receive two or three days released time from work to facilitate studying.

The substitution of part time work and study for full time education in secondary day schools had, from Khrushchev's point of view, two advantages. First, it would instill in the younger generation a respectful attitude toward physical labor. Second, it would equalize access to higher

---

[4]See *Pravda,* Sept. 21, 1958.

education. The secondary day schools had become the province of children from the urban intelligentsia. Evening and correspondence schools, on the other hand, recruited most of their students from worker and peasant families. The difference in the quality of education offered by these two divisions gave the day school graduate an obvious advantage. By fusing the two channels into one undifferentiated system, Khrushchev hoped to eliminate the class bias in Soviet education. The road to a higher education would be the same for all irrespective of the positions or jobs which the parents held in society.

Study in higher educational institutions was also to be put on a part time basis. The student would acquire the first two or three years of his college education through evening or correspondence courses. Thereafter he could complete his training on a full time schedule. Moreover, no individual was to be granted admission to higher education unless he had already worked full time after completing secondary school. Once again we see Khrushchev's determination to deemphasize the purely academic side of education and to enhance the importance of work experience.

If we compare Khrushchev's September Memorandum with the actual law adopted in December 1958 we find that the two differ not only in detail but in basic principle. To begin with, the old secondary day school was preserved more or less intact both in form and content. Khrushchev's demand that work be combined with study had received token satisfaction by increasing the number of hours devoted to polytechnical training *within* the schools. But the quantity and quality of academic subjects had in no way been sacrificed. The law established an eleven year day school to replace the old ten year day school system. The addition of another year permitted greater emphasis upon labor training without simultaneously diluting the quality of academic education. Indeed, the number of hours devoted to purely academic subjects proved to be *exactly the same* under the new system as it had been under the old.

The maintenance of continuous secondary full time education must be seen as a rebuff to Khrushchev's demands. When the new law went into effect, it became apparent that nearly all the former ten year schools would continue to operate as part of the new eleven year system. Some figures also suggest that the number of students enrolled in the new system was comparable in size to the two senior grades of the old ten year school.[5] It is true that Khrushchev recognized in his memorandum the need for *some* full time day schools. But he envisaged that they would operate only during a

---

[5]The actual law left this point unclear but later developments indicated that just as many children—about a third of the total—would attend full time high schools as had been the case before the reform. Sèe Thomas Bernstein, "Soviet Educational Reform," (M.A. Thesis, Columbia University, 1962), p. 111, and articles in *The New York Times*, Sept. 2, 1959; *Wall Street Journal*, June 29, 1960.

transitional period and he expected their number to be sharply reduced right from the beginning of the reform.

While the eleven year system might have satisfied the demand that work be combined with study, it could not possibly have achieved Khrushchev's other expressed purpose—the elimination of privilege and inequality. The perpetuation of a bifurcated full time and part time school system insured that inequality would persist. Nevertheless the disadvantages faced by the evening and correspondence student might have significantly diminished had the law incorporated Khrushchev's suggestion regarding released time for study. Yet in this area as well important modifications were made. The reorganization decree left this question open and subsequent legislation resulted in a far less liberal policy.[6] Under these circumstances the vast majority of college students would continue to come from the full time secondary schools and an inevitable by-product would be the continuation of class bias in higher education.

The provision for admission to and study in higher educational institutions likewise markedly deviated from Khrushchev's suggestions. Instead of *absolutely* requiring full time work before admission, the law merely stipulated that *priority* would be granted those with the record of employment or military service. But precedence for people with production experience already existed before the reorganization of the school system. Thus the wording of the law gave only formal recognition to an on-going practice. It cannot be interpreted as a "concession" to the demands made by Khrushchev in his memorandum.

His insistence upon part time study during the first few college years appears to have been more successfully realized. At least the law accepted it in principle. However, even here some important alterations occurred. The law explicitly exempted from this requirement all students in difficult theoretical disciplines. Similarly, the requirement would be inoperative in both non-technical higher educational institutions and in arts faculties at universities since "factory work for students cannot in these cases be connected with their future job."

Generally speaking, the education reform failed to implement the most important goals and purposes which Khrushchev had articulated in his memorandum. What factors can account for the observable disparity between the September proposal and the December law? To answer that question we must look briefly at the discussion which ensued during this period of time. The content of that debate clearly revealed that different societal groups, or at least some members of them, opposed Khrushchev's reform.

Teachers and administrators identified with the ten year school

---

[6] Instead of the two to three days released time from work as suggested by Khrushchev, students in evening schools received only one additional free day for study.

obviously wished to preserve and protect their institutional bailiwicks. But a frontal assault on the First Secretary's ideas would not have been good politics. Instead they opposed the reform more deviously. Essentially they argued that to prepare youth for manual labor it was not necessary to send them after the eighth grade to factories or farms. A much better way would be to bring the factories and farms into the schools by setting up first class workshops. Under these conditions it would be possible to teach pupils the same skills they could learn by entering the labor force. To substantiate their case the proponents of this approach assumed the initiative even *before* the appearance of Khrushchev's September memorandum. Prior to the opening of the school year in 1958, Y. I. Afanasenko, Minister of Education for the Russian Republic, announced that the number of schools giving training in industrial and agricultural skills would double. He further announced that the Russian Republic had begun to experiment with extending secondary schools from ten to eleven years. Under the extended program students would spend half of their time at school and the other half at jobs on farms, in factories, or at construction sites. He mentioned that fifty schools with this program had operated the last year and this number would increase to two hundred this year. Here, in embryonic form, was the eleven year school system that became law in December of 1958. Thus, through word and deed, those occupational groups associated with full time secondary education sought to protect the organization they had built with effort and care.

Other groups opposed to the reform included higher educational and scientific personnel. Their arguments were perhaps more telling. They warned that it would be impossible under the new system to ensure the supply of highly qualified cadres for economic and societal growth. How can we, they asked, perfect and advance scientific knowledge when new entrants to higher educational schools would have only eight years of regular schooling behind them and who, in the following years, would have forgotten the little they had once learned. Several prominent educators and scientists went so far as to assert that a hiatus between incomplete and complete secondary school as well as between complete secondary school and higher education would result in irreparable damage to the state. For creative work in scientific research often manifests itself when the individual has reached his mid-twenties and the acquisition of theoretical knowledge on a large scale demands uninterrupted study.

The warning of experts reinforced grave doubts raised by many parents. The basic argument of the latter was that a shortened basic school program would adversely affect the physical and intellectual maturation of adolescents. Furthermore, it was said that channeling young people into production at an early age does not give them a chance to adequately choose a skill which best suits them. While both of these points had merit, parental views were somewhat suspect because other motives could be readily discerned. As Khrushchev himself pointed out, many parents were determined that their children receive opportunities for maximum education. They saw his plans as a threat to that opportunity and responded by attacking it. To the extent that pedagogical experts echoed parental concerns, as some did, they served as a linkage between public opinion and political decision makers. By articulating the interests of an amorphous group in technical terms, the experts transformed their claims into a politically relevant issue.

A few words must also be said about the attitudes of factory managers. Although their opposition did not find explicit expression in the debate, their behavior left few doubts as to where they stood on the issue. Long before the question of reform had arisen, managers had displayed a reluctance to hire and train juvenile workers. Under the new arrangements they would become responsible for all sorts of educational functions for which the factory was ill prepared. Moreover, the large influx of school children and the necessity to train them would inevitably divert managers from their own duties of production and plan fulfillment. In light of this fact it is not surprising that the reform act failed to implement Khrushchev's suggestions regarding released time from work. That would have greatly complicated the managers' tasks and we can assume that their views were transmitted to the proper authorities.[7]

At this point, our task is to account for the role of groups in forming educational policy in this instance by interpreting a number of facts. The objective facts we must work from are, in summary, that Khrushchev made a far-reaching proposal to deal with a number of educational problems facing the regime, and that the substance of the proposal was radically modified. The major proponent of the reform was obviously Khrushchev himself. The most important—indeed the only—opponents of the changes we can identify are the social groups cited above.

Here we should note that if one quantifies the number of articles which appeared during the debate, the oppositional point of view is clearly a minority. It is quite possible that a "war of memoranda" may have been raging behind the scenes and that during this exchange the minority position was in fact the majority point of view.[8] Whatever may have been the case,

---

[7] For a scathing criticism of managerial attitudes toward juvenile workers see the lead editorial in *Pravda*, Sept. 25, 1957.

[8] There is some evidence that the opposition was far greater than one would gather from simply reading the official press. For example, relatively few parental criticisms found their way into print. But during 1963-64 when the first author of this paper was conducting interviews in the Soviet Union, it was learned that a very large number of urban middle class parents had strongly criticized Khrushchev's proposals at "PTA" meetings held during the reform debate period. Similarly, Professor William Johnson of the University of Pittsburgh told the same author that opposition among educational officials was far more widespread than the official press revealed. Professor Johnson was in the Soviet Union at the time of the debate and is known to have extensive contacts with Soviet educators.

it is undeniable that the oppositional arguments were closer to the form of the finally enacted law.

There are several possible interpretations which would explain the outcome of the educational reform debate. One might argue, for example, that the disparity between the September memorandum and the December law resulted from Khrushchev changing his mind. Once the technocratic elites had pointed out the potentially dangerous consequences inherent in Khrushchev's proposals, the First Secretary simply revised his original position. There is no way, of course, to verify or falsify this interpretation. Since we have no knowledge of Khrushchev's preference schedule or to whom he would most likely listen, we must allow for the possibility that anyone who had a position and stated it prior to the outcome might have influenced Khrushchev. If we accept this interpretation, however, we must resolve certain questions which detract from its credibility.

When Khrushchev spoke to the Komsomol Congress in April, 1958, he stated, that the Party Central Committee had, *for some time*, been discussing the improvement of public education. Presumably, experts had been consulted during the course of such discussions. We might also presume that Khrushchev sounded out experts between April and September when he was preparing a detailed proposal for educational reform. In light of this, it seems unlikely that Khrushchev changed his mind because he heard convincing arguments which had not been made in the far longer period which preceded publication of his memorandum.

It is also important to recall that Khrushchev clearly identified himself personally with the issue of educational reform. He placed his public prestige squarely upon the line. As Richard Neustadt has pointed out, chief executives cannot afford to make indiscriminate public pronouncements. If they are sensitive to the prerequisites of power and influence, they must carefully weigh the consequences which flow from what, when and how they say things.[9] All the evidence we have on Khrushchev's career suggests that was highly sensitive to the requisites of power and influence. Thus not only did the First Secretary have ample opportunity to consult expert opinion on the educational question, but he also had a vested political interest in doing so before publicly stating his position.

Our own inclination then is to discount, though not categorically reject, the possibility that Khrushchev simply changed his mind between September and December. An alternative interpretation is that bureaucratic groups prevailed over the First Secretary and forced him to act against his will.[10] To accept this, however, would demand a rewriting of the literature on political power and resources in the Soviet Union that we think is neither necessary

---

[9]Richard Neustadt, *Presidential Power* (New York 1964).

[10]For an analysis of the reform with this type of implication see David Burg, "Some thoughts on the Soviet educational reform," *Bulletin* 6 (Mar. 1959), pp. 32-36.

nor appropriate. It is quite easy on the other hand to imagine more important actors prevailing over Khrushchev with the social groups associating themselves spuriously, so to speak, with the stronger actors. In suggesting this interpretation we must argue inferentially because the only direct evidence we have about opposition to the proposal relates to the groups. In the section below we will attempt to account for what happened and to assess the role of the social groups in it.

II. THE ROLE OF SOCIAL GROUPS IN SHAPING THE ACT

Brzezinski and Huntington express the orthodox interpretation in arguing that the key political resource in the Soviet Union is control of the party organization, and that such control can be shared only at the top.

> Thus, insofar as there are limits on the power of the top leader in the Soviet Union, they stem from his sharing control of the *apparat* with a small number of colleagues . . . the principal limits on the power of the Soviet leader are inside the Kremlin.[11]

We agree, and we feel that those colleagues were crucially important in defeating Khrushchev's proposal. But the opposition of the groups identified above was not coincidental. We submit that the groups were mobilized after the dispute was left unresolved at the top.

Such an argument forces us to take sides in a dispute among Soviet scholars about whether or not there is conflict within the Soviet leadership at times other than succession crises. It is the position of the "conflict" school that policy issues such as those on agriculture, heavy industry, consumer goods, foreign affairs, Stalinism, economic reorganization and education are continuous sources of dispute among the top leadership. When one issue is resolved, another is likely to take its place. We think there is strong evidence for this viewpoint, which became more compelling than ever with Khrushchev's political demise in October, 1964.[12]

In this specific case, Khrushchev stated in April, 1958, that the Party Central Committee was presently engaged in preparing a resolution on the improvement of public education. But the September "theses" proved to be simply a note by Khrushchev with the "approval" of the Central Committee, instead of a formal resolution by that august body. This suggests that

[11] Brzezinski and Huntington, *op. cit.*, p. 145.
[12] See, for example, Carl A. Linden, *Khrushchev and the Soviet Leadership 1957-1964* (Baltimore 1966).

Khrushchev's educational reform was a highly personal document which lacked support among a substantial element of the top political leadership. Esoteric evidence to support this thesis is provided by the unusual silence of the top political leadership during the educational reform debate. Khrushchev appears to have been the only Praesidium member to have played a significant role in the reform discussions and to have clearly and publicly expressed his attitudes. Sidney Ploss has argued that in the context of Soviet politics the silence of leaders on a topical issue must be construed as disagreement with the expressed viewpoint of their colleagues.[13] It is also significant that major amendments to Khrushchev's plan were reflected in the Central Committee resolution on education reform which was finally issued on November 16, 1958.[14]

If, as we have argued, the important conflict was on the top leadership level, and if the persons on that level have the power to determine policy outcomes, what role did the social groups play? The answer hangs on the nature of conflict among the leaders. It is well known that such conflict involves elements of power struggle and elements of dispute over policy alternatives.[15] Sometimes these elements operate independently of one another; more often they intertwine. Since Khrushchev had decisively defeated his rivals for power in 1957, we can assume that in the case of the education reforms of 1958 the elements of power struggle were less important than at almost any time since Stalin's death, and that the elements of unadulterated policy dispute were correspondingly more important. Indeed, it is unlikely that Khrushchev would have survived such a defeat as this had this policy dispute involved much power struggle.

Insofar as this was really a policy dispute, it involved numerous problem-solving considerations, as we emphasized above. The problems and policy positions associated with them involved a number of questions of judgment about what courses of action would solve the problem, and what the consequences of such action would have for other goals of the regime. It is here that the groups play an important role. Numerous groups have recognized expertise about what problems are in their own area. The ten year school personnel had an authoritative position for a judgment that students could get work experience without radically changing the school organization and curriculum. The scientific community had good claim to special insight into the needs of training scientists. Parents may be viewed as having some legitimate judgment about the needs of adolescents, although this is less apparently expertise. One student of the reform debate has argued that

[13] See *Conflict and Decision-Making in Soviet Russia* (Princeton 1965), p. 17-18.

[14] For an analysis of these amendments see Rudolph Schlesinger, "The Educational Reform," *Soviet Studies* 10 (Apr. 1959), pp. 432-444.

[15] See Brzezinski and Huntington, *op. cit.*, pp. 267, 269-283, 295-300.

The most important factors responsible for the change in Khrushchev's original proposals probably were the arguments of experts—the function of expert opinion was to point out to the leadership the possibly harmful consequences to Soviet society of the literal adoption of Khrushchev's original plans.[16]

It is hard to identify any concrete resource other than their own recognized expertise which the groups might have used in the dispute. Neither money, votes nor popularity were relevant to its resolution. Only the expert judgment was clearly relevant. The only reasonable alternative would seem to be that the regime may have accorded the positions of these groups a certain legitimacy just because they were group preferences, much as an American public official might yield to a constituent's demand simply because he views it as legitimate and because he may view his job as one of servicing such demands when they are legitimate and do not conflict with other goals. We have no reason to believe that Soviet officials view their jobs this way. Communist ideology, unlike democratic ideology, supplies its own policy goals, rather than depending on public expressions of preference to define them. Besides, we have already seen that the goals of these groups conflicted with the goals of none other than the First Secretary of the Communist Party. It does seem apparent that insofar as groups influenced the outcome of this issue it was through the communication of their expert judgments to people at the top of the hierarchy who *were* in a position to influence outcomes. The expertise became a resource to be used in making a case that more harm than good would result from the proposed reform.[17] We contend that in the Soviet Union policy issues are often decided on the basis of such debates. If such is the case the arguments of persons who are recognized as being knowledgeable can be an important resource for the proponent or opponent of a policy proposal.[18]

One can see elements of ambiguity in this interpretation of the role of these groups as articulators of expert judgment. It may appear, for example, that the ten year school personnel are looking out for themselves when they oppose changes in their institution. The position of the parents seems even

[16]Bernstein, *op. cit.,* p. 119. See also Brzezinski and Huntington, p. 214.

[17]In this instance, many political leaders may have been especially inclined to "believe" these arguments. As primary members of the new class, Communist Party cadres had good reason to support the educational *status quo.* They were among the chief beneficiaries of the existing system. Their children enjoyed advantageous access to full-time secondary and higher education. There is no question that such cadres hoped to perpetuate the provision of such education for their children. Khrushchev's proposals surely must have caused consternation among party cadres which other top party leaders would readily have been conscious of. In this respect the party itself was probably an important constituent pressure group which reinforced the doubts Khrushchev's colleagues had about the wisdom of his proposals.

[18]For a view of government as problem solving and adapting to environments in which communications play a crucial role, see Karl W. Deutsch, *The Nerves of Government* (New York 1963).

more transparent. There may even have been some self-interest involved in the position of the scientists. The point is that there is no objective way for either Soviet leaders or American scholars to clearly separate the elements of self-interest from those of expert predictions of dire consequences. We would argue that in western democracies as well there is often an almost indecipherable mixture of preference and prediction in policy debate. For example, social welfare policies in the United States are commonly defended in terms of the prospects of contraction and recession if welfare funds are not fed into the economy. The very ambiguity between preference and prediction may serve to enhance the prospects of group influence through the pressing of interests with the support of expert judgments. The congruence of one's interests with one's predictions is probably less important than the persuasiveness of the predictions and the acknowledged expertness of predictors, no matter whose interests they seem to support.

This almost inevitable mixture of self-interest and expertise provides a channel through which groups in the Soviet Union *may* influence policy when higher powers seek their judgment. We do not know how common this occurrence is, but we are confident that expertise is not used in this way to resolve all policy disputes. We will devote the remainder of this paper to an assessment of conditions leading to such a state, and to hypotheses about when to expect it. Our first set of hypotheses deal with what conditions within the current post-Stalin regime will be associated with such group influence. The second set will attempt to identify what it is about post-Stalinist Russia that makes this possible in contrast with the Stalin era.

III. SOME HYPOTHESES

Leadership conflict has already been cited as an important factor in leading top officials to look to group expertise. It is more than conceivable that monolithic leadership would itself seek expert advice, but we expect that it would do so more surreptitiously than through semi-public debate. More importantly, it could ignore the advice when it chose to rather than in effect being reversed by it. Under conditions of leadership conflict, unresolved disputes may lead some of the participants to broaden the scope of conflict by involving policy groups who might shift the balance. The dynamic involved may be something like the following. There is a split, for example, among the Politburo, wherein the First Secretary is about to prevail. Holders of the minority position may react to their imminent defeat by contacting their sympathizers among the "policy groups" and urging

[19]See Ploss, *op. cit.*, pp. 61, 84, 286, for other examples and a discussion of changes in the scope of conflict in the Soviet Union.

them to state their position on the issue in their specialized publications, in hopes that the balance of power will shift in their favor when more actors are involved. Broadening the scope of conflict may change the outcome.[19]

> We hypothesize that the more and greater the disputes on the top policy making level, the more likely it is that policy groups will be involved and listened to.

Brzezinski and Huntington point out that policy-makers are "more responsive to the demands or aspirations of groups" during a struggle for power, which would seem to bear out our point.[20] They use Khrushchev's struggle as an example but they themselves point out elsewhere that victors in power, struggles often reverse themselves and adopt the policies advocated by their opponent.[21] This pattern would seem to reduce the long term impact of group influence in a power struggle. Our own example is of an unreversed policy decided in a period when the heat of the struggle for power had diminished, whether it had completely died or not. Indeed the absence of a threat to his power may well have made Khrushchev more willing to yield. Brzezinski and Huntington say that while policy is the means to power in succession struggles,

> In stable dictatorial conditions, however, the leader may sometimes exercise power in matters that do not affect the security of his position. Then, as with the education reform of 1958, he can tolerate substantial amendments to his original proposal.[22]

It may be, then, that conditions of tranquility lend themselves more effectively to more or less permanent and far-reaching group influence than do power struggles. Leaders are probably more eager to solicit the support of groups when they are trying to secure power or ward off threats to their position, but group influence may be more permanent and real outside of power struggles. We are not prepared to predict that group influence over policy will be greater under power struggles or more ordinary policy conflicts, but we are prepared to argue that under either of these conditions of leadership conflict group influence will be greater than when leadership is relatively monolithic. Such an hypothesis is at the core of our whole argument.

Bauer, Inkeles and Kluckhohn observe that the failure of a policy may lead the Politburo to adopt an approach that they recently opposed.[23] Our example does not directly support this observation, although of course it does not conflict with it, but the important point suggested by it is that the nature of the issue may be an important variable. Pursuing the rationale for

[20]*Op. cit.*, p. 198.
[21]*Ibid.*, pp. 193, 240-252.
[22]*Ibid.*, p. 270.
[23]Raymond A. Bauer, Alex Inkeles and Clyde Kluckhohn, *How the Soviet System Works* (New York 1956), p. 98.

our argument of group influence in the educational reforms it is apparent that the problematic character of the issue and the fact that the consequences of a shift were not known with certainty made the judgment of policy groups more important than they would have been otherwise. The obvious implication of this is that the more problematic the consequences of a given course of action the more likely it is that groups would be involved.

A related point that is derived from interest groups politics in western democracies is that groups are likely to be more influential in policy outcomes when the issue is narrow and technical than when the issue is broad and general.[24] In democratic polities, this is partly because other publics are less likely to be paying any attention or to care when the issue is technical. Thus the field is left relatively open for the interested group. A further rationale would be pertinent in the Soviet Union. It is not so much that other actors are or are not concerned; it is rather that technical advice and opinions are at a premium on technical issues.

We hypothesize that the more problematic and technical the issue, the more dependent on expert judgment elites will be. Consequently they will be more likely to consult policy groups, who will thereby be more influential on such issues.

While we hope that the above hypotheses help account for conditions varying *within* the current post-Stalinist regime which we associated with such group influence as we have illustrated, we do not argue that such influence ever occurred in the Stalin era. We know of no such prominent examples. In this final section we will identify several underlying conditions which in part distinguish the two eras and make groups more important in policy formation, or at least potentially so, in the present.

One important change is that the rigid dictatorial one-man rule of the Stalin period has given way to collective leadership. While there may be one dominant leader, his power is shared among several key figures at the apex of the political structure. Under conditions of a diffused power structure, group influence is far more likely.[25] When power is exercised in an autocratic manner, groups must gain the ear of the all-powerful leader if they are to influence the policy process. During a period of collective leadership the access routes to points of decision making become more numerous. Indeed,

---

[24]See Harry Eckstein, *Pressure Group Politics* (Stanford 1960).

[25]Dispersion of decision making can assume a "personalized" as well as an institutional form. Instead of separation of powers between executive, legislative, and judicial groups one may find a separation of powers between leaders at the top of an outwardly monolithic political structure. See Ploss, *op. cit.,* p. 286. On the relationship between group influence and a diffusion of power see Harry Eckstein, "Group Theory and the Comparative Study of Pressure Groups," *Comparative Politics,* edited by Harry Eckstein and David Apter (New York 1963), p. 396.

the very nature of collective leadership may make political leaders more responsive to group demands.

Carl Linden has argued that the transition from autocracy to oligarchy brings with it a constant struggle for political primacy at the very top. Since no individual is automatically assured of predominant power he must secure that position by winning and holding the support of a combination of societal groupings. His actual or potential rivals, on the other hand, can build their own constituency coalitions by identifying with those elements discontented with an incumbent leader's policy. The politics of leadership struggle then intertwines with the politics of group conflict. It is this interdependence which facilitates group influence on the policy process.[26]

> We hypothesize that the larger and more collective the top leadership, the greater the prospects for the sort of disputes that can lead to the involvement of social groups in policy formation.

The attitudes of those leaders and their methods of social control will also have an important bearing on the prospects for group influence. Under a system of terror individuals are frightened into silent submissiveness and live in an atomized state. Unaware that others share common attitudes, grievances and interests, the terrorized citizen accepts his lot and does not attempt to influence the behavior of decision makers.[27] Only when terror subsides does this condition of "pluralistic ignorance" end and the opportunity for interest articulation emerge. For now communication, both through the formal mass media and through informal personal interaction, assumes a more candid and realistic nature. Under these new conditions the communication process itself facilitates group influence. It serves to generate widespread awareness of commonly shared attitudes which in turn becomes a powerful factor inducing groups to influence policy outcomes in their favor.

The leashing of terror enhances the prospect for group influence in other ways as well. David Easton points out that not all societal claims and demands are converted into policy outputs. Only those which become public issues have this possibility.[28] In any polity this requires the patronage and support of some political authority figure. In a system where terror is no longer all-pervasive individuals may be far more likely to risk identification with unresolved issues since the consequences of poor choices are far less serious. At best it may mean that one's power position remains static. At worst it may mean a diminution in political power and perhaps even demotion. But it does not mean internment or execution as it so often did

[26]*Op. cit.*, pp. 20-21.

[27]This condition of "pluralistic ignorance" is discussed in Bauer and others, *op. cit.*, p. 263.

[28]David Easton, "The Analysis of Political Systems," *Comparative Politics: Notes and Readings*, edited by Roy C. Macridis andd Bernard E. Brown (Homewood 1964), pp. 94-95.

during the Stalinist period. The individual has lost a political battle but not necessarily the war. He remains on the scene with the possibility of recouping his losses and rising once again to top political positions.

We hypothesize that groups will be influential as technocratic spokesmen only when terror subsides and the regime accords them legitimacy of expression of their point of view.

The kind of expert judgment involved in the interest articulation we have described is a function of the nature of the society. Harry Eckstein has noted that modernization increases the significance of groups in the political process.[29] We suggest that the modernization of Russia positively relates to potential group influence in several ways. First, it introduces a functional specialization and differentiation into the society which in turn generates a diffusion of interests competing with one another to write the laws of society to their advantage. During the early stages of Soviet rule the party preempts interest articulation not only because it wants to but also, to some degree, because it has to. The society which the Bolsheviks inherited was largely composed of an undifferentiated mass of peasants who had traditionally played a politically passive role. Thus the task of identifying and articulating interests fell to the party by default.

This is not to say that at the time of Bolshevik ascendancy there were no functionally specialized groups with political experience in the protection of their interests. They existed but they were far fewer and far less significant than in the present period. Furthermore, those groups tended to be stigmatized by their identification with the old regime. Thus any demands put forth by them lacked an essential ingredient for success—the presumption of legitimacy. The *a priori* belief of the party that such individuals were disloyal deprived them of any political currency which could be used in the process of trading support for recognition of their demands.

The modernization of Russia has fundamentally altered this situation. Not only has it generated a complex economic and social pluralism but it also has provided new cadres to staff these skilled groups.[30] Those who possess scarce technical capabilities are far more likely to exert influence today than in the past. Such technocrats are products of the new system (the new Soviet man) and their loyalty is not impugned. Consequently, their attempts to influence the political process is perceived in legitimized rather than counter-revolutionary terms. The arguments of scientific, educational, and managerial experts may have been motivated by selfish concerns. But, as

---

[29]"Group Theory and the Comparative Study of Pressure Groups," *Comparative Politics, op. cit.*, p. 395.

[30]For an interesting suggestive article on the growth of pluralism in Russian society see Henry L. Roberts, "The Succession to Khrushchev in Perspective," *Proceedings of the Academy of Political Science* 28 (Apr. 1965), pp. 2-12.

we noted earlier these arguments were made in the context of what would best serve the interests of the Soviet Union. Given the fact that these experts are the products of the Soviet period, their counsel cannot be ignored on the grounds that the purveyors of such ideas are politically suspect. The handicap which afflicted old specialists simply does not operate in the contemporary period.

Stalin's transformation of Russia insured the increased importance of groups in the policy process in yet another way, although the full impact of this development had to await the dictator's death. It was during the thirties and forties that the politicization of society reached totalitarian dimensions. As politics came to predominate in all areas of life individuals realized that the protection of their interests could be achieved only by gaining access to and influencing the political structure. Unlike western political systems where many issues are resolved in the private sector of the society, the struggle over who gets what when and how in the Soviet Union takes place entirely within the public domain.[31] Thus individuals and groups are perforce compelled to focus their attention and pressure on the decision-making process if they hope to maintain or improve their status.

The fourth contribution of modernization stems from the fact that a complex technological society requires stable occupational group membership. As we have already suggested the behavior of managers, teachers, educators and scientists was motivated in part by their desire to protect interests derived from their occupational roles. Such a phenomenon occurs, however, only when individuals have an opportunity to firmly anchor themselves in one occupational role so that it becomes for them an important reference group. This connotes, in turn, an absence of the recurring purge so characteristic of the Stalinist period. Stalin purposefully removed leading strata of important groups lest they become too closely identified with the interests of those groups and more specifically lest they use the economic, social and political resources inherent in those groups for the purpose of delimiting the decision making power of the leader.

Now this is a very costly procedure and one that a developed society cannot afford to engage in for very long. Managers, teachers, scientists and other specialists are not created overnight and their summary purge means not only a loss of experienced and skilled personnel but also the forfeiture of scarce economic resources invested in their education and training. As Soviet

---

[31]We are identifying here a difference of degree. As Eckstein notes, pressure groups have become very active and significant in the postwar political systems of Britain, France, etc., for similar reasons. "One rather obvious reason for this development is the growth of the social service state—of positive government regulating, planning, directing, or entirely drawing into itself all sorts of social activities. This trend has given social groups a greater stake in politics and therefore mobilized them to a much greater extent while making government increasingly dependent on the collaboration and advice, technical or otherwise, of the groups." *Comparative Politics, op. cit.,* p. 395.

society has become more complex and sophisticated this type of gross economic waste proved intolerable. We do not imply, of course, that high ranking Soviet personnel are no longer removed from their positions. The official press is full of accounts concerning the removal of such personnel. We do argue, however, that "the purge" today significantly differs from its Stalinist predecessor. At present leading occupational strata are not removed in the wholesale manner reminiscent of the thirties and forties. More importantly their removal is seldom if ever accompanied by internment or execution. Most often they seem to be demoted to a less prestigious and influential job but within the same area of expertise.

We hypothesize that the more modern the society, the more dependent it is on technical expertise, which in turn improves the prospects that groups may influence policy when higher powers seek their judgment.[32]

We have attempted in this article to illustrate that under some circumstances social groups can influence policy formation in the Soviet Union. We have specified those circumstances as clearly as we could, providing hypotheses according to which we expect group influence to vary. If our analysis is sound and valid, we hope that it may provide some guidelines for further research on group influence in the comparative study of Communist political systems.[33] Indeed, we hope that some parts of our analysis may be relevant to the study of the role of groups in policy formation in non-communist political systems as well.

---

[32]See S. N. Eisenstadt, *The Political Systems of Empires* (New York 1963), for a suggestive analysis of the role of skill groups in historical bureaucratic empires.

[33]See Robert C. Tucker, "On the Study of Comparative Communism," *World Politics* 19 (Jan. 1967), pp. 242-257.

E

MASS PARTICIPATION, REPRESENTATION, AND SUPPORT

19

Political Participation and Strategies of Influence: A Comparative Study

Sidney Verba

Democracy refers in some rough way to the degree to which power and influence over significant decisions for a society is diffused throughout that society. Political participation, therefore, will increase the extent to which a nation is democratic only insofar as such participation involves at some point influence by the participant over governmental decisions. Participatory acts whose main function is to express support for the government are important, but not as crucial to democracy as are acts that involve influence.

The influence of a group or individual over a governmental decision may be defined as equal to the degree to which governmental officials act to benefit that group or individual because the officials believe that they will risk some deprivation (they will risk their jobs, be criticized, lose votes) if they do not so act. Thus influence involves both the outcome of the decision (it will, to some extent, be more advantageous to the influential groups or individual than it would have been if that group or individual has not been influential), and the motives of the decision-makers (they act to benefit the

"Political Participation and Strategies of Influence: a Comparative Study" by Sidney Verba is reprinted from *Acta Sociologica,* 6 (1962), 22-42, by permission of the author and journal.

This article is part of a larger comparative study of attitudes toward politics and citizenship in Germany, Italy, Mexico, Great Britain, and the United States carried out under the direction of Gabriel A. Almond and the author. The main publication is *The Civic Culture: Political Attitudes and Democracy in Five Nations* (Princeton: Princeton University Press, 1963). The study was sponsored by the Center of International Studies of Princeton University and supported by a grant from the Carnegie Corporation of New York. The material reported is based on approximately 1000 interviews carried on in each nation using a national, multi-stage probability sample.

Footnotes are abridged.

group because they believe they will otherwise suffer some deprivation). The latter criterion is important. Officials may act to benefit a particular group for a variety of reasons; out of a feeling of paternalism, for instance. But it is only when officials act because they fear the consequences of not so acting, that a group may be considered to be influential and a participant in the decision.

Influence, and consequently democracy, are defined in terms of the way in which governmental elites make decisions. But the problem of studying the way in which such decisions are made is enormous, especially when one is dealing with an entire nation, or as in this paper, with five nations at once. No such attempt is made here. Rather, this paper concentrates not upon the perceptions and behaviors of governmental elites but upon the perceptions and behaviors of governmental elites but upon the perceptions and behaviors of the ordinary citizen. It will report some preliminary results to a series of survey questions on the amount of influence individuals believe they can exert over the government, and the ways in which they would go about it. The paper will concentrate on differences among the five nations surveyed—the United States, Britain, Germany, Italy, and Mexico. In subsequent publications, attempts will be made to explore and explain those differences further.

We are interested in the perception of the ordinary man as to how much influence he has over the decisions of his government. Thinking that one can influence the government or even attempting to influence government is not the same as actually influencing it. An individual may think he has influence over decisions or he may attempt to exert influence over decisions, and the government official may be unmoved. Conversely, he may believe that all government decisions are made without any consideration of his needs and desires and of the needs and desires of his fellow citizens, when, in fact, government officials constantly try to calculate the reactions of groups to their acts. In the latter case, an individual will exert influence without being aware he is doing so.

If the degree to which individuals believe they can influence the course of governmental decisions is not necessarily related to their actual level of influence, why study their subjective views as to their competence? There are several reasons. The perception that one can participate furthers such participation: if an individual believes he has influence, he is more likely to attempt to influence the government. A subjectively competent citizen, therefore, is more likely to be an active citizen. And if government officials do not necessarily respond to active influence attempts, they are more likely to respond to such attempts to influence than to a passive citizenry that makes no demands. If the ordinary citizen, on the other hand, perceives government policy as being far outside of his sphere of influence, he is unlikely to attempt to influence that policy and government officials are unlikely to worry about the potential pressure that can be brought to bear on them. Thus the extent to which citizens in a nation perceive themselves as competent to influence the government should be closely related to the extent of democracy in that country.

A good deal of the influence that individuals and groups exert over their government may not involve any conscious attempt on their part to influence. As our concept of influence specifies, governmental officials are being influenced if they respond to what they consider a possible deprivation. This implies that the citizen or group of citizens from whom they fear some deprivation may, at the time the government officials are acting, neither have attempted to influence these officials nor intend so to attempt. The government officials act in anticipation of certain consequences if they do not so act. They believe that if they do not act to benefit a group, that group will at some point in the future withdraw its support or its vote. In many respects a good deal of the influence that the ordinary citizen has over the decisions of the government officials may be of this anticipatory type.

But if one is interested in the extent of the perception that one can influence the government, one will have to concentrate on more overt and conscious attempts to affect actions of the government. Several questions may be asked about conscious attempts to influence the government:

1. Under what circumstances will an individual make some conscious effort to influence the government? Direct political influence attempts are rare. For the ordinary citizen, the activities of government—even local government—may seem quite distant. At the time that a decision is being made, the citizen will not be aware that it is being made or of what its consequences for him are likely to be. It is likely then, that only in situations of some stress in which a government activity is perceived to have a direct and serious impact upon the individual will a direct influence attempt be triggered off.

2. What method will be used in the influence attempt? Some major dimensions along which the method used can vary include: whether or not the attempt is made through legitimate channels; whether the attempt is violent or non-violent; whether the individual attempts to influence the government alone or attempts to enlist the support of others; and, if he seeks support, whose support does he seek.

3. What is the effect of the influence attempt? The problem of the extent to which the government official changes his behavior in response to some influence attempt on the part of a citizen is beyond the scope of this study. However, since it concentrates on the perspectives of the citizen, we shall consider his view as to the likelihood that an attempt made by him to influence the government would have any effect. That, after all, is a key question.

The distribution of subjective competence: Does an individual feel he can influence his government? How would he go about it? Would it make any difference? Respondents were asked questions that attempted to place them in hypothetical stress situations. Each respondent was asked to suppose that a law were being considered by the national legislature that he considered very unjust and harmful. Could he do anything about it and, if so, what? He was then asked how much effect he thought any action he took would have, and how likely it was that he actually would do something. A similar set of questions was asked about an unjust and harmful regulation being considered by the most local governmental unit.[1] These questions attempted to get some notion of the respondent's views as to the extent of his political competence and, more important, of the strategy of influence open to him.

The question as to the amount of influence the ordinary man has is a fundamental political one and the response to it reflects an individual's perception of the nature of his government and of his own role as a citizen. Let us look at responses as to how amenable to influence is a local government. This is a good place to start because the impact of local government tends to be more immediate. And, for obvious reasons, people in all countries tend to think that one can do more about a local regulation than about a law considered by the national legislature. But what is striking are the sharp differences among nations in the number who think they can do something and in what these people think they can do. In response to the question on whether one can do anything about a local law that is unjust American and British respondents most frequently say that there is something they can do. More than three-quarters of the people interviewed in each of these two countries express the opinion that they have some recourse if they believe the local government is planning a law they consider unjust. (The data on what individuals say they can do about a local regulation is reported in Table 1. The figures we are considering here are near the bottom of the table.) In each country, only 17% say that there is nothing they can do. In the other three countries over 30% of those interviewed report that there is nothing they can do in such a situation. In Germany more people (62%) say they can do something than in Mexico and Italy (52% and 51%). In the latter two countries, respondents are more likely to say they do not know what they can do. Clearly then the images that citizens have of

[1]The exact question wording on the national government was: Suppose a law were being considered by (appropriate national legislature specified for each nation) which you considered to be unjust or harmful, what do you think you could do? If you made an effort to change this law, how likely is it that you would succeed? If such a case arose, how likely is it you *would actually* try to do something about it? The exact question wording on the local government was: Suppose a regulation were being considered by (most local governmental unit: Town? Village? etc. specified) which you considered very unjust or harmful, what do you think you could do? If you made an effort to change this regulation how likely is it that you would succeed? If such a case arose, how likely is it that you *would actually* do something about it?

Table 1.   What citizens would do to try to influence their local government, by nation.

	U.S.	U.K.	Germany	Italy	Mexico
Some citizens would try to enlist the support of others by: Organizing some informal group; arousing their friends and neighbors, getting them to write letters of protest or to sign a petition	56%	34%	13%	7%	26%
Working through a political party.	1	1	3	1	—
Working through some other formal group of which they are a member: union, church, professional group	4	3	5	1	2
TOTAL WHO WOULD ENLIST SUPPORT OF OTHERS*	59%	36%	22%	8%	28%
Other citizens would, as individuals: Directly contact political leaders (elected officials) or the press. Write a letter to, or visit a local political leader	20%	45%	15%	12%	15%
Directly contact administrative officials (non-elected officials)	1	3	31	12	18
Consult a lawyer; appeal through courts . .	2	1	3	2	2
Vote against offending officials at next election	14	4	1	1	—
Take some violent action	1	1	1	1	1
Just protest	—	—	—	12	—
Other.	1	2	—	3	5
TOTAL WHO WOULD ACT AS INDIVIDUALS**	18%	42%	40%	43%	25%
TOTAL WHO WOULD DO SOMETHING WITH OTHERS OR AS INDIVIDUALS*	77%	77%	62%	51%	52%
Other respondents say they can do nothing	17%	17%	31%	31%	32%
Others say they do not know if they can do anything	6%	5%	7%	18%	15%
TOTAL (respondents)	100%	100%	100%	100%	100%
TOTAL (responses)	123%	115%	111%	101%	118%
Number of cases.	970	963	955	995	1295

 * The total percentage is less than the total of the individual cells since some respondents gave more than one answer.
 ** This row includes only the respondents who replied that they could do something, but did not mention working with others. Hence, the total is less than some of the individual categories which contain respondents who may have mentioned both group activity and an individual activity.

their roles and potentials differ from nation to nation. Britons and Americans are more likely to think of themselves as competent to influence their local government than are people in the other three countries.

That an individual believes there is something he can do if the government is planning an unjust or unfair act does not mean that he will in fact try to do something. This was a hypothetical situation and, of course, one does not really know what respondents would do if they ever were in fact faced with such a challenging situation. But they were asked for their opinions on whether or not they actually would act. In all countries many who say they can do something about an unjust regulation report that in fact they probably would do nothing. But the number who report that there is at least some likelihood that they would make an effort, reflects the same national pattern reported above. 58% of the American respondents and 60% of those in Britain say that there is some likelihood that they would actually make an effort to influence an unjust regulation. In Germany 44% made some such affirmation, while in Italy 41% of the respondents say that they might act in these circumstances. (The question was, unfortunately, not asked in a comparable form in Mexico.) The American and British respondents express a willingness to act much more frequently than do the respondents in Germany and Italy.

Lastly, there is some evidence that the subjective estimate of one's propensity to act in such a challenging political situation is not completely unrelated to actual attempts to influence the government. In all five nations a substantially larger proportion of those respondents who say there is something they can do about a local unjust regulation (let us, for convenience, call them "local competents") report some experience in attempting to influence the local government than is reported among those who say there is nothing they can do. These data are reported in Table 2.

At this point we are merely describing differences among nations in the political attitudes of respondents. In this connection it is clear that the frequency with which individuals report that they could have some effect upon a law contemplated by the local government differs from nation to nation. The explanation of these differences is more difficult. At least part of the explanation of the differences in the degree to which individuals believe they are politically competent rests upon the differing structures of government. The individual who says he can do nothing to oppose the local government may be making a quite realistic appraisal of his potentialities. Thus the lower frequency of subjective political competence in Italy, for instance, may be largely a reaction to a political structure—the Italian prefecture system—that does not allow the individual to be politically competent. It is not that individuals choose to be uninfluential. It may be that they have no choice.

The frequency with which individuals say they could exert some influence over the local government is clearly a case in which attitudes are affected significantly by governmental structure (although there is evidence that they are not completely determined by these structures). Let us turn to a more significant aspect of political competence than the extent to which individuals believe themselves competent; an aspect of competence that is not as clearly affected by the structure of the local government. This is the strategy an individual would use in attempting to influence the government. The way in which those individuals who report that they *could* influence the government report they *could go about* exerting this influence is, of course, important. It makes a difference whether an individual has, on the one hand, only the vaguest notion as to what he can do in such a situation or on the other, a clear and explicit view of the channels open to him for expressing his point of view. It also makes a difference what resources he believes he has available to use in such a situation. Furthermore, the strategy that an individual would use will naturally have an effect on the extent to which his subjective view of his ability to influence will represent real influence potential—that is, represent the sort of activity that has some chance of changing the behaviors of the government officials. Lastly, by concentrating on how those who think they can have influence would go about exerting that influence, we can partially eliminate (but only partially) the effect of the differing degrees to which local governments are amenable to influence. We shall deal primarily with those who think they have influence, the "local competents", and ask how they would exert that influence.

Table 2. Proportion of those respondents who say they have attempted to influence the local government among local competents and local non-competents.

Proportion of respondents who have attempted to influence the government.

	Among local competents	*Among local non-competents*
U.S.	33% (745)	10% (225)
U.K..	18% (748)	3% (217)
Germany	21% (590)	2% (355)
Italy.	13% (508)	4% (487)
Mexico.	9% (677)	2% (618)

(Numbers in parentheses refer to the base upon which percentage was calculated.)

The strategy of influence: The strategies of influence that individuals report they would use are summarized in Table 1. Consider first the question of what social resources the individual feels he has available to him in attempting to influence the local government. When one looks at the individual and his government, one is tempted to see him as lonely, powerless, and somewhat frightened by the immensity of the powers he faces. Whatever the validity of this view may be in terms of the actual amount of power the average man has and the social resources available to him, our data suggest that a large number of our respondents think of themselves neither as powerless nor, what is more important, as alone, in their relationship to the government.

This fact is reflected in the data reported in Table 1. A number of respondents believe that they can enlist the support of others in their attempts to influence the government. What is most striking is the variation from country to country in the numbers who feel they can call on others to aid them. In the United States, 59% of the respondents indicate that they would attempt to enlist the support of others if they wish to change a regulation they consider unjust. At the other extreme, only 8% of the Italian sample mention the use of this social resource. In the other countries, the percentage reporting that they would try to enlist the support of others varies from 36% in Britain, to 28% in Mexico, to 22% in Germany.[2]

Who is it that citizens would enlist to support them? Individuals as we know are members of a large number of social structures. They are not merely citizens of their nations; they are members of families, communities, churches, voluntary associations, trade unions and a myriad of other groups and organizations. Much has been written about the important role of formal organizations in the political process—in particular, the role of political parties and formal associational interest groups. But what the data show most strikingly is that when it comes to the support that individuals believe they could enlist in a challenging political situation, they think much more often of enlisting the support of the informal face-to-face groups of which they are members than they think of enlisting the support of the formal organizations with which they are affiliated.

In all countries, the numbers are few who say that they would work through their political party if they were attempting to counteract some unjust regulation being considered by the local government. Less than 1% of the respondents—with the exception of Germany, where the figure is about 3%—mention that they would work through their political party. Clearly, no matter how important the role of political parties may be in democratic societies, relatively few citizens think of them first as the place where support may be enlisted for attempts to influence the government.[3]

---

[2]Since question wording can seriously affect responses, it is important to note here that the notion that one can enlist the support of others was in no way suggested by the question or by the interviewer's probing of the question. Interviewers were carefully instructed not to ask such questions as: "Is there anyone you could get to help you?" or "Would you attempt to do this alone or with other people?"

[3]To some extent the infrequent mention of a political party in this context probably understates the role of parties in this influence process. Many more respondents mentioned contacting government officials. If they explicitly mentioned that the partisan affiliation of the official was

In all countries, more individuals report that they would attempt to work through other formal organized groups than would attempt to work through political parties. But even when one considers the entire range of formal organizations to which people may belong, the numbers who report they would enlist the support of these organizations is small, in no country going above 5% of all the respondents (as seen on Table 1) or 9% of the local competents.[4] Of course, not all respondents have some formal organization at their disposal. Such organizations are more frequent in some nations than in others. And the percentage who report membership differs substantially from country to country. Furthermore, not all formal organizations are equally politically relevant. But even if one considers only those respondents who belong to some formal organization that they report is involved in politics, the percentage invoking such membership in a stress situation is much smaller than the percentage who are members. In the United States where such memberships are most frequent, 228 respondents report membership in some organization that they consider to be involved in some way with government or politics, but only 35 Americans report that they would work through such an organization if they were trying to influence a local regulation. In Italy where such memberships are least frequent, we find the same pattern. Fifty-six Italians belong to some organization they believe is involved in political affairs, but only 13 Italians would work through a formal organization if they were trying to influence a local regulation. The greatest frequency of mention of formal organization is found in Germany, but it is still only half as frequent as the frequency of membership in a politically relevant organization.

That formal organizations are rarely invoked as the resource that individuals would use if they were trying to enlist some support for their attempt to influence the government does not mean that these organizations are unimportant politically. They still operate on what we have called the passive level—that is, the citizen has influence over government officials by being a member of such a group, but he does not necessarily make any overt attempt to influence the government. And this sort of influence is of a great significance, perhaps of greater overall significance than the overt influence attempts that citizens from time to time will make. Furthermore though

relevant in giving them access to him, they would be coded as working through a party. But many may have considered this affiliation relevant, even if it was not mentioned.

[4]The percentage of respondents mentioning a particular strategy of influence can be computed either as a percentage of the entire population or as a percentage of the local competents—in this latter case, that is, as a percentage of those who feel there is something they can do. Both figures are important. The first figure reflects frequency of certain types of political behavior in a nation. But if we are interested in how nations differ in the strategies their citizens will use, we must use the second figure—the percentage of local competents who would use a particular strategy—for, otherwise, differences between nations in the percentage choosing a particular strategy might be merely a reflection of the fact that there are more in one country than another who report that there is "nothing" they could do.

individuals would not use their formal organizations as the means to influence the government directly, such formal membership enhances the prospects that an individual will believe himself capable of influencing the government and will in fact make some such attempt. Thus, even though he does not directly use his group membership in attempting to influence the local government, an individual may, for a variety of reasons, develop greater self-confidence in his own political competence through organization membership.

Cooperative political behavior: If one is interested in who it is that citizens believe they can enlist to support them if they are trying directly and consciously to influence an act of their local government, one must turn to the informal face-to-face groups to which they belong. In all countries, respondents more frequently mention enlisting the support of such groups—arousing their neighbors, getting friends and acquaintances to support their position, circulating a petition—than they mention using some formal organization. This is seen in the top row of Table 1. The differences among nations are quite sharp here. These differences are highlighted if one considers the proportion of local competents (i.e., those who believe they can influence the local government) who say they would cooperate with their fellow citizens in attempting to influence the government: 73% of American local competents would use informal groups, whereas only 13% of Italian local competents and 22% of the German would do so. In Mexico, though the proportion of local competents is relatively low, the proportion of these local competents who would work through informal groups is quite high—50%. And in Britain, the proportion of local competents who say they would seek the cooperation of others is about as great—43%.

The belief that cooperation with one's fellow citizens is both a possible political action and an effective one, it may be suggested, represents a highly significant orientation from the point of view of a democratic political system. The diffusion of influence over political decisions by which we define democracy implies some cooperative ability among the citizenry. This cooperation would appear to be necessary in terms both of the amount of influence the ordinary man could otherwise expect to have and the results of the influence of the ordinary man on governmental decisions. By definition, the "average" man's influence over the government must be small. Compared with the forces of the government and the state he is a frail creature indeed, and this would apply to local as well as national government. If the ordinary man is to have any influence vis-à-vis the government, it must be in concert with his fellows. Secondly, uncooperative and completely individualistic influence attempts could only lead to dysfunctional results from the point of view of the output of a democratic government. Every individual demand cannot be met or the result will be chaos. If the government is to be responsive to the demands of the ordinary man, those demands must be aggregated, and the aggregation of interests implies cooperation among men. The aggregation of interests involved in the cooperation of groups of like-minded individuals is aggregation on a rather low level, but it does suggest a propensity to work together with one's fellows that is relevant for larger political structures as well. In any case, one may suggest that the citizen who believes that he can work cooperatively with others in his environment if he wants to engage in political activity has a quite different perspective on politics from the individual who thinks of himself as a lone political actor.

Furthermore, the notion that one can affect a government decision by bringing one's peers into the dispute is a highly political notion. It represents a fairly clear attempt to use political influence in one's relations with government officials. The invocation of others in the dispute indicates that in this way the individual hopes to bring pressure on the officials, to threaten them with some deprivation if they do not accede to his demands. The threat that many make—whether it be the threatened loss of votes or of support, or the threat of public criticism—is, other things being equal, greater than the threat that one can make. Thus the individual who mentions getting others to join him in his dispute with the government is more likely to be an individual who sees himself as able to influence his government. And the variation among the five nations in the frequencies with which such groups are mentioned reflects a varying distribution of such citizen competence.

Lastly, the importance of this propensity toward cooperation with one's fellow political actors is stressed not merely because such behavior has significant consequences for a political system, but because it is a type of behavior which cannot be understood and explained solely in terms of differences in the structure of local government. The difference between the individual who responds that he would write a letter to the local council and the individual who responds that he would write a letter to the local council *and try to induce his friends to do likewise* cannot be explained by differences among nations in the structure and powers of their respective local councils.[5] Furthermore, as we shall see shortly, the propensity to cooperate politically can not be explained in terms of differing levels of social and economic develop-

[5]This is not completely true. 'Governmental structure may be more amenable to group influence in some countries than in others. But this is more likely to be the case because of experience in the past with such groups rather than formal structure. On the other hand, there is no doubt that certain structures of government foster such "banding together" protests more than others. Structures where power is diffused among a large number of autonomous or semi-autonomous boards and councils and the like (especially elected boards and councils) are more likely to foster such protest than structures dominated by a centrally appointed official whose domain includes a larger area (as with the Italian prefect system). But this is an example of the general proposition that there will be an interaction between political orientation and political structure. In this case, however, the explanation of the origins of this group-forming attitude in terms of formal structure alòne would be quite hard. One has to look beyond the structure of the local government.

ment in the five nations. The origin of this propensity toward political cooperation must be sought elsewhere.[6]

Though the use of primary groups as a resource for influence is most common in the United States, Britain and Mexico, several interesting differences between the United States and Britain on the one hand and Mexico on the other in this respect must be mentioned. The notion that one can mobilize an informal group to aid one in the process of attempting to influence the government, appears to be of greater significance for the actual exercise of influence in the former two countries. Earlier it was pointed out that those who report they can do something about an unjust local law (the local competents) are much more likely also to report some experience in attempting to influence the government. If we look only at the local competents and ask how those who would work through groups and those who would attempt to influence the government alone differ in terms of the extent of their experience in attempted influence, we find that in the United States and Britain those who would work through groups are more likely to be those who have had experience in attempting to influence their local government. In the United States 36% of those who report they would work through informal groups (n: 547) report experience in influence attempts, whereas only 25% of those local competents who would use some other strategy (n: 198) report such experience. In Britain the parallel figures are 23% for those who mention informal groups (n: 315) and 15% for other local competents (n: 414). On the other hand, in Mexico, those who mention informal groups are a bit less likely to be the experienced respondents—7% report experience of those who mention informal groups (n: 339) as against 10% of the other local competents (n: 344).[7]

Furthermore, in the former two countries, the use of informal groups as a means of influencing the government is seen not only as a means to protest

[6]That one can show the relationship between social grouping and the propensity to form groups as well as attempt an explanation for this propensity in terms of other attitudes illustrates the advantage of "discovering" this group-forming propensity through the sort of keen but unsystematic observation of a writer like Tocqueville—who certainly noticed and was impressed by the way in which political groups could be easily formed when needed in the United States. In the first place, one now knows about the relative propensities to form groups in a new way. Those of us who work on studies of this sort like to think that the data are more reliable when systematically gathered. Secondly, the knowledge is more precise. One cannot only distinguish among nations more finely, one can specify who it is within the nation who is likely to think of forming groups of this sort. And lastly, one can explore the roots of this group-forming propensity by seeing the ways in which those individuals who think of forming such groups differ from other respondents who do not. Thus, not only is the knowledge more precise, it is more useful since it can lead to further knowledge.

[7]In Germany, those local competents who mention informal groups are somewhat less likely to be experienced. 17% of those who mention informal groups (n:126) report experience as against 23% of local competents who do not mention such groups (n:460). In Italy, those local competents who mention groups are slightly more likely to be experienced: 16% (n:67) as against 13% (n:438) of those who do not mention groups.

but as the key to effective protest. In order to test the extent to which individuals felt they could influence their local government, respondents were asked another question: "If you made an effort to change this regulation, how likely is it that you would succeed?" Of interest to us here is that a large number of American and British local competents volunteered the statement that their protest would have some likelihood of success only if others joined with them. (The percentages were 30% in the United States and 20% in Britain.) In Mexico, though a good percentage felt that there was some likelihood that they would succeed if they attempted to influence their local government, fewer than 10% of the Mexican respondents suggested that this would only be the case if they had the support of others. Thus, though the use of informal groups is perceived as a means of influence in Mexico, it is not yet perceived as the key to effective influence.[8]

One further difference deserves mention. In the United States and Britain, the use of informal groups as a means of influencing a governmental decision is considered much more appropriate on the local level than on the national level. In the United States 73% of the local competents report that they would work through informal groups in attempting to influence the local government, whereas only 38% of the national competents (i.e., those who believe they could do something if the national government were considering a law they thought unjust) would work through such groups. In Britain, similarly, 43% of the local competents would work through informal groups, while only 28% of the national competents would do so. On the other hand, in Mexico, the proportion of local and national competents who would use informal groups is about the same—50% of local competents mention informal groups as the means they would use to influence the local government and 46% of national competents say that this is the means they would use to influence the national government. The fact that the use of such groups is more closely related both to experience and to expectations of success in Britain and the United States than in Mexico, coupled with the fact that such strategy is considered more appropriate in connection with the local government in the former two countries suggests that such informal group strategy is based on a more realistic appraisal of the potentialities of such a strategy—a realistic appraisal deriving from actual experience with such groups on the local level. In Mexico, this influence strategy is less well grounded in actual local experience.

Individual activities: Among those respondents who spoke of themselves as acting as individuals in an attempt to influence the government there is some variation, as Table 1 indicates, in the strategies they mention. In the United States and Britain respondents are more likely to say that they would

---

[8]In Germany the percentage of local competents who mentioned that they would succeed only if others joined them was 12%; in Italy it was 5%.

approach an elected government official rather than an appointed official of the bureaucracy. In Mexico and Italy, respondents are as likely to say they would direct their protest toward one type of official as toward the other. In Germany, in contrast, more respondents mention appointed officials than mention elected officials as the target of their protest. It is tempting to consider these results to be a reflection of a more highly developed political competence in the United States and Britain. A protest to an elected official would appear to be inherently more of a political protest in the sense of involving an implied threat of deprivation to the official if he does not comply—since the loss of the vote is the most usual deprivation with which the individual can threaten an offending official. To some extent this may be an explanation of the differences among the nations in the chosen targets of influence attempts, but it is more likely that these differences merely reflect differences in the relative position and importance of elected and appointed officials within the structures of local governments in the respective nations.

Lastly, in considering the strategies that local competents say they would use, it is important to note that not all those who say they could do something about a local regulation they consider unjust have any clear strategy in mind. As Table 1 indicates, 12% of the Italian respondents say that they can "protest" if faced with a regulation they consider unjust, but when asked how or to whom they can protest, give no more specific reply. The 12% who would "protest" represent about one-fourth of all Italian local competents. While this answer shows a higher level of subjective competence than the answer that one could do nothing (the right to gripe and complain being perhaps one of the last and most basic of democratic rights), it certainly reflects little awareness of the political channels through which one might effectively approach the government.

Distribution patterns of influence and influence strategies: The data presented so far indicate some rather sharp differences among the nations. But the data are rather crude, representing, as they do, national totals. One would want to go further and seek some explanation for these differences. This will not be attempted in this paper, but the question will be considered of the extent to which such differences are explicable in terms of differences in the social class compositions of the samples for the various nations (and, since these were national samples, in the social class compositions of the nations.) We shall consider three questions: the extent to which the attitudes reported in the previous section are related in similar ways to social groups in the five nations (does, for instance, perceived influence increase with social class in all five nations?); the extent to which differences among nations diminish when one compares similar social groups; and the extent to which differences among differing social groups within a single nation are greater or less than differences among similar social groups across the nations. The answer to the last question, of course, depends on the first two. If, when one controls for some social class variable, one finds that the frequency of a political attitude varies sharply and in a similar manner with that variable from nation to nation and that the differences among nations tend to disappear, one will then find that differences among groups within a nation are greater than differences among similar groups across the nations.

The answers to these three questions will help us decide if the differences in political attitudes discussed in the earlier part of the paper are, in some sense, "real" differences in political style among the nations, or if they are explicable in terms of differing levels of social and economic development in the various nations—in terms, for instance, of the fact that there are many more respondents with no education in our Italian and Mexican samples than in the other nations. If a political attitude varies sharply with a social attribute in all the nations, if the differences among the nations tend to diminish when one controls for the social attribute, and if those of a particular social group are more like others of a similar social group in other nations than they are like their fellow citizens of a different social group one probably has a political attitude less intrinsic to the political style in a particular nation and more dependent on the level of social and economic development in the nation. On the other hand, if the attitude is not closely related to social grouping, if all groups in a nation are likely to respond the same way, and in ways that differ from similar groups in other nations; if therefore, an Italian from the upper class is more likely to respond like an Italian of the lower class than like a German of the upper class, one is probably dealing with an aspect of political style more intrinsic to a particular nation.

As an indicator of social group, we shall use the respondent's educational attainment. This is selected because it is a social attribute that is closely related to political attitudes and that differs sharply in its distribution from nation to nation. (For instance, 35% of the sample in the United States did not go beyond primary school education, in contrast with 69% of the Italian sample.) It will not be possible to report data for other social attributes, but suffice to say that the pattern of attitudes one would find if one considered such characteristics as occupation or income would be almost identical.

As Figure 1 clearly points out, in all countries the more education an individual has, the more likely is he to consider himself capable of influencing the local government; that is, to be what we have called a local competent. (The percentage of individuals who say they could affect a local law is measured on the vertical axis; the level of education on the horizontal.) Fifty-eight percent of those who did not get beyond primary school are local competents in the United States; 94% of those with some college education are. And the pattern repeats itself in each country. This then is a clear uniformity across national lines. No matter what the frequency in a nation of local competence, the incidence of this competence is greater among those with higher education.

Figure 1. Percentage of respondents who say they can do something about a local regulation they consider unjust, by nation and education.

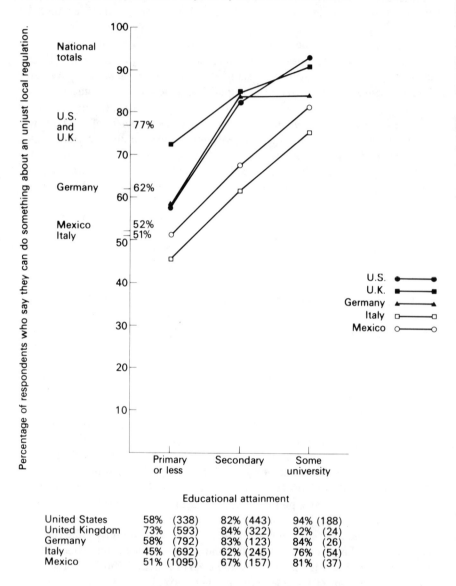

	Primary or less	Secondary	Some university
United States	58% (338)	82% (443)	94% (188)
United Kingdom	73% (593)	84% (322)	92% (24)
Germany	58% (792)	83% (123)	84% (26)
Italy	45% (692)	62% (245)	76% (54)
Mexico	51% (1095)	67% (157)	81% (37)

What about the question of the differences among and within nations? The question is a bit harder to answer for differences exist both among educational groups within the same country (as the slopes of the lines indicate) and within similar educational groups among nations (as the different lengths of the lines indicate.) Some differences among nations diminish significantly within matched educational groups. For instance, though the national totals for local competents are quite different as between the United States and Germany, the differences between the two countries almost disappear when similar educational groups are compared. On the other hand, the two pairs of nations that are most similar in terms of the national totals, the United States and Britain, on the one hand, and Mexico and Italy on the other, differ somewhat more from each other within matched educational groups than they do on the national level. This is the case among those with primary school education in the case of the United States and Britain, where Britons show a higher rate of citizen competence, and in all educational groups for Italy and Mexico, with the Mexicans showing somewhat higher competence on the lower two levels and somewhat lower competence on the higher level.

What about the problem of which are greater, national differences or educational differences? The measure of this is rough, but if one compares the range between the highest and lowest nation within each educational group with the range between the highest and lowest educational group within each nation, the results suggest that there is certainly as much if not, on the average, more variation among educational groups within a single nation than among those with similar educational attainment in different nations. The range between the nation with the greatest frequency of local competents and the nation with the smallest frequency is 28 percentage points (between Britain and Italy) on the elementary school level, 22 percentage points (again between Britain and Italy) on the secondary school level, and 18 percentage points (between the United States and Italy) on the university level. Within each nation, on the other hand, there is about as much if not more difference among the differing educational levels in the frequency with which respondents believe themselves competent to influence the government. The ranges between the educational group that most frequently reports itself competent to influence the government (those with some university education in each nation) and the group that least frequently reports such competence (those with only primary education or no education in each country) are: United States, 36 percentage points; Britain, 19 percentage points; Germany, 26 percentage points; Italy, 31 percentage points; and Mexico, 30 percentage points. These figures compare extremes in terms of education and in terms of nation. But they do suggest that in terms of overall local competence, similar educational groups compared cross-nationally are at least as similar and perhaps more similar than are different educational groups within a nation.

So far we have considered the extent to which individuals believe they can influence a local unjust regulation. But the strategy an individual would use may be more important than the simple distinction of whether or not he thinks he can do anything. In particular the belief that one can cooperate with one's fellow citizen as a means of influencing the government appears to

Figure 2.   Percentage of local competents who would enlist the support of an informal group in order to influence a local regulation they consider unjust, by nation and education.

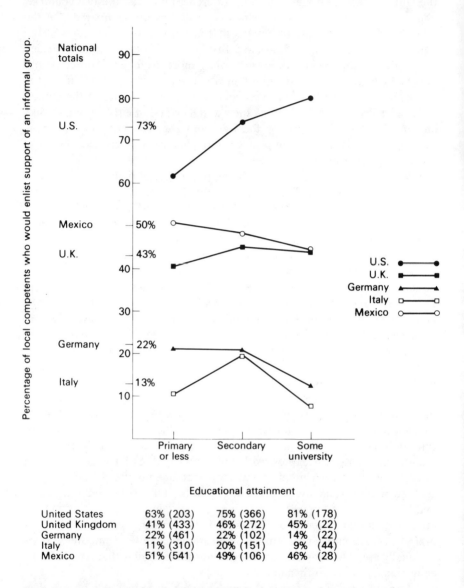

Educational attainment

United States	63% (203)	75% (366)	81% (178)
United Kingdom	41% (433)	46% (272)	45% (22)
Germany	22% (461)	22% (102)	14% (22)
Italy	11% (310)	20% (151)	9% (44)
Mexico	51% (541)	49% (106)	46% (28)

be important. Does this particular political strategy depend to as large an extent upon educational attainments as does the existence of local competence? The data in Figure 2 suggest that this is not the case. The percentage of local competents who would work through informal groups varies sharply from country to country even within each educational group, but varies very little among educational groups within the individual countries.[9] Only in the United States does the frequency with which such activity is mentioned vary directly with educational attainment, and even in this case the relationship is not as strong as that between education levels in terms of local competence in general. Consider again the contrast between the United States and Germany. When we consider similar educational groups, German and American respondents hardly differ in the frequency with which they say that there is something they can do about a local unjust regulation. But if we compare the percentage of the local competents who would cooperate with their fellow citizens, we see that on each educational level, German respondents are much less likely to mention such activity. Furthermore, more highly educated German respondents are no more likely to talk of such activity than are less highly educated ones. In general, unlike the situation in relation to overall local competence where the range of difference among nations was no greater and perhaps a little less than the range of variation among educational groups, the variation among nations in the frequency with which political cooperation is mentioned is much greater on all educational levels than in the variation among educational groups within a nation.[10] Here, then, may be a pattern of political behavior whose existence is independent of the educational level in a nation. Education, the data suggest, may lead individuals to believe that they can influence their government, no matter what country they live in (providing, of course, that there is at least some institutional structure to support this). The data also suggest that as the overall educational levels of nations rise, they will become more similar in this respect. But education does not necessarily increase the potentiality that individuals will create groups to support them. The ability to create political structures through cooperation with one's fellow citizens in time of stress seems to be typical of some nations and not of others. It is an element of political style, not a result of educational attainment.

The data on differences among social groups in citizen competence suggest that it makes a great deal of difference who you are within your own country whether or not you believe yourself able to influence a local regulation. If you have more education, a higher status or are male, you are clearly more likely to consider yourself competent. In this sense, one's self-perceptions of one's role as a citizen vary greatly with one's social position within a nation. But whether or not the local competent believes that his friends and neighbors are available to help him in a situation of this sort depends relatively little on his social position within a nation, but depends

---

[9]The data are calculated as a percentage of local competents, not of the total population. This is to isolate the political strategy that competents would use from the fact that the frequency of competents differs from country to country.

[10]The difference between the pattern in relation to the extent to which individuals think they have influence and that in relation to their strategy of influence is quite striking if one compares Figures 1 and 2.

heavily on what nation he happens to be in. Political competence, thus, grows with higher education or occupational status, but the style of political competence seems to be rooted more in general political culture.[11]

[11]As mentioned earlier, a similar pattern would appear if one controlled for other indicators of social group. The intriguing question is, of course, how does one explain the differences in propensity to form groups if such social variables do not explain it.

20

Social Structure and Political Participation: Developmental Relationships

Norman H. Nie, G. Bingham Powell, Jr.,
and Kenneth Prewitt

Economic development has consequences for many aspects of social life. Some of these social consequences, in turn, have an impact on a nation's political life. Studies of social mobilization, for example, have demonstrated that economic development is associated with sharp increases in the general level of political participation.[1] These studies report strong relationships between aggregate socio-economic measures such as per capita income, median level of education, and percentage of the population in

Author's abridgement reprinted by permission of the authors and the American Political Science Association from Norman H. Nie, G. Bingham Powell, Jr., and Kenneth Prewitt, "Social Structure and Political Participation: Developmental Relationships," *American Political Science Review* 63, pp. 361-378, June 1969, and 63, pp. 808-832, September 1969, using only pp. 361-370, 372-374, 811-814, 819-820, 824-828. Space limitations have necessitated deleting portions of this two-part article, including extensive methodological comments and explanations. The interested reader will find page references to the omitted material in the text and footnotes. Article revised and abridged by Norman Nie. The authors are listed alphabetically to indicate equal co-authorship.

[1] Karl W. Deutsch, "Social Mobilization and Political Development," *American Political Science Review*, 55 (Sept. 1961), pp. 493-515. Also, particularly, Daniel Lerner, *The Passing of Traditional Society* (New York: Free Press of Glencoe, 1958). For important analysis which in part contradicts the social mobilization hypothesis, see Walter Dean Burnham, "The Changing Shape of the American Political Universe," *American Political Science Review*, 59 (March 1965), pp. 7-28. Burnham indexes political participation with voter turnout; we deliberately exclude voting from our scale of participation. It is not clear, therefore, whether our general findings are in opposition to Burnham's. There is some reason for presuming that voting and other types of political participation are much more independent than a previous generation of scholarship has assumed.

urban areas, on one hand, and aggregate measures of political participation, such as voting turnout, on the other. Simultaneously, scholars conducting surveys of individual political participation consistently have reported that an individual's social status, education, and organizational memberships strongly affect the likelihood of his engaging in various types of political activities.[2]

In spite of the consistency of both sets of findings across many studies and although the findings appear frequently in analysis of political stability, democracy, and even strategies of political growth,[3] we know little about the connections between social structure and political participation. With few exceptions the literature on individual participation is notable for low level generalizations (the better educated citizen talks about politics more regularly), and the absence of systematic and comprehensive theory. While the literature on the growth of national political participation has been more elaborate theoretically, the dependence on aggregate measures has made it difficult to determine empirically how these macro social changes structure individuals' life experiences in ways which alter their political behavior.

I. THE PROBLEM AND THE APPROACH

The task is to identify the significant social experiences which explain the growth of political participation in economically advanced nations. Having identified these social concomitants of economic development, it is also necessary to fill in the *causal* links between macro socioeconomic processes and citizen political participation. These links, we hypothesize, are the resources, the attitudes, and the needs of individual citizens.

Multi-level analysis requires data about individuals and about nations. Such data is available in the form of the survey research data from the Almond-Verba five-nation study and aggregate statistics on the level of economic development in these five nations.[4] The theoretical assumptions we explore require a technique showing the relationships between socioeconomic attributes, intervening attitudinal characteristics and rates of political participation; such a technique is provided by causal modeling, which is applied to the analysis . . . [below].

---

[2] Gabriel A. Almond and Sidney Verba, *The Civic Culture* (Princeton: Princeton University Press, 1963); Robert A. Dahl, *Who Governs?* (New Haven: Yale University Press, 1961), pp. 282-301; V. O. Key, *Public Opinion and American Democracy* (New York: Alfred A. Knopf, 1961); Lester W. Milbraith, *Political Participation* (Chicago: Rand McNally Co., 1965).

[3] For example, Samuel P. Huntington, "Political Development and Political Decay," *World Politics* 17 (Apr. 1965), pp. 386-430.

[4] Some of these data were analyzed by Almond and Verba, *op. cit.*

II. SOCIAL STRUCTURE AND ECONOMIC DEVELOPMENT

The process of economic development drastically alters the social structures of a nation, and consequently, the social life of its citizens. The effects of social change on political behavior and on the operation of the political system are numerous and complex. In a given nation the political consequences of economic development cannot easily be separated from such issues as historical social cleavages, existing social patterns, and the timing of the developmental process itself.[5] The complexity and variations notwithstanding, some changes in social life appear inevitably to be brought about by the process of economic development. It is these persistent changes which, we hypothesize, have a universal and predictable impact on citizen participation in political life.

Economic development and changes in the class structure. As a nation develops economically, the shape of its social stratification structure is substantially altered. There are increased requirements for trained labor, a growth of opportunities for social mobility, and expanded facilities for formal education. As a consequence, the pyramidal class structure associated with peasant and peasant-worker societies changes to a more diamond-shaped structure. The middle stratum expands and eventually becomes the majority class as great numbers of citizens, whose parents were agricultural or unskilled workers, find jobs in the service industry or otherwise become members of the educated white-collar class.

Economic development and changes in organizational structure. As a nation develops economically, its organizational infrastructure becomes increasingly complex. Differentiation and specialization occur. Social life becomes more organized; work groups (such as trade unions and professional societies), leisure groups (such as youth organizations and voluntary associations), and special task groups (such as civic associations) expand in number and take over duties formerly carried out by the extended family or the small, face-to-face social group. Additional organizations become necessary to coordinate activities of an increasingly interdependent social and economic life. There is a corresponding growth of membership in secondary organizations. The group life structure of a society cannot avoid being substantially affected by the development process.

Economic development and changes in residence patterns. As a nation develops economically, it becomes more urban. Youths leave the farms and

[5]See, for example, the introductory chapter in Seymour M. Lipset and Stein Rokkan, *Party Systems and Voter Alignments* (New York: Free Press, 1967).

small towns in search of education or better paying jobs in the nation's cities. Industry expands where there is population concentration, and availability of jobs attracts yet more people. Larger proportions of the population seek employment and establish homes in urban areas as a consequence of development.

Thus, along with Deutsch and other students of development, we identify three areas of social life known to vary with level of economic development: social stratification, organized economic and secondary associations, and urbanization. The research task is to move from these macro variables to an explanation of whether a given individual citizen will engage in political activity. To carry out this research task, we proceed in three steps:

1. We determine the strength and the cross-national consistency of correlations between the citizen's class position, his organizational involvement, his place of residence (i.e. urban versus rural) and his level of political participation.

2. We integrate the survey data with aggregate information available for the five nations in order to clarify and evaluate the effect that the individual level correlations have on the larger relationship between economic development and national rates of participation. . . .

3. Finally, with the aid of causal modeling, we examine the role played by several cognitive and attitudinal variables in explaining the persistent relationship between socio-economic attributes on the one hand and political participation on the other. In so doing we attempt to refine further the linkages between national economic development and individual acts of political participation.

III. THE PRIMARY VARIABLES: IDENTIFICATION AND CORRELATION

The impact of economic development on class structure, secondary group structure, and residence patterns has been documented.[6] However, in an attempt to assess their impact on levels of participation, we

---

[6]For the relationship between economic development indicators and various indices of urbanization and class structure, see the data in Bruce M. Russett, *et al., World Handbook of Political and Social Indicators* (New Haven: Yale University Press, 1964). Also see Donald J. McCrone and Charles F. Cnudde, "Toward a Communication Theory of Democratic Political Development," *American Political Science Review*, 61 (March 1967), pp. 72-79. The literature on general processes of change in the social structure during modernization is, of course, very large. See, among other analyses, S. N. Eisenstadt, "Social Change, Differentiation, and Evolution," *American Sociological Review*, 29 (June 1964), pp. 375-387; and Talcott Parsons, "Evolutionary Universals in Society," *American Sociological Review*, 29 (June 1964), pp. 339-357.

need some means of determining whether they are independent phenomena or a package of relationships which are so tightly intertwined as to be inseparable in terms of their impact on citizens' participation in politics. If, for example, the changes in social class structure take place only in the urban population centers, and if only urban middle and upper class citizens are active in a nation's organizational life, then there would be only one major dimension of social structural change important for this study—urbanization.

In order to answer these questions, we set forth an extensive list of socio-economic items presumed to be related to the social structural changes. We subjected these items to a factor analysis in each nation and then for all five nations grouped together as a single population. In both cases there emerged two relatively independent and very consistent clusters of items. Other items, fewer in number, were consistently unrelated to each other or to either cluster.

The two clusters and two unrelated items are analogs for the individual citizen of the structural variables outlined above. One cluster includes items which measure socio-economic status: education, income, occupation, and an interviewer's rating of social status. The second cluster includes items which measure organizational involvement: number of organizational memberships, amount of organizational activity, involvement in the economic market-place, and involvement in group-related leisure time activities. Thus, there is a cluster which corresponds to the social stratification system and a cluster which corresponds to the organizational infrastructure of the society. Unrelated to these clusters were two items corresponding at the individual level to urbanization; size of present community and length of residence there.

Three summary indexes were constructed: social status, organizational involvement, and size of place of residence. A political participation scale was also constructed, including the following items: talking politics, contacting local authorities, contacting national authorities, involvement in electoral campaigns, and membership in political organizations and political parties. Table 1 presents pertinent correlation coefficients.

The relationships in Table 1 are clear and remarkably consistent from nation to nation. Although problems in the design of the samples are such that significance tests must be used with care, the following inferences are warranted: (1) Organizational involvement is the predictive variable with the most strength. Within each of the five nations the citizen who is an active member of social groups is more likely to be a political participant than the citizen with few or no organizational involvements. The relationships observed in Table 1 are extremely strong for data of the type available.[7] If the

---

[7] For readers unfamiliar with correlation coefficients in assessing the strength of relationships, Table 4 (p. 371) of the original article presents some of the same patterns in terms of differences between percentages. The reader may wish to review that Table.

correlation coefficients are squared, using the general rule of estimate, organizational involvement alone predicts approximately 25 percent of the variation in participation. The strength of this relationship is consistent across the five nations. (2) In addition, as expected, the citizen's tendency to be politically active is related to his social status; however, and not fully expected, the relationship between social status and political activity is weaker and less consistent cross-nationally than the relationship between organizational involvement and political activity.[8]

Table 1. Social Structure and Political Participation: Product-Moment Correlation Coefficients in Five Nations

| | Nation | | | | |
Correlation Relationship	U.S.	U.K.	Germany	Italy	Mexico
Urban Residence with Participation Scale	.068	—.023	—.022	—.002	.073
Social Status with Participation Scale	.431	.303	.181	.283	.238
Organizational Involvement Scale with Participation Scale	.523	.480	.480	.490	.515
Urban Residence with Social Status	.159	.040	.166	.175	.118
Urban Residence with Organizational Involvement Scale	—.010	.043	—.011	—.021	.017
Social Status with Organizational Involvement Scale	.435	.313	.213	.304	.227

On balance, these findings are familiar ones. The educated, wealthy and occupationally skilled citizen participates in political life at a greater rate than the uneducated, poor and occupationally unskilled.[9] It is well known that social and economic resources provide a citizen with currency he transfers to the political sphere. To turn the statement around, political influence is not randomly distributed across social categories but, rather,

[8]It is interesting that social status is a stronger predictor of political participation in the United States than in any of the other nations. However, it still lags behind organizational involvement. For all the nations, of course, the status measure and the involvement measure are moderately correlated, with the U.S. showing the strongest relationship.

[9]When the individual items composing these summary indices were correlated with political participation, the coefficients obtained were almost always considerably lower than those shown in Table 1. Further, no single item accounts for a disproportionate amount of the correlation between the summary indices and the participation scale. This indicates (1) that the unidimensionality indicated by the factor loadings is justified and (2) that no single variable, such as education, for instance, is the "real" explanation for the strong correlations which appear in Table 1. Social Status, in other words, seems to be the common dimension being tapped by the varied findings linking participation to education, income, and the like.

tends to concentrate in very disproportionate amounts among the well-to-do and socially involved. Perhaps, however, the difference between social status and organizational involvement as predictive variables is not as familiar. We will have much more to say about this difference.

Urbanization and political participation. The least expected pattern in Table 1 is the consistent *absence* of any relationship between urban residence and political participation. Only in two nations (the U.S. and Mexico) is the relationship significant at the .05 level, and even in these nations the relationship is weak, explaining less than one percent of the variance in participation. For nations as developed as the five reported on in Table 1, the tendency for urbanization and mass political activity to co-vary is *not* because city-dwellers are more active than country-dwellers. The absence of a relationship between urban residence and activity rates at the individual level may, thus, help to erase from the literature on political development an ecological fallacy.[10]

We reason as follows: as nations develop economically, two things increase, the proportion of urban-dwellers and the proportion of active political participants. However, the ecological correlation between urbanization and mass political participation is spurious, as is indicated by the absence of a relationship between urban residence and participation *within* each nation to further investigate the inconsistency between the widely reported ecological correlation and the absence of the correlation at the individual level, we merged the file from the five nations. The correlation between urban residence and activity for the merged file is positive and significant and thus is consistent with the relationship found when aggregated data are used.

It is evident that the ecological correlation is a derivative of the greater levels of urbanization and political participation in more advanced nations. For when the aggregate correlation is decomposed, as in Table 1, political activity is seen to vary hardly at all by urban-rural differences. The fourth and fifth lines in Table 1 suggest part of the reason: while urbanization is somewhat associated with social status, it is not at all related to organizational involvement. As we have seen, in every nation organizational involvement is the strongest predictor of participation.

In making these initial observations we were troubled by the fact that the five nations being studied would be clustered toward the top end of any development continuum on which all nations of the world could be

[10]For a discussion of the general problem of ecological fallacies see W. S. Robinson, "Ecological Correlations and the Behavior of Individuals," *American Sociological Review* 15 (1950), pp. 351-357. Also see Hayward R. Alker, "A Typology of Ecological Fallacies: Problems of Spurious Associations in Cross-level Inferences," International Social Science Council: Symposium on Quantitative Ecological Analysis in the Social Sciences, Evian, France, September, 1966.

arrayed. Even Mexico, the "low" case, ranks well above the median. What was needed was a nation, with a democratic form of government, much less developed than those studied in the Five-Nation study. Such a nation would provide a "hard test" for the inferences drawn from the patterns in Table 1. As a matter of scientific interest and personal generosity, Professors Sidney Verba, Rajni Kothari, and Bashiruddin Ahmed made available data from a forthcoming study of political participation in India for our purposes. These data, which suit our needs ideally and which have been preliminarily analyzed by Nie, are from the "Cross National Research Program in Social and Political Change."

The India data provide a striking confirmation of the findings presented in Table 1. The correlation between political participation and organizational membership is .420; between participation and social status, .300.[11] These correlations are of the same order of magnitude as those reported in Table 1, although the former is slightly lower.[12] Social status and organizational involvement appear to be similar in their explanatory power even in the much less developed nation of India.

The India data also confirm our inferences about urbanization and political participation. As is to be expected, citizens of high social status and high organizational involvement are more concentrated in urban areas in a nation at India's developmental level than in the more advanced nations. The correlation between urban residence and social status is .339, much higher than in the five more developed nations; the correlation between urban residence and social involvement is .127, again much higher than the other nations. In spite of the greater concentration of persons with social and organizational resources in the cities of India, the correlation between urban residence and political participation is an insignificant .035. Place of residence is no predictor of political activity.

Urbanization and local vs. national political participation. The literature about the effects of urbanization on political participation reveals an interesting anomaly [which should be further explored]. First, stemming largely from Deutsch, there are theoretical notions found in the studies of social mobilization and modernization. Urbanization, it is stressed, creates among citizens new ties to the national scene, increases the amount of

---

[11]Although the effort was to tap the same basic variables of social status, organizational involvement, and participation as in the 1960 study, different specific questions were believed appropriate to the Indian context. The Indian sample is also particularly useful for testing urbanization hypotheses because interviews were conducted in towns as small as 200 persons.

[12]The slight falling off of the relationship between participation and organization membership might be due to the differences in the measures used in India, on the one hand, and the original five nations, on the other. In India, only information on number of memberships was available and this had to be used in place of a composite involvement scale. The correlations between participation and organizational membership only in the five nations are comparable to the correlation produced by the India data.

political communication, and leads to greater awareness of social and political needs. In short, urbanization is one of the processes of modernization which shifts the political orientations of citizens from parochial to national and participant.[13]

Second, using individual survey data rather than national aggregate data, other investigators have noted that the process of urbanization weakens the ties between individual and community. Presumably one consequence of this has been to decrease citizen participation in local politics. For instance, Dahl writes how living in large political communities can lessen the likelihood of political participation:

> Yet, the larger and more inclusive the unit with a representative government, and the more complex its tasks, the more participation must be reduced for most people to the single act of voting in an election.
> Conversely, the smaller the unit, the greater the opportunity for citizens to participate in the decisions of their government . . .[14]

These seemingly contradictory observations about urbanization and political participation are not actually in direct conflict. The social mobilization literature refers to national participation and mainly uses voter turnout to support the hypothesis. The Dahl thesis refers to local participation and deliberately excludes the act of voting from the consideration.

However, the two observations do present us with difficulties. The operational procedures used in Table 1, which show little to no relationship between urbanization and political participation, combine both national and local items in the participation scale. Thus it is possible that both the Deutsch and Dahl views are correct and that our data manipulation hides two opposing effects, urbanization is increasing national participation and decreasing local participation. To check this possibility, we decomposed the participation scale and separately correlated urban residence, controlling for social status and organizational involvement, with *national* and *local* acts of political activity.[15] . . .

The results of this analysis[16] tend to confirm the conflicting implications

[13]See citations under footnote 1 above.

[14]Robert A. Dahl, "The City in the Future of Democracy," *American Political Science Review* 61 (Dec. 1967), p. 960. For a very different perspective on size of city and citizen representation in local matters, see Kenneth Prewitt and Heinz Eulau, "Political Matrix and Political Representation: Prolegomenon to a New Departure from an Old Problem," *American Political Science Review* 63 (June 1969), pp. 427-441.

[15]Methodologically it is quite possible and, for that matter, common for items to demonstrate a strong relationship to a principal factor (e.g., participation level) and at the same time contain uncorrelated portions which are strongly related to different orthogonal factors. This may be what is taking place with the local-national distinction.

[16]For the table presenting these results and a more detailed discussion of them, the reader is referred to Table 2 and pp. 367-68 in Part I of the original article.

of urbanization for political participation. The citizen living in the city is likely to have the social status and, in less developed nations (if India is a representative case) the organization involvement which leads to political participation. But the city-dweller loses the facilitating effect of small town life on local participation. The general problem sketched out by Dahl appears to be confirmed by these findings: with respect to participation in local matters there is an "optimal" size for cities. However, the effects of city size are not strong, especially when compared with the impact on participation of social status and organizational involvement. In no case does urbanization explain more than two percent of the variance in rates of participation; in most cases it is less than that. This compares to about ten percent of the variance explained by social status and about twenty-five percent explained by organizational involvement. The comparative weakness of urbanization as a predictive variable leads us to pay much less attention to it than to the other two variables in the remainder of the analysis.

IV. POLITICAL PARTICIPATION: SHIFTING FROM INDIVIDUAL CORRELATES TO NATIONAL PATTERNS

Analysis presented thus far shows: first, within each of the five nations a citizen's tendency to be politically active strongly varies according to his social status and his organizational involvement; and second, the citizen's tendency to be politically active is but slightly affected by his place of residence, and this weak relationship masks two counter trends. Living in an urban environment depresses the likelihood of local participation while not significantly altering the likelihood of national participation.

We infer from these findings that economic development increases mass political participation *because* associated with economic development are greater numbers of citizens in the middle and upper social classes and greater numbers involved in organizations. From data presented thus far this can only be an inference. We have yet to examine in a direct manner how economic development affects political participation. It is to this issue that we now turn.

With only five cases it is not possible to devise a single definitive test which would substantiate a hypothesis linking economic development with national rates of political participation. What is possible is to carry out a number of smaller tests, each of which can confirm or reject a part of the more inclusive theory. If each of the independent tests confirms the general theory, the cumulative effect will provide some rationale for considering the theory verified.

If true (a) that economic development is the major determinant of national rates of participation; and (b) that this relationship is largely the result of how development affects society's class structure and organizational infrastructure, then data should demonstrate the following:

1. Strong covariance between a nation's level of economic development and its rate of mass political participation.

2. The disappearance of this relationship when social class and organizational involvement are controlled.

3. The lack of strong relationships between mass political participation and non-development-associated variables.

4. Similar *absolute* rates of participation among citizens of similar social class and organizational involvement irrespective of nation, as well as the same *relative* differences from one nation to the next already indicated by the coefficients in Table 1.

Comparing national rates of political participation. Comparing rates of political participation among the five nations shows that the United States and Great Britain have the highest rate; Germany is slightly lower; Mexico and Italy follow in that order and have considerably lower rates of participation than the three more developed nations.[17] With the exception of the reversal between Italy and Mexico,[18] this ranking corresponds with an economic development ranking constructed from aggregate statistics.

Five cases "prove" nothing, but the predictive pattern is apparent. The correspondence in rankings of economic development and mass political participation, based in the present case on survey and aggregate data from five nations, does conform to the rankings reported in studies using only aggregate data but based on many more than five cases. It is consistent with Deutsch, Lipset, Lerner, and others to conclude that national rates of political participation covary with levels of economic development.

The component variables: social class and organizational life. It comes as no surprise to learn that a nation's level of political participation covaries with its level of economic development. The more difficult task is to identify what components of economic development account for the growing numbers of citizens who become active in political life. The theory which guides our analysis points to two component variables: social class and organizational life. These variables are chosen from a long list of social factors know to be affected by development for two reasons. Findings about

[17]The ranking was achieved by calculating the national means on the participation variable. This is the same variable used in Table 1. Medians were also calculated and in no case did this alter the ranking.

[18]The Mexican sample contains no respondent from communities with populations less than 10,000. The .232 correlation between size of place of residence and social status in Mexico may account for the reversal in rankings between Italy and Mexico. Indeed, the means are so close at present that it is highly probable that they would reverse with a representative Mexican sample.

individual political behavior indicate that status and organizational membership are strongly related to political activity. Further, at the national level, social class composition and organizational life change in highly predictable ways during the process of economic development. It is on the importance of these variables at the individual *and* the national level that our theory depends.

What is needed is some manner of determining whether social class and organizational structure are indeed the components of economic development which predict rates of mass political participation. The theory is strengthened if it can be shown that other components of development are not associated with participation. Although the data available impose constraints on us, and we cannot directly examine the possible impact of additional variables, one simple test can be performed. The relative importance of the two structural variables can be compared to all remaining development-associated variables taken as a residual group.

This can be accomplished by correlating economic development with political participation while controlling for social status and organizational involvement. To accomplish this each respondent was given a score based on his nation's level of economic development. Thus each respondent in the U.S. was scored 5, each British respondent was scored 4, each German 3, each Italian 2, and each Mexican 1. This variable was added to each respondent's data record and the files from the five nations were merged. Level of economic development, now treated as a property of the individual, was correlated with political participation.

Table 2 presents the results. The now familiar hypothesis derived from social mobilization literature is confirmed. There is a significant relationship between national economic development and individual political participation, as the uncontrolled relationship indicates. The simple correlation between political participation and economic development is .133.

The question we ask, then, is how much of this relationship can be attributed to national patterns of social class and organizational involvement and how much of it can be attributed to other factors associated with economic development. To answer this question we compute the partials, controlling first for social class, then for organizational involvement, and finally simultaneously controlling on both class and organizational involvement. Controlling for social class, the .133 correlation is reduced to .048; controlling for organization involvement it is reduced to .015; controlling for both (the second order partial), it is essentially zero, a nonsignificant −.012.[19]

---

[19]As an additional check stemming from our concern for the accuracy of the rankings among the more developed nations a second dichotomous variable was created giving each respondent in the three developed nations a score of "2" and those in the two less developed nations a "1." The same analysis was then performed on this variable.

The results of this analysis are similar to those reported in Table 2. The simple correlation

If other factors associated with economic development were independently affecting levels of citizen political participation, then some significant relationship should have remained when the effects of status and organizational membership were partialed out. However, this clearly is not the case. The partial correlations show that *the two variables alone account for all of the difference between the participation levels of citizens in the more and the less developed nations.*

Table 2. Residence in Nations at Different Levels of Development and Political Participation: Simple and Partial Correlations Controlling for Social Status and Organizational Involvement

Correlation relationship	Control	Residence according to national level of economic development
Residence in nations at different levels of development *with* political participation	NONE	.133 [a]
	SES (only)	.048
	ORG. IN. (only)	.015
	SES and ORG. IN.	—.012

[a] Sample size is about 4000. The zero-order correlation is, of course, significant at better than .001.

This finding can be rephrased in terms of the general theory being advanced in this paper. Economic development leads to greater rates of political participation *because* associated with economic development is an expanding middle-class and an expanding organizational infrastructure. Social class and organizational life are the components of economic development which most strongly affect mass political participation.

Since we have only five nations and since there can be nation to nation differences not attributable to economic development, the test we devise is hardly a conclusive one. The test is adequate, however, for us to conclude that the inference about economic development and political participation withstands this particular attempt to falsify it. We are unable to show any

between the development index and level of participation is .142. The partial for this relationship controlling only for SES is .073. That controlling for only organizational involvement is .030. The second order partial controlling for both SES and ORG. IN. is an insignificant .002.

relationship between development and rates of participation which cannot be explained by reference to the two important social structural variables— social class and organization involvement.

[The analysis so far has left two important questions unanswered. First, do persons of similar social status or organizational involvement differ in their levels of participation from country to country? The theoretical orienta- tion guiding this discussion would suggest that such cross-cultural differences would be minimal. That is, it would predict that a laborer in Mexico would participate at approximately the same level as a laborer in Germany. So too, the level of political activity of a German citizen active in a number of organizations would resemble that of a Mexican citizen similarly involved. The second question is a corollary of the first. Are there historical or cultural factors particular to a nation which, independently of that nation's level of economic development, affect how politically active its citizens are? Again, the theoretical thrust of this paper suggests that the effects of discrete national experiences would be minimal. A comparison of levels of participation of persons of similar social class and organizational involvement in the five countries studied would answer both questions. For if we find that individuals at the same level of social class and organizational involvement are approximately equal in their political participation from one nation to the next, it is unlikely that unique cultural, historical, or political variables are causing different rates of mass political participation. Such a cross-cultural comparison (see Part I of the original article, pp. 370-72, Table 4, p. 371, and footnote   23, p. 373) suggests that important idiosyncratic differences between countries do exist, but they are very small when compared to the extremely strong effects of differences in social status or organizational involvement. With a few significant exceptions individuals with similar social statuses and similar organization involvement display similar absolute levels of political participation no matter in which of the five nations they live.]

Three types of data have now been presented: (a) individual correlations showing the association between social status, organizational involvement, and urban residence, on the one hand, and political participa- tion, on the other; (b) rankings of national levels of economic development and of aggregate measures of political participation; (c) partial correlations showing the effect of economic development on political participation when social class and organizational involvement are controlled. These data, from different perspectives, tend to confirm the general hypothesis that economic development alters the class and organizational structures of societies which in turn increases the level of mass political participation. No single test is conclusive, but taken together they present a strong case for the theory. Each of the following sections . . . present additional analysis further testing and clarifying these relationships. . . .

V. THE LINKING VARIABLES: POLITICAL ATTITUDES AND THE DEVELOPMENTAL PROCESS

Examining general relationships between social structures and political participation can take us only so far. To explicate more fully how economic development relates to political participation it is necessary to complicate the causal model. Up to this point, we have utilized the model suggested by Deutsch and others which looks as follows:

Economic → Changes in the → Increased Political
Development   Social Structures   Participation

Discussions involving this model suggest that changes in the social structure affect political participation *because* citizen attitudes about politics are altered. Numerous survey studies in the U.S. and elsewhere show, for example, that persons who feel confident of success in influencing decisions are more likely to be political participants, and that middle class persons are more likely to feel confident.[20] Hence, increasing the number of middle class citizens increases the number of confident citizens, and this, in turn, increases political participation.

The causal model with the intervening attitude component looks as follows:

Economic → Changes in the → Changes in the Distribution → Increased Political
Development   Social Structures   of Certain Political Attitudes   Participation

There may be feedback loops in this process. Successful political participation, for instance, promotes greater confidence; successful participation may even alter the political structures of society so that participation itself is facilitated (expanding the franchise, for instance). However, for the moment we set aside the problem of feedback effects and limit attention to testing the basic assumptions of the model.

Questions included in the Five Nation study allow us to explore this causal model in a limited way. We begin by identifying five attitude sets which frequently are cited as the likely intervening variables explaining how socio-economic attributes predict rates of political activity. The five are: 1) sense of citizen duty, 2) basic information about politics, 3) perceived stake in political outcomes, 4) sense of political efficacy, and 5) attentiveness to political matters.

We examine the relationship of these intervening variables to the general theme of economic development and political participation in two

[20]See, for example, Dahl, *Who Governs?*, *op. cit.*

steps. First, at the nation-state level, we examine the relationship between measures of economic development and aggregate scores for the five attitude sets, and between the attitudes and general rates of political participation. Second, using causal modeling techniques, we investigate the importance of these attitude sets in linking socio-economic attributes and political participation.

Table 3 presents data pertinent to the first step. The five nations are ranked by level of economic development. Then, in column B, the nations are ranked in terms of mean level of organizational involvement and social status. The next five columns (C) present the rankings of the various political attitudes (again using mean level). The final column shows the mean level of political participation for the five nations.

Table 3. Economic Development, Social Structure, Attitude Structure, and Political Participation

A	B		C						D
Economic Development	Social Structure		Attitude structure						
Rank order of countries with respect to measures of economic development	Social status	Social involvement	Citizen duty	Political information	Impact of politics	Political efficacy	Political attentiveness	Political participation
United States	1 (1)	1	1	2	1	1	1	1.5
United Kingdom	2 (2)	2.5	3	3	3	2	3	1.5
Germany	3 (3)	2.5	2	1	2	3	2	3
Italy	4 (4)	5	5	4	5	4.5	5	5
Mexico	5 (5)	4	4	5	4	4.5	4	4

Kendall Coefficient of Concordance W = .859 Sig. ⟩ .001.

Although there are various methodological difficulties in such absolute rankings (and we especially must recall the bias in the Mexican sample),[21] Table 3 does confirm the reasoning outlined. Across Table 3, the three more developed nations *always* rank above the two less developed. The Kendall coefficient or concordance, or W, which measures the amount of agreement among multiple rankings, is .859 and is statistically significant at the .001 level. (The maximum observable value of Kendall's W is 1.0.)

[21] See footnote 18 above.

Table 4. Path Components of Relationship Between Two Independent Variables and Political Participation as Percentages of Total Correlations[a]

	Independent Variables									
	Social Status					Organizational Involvement				
Proportion of Correlation Attributable to:	US	UK	Ger	It	Mx	US	UK	Ger	It	Mx
(1) Direct link to participation	20%	−8%	−33%	−15%	−1%	57%	62%	61%	51%	68%
(2) Paths thru other independent (1 or 2 variable only)	30	30	35	27	34	7	−2	−3	−2	0
(3) Paths thru other ind var *and* attitude variables	10	12	20	21	13	14	12	6	12	6
(4) Paths thru attitude variables only	40	61	78	67	54	20	25	35	40	26
Total percentage	100	95	100	100	100	98	97	99	101	100
Basic correlation between ind var and participation	.431	.303	.181	.283	.238	.523	.480	.486	.490	.515

[a]The correlations are equal to the sum of all pathways from independent to dependent variable. The pathways are computed by multiplying all path coefficients along the given path. Negative scores arise from negative path linkages. For those percentages, each independent variable is treated as if it were the first, undetermined, variable in the chain. Key: US = United States; UK = United Kingdom; Ger = West Germany; It = Italy; Mx = Mexico.

Economic development alters the social class structure and the organizational infrastructure of a society. One consequence of these alterations is the greater proportion of citizens who have social attributes—education, stable incomes, white-collar jobs, organizational memberships—which, as already shown, relate to political participation. Further, the more developed nations have more citizens holding the views normally associated with political activity. Greater proportions of Americans, British, and Germans than Mexicans or Italians have a sense of civic duty, are politically informed, see the impact of public policies on their lives, feel politically efficacious, are attentive to politics—and, finally, actively participate in political life.

We should emphasize again that there are national differences in political attitude scores which cannot be explained by differences in developmental levels alone. Obviously cultural heritages and specific national experiences or diverse system arrangements leave their particular impact on national attitude patterns. Germany ranks higher than the United States on mean level of political information, even though its general level of development is lower. An exploration of other attitude patterns, especially those associated with affect towards national institutions and inter-group perceptions and evaluations would reveal further differences.[22] Many of these were pointed out by Almond and Verba in their initial analysis and we shall not explore them here.[23] Nonetheless, we wish to emphasize that insofar as attitudes bearing on individual political involvement and attentiveness and personal political competence are concerned, the development-associated patterns seem to be extremely powerful. Future analyses of cross-national differences should be sensitive to the often over-riding power of these relationships.

We can summarize the theoretical argument briefly: economic development alters social structures, particularly the class structure and the secondary group structure. Expanding the middle class and increasing the

---

[22]Further research will have to distinguish, of course, between the different dimensions of the variables here considered. For example, the "information" questions here only cover very basic items like the names of national party leaders. It might be that detailed information would tend to follow, rather than precede, participation. The various dimensions of political efficacy are also a matter for investigation. At a very abstract level, efficacy seems to become more related to general national affect items. At the more concrete and personalistic level, it follows the pattern here outlined: linked to personal status and involvement, varying little by national pattern. Thus, the only item on which an underdeveloped nation scored higher than a developed one was on an estimate as to whether possible national participation might succeed in influencing outcomes. Here, Mexicans scored higher than Germans, although very few felt they understood local or national events, or could name any potential strategy of influence. Again, the factor analysis justifies the dimension of the scale, but there are obviously additional dimensions to explore.

[23]Almond and Verba, op. cit.

organizational complexity of society changes political socialization patterns; greater proportions of citizens have those politically relevant life experiences which lead to attitudes such as political efficacy, sense of civic duty, etc. These attitudes motivate the citizen to participate in politics, sensitize him to available opportunities, and provide him with political resources. Thus it is that economic development increases the rate of mass political participation.

The many implicit hypotheses in this causal model cannot be directly examined in a table reporting aggregate measures. To investigate systematically the pathway from development to political participation we must examine the extent to which individual traits associated with position in the class structure and with involvement in organizational life do in fact affect political attitudes and the extent to which political attitudes are intervening variables between socio-economic characteristics and political participation. . . .

A. The Findings: Differences in the Causal Linkage Patterns of Social Status and Organizational Involvement.

We begin with the very general hypothesis that the causal relationship between social status and organizational involvement, on the one hand, and political participation, on the other, can be traced through intervening political attitudes. Figure 1 and Table 4 present data relevant to this hypothesis. . . . [Our discussion will focus on the differences in the causal linkages of the two independent variables, SES and organizational involvement. For discussion of the individual attitudes used as intervening links in the causal chain see Part II of the original article, pp. 814-18.]

Initial examination reveals one pattern of overwhelming strength and consistency: social status and organizational involvement operate through quite different causal paths in their impact on political participation. This finding holds true in all five countries and remains the case in spite of various manipulations of the data, alteration of the order of the intervening variables, changing the number of the intervening variables, and the like.

The basic finding is both simple and important. Virtually all the relationship between social status and political participation is explained by the intervening linking attitude variables. The high social status citizen does not *just* participate in politics; he does so only when he has the attitudes such as efficacy and attentiveness which are postulated as intervening variables. Social status, then, affects rates of political participation through its effect on political attitudes. This does not mean, it must be emphasized, that the correlation between status and participation is spurious; on the contrary, it means that intervening attitude variables explain *how* a citizen's social status affects his political activity.

On the other hand, a very large part of the relationship between organizational involvement and participation *is unexplained by any variable in this model*. In every case, about 60 percent of the correlation between organizational involvement and political participation is accounted for by the direct link, that line that does not pass through social class or the attitudinal variables. (See link 2 → 8 in Figure 1).

Figure 1. Eight variable causal model: paths from status and organizational involvement to political participation

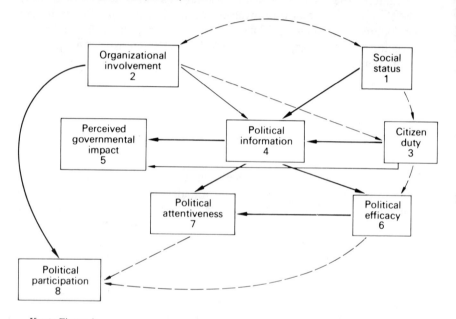

Key to Figure 1:

(1) No arrow between variables indicates that the path coefficients are less than .150 in at least three of the five nations. There are 13 paths *not* shown in the figure.

(2) Heavy arrows between variables indicate path coefficients greater than .250 (about 5 times the average standard error) in at least three of five national samples. Light arrows between variables indicate path coefficients between .150 and .250 in three or more of the five national samples.

(3) Unbroken arrows (both light and heavy) indicate *difference* between largest and smallest of the five coefficients is *less* than .150 (about 3 standard errors). Broken arrows between variables indicate a difference greater than .150.

The strength and cross-national consistency of this pattern is shown as well in Table 4. In a causal model of this type, the raw correlation (Pearson Product-Moment) between independent and dependent variable equals the sum of all pathways down the causal chain from independent to dependent variable.[24] The score of a "pathway" in this sense is the product of all path coefficients along the chain. Table 4 presents the percent of the raw correlation between social status and organizational involvement, on the one hand, and political participation, on the other, accounted for by: (1) the direct relationship only, unaccounted for by other variables in the model; (2) the path through the other independent variable only; (3) the paths going first through the other independent variable and then through the attitude variables; and (4) the paths going directly from each independent variable through the attitude variables to political participation. For example, the correlation between organizational involvement and political participation in the United States is .523. Fifty-seven percent of *this* is accounted for by the direct path between these two variables (that is, the path that passes through no other variable in the model). Seven percent of the correlation between these two variables is accounted for by the path from organizational involvement to social status and then directly to participation; 14% of the correlation is explained by the path from organizational involvement through social status and then through the intervening attitude variables; and the remaining 20% of the correlation is accounted for by the path from organizational involvement through the various attitude variables but by-passing the social status variable.

The structure of the components of the organizational involvement relationship are almost uncannily consistent from nation to nation. The social status to participation relationships are less consistent, with the U.S. having a fairly large proportion accounted for by the direct link (although the path coefficient is less than twice the standard error and would not usually be considered statistically significant). In Germany the direct link between social status and participation has a high negative score, although the percentage is exaggerated by the weakness of the total correlation (and the score is also less than twice the standard error).[25] The basic pattern,

---

[24]In the eight variable causal model there are 54 paths from status to participation. No paths moving back along the model at any points are allowed by the constraints imposed. The method employed here has been termed "path analysis" by Otis Dudley Duncan, "Path Analysis: Sociological Examples," *American Journal of Sociology* 72 (July 1966), pp. 6-7. For an explication of the method, the statistical assumptions which it employs and its limitations, see the discussion and references in footnotes 4 and 5 in Part II of the original article.

[25]At an earlier stage in the analysis, scales were built with consistency checks on the SES dimension. Persons high on one status item and very low on another were deleted. This procedure increased correlations, but decreased the size of the valid sample, and was not, therefore, used in this analysis. It is especially noteworthy that while only about 10% of the original samples in the US, UK, Italy, and Mexico failed to meet the SES dimension consistency check, about 50% of the German sample failed to meet it. This suggests the disruption of the social stratification system in Germany as a consequence, no doubt, of the historical upheavals. The strong wage position of workers in the post-war boom, following the leveling impact of World War II and the Third Reich, may also be a contributing factor. See the comments by Lewis J. Edinger, *Politics in Germany* (Boston: Little, Brown, 1968), pp. 19-30.

nonetheless, is clear, and we suspect inconsistency reflects in part, at least, some of the problems in adequate measures of social status, or its sub-dimensions.

The general pattern for social status finds about 60 percent of the relationship going through the attitude variables, about 30 percent going directly through organizational involvement, and about 10 percent going through the attitude variables by way of involvement. The general pattern for organizational involvement shows about 60 percent accounted for by the direct link, about 30 percent going through the attitude variables only, and about 10 percent going through social status and then the attitude variables.

Thus, a large part of the relationship between organizational involvement and political participation cannot be explained by reference to other variables included in the model. It is clear that those who are organizationally involved participate in politics at rates far greater than citizens who are not involved. In addition, and of considerable importance, many citizens whose organizational involvement propels them into political life are *not* more politically informed, politically efficacious, or politically attentive than the non-participants. Unlike political participation stemming from high social status, participation stemming from organizational membership does not necessarily imply those attitudes normally thought to be associated with democratic political participation. We return later to the implications of these findings.

There are two alternative, though not mutually exclusive, explanations for why the organizationally involved are politically active even though they lack certain attitudes. First, organizations can mobilize their members toward political goals; and this can occur without an intervening state of changes in attitudes by the members. The organizations might provide inducements and gratifications to their members, such as sociability, which though producing political activity have nothing to do with political information, awareness, and so forth. Further, the organizations can mobilize members for relatively specific, short-term issues, a mobilization which again does not depend upon any facilitating attitudes other than a willingness to follow the lead of the organization leadership. A professional or business group circulating a petition to be signed or a union enjoining their members to vote are examples of such mobilization.

Second, both organizational and political involvement might be strongly affected by an underlying personality attribute or cultural norm. For instance, both types of activity might be related to a general propensity toward social activism which is unrelated to social status. This explanation implies that joining an organization, becoming active in it, and getting involved in politics are subsets of a more general social behavior which, for reasons of personality attributes, is more attractive to some citizens than others. It is an explanation stressing self-selection.

This is not the place to explore the merits of these alternative explanations—and the data available permit no direct test—but we do suggest that the former explanation has more merit than the latter. The self-selection hypothesis is weakened since we would expect a self-selective tendency to correlate with attitudes such as political efficacy and attentiveness. The absence of strong relationships between organizational involvement and these attitudes makes us suspicious of the self-selection explanation. The first explanation, that organizations are mobilizing their members, is intuitively more persuasive and has been supported by additional research. Data collected in the United States show that membership in organizations which have some relationship to public affairs and which have formal or informal discussions of politics at meetings, greatly increases the likelihood of being politically active. In contrast, members who belong to more apolitical organizations are only slightly more likely than non-members to participate in politics. . . .[26]

B. Social Structure and the Participation of Class Groups [27]

Individuals vary in their political participation according to their social status and according to their organizational involvement, with the latter social characteristic having the stronger impact on political participation. This finding is consistent from one nation to another. Further, and because there is cross-national consistency, both social status and organizational involvement remain strongly related to political participation when we shift from the individual to the nation as a unit of analysis. That is, nations vary in their level of mass political participation according to the proportion of citizens in the middle and upper classes and according to the density and complexity of organizational life.

In addition, organizational involvement may represent an alternative channel for political participation for socially disadvantaged groups. The rural peasant, the industrial laborer, the disadvantaged black may become politically active through his organizational involvement even though he may otherwise lack the status resources for political participation. In these ways the class structure and the organizational structure of societies determine

[26]This research, carried out by Sidney Verba and Norman Nie, shows that a great majority of all types of voluntary organizations in the U.S. have an interest in public affairs and members engage in political discussions; this accounts for the strong relationship between organizational involvement and participation even when not controlling for the type of organization. These findings are based on preliminary analysis of the U.S. data from the "Cross National Research Program in Social and Political Change."

[27]We are indebted to Mr. Jae-On Kim for help with some of the methodology required for our analysis in this section.

both the overall rate of participation and the relative amount of participation coming from various social groups.

We have argued that economic development changes both the class and organizational structures of a society. This is true, but other factors may also promote such changes. The class structure is, of course, intimately tied to the long-term development of human and capital resources. Governments may establish massive education programs and engage in forceful income redistribution. These efforts may well affect participation patterns. However, obviously major changes in the status structure, involving occupation, education, and income patterns, are extremely difficult to bring about. We suspect that the organizational structure may be susceptible to more direct and short-term manipulation. Assuming that our organizational correlations reflect causal patterns, rather than the operation of self-selection mechanisms (an assumption we feel is tenable), then the great influence of organizational structure on participation suggests important possibilities for political change.

Although there are few systematic and comparative studies of the process of organizational development, there are numerous examples of efforts by governmental and extra-governmental bodies to generate organizational structure. Religious groups, for example, have spawned an enormous variety of organizations. Governments have fostered—and impeded—the development of both political and non-political organizations such as farmers' associations, professional societies, trade unions, and youth groups. The European socialist movements and the accelerating actions of civil rights groups in the United States in the past few years are additional examples of group mobilization only partially related to economic development patterns. We should not underestimate the complexity of the problems. The new African states have discovered the difficulties in penetrating a pre-mobilized economic structure even with a mass political party, as the numerous coups in recent years illustrate. And the history of socialist and labor movements suggest the frequency of middle class leadership in initial generation of working class movements. Nonetheless the historical examples suggest a potential manipulability of the organizational structure, as well as a potential for mediating the effects of social class, which make it a central variable in the analysis of participant societies.[28]

The shape of the class structure, the extent of organizational involvement, and the relationship between social status and organizational membership are only partially determined by economic development levels.

[28]It may also be true that the development of different types of national industries may create differential needs for economic organizations depending upon industry requirements to coordinate production, transportation, marketing and the like. See, for example, Barrington Moore, Jr.'s discussion of the differential impact that varying types of national industry have on the social structure, in *Social Origins of Dictatorship and Democracy* (Boston: Beacon Press, 1966).

And these three factors have a complicated but identifiable impact on the overall rate of participation as well as on the amount of participation coming from the various social classes. In this section we examine how different mixtures of these factors affect the degree to which class groups will be under- or over-represented in the "stratum" of political participants in a society. An example illustrates what is meant by these terms as we employ them. Suppose that one-fourth of the citizens are active participants (by some explicated criterion) in the political life of their society. Suppose further that lower class peasants and industrial workers numbered half of the total society. Also suppose that a very limited proportion of this group were members of organizations. All of our previous analysis would therefore suggest that while this class group represented 50 per cent of the total society, it would probably represent a *much* smaller proportion of the 25 per cent who are active political participants. We would conclude that the peasants and workers were "under-represented" in the political stratum. . . .

[Table 5 provides some suggestive evidence on this point. For each of the five nations in the study, the table indicates the proportion of persons in the lower, middle, and upper classes, the class-organization correlation, the proportion of those who are politically active who come from each of the social classes, and an index of under-representation for the lower class. With one exception, the cutting points for these variables are identical from nation to nation.[29] The patterns in the table suggest first that the higher the correlation between status and organizational membership, the more under-represented the lower class becomes. (Compare Germany and Mexico with the other nations. Note especially Germany and Britain which appear quite similar in class structure but which differ sharply in their degree of lower-class under-representation.)

[The most striking though related finding is the extent to which the lower class is under-represented among the politically active citizens in the United States; the lower class is more severely under-represented there than is true in any of the other nations. The severe under-representation in the United States seems to result first from the fact that the lower class is confronted with a basic correlation between class and participation which is

[29]Since our scales were derived to give intra-nation distributions of maximum utility, their validity for cross-national absolute comparisons is somewhat limited. Nor is it entirely clear how one should treat an indicator like "years of education" as a social status indicator on a cross-national basis. The meaning of such absolute measures, like the real buying power of formal income equivalents, depends considerably on the distribution of the commodity within the society. Nonetheless, the chosen cutting points fitted four of the societies in fairly plausible fashion. Actual distribution of education in the United States, for example, reported in the 1959 census was about 17% college educated, 48% 9-12 years of education, and 35% with 8 years or less. (Compare the class distribution in Table 5.) Only in Britain was a slightly different scale cutting point used—the division between lower and middle class was lowered by one level to show 46% in the lower class rather than 60%. This seemed a more plausible distribution in comparable terms, although it does not greatly affect the class analysis.

higher than average. (Although it is not a powerful part of the phenomenon, the partial correlation between status and participation, controlling for organizational membership, remains higher in the U.S. than in the other nations. We have no explanation for this fact.) Secondly, the high correlation between social class and organizational involvement (.44) eliminates the potential help offered by the organizational structure. (See Column II.)[30]]

Table 5.   Social Structure and Class Group Participation: Five Nations

Nation	Given Conditions		Participation Patterns	
	Class structure of society: proportion in low, middle, upper classes	Class-organization correlation	Class structure of politically active[a] proportion in low, middle, upper classes	Index of under-representation for lower classes[b]
United States	30%—45%—25%	.44	16%—47%—37%	—47
Britain	46 —38 —16	.31	32 —43 —25	—30
Germany	44 —41 —15	.21	41 —36 —23	— 7
Italy	54 —32 —14	.30	42 —39 —19	—22
Mexico	77 —16 — 7	.23	64 —25 —10	—17

[a] Being classified as "politically active" is roughly equivalent to discussing politics at least once a week, or more active involvement, as measured by our original scale items.

[b] Computed by (1) subtracting the per cent of lower class among active participants from the total per cent in the lower class, and (2) dividing the difference by the latter.

It seems likely that the high correlation between social class and organizational involvement in the United States reflects the fact that in the three European countries there existed historical efforts by political parties to mobilize the lower class and, especially in Germany, to create an organizational structure deliberately parallel to that which had traditionally evolved among the established strata. Even where there may have been a considerable subsequent disengagement of the parties from organizational

[30]These findings are both illuminated and somewhat strengthened by their close accord with a series of simulations which sought to reproduce the structure of political activity in "model societies" based on hypothetical values for the shape of the class structure, the proportion of those in the whole society who were members of organizations and the class-organization correlation. For further discussion of the methods employed in constructing the simulations and their implications for the role of organizations in political mobilization, see pp. 820-823, Table 5, and Appendix IX in Part II of the original article.)

domination, the effects of such mobilization may have continuing consequences. Lipset and Rokkan have suggested the importance of the political organizational structures initially established during the social mobilization of the society in setting the party alternatives for the society in subsequent years.[31] Their analysis may well apply to the initial formation of organizational infra-structures more generally. In Mexico, the political regime itself has engaged in a protracted attempt to create a lower class infra-structure. For various reasons, such deliberate attempts at group formation in the United States have been more limited, and particular socio-economic features may have also inhibited the development of lower class organizations.[32] Explanation of these historical patterns is beyond the scope of our analysis. But it is at least clear from the American case that the growth of a lower class organizational structure is *not* part of the natural process of economic development. In fact, the consistent positive correlation between organizational involvement and social class points just in the opposite direction. As Olson and other theorists of the costs of organizational development have suggested, the consequent "natural" evolution has limited the formation of mass organizations among groups with low resources.[33]

The evidence presented here, both actual data and the simulation, suggest a basis for analysis of trends in political participation and group representation. If, for instance, it proves to be the case, as recent data suggest, that the American lower class black population is developing a secondary group structure more rapidly than other similarly located groups in society, one should expect an emergent pattern of broader based representation in the political stratum. More complete understanding of these processes, *and* of the reliability of the relationships under differing conditions, might enable us to foresee some of the outcomes of patterns of social change in various national settings.

However, although alerting us to conditions which affect the rates of political participation and the relative contribution of different social groups to the participant stratum, the simulation as presented ignores the issue of

---

[31]Seymour M. Lipset and Stein Rokkan, *Party Systems and Voter Alignments* (New York: Free Press, 1967), pp. 50-56.

[32]A wide range of possible reasons for this failure of group mobilization of the American lower classes has been suggested. These include the presence of the frontier, the general belief in social mobility and economic progress, the tremendous linguistic, ethnic, and religious differences during the period of immigrations, and the lack of traditional social structures such as guilds. Others have suggested more specifically political factors. For example, Walter Dean Burnham, "The Changing Shape of the American Political Universe," *op. cit.*, p. 24. A unified interpretation is obviously beyond the scope of the present discussion.

[33]Mancur Olson, *The Logic of Collective Action* (Cambridge: Harvard University Press, 1965). The organizational membership cutting points are the same from nation to nation; they correspond closely to the percentage of citizens in each nation reporting membership in one or more organizations (U.S. 57%; U.K. 47%; Germany 44%; Italy 30%; Mexico 24%), although our scale is composed of several items, rather than membership alone.

the "quality of participation." We saw in the previous section that persons mobilized into a politically active role through their organizational involvement need not share the attitudes normally thought conducive to "rational" political involvement. In the conclusion we attempt to sort out some of the issues connected with the costs and benefits of more equitably distributed access to the participant stratum.

VI. SUMMARY AND CONCLUSIONS

Evidence from five nations indicates that the relationship between economic growth and increases in mass political participation is largely explained through two changes in the social structure of society: larger numbers of upper and middle class persons, in both relative and absolute terms; and the emergence of organized economic and social groups. Stating the relationship between economic development and mass political participation in terms of structural changes in society provides strong empirical correlations and leads to inclusive social theory. The frequently cited correlations between such individual traits as years of education or number of organizational memberships and the citizen's specific acts of political involvement can be subsumed into the more general theory advanced in this study.

At the national level economic development is associated with urbanization, with the growth of secondary groups, and with the expansion of the white-collar class. Each of these variables has been cited as producing mass political participation. We find, however, that at the individual level urban residence has little effect on participation. Living in larger cities has some *negative* impact on *local* participation, but the total amount of variance explained is slight. An even weaker relationship between urban residence and national participation seems purely a function of the concentration of status resources in urban areas in these systems.

There is less of a correlation between social status and organizational involvement than is sometimes supposed. In their impact on political participation, these characteristics clearly can operate independently of one another. In addition, social status and organizational involvement are differentially linked to participation by intervening political attitudes.

Social status tends to affect political participation through its impact on political attitudes and cognitions which, in turn, facilitate political activity. Although the findings are tentative, the data do suggest that the most important causal link is the creation of *attitudinal resources* that sensitize an individual to political messages and provide him the sense of competence needed to engage in political behavior. There is also evidence indicating that higher status exposes the citizen to learning situations in which the duty to participate is stressed. Acquiring this normative predisposition leads the citizen to acquire other attitudinal resources, such as information and competence, which further increase his probability of political participation. (There is, however, wide variance from nation to nation in the importance of an attitude of civic duty and we present these remarks very tentatively.) Finally, the data tend to reject the hypothesis that the well-to-do citizens participate more frequently in politics because they perceive a higher stake in the day-to-day conduct of political affairs. Correlations between such views and participation appear to be spurious.

Involvement in organizations can also produce the attitudinal resources which facilitate political participation. In some cases, at least, organizational involvement is a source of the sense of a normative obligation to participate (in Germany, a stronger source than status). However, in the main the extremely strong relationship between organizational involvement and political participation does not operate through the acquisition of attitudes and cognitions which facilitate participation.

The causal links connecting social status with political participation, links which create attitudinal resources enabling the individual to participate when opportunities occur, are a minor part of the causal impact of organizational involvement. There is either some sort of self-selection effect which ushers the same citizens into both political activity and organized group life, or there is a strong role played by organizations in mobilizing group members for political activity. The latter interpretation is the more likely, although the two are not mutually exclusive. But such mobilization, if it occurs, does not necessarily result in or reflect higher levels of general political information or awareness. Apparently mobilization opens direct lines to participation, or provides attitudinal resources relevant to specific problems only. There might be, for instance, group-initiated political discussion, group-organized contacts with political authorities, or group-related political information relevant to a specific issue.

Implications. The findings reported in this research paper have implications more far-reaching than those thus far discussed. The findings are, of course, closely related to an understanding of some of the stresses and strains in mass democracies. A research report of this type is not the most useful vehicle for speculating about issues of democratic theory, but insofar as our data suggest some observations, we would be remiss to ignore them completely. Let us at least consider what the patterns may imply about one particularly critical problem: the paradox of mass involvement in political life.

First, the data confirm one well-known finding: Even in industrialized nations a majority of citizens do not participate very actively in politics and do not have the attitudinal resources which lead to citizen control of public policies.

The data support social theories which suggest that industrialization is a necessary condition for the establishment of mass involvement in democratic politics.[34] A key component in this theory is the observation that the tendency to get involved in politics, and the attitudes associated with involvement are not randomly distributed in society. Rather, these tendencies and attitudes tend to cluster in the middle and upper classes. Political life styles of citizens will not be markedly changed until extensive industrialization alters the status structure of society, and thereby increases the overall level of political information, attentiveness, efficacy, and so forth.

Second, the data suggest the critical role which the structure of organized group life may play in the overall level of mass political participation. It appears that the richness and complexity of organizational life might be altered somewhat independently of economic development. Deliberate governmental policies, for instance, can increase the number of citizens who are politically active. Mobilization parties in the single-party states of Africa are one example of how this might happen. Unionizing the labor force, even if comprised of peasant farmers, is another illustration. That is, although historically the growth of secondary groups has been associated with economic development, mobilization politics need not await industrialization. New stimuli to group organization may provoke new patterns of growth, although we observe that complexities and difficulties (beyond this analysis) have met such efforts in practice.

Organizational membership, then, could be a political resource for the lower classes. Were this resource equitably distributed, the criteria for pluralistic democracy advanced by Dahl, Key and others would be more nearly met.[35] That is, all social strata in the society would participate in those political processes which presumably lead to control of political leadership and through this control to influence over public policy. Group mobilization could attract into political life larger numbers of those persons who presently are political isolates. These citizens need not have the enabling antecedents, such as higher levels of education, now thought to be necessary conditions for political participation. Alterations in the organizational structure, then, can serve to correct the tendency for even the most democratically organized

---

[34]For example, Seymour Martin Lipset, *Political Man* (Garden City: Doubleday and Co., 1960), pp. 27-63. Also see Philip Cutright, "National Political Development," in Nelson W. Polsby, Robert A. Dentler, and Paul L. Smith (eds.), *Politics and Social Life* (Boston: Houghton Mifflin Co., 1963), pp. 569-582. In his critical analysis of Lipset and Cutwright, Deane Neubauer argues that economic development may be a necessary condition for democracy, at least to some threshold, but that the relationship is not linear, and does not seem to hold within the subset of more developed systems he examines. See Deane Neubauer, "Some Conditions of Democracy," *American Political Science Review* 61 (Dec. 1967), pp. 1002-1009.

[35]Robert A. Dahl, *A Preface to Democratic Theory* (Chicago: University of Chicago Press, 1956); Key, *op. cit.;* and see the exchange between Jack Walker, "A Critique of the Elitist Theory of Democracy," and Robert A. Dahl, "Further Reflections on the 'Elitist Theory of Democracy,'" *American Political Science Review* 60 (June 1966), pp. 285-305, and Communications to the Editor.

societies to allow a disproportionate amount of political influence to be exercised by the well-to-do.

These observations about the organization-related potential for increasing political participation should be advanced cautiously, however. For one thing, we reemphasize that in every nation examined social status and organizational involvement were somewhat correlated, though the relationship is not determinate. Indeed, it is important for the student of American politics to note that the distribution of organizational resources is more intertwined with the distribution of status resources in the United States than in any of the other four nations in the study. The natural growth of organizations, as Mancur Olson has suggested, seems to be one which places at a disadvantage very large potential groups when the individuals who might make up those groups have limited individual resources.[36] The cost to each individual of organization building is discouragingly great. It is probably no coincidence that those nations in which both political parties and governmental bureaucracies have been most active in encouraging secondary group formation show less upper class domination of the organized life of the society. What must be concluded is that processes of economic development will not automatically help redress class participation imbalances through the growth of secondary groups.

Another note of caution must be voiced as well. One cannot be certain, particularly on the basis of data presented here, about the quality of organization-based political participation. The individual mobilized by his group membership lacks the attitudes usually associated with political involvement. This may mean that the content of his effort to influence will be largely determined by the mobilizing leaders, a possibility suggesting that organizations are more the base of a "counter-elite" than a source of broader and more democratic patterns of political influence.

Whereas our findings suggest a potential for participatory democracy which is in optimistic contrast to most modern empirical studies of mass participation, these same findings raise again the specter of mass "irrationality" and "ignorant" involvement which has haunted democratic theorists since the Greeks. Organizations mobilizing their members and providing resources for their leaders present the possibility of large numbers of political activists who do not have the attitudes usually assumed to be associated with involvement in political life. Political information, a sense of civic duty, political attentiveness, and a sense of political efficacy are not preconditions for political participation among the organizationally involved.

Just what this implies is not entirely clear from the data at hand. While some modern American theorists have placed great stock in the moderating influence of norms of tolerance and accommodation, and of the gate-keeper role of those thoroughly socialized into recognition of democratic procedures

---

[36]Olson, *op. cit.*

and processes,[37] it is not evident that such norms are necessarily the property of elites rather than masses. If American data showing the informed substratum to be more tolerant and democratically oriented, although also more split on political issues, are correct, then group mobilization in this system is likely to be associated with higher levels of conflict and intolerance.[38] On the other hand, there is some evidence that in systems with a more ideological and conflict-ridden history, the better informed and more active citizens may possess belief systems into which deeply rooted hostility and suspicion of the opposition, as well as intransigent issue positions, are firmly integrated.[39] Such would seem to be the case in nations such as France, Austria, and Italy. In these circumstances, group mobilization of a certain type might draw into the system citizens oriented more pragmatically to specific issues and problems, who might press elites to abandon traditional attitudes of rigidity.

The problem is further complicated by the facts that (1) the relationship between basic attitudes, such as information and attentiveness, and the specific affective and normative content of opinions, has not been established; and (2) the possibility that under some conditions group activity itself may structure affective attitudes must be brought into the analysis. In nations where organized groups are linked to partisan camps, and few groups cut across party, class, and religious lines, then involvement itself may reinforce suspicions and hostilities. Thus, in nations such as Italy and Austria, where group members and leaders seem to be more distrustful of the opposition than citizens at large,[40] the mobilization of ever greater numbers of participants through this same group structure may only increase the number of distrustful participants, neither easing nor exacerbating the hostility among political elites, but generally intensifying the political interactions in the system.

---

[37]Dahl, *op. cit.*; and Key, *op. cit.*

[38]James W. Prothro and Charles M. Grigg, "Fundamental Principles of Democracy," *Journal of Politics* 22 (1960), pp. 276-294; Samuel Stouffer, *Communism, Conformity, and Civil Liberties* (New York: Doubleday and Co., 1955); Herbert McClosky, Paul J. Hoffmann, and Rosemary O'Hara, "Issue Conflict and Consensus among Party Leaders and Followers," *American Political Science Review* 59 (June 1960), pp. 406-427.

[39]See, for example, Duncan MacRae, Jr., *Parliament, Parties and Society in France, 1946-1958* (New York: St. Martin's Press, 1967). Also, for suggestive data from a single community, G. Bingham Powell, Jr., *Fragmentation and Hostility in an Austrian Community* (Stanford: Stanford University Press, 1971.

[40]See the general discussion of organizational fragmentation; as well as the data on Italy, in Sidney Verba, "Organizational Membership and Democratic Consensus," *Journal of Politics* 27 (1965), pp. 467-497. Also see the discussion and data of Powell, *ibid.*, Chapters I and IV; Arend Lijphart, *The Politics of Accommodation* (Berkeley: University of California Press, 1968), Chapter I; and Rodney P. Stiefbold, "Elite-Mass Opinion Structure and Communication Flow in a Consociational Democracy (Austria)," paper presented at the 1968 Annual Meeting of the American Political Science Association.

In short, the place of participation in the nature of democratic processes is a complex one, and the effect of increases in participation, particularly through operation of organized groups, depends on a number of other factors. Even such implications as we have suggested must be advanced only as speculations in no way tested by our data. What we have shown is that the relationship between individual political activity and mass political participation has some properties not heretofore recognized. It is a separate research task to specify how different bases of political participation produce different politics.

21

Policy Demands and System Support: The Role of the Represented

John C. Wahlke

Discontent with the functioning of representative bodies is hardly new. Most of them were born and developed in the face of opposition denying their legitimacy and their feasibility.[1] Most have lived amid persistent unfriendly attitudes, ranging from the total hostility of anti-democrats to the pessimistic assessments of such diverse commentators as Lord Bryce, Walter Lippmann, and Charles de Gaulle.[2] Of particular interest today is the discontent with representative bodies expressed by the friends of democracy, the supporters of representative government, many of whom see in recent history a secular 'decline of parliament' and in prospect the imminent demise of representative bodies.[3]

Much of the pessimism among the friends of representative government appears, however, to be very poorly grounded. The notion that we are witnessing 'the decline of parliament', it has been observed, 'has never been

Reprinted from *British Journal of Political Science*, Vol. I, pp. 271-290, by permission of Cambridge University Press. This is a revised version of a paper originally presented at the Seventh World Congress of the International Political Science Association in Brussels, Belgium, September 18-23, 1967.

[1] The best analytical surveys of representation theory are those of A. H. Birch, *Representative and Responsible Government* (Toronto: University of Toronto Press, 1964), and Alfred de Grazia, *Public and Republic* (New York: Alfred A. Knopf, 1951).

[2] Bryce's views are expressed, for example, in *Modern Democracies* (New York: The Macmillan Co., 1921), vol. II, pp. 335-357. Lippmann's can be found in *Public Opinion* (New York: Penguin Books, 1946), especially pp. 216-220. While General de Gaulle has, of course, not contributed formally to literature of this kind, Gaullist views are well known from various speeches, debates, and publication preceding the creation of the Fifth French Republic. They are conveniently discussed in Roy C. Macridis and Bernard E. Brown, *The de Gaulle Republic* (Homewood, Ill.: Dorsey Press, 1960), pp. 124-131.

[3] Joseph P. Clark, *Congress: The Sapless Branch* (New York: Harper & Row, 1964); *The Senate Establishment* (New York: Hill & Wang, 1964).

based on careful inquiry into the function of parliaments in their presumed golden age, nor into their subsequent performance.'[4] Neither had it rested on careful inquiry into the functions and roles of citizens, individually and collectively, in a representative democracy. Indeed, it is both possible and likely that, 'If there is a crisis, . . . it is a crisis in the theory of representation and not in the institution of representation.'[5] This paper suggests how (and why) we might begin to reformulate representation theory and to identify the critical questions which research must answer.

I

         Much of the disillusionment and dissatisfaction with modern representative government grows out of a fascination with the policy decisions of representative bodies which, in turn, reflects what may be called a 'policy-demand-input' conception of government in general and the representative processes in particular. Theorists and researchers alike have long taken it for granted that the problem of representative government centers on the linkage between citizens' policy preferences and the public-policy decisions of representative bodies. Almost without exception they have conceived of the public side of this relationship in terms of 'demands' and the assembly side in terms of 'responses'. Julius Turner, for instance, has said that, 'the representative process in twentieth-century America involves . . . the attempt of the representative to mirror the political desires of those groups which can bring about his election or defeat.'[6] Almond and Verba, in the course of explicating new dimensions of civic behavior (to which we shall return) take the making of demands to be the characteristic act of citizens in democratic systems: 'The competent citizen has a role in the formation of general policy. Furthermore, he plays an *influential* role in this decision-making process: he participates through the use of explicit or implicit threats of some form of deprivation if the official does not comply with his demands.'[7]

[4]Gerhard Loewenberg, *Parliament in the German Political System* (Ithaca, New York: Cornell University Press, 1967), p. 1.

[5]Heinz Eulau, 'Changing Views of Representation', 53-85 in Ithiel de Sola Pool, ed., *Contemporary Political Science: Toward Empirical Theory* (New York: McGraw Hill Book Co., 1967), p. 55.

[6]Julius Turner, *Party and Constituency: Pressures on Congress,* Johns Hopkins University Studies in Historical and Political Science, vol. LXIX, No. 1 (Baltimore, Maryland: Johns Hopkins University Press, 1962), p. 178. Italics added.

[7]Gabriel A. Almond and Sidney Verba, *The Civic Culture* (Princeton, New Jersey: Princeton University Press, 1963), p. 214. More recently Almond has specifically identified this kind of model as a sort of paradigm for developed representative political systems, listing 'responsiveness' (to demand inputs) as a capability of the most developed political systems. Gabriel A. Almond, 'A Developmental Approach to Political Systems', *World Politics* XVII (1965), pp. 183-214, especially 197 ff.

The Simple Demand-Input Model

The basic elements in the general policy-demand-input conception can be described, in necessarily oversimplified form, as follows. The principal force in a representative system is (as it ought to be) the conscious desires and wishes of citizens, frequently examined in modern research on representation under the heading of 'interests'. Interests are thought of as constituting 'policy demands' or 'policy expectations', and the governmental process seems to 'begin' with citizens exerting them on government. Government, in this view, is essentially a process for discovering policies which will maximally meet the policy expectations of citizens. There are several points at which emphases or interpretations may vary in important respects, but the critical assumptions of this view and the points at which such variations may occur can readily be outlined.

In the first place, the interests which constitute the fundamental stuff of democratic, representative politics are most often thought of in terms of specific policy opinions or attitudes, i.e., preference or dislike for particular courses of government action. But it is also common to envision citizens holding less specific policy preferences, in the form of ideological orientations or belief systems.

Although 'interests' are taken to be rooted in individual desires, they may be expressed in the form of either individual policy opinions (often aggregated by opinion analysts as 'public opinion' or the opinion of some segment of the public), or organized group or associational opinion, usually thought to be expressed on behalf of the individuals by group agents or spokesmen, or, of course, in both forms simultaneously.

Analytically, the core of the representative process is the communication of these various forms of interest to governmental actors, which is thought to occur in either or both of two principal ways. It may take place through constituency influence, i.e., the communication of aggregated individual views by constituents to their 'representatives'. (The latter term theoretically includes administrative agency personnel, police officials, judges, and countless other governmental actors, but we shall deal here only with members of representative bodies.) Communication may also occur through group pressure or lobbying activities, conceived of as communication by group agents who are intermediaries between representatives and the aggregates of citizens for whom they (the group agents) speak.

The critical process for making representative government democratically responsible is, of course, election of the representatives. Elections are the indispensable mechanism for ensuring a continuing linkage between citizens' public-policy views (interests) and the public policy formulated by representatives (in cooperation, needless to say, with executives and administrators). The mechanism works in one or both of two ways. It may provide representatives with a mandate to enact into public policy at an early date the policy views expressed in the elections. It may also serve to legitimize, by stamping the *imprimatur* of citizen acceptance on, the policies most recently enacted by the representatives.

However logical and obvious such a conception of democratic representative governmental processes may seem, the observed behavior of citizens is in almost all critical respects inconsistent with it. Some of the more important established propositions about observed behavior which conflict with assumptions about the role of policy-demand inputs in politics may be listed here, even though there is no room to list in detail the evidence supporting them. They are, in most instances propositions which are well known, although not normally brought to bear in discussions of representation:[8]

1. *Few citizens entertain interests that clearly represent 'policy demands' or 'policy expectations', or wishes and desires that are readily convertible into them.*

2. *Few people even have thought-out, consistent, and firmly held positions on most matters of public policy.*

3. *It is highly doubtful that policy demands are entertained even in the form of broad orientations, outlooks, or belief systems.*

4. *Large proportions of citizens lack the instrumental knowledge about political structures, processes, and actors that they would need to communicate policy demands or expectations if they had any.*

---

[8]See, for example, the familiar discussion in Bernard R. Berelson, Paul F. Lazarsfeld, and William N. McPhee, *Voting* (Chicago: University of Chicago Press, 1954), pp. 305-323. The particular propositions listed here are supported, in every instance, by survey data from various political systems collected at various different times. Although systematically analyzed in the original research for this paper, the data are not reported here because of limitations of space. The more relevant compilations and commentaries include the following: Hadley Cantril, *The Pattern of Human Concerns* (New Brunswick, New Jersey: Rutgers University Press, 1965), pp. 167-171; Hadley Cantril & Mildred Strunk, *Public Opinion 1935-46* (Princeton: Princeton University Press, 1951); Angus Campbell, Philip E. Converse, Warren E. Miller, and Donald E. Stokes, *The American Voter* (New York: John Wiley & Sons, Inc., 1960); Philip E. Converse and Georges Dupeux, 'Politicization of the Electorate in France and the United States', reprinted from *Public Opinion Quarterly*, XXVI (1962) in Angus Campbell *et al., Elections and the Political Order* (New York: John Wiley & Sons, Inc., 1966), pp. 269-291; Philip E. Converse, 'New Dimensions of Meaning for Cross-Section Sample Surveys in Politics', *International Social Science Journal* XVI (1964), 19-34; Raymond A. Bauer, Ithiel de Sola Pool, and Lewis Anthony Dexter, *American Business and Public Policy* (New York: Atherton Press, 1963); Donald E. Stokes, 'Spatial Models of Party Competition', reprinted from *American Political Science Review*, LVII (1963), in Angus Campbell *et al., Elections*, pp. 161-179; Robert Axelrod, 'The Structure of Public Opinion on Policy Issues', *Public Opinion Quarterly* XXXI (1967), pp. 51-60; Elisabeth Noelle and Erich Peter Neumann, eds., *Jahrbuch für öffentliche Meinung, III (1958-64)*, (Allensbach und Bonn: Verlag für Demoskopie, 1965); William N. McPhee and William A. Glaser, eds., *Public Opinion and Congressional Elections* (New York: Free Press of Glencoe, 1962); Leon D. Epstein, 'Electoral Decision and Policy Mandate: An Empirical Example', *Public Opinion Quarterly* XXVIII (1964), 564-572; and William Buchanan, 'An Inquiry into Purposive Voting', *Journal of Politics* XVIII (1965), pp. 281-296.

5. *Relatively few citizens communicate with their representatives.*
6. *Citizens are not especially interested or informed about the policy-making activities of their representatives as such.*
7. *Nor are citizens much interested in other day-to-day aspects of parliamentary functioning.*
8. *Relatively few citizens have any clear notion that they are making policy demands or policy choices when they vote.*

None of this, of course, is new or surprising information. But it is sometimes forgotten when working from slightly less naïve models of the representational system than the one sketched out above. Each of the alternative models familiar to students of representative bodies, however, must sooner or later reckon with these facts.

A Responsible-Party Model

Whatever else they are doing in the electoral process, voters in most political systems are certainly choosing between candidates advanced by political parties. It is therefore easy to assume that electoral choice between party-candidates is the vehicle for making policy-choices and to derive logically plausible mechanisms by which that choice might be made. For such mechanisms of demand-input to operate, several requirements would have to be met. In the first place, there must be a party program formulated and it must be known to the voters. Second, representatives' policy-making behavior must reflect that program. Third, voters must identify candidates with programs and legislative records, and base their choices on reaction to them.[9] The arguments against the American party system and in favor of the British on grounds of systemic capacity for meeting these requirements are well known.[10]

In most American contexts, the failure of party and legislative personnel to provide appropriate policy cues makes the applicability of the responsible-party model dubious to begin with, no matter what voters might be doing. But there are also signs of voter failure to respond appropriately to whatever such cues might be available. In one American state (Washington), for example, far less than half the public knew which party controlled either house of the state legislature at its most recent session (41 per cent in the case of the lower, 27 per cent for the upper house).[11] Shortly after the 1966

[9]Donald E. Stokes and Warren E. Miller, 'Party Government and the Saliency of Congress' *Public Opinion Quarterly* XXVI (1962), pp. 531-546. Reprinted in Campbell *et al.*, *Elections*, pp. 194-211.

[10]Committee on Political Parties of the American Political Science Association, 'Toward a More Responsible Two-Party System', Supplement, *The American Political Science Review* (September 1950).

[11]Morris Showell, 'Political Consciousness and Attitudes in the State of Washington', *Public Opinion Quarterly* XVII (1953), pp. 394-400.

election in the United States, 31 per cent of the electorate did not know (or was wrong about) which party had a majority in Congress just before the election; more striking still, 34 per cent did not know which party had won most seats in that election and another 45 per cent misinterpreted Republican gains to believe the Republican Party had won a majority![12] With respect to public reaction to party at the national level, Miller and Stokes have demonstrated that party symbols are almost devoid of policy content, which is not surprising in view of what they call the legislative party 'cacophony'.[13] And Converse, in one of the few relevant studies using panel data, found that party identification was far more stable among American voters sampled in 1958 and 1960 than their opinions on any 'issues'.[14] We can only conclude, at least for the American case, that, with or without policy content, party symbols do not serve the American voter as the responsible party model would wish.

Of somewhat greater interest, however, is the situation in those countries where it seems more likely that party and legislative leaders provide voters the conditions under which they could, if they chose, behave as the responsible-party model would have them. The British political system is usually cited as the classic example. What, then, are the facts about the connection between voting and policy preferences of British voters? Perhaps because it has been so commonly taken for granted that every General Election in Britain constitutes an electoral mandate or at least an unfavorable judgment on past policy performance, surprisingly little evidence is available. The most direct testimony, from a nationwide survey of 1960, is that, given a question asking them to differentiate between the two major parties with respect to sixteen political ends or party traits, on only four of the statements did as many as two-thirds of the sample attribute a clear-cut goal to either party, and these were not stated in policy but in group (e.g., 'middle class') or personal terms; on four, some one-half or more were unaware of any difference between the parties, and on the remaining eight, between 33 per cent and 45 per cent detected no differences.[15] There is strong reason, then, to doubt the applicability of the responsible-party model even in Great Britain.

But the most persuasive reason for questioning that model is what we know about the phenomenon of party identification itself. For the mere fact

[12]University of Michigan Survey Research Center Study 0504, Preliminary Code Book, 1967, Deck 02, Columns 51, 52. I am grateful to Professor Warren E. Miller and the Inter-University Consortium for Political Research for their permission to cite this and other preliminary marginal tabulations.

[13]Stokes and Miller, 'Party Government and the Saliency of Congress,' p. 209.

[14]Philip E. Converse, 'The Nature of Belief Systems in Mass Publics', pp. 206-261 in David E. Apter, ed., *Ideology and Discontent* (New York: The Free Press of Glencoe, 1964).

[15]Mark Abrams, 'Social Trends and Electoral Behavior', reprinted from *British Journal of Sociology* XIII (1962), pp. 228-242, 129-144 in Richard Rose, ed., *Studies in British Politics* (New York: St. Martin's Press, 1966). Quoted on p. 136.

that one political party (or coalition) is replaced in government by another as a result of changing electoral fortunes, together with the fact that voters are making electoral choices between parties, does not in itself demonstrate anything at all about the relationship between election results and the public's views about party programs or policy stands. There is abundant evidence, on the contrary, that in many political systems voters identify with a political party much as they identify with a baseball or soccer team. Many voters in many lands are better described as 'rooters', team supporters, than as policy advocates or program evaluators. The authors of *The American Voter* have acquainted us with the importance of that phenomenon in the United States.[16] Of special interest here is their finding that, far from serving as a vehicle for the voter to express prior formed policy views, it is more likely that 'party loyalty plays no small role in the formation of attitudes on specific policy matters.'[17] More recent studies seem to show that party identification of German voters is in some respects similar.[18] The very great stability of party loyalties in Great Britain suggests strongly the operation of similar mechanisms there:

> Not many people switch their votes in the course of their whole lives; therefore, the number changing in the short period between any two successive elections is necessarily small. On this definition, only 4 per cent of the electors in the Bristol sample [Bristol Northeast, 1951] were floaters: . . .[19]

It can hardly be said, then, that the responsible-party model solves any of the theoretical problems encountered in the elementary atomistic model of representative democracy. If anything, it raises further and more serious ones.

Polyarchal and Elitist Models

Historically, the awareness that few human beings are politically involved or active was at the core of many anti-democratic theories. More recently it has been the starting assumption for various elitist conceptions of power structure, particularly at the level of local communities.[20] Still more recently the empirical accuracy of the assumption as

---

[16]Campbell *et al.*, *Elections*, especially pp. 68-75.

[17]Campbell *et al.*, *Elections*, p. 169.

[18]Werner Zölnhofer, 'Parteiidentifizierung in der Bundesrepublik und den Vereinigten Staaten', pp. 126-168 in Erwin K. Scheuch and Rudolf Wildenman, eds., *Zur Soziologie der Wahl. Sonderheft 9/1965, Kölner Zeitschrift für Soziologie und Sozialpsychologie* (Köln und Opladen: Westdeutscher Verlag, 1965).

[19]R. S. Milne and H. C. MacKenzie, 'The Floating Vote', reprinted from *Political Studies*, III (1955), pp. 65-68, 145-149 in Richard Rose, ed., *Studies in British Politics* (New York: St. Martin's Press, 1966). Quoted from p. 145.

[20]Floyd Hunter, *Community Power Structure* (Chapel Hill: University of North Carolina Press, 1953). For a general commentary on this line of studies see Nelson W. Polsby, *Community Power and Political Theory* (New Haven: Yale University Press, 1963).

well as the justifiability of 'elitist' conclusions drawn from it have been questioned and subjected to empirical research.[21]

Our concern here is not with the general theoretical problems raised by such approaches, however.[22] It is rather with their implications for the demand-input conception of representative processes. The chief implication, of course, is that policy demands and policy expectations are manifested by a relative few and not by citizens in general. This implication is hardly to be questioned. Summarizing relevant knowledge on the point, one article noted that 'Most recent academic studies of public attitudes . . . indicate differences between the political attitudes of elite groups and attitudes reflected in mass samples.'[23] And Converse and Dupeux have said that 'It appears likely that the more notable [Franco-American] differences stem from the actions of elites and require study and explanation primarily at this level, rather than at the level of the mass electorate.'[24]

The crucial question, then, concerns the extent to which and the mechanisms by which elites' policy-demanding activities are connected to the representational activities of the mass public. One possibility is that there is competition for different policy satisfactions among different elites, that this competition is settled initially in the governmental process, much as Latham has described the group process:

> The principal function of official groups is to provide various levels of compromise in the writing of the rules, within the body of agreed principles that forms the consensus upon which the political community rests. In so performing this function, each of the three principal branches of government has a special role.
>
> The legislature referees the group struggle, ratifies the victories of the successful coalitions, and records the terms of the surrenders, compromises, and conquests in the form of statutes.[25]

What Latham leaves unsaid is how members of the voting public enter into this process 'within the body of agreed principles that forms the consensus upon which the political community rests.' Does it, by electoral decision, provide the ultimate ratification of policies formulated in the process of compromise among elites (groups)? At the very most, one might look for some 'potential' power in the hands of the general public which it could use, if it

[21]Robert A. Dahl, *A Preface to Democratic Theory* (Chicago: University of Chicago Press, 1956), especially Chapter 3, and *Who Governs* (New Haven: Yale University Press, 1961).

[22]Such problems are discussed in 'Electoral Studies and Democratic Theory: I. A British View', by John Plamenatz, and '. . . . II. A Continental View', by Giovanni Sartori, *Political Studies* VI (1958), pp. 1-15; Jack Walker, 'A Critique of the Elitist Theory of Democracy', *American Political Science Review* LX (1966), pp. 285-295, and the reply by Robert A. Dahl, 'Further Reflections on "The Elitist Theory of Democracy" ', *Ibid.*, pp. 296-304; and Peter Bachrach, *The Theory of Democratic Elitism: A Critique* (Boston: Little, Brown & Co., 1967).

[23]Sidney Verba *et al.*, 'Public Opinion and the War in Vietnam', *American Political Science Review* LXI (1967), pp. 317-333, p. 318.

[24]Converse and Dupeux, 'Politicization of the Electorate', p. 291.

[25]Earl Latham, *The Group Basis of Politics* (Ithaca: Cornell University Press, 1952), p. 35.

wished, to ratify or reject policies and programs thus put before it. But all the considerations which made the simple atomistic and responsible-party conceptions implausible apply with equal force and in identical fashion against such an interpretation.

Thus, when we look for public participation through electoral choice among competing elites, we encounter the same difficulties we have encountered before. So-called polyarchal or elite-democracy models are no more helpful in connecting policy-making to policy demands from the public than were the atomistic and party models.

II

Demand-input emphases have tended also to color our views of what constitutes responsible behavior by elected representatives. Since the kind of findings just surveyed are well known, few modern studies consider Edmund Burke's 'instructed delegate model' appropriate for modern legislators.[26] Most report without surprise the lack of connection between any sort of policy-demand input from the citizenry and the policy-making behavior of representatives.

Nevertheless, most empirical studies of representative behavior accept the premise that conformity between legislators' actions and the public's policy views is the central problem of representative government, usually envisioning some kind of role-conception or normative mechanism through which the agreement comes about. Thus Jewell and Patterson argue that high concern of representatives for their constituency is plausible in spite of the fact that legislators have low saliency in constituents' eyes.[27] And Miller and Stokes suggest still more specifically that, in spite of these facts, 'the idea of reward or punishment at the polls for legislative stands is familiar to members of Congress, who feel that they and their records are quite visible to their constituents.'[28] A study by John Kingdon suggests one interesting mechanism through which the moral obligation to represent constituency views might work: what he terms the 'congratulation-rationalization effect' leads winners of Congressional elections to have higher estimates of voters' interest and information than do losers, and to attribute less importance to

[26]John C. Wahlke, Heinz Eulau, William Buchanan, and LeRoy C. Ferguson, *The Legislative System* (New York: John Wiley & Sons, Inc., 1962), pp. 267-286; Warren E. Miller and Donald E. Stokes, 'Constituency Influence in Congress', *American Political Science Review* LVII (1963), 45-56, reprinted in Campbell *et al.*, *Elections*, pp. 351-373; and Donald E. Stokes, 'A Variance Components Model of Political Effects', 61-85 in John Claunch, ed., *Mathematical Applications in Political Science* (Dallas, Texas: The Arnold Foundation of Southern Methodist Univ., 1965), p. 62.

[27]Malcolm E. Jewell and Samuel C. Patterson, *The Legislative Process in the United States* (New York: Random House, Inc., 1966), pp. 351-352.

[28]Miller and Stokes, 'Constituency Influence in Congress', p. 368.

party label and more importance to policy issues in voters' actions at their election than do losers. Therefore,

> The incumbent is more likely than if he lost to believe that voters are watching him, that they are better informed, and that they make their own choices according to his own characteristics and even according to the issues of the election. Because of the congratulation-rationalization effect . . .[he] may pay greater attention to the constituency than otherwise, because he believes that his constituents are paying greater attention to him than he might think if he had lost.[29]

Perhaps the most persuasive explanation of the mechanism linking public views to legislative policy is that offered by Miller and Stokes. They compared representatives' votes in several policy domains to constituency opinion, representatives' personal opinion, and representatives' perceptions of their constituency's opinion, in order to determine the proportionate contribution of each to his voting. In brief, they found that constituency policy views play a large role for Congressmen in civil rights issues, but a negligible role in domestic welfare issues and no role in foreign policy issues. Cnudde and McCrone, extending this line of research, demonstrated the primary importance of the Congressman's perceptions of his constituents' opinion in establishing whatever link there is from constituency through to legislative voting. That is, in civil rights issues, Congressmen appear to shape their attitude to fit the opinions they think their constituency holds.[30]

These findings, while in some respects striking, are nonetheless ambiguous. From the standpoint of our understanding of representative government, the results of studies of the behavior of representatives are as unsatisfactory as the studies of citizen behaviour seem disquieting. Many important questions are left unanswered, theoretically or empirically. Often the differences on which theoretically important distinctions are based are found to be small. Above all, in spite of the fact that legislative policy decisions are universally taken to be the most important type of legislative output, we know almost nothing about the character, let alone the conditions and causes, of how they vary in content. We now turn briefly to this problem.

III

'Policies' have been described as the most important variety of political output, and legislative policy decisions are commonly understood to

---

[29]John W. Kingdon, 'Politicians' Beliefs about Voters', *American Political Science Review* LXI (1967), pp. 137-145, p. 144.

[30]Warren E. Miller and Donald E. Stokes, 'Constituency Influence in Congress'; Charles F. Cnudde and Donald J. McCrone, 'The Linkage between Constituency Attitudes and Congressional Voting Behavior: A Causal Model', *American Political Science Review*, LX (1966), pp. 66-72.

be the most important type of legislative output.[31] It has been argued, therefore, that a major problem for legislative research is 'to achieve adequate conceptualization of legislative output, i.e., to specify the dimensions or variables of legislative output which are related to different consequences of that output.'[32] So it is rather startling to discover that the term 'policy' remains almost totally unconceptualized, i.e., that the literature provides 'no theoretically meaningful categories which distinguish between types of policies.'[33]

There is, however, a recent series of methodologically sophisticated but theoretically unstructured inquiries into possible variations in public policy which tends still further to challenge the relevance of demand-input conceptions to understanding the representative process. Most of these studies utilize the readily available masses of quantitative data about American states to analyze relationships among policy outputs and many possible correlates. Variations in policy output have usually been measured by the amount of money spent by a system on different categories of substantive policy or program, such as public highways, health programs, welfare, etc. Political variables investigated have usually been 'structural' in nature—for example, degree of two-party competition, degree of voter participation, extent of legislative malapportionment, and so on. Socioeconomic environmental (or 'background') variables have included such things as degree of urbanization and industrialization, or education level.

It is the general import of these studies that, with only rare and minor exceptions, variations in public policy are *not* related to variations in political-structure variables, except insofar as socio-economic or environmental variables affect them and public policy variations together. Variations in policy output can be almost entirely 'explained' (in the statistical sense) by environmental variables, without reference to the variables supposedly reflecting different systems and practices of representation. Most far-reaching of such studies is Dye's examination of the effects of economic development (industrialization, urbanization, income, education) and political-system (party division, party competition, political participation, and malapportionment) on ninety policy variables in four different policy fields. His conclusion:

> . . . system characteristics have relatively little *independent* effect on policy outcomes in the states. Economic development shapes both political systems and policy outcomes, and most of the association that occurs between system characteristics and policy outcomes can be attributed to the influence of economic development.[34]

[31] David Easton, *A Framework for Political Analysis* (Englewood Cliffs, N.J.: Prentice-Hall, Inc., 1965), p. 125; *A Systems Analysis of Political Life* (New York: John Wiley & Sons, Inc., 1966), pp. 353 ff.

[32] Wahlke *et al.*, *The Legislative System*, p. 25.

[33] Lewis A. Froman, Jr., 'An Analysis of Public Policies in Cities', *Journal of Politics*, XXVIII (1967), pp. 94-108.

[34] Thomas R. Dye, *Politics, Economics and the Public: Policy Outcomes in the American States* (Chicago: Rand McNally & Co., 1966), p. 293.

It is possible, of course, that these remarkable findings are unique to the American political system. That such is not the case, however, is strongly suggested by Cutright's discovery that variations in the national security programs of seventy-six nations appear to be explainable directly in terms of economic-development level and to be unrelated to differences in ideology or type of political system (including differences between communist and capitalist systems).[35] There is a curious hint of similar findings in a study suggesting that changes in foreign policy do not seem to be associated with instances of 'leadership succession' so far as voting in the U.N. General Assembly is concerned; that is, there is apparently substantial continuity of foreign policy in any given system despite changes in political regime.[36]

In sum, then, the policy-environment correlation studies imply that stimuli which have been thought to be policy demands are really just automatically determined links in a chain of reactions from environment to policy output, a chain in which neither policy demands, policy expectations, or any other kind of policy orientation plays any significant role. There is no room, in other words, for any of the policy-related behaviors and attitudes of citizens which we examined in the preceding section of this paper to enter into the policy process.

IV

The foregoing arguments are not especially 'anti-democratic' or 'anti-representative'. They are just as damaging to much antidemocratic theory and to elitist criticisms of representative democracy. It is not only policy-opinions of citizens in the mass public which are demoted in the rank order of policy determinants but policy opinions of elites and group leaderships as well. The principal implication is that 'policy-process' studies whose aim is primarily to discover the political bases of policy decisions conceived of as choices between policy alternatives contended for by divergent political forces, or to explain why a particular decision went one way instead of another, comprehend too little of the political life of man, and that the part they do comprehend is probably not its most vital. The appropriate conclusion is not the grandiose notion that representative democracy is chimerical but the limited recognition that our conceptions of government, politics, and representation are somehow deficient, that 'policy making' plays a different and evidently smaller role in the governance of society than we thought.

Precisely what role we cannot yet say, for neglect to study the political consequences of policy making is 'a practice very much in line with the

[35] Philips Cutright, 'Political Structure, Economic Development, and National Security Programs', *American Journal of Sociology* LXX (1965), pp. 537-548.

[36] David H. Blake, 'Leadership Succession and Its Effects on Foreign Policy as Observed in the General Assembly', Mimeographed paper prepared for the Annual Meeting of the Midwest Conference of Political Scientists, Indiana, April 27-29, 1967.

tradition of political science.'[37] Research on representation has tended toward preoccupation with the results of legislative roll calls and other decisions, or the results of elections and series of them. It has concentrated on the antecedents of legislative 'output' and left unexamined the political 'outcomes' which above all make output an appropriate object of political study.[38] It has explored the possible sources of variations as small as a few percentage points in the influence of 'factors' influencing legislative and electoral decision, but ignored the relationship, if any, between legislative output and the incidence of discontent, riots, wars, civil wars, *coups d'état,* revolutions, and decay or integration of human groups. Its focus has been determined by 'political theories of allocation', in almost total disregard of the perspectives opened up by 'theories of systems persistence'.[39] This is an essential part of de Jouvenel's charge that political science has not so far had the 'dangerous' impact it might because it has so far been content to investigate only 'weak political behavior'.[40]

A plausible working hypothesis which directs the study of representation toward 'strong political behavior' is provided by Easton's discussion of 'support'. Viewed from this perspective, previous studies are seen to presume that political systems stand, fall, or change according to the 'specific support' accorded them, the 'consent' granted 'as a consequence from some specific satisfaction obtained from the system with respect to a demand that the members make.'[41] But the arguments above show that specific support, the support attaching directly to citizens' reactions to policy decisions, does not adequately describe the relationship between citizen and government. We must also recognize and take into account what Easton calls 'diffuse support', the support constituted by 'generalized attachment to political objects, . . . not conditioned upon specific returns at any moment.'[42]

---

[37]Eugene J. Meehan, *Contemporary Political Thought* (Homewood, Ill.: The Dorsey Press, 1967), p. 180.

[38]Easton describes this distinction as that between 'a stream of activities flowing from the authorities in a system' (outputs) and 'the infinite chain of effects that might flow from an authoritative allocation' (outcomes). *A Systems Analysis,* pp. 349, 351.

[39]Leon Lindberg, 'The Role of the European Parliament in an Emerging European Community', pp. 101-128 in Elke Frank, ed., *Lawmakers in a Changing World* (Englewood Cliffs, New Jersey: Prentice-Hall, Inc., 1966), p. 108. The same point has been made in John Wahlke, 'Behavioral Analyses of Representative Bodies', pp. 173-190 in Austin Ranney, ed., *Essays in the Behavioral Study of Politics* (Urbana: University of Illinois Press, 1962), and is indirectly made by Malcolm E. Jewell and Samuel C. Patterson, *The Legislative Process in the United States* (New York: Random House, Inc., 1966), pp. 528-531.

[40]Bertrand de Jouvenel, 'On the Nature of Political Science', *American Political Science Review* LV (1961), 773-779, p. 777.

[41]Easton, *A Systems Analysis,* p. 268.

[42]Easton, *A Systems Analysis,* pp. 272, 273. Easton himself later (434n.) makes the much stronger assertion still that, 'Under some circumstances the need for outputs to bolster support may be reduced to the vanishing point.'

There is good warrant for the working hypothesis that,

> Except in the long run, diffuse support is independent of the effects of daily outputs. It consists of a reserve of support that enables a system to weather the many storms when outputs cannot be balanced off against inputs of demands. It is a kind of support that a system does not have to buy with more or less direct benefits for the obligations and responsibilities the member incurs. If we wish, the outputs here may be considered psychic or symbolic, and in this sense, they may offer the individual immediate benefits strong enough to stimulate a supportive response.[43]

The plausibility of such a starting point has been intimated by other observers. Edelman's instructive discussion of the importance of 'symbolic' as compared with 'instrumental' satisfactions deriving from the administration of public policies clearly argues for it.[44] More directly concerning representative functions, Thomas Anton has shown, with respect to the roles of agency spokesmen, budget, officers, legislators, and citizens in the budgetary process of American states that 'what is at stake . . . is not so much the distribution of resources, about which state actors have little to say, but the distribution of symbolic satisfaction among the involved actors and the audiences which observe their stylized behavior.'[45] And Alfred de Grazia has discussed the ways in which 'the election process is symbolic and psychological in meaning, rather than a device for the purpose of instructing delegates.'[46]

That the problem of support is a proper springboard for representation research is suggested also by some commentators on the functions of representative bodies. Almost thirty years ago, T. V. Smith spoke of the 'cathartic function' of legislatures, which by themselves appearing as scapegoats, harmlessly conduct away disaffections that otherwise 'might well totalize into attacks upon public order.'[47] More recently, Eulau and Hinckley have pointed out that representative bodies perform 'such latent functions . . . as consensus-building, interest aggregation, catharsis for anxieties and resentment, the crystallization and resolution of conflicts, and the legitimization of decisions made elsewhere in the political system.'[48] With respect to Great Britain, Beer has described the main parliamentary task as that of 'mobilizing consent', 'certainly not the representative function by which in greater

---

[43]Easton, *A Systems Analysis*, p. 273.

[44]Murray Edelman, *The Symbolic Uses of Politics* (Urbana: University of Illinois Press, 1964).

[45]Thomas J. Anton, 'Roles and Symbols in the Determination of State Expenditures', *Midwest Journal of Political Science* XI (1967), 27-43, p. 39.

[46]Alfred de Grazia, *Public and Republic*, p. 170.

[47]T. V. Smith, 'Two Functions of the American State Legislator', *Annals of the American Academy of Political and Social Science*, CXCV (1938), p. 187.

[48]Heinz Eulau and Katherine Hinckley, 'Legislative Institutions and Processes', pp. 85-189 in James A. Robinson, ed., *Political Science Annual*, 1 (1966), pp. 85-86.

or lesser degree the legislature brings the grievances and wishes of the people to bear upon policy-making.'[49] And Patterson has asserted that,

> A legislature is much more than a law-making factory. It is a symbol of representative, democratic government. Its symbolic 'output' may be related to the kinds of policies it makes, but it is related also to the representative adequacy of the legislature, to the respect citizens can have for individual legislators, and to the pride citizens can take in their legislatures.[50]

David Truman has drawn important implications from such a view for the behavior of representatives, arguing that the primary skill lying at the heart of representative government is not substantive, technical skill, but in combination with that,

> a special skill. This is skill in assaying what is asked or done in the name of substantive expertise and in reconciling or combining such claims or acts with the feasibilities that exist or can be created in the electorate, in the extra-governmental world in all its configurations.[51]

The shift of attention from 'demands' to 'support' which all these insights suggest calls for a corresponding shift of research emphasis from the behavior of representatives which has hitherto preoccupied most of us, to the perceptions, attitudes, and behaviors of the people whom representatives collectively represent, about which as yet we really know very little. The most immediate task is a primarily conceptual one—to identify the dimensions of support behavior, to map the incidence and variations of support in specific systems, and through comparative analysis of support mechanisms in different systems, to formulate hypotheses about its conditions and correlates.

V

David Easton's definition of support as affective orientation toward political objects, and his analytical distinction of political community, political regime, and political authorities as the three principal categories of such political objects is a useful starting point.[52] We can probably assume, to begin with, that support for the political community is the

[49]Samuel H. Beer, 'The British Legislature and the Problem of Mobilizing Consent,' Elke Frank, p. 31.

[50]Samuel C. Patterson, *Midwest Legislative Politics* (Mid-America Assembly on State Legislatures, Participants' Edition, 1966), p. 114.

[51]David B. Truman, 'The Representative Function in Western Systems', pp. 84-96 in Edward H. Buehrig, ed., *Essays in Political Science* (Bloomington: Indiana University Press, 1966), p. 90.

[52]'Political community,' refers to 'some minimal readiness or ability (of a group of people) to continue working together to solve their political problems'. (*A Systems Analysis,* p. 172) 'Political Regime: refers to the values and principles, norms ("operating rules and rules of the game") and structures of authority (authority-*roles*) by which, over a period of time authoritative decisions are made in the political community.' (*A Systems Analysis,* 190-211). Political authorities are the persons who occupy the authoritative roles at any given point in time. (*A Systems Analysis,* pp. 212-219).

most pervasive, general (diffuse), and stable element in the overall support
mechanism of any political system. Basic group-identification, the sort of
'pre-political' sentiment giving all segments of the community 'a we-feeling
. . ., not that they are just a group but that they are a political entity that
works together and will likely share a common political fate and destiny,'[53] is
surely a major dimension of this level of support. Everything we know about
the historical evolution of nation-states, tribal societies, and all other political forms, as well as everything modern research tells us about the processes of political socialization indicates that the loyalties, identifications,
and cognitive-affective structures which make up this communal-loyalty
dimension are acquired and shaped in early childhood and are affected
little, if at all, by any political events, let alone such little salient events as
the functioning of representative bodies. The indispensability of this kind of
support for any political system was noted by V. O. Key: 'A basic prerequisite is that the population be pervaded by a national loyalty. Or
perhaps, more accurately, that the population not consist of segments each
with its own sense of separateness.'[54] Almond and Verba, whose concept of
'systems affect' approximates the concept of support for political
community, likewise appear to take for granted (at least in the five countries
they studied) the existence of a nationality sentiment or similar community
sense defining a political community toward which members respond with
varying effect.[55]

But what if no sentiment of political community binds together a group
of people who are, in fact, being governed (as is the case in many new African
nations, to give an obvious example? Or if segments seem increasingly to
develop 'each with its own sense of separateness' (as may well be the case in
Canada or Belgium)? Can we be sure that 'the sense of community must also
be in part a product of public policy?'[56] If not 'policy', what aspect then of
governmental activity, and especially of representative bodies' activity,
affects it? At this stage we can only wonder—and begin to design research to
find out.

A second major dimension of political community support is suggested
by Almond and Verba's typology of political cultures, comprising what we
may interpret as the political roles of 'parochial', 'subject', and 'participant'.
The authors' original formulation differentiates these three types primarily
in terms of their relative participation in demand-input activities.[57] There is
justification even in the original formulation, however, for viewing these roles

[53]Easton, *A Systems Analysis*. p. 332.

[54]Key, *Public Opinion and American Democracy* (New York: Alfred A. Knopf, 1961), p. 549.

[55]Almond and Verba, *The Civic Culture*. pp. 101-105.

[56]Almond and Verba, *The Civic Culture*. p. 551.

[57]The 'participant' is 'an active participant in the political input process,' the 'subject' hardly
at all oriented toward input objects but positively (if passively) oriented affectively 'toward the
output, administrative, or "downward flow" side of the political system', and the 'parochial'
detached from political roles of every sort, on both input and output sides. Almond and Verba,
The Civic Culture. pp. 161, 19, 17, respectively.

as differentiated also by the extent of conscious support for the political community, or 'the gradation from "public" to "private" ': 'The overwhelming
majority of the members of all political systems live out their lives, discover,
develop, and express their feelings and aspirations in the intimate groups of
the community. It is the rare individual who is fully recruited into the political system and becomes a political man.'[58] Viewed this way, the second
component of community support, which might be labelled 'political
commitment', appears as an autonomously defined political variable, a kind
of participation through sensitivity and alertness to political events and
objects as well as participation in civic and political roles—participation in
politics per se, not necessarily in the sense of power seeking, however, and
not participation in primarily instrumental activities. It is a kind of 'political
interest', but, '. . . it is interest not in the form of gains in material well-
being, power, or status, but it is rather in personal satisfaction and growth
attained from active engagement in the political process.'[59]

A number of familiar concepts bear on this second dimension of poli-
tical-community support. Most of the phenomena usually treated under the
heading of 'political alienation', for example, represent an extreme negative
value, ranking above only such anti-supportive positions as rebellion itself.
'Political apathy', in a sense related to Almond and Verba's 'parochialism',
is more supportive than alienation but less so than 'compliance'. More supportive still is active 'interest and involvement', although one must be careful
to remember that support for the political community here is perfectly compatible (perhaps often associated?) with failure of support for regime or
authorities. Beyond active spectator interest there is participation of varying
degrees—ranging from nothing more than sporadic voting to regular and intensive political communication, to participation in authority or other 'trans-
civic' roles.

Such a conception of supportive political commitment seems perfectly
consistent with what we do know about the relevant behavior of citizens. For
example, once-depressing statistics about 'low levels' of citizen interest take
on quite different meaning in this light. The finding that 'only' 27 per cent of
the American public could be considered politically active,[60] that during
1945 and 1946 sometimes 'as few as' 19 per cent and 'never more than' 36
per cent of the American Zone population in West Germany claimed to be
personally interested in politics,[61] that in 1958 35 per cent of the West Germans had no interest at all in attending Bundestag sessions even if it cost

[58]Almond and Verba, *The Civic Culture*, p. 143.
[59]Peter Bachrach, *Theory of Democratic Elitism*, p. 38.
[60]Julian L. Woodward and Elmo Roper, 'The Political Activity of American Citizens',
American Political Science Review XLIV (1950), pp. 872-885.
[61]OMGUS, 26 October, 13 December, 1945; 31 January, 7 June, 9 August, 3 September,
1946. Reported in Cantril and Strunk, *Public Opinion 1935-46*, pp. 582-583.

them nothing,[62] or the countless similar readings of political interest and involvement in other political systems, must now, if there is no other different evidence on the point, be read not as sure signs of 'apathy' or 'negativism' but as probable indications of moderate support for the political community.

Still, on balance, we know much less than we should about the dynamics of support for the political community. Though we can recognize that communal loyalty and political commitment constitute important dimensions of it, we do not know how one dimension relates to the other, or how the day-to-day functioning of government, including the input-output functioning of representative institutions, relates to either.

The situation is not much different when we consider the problem of support for the 'political regime'. One major dimension here appears to be the level of conscious support for broad norms and values which apply to the political world generally, i.e., to 'rules-of-the-game', or standards by which regimes are judged. But the meaning of what information we have here is ambiguous. How much consensus, in the sense of 'agreement on fundamentals,' may vary, and what is the effect of such variation, are questions which do not yet have clear answers.[63]

The level of support for the institutional apparatus of government seems to be another major dimension of regime support, empirically distinguishable from generalized 'agreement on fundamentals'. Citizens are apparently able to dislike something or other about the actions of government and at the same time support its continuation institutionally unchanged, and their levels of support in this respect apparently fluctuate over time. An instructive example is the differences in French responses to identical questions put at different times concerning which political regimes seemed to be functioning better or worse than the French regime. From January 1958, to January 1965, the percentage saying each country named worked better than the French dropped in every case and the percentage saying the French regime worked better increased in every case.[64] Again, although 41 per cent of a sample in a small midwestern American city said, in 1966, that there were things Congress had done which they did not like (about some of which they

---

[62] Noell and Neumann *Jahrbuch für offentliche Meinung*, July, 1958, p. 265.

[63] Key's discussion (*Public Opinion*, 30 ff) of 'supportive', 'permissive', 'negative', and 'decisional' consensus is most instructive here. See also Herbert McClosky, 'Consensus and Ideology in American Politics,' *American Political Science Review* LVIII (1964), 361-382, and James W. Prothro and Charles W. Grigg, 'Fundamental Principles of Democracy: Bases of Agreement and Disagreement', *Journal of Politics* XXII (1960), pp. 276-294.

[64] Drop in proportion saying other regime better than France, 25 per cent for G.B.; 28 per cent for U.S.A.; 7 per cent for Italy; 31 per cent for West Germany; 16 per cent for U.S.S.R. Increase in proportion saying French worked better; 15 per cent for G.B.; 13 per cent for U.S.A.; 1 per cent for Italy; 14 per cent for West Germany; 9 per cent for U.S.S.R. *Sondages*, XXVI (1), (1966).

claimed to feel strongly), only 20 per cent of them thought any proposals for changing Congress should be given serious attention; although 44 per cent said the city council had done something they particularly disliked, and only 20 per cent thought the council was doing a good or excellent job, less than a third thought the form of government should be changed.[65] This perspective also leads us to view not as deviant, undemocratic views, but as probable indicators of probably normal regime support, the fact that more Americans think the majority of people usually *in*correct in their ideas on important questions (42 per cent) than think the majority correct (38 per cent), or that Congress is thought more correct than 'the people' in its 'views on broad national issues', (42 per cent as against 38 per cent).[66] Similarly, it becomes understandable why, when only half the American public thinks it makes much difference at all which party wins the election, some two-thirds to three-fourths of them make a point of voting at all elections, whether or not they have any specific interest in them,[67] and almost nine-tenths of them (87 per cent) think having elections makes government pay some or a good deal of attention to what the people think.[68] Although Almond and Verba consider such indicators as these under the heading of 'input affect', meaning essentially demand-input ('the feelings people have both about those agencies and processes that are involved in the election of public officials, and about the enactment of public policies'),[69] they seem much more intelligible viewed under the heading of regime support, i.e., support for the apparatus of government in general.

Our information about regime support phenomena, then, is no more adequate or satisfactory than our information about support for the political community. What there is of it, however, does seem to indicate that symbolic satisfaction with the process of government is probably more important than specific, instrumental satisfaction with the policy output of the process. Thus Thomas Anton has noticed, concerning the budget process, that 'it is not the document which creates satisfaction, but the process of putting it together. . . . [The] budget, as document and process, creates symbolic satisfaction built upon the idea that affairs of state are being dealt with, that responsibility is being exercised, and that rationality prevails.'[70] Dye's conclusion after studying a voluminous array of the content of policy outputs, was that 'The *way* in which a society authoritatively allocates values may be an even

[65]Iowa City Form of Government Study, 1966, Code Book. University of Iowa Laboratory for Political Research.

[66]A.I.P.O. 17 July 1939, and 8 August 1939, reported in 'The Quarter's Polls,' *Public Opinion Quarterly*, X (4), p. 632. The remainder of responses in each instance were DK and NA.

[67]49 per cent and 51 per cent in two separate polls in September 1946, for example. A.I.P.O. reported in 'The Quarter's Polls', *Public Opinion Quarterly*, III (4), p. 580.

[68]Survey Research Center, 1966, SRC Study 0504, ICPR Preliminary Code Book.

[69]Almond and Verba, *The Civic Culture*, p. 101.

[70]Anton, 'Roles and Symbols', pp. 39-40.

more important question than the outcomes of these value allocations. Our commitments to democratic processes are essentially commitments to a mode of decision-making. The legitimacy of the democratic form of government has never really depended upon the policy outcomes which it is expected to produce.'[71] And deGrazia has said, more poetically, '. . . the whole *process* of representation becomes an acting out of a play in which the actors are independent within the limits of the state, the setting, and the changing tastes of the audience. Their role is meaningful but it has no direct connection with the ticket the audience files for admission.'[72]

Whereas political research has by and large neglected to study support for the political community and the political regime, it has paid considerable attention to support for 'political authorities'. Elections, of course, are considered an indispensable feature of representative government by anybody's definition, and election results in representative systems are almost universally interpreted as indices of support for incumbent authorities. The innumerable public opinion polls between elections which ask the level of voters' satisfaction or dissatisfaction with the ruling Government's performance in general, with the performance of various individual office holders or agencies, or with the handling of particular problems, are likewise taken as indicators of the rising and falling level of support for authorities.

No doubt such data are properly interpreted as measures of such support. But the question is, what should be read into them beyond that simple indication? 'Democracy', says Schumpeter, 'means only that the people have the opportunity of accepting or refusing the men who are to rule them.'[73] Our earlier discussion of the role of issues and policies in elections cautions us not to hastily assume voters are voting up one set of policies and voting down another when they go to the polls.[74] A unique series of data about British opinion in 1966 strongly intimates we ought not even assume that they are voting up one set of officeholders and voting down another in quite the simple, straightforward, preferential fashion we have always taken for granted. The data shown in Figure 1 clearly demonstrate that, at least in Britain in 1966, many voters seem to be giving or withdrawing support from the whole apparatus of government officialdom and not, as one might at first think, transferring support from one set of authorities to another. To a remarkable degree, support for Government goes up as support for Opposition goes up, and support for Opposition goes down as support for Government goes down. One is strongly tempted to conclude, though it may be premature, that the support for authorities is much more closely related

[71]Dye, *Politics, Economics and the Public,* p. 30.

[72]de Grazia, *Public and Republic,* p. 170. Italics not in original.

[73]Joseph A. Schumpeter, *Capitalism, Socialism, and Democracy* (New York: Harper & Brothers, 1947), p. 285.

[74]See text above.

Figure 1.   Trends in Support for British Government and Opposition Leaders, 1966.

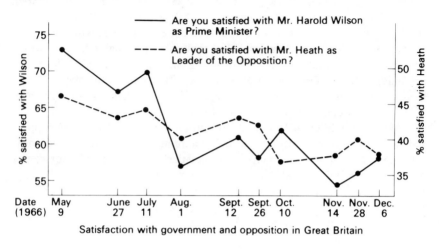

Satisfaction with government and opposition in Great Britain

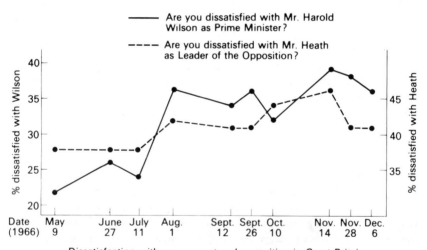

Dissatisfaction with government and opposition in Great Britain

Source: Polls II (4), p. 44 (Sum. '67)

to regime support and much less related to individual voter preferences for individual authority figures than anyone has hitherto suspected.[75]

[75]For a summary of the implications of available studies on the dynamics of support and suggestions for further cross-national study of the problem see G. R. Boynton, Samuel C. Patterson, and John C. Wahlke, 'Dimensions of Support in Legislative Systems,' a Paper prepared for the Quail Roost Conference on Comparative Legislative Research, Rougemont, North Carolina, 25-27 February, 1970.

VI

The conceptualization of support sketched out here is only that. It is not a theory, nor even a few hypotheses. Indeed, it is not even a very complete conceptualization, since many important questions are left open—how do we visualize support in a complex, multi-level, pluralistic government? What is the connection between support for local as against national (and, in federal systems, intermediate) authorities, regime, and political community? Between support for different segments of the regime at different levels? What is the relevance of the notion to supranational and intergovernmental politics?

What bearing has all this on representative government? Surely it does not suggest that to maintain representative democracy is more difficult, or that representative democracy is less desirable, just because it might seem to depend less on support deriving from mechanically satisfying demand-inputs than it does on the generation of support through quite different mechanisms. The question still is, how do representative bodies contribute to the generation and maintenance of support? In what respects and for what particular aspects of the task are they superior to non-representative institutions? These are questions to be answered by empirical research.

22

Citizen Demands and The Soviet Political System

James H. Oliver

Political scientists interested in non-Communist systems have paid considerable attention to demands (expressions of opinion that an authoritative allocation with regard to particular subject matters should or should not be made by those responsible for doing do)[1] coming from the intra-societal (domestic) environments of these political systems. The importance of intra-societal demands, including citizen demands, for non-Communist systems is well established. Researchers interested in the Soviet political system have paid relatively little attention to intra-societal demands, especially demands coming from those whom David Easton would call citizen gatekeepers, i.e., citizens who convert their wants into demands by articulating them.[2]

The reasons for the neglect of research in this area are obvious enough. Quite apart from the problem of gathering useful data, there exists the question of whether demands from the intra-societal environment, and in particular citizen demands, are really important for a "totalitarian" system. Nothing like the politically autonomous interest groups of the Western democracies exist in the Soviet Union. Whatever demands come from the intra-societal environment are therefore largely grassroots demands from the populace, and there is reason to doubt that Soviet authorities feel compelled to heed such demands when formulating policy. Lenin's assertion that the

Reprinted by permission from *American Political Science Review*, LXIII (June 1969), 465-475. Text and footnotes are abridged by permission of the author (references to documents in Russian omitted). The author wishes to thank Prof. John A. Armstrong for his comments on an earlier version of this paper. He also expresses his gratitude to the Inter-University Committee on Travel Grants for their support of his research in the Soviet Union.

[1] I will use the term "demand" only in this restricted sense. For a full discussion of the concept see David Easton, *A Systems Analysis of Political Life* (New York: John Wiley & Sons, 1965), part II.

[2] For a discussion of citizen gatekeepers see Easton, *op. cit.*, pp. 93-94.

Party is the vanguard of the proletariat was clearly a rejection of the idea that the masses should direct the Party. His successors have continued to assert that the Party leads the masses, and not the masses the Party. Stalin argued:

> The Party cannot be a real party if it limits itself to registering what the masses of the working class feel and think. . . . The Party must stand at the head of the working class; it must see farther than the working class; it must lead the proletariat, and not follow in the tail of the spontaneous movement.[3]

The 1961 Party Program clearly reasserted the doctrine of the primacy of the Party as the guiding force in society.

> The period of full-scale communist construction is characterized by a *further enhancement of the role and importance of the Communist Party* as the leading and guiding force of Soviet society.[4]

The directing element of the Party is much narrower than its total membership. Although Western scholars' estimates vary from under 1,000 to several thousand, they agree that the number of persons who really count in the formulation of policy in the Soviet Union is small.[5] Furthermore, Soviet leaders have promoted not merely programs that were clearly contrary to the wishes of important segments of the general populace—collectivization—but also programs contrary to the wishes of segments of the elite—Khrushchev's bifurcation of the Party.

I. SOME HYPOTHESES CONCERNING DEMANDS OF SOVIET CITIZENS

The existence of an apparently limited political community, the lack of independent associational interest groups, the leadership's apparent contempt for mass opinion, the marked centralization of decision-making all suggest that demands from what Easton calls the intra-societal environment are far less important in the Soviet system than in the Western democracies, and even in many of the non-democratic but non-Communist states.

[3]J. V. Stalin, "Foundations of Leninism," *Problems of Leninism* (New York: International Publishers, 1928), p. 73, as quoted in Merle Fainsod, *How Russia is Ruled* (Cambridge: Harvard University Press, 1963), p. 137.

[4]Program of the Communist Party of the Soviet Union, reproduced from a supplement of *New Times* (No. 48), Nov. 29, 1961, in Leonard Schapiro (ed.), *The U.S.S.R. and the Future* (New York: Frederick A. Praeger, 1963), p. 310. Emphasis in the original.

[5]Compare Merle Fainsod, *op. cit.*, p. 205; Derek J. R. Scott, *Russian Political Institutions* (New York: Frederick A. Praeger, 1961), p. 54; and Wolfgang Leonhard, *The Kremlin Since Stalin*, trans. Elizabeth Wiskemann and Marion Jackson (New York: Frederick A. Praeger, 1962), pp. 11-15. See also John A. Armstrong, *The Soviet Bureaucratic Elite* (New York: Frederick A. Praeger, 1959), Chapters I and II.

Certainly much of the work of Soviet-area specialists supports Easton's contention that although "there is still room for articulation of political demands" within totalitarian systems despite "the severe restrictions upon popular participation,"[6] the number and variety of gatekeepers—those who convert wants into demands by articulating them—is so restricted that input overload is not "likely to occur or even threaten."[7] He contrasts "modern totalitarian or dictatorial systems" with democracies, which, "within the limits imposed by other aspects of the political culture," encourage every citizen to participate in the system by tending his own gate, that is, by converting his own wants into demands by directing statements concerning the allocation of values to authorities.[8]

The hypotheses that in the Soviet Union (1) citizens are not encouraged to tend their own gates; (2) the number of gatekeepers is so restricted that input overload is unlikely to occur or even threaten; (3) demands from the intra-societal environment, and in particular citizen demands, are of little importance, seem tenable. I will try to show that these hypotheses, if not false, are true only in a very limited sense. In the course of my argument I also will attempt to clarify the way in which these demands are processed, and indicate some of the problems that arise in conjunction with their processing.

II. SOVIET CITIZEN GATEKEEPERS AND THEIR DEMANDS

Evidence that Soviet citizens tend their own gates and that higher officials require local officials to pay attention to the resulting citizen demands has existed ever since Merle Fainsod published his study of the Smolensk Province Party Archives in 1958.[9] In this chapter on the right of petition he noted that this right existed prior to World War II and that the citizens of Smolensk Province vigorously exercised it.[10] Fainsod also noted that citizen petitions had at least two functional consequences. First, the petitions (demands in Easton's terminology) served to expose and, therefore, inhibit misconduct at the lower administrative levels. Second, they tended to diffuse popular discontent and direct it from the center to local officials.[11]

The inaccessibility of Party archives, other than the captured Smolensk Archives, makes a replication of Fainsod's study impossible. Nevertheless,

[6]Easton, op. cit., p. 110.
[7]Ibid., p. 93.
[8]Ibid., pp. 93-95.
[9]These archives were captured first by the German army during World War II and subsequently by U.S. forces. They are the only party archives open to non-Communist scholars.
[10]Merle Fainsod, Smolensk Under Soviet Rule (New York: Vintage Books, 1963), chap. XX.
[11]Ibid., p. 408.

data available for Moscow and Leningrad clearly show that Soviet urban citizens in the 1950's and 1960's continued to make their demands known to local authorities, just as their rural counterparts had done during the pre-war period in Smolensk Province. By the 1960's thousands of citizen demands were pouring into the city raion (borough)[12] agencies and organs, either directly from the citizens or via higher officials who simply sent any demands within the jurisdiction of a raion to that raion in the individual raw form in which the citizen had submitted it.

Whatever the route of the demands, the number was astounding. In the first four months of 1962 some 11,803 citizen demands poured into the offices of the Kirov raion of Moscow. In the first half of 1963 officials of a single raion in Leningrad received over 15,000 letters and visits from the populace involving demands of various sorts.

The demands themselves cover nearly the entire range of activities under the jurisidiction of the city governmental apparatus. The citizens complain about the quality of new construction; request additional housing space; and complain about the slowness of housing repairs and their quality. They make demands concerning the quality, assortment and availability of goods in stores and shops and the location of retail outlets and restaurants. They complain about the quality of service in retail outlets, restaurants, and consumer service facilities. They complain about taxi service; they make demands concerning mass transportation facilities. They express their concern about health facilities, about poor street lighting, about unkept parks, about cultural facilities, and about the condition of streets and sidewalks. They complain about the behavior of officials, and they complain about the activities of their neighbors. The regime that has undertaken, with great pride and deliberate purpose, more activities than any in modern

---

[12]Moscow and Leningrad are divided into a number of raions (city boroughs). Each raion has its "popularly" elected legislative assembly (soviet); executive committee (borough council), which is "elected" by the soviet; and numerous governmental administrative agencies. According to the legal theory of dual subordination, the raion soviet is subordinate to its electors and the "popularly" elected city soviet. The raion city executive committee is subordinate to its soviet and the city executive committee, and the raion administrative agencies are subordinate to their executive committee and the corresponding city administrative agency. Similar dual subordination exists for city organs and agencies, the next higher level for Moscow and Leningrad being the RSFSR.

In each raion there is a raion party organization consisting of the large raion party committee (raikom), which is "elected" by the larger raion party conference; the bureau of the raikom, which is "elected" by the raikom; and the party administrative agencies. The raion party organizations are subordinate to the city party organization, which also has a conference, city party committee (gorkom), bureau, and administrative agencies.

At each level the governmental organs and agencies are subordinate to their appropriate party organs and agencies. Candidates to governmental offices are selected, or at least approved, by the appropriate party organizations and by higher state organs and agencies. Party officials must be approved by higher party organizations.

history is confronted with demands covering a wider range of subjects than any regime in history.

The vast majority of citizen demands, whatever their topic, have certain common characteristics. They are specific demands from individual citizens involving limited and usually individual or neighborhood needs and wants. They are, in other words, raw demands. Because large autonomous interest groups, which exist in other modern societies are not permitted in the Soviet Union, these raw demands must be processed within the political system without the benefit of any prior efforts to sort, combine and consolidate them into general proposals for political action, but more about this later.

Most of the demands examined in this study are also apparently spontaneous and processed within the governmental apparatus. This obviously is not true of all demands. Fainsod's Smolensk study revealed that during the 1920's and 1930's some processing of citizen demands also went on within the party apparatus. No doubt it still does, although the inaccessibility of party records makes impossible a detailed discussion of party processing for any later period.

I can, however, state that the Party does play a considerable role in the processing of demands included within the electoral mandates, which are lists of demands that are binding, at least formally, on the local governmental officials to whom they are addressed. Furthermore, these demands often are not spontaneous.

To be included within an electoral mandate, a demand must be presented in a particular manner and meet certain criteria. It must be presented in a meeting called either to nominate deputies to the soviets or to present candidates for deputy seats to the electorate; it must be discussed by those present at the meeting with respect to its expediency and practicality; it must be adopted by a majority vote; it should involve matters of common concern to the electors; and it should be substantial enough to require inclusion in the plan for fulfillment.

At the proper meeting a citizen may offer a demand for inclusion in the mandate, but frequently demands offered have been discussed first in the organs of public and voluntary associations. These organs, of course, are dominated by party members. Furthermore, subjecting the proposed demands to public discussion may eliminate some of them. Discussions at public meetings are often rather open, vigorous and frank; but whether any resolution opposed by the party group present at such meetings stands any chance of being adopted is doubtful. The influence of the Party on the mandate has been clearly indicated by two Soviet jurists who state that the Central Committee considers the mandate an important means by which the Party sets tasks for the organs of state authority.

III. FAILURES IN HANDLING CITIZEN DEMANDS

The thousands of raw demands pouring into the system create serious problems for local officials, especially the raion officials. They are in close contact with the populace and receive the major portion of citizen demands. The failure of hard-pressed raion officials to respond to many of the demands encourages citizens to route them through higher authorities in the hope that demands so routed have a better chance of attracting the attention of lower officials. Even so, a response is by no means certain. Between 1958 and 1960, 40 per cent of the demands received by officials of the Sokol'nicheskyi raion in Moscow had been sent via higher authorities, many of them, according to the city executive committee, for the second time. Of these 50 per cent had not been disposed of within the required 20-day period.

The failure of officials to fulfill citizen demands extends even to those legally binding demands included in the electoral mandate. Although their own record is not flawless, city officials often criticize raion officials for failures in this area. Many things go wrong. Sometimes officials simply ignore certain items in mandate, failing even to discuss them. Sometimes officials sacrifice items in a mandate in order to fulfill more important items in the plan. The plan has its priorities; and whatever standing mandate items may have in law, many of them do not enjoy much priority in the plan. Sometimes local executive committees fail to set a specific date for the fulfillment of some mandate demands, thereby making control over fulfillment difficult. Other times the executive committees find themselves without the resources needed to fulfill a mandate.

Although the decrees of the raion soviets and city executive committees clearly show that local officials, especially raion officials, have trouble coping with the flow of citizen demands, little or no effort is made to stem the flow. On the contrary, evidence indicates that higher officials may view large number of demands flowing into the raions with enthusiasm. In 1962 the Moscow city executive stated it considered a large number of citizen demands on raion officials as desirable insofar as the demands indicated increased citizen activism. In the same decree the executive committee also stated it viewed large numbers of such demands as evidence of the raion officials' neglect of citizen needs. Apparently, the city officials view a high volume of demands as a negative indicator for the performance of raion officials and a positive indicator for the existence of citizen support. This makes some sense. Certainly, an unusually high level of demands in one raion might indicate poor performance by raion officials, but at the same time indicate that citizens have confidence in the system's ability to satisfy their needs and wants.

Within the past decade the difficulties of the raion officials may have been aggravated by the demand of higher authorities that the raion officials adopt practices likely to increase both their work load and the flow of citizen demands. For example, city officials urged raion executive committees to hold "circuit" meetings at places where citizens work or live in order to facilitate citizen participation in the discussion of raion problems. They also urged raion officials to send out advance publicity on sessions of the raion soviets in order to give the citizens an opportunity to send in complaints and suggestions concerning questions on the agenda. The raion officials were supposed to consider these for inclusion in the draft resolutions submitted for adoption by the raion soviet. Authorities also ordered raion executive committee officers and raion agency heads to make periodic reports at public meetings and to use the meetings as opportunities to gather additional citizen demands.

The city officials and higher authorities claimed these practices brought officials into closer contact with the masses and improved their understanding of the masses' needs. The reluctance of some raion officials to adopt such practices suggests that they were not unaware that adoption would increase their work loads at a time when they were already having problems handling citizen demands.

IV. THE PERSISTENCE OF THE THREAT OF INPUT OVERLOAD

The city and raion officials have only a limited ability to reduce the threat of input overload by correcting the conditions that give rise to the deluge of citizen demands. If the demands concern such limited problems as a specific street in poor repair, a dirty park, poor street lighting in a certain neighborhood, etc., the local officials can often effectively reduce the input load by correcting the conditions that give rise to the demands. Such corrective action ordinarily involves only the proper allocation and distribution of available resources, and this is within the capabilities of local officials.

When demands arise from conditions created by centrally determined investment and allocation priorities or certain basic characteristics of the economy, local officials can do little. For example, city officials can do something about demands concerning the poor quality of food in restaurants insofar as its quality depends on preparation and handling. They can satisfy the demands of citizens in a particular neighborhood for a restaurant in that neighborhood by using some of the limited resources available for such purposes to build a restaurant in that part of the city. However, they can do nothing to reduce effectively the flow of demands resulting from the general lack of restaurants or other service facilities because this lack results from investment decisions falling outside their jurisdiction.

In such cases city officials can fight for their share of a small pie; they can lend what support they can to whatever reforms are being discussed at higher levels; they can reassure the citizen that they are aware of the problems and are trying to do something to ameliorate the general conditions; and in individual cases they can provide some material relief. But the officials cannot change the basic conditions; consequently, they can do little that might reduce the input of demands resulting from those conditions.

As a result, many of the demands voiced by citizens in 1968 were the same as the demands voiced years earlier. This is occasionally revealed in local decisions. Thus, in 1963 the Leningrad soviet noted improvement in the work of service enterprises between 1958 and 1963, and pointed with considerable pride to expanded facilities. In the same decision the soviet noted that complaints from citizens had also increased. The reason is to be found in the growth figures reported in the decision. The per capita volume of services had increased by only 1.3 per cent over the reported period.

V. DISAPPROVED RESPONSES

Confronted with a difficult situation, the local officials resort to various disapproved tactics in an effort to conceal their failures in handling the deluge of citizen demands or to reduce it. Some simply falsify their reports by untruthfully claiming to handle properly a substantial proportion of received demands. Some try to reduce the flow by curtailing reception hours for citizens wanting to make oral demands. Other officials bury the demands by sending complaints for verification to those very persons against whom the citizens lodged them. Still others simply ignore citizen demands. These tactics provide some temporary relief, but at the risk of censure from higher authorities.

The citizens' perception of the inability of local officials to meet many citizen demands causes citizens to turn to disapproved devices for the satisfaction of their wants and needs. This fosters the rise of various small "businessmen," whose activities are both illegal and ideologically objectionable. Whereas demands addressed to authorities provide the regime with information on popular attitudes and official performance and with an opportunity to build support, the disapproved devices provide neither. They do, however, provide satisfaction for the citizen.

The disapproved devices may also serve some of the needs of local officials. No way exists to discover the motives behind the local officials' toleration of disapproved devices, but that they tolerate them is beyond doubt. The toleration may be indicative of actual corruption or simply a desire not to harass unnecessarily local citizens. Local officials also may tolerate formally disapproved devices because they see them as reducing their input load by providing an alternative way of satisfying citizens needs and wants. . . .

Although the use of disapproved devices by citizens and the collusion of local officials pose serious problems for those seeking to impose the official norms, these problems should not be permitted to obscure the possible, if unintentional, beneficial consequences for the regime. If the regime successfully suppressed these practices, which so clearly violate officially prescribed norms, and if, as a result, citizens and local officials could no longer resort to them to satisfy their felt needs and wants, the level of popular dissatisfaction with the political leadership, its policies and the institutional structure it has established might sharply increase.

Propaganda and coercion may contribute to mass conformity to officially prescribed norms. However, the regime's willingness to tolerate (within limits) citizen gatekeepers and its inability to close off all officially disapproved means by which citizens can obtain satisfaction of needs and wants the regime is unable or unwilling to satisfy, may, by making life more tolerable, be no less important for the maintenance of popular acceptance or acquiescence in the system. Ironically, the use of disapproved devices by citizens, may, by reducing dissatisfaction, make less likely any challenge of what the ruling oligarchy regards as a legitimate right: namely, the right to impose on the people policies that the oligarchy allegedly believes to be in the best interest of the people, even when the people disagree.

VI. APPROVED RESPONSES

There are approved means for reducing the demand input load. City officials may properly refer many of the demands they receive to raion officials for final action; but the raion officials are not so fortunate. They can refer some to public or voluntary associations such as the trade unions, the parents' committees attached to schools, apartment house committees, shoppers' councils, etc. These organizations may also directly absorb a certain number of demands. The trade unions devote some attention to working conditions and safety standards at places of employment. Parents' committees provide some material aid to children of needy families.

However, the ability of these organizations to handle or absorb demands is not very great. In fact, the small local voluntary associations—the parents' committees, apartment house committees, shoppers' councils, etc.—are likely to add to the flow of demands on raion officials. These groups are valuable primarily because they involve citizens in civic work, which helps build civic pride and support, and because they provide free labor for small civic projects such as clean-up and shrubbery planting campaigns. To a considerable degree, the effectiveness of the volunteer organizations depends on the amount of organizational aid the local officials are willing to give them. Therefore, the organizations are as likely to increase the work load of local officials as they are to reduce it. Some volunteer groups have become moribund for the lack of such aid, which suggests that some local officials may find the groups require more time and work than they are worth. . . .

In addition to the use of volunteers, city officials have urged the raion officials to reduce the red tape and paper shuffling that so often accompanies the handling of citizen demands. The available data indicate that many raion officials quite needlessly add to their own burdens. In February of 1963 the Moscow city executive committee noted that despite a 1960 decision ordering raion officials to cease demanding numerous unnecessary forms, certificates, and notarized documents from citizens before undertaking such routine administrative matters as changes in residence, school registration and the issuance of passports, the practice continued, especially in Kuybyshev, Sverdlov and Timiriazev raions. The demand for notarized documents was so great that in a 21-month period one notary office in one of the raions notarized over 625,000 documents. The housing exploitation office of the Sverdlov raion had demanded and received in a single year over 75,000 certificates of various sorts from the citizenry. In the same raion a citizen wishing to acquire better housing had to present not only various forms, certificates and documents, including a personal financial report, but also fill out a seven-page questionnaire containing nearly 200 questions. In view of the small size of the raion staffs such figures are astounding. The executive committee decision gives no indication of why the raion officials persisted in the use of procedures that increased their own work load despite contrary orders from higher authorities. Such procedures apparently had been standard at an earlier date. Perhaps some raion officials believed a large amount of documentation provided them with a ready defense against charges from above that they were giving housing or other material goods or services to unqualified applicants.

VII. THE USE OF DEPUTIES

Higher officials have encouraged raion officials to work with the deputies "popularly elected" to the soviets and to weld them into an effective work force. This also may increase the work load of raion officials. The effective use of deputies requires considerable organizational work and other aid from the raion executive committees and their administrative agencies. Furthermore, one of the major jobs of the local deputy is to transmit his constituents' demands to the local officials. Therefore, an effective deputy can add significantly to the total input of citizen demands.

On the other hand, the deputy can also relieve the local officials of some of their burdens by undertaking the initial investigation of demands, and the verification of the fulfillment of official decisions concerning them. Deputies also can organize the citizenry to work for the satisfaction of their own demands on a self-help basis. This activity is very helpful to local officials when they find themselves in the awkward position of not having the resources to meet citizen demands, especially the legally binding ones included in the electoral mandate. For example, deputies in one raion, faced with the prospect of having to tell their constituents that the raion had no resources to build a shop that had been included in the mandate, organized the citizens, issued appeals to enterprises for material aid, and led the citizens in the construction of the shop.

The deputy does not confine his activities to the electoral mandate. He is expected to hold office hours in public places for the collection of demands from his constituents. He must periodically report to them on his work and hear their demands at public meetings. He also receives numerous letters from constituents. The citizen demands may involve matters of concern to the entire district, such as those pertaining to the quality of food in local restaurants, the need for new shops, or the lack of adequate cultural and re-creational facilities. Other demands may be highly personal and relate to such matters as the enrollment of children in special schools, or disputes with neighbors, or even trouble within the family. No problem is supposed to be too personal or too small to take to the deputy. He is supposed to take the same interest in the personal affairs of his constituents as the old ward politician did in American cities. The reason is probably the same in both cases. Personal attention builds popularity and support for the administration. Once the deputy receives a demand, he should investigate it, present it to local authorities if it has merit, and make certain that the citizen gets some sort of response from the officials, even if only a verbal one.

VIII. DESIRABLE AND UNDESIRABLE CITIZEN DEMANDS

The demands discussed up to this point have been ones that the authorities, at least the higher authorities, regard as desirable and think should be given some measure of gratification, either material or psychic. The authorities undoubtedly regard many of them as legitimate and routine claims for goods or services—housing, housing repairs, pensions, etc.—to which the claimants are officially entitled. Authorities may find other demands desirable because they provide feedback on regime policies, reveal popular attitudes, or provide information on the performance of lower level functionaries. The authorities may value some merely as acceptable means for people to vent their frustrations.

Certainly, local officials who try to suppress or conceal demands of this sort run the risk of censure from above. The higher authorities' obvious desire that desirable demands receive some type of satisfaction is understandable. By satisfying the demands the authorities build support and cultivate in the minds of the citizens the belief that their demands are efficacious. This sense of efficacy itself may lead to greater support, and it almost certainly encourages citizens to submit additional desirable demands. This provides additional opportunities to build support and assures the continued flow of needed information to the authorities. The very fact that the citizens use official channels, rather than the disapproved but available means, to satisfy their needs and wants is itself an indication of support.

Undoubtedly, the authorities do not regard as desirable all citizen demands flowing into the system. The sources used in this study contain no information on whatever directives may exist concerning the handling of undesirable citizen demands. Consequently, any discussion of undesirable demands must be speculative.

Soviet citizens are more or less aware of the extent to which the regime is willing to act at a given time to meet certain kinds of demands. Whatever shortcomings the Soviet mass media may have as general news sources, they quite carefully provide information concerning official policy lines on the various subjects for which established policy lines exist. Research on Western political systems has shown that political participation is related to a sense of efficacy. No way exists to verify this hypothesis in the Soviet Union; but it seems reasonable to assume that there, too, active participation such as stating demands will vary according to the citizen's perception of the efficacy of his actions. . . .

IX. THE LIMITED IMPACT OF CITIZEN DEMANDS ON OFFICIAL DISCUSSION

The impact of citizen demands, or more precisely the impact of the data that results from the aggregation of citizen demands by local officials, on the deliberations of local decision-makers is difficult to determine because of the lack of access to the minutes of the most important local decision-making bodies: the city executive committee and the bureau of the city party committee. Nevertheless, a few observations, based on the local press reports of meetings of the full city party committees of Moscow and Leningrad from 1953 to 1967, are possible.

These reports have certain shortcomings. They are not verbatim accounts, but extended summaries. No way exists to determine the effects of censorship on the reports. Nevertheless, the reports are extensive summaries, attributing specific remarks to specific speakers. The speakers themselves constitute a fair cross-section of that part of the local elite with an interest in the matter under discussion. Finally, the press reports provide the only accessible source of information on the deliberations of the local elite.

The city party committees discussed various topics, among which were the state of housing construction, consumer goods production, and the state of retailing and various consumer and communal services. These were areas of governmental activity that gave rise to numerous citizen demands. During the course of these meetings, speakers sometimes stated that citizen needs, wants, complaints, or requests in some area were not being met. However, the speakers usually attributed the failure to meet citizen demands to the poor performance of some particular agency, institution, enterprise, or branch of the economy and never to centrally established policies and priorities. In other words, speakers occasionally used aggregated data on citizen demands to raise more general demands, but the more general demands themselves were limited. Speakers used the citizen demands as an indicator of how well some agency, institution, or branch of the economy satisfied the needs or demands of the populace within the limits set by centrally established policies and priorities.

Even this limited use of citizen demands has not been common. The members of the local elite are subject to various pressures; but of these pressures, the pressure of public opinion is not among the strongest. As a result the local elite is not very responsive to it. The Party leads the masses, not the masses the Party. The aggregated data on citizen demands are treated like any other aggregated data on performance. The information provides an opportunity to act and is taken into account, but it provides no compulsion to act. Indeed, aggregated data on unmarketable stocks of consumer goods may seem more compelling than aggregated data on consumer complaints about goods purchased. The speakers from the various agencies, institutes, and organizations have their own particular demands to promote. They are spokesmen not for the citizenry, but for some segment of the governmental, party, or economic apparatuses; and they usually use aggregated data on citizen demands only when the data supports their own particular perceived interests.

To assert that the party and governmental officials have no regard for public opinion or the welfare of the citizenry would be incorrect; but even the highest ranking city officials—the secretaries of the city party committee—have only a limited ability to cope with the more general problems implicit in the aggregated citizen demands. They can provide some satisfaction for the demands by calling on the government agencies fulfilling the housing construction program to build better housing. They can call on enterprises to produce more and better consumer goods. They can support the requests of the city construction agency, the city trade agency, or the city consumer services agency for more resources. The city party officials' demands directed to the center are, no doubt, often influential because of their political standing in the system. However, even they can call only for the most efficient use of available resources to attain centrally determined goals; goals that might or might not be consistent with the satisfaction of citizen demands.

X. THE IMPORTANCE OF DEMAND PROCESSING

The lack of any autonomous groups in the intra-societal environment capable of aggregating and processing the specific raw citizen demands into a program for political action that can serve as an alternative to the one advanced by the ruling oligarchy weakens the impact of citizen demands on official deliberations and policy making. In the Soviet Union the raw citizen demands are processed entirely within the political system. This imposes a burden on officials, but it also assures the leadership a greater amount of decision-making autonomy by sharply reducing the pressures of public opinion. At the same time it assures the leaders opportunities for building support and a flow of needed information.

This deserves further elaboration.[13] One may argue that in any society the political system's institutional structure, the composition of the political leadership and public policies generate frustration, anxiety and dissatisfaction among the people. The people respond in various ways, among which is the articulation of demands by individual citizens. In many societies this is followed by a collective redefinition of demands by various organizations involved in the political process. Many of these organizations are independent of the regime and some stand outside the political system, although linked to it. Thus political parties, both those participating in the government and those in opposition, pressure groups, and other organizations take raw citizen demands along with other materials and aggregate and process them into alternative programs and policies. This leads to activities, protests and movements seeking to implement new policies, to capture and even to modify or overthrow the existing institutional structure for political decision-making. The result is civil debate and conflict. Citizen demands do not merely offer rulers useful information and opportunities to build support, but generate additional strain within the

[13] The following discussion is based on an adaption of a "Simplified Systematic View of the 'Collective Behavior' Approach to a Theory of Institutionalism" presented by Walter Buckley, *Sociology and Modern Systems Theory* (Englewood Cliffs, N.J.: Prentice Hall, 1967), p. 138.

society and pressure for changes in public policy, leadership composition, and institutional structure.

In the Soviet Union the process is short-circuited at a critical point. Strains are generated; frustration, anxiety and dissatisfaction within the general populace exist; and citizens do articulate demands. However, these demands feed directly into the political system to be processed by members of the governmental and party apparatuses serving the ruling oligarchy. The lower level officials process and make use of citizen demands in ways that are useful to themselves, but they cannot, according to the norms they observe in self-interest and which they probably regard as legitimate, process the citizen demands into more general proposals that challenge the existing institutional structure, the policies and priorities of the leaders—unless given a signal that discussion of such matters is desired by the leaders—or the composition of leadership. In fact, established norms prohibit even the leading members of the politburo from freely appealing to the public or groups for support on controversial matters.[14] Consequently, the potential of citizen demands for generating additional strains and pressures for change is sharply reduced. On the other hand, the toleration and encouragement of citizen gatekeepers provide the officials and ruling oligarchs with opportunities to build support and a flow of information useful in adapting the system's structure and policies in ways the *leadership* believes appropriate, plus a means of reducing the erosion of support that may result from policies adopted and pursued with little regard for public opinion.

XI. CONCLUSION

Soviet citizens clearly tend their own gates and the quantity of citizen demands is sufficient to pose a serious threat of input overload at the lower administrative levels. The attempt to distinguish the Soviet political system from those of Western democracies on the basis of the absence of numerous citizen gatekeepers in the former and their existence in the latter is erroneous. Distinctions must be based on the kinds of demands that may be raised by these gatekeepers; the absence in the Soviet Union of institutions independent of the regime that can aggregate these demands; and the impossibility in the Soviet Union of using demands to create an alternative program to that advanced by the ruling oligarchy.

Citizen gatekeepers may be either an inevitable consequence of democracy or a necessary condition for it; but they are not a sufficient condition.

---

[14]For a discussion of this point in the context of high level disputes over agricultural policy see Sidney I. Ploss, *Conflict and Decision Making in Soviet Russia: A Case Study of Agricultural Policy, 1953-1963* (Princeton, N.J.: Princeton University Press, 1965), p. 84.

In the absence of other democratic institutions, they may serve the interests of a dictatorship as well as they have ever served the interests of a democratic regime. They provide both with needed information and opportunities to build support.

This support may be built very cheaply. Not all demands need be given actual material satisfaction. The mere acceptance of a demand by local officials, some expression or indication of interest and concern (even if this amounts to nothing more than helpless thrashing about), can create support. The citizen is able to vent his grievances and make his wishes known. He may derive some release of hostility merely from seeing the discomfort of local officials as they struggle to meet his demands and suffer the criticism of higher authorities. Even this useless effort may make the regime seem more human and interested in the welfare of the ordinary citizen. The more limited, the more private the demand and the more personal its handling by local officials, perhaps the greater the support generated for the regime, even though the regime persists in the policies that created the conditions that gave rise to the demand.

23

Problems of Parliamentary
Democracy in Europe

Karl D. Bracher

I. THE DILEMMA

The phrase "crisis of parliamentarism" is nearly as old as the phenomenon of modern parliamentary democracy. It is closely bound up with the deeply rooted social and intellectual transformations in which the process of emancipation—first with a liberal, then with a socialistic stamp—broke the framework of constitutional government based on privileged estates, and in which the principle of full representation and participation of all citizens in a parliament chosen in a general and equal election was carried out. This development reached its critical peak after World War I. For the concept of parliamentary democracy the moment of apparently complete victory over the autocracies of old Europe signified at the same time the beginning of a structural crisis which particularly affected the newly created parliamentary democracies of Europe and which aided the strongly anti-parliamentary dictatorial movements toward a quick rise.

With the exception of Czechoslovakia and Finland this crisis quickly displaced and destroyed all new parliamentary democracies: in Russia and the Baltic states; in Poland, Hungary and the Balkan countries; in Italy, Germany and Austria; in Spain and Portugal. Everywhere in this area the parliamentary system seemed to prove itself unworkable; almost nowhere did it seem capable of absorbing the political and social tensions of the "age of the masses" in a democratic order that was both stable and flexible. The transition from the old liberal parliamentarianism of well-to-do individuals (*Honoratiorenstaat*) to egalitarian party-state parliamentarianism led to serious functional disturbances even in the tradition-bound older

Reprinted by permission from *Daedalus,* Journal of the American Academy of Arts and Sciences, Boston, Massachusetts, Volume 93, No. 1 (Winter 1964), 179-198.

democracies of Europe. In England, to be sure, it was possible to absorb the effects of these disturbances by thorough-going changes in the system of parliamentary rule; in France the Third Republic was able to sustain itself, but only with difficulty. Even in the Scandinavian countries, spared by the World War and apparently sheltered against the European crises, minority governments were often only provisionally able to contain the tensions; even they scarcely provided a proof of the workability of the parliamentary system.

The second postwar epoch of the European parliamentary democracies is of course significantly different from this first crisis period, which ended in the catastrophe of another world war. On the one hand it was still confronted with those basic problems of democratic structural change which the nineteenth century had laid in the cradle of European parliamentarianism. But on the other hand conditions had deeply changed, giving a new profile to the attempts at reconstruction or new construction of parliamentarianism in western Europe after 1945. On three levels these new perspectives were opened.

1. *Constitutional:* The experience of the twenties and thirties directed attention to possible precautionary measures and modifications in the parliamentary system for the protection of its substance and its efficiency. The West German "chancellor democracy" and even more the half-parliamentary presidential regime of the Fifth Republic in France are examples of this attempt at a limitation of parliamentarianism.

2. *Sociological:* At the same time the process of realignment and leveling of society—the product of the radical changes of the war and postwar period, a tendency away from ideologizing and toward pragmatizing of the parties—fostered the concentration of parties and finally the approach to a two- or three-party system, which was strengthened and hastened by constitutional and technical electoral provisions. West Germany was the most strongly affected by this process, in the course of the immigration and absorption of well over ten million displaced persons. But the tendency characterized much too simply as "Americanization" of party and parliamentary life was strong in the rest of Europe as well. This development seemed to simplify the formation of an administration and an opposition, to clarify political alternatives and to allow the parliamentary process to become less hindered by the formation of ideological fronts.

3. *Foreign Affairs:* The decisive phase of European political change at the end of the forties was marked by an increasingly firm opposition to the dynamics of Soviet Russia's European politics. The American politics of restraint, the Marshall Plan, the establishment of NATO placed western Europe within the framework of a broader international cooperation. It opened aspects of a supranational integration which could have an incomparably more lasting effect on the internal politics and structure of the European states than the League of Nations had once had. The idea and the

weight of a European and Atlantic community formed, first of all, a kind of protection for the new parliamentary democracies; insofar as they were still limited by powerful groups hostile to democracy—as in the case of France and Italy with their strong Communist parties—the growing inter-dependence meant a supplementary support.

The starting conditions for the "new Europe" thus seemed more favor-able than in 1918. The attempt at a self-limitation of sovereignties had taken the place of a confusion of national ambitions, which at that time had made the rise and triumph of nationalistic dictatorial movements possible. The East-West conflict seemed to outweigh the internal explosive forces of national parliamentarianism. In the foreground stood the overlapping problems of political cooperation, economic and military networks, and the overcoming of the colonial age. In the face of such problems intrastate tensions tended to diminish in sharpness and importance or at least to recede to a deeper level of confrontations more specific and more suited to com-promise. Such a prognosis seemed especially plausible from the German point of view. Had not Germany immediately after the occupation joined, as the Federal Republic, the European and Atlantic politics of alliance, within whose frame the West German parliament system could develop and stabilize itself almost without hindrance? Indeed, the experience of a parlia-mentary democracy operating with political and economic success was some-thing entirely new in the history of German political thought, which had learned from the catastrophes of 1848, 1918 and 1933 to identify parliamentary politics with crisis and collapse.

But these positive perspectives reflect only the external, superficial image of the reconstruction period. They say nothing about the real stability and functional capability of the reconstituted parliamentary democracies of western Europe. Upon closer inspection it has quickly become apparent not only that the old problems of parliamentary politics continued to exist unsolved under the double protection mentioned, but also that the new conditions of the postwar period, with their revolutionizing consequences in the economic, social and intellectual areas, necessarily led to new crises of adjustment in the political system. It became a question whether and how, in the light of the changes cited, the individual parliaments would be able to carry out their role—which was still conceived in the classical sense of control and "decision-making"—in the actual practice of national politics. The increasingly complicated network of the modern industrial state con-fronted them with a dismaying array of new problems for which political common sense and the old parliamentary practice no longer seemed adequate. These problems threatened to undermine the competence and decision-making ability of the individual member of parliament, to strengthen at the cost of parliament the power of committees, experts and the bureaucracy of the executives and to lead toward an undermining of the parliamentary system of government from within.

As a result a series of surprisingly similar basic questions came to the fore in all of the western democracies. Is a parliament as such still capable, under such circumstances, of exercising an effective control of politics, not even to mention active participation in the formulation of political desires? Further, is it possible any longer to defend the submission of complicated economic, social and military decisions, which demand precise planning, to the tedious discussion procedure of technically incompetent large assemblies, considering that the deliberations of a small circle of committee experts are simply repeated in these sessions? And under these circumstances is it at all possible to continue upholding the classical basic principle of parliamentarianism—to combine democratic representation and the correct decision of all questions—or does not the parliamentary process become reduced to a formality in the face of the incompetence of the mass of the representatives?

A further consideration derives from the fact that precisely the supra- and international network of those technical decisions transcends the capacities of the national parliaments and at the same time must impose sensitive limitations upon them. The development of European institutions has demonstrated in recent years what a great effect this consideration has had in shifting politics from the parliamentary level to that of administration and bureaucracy. A European bureaucracy of a new character has gained a decisive advance upon the parliamentary organs in those institutions; the supranational formation of politics has been shifted extensively to an extra- or superparliamentary area of competence handled by experts and governments; in the face of this power the merely advisory function of the European "parliaments," which moreover have possessed only a derivative legitimation, not a direct one through direct European elections, has had little effect.

In view of these problems our diagnosis of parliamentarianism in western Europe will consider the following elements. We shall inquire about the model, the reality and the structural transformation of "classical" parliamentarianism, which has also been the point of departure for the parliamentary democracies of postwar Europe. We shall analyze the most important factors and arguments that form the basis of this structural change. What are their consequences: the transformation or the decline of parliamentary politics? Last, we shall endeavor to ascertain what efforts toward reform, substitute forms and future perspectives can be recognized within the national and supranational framework. Although the examination will proceed from Germany to the particular conditions of the various countries, attention will be devoted principally to the typical instances of those problems which today more than ever bear a general European character, both in positive and in negative regards.

II. STRUCTURAL TRANSFORMATION OF DEMOCRACY

The "crisis of parliamentarianism" figured, immediately following World War I, as the central theme of countless conferences of the Interparliamentary Union—in Washington, Ottawa, Geneva, Paris, Prague and Berlin. The discussion probed deeply into essentials. It dealt with the actual and necessary adjustment to the new European situation; it vacillated between a modernization or a limitation of parliamentarianism. At the same time it became increasingly clear that parliamentarianism had undergone an actual structural transformation which also needed to be put into effect constitutionally and institutionally.

Indeed the language of the constitutions and of their interpreters—insofar as it referred to the original model of the "classical" parliamentarianism, developed according to the idealistically elevated English pattern—was so far from reality that it appeared to be more and more fictitious. Whereas constitutional theory held to the concept of the independent member of parliament, responsible only to his conscience, in reality the representative found himself to be working within a network of social and political ties, a network which had become increasingly dense with the complication of modern industrial society and with the organizational consolidation and increase in importance of parties and organized interest groups. The result was that the member of parliament, contrary to the postulates of the constitutions, was subjected increasingly, whether consciously or unconsciously, to an "imperative mandate" by party interests and other joint interests. His role as representative of the people as a whole had thereby become unreal. The classical-liberal form of representative parliamentarianism gave way to a parliamentary democracy determined by plebiscite and party politics, a democracy which also brought about far-reaching changes in the process of forming political opinion and the function of the parliament as an organ for decision and control.

The interrelationship of this "structural transformation of democracy" (Leibholz) with modern party history has meanwhile been thoroughly analyzed. After World War II some of the European constitutions tried to give the new reality its due—though only in a makeshift way and rather incidentally—by dedicating a few articles to the role of the parties and their structure. Probably the most prominent instance of this was in the Basic Law of the Federal Republic of Germany, the West German constitution of 1949, in which (contrary to the Weimar Constitution) not only is the participation of the parties in determination of political policy emphasized, but their democratic structure and their agreement with the ordinances of the constitution are also specifically required. To be sure the old postulate of representative democracy was also preserved. The deputies are considered the "representatives of the people as a whole, not bound to specific commissions and directions, and subject only to their consciences" (Art. 38); thus they are supposed to be free of the "imperative mandate" to which they are in fact so thoroughly bound by the manner of nomination of candidates, electoral modes, parliamentary practice and party coercion.

The whole tension between theory and practice continues in these introverse stipulations. In other European countries the situation appears to be scarcely any different. In the merely laconic, usually meaningless reference to the parties there still prevails that "conspiracy of silence" (Loewenstein) with which the constitutions hold to the fiction of partyless parliamentarianism and the superparty parliament member. This is true of the Italian constitution (Art. 49) as well as of the French constitutions of the Fourth and Fifth Republics, even though the beginnings of a transformation are visible and in the practice of constitutional interpretation there is a growing attempt to give the political reality of party democracy its due. It is expected that this reality will be taken into account still more thoroughly by the new Swedish constitution, which has been in preparation for years with the authoritative participation of political science.

There is, however, a further aspect of that structural change which, although so far it has enjoyed less attention, has a more fundamental, comprehensive significance than the constitutional-political reform of the relationship between party, parliament and government. This is the expansion of the organized interest groups on the one hand and of public administration on the other hand. The consequence of both is that "unpolitical" experts and superparty planning confront the parliament's claim to power of decision and control with an increasing claim to primacy, attempting to undermine or even displace the parliament. The reasons for this development are as various as they are obvious. They lie in the need for continually improved, rational organization and planning in a complex, highly differentiated, sensitive society which can no more afford mere improvisation and dilettantism than can modern economics and industry.

But at the end of this development, which opposes to the political process of parliamentary democracy the greater effectiveness of the "unpolitical" experts, the objectively planning and rationally functioning, specialized bureaucracy in state and society, there appears the frightful image of a mere technocracy, a rule by the managers and functionaries, which would evade control and the entire realm of democratic-parliamentary decision-making. Thereby the balance of power would be seriously disturbed and a new form of dictatorship would be coldly brought into being. It is this opposition between highly specialized expertise and the principle of democratic participation that appears as the central structural problem of all western parliamentary democracies. To be sure this dilemma is also by no means new, however sharply it confronts us today on all sides.

Bureaucratization and specialization, no less than liberal and social emancipation movements, accompanied the development of parliamentary democracy at an early stage and continue to do so to an increasing degree. They have governed its forms and at the same time complicated them. The development of the apparatus of government has meant more than an expansion of its political functions. It has fostered the rise of the modern professional bureaucracy, which especially in nineteenth-century Germany was most closely tied to the continuation of absolutistic and authoritarian-official (*obrïgkeitsstaatliche*) elements in the structure of state and society. This became especially apparent after the establishment of the Weimar Republic, which tried, with the army and the state bureaucracy, to incorporate the great, allegedly indispensable supports of political continuity into the new order of parliamentary democracy—an attempt which is known to have been a huge failure. The collapse of the first German democracy was to a considerable degree a result of the unsolved tension between parliamentary and bureaucratic-authoritarian elements of structure; this tension was already prepared for in the dualism of the Weimar Constitution; it finally ended with the victory of a bureaucratic presidial dictatorship and its pseudo-democratic manipulation and subjugation by Hitler.

To be sure, the cause for this was not simply a faulty construction of the constitution. Rather, the problems of the first German republic showed how unavoidable was a clarification of the relation between the conflicting elements. Max Weber had already recognized at the end of World War I the tendency toward bureaucratization and expertise in the leadership of the state as a dominating sign of the age; according to him there remained only the choice between bureaucratization and dilettantizing. Later Karl Mannheim saw our "period of social change" to be essentially determined by the fact that great "strains" arose "out of the contiguity of the principle of competition and the principle of regulation and planning," strains which could be solved only by a system of "planning for freedom."

This problem certainly did not apply exclusively to the democracies. The authoritarian and totalitarian regimes were also unable to solve the strain, even after eliminating the parliaments; it continued to exist almost undiminished in the dualism of state and party, especially visible in the "Third Reich." And finally it became apparent in postwar France and Germany how great an importance is possessed by the continuity and the growing weight of the elite of experts in organized interest groups or unions and in state bureaucracy as opposed to the politically-parliamentary dynamics. Only recently it was once more pointed out, by Maurice Duverger, that the bureaucracy of experts in France plays a stabilizing role that alone makes government possible. The Fifth Republic deduces from this fact the consequence—albeit a disputed one—of a restriction of parliament, which ultimately aims at a *gouvernement de legislature* in which the parliamentary and the presidial systems would be merged. This, however, could be the end of real parliamentarianism and the victory of rule by executive mandate with a plebiscitary façade.

In West Germany, which with controversial arguments held to the continuity of the political apparatus beyond the period 1933-1945, the development proceeded somewhat differently. Here the "chancellor democracy" commanded a continually growing governing and steering apparatus whose complication and indispensability in the modern bureaucratic state works against a change of government. Now that it has outlasted several parliamentary periods this apparatus is far superior in technical knowledge to the parliamentary agencies of power, which in the Bonn system are curtailed anyway. In addition there is the fourteen-year duration of the political constellation, which is modified only by the federalistic structure. Here the danger of instability of the government is averted at the cost of disempowering the parliament, whose capability for control becomes inferior to the claim to expert knowledge and the stability of the political apparatus. The head of the government himself was able, thanks to his constitutionally assured position and to the special authority of Adenauer as Chancellor and party head, to extend the executive power far into the parliament, which then converts his will into laws prepared for him by the government bureaucracy.

In both cases, even though by different courses, the consequence of the unsolved strain is a tendency toward authoritative remodeling of parliamentary democracy. Of course in both cases the concrete form owes much to a personal element. It may not outlast de Gaulle and Adenauer. But the development itself would scarcely be thinkable without the factual and structural problems which lie at the basis of the crisis of parliamentarianism in the industrial and mass state of the twentieth century.

III. BETWEEN CRISIS AND REFORM

In the following survey we shall try therefore to summarize the most important points of view and arguments which characterize the critical discussion of parliamentarianism in Europe.

In the representative system the direct contact with the will of the people is lost, since in the large modern state the parties of rank have become mass parties, and elections based on personality have become impersonal, machine elections. One consequence is the stronger demand for plebiscitary arrangements, which correspond to a more general tendency toward "supraparty" ties. Just recently de Gaulle, who set the Fifth Republic on this course, criticized the lack of such arrangements in the Bonn democracy. All the recent experiences indicate, however, that they are feasible only in the smaller framework of a direct democracy (such as Switzerland still is), if the danger of uninformed demagogy or even of a new autocracy is to be avoided.

The prestige of the members of parliament has fallen precipitously since they no longer have to resist an autocratic principality and are enjoying a career that is almost without risks. To the public they seem to be dispensable: a constitutional state and a functioning government are already insured by good organization and efficient development of the political apparatus.

The organization of parliamentarianism, originally created for political problems, is not suited to deal with the penetration of economic and social problems into the concerns of government. Lawmaking has extended its boundaries considerably. It embraces almost all areas of social existence and it makes too great demands on the abilities of the members of parliament, both technically and temporally. The results are extended periods of session and necessary specialization. The participating citizen is replaced by the professional politician, who himself becomes a bureaucrat, a functionary, without having the experience and the specialized training of the state official.

Thus the continual broadening of functions of the state threatens traditional parliamentarianism, which is thereby alienated from its real function and fragmented in its effectiveness. On the other hand, a limitation of the extent of parliamentary control, especially in the economic area, has proved fatal, the more complicated the economic and social organism of the modern state has become and the more it has called for coordination and planning. But one is confronted with the facts that the state is seldom a capable entrepreneur and that the parliament is not a good organ of control of economic undertakings, especially since in this case it will transfer its prerogatives to a great extent back to the political bureaucracy. A system of decentralization scarcely offers the satisfying solution either. Federalism can of course unburden parliamentarianism, given the appropriate historical premises (as in Germany or Switzerland) by disseminating responsibility and control more broadly. But thereby coordination and planning become more difficult and complicated.

As the expansion of the state places too great demands on the abilities of the members of parliament, it at the same time lowers their position and the importance of their activity. An elected representative cannot, by the nature of the thing, be equal to the many-sided detailed problems with which society and bureaucracy confront him. The fact that he has to make pronouncements and decisions and exercise control in these matters, as if he were an expert, contributes to the lessening of the prestige of parliamentarianism in the eyes of the public and makes the member of parliament himself vulnerable, insecure and resigned in the face of the real or alleged specialists inside and outside of the political institutions. It also does not help to make his activity more attractive to the really suitable persons. At the same time that technical and political competence is concentrated in a minority within the parliamentary parties, the representative become dependent on an apparatus of reporters and specialists, and parliamentary debate is reduced to a mock struggle in the foreground behind which work those anonymous and nonresponsible apparatuses upon which the member of parliament is dependent to a great extent in technical matters.

The consequence is not only a weakening of the parliamentary debates but also that loss of substance and interest which has become characteristic for the greater part of parliamentary activity, with the exception of the few debates over matters of principle; this is also especially true of that domain particularly proper to parliament, which has become so complicated—household politics. The attendance in the parliament chamber is often meager; the parties function as mere voting machines; their activity seems to the critical public to be an expensive waste and complication; derogatory remarks against the conduct of parliament, whether they come from the government and the bureaucracy or from the interest groups, fall upon fruitful ground; finally, the institution itself is no longer taken seriously and it is overriden wherever possible and led into error. Overtaxed in its assignments, the parliament limits itself to topics that have an effect on the elections and abandons important decisions in practice to the planning and formulating bureaucracy. Thus their roles are often exactly reversed. Lawgiving is transferred to the apparatus of administration and parliament loses its authority to a quasidictatorship of the executives. Finally the will of the experts triumphs over the parliamentary art of submitting technical decisions to political decision and control; the decisions have already been made.

The structural transformation into the party state has sharpened these problems still more. The advance determination of decisions in the party committees so extensively binds the parliamentary member, whose parliamentary existence rests upon the party's favor, that even without express party coercion his parliamentary flexibility is extremely limited. Discussion, the basic element of democracy, no longer takes place chiefly on the parliamentary level but in the preparliamentary area of party politics, and largely to the exclusion of the public. Parliamentary decisions are prefabricated there and become a mere matter of form, since the voices are previously counted; the minority, that is usually the opposition, is left with mere resignation—until the next election—or with increasing anger, which can become intensified to enmity toward the regime itself, to a revolutionary mood. Old and new attempts to put an end to this development—for instance by prohibiting the "imperative mandate"—are of course condemned to failure. But the consequences can be lessened, above all under two conditions: by the loosening effect of decentralization and federalism and by a greater flexibility and elasticity of the parties themselves if they are no longer strictly bound to certain classes and programs and if there is a continuation of the process of leveling and pragmatization, which is so characteristic for the postwar development, especially that of Germany. On the other hand, here as in Italy and other countries the phenomenon of the "Christian party" has been thwarting this process and has added a new chapter to the European history of the (ideological) "Weltanschauung" parties.

The selection and education of the members of parliament is not holding pace with the complication of political tasks. Even the process of selecting the candidates seems inadequate from this point of view. The central dilemma of modern parliamentarianism becomes apparent here. A strong influence of the central party leadership is the only guarantee for the nomination of objectively suited, specialized candidates for parliamentary and party work; but this method endangers precisely that immediate contact with the constituency which seems to be possible only by way of local electoral committees, through a decentralized party organization. The technical question of the electoral system is secondary to this. The point of view of the continental backers of the majority election, in so passionately supporting the reform of parliamentarianism by a "personality election," is still oriented to the older model of parliamentarianism. However, empirical observations in England have confirmed that with the change from prestige democracy to party democracy, the elections have also changed from personality elections to party elections regardless of the electoral system.

It is felt especially urgent, therefore, that the representatives to parliament be better informed and equipped. An advance technical examination of the candidates, such as has been called for again and again, can be neither politically justified nor technically realized; it seems impossible to set up suitable standards. On the other hand, an expansion of the apparatus for information and assistance is under way everywhere. Assistants, experts, forces of aid of all sorts are to see to it that the balance of power between the government apparatus and the parliament, which is supposed to control the government apparatus, does not become too unequal in the conduct of affairs. But precisely this may give rise to another problem. A second big apparatus is created which is scarcely less subject to the tendencies of bureaucratization than is the government apparatus. Such a bureaucratization of parliamentarianism once more calls up, only on a different level, the old danger that the member of parliament is overriden by or becomes dependent upon extraparliamentary, nonresponsible experts. The collaboration of government officials, experts and members of parliament in committees of experts does increase the possibilities for objective information and controls, but it also considerably complicates the course of government and committee activity and in addition confuses the executive and legislative competences. One way out is the formation of commissions of experts in the government, as they are used in England with some success; thereby the technical knowledge of the organized interest groups is drawn especially into economic and social planning. But that does not essentially foster either a solution of the control problem or the reactivation of parliamentarianism as a whole; it only shifts, and probably sharpens, the tendencies to "expertocracy."

In all of this it is the ponderousness of the parliamentary system that is especially exposed to criticism. The first principle of modern government and economy, the principle of rationality and effectiveness, is apparently contradicted by the existence and practice of the parliaments so strikingly that the critics question not only their ability to function but also their justification for existence. Important decisions—as in Germany a new penal law, the social reform or the party law expressly required in the constitution —and also a plethora of detailed tasks are often postponed over several periods of sessions or remain entirely unsettled. For the greater part of the representatives the sessions mean up to 90 per cent idle time; for the public they mean a waste of valuable working power. This too scares many a qualified person away from the parliamentary career. Therefore recommendations have been put forward again and again for the technical rationalization of parliamentary procedure, which is still in the state it was in the eighteenth and nineteenth centuries. For example, time-wasting sessions might well be curtailed by the exchange of opinion and voting in writing or by telephone, extensive use of electric brains and other methods. But there are still narrow limits set to the simplification and shortening of the procedure. It is precisely the nature of the parliamentary system, as distinct from and contrary to bureaucratic procedure, to achieve a more comprehensive basis and sharper control of political decision through more extensive proceedings.

The idea of a second chamber of experts to bridge the gap between expert knowledge and political power has been playing a significant role right up to the present. Made up on the basis of technical suitability and professional grouping from the various provinces of economic and social life, such a "parliament of experts" could contribute as an auxiliary organ of the parliament and government to the objectification of the political process. To be sure, it has proved an insolvable difficulty to decide in what way and according to what key such an institution could be recruited. All previous attempts have also either run aground in useless technical discussions, as in the economic council of the Weimar Republic, or have been misused for the purpose of deposing the parliamentary system by authoritarian regimes, as in Mussolini's *stato corporativo* and similar institutions in Greece, Poland, Austria and Portugal in the thirties. In France since 1945 and especially in the Fifth Republic the idea of an economic council has been institutionalized; but this coincides again with a threat to parliamentary democracy.

Theoretically the auxiliary function of such an agency, which makes it possible to incorporate technical-economic expertise into the political process, should be hailed as a support of parliamentarianism. But the practical realization of it appears to be incomparably more difficult than the formation of commissions and councils, which according to the English example of the royal commissions and committees would have to bridge expert knowledge and politics and simultaneously curb and channel the pressure of interest groups. A chamber of professionals and experts seems to be not only historically discredited but also a danger in the present. The interest groups' influence on politics, which is already almost too strong, would have in such a chamber an additional vehicle and instrument. Therefore as a guarantor of objectivity it would be scarcely better qualified —indeed, its members would be still more subjectively tied to particular interests than the members of parliament, who have to represent various interests at once and therefore are more predestined for a comprehensive manner of making decisions. The primacy of politics is also indispensable in all matters of technical decision.

An especially weighty argument of the critics is finally the lack of stability of parliamentary governments. This was especially true of the unbridled parliamentarianism of the period between the wars. The twenty-one administrations in the fourteen years of the Weimar Republic were a frightening example. Even after World War II the French Fourth Republic exhausted twenty-five administrations in the space of thirteen years. It is true that the rapid change of cabinets was mitigated by the fact that often there were only minor shifts in the personnel component. But without a doubt, not only the total triumph of Hitler (and the assent of broad circles in Germany) but also the more moderate victory of de Gaulle over parliamentary democracy are to be ascribed in no small way to discontent about the discontinuity of parliamentary state politics. This discontinuity has been particularly consequential in periods of economic and political crises, which have needed the more far-sighted objective planning and persistent execution of a course of consolidation to a greater extent. Parliamentarianism appears to be not only a particularly cumbersome but also an unreliable form of government which, because it is entirely bound up with the transitory present, is incapable of demanding unpopular sacrifices for more far-reaching politics from a short-sighted "will of the people."

Thus the tendency of European democracy is toward a modification of the parliamentary system of government. Its particular goal is to lengthen the duration of periods of government and to render more difficult the overthrow of cabinets and the dissolution of parliaments. This of course has always implied the danger of lessening or even blocking political dynamics, the flexibility and capability for decision of the political forces. The rigidifying chancellor democracy of Adenauer and the pseudo-presidential regime of de Gaulle are examples of this problem, which can result in the undermining and displacement of a lively parliamentarianism rather than in reform. There are various forms of this modification. The Fifth Republic has established a dualistic system, which runs on two tracks by placing representative and plebiscitary execution of the popular will in a parallel position and thus producing a peculiar system of balance in which finally the presidial-plebiscitary element dominates. From the German point of view this recalls all too vividly the faulty construction of the Weimar Republic; a decision for genuine presidential democracy or for the restitution of parliamentary democracy will not be avoidable when the present special form is no longer potected by the peculiar phenomenon of de Gaulle.

But the forms of modification in the Bonn democracy are also disputed. Undoubtedly an astonishing stability of the political constellation has been brought about by the elimination of splinter parties by the 5-per-cent clause, by the officially privileged position of the parliament parties by state financing, by hindrances put in the way of the overthrow of government by the "constructive vote of lack of confidence"; at the same time the dissolution of parliament is impeded, owing to a weakened position of the federal president. But the other weaknesses of parliamentarianism enumerated above have appeared all the more prominently. And more particularly the government, the bureaucracy and the interest groups, protected by the stable parliamentary conditions, have achieved such a great weight that many clear-sighted critics characterize the Bonn democracy as an actual government by bureaucracy and interest associations. This parliamentary democracy also will not have to stand its test until the moment of a change of administration; the end of the Adenauer era leaves many questions open, even though it seems to be less dramatic than the transition to the post-de Gaulle era.

This summary of the critical points in European parliamentarianism, as incomplete as it is, nevertheless indicates the central significance of the inquiry into the relation between politics and technical knowledge with regard to the future of European parliamentary democracy. This problem should now be pursued first in the national, then in the supranational, contexts.

IV. PERSPECTIVES TOWARD A SOLUTION

Three main directions are taken in the attempts to solve—without a loss of democratic substance—the sharpened conflict between parliamentary politics and technical planning in the expanding industrial state of present-day Europe. The first direction is pursued especially in England and in the Scandinavian countries. It is the attempt to democratize the growing phenomenon of specialists and experts by making it useful and at the same time bringing it under control within the framework of, or in association with, the apparatus of government. This attempt proceeds from the insight that the activity of the interest groups cannot be separated from the political process and abandoned or consigned to a fictitious neutrality of the experts. In England the development of the royal commissions and similar institutions is significant in this line and at the same time poses a counterbalance to the rule of an isolated state bureaucracy. To be sure, new problems are created by the expansion of such commissions, which advise the government and administration in economic, social and cultural-political questions with technical competence, but also with their own interests prevailing. The importance of the experts has been fostered, the "anonymous empire" (S. Finer) of interest groups becomes institutionalized, but the parliaments' loss in substance has progressed further while the cabinet system, which is founded on parties and the administrations, has grown stronger.

A second course proceeds by way of the attempt *to submit parliamentarianism itself to the tendencies toward technology and rationalization* which have led to the advance of the expertise-and-planning system. This course has been pursued most decisively in France by means of the unburdening of the parliament (which of course also means its loss of importance), and by means of the institutionalizing of the system of expertise in large planning commissions. Another variation of this "rationalization" of parliamentarianism is the progressive shifting of technical decisions from the plenum to the commissions of the parliament, as is especially characteristic of the German development. The plenum retains little more than the sanctioning of the decisions that the members of the commissions bring before it. Therefore the selection and incorporation of the experts into the parliamentary party groups becomes the principal content of parliamentary activity. Here too the "rationalization" results in a loss of substance and significance of the actual parliamentary discussion. The system of *hearings*, which could steer this development, is lacking in the European parliamentary democracies with the exception of the Swiss democracy, which has a different form. Substitutes such as the interrogation hour of the Bonn system, in which the ministers must answer critical questions before parliament, are hardly sufficient, although in some cases (as the Spiegel affair) it proved quite important. But the basic principle remains in danger —the principle that decision is the prerogative of the politically responsible, elected officials of the parliament and of the government, and that it is not to be relegated to the bureaucracy or to the experts, with or without an interest-group slant.

All the more important are the efforts toward a new delimitation of the altered functions of parliament, government, administration and the organized interest groups which are undertaken in view of this dilemma. Their premise is that in view of the general tendency to bureaucratization the future of democracy depends upon whether objectivity and expertise can also be exercised outside of bureaucratic areas of organization. A clear separation of political decision (parliament) and technical planning (bureaucracy) is not possible; it would finally lead to the hypertrophy of the administrative state, to the victory of the hierarchy of officials over open democracy. To equate bureaucracy with expertocracy could appear as the tempting solution to the problems. But it contains serious dangers; it implies an evasion of democratic control and creates a new gap between the state and the citizens; it sharpens their dependence and helplessness in the face of the political-social process and degrades them to subjects facing a highly specialized, uncontrollable network of rule without comprehension. The result could be indifference and resignation; the political answer could become an erroneous reaction such as that of 1933 in Germany, if in place of a political solution to the problems a bureaucratic one were to prevail.

It is indisputable that the number of the actual decision-bearers in the modern state is becoming steadily smaller and the tendency toward rule by experts is becoming steadily harder to control. Thus the future of democracy depends all the more on whether it becomes possible to open up new ways for the citizens to participate in political and social affairs and thus to rise above the role of mere observers. Parties, organized interest groups and self-rule offer possibilities to create a counterweight against the threatening depolitization; an improved political education seems to be its precondition. This is true at the same time for the expert in the planning and steering committee. His "democratization" and control is most likely to become feasible if every kind of monopoly and hierarchy of the agencies of competence is avoided and if room is made for the principle of free competition in the sense of competition for achievement.

The basis for all attempts at solving the problem is therefore the insight that there must be no necessary opposition between expert knowledge and politics, between expertise and democracy. The primacy of politics must be maintained. The question is only what place parliamentarianism is to retain here, in what form it is to be brought into accord with the changed conditions of modern state, social, economic and military politics. The parliament and the parties which support it still have the double function of first working for contact and conjunction between the various areas of expertise, interests and politics, thereby guaranteeing the openness, readiness for compromise and competition; and second of control of technical counseling and technical planning, re-examining them in the discussions between administration and opposition and relating them to concrete political reality.

For both tasks—the uniting of political determination and technical planning on the one hand; the critical examination of the interest associations and also those of the experts on the other hand—the European democracies now as before need parliamentary institutions that are capable of functioning. We have indicated what possible modifications are being discussed and also to some extent realized to reduce the disadvantages and crises of parliamentarianism and to consider the structural changes of society and state. These modifications are resulting everywhere—not only in France—in a limitation of the "classical" parliamentary rule. But at the same time they aim at an intensification and rationalization of parliamentarianism in its indispensable functions. Improvement of the channels of information, expansion of the system of commissions, more conscious policy in the selection of their own experts on the part of the parliamentary parties and incorporation of the specialists into the work of the parliament are the means of this rationalization. Its goal continues to be to work as a clearing house and counterweight to the technical claims of the bureaucracy of government as well as of interest groups, and to provide the comprehensive impetus for the primacy of political decision.

This is particularly applicable to the new problems that have been brought forward by the international network and the creation of *supranational* institutions. Today an isolated view of intrastate parliamentarianism is no longer possible. It is superseded by the comprehensive question as to how the separation of politics and planning, of democracy and expertocracy can be bridged in the sphere of the European network, and partly also in the Atlantic network. Here too only an inadequate political control by the governments confronts the forward-moving, expanding bureaucracy of administrators and specialists. Commissions and ministerial councils of the European economic community incorporate this tendency as do the other European administrative offices. And here too the parliamentary institutions have remained far behind. As qualified as some of their members are and as favorable as the supranational exchange of thought is, European parliamentary institutions have little actual weight as long as they lack legitimation through direct European elections and as long as they carry out only insignificant advisory functions. Here too it must be recognized that technical planning needs political planning and control if it is to be both effective and democratic.

The danger of self-satisfied expertocracy is heightened still more by the economic and technical successes of cooperation on the level of bureaucracy. The collapse of negotiations between the Common Market and England fits into this complex. If England can be counted as a model of a parliamentary democracy that has succeeded in adjusting to the changed conditions without a breach of the basic principles, then England's inclusion would without doubt shift the politics of European unification from the bureaucratic level to the parliamentary level. Therein—and not only in a French claim to leadership—lies one of the reasons for the resistance of de Gaulle, who may fear the disturbing effect of such tendencies on the economic-technical development of the European cooperation. But therein also lies the reason for the all too long hesitation of England, which regards with mistrust the reciprocal effect on the tested institutions of its own political system.

Not only in Italy and the Benelux countries but also in Germany these political aspects of the problem—along with the economic and military ones —have in the meanwhile come into such prominent awareness that the French standpoint appears considerably isolated. The Fifth Republic is considered a special case, not a model for the solution of the problems of European parliamentarianism. Precisely at a moment in which a Europe of reduced sovereignties is considering its strengthened role in the world, a retreat into national, or even regional, small-European isolation has become unthinkable. This is not only a question of economic and military potential. It is still more a political question. The danger that threatens the European democracies externally because of their geographical position, and internally still more because of the multifariously broken tradition of their parliamentarianism, also has not been averted by their rapid reconstruction. In the search for security and necessary reform the European states need not only close association among themselves but also with the Anglo-Saxon democracies, which command the strongest traditions and experiences in the art of the adjustment of a firmly established parliamentarianism to the new conditions of the industrial world.

V. CONCLUSION

While there are striking parallels and similarities in the appearance and problems of parliamentarianism in present-day Europe, the differences between the national forms of its realization still seem very great. In Germany, the experience of the Weimar Republic and the causes of its fall form the exit-point for all discussions about the relation of parliament, government and bureaucracy. The pseudo-presidential experiments of 1930-1933, which led to the dictatorship of Hitler, seem to justify the widespread mistrust against all attempts to minimize the position and function of parliament in favor of bureaucracy. In France, under the impact of the failure of classical parliamentarianism in the Fourth Republic, the experiences influencing public opinion and discussion support a very different view, almost contrary to the German version of a parliamentary party state. While in both of these cases, however, the main tendency goes toward a modification of parliamentary democracy, in Italy the older type of a multi-party system still prevails, confronted with the classical problems of a parliament which is split up in many political groups hardly able to form stable coalitions.

Such profound differences in the domestic scene of the European states must be considered if the prospects of coordination and integration of the national systems into a "new Europe" are examined. Besides strong remnants of the past—including very different experiences—it is a question of how to combine strong government and executive authority with effective control, which has led to individual solutions of the problems of parliamentarianism; decentralization and federalism—as traditional in Germany —are further elements of difference. The quest for European integration may as well complicate these problems as it tends to neglect them. It is also for such reasons that the position of a European parliament as a legislative body seems still very uncertain.

If the relation between parliament, government and bureaucracy demands new answers on the national as on the supranational level, this applies even more to the role of parties, interest groups and expert commissions within the institutional framework of parliamentary democracy. Beyond all national differences, two main tendencies are discernible: the growing importance of pressure groups, tending even to a *Verbände-Staat;* at the same time, the decline of ideological parties. This process, to be sure, is modified by the existence of strong Christian parties which may work as integration factors in a biconfessional society, as in Germany; but it may simultaneously block the tendency to open two-party systems, as does the unbroken strength of Communist parties in Italy and France.

In summing up, the development of democracy in western Europe, showing so many different traits and tendencies, has posed many new questions. On the level of domestic politics, there are as yet no common answers in terms of a "new Europe." This will be the future task of interstate compromises which may result in the creation of a European parliament. In spite of the experiments of the French Fifth Republic, however, the substantial form of European governments has remained that of parliamentary democracy, though modified: a fundamental change in the direction of a presidential system seems outside of all possibilities. On this point, the difference between Europe and the United States, whose peculiar political system seems not fit for export, remains a reality which in its importance for European and Atlantic politics should not be overlooked.